Communications in Computer and Information Science

2845

Series Editors

Gang Li, *School of Information Technology, Deakin University, Burwood, VIC, Australia*

Joaquim Filipe, *Polytechnic Institute of Setúbal, Setúbal, Portugal*

Zhiwei Xu, *Chinese Academy of Sciences, Beijing, China*

Rationale

The CCIS series is devoted to the publication of proceedings of computer science conferences. Its aim is to efficiently disseminate original research results in informatics in printed and electronic form. While the focus is on publication of peer-reviewed full papers presenting mature work, inclusion of reviewed short papers reporting on work in progress is welcome, too. Besides globally relevant meetings with internationally representative program committees guaranteeing a strict peer-reviewing and paper selection process, conferences run by societies or of high regional or national relevance are also considered for publication.

Topics

The topical scope of CCIS spans the entire spectrum of informatics ranging from foundational topics in the theory of computing to information and communications science and technology and a broad variety of interdisciplinary application fields.

Information for Volume Editors and Authors

Publication in CCIS is free of charge. No royalties are paid, however, we offer registered conference participants temporary free access to the online version of the conference proceedings on SpringerLink (http://link.springer.com) by means of an http referrer from the conference website and/or a number of complimentary printed copies, as specified in the official acceptance email of the event.

CCIS proceedings can be published in time for distribution at conferences or as postproceedings, and delivered in the form of printed books and/or electronically as USBs and/or e-content licenses for accessing proceedings at SpringerLink. Furthermore, CCIS proceedings are included in the CCIS electronic book series hosted in the SpringerLink digital library at http://link.springer.com/bookseries/7899. Conferences publishing in CCIS are allowed to use our online conference service (Meteor) for managing the whole proceedings lifecycle (from submission and reviewing to preparing for publication) free of charge.

Publication process

The language of publication is exclusively English. Authors publishing in CCIS have to sign the Springer CCIS copyright transfer form, however, they are free to use their material published in CCIS for substantially changed, more elaborate subsequent publications elsewhere. For the preparation of the camera-ready papers/files, authors have to strictly adhere to the Springer CCIS Authors' Instructions and are strongly encouraged to use the CCIS LaTeX style files or templates.

Abstracting/Indexing

CCIS is abstracted/indexed in DBLP, Google Scholar, EI-Compendex, Mathematical Reviews, SCImago, Scopus. CCIS volumes are also submitted for the inclusion in ISI Proceedings.

How to start

To start the evaluation of your proposal for inclusion in the CCIS series, please send an e-mail to ccis@springer.com

Fernando Ortiz-Rodríguez · Pramod Patil ·
Shubhangi Suryawanshi · Kailash Shaw ·
Shishir Shandilya

Editors

Business Intelligence, Computational Mathematics, and Data Analytics

Second International Conference, IBCD 2025
Pune, India, September 26–27, 2025
Proceedings

 Springer

Editors
Fernando Ortiz-Rodríguez
Universidad Autónoma de Tamaulipas
Ciudad Victoria, Tamaulipas, Mexico

Pramod Patil
Dr. D. Y. Patil Institute of Technology
Pune, Maharashtra, India

Shubhangi Suryawanshi
Dr. D. Y. Patil Institute of Technology
Pune, Maharashtra, India

Kailash Shaw
Vishwakarma Institute of Technology
Pune, Maharashtra, India

Shishir Shandilya
Devi Ahilya Vishwavidyalaya
Indore, Madhya Pradesh, India

ISSN 1865-0929   ISSN 1865-0937 (electronic)
Communications in Computer and Information Science
ISBN 978-3-032-20906-1   ISBN 978-3-032-20907-8 (eBook)
https://doi.org/10.1007/978-3-032-20907-8

This Springer imprint is published by the registered company Springer Nature Switzerland AG
The registered company address is: Gewerbestrasse 11, 6330 Cham, Switzerland

If disposing of this product, please recycle the paper.

Preface

The Second International Conference on Business Intelligence, Computational Mathematics, and Data Analytics (IBCD 2025), emphasized the role of advanced technologies in shaping the future of business, industries, and society. It highlighted the power of business intelligence, computational mathematics, and data analytics in driving innovation, optimizing processes, and creating impactful solutions. The conference aimed to provide a platform for researchers, academics, and professionals to share and discuss the latest advancements and innovations in the fields of business intelligence, computational mathematics, and data analytics.

The main scientific program of IBCD 2025 comprised 38 research papers, carefully selected from 343 reviewed submissions, resulting in a competitive acceptance rate of 11.07%.

The General and Program Committee Chairs extend their sincere appreciation to all individuals who contributed to the success of IBCD 2025. Our special thanks go to the session chairs and reviewers for their diligent efforts in maintaining a rigorous review process, which included three double-blind reviews per paper, ensure the selection of high-quality research contributions and the development of an excellent scientific program.

We also express our gratitude to the Springer team for their invaluable support in publishing and organizing this edition of the conference. Finally, the editors wish to acknowledge the distinguished keynote speakers, the enthusiastic authors whose contributions made the event truly international, and the local students and Organizing Committee members for their dedication in making IBCD 2025 a memorable and successful event.

October 2025

Fernando Ortiz-Rodríguez
Pramod Patil
Shubhangi Suryawanshi
Kailash Shaw
Shishir Shandilya

Organization

General Chairs

Fernando Ortiz-Rodríguez	Universidad Autónoma de Tamaulipas, Mexico
Pramod Patil	Dr. D. Y. Patil Institute of Technology, India
Shubhangi Suryawanshi	Dr. D. Y. Patil Institute of Technology, India
Kailash Shaw	Vishwakarma Institute of Technology, India
Shishir Kumar Shandilya	Devi Ahilya Vishwavidyalaya, India

Program Committee Chairs

Fernando Ortiz-Rodríguez	Universidad Autónoma de Tamaulipas, Mexico
Pramod Patil	Dr. D. Y. Patil Institute of Technology, India
Shubhangi Suryawanshi	Dr. D. Y. Patil Institute of Technology, India

Steering Committee

Sonali Patil	Dr. D. Y. Patil Institute of Technology, India
Pallavi Thakare	Dr. D. Y. Patil Institute of Technology, India
Sarika Pabalkar	Dr. D. Y. Patil Institute of Technology, India
Maheshwari Diwate	Dr. D. Y. Patil Institute of Technology, India
Vina Lomte	Dr. D. Y. Patil Institute of Technology, India
Ujwala Salunkhe	Dr. D. Y. Patil Institute of Technology, India
Shital Gajbhiye	Dr. D. Y. Patil Institute of Technology, India
Subhash Nalawade	Dr. D. Y. Patil Institute of Technology, India
Jyoti Asabe	Dr. D. Y. Patil Institute of Technology, India
Prateek Malwe	Dr. D. Y. Patil Institute of Technology, India

Program Committee

Pankaj Kolhe	Kolhe Kognitech, Germany
Parag Kulkarni	Tokyo International University, Japan
P. M. Mohite	Indian Institute of Technology Kanpur, India
Abhiram Ranade	Indian Institute of Technology Bombay, India
Manesh Kokare	Shri Guru Gobind Singhji, India

Dhananjay Kulkarni	BITS Pilani, India
Hitesh Vasudev	Lovely Professional University, India
Bharat M. Deshpande	BITS Pilani, India
Suresh Gosavi	Savitribai Phule Pune University, India
Aditya Abhyankar	Savitribai Phule Pune University, India
P. K. Sinha	International Institute of IT Kharagpur, India

Additional Reviewers

Abhaar Gupta	Anchorage Digital, USA
Abhishek Sharma	LNM Institute of Information Technology, India
Amol Bhosle	MIT ADT University, India
Amreen Khan	MIT ADT University, India
Anamika Wasnik	Amity University, India
Anil Lokesh Gadi	Cognizant, USA
Anupam Bonkra	Chandigarh Engineering College, CGC, India
Apurva Kandelkar	Lovely Professional University, India
Archaana Randive	AISSMS College of Engineering, India
Arpit Garg	CGI Inc., USA
Ashwini Gavali	S. B. Patil College of Engineering, India
Chetana Shravage	Dr. D. Y. Patil Institute of Technology, India
Dattatray Kale	MIT ADT University, India
Deeksha Mishra	Meta Inc., USA
Deepak Panwar	Manipal University, India
Deepti Vadicherla	G. H. Raisoni University, India
Dikshendra Sarpate	Zeal College of Engineering and Research, India
Disha Sengupta	Dr. D. Y. Patil Institute of Technology, India
Madhavi Nimkar	MIT Academy of Engineering, India
Seema Patil	Ashokrao Mane Group of Institutions, India
Kanhaiya Sharma	Symbiosis Institute of Technology, Pune, India
Swati Bhonde	Amrutvahini College of Engineering, India
Pramod Dhamdhere	Marathwada Mitra Mandal's Institute of Technology, India
Rohini Patil	Terna Engineering College, India
Suvarna Joshi	MIT ADT University, India
Suvarna Pawar	MIT ADT University, India
Ganesh Jadhav	Vishwakarma Institute of Technology, India
Gayatri Mirajkar	Arvind Gavali College of Engineering, India
Girish Kotte	QliqSOFT, Inc., India
Gunjan Paliwal	Meta Inc., India
Hemangi Patil	Dr. D. Y. Patil Institute of Technology, India

Ifrah Sutar	Dr. D. Y. Patil Institute of Technology, India
Jagannath Nalavade	MIT ADT University, India
Jagjot Bhardwaj	United Health Group, USA
Jaya Mathur	Dr. D. Y. Patil Institute of Technology, India
Jyoti Asabe	Dr. D. Y. Patil Institute of Technology, India
Jyotsna Barpute	Dr. D. Y. Patil Institute of Technology, India
Leela Krishna Potluri	Enliven Technologies Inc., USA
Lingaraj Hadimani	KIT's College of Engineering, India
Maheshwari Divate	Dr. D. Y. Patil Institute of Technology, India
Mandeep Singh Devgan	Chitkara University, India
Mangesh Salunke	Marathwada Mitra Mandal's Institute of Technology, India
Manik Patil	Birla Institute, India
Manisha Mane	Dr. D. Y. Patil Institute of Technology, India
Manoj Wakchaure	Amrutvahini College of Engineering, India
Mayuri Kulkarni	SVMK's Institute of Technology, India
Meghjeet Vartak	TransUnion, USA
Minal Zope	Kalinga University, India
Minal Jungare	Indira college, India
Mohit Mittal	NASCO, USA
Monali Bachhav	Dr. D. Y. Patil Institute of Technology, India
Mrudul Arkadi	SVKM DJ Sanghvi, India
Naveen Chatlapalli	Ashling Partners, USA
Neetika Gupta	MMEC MM University, India
Neha Patil	AISSMS College of Engineering, India
Nilesh Ghavate	Dwarkadas Jivanlal Sanghvi, India
Nishant Pachpor	G. H. Raisoni University, India
Nitin More	MIT Art, Design and Technology University, India
Nitin Shivale	Nirwan University, India
Nutan Deshmukh	Cummins College of Engineering for Women, India
Pallavi Thakare	Dr. D. Y. Patil Institute of Technology, India
Pardeep Singh	CGC, India
Pooja Baravkar	Dr. D. Y. Patil Institute of Technology, India
Prachi Karale	Dr. D. Y. Patil Institute of Technology, India
Praful Sambhare	Dr. D. Y. Patil Institute of Technology, India
Prajwal Gaikwad	Kalinga University, India
Praneetha Kotla	ERP Smartlabs, USA
Pranjali Bahalkar	Dr. D. Y. Patil Institute of Technology, India
Preeti Gupta	Narsee Monjee Institute of Management Studies, India

Priya Metri	Dr. D. Y. Patil Institute of Technology, India
Priyanka Pawar	Dr. D. Y. Patil Institute of Technology, India
Rajani Sajjan	MIT ADT University, India
Rajesh Gadipuuri	Meta Inc., USA
Rajkumar Modake	Bank of New York, USA
Ram Joshi	The Climate Corporation, USA
Rashmi Badave	Dr. D. Y. Patil Institute of Technology, India
Ravindra Apare	Trinity College India
Reena Sahane	Dr. D. Y. Patil Institute of Technology India
Reva Patil	Rajarambapu Institute of Technology, India
Rutumaben Shah	JPMorgan, USA
Sachin Kolekar	Sandip University, India
Sai Krishna Reddy Reddy	JPMorgan, USA
Salim Shaikh	Anjuman-I-Islam's Kalsekar Technical Campus, India
Sana Zia Hassan	New York University, USA
Sandeep Sharma	Uttaranchal University, India
Sanjay Patil	AGTI's Dr. Daulatrao Aher College of Engineering, India
Sanjeevkumar Angadi	Nutan Maharashtra Institute of Engineering and Technology, India
Santosh Chobe	Pimpri Chinchwad College of Engineering & Research, India
Santosh Todkar	Shivaji University, India
Sarika Pabalkar	Dr. D. Y. Patil Institute of Technology, India
Sarita Kalokhe	Dr. D. Y. Patil Institute of Technology, India
Shailesh Sangle	Thakur College, India
Sharad Adsure	Dr. D. Y. Patil Institute of Technology, India
Shatakshi Kokate	G. H. Raisoni University, India
Shital Gajbhiye	Dr. D. Y. Patil Institute, India
Shivaprasad Sankesha	SAIPTIST INC, India
Shrinivas Sonkar	Amrutvahini College, India
Shubhangi Solanki	Sinhgad Institute, India
Shubhangi Vairagar	Dr. D. Y. Patil Institute of Technology, India
Shweta Sharma	Manipal University, India
Smita R.	Fr. Conceição Rodrigues Institute of Technology, India
Sonali Gavali	Dr. D. Y. Patil Institute of Technology, India
Sonali Sawardekar	Dr. D. Y. Patil Institute of Technology, India
Sonali Patil	Dr. D. Y. Patil Institute of Technology, India
Sonam Singh	Dr. D. Y. Patil Institute of Technology, India
Sravan Chittimalla	Enliven Technologies Inc, USA

Srinivasa Reddy Vuyyuru	L.L. Bean, USA
Subhash Rathod	Marathwada Mitra Mandal's Institute of Technology, India
Sukriti Mittal	Amazon, USA
Sunita Patil	Dr. D. Y. Patil Institute of Technology, India
Supriya Bhosale	Nutan Maharashtra Institute of Engineering and Technology, India
Suraj Sawant	College of Engineering, Pune, India
Surbhi Pagar	Dr. D. Y. Patil Institute of Technology, India
Sushma Vispute	Poornima University, India
Suvarna Bahir	Trinity Academy of Engineering, India
Swapnil Pawar	K. J. Somaiya College of Engineering, India
Tanmaykumar Shah	JPMorgan, USA
Tejendra Patel	Snapchat, USA
Trupti Farande	Shree Ramchandra College of Engineering, India
Ujwala Salunke	Dr. D. Y. Patil Institute of Technology, India
Umesh Ghorpade	Dnyanshree Institute of Engineering and Technology, India
Vaibhav Suryawanshi	Nutan Maharashtra Institute of Engineering and Technology, India
Vaidehi Sharma	Dr. D. Y. Patil Institute of Technology, India
Vanita Kshirsagar	Dr. D. Y. Patil Institute of Technology, India
Venkat Mounish Gundla	Verana Health, USA
Venubabu Paruchuri	FIS Management Services LLC, USA
Vidhya Gavali	Dr. D. Y. Patil Institute of Technology, India
Vina Lomte	Dr. D. Y. Patil Institute of Technology, India
Vineet Jain	Genpact, USA
Vivek Ware	Symbiosis University, India
Yugal Jindle	Meta Inc., USA

Contents

Robust Swin Transformer and ArcFace Framework for Closed and Open Set Ox Face Recognition in Precision Livestock Management

D. Swaroop$^{(\boxtimes)}$, D. S. Guru , D. Nandini , and K. Samruddh

Department of Studies in Computer Science, Manasagangotri, University of Mysore, Mysore 570006, Karnataka, India
swaroopdevaraju@gmail.com, dsg@compsci.uni-mysore.ac.in

Abstract. This study proposes a robust ox face recognition system based on the Swin Transformer (Tiny) architecture combined with ArcFace loss to generate highly discriminative 512-dimensional embeddings. As a contribution a custom dataset of 427 oxen with 3,843 training and 2,562 validation images is created and augmented to reflect real-world scenarios. The proposed model achieved 98.44% closed-set recognition accuracy which out performs ViT-Small and ResNet-50, with precision and ROC-AUC of 98.57% and 99.79%, respectively. Additionally, this study also supports both closed-set identification and open-set verification using cosine similarity thresholds, addressing the challenges related to scalability, dataset scarcity, and cross-pose variation thus offering a practical solution for automated ox identification and secure livestock management.

Keywords: Swin Transformer · Ox face recognition · ArcFace Loss · closed-set recognition · open-set verification · livestock identification · animal biometrics · deep learning · cosine similarity

1 Introduction

Artificial Intelligence has now converted oxen identification by providing accurate, non-invasive alternatives to traditional tagging plus branding methods that are often error-prone and stressful. Despite the benefits for theft prevention, livestock tracking and health monitoring challenges like facial difference, limited datasets and occlusion, persist. Early methods like RFID, tattoos evolved into biometric approaches via muzzle pattern recognition, achieving 89.2% accuracy [1]. Classical ML [3] models like LBP-SVM increased robustness by 92.5% but remained alignment-dependent. [4] has utilized deep learning advanced the field CattleFaceNet combined RetinaFace-MobileNet and ArcFace with 91.3%, while [6] has used hybrid CNNs and SSD with FaceNet exceeded 94%. Transfer learning and multimodal fusion (Face, Muzzle, Ear Tag) further enhanced accuracy up to 95.74%. [5] utilized Transformer-based systems like ViT-Sheep and [7] has worked with Bi-Level Routing ViT has achieved over 98%, with MobileViTFace (97.13%) offering real-time performance, and DETR with Swin Transformer reaching 88.03%

F. Ortiz-Rodríguez et al. (Eds.): IBCD 2025, CCIS 2845, pp. 1–12, 2026.
https://doi.org/10.1007/978-3-032-20907-8_1

[2]. However, cross-breed variability, data scarcity, and environmental sensitivity still limit deployment. Recent advances include a Parallel Attention Network for improved accuracy [8], an attention-based framework for multi-breed recognition under complex conditions [10], and a two-stage model integrating detection and recognition networks for robust identification [9]. To address this, we propose a Swin Transformer (Tiny) + ArcFace model, which combines hierarchical attention for robust feature extraction with angular margin loss for fine-grained oxen face discrimination.

The major contributions of this study are summarized as follows:

- A Novel Large-Scale Ox Face Dataset is created which is comprises 427 oxen with 3,843 training and 2,562 validation images captured under real-world farm conditions.
- The Proposed study adopted a Swin Transformer (Tiny) with ArcFace loss ($s = 49.452$, $m = 0.6859$) to generate 512- feature Dimension embeddings for precise ox identification.
- The proposed study out performs ViT-Small and ResNet-50 baselines by Achieving 98.44% accuracy, 98.57% precision, and 99.79% ROC-AUC.
- To improve the resilience to environmental variations and pose robust Data Augmentation is applied via cropping, flipping, rotation, color jitter, and affine transforms.
- This study provides the flexibility by Closed- and Open-Set verification using cosine-similarity thresholds for practical farm deployment.
- The proposed model is employed via AdamW optimizer, cosine annealing, early stopping, and dropout (0.1) as efficient training methods to enhance generalization and scalability.

2   Materials and Methods

2.1   Dataset Collection and Experimentation Setup

Creating a novel dataset of Ox with 6,405 facial images from 427 oxen, each contributing 15 curated images captured under real-world farm conditions to address the absence of standard datasets for ox identification. The dataset is split 60:40 ratio where 3,843 images for training and 2,562 images for validation. Data were collected from 500 oxen across farms in Chamarajanagar, Mandya, and Mysore districts.

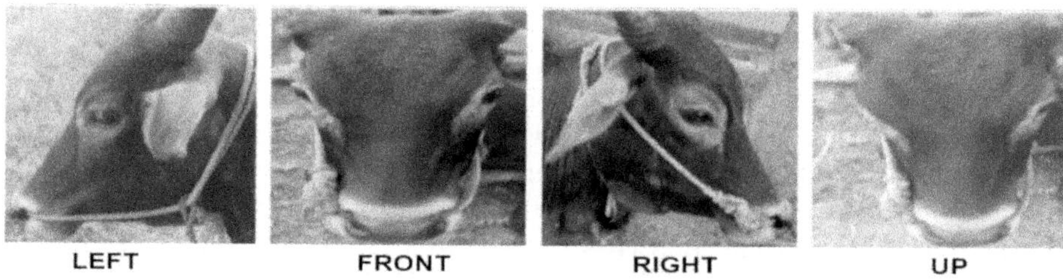

Fig. 1. Illustration of oxen face images which are captured from multiple views.

which covers four facial angles (front, left, right, upward) to ensure pose diversity as in Fig. 1. Images were taken from different device using 13–48 MP Android smartphones

(OPPO A5, REDMI 9A, Samsung M21, Vivo S), representing practical, low-cost field conditions. This design ensures variability in lighting, angle, and quality, supporting both closed-set classification and open-set verification tasks.

2.2 Video-Based Frame Extraction

The proposed created the dataset of 427 oxen from 500, which comprises 4 static images (left, right, up, front) and 11 high-quality video frames per subject, and selected from 20 initial frames after removing duplicates plus low-quality samples. Images were captured using Android smartphones (13–48 MP) under varied conditions. With a 60:40 split, the dataset includes 3,843 images for training and 2,562 images for validation covering diverse angles, lighting, and poses, supporting robust closed-set and open-set ox face recognition for scalable livestock tracking, theft prevention, and health monitoring in resource-limited farms.

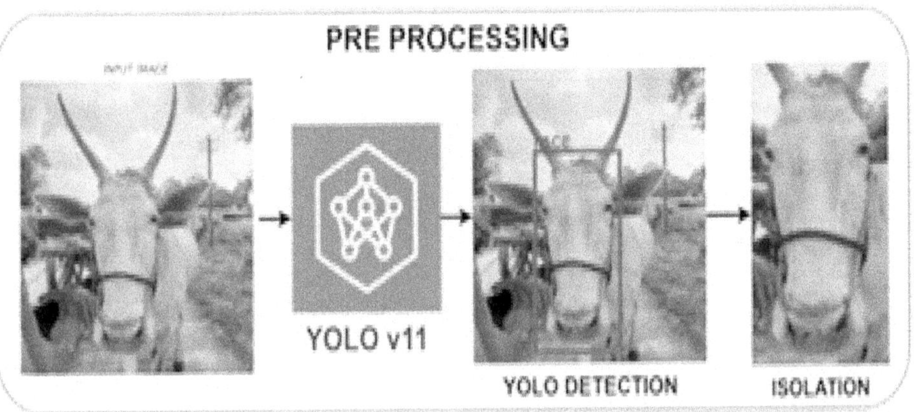

Fig. 2. YOLOv11 Segmentation Outputs – Original, Masked, and Segmented Regions.

2.3 Pre-processing

A streamlined preprocessing pipeline is standardized for ox face images for recognition. Tailored YOLOv11 model is trained on 1,600 annotated images where 1,280 images for training and 320 images for validation via 150 epochs, accurately detected facial regions across varied poses, lighting, and 13–48 MP resolutions. The Detected faces are cropped and resized to 224×224 to input for Swin Transformer-Tiny model. Augmentations via random cropping, flipping, $\pm 15°$ rotation, color jitter, and affine transforms to enhance generalization, while validation images are resized and normalized. The proposed YOLO-based preprocessing reduced background noise, emphasized key facial cues (muzzle texture, ear shape), and contributed to 98.44% recognition accuracy in closed- and open-set livestock identification. Where the segmentation flow is shown in Fig. 2.

2.4   Proposed Methodology

The proposed study utilized Swin-Tiny Transformer model via ArcFace loss for ox identification, integrating customized preprocessing, feature extraction, classification, and a tailored training setup to enhance discriminative learning is illustrated in Fig. 3.

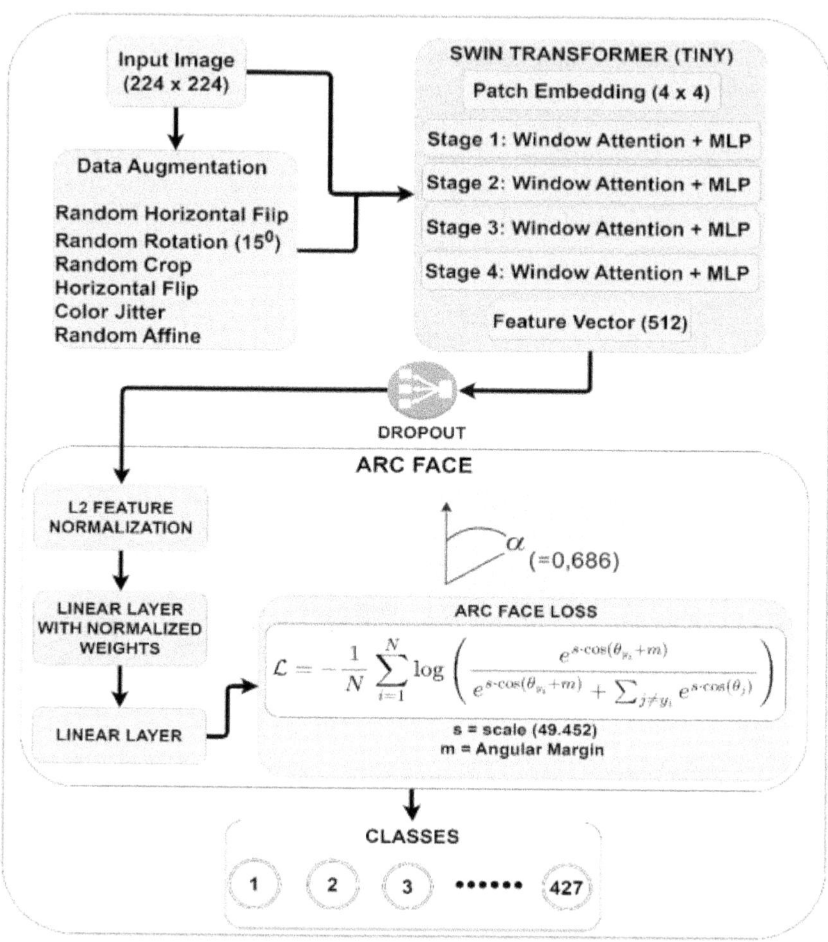

$$\mathcal{L} = -\frac{1}{N}\sum_{i=1}^{N}\log\left(\frac{e^{s\cdot\cos(\theta_{y_i}+m)}}{e^{s\cdot\cos(\theta_{y_i}+m)}+\sum_{j\neq y_i}e^{s\cdot\cos(\theta_j)}}\right)$$

Fig. 3. Simple Generalized Architecture of Proposed Model.

2.5   Input Image Preparation and Data Augmentation

Initially all the input images are pre-processed to a fixed resolution of $224 \times 224 \times 3$ pixels to standardize the facial region and aligning with the model's requirements. And these images are derived from tailored YOLO-based face detection and then cropping, ensures a focused view of ox facial features while minimizing background noise.

To enhance the proposed model robustness and generalization, variety of data augmentation techniques are integrated during the time of training, via including random cropping, horizontal flipping, rotation ($\pm 15°$), color jitter, and affine transformations as depicted in Fig. 4. These methods simulate the orientational, spatial, lighting, and geometric difference for enabling the model to effectively handle the diverse real-world conditions such as varying poses and image quality.

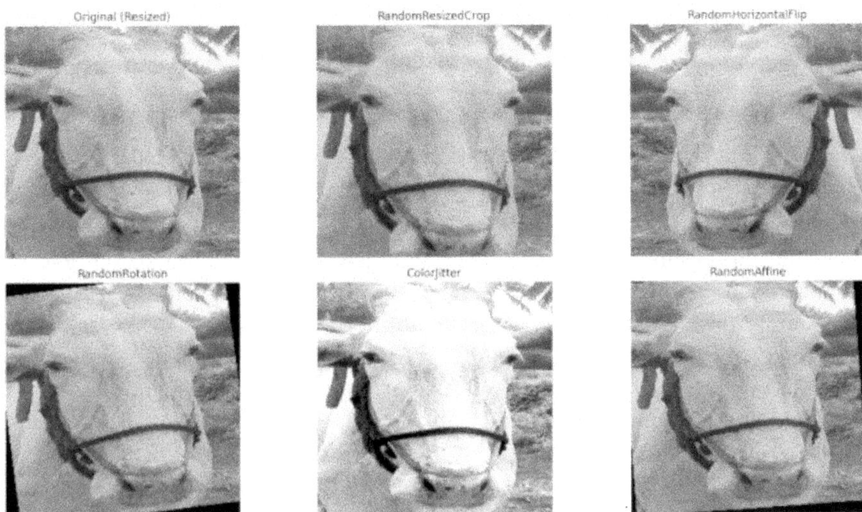

Fig. 4. Presents the images after data augmentation process.

Feature Extraction

After pre-processing step, the Swin Transformer-Tiny (swin_tiny_patch4_window7_224) are utilized to extracts a 512-Dimention feature vector for ox identification efficiently. Initially, at the Stage 1 produces $56 \times 56 \times 96$ size features vector via two blocks with W-MSA and SW-MSA (7×7 windows) to capture the local textures and broader facial relations. Then in Stage 2 the patches are merged to $28 \times 28 \times 192$ feature dimensions, for abstracting mid-level semantics while preserving local detail. After this stage the stage 3 downsamples to $14 \times 14 \times 384$ features with six blocks for compact representations of subtle inter-class variations. Finally at Stage 4 downsamples it to $7 \times 7 \times 768$ feature dimensions, to aggregates global cues, and then this applies global average pooling to a 768-D vector and which are then projected to 512-Dimentions for classification the whole process proposed of feature extraction is showed at Fig. 5.

Classification Head: ArcFace Module

The proposed method utilized an ArcFace-based loss function for the classification head to convert 512-D features into discriminative predictions across 427 ox identities, which enhances the angular separability.

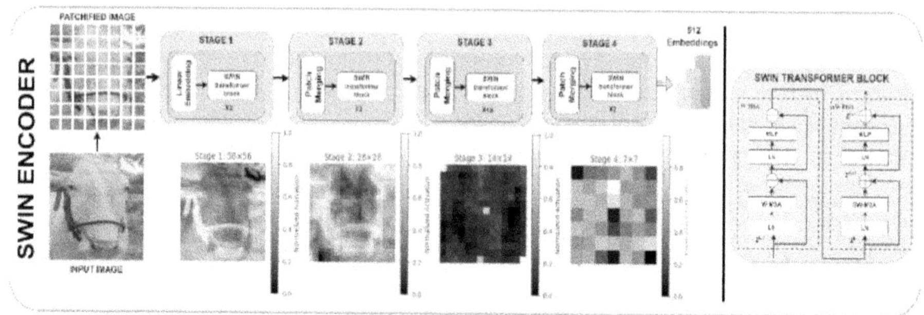

Fig. 5. Feature extraction process using Swin Transformer Model.

A dropout layer (0.1) is given to improves robustness by randomly deactivating neurons during the time of training. Then the features are L2-normalized onto a unit hypersphere, and a linear layer with normalized weights maps them to class space via cosine similarity. The ArcFace loss via scale factor = 49.452, and angular margin = 0.686 are given to optimized via Optuna. Which intern introduces an angular penalty $(\cos(\theta y + m))$ to tightening the intra-class clusters and enlarging inter-class gaps, for ensuring reliable identification under illumination, pose, and occlusion difference while boosting accuracy.

Training Configuration

To ensure the robust convergence and high accuracy of the proposed model, the Swin Transformer–ArcFace framework utilized a carefully designed training methodology via advanced optimization and regularization. The network is trained under AdamW with LR = 1e−4, weight decay = 1e−2 inputs. And then a CosineAnnealingLR scheduler are used to adjust learning rates for efficient convergence. As a Early stopping halts the training, if the validation plateaus for five epochs are used for enhancing generalization. This strategy, are combined via hierarchical feature extraction with discriminative margin learning, for the accuracy of 98.44% at closed-set, effectively distinguishing 427 ox identities despite intra-class and environmental variations.

3   Results and Discussion

This section evaluates the proposed ox face recognition framework (Fig. 6), including YOLOv11-based face detection, closed-set identification, open-set verification, and comparative analysis. The model was trained on 427 oxen (15 images each; 3,843 training, 2,562 validation). Data augmentation (flipping, rotation, affine, color jitter) was applied to training images, while validation images were resized to 224 × 224 and normalized.

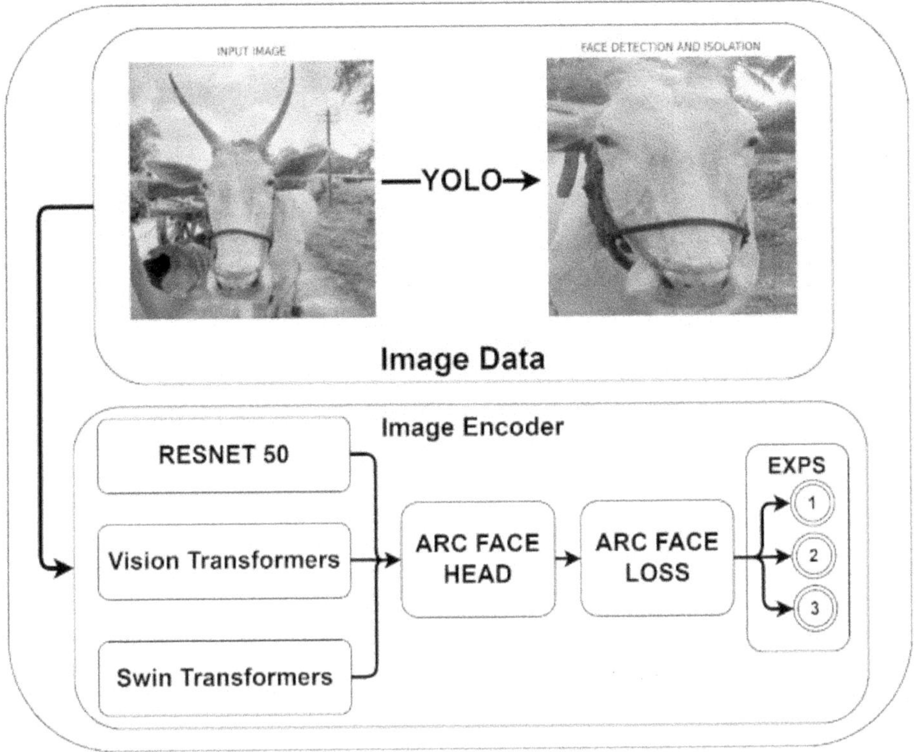

Fig. 6. Illustration of the experimental workflow.

3.1 Oxen Face Detection and Segmentation with YOLOv11 Performance Analysis

A YOLOv11 model, trained on 1,600 labeled ox face images (1,280 training, 320 validation), achieved robust detection across diverse poses, lighting, and occlusions, accurately localizing facial landmarks in 13–48 MP images. The mAP@50 improved from 0.68 to 0.76–0.78 by epoch 50, with a confusion matrix confirming precise localization. Dataset analysis showed consistent single-class ("face") annotations, with bounding boxes tightly centered and moderately varied in size, ensuring balanced and effective detection.

3.2 Recognition Performance

The ox face recognition model, trained with ArcFace loss to generate 512-D embeddings, was evaluated in closed- and open-set settings for livestock management tasks. Closed-set recognition classifies images among 427 known identities, while open-set verification uses cosine similarity (0.8–0.9 threshold) to determine matches, including unseen animals, ensuring robust real-world performance. Figure 7 shows the evaluation flow.

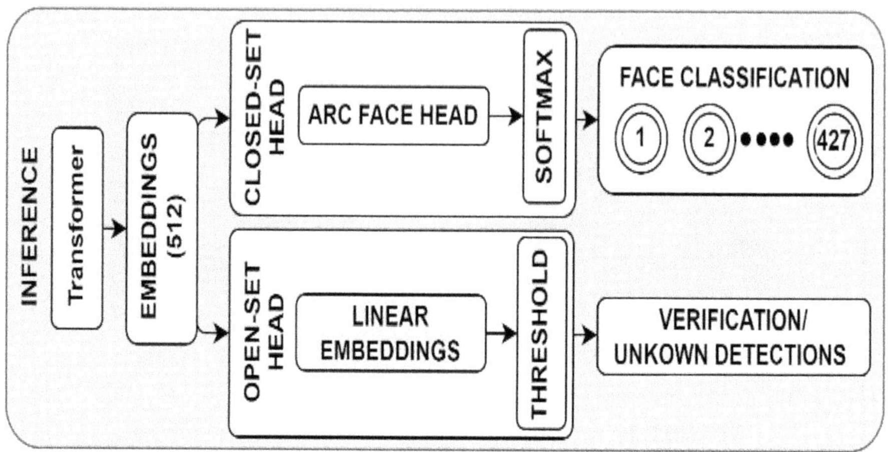

Fig. 7. Shows the illustration of open set and close-set evaluation.

Closed-Set Classification

The Swin-Tiny + ArcFace model (Fig. 8) achieved peak closed-set recognition at epoch 33 with 98.44% accuracy, 98.57% precision, and 99.79% ROC-AUC (Table 1), indicating near-perfect identification. Comparisons with ViT-Small and ResNet-50 confirmed Swin-Tiny's superiority, due to its hierarchical feature extraction and shifted-window design, effectively capturing local and global facial patterns.

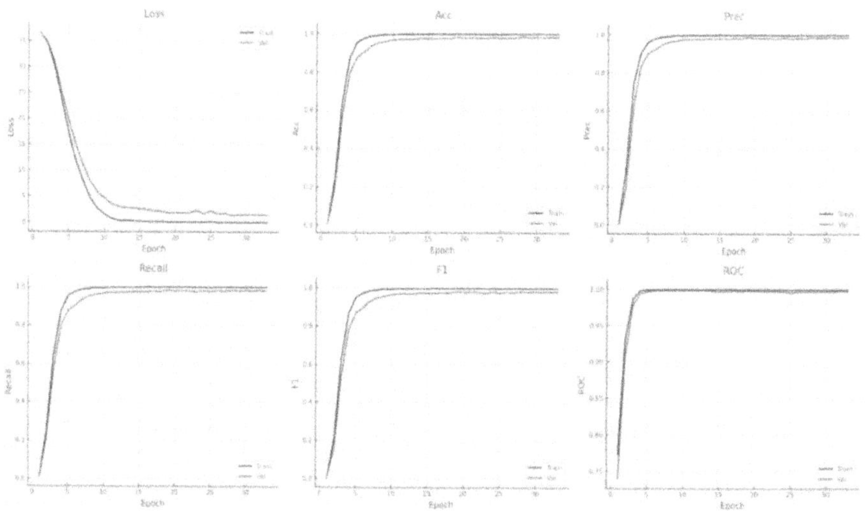

Fig. 8. Training and validation performance metrics of the proposed model, showing trends in loss, accuracy, precision, recall, F1-score, and the ROC curve.

Table 1. Comparison of Model Performance on Ox Face Dataset.

Model	Accuracy (%)	F1(%)	ROC-AUC (%)
ResNet-50	96.31	96.22	99.91
ViT-Small	98.29	98.25	99.86
Swin-Tiny (Proposed)	98.44	98.40	99.78

Open-Set Verification

The model was also tested in open-set verification to simulate real-world ox identification, including unseen individuals. Using ArcFace loss, it effectively clusters same-identity images and separates different ones key for tasks like theft prevention and ownership verification.

Verification Procedure

For open-set verification, 3122 ox face images formed 1600 genuine and 1522 impostor pairs. ResNet-50, ViT-Small, and Swin-Tiny models are evaluated using cosine similarity across different thresholds from 0.10 to 0.90. And all these models achieved zero false acceptance rate (FAR) which indicates the strong impostor rejection. And the Table 2 show performance metrics of the proposed model across different thresholds.

Table 2. Open-Set Verification Performance Across Thresholds.

Threshold	Swin-Tiny Acc	Swin-Tiny FRR	Swin-Tiny TPR	ViT-Small Acc	ViT-Small FRR	ViT-Small TPR	ResNet-50 Acc	ResNet-50 FRR	ResNet-50 TPR
0.10	0.9958	0.0051	0.9949	0.9963	0.0039	0.9961	0.9982	0.0019	0.9981
0.20	0.9939	0.0074	0.9926	0.9919	0.0086	0.9914	0.9908	0.0097	0.9903
0.30	0.9914	0.0105	0.9895	0.9893	0.0113	0.9887	0.9786	0.0226	0.9774
0.40	0.9878	0.0148	0.9852	0.9864	0.0144	0.9856	0.9568	0.0455	0.9545
0.50	0.9837	0.0199	0.9801	0.9812	0.0198	0.9802	0.9284	0.0754	0.9246
0.60	0.9773	0.0277	0.9723	0.9745	0.0268	0.9732	0.8809	0.1256	0.8744
0.70	0.9696	0.0371	0.9629	0.9657	0.0362	0.9638	0.8086	0.2018	0.7982
0.80	0.9596	0.0492	0.9508	0.9517	0.0509	0.9491	0.6894	0.3274	0.6726
0.90	0.9279	0.0878	0.9122	0.9137	0.0910	0.9090	0.4607	0.5684	0.4316

Performance Across Thresholds

The proposed model achieved an zero FAR and FPR across all different thresholds as showed in Fig. 9, which showcases the ArcFace loss's effectiveness in producing distinct embeddings in crucial for open-set verification. As thresholds increased, accuracy and TPR decreased while FRR rose, due to stricter acceptance. At low thresholds (0.10–0.30), all models performed excellently with >97% accuracy and <2.3% FRR; ResNet-50 slightly led at 0.10 with 99.82% accuracy. At moderate thresholds (0.40–0.60), Swin-Tiny and ViT-Small maintained >97% accuracy, while ResNet-50 dropped to 88.09% at 0.60. At higher thresholds (0.70–0.90), Swin-Tiny and ViT-Small still performed well (~92% at 0.90), but ResNet-50 fell sharply to 46.07% accuracy and 56.84% FRR.

Model Comparison and Implications

The Swin-Tiny ArcFace model achieved a 98.44% accuracy on 427 ox identities, surpassing models like Bi-Level ViT (98.36% on 200 cattle) and others such as PANet and Cattle-FaceNet (<92% accuracy), due to its hierarchical attention capturing both local and global features, outperforming ViT-Small's global self-attention and ResNet-50's local feature reliance, especially at stricter thresholds (Fig. 10). While ResNet-50 suffices at low thresholds (0.10–0.30) for minimal false rejections, Swin-Tiny excels in high-accuracy, low-FRR scenarios with no false accepts, making it ideal for secure, field-ready ox identification in large-scale livestock management.

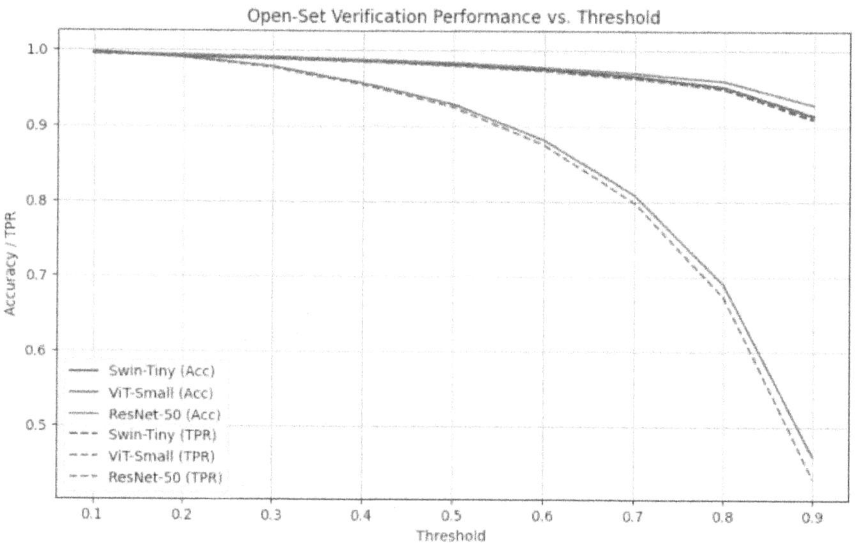

Fig. 9. Visualizes the accuracy and TPR as a function of the threshold for each model.

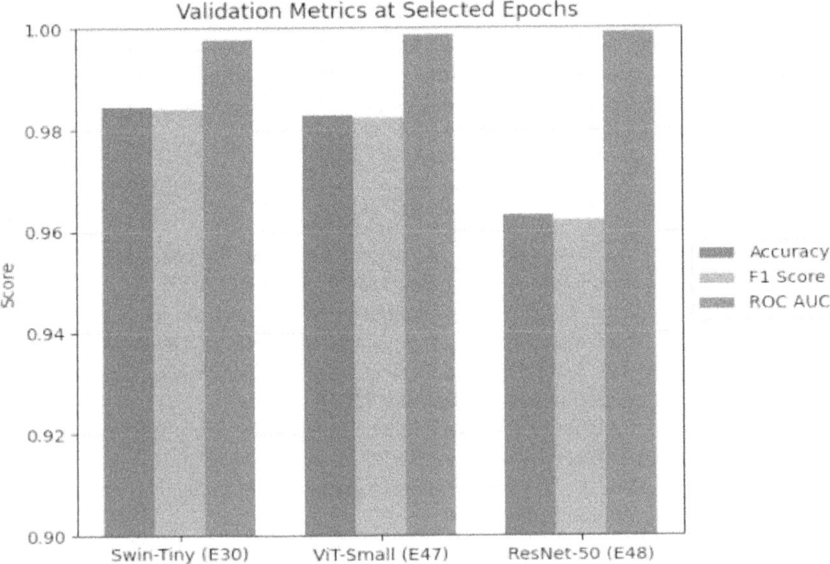

Fig. 10. Graphical comparison of the performance between the proposed model and other models.

3.3 Overall Analysis and Implications

The transition from ResNet-50 to ViT-Small and Swin-Tiny highlights evolving requirements for fine-grained ox face recognition. ResNet-50 (96.31% accuracy) captured local features but missed subtle inter-class differences. ViT-Small improved accuracy (98.29%) and learning speed via global attention but lacked locality bias. The Swin-Tiny integrated via local and global attention achieves an accuracy of 98.44% in 33 epochs which balancing fine detail and contextual understanding.

This progression which highlights the value of hierarchical transformers in livestock identification, where in which both fine and holistic features matter. The proposed tailored YOLO-based model enhances the detector results via 0.78 mAP@0.5, the proposed system ensures the face localization accurately. As a final model, which integrats Swin Transformer with ArcFace loss, robustly handles, occlusion, pose variations and lighting inconsistencies under different farm conditions. Which intern supports both closed-set and open-set evaluations, applicable in scenarios like animal monitoring, theft prevention and welfare tracking, with potential integration into existing farm systems for scalable use in precision agriculture.

4 Conclusion

The successful attempt made in this study presents a robust ox face recognition framework, by achieving 98.44% of accuracy across 427 oxen using a Swin-Tiny Transformer and 0.78 mAP@0.5 is achieved with a tailored YOLO-11 based face detector. This integration of hierarchical vision transformers and precise detection proves effective for fine-grained livestock identification. Intern This approach shows strong potentiality for real-world applications like ownership and animal tracking verification. As a future work the proposed study will explore extending the system to other species, optimizing for mobile deployment, and enhancing robustness with 3D-aware recognition.

References

1. Barry, J., Kennedy, E., Jones, R.: Muzzle pattern matching for cattle identification using fingerprint-inspired techniques. J. Agric. Sci. **151**(5), 678–689 (2013)
2. Liu, Y., Zhang, H., Chen, L.: Cow face recognition in wild environments using DETR and Swin-Transformer. IEEE Trans. Pattern Anal. Mach. Intell. **46**(3), 1892–1905 (2024)
3. Rajankar, S.O., Mankar, V.H.: Cattle identification using local binary pattern and support vector machine. Int. J. Comput. Appl. **182**(39), 12–18 (2019)
4. Xu, B., et al.: CattleFaceNet: a cattle face identification approach based on RetinaFace and ArcFace loss. Comput. Electron. Agric. **193** (2022). Article 106675
5. Zhang, L., Wang, J., Liu, X.: ViT-Sheep: vision transformer for sheep face recognition. Anim. Sci. J. **94**(1) (2023). Article e13845
6. Zhou, Q., Xu, H., Li, J.: Multi-modal cattle identification using decision-level fusion of face, muzzle, and ear tag features. Comput. Electron. Agric. **208** (2024). Article 107789
7. Zhou, Q., Zhang, Y., Li, H.: Bi-level routing vision transformer for cattle face recognition. Pattern Recogn. **145**, Article 109876 (2024)
8. Li, J., Zou, X., Wang, S., Chen, B., Xing, J., Tao, P.: A parallel attention network for cattle face recognition. arXiv preprint arXiv:2403.19980 (2024)
9. Zheng, P., Deng, M., Gong, J., Li, G., Yin, Y.: A two-stage cattle face recognition method based on target detection and recognition network. Inf. Technol. Control **54**(2), 536–559 (2025)
10. Xiao, Z., Dai, W., Li, C., Liang, W., Chen, X.: Enhanced multi-breed cattle face recognition in complex environments using attention-based deep learning. Vis. Comput. 1–20 (2025)

Improvement of Human Health Lifespan with Hybrid Group Pose Estimation Methods

Arindam Chaudhuri[(✉)] [iD]

Samsung R & D Institute, Noida 201304, Delhi, India
`arindamphdthesis@gmail.com`

Abstract. Human beings rely heavily on estimation of poses in order to access their body movements. Human pose estimation methods take advantage of computer vision advances in order to track human body movements in real life applications. This comes from videos which are recorded through available devices. These paradigms provide potential to make human movement measurement more accessible to users. The consumers of pose estimation movements believe that human poses content tend to supplement available videos. This has increased pose estimation software usage to estimate human poses. In order to address this problem, we develop hybrid ensemble-based group pose estimation method to improve human health. This proposed hybrid ensemble-based group pose estimation method aims to detect multi-person poses using modified group pose estimation and modified real time pose estimation. This ensemble allows fusion of performance of stated methods in real time. The input poses from images are fed into individual methods. The pose transformation method helps to identify relevant features for ensemble to perform training effectively. After this, customized pre-trained hybrid ensemble is trained on public benchmarked datasets. This is followed by evaluation with test datasets. The effectiveness and viability of proposed method is established based on comparative analysis of group pose estimation methods and experiments conducted on benchmarked datasets. It provides best optimized results in real-time pose estimation. It makes pose estimation method more robust to occlusion and improves dense regression accuracy. These results have affirmed potential application of this method in several real-time situations with improvement in human health life span.

Keywords: Decision support · social media · pose estimation · accuracy · assessment · development · decision making · inductive research

1 Introduction

In current digital media age, huge data volumes are produced on social media platforms on daily basis. This media data is continuously created, viewed, modified and distributed through electronic devices which doubles almost every month. These massive data chunks are used by researchers regularly for analysis and decision making. The majority of this data comprises of images and videos [1]. However, there remains a

F. Ortiz-Rodríguez et al. (Eds.): IBCD 2025, CCIS 2845, pp. 13–24, 2026.
https://doi.org/10.1007/978-3-032-20907-8_2

challenge in understanding available objects in these data. This process of understanding objects in images and videos is known as pose estimation. It is an important activity in artificial intelligence and computer vision. It involves tracking position, detection and human body parts orientation in images and videos [2]. The accurate detection and tracking of human movements call for their quantitative measurements [3]. Some common examples include scrutiny by sports' judges and performance of figure skaters', measures by physical therapist to access patient's speed, inspections by running coaches etc. These movements are interpreted by humans in order to communicate and make emotional state inferences through body language reading [4].

Human pose estimation data can have either single person or multiple persons. The multiple persons pose estimation has attracted attention of researchers for decades. There has been wide spectrum of applications [5] in areas of augmented reality, human computer interaction and virtual reality. The most popular pose estimation applications [6] in past few years include human activity estimation, motion transfer, motion capture for training robots and motion tracking for consoles. Considering an image, prime objective is to localize 2D key point positions for every person in image. Several methods have been developed in this area [7–9]. Inspite of this it remains challenging and intractable problem for situations with heavy occlusions, hard poses and diverse body part scales. Human pose estimation has often been considered as method which helps in measurement of human movement kinematics. Pose estimation methods helps people to identify important landmarks in human body. These are recorded through devices as shown in Fig. 1. The pose estimation task needs to focus at local and global dependencies which work for human and key point levels respectively. These dependencies lead to normalization of body parts. Here concentration is attributed to semantic granularity.

Fig. 1. The movement kinematics measured with basic pose estimation workflow

Considering the success received from recent end-to-end object detection methods, there are related methods which regard human pose estimation as direct set prediction problem. The two stage methods or DETR [10] suffers because of slow convergence in training. In [11] off-the-shelf detector obtains bounding boxes where individual estimation of pose is performed for each person. In real world pose estimation methods can be used for purpose of entertainment [12].

This research concentrates to develop hybrid ensemble-based group pose estimation method to identify human poses with transformation involved. Here poses detection method is considered as regression problem. Based on motivation from [13] and [14], a novel hybrid ensemble-based group pose (HEGPosEs) [15] for end-to-end multi-person pose estimation is presented. This computational system consists of (a) modified group pose estimation (MGPosEs) and (b) modified real-time multi-person pose estimation (MRTMPPosEs). MGPosEs and MRTMPPosEs focus on estimating poses at individual levels. The outputs received from these methods are subjected to pose transformation which helps to identify relevant ensemble features such that training is effectively performed. Then pre-trained customized hybrid ensemble is trained on public benchmarked datasets. The ensemble performance is assessed on test datasets. HEGPosEs is an end-to-end real time method. In order to validate strength of this method two benchmarked datasets are used viz DensePose-COCO [16] and MPII Human Pose [15]. In this research feasibility is provided considering occlusion to improve dense regression accuracy alongwith optimization benefits. This results in more profitable, efficient and sustainable multi-person pose estimation with improvement in human health life span. We have structured this paper as follows. In Sect. 2, work done in pose estimation is presented. The different components of proposed methodology are highlighted in Sect. 3. In Sect. 4, proposed method is illustrated with contextual dataset. The experiments and analysis are discussed in Sect. 5. Finally, in Sect. 6 conclusion is given.

2 Related Work

In this section recent work related to pose estimation is discussed. There has been a constant increase in readily available softwares which have helped in pose estimation. This has raised questions on credibility of poses obtained [17]. The situation becomes more challenging because of human visual appearance and host of other factors. Pose estimation methods are categorized as top-down and bottom-up. Top-down methods have body detectors which help in determination of body joints with bounding boxes. Bottom-up methods perform evaluation of each body joint and compose poses which is having unique nature. The primary output of any pose estimation process consists of two-dimensional pixel coordinates. There are different methods from 2D pixel coordinates [13, 14, 16]. The 3D human movement kinematics are reconstructed from videos with many viewpoints [15]. During past decade, human pose estimation in multi-person situations has attracted high interest among researchers [4, 5, 16]. The two stage non-end-to-end methods include top down [11, 16] and bottom up methods [6]. The current end-to-end multi-person pose estimation methods are developed with [10] and its variants [18, 19]. QueryPose [20] and EDPose [21] are adapted to end-to-end method. Earlier pose estimation methods consider keypoint localization as coordinate regression [21] or heatmap regression [15]. Transformer architectures [22] have been successful in vision applications.

3 Designing Group Pose Estimation

In this section we give description of proposed pose estimation method. Figure 2 shows detailed HEGPosEs architecture. In order to detect robust poses, HEGPosEs [15] analyses different human body movements. It is an ensemble of MGPosEs and MRTMPPosEs. Both of these models are optimized for variety of poses. These model [4] variety of human body configurations. HEGPosEs has wide variety of applications in multi-person human pose estimation [15]. It does not estimate poses accurately with direct inputs and identify features well in isolation. In order to achieve better results from HEGPosEs, proper feature extraction is required. This is achieved with pose transformation method with PoseTrans [23] which is next discussed.

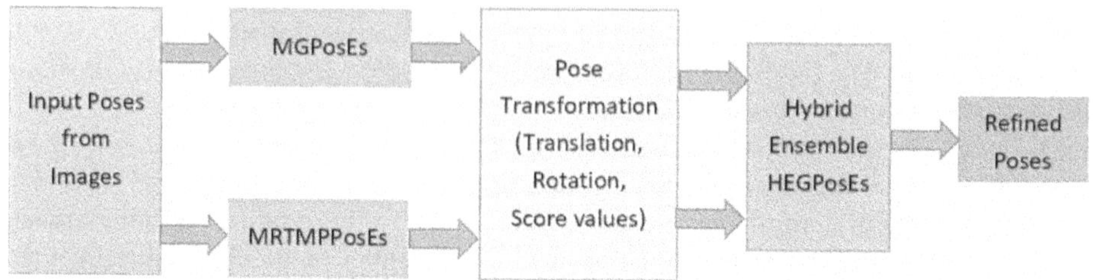

Fig. 2. HEGPosEs architecture to identify most efficient pose transformation method

3.1 Pose Transformation Method

Figure 3 shows PoseTrans from where new training samples are generated with diverse posesets. PoseTrans is used because best results are achieved for JPEG images. It consists of transformation alongwith discriminator and clustering modules. We consider (x, y) as training sample which has human image x and annotation y. Pose transformation creates new training sample $(x\prime, y\prime)$ where affine transformation is applied on human limbs. We filter out implausible samples with discriminator module in order to maintain plausibility. PoseTrans uses transformation module till plausible poses are developed. Clustering module clusters poses into different categories. It calculates probability of belongingness to each cluster for poses generated. The best is selected from this to be added as new training sample. Clustering module is refit after each training epoch.

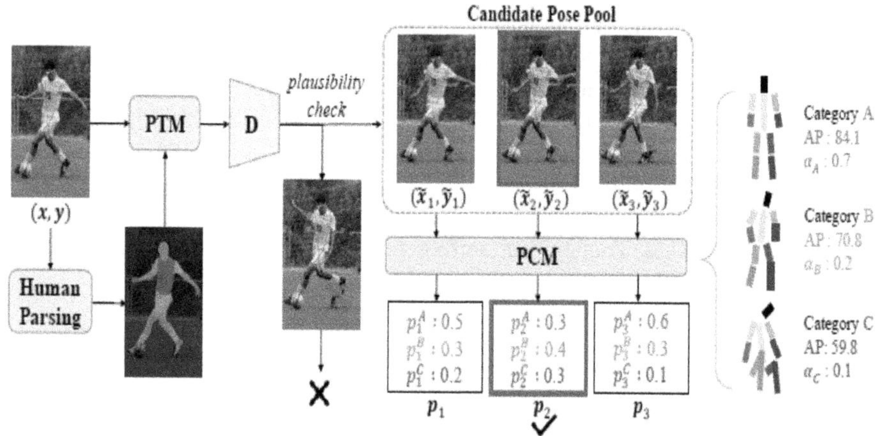

Fig. 3. PoseTrans generates new training samples with diverse posesets

If we generate poses randomly some implausible poses may crop in. This can also violate biomechanical structure present in human body. This is addressed with optimization functions such that meaningful poses appear. Clustering module measures rarity in poses and identifies poses to be used in data augmentation. It is built with components based gaussian mixture models. The poses are first normalized and kept in training set.

All human instances are normalized at same time. Clustering module is fitted with normalized human poses. The poses with maximum probability are mapped with gaussian components. With clustering module poses are clustered into different categories with gaussian components. Here weights are identified and assigned to each component so that best possible results are achieved. The outputs from MGPosEs and MRTMPPosEs are transformed and passed to HEGPosEs. The various steps are shown in Fig. 4. Here objective is to produce best transformation results. We divide transformed pose images into ratio of 80:20 to perform training and validation. With 50 epochs and batch size of 200 this model is trained and validated. Benchmarked datasets [16, 24] are used to increase model performance. The model's performance is also improved with transfer learning [15]. The transfer learning helps to identify weightage factor to each individual pose estimation component. In HEGPosEs, pre-trained models are used simultaneously for transfer learning. The domain specific classification backbone used here is ResNet50 [25] and task specific keypoint model is Mask R-CNN [26]. The feature concatenation is performed through shallow feature converters learning. The model overfitting is resolved with early stopping. In Fig. 5 steps are demonstrated which incorporates transfer learning with HEGPosEs.

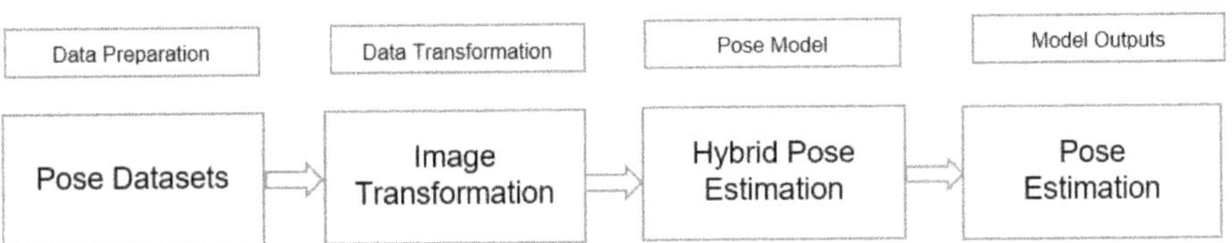

Fig. 4. Block diagram for pose transformation method identification

3.2 Design and Implementation

Identification of best deep learning method for pose estimation is difficult. Keeping this in view, method proposed learns when stated algorithm is superior [15] with respect to another algorithm. This helps to develop robust multi-person ensemble method. This ensemble allows fusion performance of different methods. The ensemble is created with bagging and stacking methods. Both ensembles depend on set of deep learning models. The results are fine-tuned through refinement of obtained human poses. Several deep architectures are trained to develop reliable results with customized vanilla pose estimation ensembles. The ensemble strategies help to develop refined poses. Each ensemble is optimized for variety of purposes. Table 1 summarizes hyperparameter values in this method. The method is benchmarked with respect to certain baseline models [13, 14]. This helps in identification of performance gain or loss. The validation is performed through metrics multi-task loss and reconstruction loss [15]. The bagging and stacking methods also helps us to arrive at optimum results of refined pose. The bagging methods are defined through mathematical integration of individual results of MGPosEs and MRTMPosEs. The stacking methods reply on certain statistical and machine learning methods to refine pose results obtained from bagging. They increase predictive performance of ensemble through consideration of best results achieved from bagging. This reduces bias and variance [27], increases model variety, and improves interpretability factor of prediction.

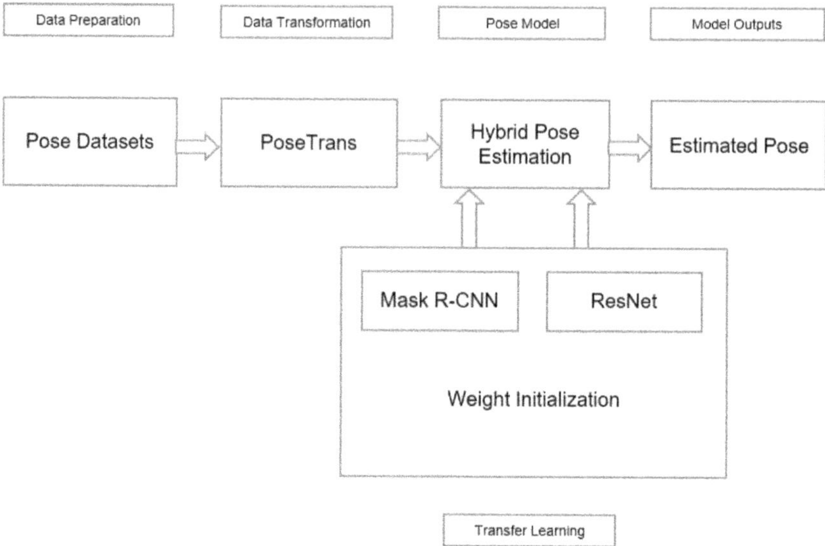

Fig. 5. Proposed method for hybrid pose estimation

Table 1. Hyperparameter values for HEGPosEs

Hyperparameters	Values
Dropout rate	0.4
Learning rate	0.004
Decay	0
Epochs	40
Batch size	200

Here bagging ensemble is represented as simple bagging and weighted bagging which take output poses of MGPosEs and MRTMPPosEs to calculate refined pose. These models provide initial predictions towards object pose. Here weighted bagging considers scores which each model which contribute towards estimation. These scores describe confidence levels of models and detection class. The stacking ensemble is a generalization method which integrates different models [17]. The training of base models is performed followed by validation. It generates new dataset which are independent from each model's output. With validation data integration model is trained. Figure 6 shows training and evaluation pipeline of model. Integration level methods integrate output of base level model results. Here integration level methods used are Ridge Linear Regression or L2 Regularization, Random Forests, XGBoost, Regularized Support Vector Regression and Regularized Multi-Layer Perceptron.

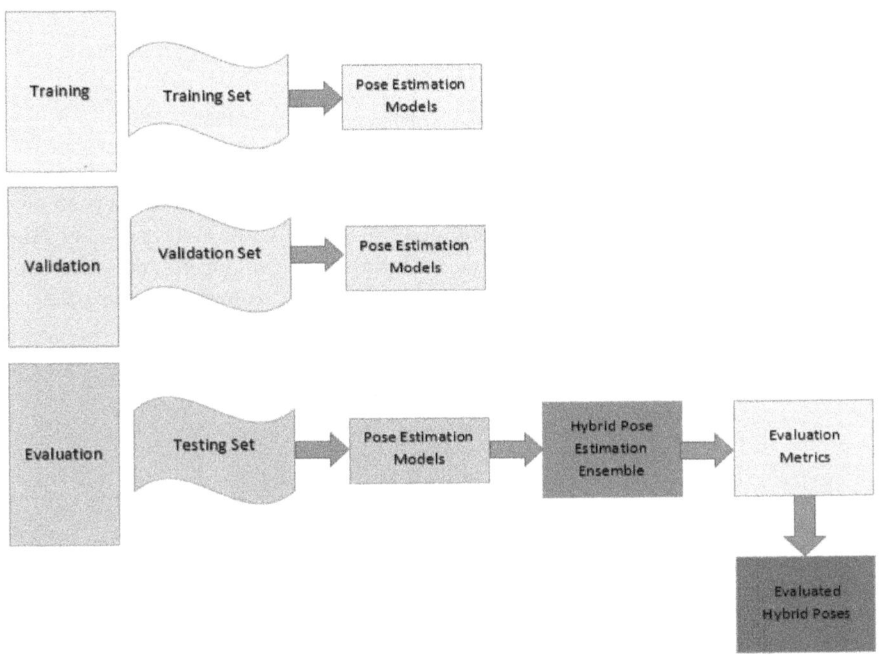

Fig. 6. Hybrid ensemble model - training, validation and evaluation pipeline

4 Illustration of Group Pose Estimation Methodology

Now we illustrate proposed group pose estimation method with DensePose-COCO [16] dataset. It is prepared by manually annotating 500 COCO based images. DensePose-COCO dataset has variety of annotations in alignment with dense correspondences. It uses ideas from bounding boxes, object detection, image segmentation and other methods. This method is tested with baselines which have semantically meaningful pose estimates. The domain experts provide their viewpoints from poses. The process flow is highlighted in Fig. 7.

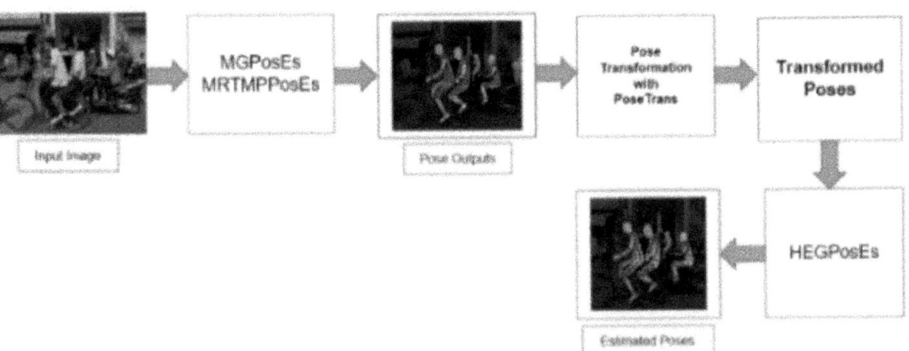

Fig. 7. Hybrid pose estimation method with DensePose-COCO dataset

Table 2. The model performance of HEGPosEs on DensePose-COCO dataset

Training Accuracy	Training Loss	Validation Loss	Validation Accuracy	Precision	Recall	F1 Score
0.9994	0.02	0.02	0.9992	0.9950	1.0	0.9975

The model performance of HEGPosEs on DensePose-COCO dataset is presented in Table 2. A close examination of PoseTrans counterparts for actual and pose images shows that there is uniformity in poses estimated for both image categories. Any difference in estimated poses helps us to differentiate authentic poses from inaccurate poses. The customized HEGPosEs takes transformed images as inputs. With 50 epochs and batch size of 20 we train and validate this model. In Fig. 8 performance matrix is presented.

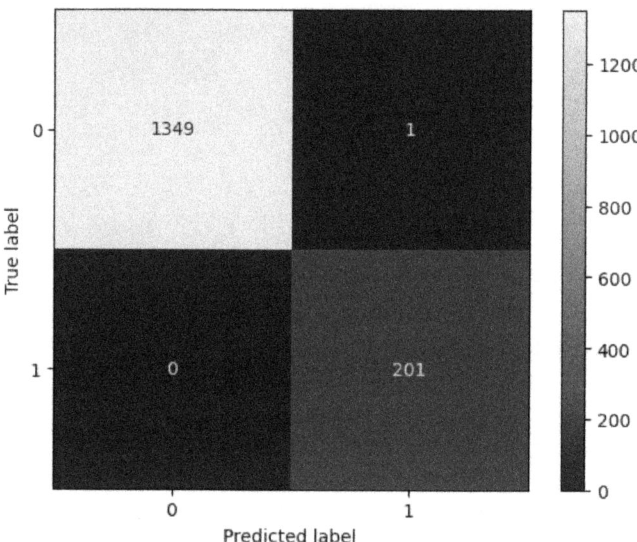

Fig. 8. Performance matrix for DensePose-COCO datasets

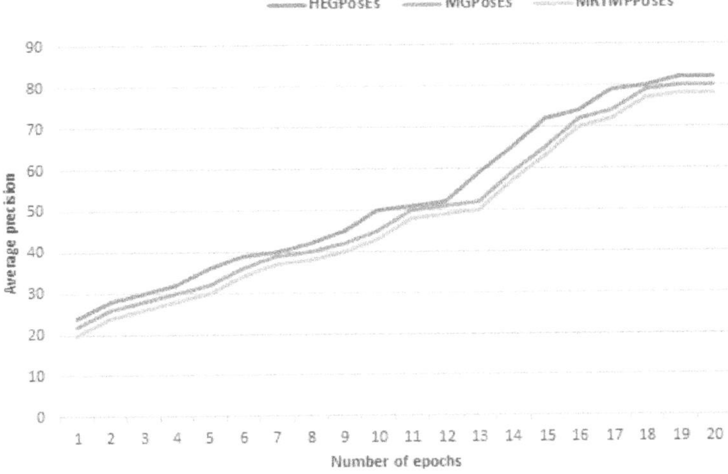

Fig. 9. Convergence curve comparison of HEGPosEs, MGPosEs and MRTMPPosEs

Table 3. Performance of HEGPosEs on MPII Human Pose in end-to-end methods

Method	Backbone	Loss	mAP	mAP_50	mAP_75	mAP_Medium	mAP_Large
PETR [9]	ResNet-50	HM + KR	67.7	87.6	76.4	62.9	77.9
PETR [9]	Swin-L	HM + KR	73.4	90.9	81.0	66.6	80.8
QueryPose [21]	ResNet-50	BR + RLE	68.9	88.7	74.5	63.9	76.6
GroupPose [13]	ResNet-50	KR	73.0	89.5	79.6	66.9	79.9
GroupPose [13]	Swin-T	KR	73.9	90.5	80.6	68.8	81.6
GroupPose [13]	Swin-L	KR	75.9	90.7	82.7	69.6	84.0
RTMPose-t [14]	CSPNeXt-t	KR	65.5	88.6	75.6	68.8	77.0
RTMPose-s [14]	CSPNeXt-s	KR	68.9	90.9	78.9	67.0	80.0
RTMPose-m [14]	CSPNeXt-m	KR	73.6	88.9	80.8	69.9	84.8
RTMPose-l [14]	CSPNeXt-l	KR	75.6	90.0	80.9	67.9	80.9
RTMPose-m [14]	CSPNeXt-m	KR	76.9	90.9	80.7	68.9	81.9
RTMPose-l [14]	CSPNeXt-l	KR	75.9	90.8	85.6	69.8	84.9
HEGPosEs	ResNet-50	KR	79.0	90.9	80.9	68.9	84.8
HEGPosEs	Swin-T	KR	80.9	93.8	84.8	69.9	81.9
HEGPosEs	Swin-L	KR	84.6	93.9	85.9	70.8	85.8

Table 4. Performance of HEGPosEs on MPII Human Pose in non-end-to-end methods

Method	Backbone	Loss	mAP	mAP_50	mAP_75	mAP_Medium	mAP_Large
Mask R-CNN [15]	ResNet-50	HM	66.5	87.5	71.1	61.3	73.4
Mask R-CNN [15]	ResNet-101	HM	66.6	87.4	74.0	61.5	74.4
PRTR [11]	ResNet-50	KR	68.6	88.2	75.2	66.2	76.2
HrHRNet [7]	HRNet-w32	HM	67.6	86.2	73.0	61.5	79.9
InsPose [9]	ResNet-50	KR + HM	64.9	86.9	68.9	59.5	70.9
HEGPosEs	ResNet-50	KR + HM	75.0	88.8	78.9	64.0	79.4
HEGPosEs	ResNet-101	KR + HM	78.9	90.5	77.9	67.1	79.0
HEGPosEs	Hourglass-104	KR + HM	80.8	88.6	70.9	58.8	76.5

Table 5. The model convergence analysis

Method	With Human Detection Detector	12e	24e	36e	48e	60e
GroupPose [13]	No	61.0	67.6	70.1	71.4	72.0
GroupPose [13]	Yes	61.4	68.1	70.3	71.6	72.2
RTMPose [14]	No	60.7	67.4	70.0	71.3	71.7
RTMPose [14]	Yes	61.9	67.5	70.2	71.4	71.9
HEGPosEs	No	62.7	68.4	73.0	73.3	73.7
HEGPosEs	Yes	64.9	69.5	73.3	73.4	73.9

5 Experiments and Analysis

In order to further strengthen our hypothesis, we present additional experimental results. Considering baselines ensemble learning methods are compared. The mean average precision (mAP) evaluation metric [15] is used to validate results. We have used 128-bit OS having x128 Intel processor with RAM of 32 GB. The method is implemented with Python 3.11.0 in Google Colab with 8 GPUs NVIDIA A100 hardware. With multiple performance scores stacking and bagging pipelines are being setup [15]. The hybrid ensemble combines prediction results which reduces predictions-based variance and generalization errors. The solution has committee of methods which gives good fit. The predictions are performed for each developed model. The actual predictions are achieved as average of predictions. During experimentation process we also varied [15] ensemble models, their combinations and training data. The models are varied with multiple runs of training along with hyper parameters tuning, snapshots, vertical representations and horizontal epochs. The combinations are varied with average and weighted average of models. The experiments are performed on publicly available human pose estimation benchmarked dataset viz. MPII Human Pose [15] which is state-of-the-art dataset and evaluates articulated human poses. Tables 3 and 4 evaluate performance of HEGPosEs on MPII Human Pose datasets for end-to-end and non-end-to-end methods with different backbones. The loss functions used provide better insights into results. With standard evaluation process, we have different thresholds. The results have confirmed that stated pose estimation method is more robust to occlusion with improvement in dense regression accuracy. Figure 9 compares convergence curves of methods with model convergence in Table 5.

6 Conclusion

In this research work hybrid ensemble group pose estimation method HEGPosEs is developed to estimate authentic human poses. Here robust pose estimation objective is reached with pose transformation PoseTrans and pre-trained models. Transfer learning with early stopping have been used for model efficiency and fast training. The pose transformation method results in best pose estimates with pose estimator. The ensemble is evaluated on test datasets. This method's viability is established based on comparative analysis of group pose estimation methods. It makes pose estimation method more adaptive to occlusion and improves dense regression accuracy. The proposed pose estimation method can also be tested on additional pose estimation datasets. The estimation of poses is significant for various reasons such as identification of human body movements for health condition, detection and classification of body joints, description of posture of person and dynamic tracking in real-time motion. The results have confirmed application of this method in several applications viz clinical sciences, human activity, media and sports with considerable improvements.

References

1. Hartanto, A., Quek, F.Y.X., Tng, G.Y.Q., Yong, J.C.: Does social media use increase depressive symptoms? A reverse causation perspective. Front. Psych. **12**, 641934 (2021)
2. Knap, P.: Human modeling and pose estimation overview. arXiv. arXiv: 2406.19290 (2024)
3. Leng, Z., Jain, Y., Kwon, H., Plötz, T.: Fine-grained human activity recognition using virtual on-body acceleration data. In: Proceedings of International Joint Conference on Pervasive and Ubiquitous Computing, New York, United States, pp. 55–59. ACM (2023)
4. Stenum, J., et al.: Applications of pose estimation in human health and performance across the lifespan. Sensors **21**(21), 7315 (2021)
5. Zheng, C., et al.: Deep learning based human pose estimation: a survey. ACM Comput. Surv. **56**(1), 1–37 (2023)
6. Wang, J., et al.: Deep 3D human pose estimation: a review. Comput. Vis. Image Underst. **210**, 103225 (2021)
7. Cheng, B., Xiao, B., Wang, J., Shi, H., Huang, T., Zhang, L.: HigherHRNet: scale-aware representation learning for bottom-up human pose estimation. In: Proceedings of IEEE International Conference on Computer Vision and Pattern Recognition, Seattle, WA, USA, pp. 5385–5394. IEEE (2020)
8. Mao, W., Ge, Y., Shen, C., Tian, Z., Wang, X., Wang, Z.: Poseur: direct human pose regression with transformers. In: Avidan, S., Brostow, G., Cissé, M., Farinella, G.M., Hassner, T. (eds.) ECCV 2022. LNCS, vol. 13666, pp. 72–88. Springer, Cham (2022). https://doi.org/10.1007/978-3-031-20068-7_5
9. Shi, D., Wei, X., Li, L., Ren, Y., Tan, W.: End-to-end multi-person pose estimation with transformers. In: Proceedings of IEEE International Conference on Computer Vision and Pattern Recognition, New Orleans, LA, USA, pp. 11059–11068. IEEE (2022)
10. Carion, N., Massa, F., Synnaeve, G., Usunier, N., Kirillov, A., Zagoruyko, S.: End-to-end object detection with transformers. In: Vedaldi, A., Bischof, H., Brox, T., Frahm, J.-M. (eds.) ECCV 2020. LNCS, vol. 12346, pp. 213–229. Springer, Cham (2020). https://doi.org/10.1007/978-3-030-58452-8_13
11. Li, Y., Zhang, S., Wang, Z., Yang, S., Xia, S.T., Zhou, E.: Token Pose: learning keypoint tokens for human pose estimation. In: Proceedings of IEEE International Conference on Computer Vision and Pattern Recognition. pp. 11293–11302. IEEE (2021)
12. Guan, J., Hao, Y., Wu, Q., Li, S., Fang, Y.: A survey of 6DoF object pose estimation methods for different application scenarios. Sensors **24**(4), 1076 (2024)
13. Liu, H., et al.: Group Pose: a simple baseline for end-to-end multi-person pose estimation. In: Proceedings of IEEE International Conference on Computer Vision, Paris, France, pp. 14983–14992. IEEE (2023)
14. Jiang, T., et al.: RTMPose: real-time multi-person pose estimation based on MMPose. In: arXiv. arXiv: 2303.07399 (2023)
15. Chaudhuri, A.: HEGPosEs: hybrid ensemble based group pose estimation for modeling human body configurations. In: Technical Report TR–6636, New Delhi, India. Samsung R & D Institute (2025)

16. Güler, R.A., Neverova, N., Kokkinos, I.: DensePose: dense human pose estimation in the wild. In: Proceedings of IEEE International Conference on Computer Vision and Pattern Recognition, Salt Lake City, UT, USA, pp. 7297–7306. IEEE (2018)
17. Sengar, S.S., Kumar, A., Singh, O.: Efficient human pose estimation: leveraging advanced techniques with MediaPipe. arXiv. arXiv: 2406.15649 (2024)
18. Zhu, X., Su, W., Lu, L., Li, B., Wang, X., Dai, J.: Deformable DETR: deformable transformers for end-to-end object detection. In: Proceedings of International Conference on Learning Representations, Vienna, Austria, pp. 1–16. OpenReview (2021)
19. Meng, D., et al.: Conditional DETR for fast training convergence. In: Proceedings of IEEE International Conference on Computer Vision, Montreal, QC, Canada, pp. 3631–3640. IEEE (2021)
20. Xiao, Y., et al.: QueryPose: sparse multi-person pose regression via spatial-aware part-level query. In: Proceedings of Advances in Neural Information Processing Systems, New Orleans, LA, USA, pp. 1–14. NeurIPS (2022)
21. Yang, J., Zeng, A., Liu, S., Li, F., Zhang, R., Zhang, L.: Explicit box detection unifies end-to-end multi-person pose estimation. In: Proceedings of International Conference on Learning Representations, Kigali, Rwanda, pp. 1–17. OpenReview (2023)
22. Xu, Y., Zhang, J., Zhang, Q., Tao, D.: ViTPose: simple vision transformer baselines for human pose estimation. In: Proceedings of Advances in Neural Information Processing Systems. NeurIPS, New Orleans, LA, USA, pp. 1–14 (2022)
23. Fan, H., et al.: MMViT: multiscale vision transformers. In: Proceedings of IEEE International Conference on Computer Vision, Virtual Modes, pp. 6824–6835. IEEE (2021)
24. Jiang, W., Jin, S., Liu, W., Qian, C., Luo, P., Liu, S.: PoseTrans: a simple yet effective pose transformation augmentation for human pose estimation. In: Avidan, S., Brostow, G., Cissé, M., Farinella, G.M., Hassner, T. (eds.) ECCV 2022. LNCS, vol. 13665, pp. 643–659. Springer, Cham (2022). https://doi.org/10.1007/978-3-031-20065-6_37
25. Li, J., Wang, C., Zhu, H., Mao, Y., Fang, H.-S., Lu, C.: CrowdPose: efficient crowded scenes pose estimation and a new benchmark. In: arXiv. arXiv: 1812.00324 (2018)
26. He, K., Zhang, X., Ren, S., Sun, J.: Deep residual learning for image recognition. In: Proceedings of IEEE International Conference on Computer Vision and Pattern Recognition, Las Vegas, NV, USA, pp. 770–778. IEEE (2016)
27. Chaudhuri, A.: HEGPosEs: reducing bias and variance in hybrid ensemble based group pose estimations. In: Technical Report TR–6637. Samsung R & D Institute, New Delhi, India (2025)

Efficient Fire Recognition from Surveillance Video Using Enhanced YOLOv5

Shubhangi Suryawanshi[1] , Umesh Ghorpade[2], Digvijay Bhosale[3]([✉]),
Jyotsna Barpute[1] , Akshada Kale[4] , and Ruchita Deshmukh[4]

[1] Department of Artificial Intelligence and Data Science, Dr. D. Y. Patil Institute of Technology
Pimpri, Pune, India
[2] Mechanical Engineering Department, Dnyanshree Institute of Engineering and Technology,
Satara, Maharashtra 415 013, India
[3] Department of Mechanical Engineering, Dr. D. Y. Patil Institute of Technology Pimpri, Pune,
India
digvijay_bhonsale@yahoo.co.in
[4] Department of Automation and Robotics, Dr. D. Y. Patil Institute of Technology, Pune,
Maharashtra 411 018, India

Abstract. Minimizing damage and improving safety in public and private areas
depend on timely and precise fire detection in video surveillance. High false favorable rates and slow reaction times are common problems with traditional fire
detection techniques, especially in visually complex environments. An improved
YOLOv5 architecture designed for effective fire recognition is proposed in this
study, which overcomes these drawbacks by increasing detection accuracy and
speed. To capture the distinct qualities of fire, such as irregular shapes, fluctuating
movement, and varying intensities, key modifications include incorporating an
improved feature extraction layer and optimised anchor box parameters. In realtime surveillance applications, experimental findings indicate that the enhanced
YOLO v5 model demonstrates superior performance compared to traditional fire
detection approaches, achieving higher precision and recall rates with minimal
computational overhead. Compared to YOLOv5s and YOLOv5x, the proposed
model achieves an improvement in mAP of 0.03 and 0.01 compared to YOLOv5s
and YOLOv5x respectively, when evaluated on a CPU thereby demonstrating
enhanced performance and speeds up inference by up to 5.47 and 21.31 FPS. As
a result, our model can be used for effective fire detection in real-world scenarios.

Keywords: Feature extraction layer · optimised anchor box parameters ·
YOLO · fire detection system

1   Introduction

Businesses and government agencies use surveillance technologies more often to supplement conventional security measures. In many places around the world, such financial
institution offices, hospitals, airport terminals, shopping malls, testing facilities, and
train stations, the number of unusual and disruptive activities and disruptive activities is

© The Author(s), under exclusive license to Springer Nature Switzerland AG 2026
F. Ortiz-Rodríguez et al. (Eds.): IBCD 2025, CCIS 2845, pp. 25–35, 2026.
https://doi.org/10.1007/978-3-032-20907-8_3

rapidly increasing these days [1]. Inside government and private surveillance technologies, human observers are frequently used to identify suspicious individuals on video footage [2, 3]. Because there are millions of people are recorded by the ones cameras, and numerous videos are produced and kept for while in various locations. The vehicles are checked for criminal activity in response to a complaint or while the videos are recorded. The enormous population requires human focus to constantly ensure that these activities are suspicious when performed directly adjacent to them since constant observation is virtually impossible. However, artificial intelligence-based methods are still in use because of their accuracy and reliability.

For video surveillance, many scientists have successfully developed classification models based on deep deep learning. The probabilistic neural network and the Radial Basis Neural network are two types of neural network models [3, 4]. Support Vector Machine, AdaBoost [4, 5], Artificial Neural Network [6], and other learning-based techniques are a few examples. Recently, there has been an increase in the use of deep learning methods to identify suspicious activity by obtaining and learning characteristics from video footage [7]. These techniques successfully addressed numerous challenges earlier systems faced, such as lighting variations, noise, shadows, occlusions, and low resolution. Scalability, resilience to adversarial attacks, dynamic changes in lighting, object shadows, out-of-focus objects, obstructions by objects, low resolution, and rapid processing are some of the main challenges in identifying suspicious activity [7].

Among the primary hazards to human life is fire. It can also quickly result in severe environmental harm and significant financial losses [13]. It is crucial to identify fires early on and provide precise early warning to reduce the damage they cause. The computer vision-based fire detection methods are preferred by researchers because of its low environmental interference, fast detection speed, and wide detection range [13, 14]. Some researchers attempt to characterize the nature of flames using manually chosen features, or they combine a shallow machine-learning technique with manual feature selection for additional training and classification [16–18]. However, the expertise and specific knowledge of the experts are required for manually selected features. As a result, the selection of features isn't popular as well as being gradually supplanted through the robotic feature extraction method utilizing neural networks [19, 20]. The convolutional neural network-based fire detection method has gained widespread usage because deep learning technology is developing so quickly [21, 22]. Deep learning-based detection techniques have a number of potential benefits over traditional computer vision-based techniques, including quick response times, broad detection ranges, high precision, and inexpensive detection costs. Many good deep learning-based models for object detection, including You Only Look Once (YOLO) [23], Resnet, Visual Geometry Group [25], Multi-box single shot detection [26], and Faster R-CNN, were utilized for fireworks identification and have shown good performance.

Limitations associated with current techniques employed are the region proposal stage is ignored as deep learning models have been mainly developed as a type of classification for fire detection. These techniques assign a single class to the entire image. But a fire only takes up just a small portion of an image. Using the feature of the full image with no suggestions for the region would decrease detection capabilities and cause a delay in the activating of the fire alarm if the fire feature is not immediately visible. Current fire detection techniques are also unsuitable for use in practical settings due to their high computational complexity. Second, there is a requirement for manual annotation in locations of fire with annotated files in the object fire datasets recognition models that are applied by multiple investigators in their work. These datasets are either uncommon or unavailable to the general public. The procedure for annotation is laborious and taking a long time, and it typically involves just one class—fire, for example—where the item being annotated is not examined. Therefore, the state-of-the-art techniques have only partially succeeded in detecting fire and have led to the incorrect classification of fire-like colours.

The contribution of study is as follows:

- Incorporated deeper convolutional layers into the YOLOv5 architecture to improve fire detection accuracy.
- Optimized anchor boxes using k-means clustering to better align with the shapes and sizes of fire regions, enhancing bounding box precision.
- Assessed the enhanced YOLOv5 model against other YOLO versions using metrics like precision, recall, and computational efficiency.

The structure of this article is as follows: Sect. 2 offers a critical review of the literature on the subject area. In Sect. 3 the methodology proposed for quick detection for fire from surveillance footage that uses the improved YOLOv5 model. Section 4 provides information about the dataset used in the study, as well as about the metrics used for performance assessment. The results and findings are shown in Sect. 5, whereas the final section contains the conclusion.

2 Literature Review

Fire detection has been a popular research field, and many papers have utilized deep learning machines in order to improving the accuracy and precision of prompt detection. This section provides a comprehensive literature outlined in this field regarding the developments and approaches in this area.

Recognition of human actions has become a difficult task, area of study for the video interpretation and evaluation, as Gul et al. investigated [9]. They use video sequences to detect abnormal activity in individuals or groups across multiple classes. The foundational You Look once (YOLO) network is the CNN model used in this investigation. Twenty-three thousand tagged images of patient behaviours were used over 32 epochs to retrain the backbone CNN model. In this investigation, the accuracy of the action recognition was 96.8%. Three key phases for the human activity detection model were introduced by Verma et al. [9, 10]. Space-time activity learning is used in the first stage with an LSTM network from RGB and two 3D CNNs [11]. SVM was trained using the tasks it had previously learned in the second phase. With the aid of two evolutionary algorithms, score fusion, and optimization are performed in the third stage. Benchmark and stand datasets have been used to confirm the designed approach. The empirical results ultimately verified that the planned strategy had improved performance. Ullah et al. [12] presented anomaly detection using an intelligent deep feature-based approach that may be effective within a monitoring system with a lower level of complexity. This architecture extracts data from video frames using a trained CNN model beforehand. Then, the bidirectional LSTM model is used to process the frames. Records of regular and unusual events, including 13 distinct anomalies like clashes, abuse, and mishaps, are included in the UCF-Crime dataset. The collection consists of 1900 surveillance recordings with 3.41% and 8.09% accuracy rates, respectively. According to Feichtenhofer et al. [13], there are now multiple methods available for identifying human activity in videos CNNs that take into both look and movement. They think of other access methods of this spatiotemporal and found that there is no performance loss if a temporal and a spatial system are fused at the layer of convolution as that of the softmax layer.

The study [28] introduces a novel YOLOv5 algorithm for early forest fire detection, adding a tiny layer for detecting targets in the neck network, improving fire image discovery of small flames when flames are obscured, offering better results than the YOLO baseline. The study [29] presents an improved model YOLO to increase the rate of detection of forest fire while improving on the visualization capabilities and global integration. It uses a global attention mechanism and re-parameterized convolutional module and weighted BiFPN which gives more precise, more remarkable recall, and mean average precision. The study [30] presents a modified YOLOv5s algorithm, namely GAM-ASFF-YOLO, which improves the efficiency of fire detection in images and videos through addition of new features such as global attention mechanism and adaptive spatial combining features to enhance the values of accuracy, recall as well as mean average precision for the detection of flame and smokes. The proposed system [31] of integrating YOLOv algorithm for the detecting smoke and fire in real time surveillance videos requires no pre-processing for high accuracy and low latency and is ideal for early warning systems and management of disaster incidents.

The study [29] develop a fire the detection system using YOLO for object detection and flickering analysis HSV color space with the mean accuracy of Fire detection 71.5% and minimize False Alarm use real fires distinguished from static-fire object on surveillance video. The study [33] describe deep learning model Fireguard for effective fire detection from surveillance videos. It uses a low-power variant of SqueezeNet architecture to cut down the amount of dense layers and uses tiny matrices in convolution layers. The model accurately classifies fire and non-fire pictures, or images, using a separate fire data set. Accuracy, precision, recall, F-measure, sensitivity, specificity of the performance is computed, and the system's effectiveness in real-time fire detection is demonstrated with a capability of sending an alert to Gmail whenever a fire is identified. The study [34] employed an improved architecture for deep learning for effective fire detection in surveillance settings, using MSAM and 3D convolution with a MobileNet. This increases the model's effectiveness of identifying appropriate features for fire scene classification and adds detail that is obtainable from aerial perspectives. Comparison with benchmarks shows superior results with average accuracy gains by 0.54%, 2.66%, and 1.20% on the FD, DFAN, and ADSF datasets, respectively.

3 Methodology

Figure 1 depicts the detailed steps involved in the proposed methodology, which are outlined below:

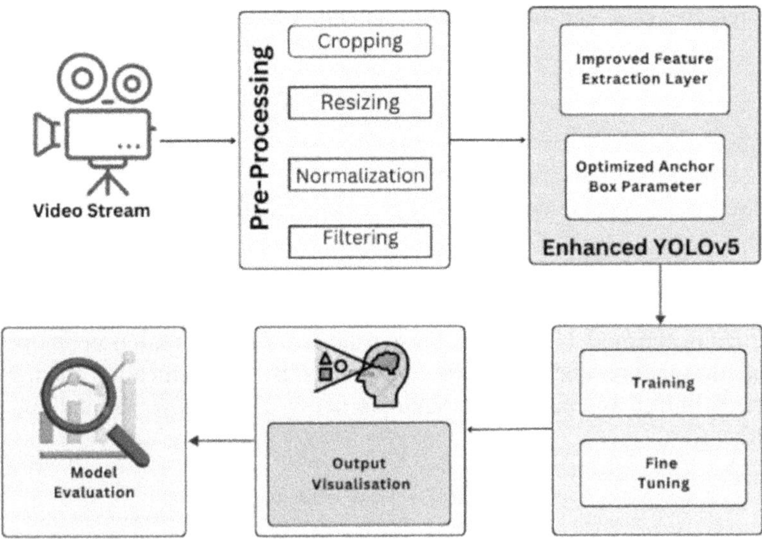

Fig. 1. Proposed workflow for the detecting fires using the enhanced YOLOv5 framework.

3.1 Step 1: Pre-Processing

In the pre-processing step, video frames are extracted from the surveillance footage at predefined intervals (e.g., one frame per second) to reduce computational load. These frames are then resized to the required input dimensions of the YOLOv5 model (typically 640×640 pixels) to ensure consistency across inputs. The values are scaled between 0 and 1 to improve the quality of the images and remove unwanted noise. The video frames are resized and denoised for efficient detection.

3.2 Step 2: Enhanced YOLOv5

To enhance the YOLOv5 model, deeper convolutional layers are used with the feature extraction network.

Improved Feature Extraction Layer:

Capturing the complex features, 10 additional convolutional layers are used to extend the backbone, CSPDarknet. Sixty-four filters are used for the first layer, the second with 128 filters, and so on, to ensure deeper feature extraction. Squeeze-and-excitation (SE) blocks are integrated into the network to recalibrate feature channels to help the model focus more on relevant features related to fire detection.

Optimized Anchor Box Parameters:

For optimization of anchor boxes, a k-means clustering algorithm means is used to better align the predicted bounding boxes with the typical shapes and sizes of fire regions. The k-means algorithm minimizes the distance between the ground truth bounding boxes and the predicted ones and can be mathematically represented as:

$$\min_{i} = \sum_{i=1}^{n} \|bi - ck\|^2$$

where b_i represents the bounding boxes and c_k denotes the canter of the $k\text{-}^{th}$ cluster.

3.3 Step 3: Training and Fine-Tuning

During training, the model is adjusted through the use of augmentation techniques such as flips, random rotations, and brightness adjustments. Both classification and localization losses are optimized as a part of the training process. This is how the total loss function L is written:

$$L = L_{cls} + L_{loc} + \lambda L_{noobj}$$

where L_{cls} is the classification loss, L_{loc} is the localization loss, and λ is a hyperparameter controlling the penalty for false positives.

3.4 Step 4: Final Output

After bounding boxes are superimposed on the original frames to visualize the results of detecting the fire regions. The bounding box coordinates are represented as B = (x, y, w, h, p) where (x, y)denotes the top-left corner, www and hhh represent the box height and width, and ppp is the degree of confidence. A confidence threshold is applied to filter out weak detections, ensuring that only strong predictions are visualized.

4 Result and Discussion

The objective of the experiment was to identify high-risk areas or situations. This would help focus risk management efforts on reducing potential threats. Another goal was to develop an alert system for quick responses to security breaches or emergencies. The study used an enhanced version of YOLOv5 and compared it with other models YOLOv5s and YOLOv5x. The findings demonstrated that the improved YOLOv5 performed more effectively than the existing models.

The proposed fire detection model demonstrates promising performance across various evaluation metrics. For all classes, this models F1 Score equals 0.62, which is received when equally prioritizing both precision and recall, as presented in Fig. 2. The Precision-Confidence Curve presents a range of precision between 0.9–1, meaning that the model has the potentiality to very much eliminate false positive cases. On the other hand, the Fig. 3 Recall-Confidence Curve shows that the used model achieves a recall of 0.72, which corresponds to the ability to recognize fire instances successfully.

Qualitative outcomes depicted in Fig. 4 exhibit the performance of model in fire region identification and localization by outlining the fire regions using bounding boxes

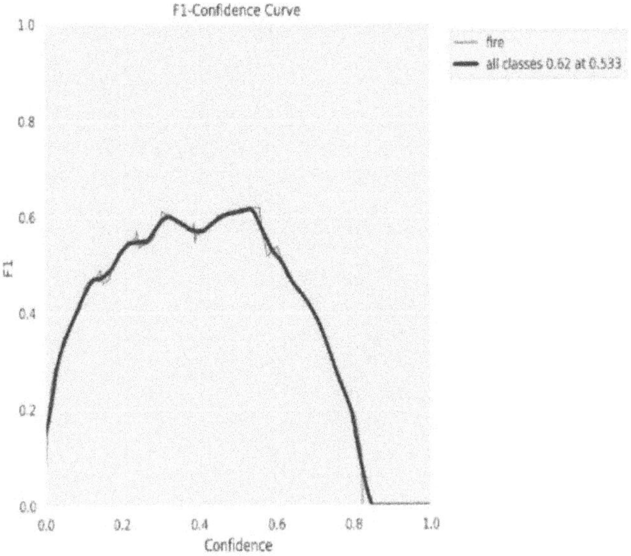

Fig. 2. F1-Score performance of the proposed fire detection model based on the enhanced YOLOv5 architecture.

in the test dataset. The suggested model achieves improved outcomes than other YOLOv5 variations, and the mAP score is slightly higher: 0.03 and 0.01 over the YOLOv5s and YOLOv5x, respectively.

Furthermore, the proposed model accelerates the speed of Inference to a greater extent. When run on the CPU, it performs faster, up to 5.47 FPS compared to YOLOv5s and 21.31 FPS compared to YOLOv5x. These improvements in performance and computation further make the model more appropriate for practical use in real-time fire detection. The experiment's findings show that the modified YOLOv5 is more effective than conventional fire detection systems in real-time monitoring scenarios. The model has a high precision and recall rate, which helps identify fire incidences with little computational load. This improved performance further underlines its practicality and usefulness in serving the purpose in practical situations.

There are specific issues to be resolved even though the improved YOLOv5 shows encouraging results regarding precision, recall, mAP score, and inference speed. For example, even though the F1 score of 0.62 indicates that precision and recall are balanced, it still shows that there is potential for improvement in detecting fire incidents in complex environments, particularly when there are occlusions, low visibility, or overlapping objects. Algorithms like Faster R-CNN, SSD, and EfficientDet may be superior to non-YOLO techniques in some situations, such as handling smaller object detections more effectively or performing more reliably in different lighting conditions. The viability of these techniques for real-time applications is constrained by their slower inference speeds and higher computational costs. For example, Faster R-CNN is less appropriate for immediate alert systems because it achieves high accuracy at the expense of slower processing speeds.

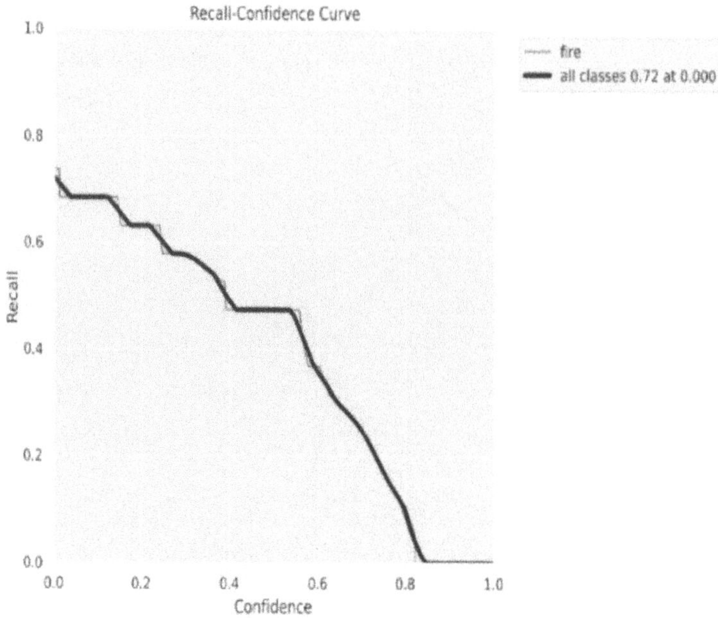

Fig. 3. Recall–Confidence curve for the fire detection model using the enhanced YOLOv5 architecture.

Future studies could look into adding features from non-YOLA approaches, like multi-scale features extraction, to improve the models ability to detect fire incidents in difficult situations. Addressing edge case limitation, like false negatives in extremely dynamic environments, will also increase the models reliability.

Fig. 4. Qualitative results of fire detection using the enhanced YOLOv5 model across diverse real-world scenarios.

5   Conclusion

This work presents a revised version of YOLOv5 tailored for fire detection in surveillance cameras with high precision and minimum error rates. The performance improvements are gained by integrating deeper convolutional layers and k-means optimized anchor boxes. A singular performance assessment of the experimental evaluation is presented with an F1 Score of 0.62 in discrete evaluation, precision of 0.9 to 1 in integer evaluation, and recall of 0.72 in floating-point evaluation. Further, the model provides a slightly improved mAP score, 0.03 and 0.01 higher than YOLOv5s and YOLOv5x, while enhancing the inference speed by up to 21.31 FPS in the CPU. These improvements validate the model as a practical and efficient way to detect fires in real time and can be implemented on practical surveillance systems. The YOLOv5 model is ideal for applications in real time because of its exceptional accuracy, precision, and inference swiftness. To increase the model's speed and reduce latency in fire detection, edge devices with GPU support are advised. By retrofitting cameras and video streams into already-existing surveillance systems, the model can be used to monitor high-risk areas continuously. A cloud-based alert system could be added to this integration to send immediate notifications to pertinent authorities or stakeholders in the event of an emergency.

References

1. Perez, M., Kot, A.C., Rocha, A.: Detection of real-world fights in surveillance videos. In: ICASSP 2019–2019 IEEE International Conference on Acoustics, Speech and Signal Processing (ICASSP), pp. 2662–2666. IEEE (2019)
2. Cao, J., Pang, Y., Xie, J., Khan, F.S., Shao, L.: From handcrafted to deep features for pedestrian detection: a survey. IEEE TPAMI **44**(9), 4913–4934 (2022)
3. Suryawanshi, S., Goswami, A., Patil, P.: CDA-PDDWE: concept drift-aware performance-based diversified dynamic weighted ensemble for non-stationary environments. Arab. J. Sci. Eng. **49**, 12989–13004 (2024)
4. Wu, C., Yue, J., Wang, L., Lyu, F.: Detection and classification of recessive weakness in super-buck converter based on WPD-PCA and probabilistic neural network. Electronics **8**(290), 1–17 (2019)
5. Geronimo, D., Sappa, A., Lopez, A., Ponsa, D.: Pedestrian detection using AdaBoost learning of features and vehicle pitch estimation. In: International Conference on Visualization, Imaging and Image Processing, 28th–30th Aug 2006, pp 1–8 (2006)
6. Emil, N., Neghina, M.: A NN approach to pedestrian detection, ICCOMP, pp. 374–379 (2009)
7. Kang, S., Byun, H., Lee, S.: Real-time pedestrian detection using support vector machines. In: First International Workshop on SVM: Pattern Recognition with SVM, pp. 268–27 (2002)
8. Wang, Y., Zhao, R., Liu, Y., Zhang, L.: Multi-modal deep learning for suspicious activity recognition in video surveillance. IEEE Trans. Inform. Forensics Secur. **18**(10), 2473–2486 (2023)
9. Gul, M.A., Yousaf, M.H., Nawaz, S., Ur Rehman, Z., Kim, H.: Patient monitoring by abnormal human activity recognition based on CNN architecture. Electronics **9**, 1993 (2020)
10. Verma, K.K., Singh, B.M.: Deep multi-model fusion for human activity recognition using evolutionary algorithms. Int. J. Interact. Multimedia Artif. Intell. (IJIMAI) **7**(1) (2021)
11. Verma, K.K., Singh, B.M.: Vision based human activity recognition using deep transfer learning and support vector machine. In: 2021 IEEE 8th Uttar Pradesh Section International Conference on Electrical, Electronics and Computer Engineering (UPCON), pp. 1–9. IEEE (2021)
12. Ullah, W., Ullah, A., Haq, I.U., Muhammad, K., Sajjad, M., Baik, S.W.: CNN features with bi-directional LSTM for real-time anomaly detection in surveillance networks. Multimed Tools Appl. **80**, 16979–16995 (2021)
13. Suryawanshi, S., Goswami, A., Patil, P.: IRBM: incremental restricted Boltzmann machines for concept drift detection and adaption in evolving data streams. In: Garg, D., Rodrigues, J.J.P.C., Gupta, S.K., Cheng, X., Sarao, P., Patel, G.S. (eds.) IACC 2023. CCIS, vol. 2053, pp. 466–475. Springer, Cham (2024). https://doi.org/10.1007/978-3-031-56700-1_37
14. Suryawanshi, S., Goswami, A., Patil, P.: Enhancing drift detection and model uncertainty handling in imbalanced streaming data using autoencoder-based approach. In: 2023 Second International Conference on Smart Technologies for Smart Nation (SmartTechCon), Singapore, Singapore, pp. 1265–1270 (2023)

15. Feichtenhofer, C., Pinz, A., Zisserman, A.: Convolutional two stream network fusion for video action recognition. In: Proceedings of the IEEE Conference on Computer Vision and Pattern Recognition, pp 1933–1941 (2016)
16. Gaur, A., Singh, A., Kumar, A., Kumar, A., Kapoor, K.: Video flame and smoke-based fire detection algorithms: a literature review. Fire Technol. **56**, 1943–1980 (2020)
17. Han, X.F., Jin, J.S., Wang, M.J., Jiang, W., Gao, L., Xiao, L.P.: Video fire detection based on Gaussian Mixture Model and multi-color features. Signal Image Video Process **11**(8), 1419–1425 (2017)
18. Peng, Y.S., Wang, Y.: Real-time Forest smoke detection using hand-designed features and deep learning. Comput. Electron. Agric. **167**, 105029 (2019)
19. Li, S.B., Yan, Q.D., Liu, P.: An efficient fire detection method based on multiscale feature extraction, implicit deep supervision and channel attention mechanism. IEEE Trans. Image Process. **29**, 8467–8475 (2020)
20. Pan HY, Badawi D, Zhang X, Cetin AE (2020) Additive neural network for forest fire detection. Signal Image Video P 14:675–682
21. Zhang, J.D., Xie, W.H., Liu, H.Y., Dang, W.Y., Yu, A.F., Liu, D.: Compressed dual-channel neural network with application to image-based smoke detection. IET Image Process **16**(4), 1036–1043 (2022)
22. Luo, Y.M., Zhao, L., Liu, P.Z., Huang, D.T.: Fire smoke detection algorithm based on motion characteristic and convolutional neural networks. Multimed Tools Appl. **77**(15075–15092), 15 (2018)
23. Saeed, F., Paul, A., Karthigaikumar, P., Nayyar, A.: Convolutional neural network based early fire detection. Multimed Tools Appl. **79**, 9083–9099 (2020)
24. Zhao, J., Wei, H.C., Zhao, X.Y., Ta, N., Xiao, M.X.: Application of Improved YOLO v4 model for real time video fire detection. Basic Clin. Pharmacol. **128**, 47 (2021)
25. Wu, Y.L., Chen, M.H., Wo, Y., Han, G.Q.: Video smoke detection base on dense optical flow and convolutional neural network. Multimed Tools Appl. **80**(28), 35887–35901 (2020)
26. Matlani, P., Shrivastava, M.: Hybrid deep VGG-NET convolutional classifier for video smoke detection. CMES-Comput. Model. Eng. **119**, 427–458 (2019)
27. Nguyen, A.Q., Nguyen, H.T., Tran, V.C., Pham, H.X., Pestana, J.: A visual real-time fire detection using single shot multibox detector for UAV-based fire surveillance. In: IEEE ICCE 2020: 2020 IEEE Eighth International Conference on Communications and Electronics (ICCE), pp. 338–343 (2021)
28. Lijuan, Q., Hengrui, Z., Tao, L., Ting, W.: Early Image Recognition of Forest Fire Based on Improved YOLOv5 Neck Network (2024). https://doi.org/10.1109/spic62469.2024.10691471
29. Lei, C., Zirui, S., Sheng, X.: Efficient forest fire detection based on an improved YOLO model. Vis. Intell./Vis. Intell. (2024). https://doi.org/10.1007/s44267-024-00053-y
30. Li, D., Jin, Z., Quanyi, L.: Improving YOLOv5s algorithm for detecting flame and smoke. IEEE Access (2024). https://doi.org/10.1109/access.2024.3442309
31. Sarthak, K.: Real time fire and smoke detection system. Int. J. Sci. Technol. Eng. (2023). https://doi.org/10.22214/ijraset.2023.54039
32. Calvin, C., Figo, A.A., Ulva, E., Fadhil, H.: Fire detection system with YOLO and flicker analysis using HSV color space masking (2024). https://doi.org/10.1109/iciss62896.2024.10751525
33. Balaji, V., Shanthini, V.S., Sri Balaji, R., Stinsha, S.L.: Fireguard: deep CNN video surveillance for efficient fire detection (2024). https://doi.org/10.1109/icstem61137.2024.10561206
34. Hikmat, Y., et al.: 4. An efficient deep learning architecture for effective fire detection in smart surveillance. Image and Vision Computing (2024), https://doi.org/10.1016/j.imavis.2024.104989

Predictive Modeling of Wear Behaviour of Ti-8Al-1Mo-1V Aero-Engine Compressor Blade Alloy

S. Jaipreetha[1]([⊠]) [iD], B. Adhitya[2] [iD], S. Karthikeyan[2] [iD], and Pooja Angolkar[3] [iD]

[1] Department of Information Technology, Thiagarajar College of Engineering, Madurai, India
sjaipreetha@student.tce.edu
[2] Department of Mechanical Engineering, Thiagarajar College of Engineering, Madurai, India
skarthikeyanlme@tce.edu
[3] Department of Robotics and Automation, Angadi Institute of Technology and Management, Belagavi, India

Abstract. The study of abrasive wear resistance of alloys used for high mechanical and thermal stress applications, particularly those used in advanced stages of jet engine compressors, involves a thorough theoretical understanding of the behaviour, as well as a robust experimental and computational analysis. The creep-resistant Ti8Al1Mo1V (Ti811) is used in compressor stages, subject to substantial amounts of abrasive wear. Based on an experimental analysis of the abrasive wear resistance of the heat-treated alloy, which involved a pin-on-disc wear test regime according to the ASTM G 99 standard, two input parameters (sliding velocity and normal load) were arrived at and were used to determine the values of the rate of wear and the coefficient of friction at low, moderate and high input values. The results of these were used as training data for four predictive models Random Forest (RF), Support Vector Regressor, XGBoost, Ensemble of RF &XGBoost) and performance of each of these was tallied against various output parameters. Judging by the performance metrics of Mean Square Error, Goodness of Fit Measure (R^2) and Mean Absolute Error, the ensemble (RF + XGBoost) model proved to be the best option for predictive modeling among the four.

Keywords: Ti8Al1Mo1V · Wear · Friction · Prediction · Random Forest · Support Vector Regression · XGBoost

1 Introduction

Jet engine spool components need to possess a variety of desirable factors to function effectively. These include a high specific strength, a good thermal resistance, high creep resistance and opposition to abrasive, erosive and general non-abrasive wear factors. Compressors, in particular, are more susceptible to wear than the later stages of the engine due to their direct contact with the environment and increased exposure to atmospheric conditions. In addition, the components within the compressor are packed in a very compact setup, in which rotary compressor blades are situated within a few hundred

F. Ortiz-Rodríguez et al. (Eds.): IBCD 2025, CCIS 2845, pp. 36–47, 2026.
https://doi.org/10.1007/978-3-032-20907-8_4

microns away from adjoining components such as stator blades and the compressor casing. This offers grounds for an investigation into the abrasive wear behaviour of compressor blade materials, whose longevity and operational effectiveness are crucial in determining the airworthiness of an aircraft.

Wear studies have been conducted on conventional materials such as Ti-6Al-4V - a commonly preferred option for compressor blades in the aerospace industry. However, the need for an alloy that exhibits good functional behaviour at operational temperatures up to 500° C, such as those observed in the high-pressure compressor stages in multi-spool engines, was recognized and forged and heat-treated Ti-8Al-1Mo-1V was found to be apt for this purpose [1]. The wear behaviour of the Ti811 was studied by performing pin-on-disc wear experiments [2] in this study. Due to limitations in the number of physical experiments that can be plausibly performed, and considering the non-feasibility of performing large numbers of trials for varying conditions, an L16 orthogonal array was used to organize four levels of two input parameters - the sliding velocity of the disc against the alloy pin, and the normal load of the pin imparted upon the disc - enforced by slotted weights connected to the interface by a pulley system. A schematic of the physical setup used for conducting the experiments is shown in Fig. 1.

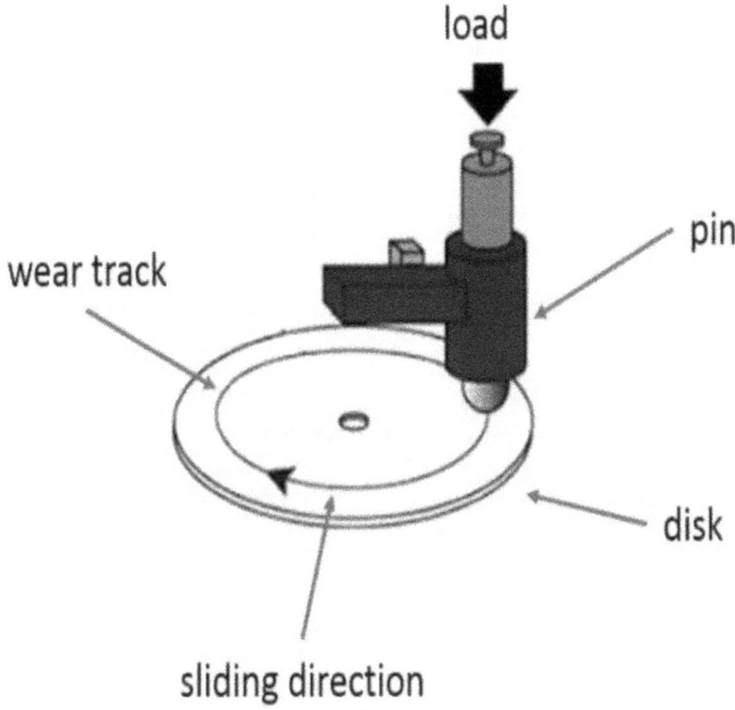

Fig. 1. Pin-on-disc tribometer and its constituents [2]

The data thus collected was in the form of two output parameters - the frictional force and the initial and final weights of the material sample. From the frictional force, the CoF was deduced and rate of wear was computed from wear volume - acquired from material weight loss values.

Physical wear experiments can yield limited results on the wear resistance of materials. The extent and scope of the results depend on the range of input parameters, such as sliding speed and loads, the number of trials that can be conducted within the resource constraints of the researchers, the type of trial characterization methods used, and the number of total trials conducted. In cases such as ours, where the subject material alloy is expensive to procure in large quantities and from which sample preparation is an extensive and time-consuming process, the number of trials may have to be kept to a minimum in the interest of cost and time. For these purposes, it is wise to turn to machine learning algorithms [7, 8, 20–26] to predict wear behavior for further simulation and analysis. In this approach, the robustness and the inherent reliability of the algorithms used must be ensured, in conjunction with worthwhile use of the available wear data [5, 6, 19].

The principal objective is to assess the wear resistance of the Ti–8Al–1Mo–1V alloy using advanced predictive machine learning approaches [11–18] and to identify the most effective algorithm [27–29] for replicating experimental wear outcomes. Comparable analysis has been done on wear properties of various materials [9, 10, 30–32]. Four predictive algorithms were used by Zhu et al. [3] to conduct an extensive evaluation of the rolling ball bearing material's wear depth: SVM, KNN, RF and XGB. They came to the conclusion that XGB outperformed the other algorithms in predicting the real wear behavior. A similar study was carried out by Altay et al. [4], wherein the wear coefficients for surface-coated ferro-alloys were predicted using LR, GPR and SVM methods. With a 96% prediction success rate in each case, they determined that SVM and GPR were the most successful of the three.

XGB, RF, SVR and ensemble of RF & XGB are all put into consideration for the analysis in this paper. These were chosen for their relative efficacy when compared to other regression techniques, as well as their capacity to operate on sparse data. Each algorithm's performance is evaluated using common evaluation measures including the Mean Absolute Error, Goodness of Fit Measure (R^2) and Mean Squared Error. Under various test settings, they are used to forecast the material's wear rate and the pin-disc interface's coefficient of friction (CoF). Performance heatmaps have been obtained to gauge the relative performances of the four algorithms with respect to the different output parameters. To demonstrate the effectiveness of the four algorithms in relation to the different evaluation measures, comparison radar has also been added. A detailed experimental procedure is presented in the following paragraphs.

2 Methodology

2.1 Dataset Preparation and Preprocessing

The chemical composition of the alloy Ti–8Al–1Mo–1V is given in the Table 1.

The alloy was solution heat-treated and aged conditions in an airfurnace. The alloy bars were machined to 30mm length and 10mm diameter pins as presented in Fig. 2. 16

Table 1. Chemical Composition

S. No	Element	Weight %
1	Titanium	90
2	Aluminium	8.0
3	Molybdenum	1.0
4	Vanadium	1.0

pins were machined for wear testing. The wear test was carried out using pin-on-disk tribometer. The input testing parameters are given in Table 2.

Table 2. Experimental Runs

Load (N)	Sliding Velocity (m/s)
10, 20, 30, 40	1.314, 2.1, 3.0,4.0

Wear loss and Coefficient of Frictions are measured. Wear Rate was calculated using wear loss.

CYLINDRICAL PIN

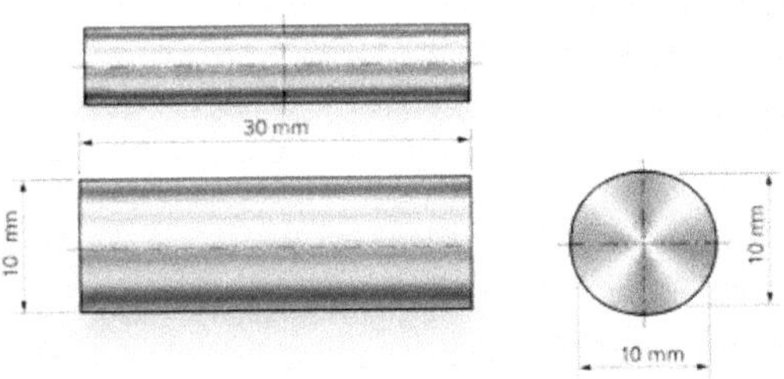

Fig. 2. Pin Specification

The dataset employed in this study was as a result of controlled tribological tests that measured the CoF and rate of wear under different operational conditions. This process included addressing missing values, normalizing the features to a uniform scale. To train and test, the dataset was partitioned. We allocated the majority (80%) of our experimental data for model training, while preserving a representative subset (20%) for rigorous final evaluation. This carefully balanced partitioning approach allows the models to learn from sufficient training examples while maintaining an independent test set that faithfully represents the full range of experimental conditions. The framework is represented in Fig. 3.

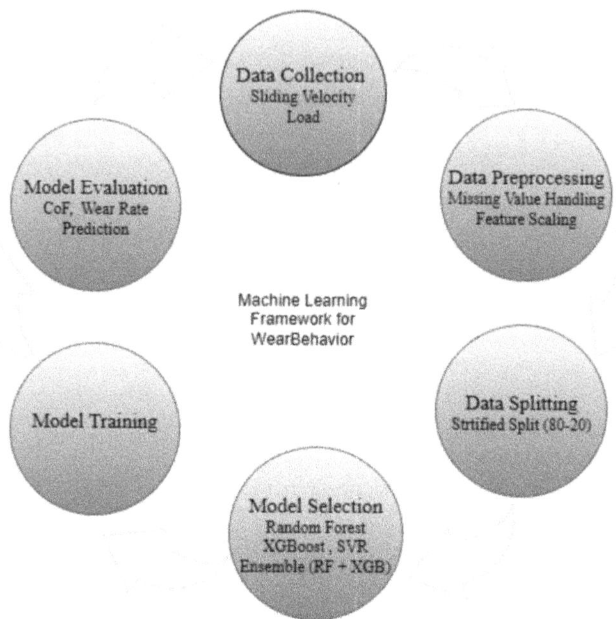

Fig. 3. Machine Learning Framework

2.2 Models Selection

The following ML models were used:

1. Random Forest (RF)
2. XGB
3. Support Vector Regression (SVR)
4. Ensemble Model (RF + XGB)

RF is a reliable technique that constructs several decision-making trees using random subsets of both the dataset and features.In this case, we set n_estimators to 100 trees and limited max_depth to 5. Setting these parameters helped us achieve an optimal tradeoff between bias and variance. This method works well with high-dimensional data, is highly resilient to noise, but can be somewhat difficult to understand because of the intricate merging of many trees.

XGBoost is an advanced and optimized form of gradient boosting that adds new trees to existing ones and fixes the errors within each tree individually. Our model reached its maximum performance when the learning rate and maximum depth were changed. With the help of the algorithm's built-in regularization, this model is efficient at detecting both linear and non-linear relationships and even reduces overfitting.

The ensemble model achieves average strength and improved precision as each prediction made by the RF and XGB models is factored into the final result. The predictive performance of the resulting model, in comparison to that of RF and XGB alone, demonstrated enhanced robustness and improved accuracy, resulting from RF's resilience to noise and XGB's adaptness at capturing complex patterns. The ensemble model is proven to extremely improve the balance, consistency and accuracy among all the tested models across different metrics.

The selected models Random Forest, XGBoost, SVR and their ensemble are well-suited for the small dataset's size, structure, and regression nature, offering strong interpretability and handling of nonlinearity, noise and feature interactions. In contrast, KNN suffers from scalability issues in high-dimensional spaces, GPR becomes computationally expensive for larger datasets due to its cubic time complexity $(O(n^3))$, and deep learning models typically require large volumes of data such as in image form, extensive tuning, and longer training times, which are redundant for the current dataset size and experimental constraints.

2.3 Model Performance Metrics

We used three metrics [13] to evaluate the model by Eqs. (1), (2), (3):

Mean Absolute Error. This metric reflects the mean absolute discrepancy between the real outcomes and the predicted outcomes. It is calculated using:

$$Mean\ Absolute\ Error = \frac{1}{n} \sum_{i=1}^{n} \left| actual_i - predicted_i \right| \tag{1}$$

Mean Squared Error.It calculates the mean squared difference between the real outcomes and the predicted outcomes.

$$Mean\ Squared\ Error = \frac{1}{n} \sum_{i=1}^{n} \left(actual_i - predicted_i \right)^2 \tag{2}$$

Goodness of Fit Measure. It shows how much of the variation in the dependent variable is explained by the independent variable.

$$R^2 = \frac{\sum_{i=1}^{n} \left(actual_i - predicted_i \right)^2}{\sum_{i=1}^{n} \left(actual_i - mean\ of\ actual\ values \right)^2} \tag{3}$$

3 Results and Discussion

For both CoF and rate of wear, the goodness of fit measure, mean squared error and mean absolute error were used to assess the predictive performance of the four machine learning models: SVR, RF, XGB & the ensemble model (RF + XGB). To show the relative performance of the models, radar chart (Fig. 5) and a heatmap (Fig. 4) are used to showcase the comparison results.

In every evaluation metric, the ensemble model (RF + XGB) fared better than the individual models. With 0.9639 for rate of wear prediction and 0.9657 for CoF prediction, it had the best R^2 values, confirming superior model fit and strong predictive reliability. In comparison, SVR showed better performance with R2 values of 0.93373(CoF) & 0.9300 (rate of wear), but slightly lagged behind the ensemble model.

The ensemble model achieved a superior performance in reducing errors in prediction that was confirmed by its lower MAE and MSE values. While XGB and SVR individually performed better than RF in predicting CoF, their performance on wear rate prediction was not as strong as the ensemble approach. Random Forest exhibited the lowest performance among the tested models, particularly in terms of R2 for wear rate.

The heatmap in (Fig. 4) makes it easy to compare how well each model performed. The brighter colored regions indicating higher R2 values for CoF and wear rate demonstrating that the ensemble model consistently delivered good results (Table 3).

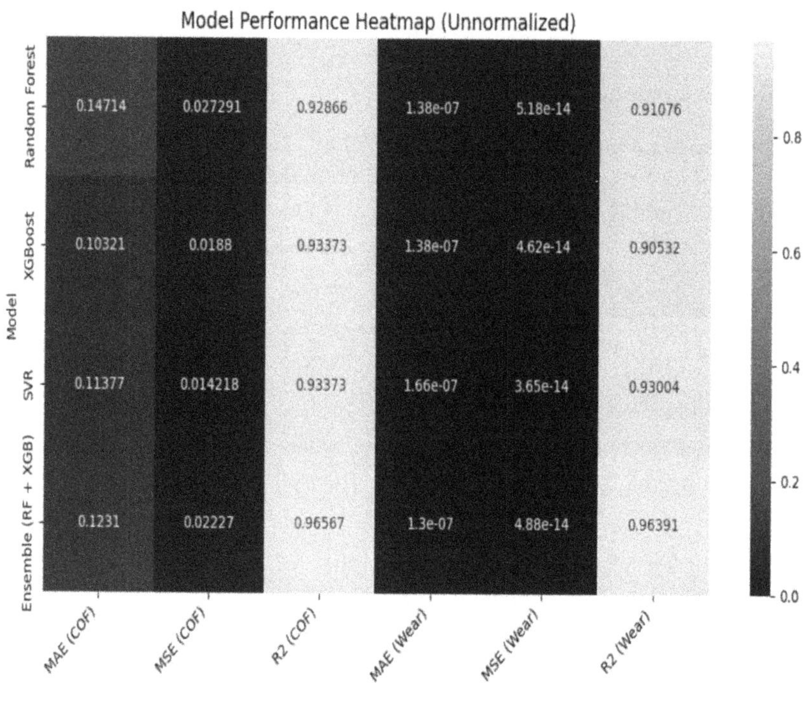

Fig. 4. Model Performance Heatmap

Table 3. Performance metrics values of each algorithm

S. No	Model	MAE (CoF)	MSE (CoF)	R^2 (CoF)	MAE (Wear)	MSE (Wear)	R^2 (Wear)
1	Random Forest	0.14714	0.027291	0.9286	1.38E−07	5.18E−14	0.9107
2	XGBoost	0.10321	0.0188	0.9337	1.38E−07	4.62E−14	0.9053
3	SVR	0.11377	0.014218	0.9337	1.66E−07	3.65E−14	0.9300
4	Ensemble (RF + XGB)	0.1231	0.02227	0.9656	1.30E−07	4.88E−14	0.9639

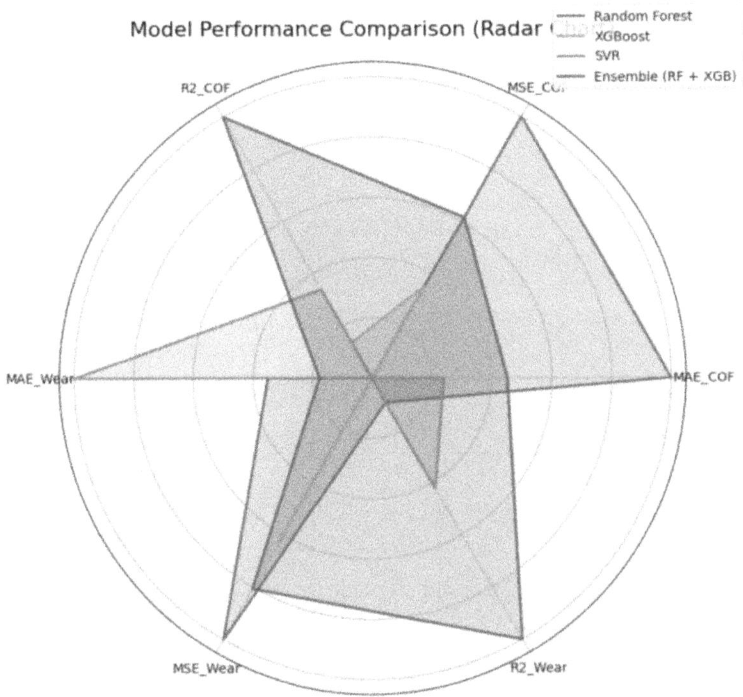

Fig. 5. Individual Performance Radar Chart

Similarly, the radar chart (Figs. 5, 6, 7) provides a comprehensive graphical comparison, where the ensemble model encloses a broader, more favourable area, reflecting its dominance across most evaluation metrics.

The experimental outcomes validate that ensemble learning strategies, which integrates multiple algorithmic approaches, lead to substantial improvements in model stability, predictive precision, and cross-condition generalization for the prediction of tribological properties of materials.

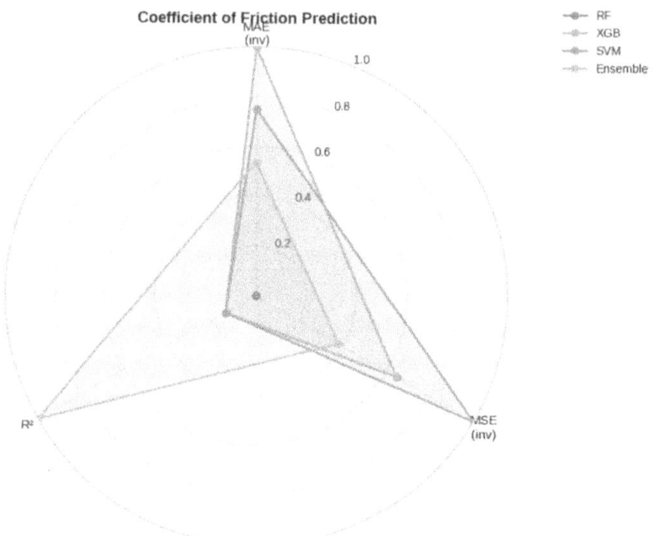

Fig. 6. Representation of CoF

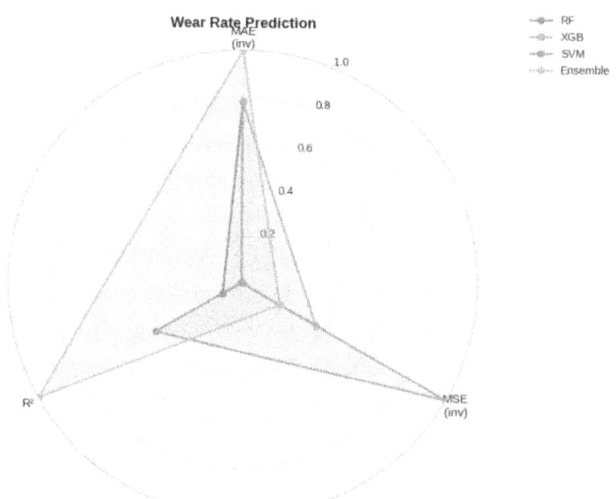

Fig. 7. Representation of Wear Rate Prediction

4 Conclusions

The Comparative assessment of four predictive modelling approaches applied to tribological data obtained from pin-on-disc testing of Ti811 produced the following key insights:

1. The highest R^2 values for CoF and wear rate were achieved by the ensemble RF + XGB model (0.965666 for CoF and 0.963905 for wear rate).
2. SVR also showed strong performance, particularly in predicting CoF (R2 = 0.9412) and wear rate (R2 = 0.9300), but was slightly less accurate than the ensemble model.
3. These results highlight the importance of hybrid ML approaches to improve model robustness and accuracy, particularly in tribological applications involving complex material behaviours.

Acknowledgment. The authors express their gratitude to the Thiagarajar College of Engineering (TCE) for supporting us to carry out this research work. Also, the financial support from TCE under Thiagarajar Research Fellowship Scheme – (File.no: TCE/RD/TRF/08) dated 27.09.2024 is gratefully acknowledged.

References

1. Saha, B., Jana, B., Yadav, J.S., Rama Krishna, C., Rao, Y.V.H., Gupta, B.: Development and certification of Ti-8Al-1Mo-1V alloy for HP compressor blades for adourengine applications. Bull. Mater. Sci. **19**, 661–669 (1996). https://doi.org/10.1007/BF02745158
2. Pin on Disk Test – About Tribology. https://www.tribonet.org/wiki/pin-on-disk-test/. Accessed 20 Mar 2025
3. Zhu, C., Jin, L., Li, W., Han, S., Yan, J.: The prediction of wear depth based on machine learning algorithms. Lubricants **12**(2), 34 (2024). https://doi.org/10.3390/lubricants12020034
4. Altay, O., Gurgenc, T., Ulas, M., Özel, C.: Prediction of wear loss quantities of ferro-alloy coating using different machine learning algorithms. Friction **8**, 107–114 (2020). https://doi.org/10.1007/s40544-018-0249-z
5. Paturi, U.M.R., Palakurthy, S.T., Reddy, N.S.: The role of machine learning in tribology: a systematic review. Arch. Comput. Meth. Eng. **30**, 1345–1397 (2023). https://doi.org/10.1007/s11831-022-09841-5
6. Sose, A.T., Joshi, S.Y., Kunche, L.K., Wang, F., Deshmukh, S.A.: A review of recent advances and applications of machine learning in tribology. Phys. Chem. Chem. Phys. **25**, 4408–4443 (2023). https://doi.org/10.1039/D2CP03692D
7. Pasha, M.B., Rao, R.N., Ismail, S., Gupta, M., Prasad, P.S.: Tribo-informatics approach to predict wear and friction coefficient of Mg/Si_3N_4 composites using machine learning techniques. Tribol. Int. **188**, 109696 (2024). https://doi.org/10.1016/j.triboint.2024.109696
8. Aydin, F., Durgut, R., Mustu, M., Demir, B.: Prediction of wear performance of $ZK60/CeO_2$ composites using machine learning models. Tribol. Int. **177**, 107945 (2023). https://doi.org/10.1016/j.triboint.2022.107945
9. Barrionuevo, G., Ramos-Grez, J., Walczak, M., Betancourt, C.: Comparative evaluation of supervised machine learning algorithms in the prediction of the relative density of 316L stainless steel fabricated by selective laser melting. Int. J. Adv. Manuf. Technol. **113**, 2335–2348 (2021). https://doi.org/10.1007/s00170-021-06596-4
10. Polmear, I., StJohn, D., Nie, J.-F., Qian, M.: Light alloys: metallurgy of the light metals. Butterworth-Heinemann (2017)
11. Mahesh, B.: Machine learning algorithms – a review. Int. J. Sci. Res. (IJSR) **9**(1), 381–386 (2020). https://www.ijsr.net/archive/v9i1/ART20203995.pdf
12. Aydın, F., Durgut, R., Mustu, M., Demir, B.: Prediction of wear performance of $ZK60/CeO_2$ composites using machine learning models. Tribol. Int. **177**, 107945 (2023). https://doi.org/10.1016/j.triboint.2022.107945

13. Zhu, C., Jin, L., Li, W., Han, S., Yan, J.: The prediction of wear depth based on machine learning algorithms. Lubricants **12**(2), 34 (2024). https://doi.org/10.3390/lubricants12020034

14. Jiang, Y., Luo, J., Liao, G., Zhao, Y., Zhang, J.: An efficient method for generation of uniform support vector and its application in structural failure function fitting. Structural Safety. **54**, 1–9 (2015). https://doi.org/10.1016/j.strusafe.2014.12.004

15. Liu, Y., Zhao, T., Ju, W., Shi, S.: Materials discovery and design using machine learning. Journal of Materiomics **3**(3), 159–177 (2017). https://doi.org/10.1016/j.jmat.2017.08.002

16. Tremmel, S., Marian, M.: Machine learning in tribology—more than buzzwords? Lubricants **10**, 68 (2022). https://doi.org/10.3390/lubricants10040068

17. Kügler, P., Marian, M., Dorsch, R., Schleich, B., Wartzack, S.: A semantic annotation pipeline towards the generation of knowledge graphs in tribology. Lubricants **10**, 18 (2022). https://doi.org/10.3390/lubricants10020018

18. Radhika, N., Sabarinathan, M., Sivaraman, S.: A comparative analysis of machine learning techniques for predicting the wear rate of ceramic coated steel. IEEE Access **12**, 146949–146967 (2024). https://doi.org/10.1109/ACCESS.2024.3473028

19. Zhao, C., Long, R., Zhang, Y., Wang, Y., Wang, Y.: Influence of characteristic parameters on the tribological properties of vein-bionic textured cylindrical roller thrust bearings. Tribol. Int. **175**, 107861 (2022). https://doi.org/10.1016/j.triboint.2022.107861

20. Jia, B., et al.: Tribological properties and machine learning prediction of FeCoCrNiAlN high-entropy coatings. Surf. Coat. Technol. **477**, 130341 (2024). https://doi.org/10.1016/j.surfcoat.2023.130341

21. Niketh, M.S., Radhika, N., Adediran, A.A., Jen, T.-C.: Enhancing high-entropy alloy performance: predictive modelling of wear rates with machine learning. Results Eng. **23**, 102387 (2024). https://doi.org/10.1016/j.rineng.2024.102387

22. Fathi, R., Chen, M., Abdallah, M., & Saleh, B. (2024, September 14). Wear prediction of functionally graded composites using machine learning. Materials (Basel), 17(18), 4523. https://doi.org/10.3390/ma17184523

23. Cavaleri, L., Asteris, P., Psyllaki, P., Douvika, M., Skentou, A., Vaxevanidis, N.: Prediction of surface treatment effects on the tribological performance of tool steels using artificial neural networks. Appl. Sci. **9**, 2788 (2019). https://doi.org/10.3390/app9142788

24. Mobarak, M.H., et al.: Scope of machine learning in materials research—a review. Appl. Surface Sci. Adv. **18**, 100523 (2023). https://doi.org/10.1016/j.apsadv.2023.100523

25. Lv, C., et al.: Machine learning: An advanced platform for materials development and state prediction in lithium-ion batteries. Adv. Mater. **34**(25), 2101474 (2022). https://doi.org/10.1002/adma.202101474

26. Ghosh, S., Dasgupta, A., Swetapadma, A.: A study on support vector machine based linear and non-linear pattern classification. In: 2019 International Conference on Intelligent Sustainable Systems (ICISS), pp. 24–28. IEEE (2019). https://doi.org/10.1109/iss1.2019.8908018

27. Himanen, L., Geurts, A., Foster, A.S., Rinke, P.: Data-driven materials science: Status, challenges, and perspectives. Adv. Sci. **6**(21), 1900808 (2019). https://doi.org/10.1002/advs.201900808

28. Shetty, S.H., Shetty, S., Singh, C., Rao, A.: Supervised machine learning: algorithms and applications. In: Singh, P. (ed.) Fundamentals and Methods of Machine and Deep Learning: Algorithms, Tools and Applications (2022). https://doi.org/10.1002/9781119821908.ch1

29. Manikanta, J.E., Ambhore, N., Dhumal, A.: Machine learning and artificial intelligence supported machining: A review and insights for future research. J. Inst. Eng. (India): Ser. C, **105**, 1653–1663 (2024). https://doi.org/10.1007/s40032-024-01118-z

30. Long, R., et al.: Tribological behavior of grooves textured thrust cylindrical roller bearings under dry wear. Adv. Mech. Eng. **13**, 16878140211067284 (2021). https://doi.org/10.1177/16878140211067284

31. Hasan, M.S., Kordijazi, A., Rohatgi, P.K., Nosonovsky, M.: Triboinformatic modeling of dry friction and wear of Aluminum base alloys using machine learning algorithms. Tribol. Int. **161**, 107065 (2021). https://doi.org/10.1016/j.triboint.2021.107065
32. Chen, C.M., Yang, C.C., Chao, C.G.: Dry sliding wear behaviors of Al–25Si–2.5Cu–1Mg alloys prepared by powder thixocasting. Mater. Sci. Eng. A **397**(1–2), 178–189 (2005). https://doi.org/10.1016/j.msea.2005.02.010

Deep Reinforcement Learning for Dynamic Energy Optimization in Data Centers

Shrivatsa Deshpande[2(✉)] [iD], Parth Gala[2] [iD], Dipti Pawade[1,2] [iD],
Avani Bhattacharjee[2] [iD], and Manan Kabra[2]

[1] Department of Computer Science and Engineering, Indian Institute of Information
Technology, Nagpur, India
dpawade@iiitn.ac.in
[2] Department of Information Technology, K J Somaiya School of Engineering, Mumbai, India
shrivatsad27@gmail.com, {gala.ps,ab2,manan.kabra}@somaiya.edu

Abstract. With data centres using 1–2% of the world's energy, efficiency in cooling is the key to sustainability. Legacy cooling technology based on static threshold values cannot adapt to dynamic workloads and climatic conditions, which causes inefficiency. In this paper, we present deep Q-learning with Experience Replay and Bellman optimization for optimal energy spending with guaranteed server safety temperatures. In a simulated data centre environment with realistic parameters, our AI model learns to adaptively adjust cooling setpoints, saving 21% energy spending compared to traditional practices. Contributions include a hybrid reward mechanism, which will be discussed in detail in the methodology, and an extensible real-time monitoring system. Variable climatic condition experiments prove the model's learnability and adaptability, resulting in a scalable, AI-based solution that realizes maximum energy efficiency over traditional techniques such as PUE. The system meets UN SDG 7 and 13 and presents actionable data centre operator and policymaker recommendations.

Keywords: Adaptive cooling · AI-based energy management · deep reinforcement learning · energy-efficient data centres

1 Introduction

Data centres are the backbone of the global digital economy that consume about 200–250 TWh of electricity annually, out of which cooling alone accounts for as much as 40% of the energy expenditures [2]. Traditionally air conditioning systems ran on strict schedules or reactive control and did not do well if workloads or environmental factors changed and consumed a tremendous amount of energy [3]. It was very explicitly stated in the 2023 IPCC report that we need to reduce the energy footprints of IT infrastructure, and this creates space for smart, AI-driven solutions to help us meet our sustainability goals. This research optimizes the problem of data centre energy consumption through a novel deep reinforcement learning (DRL)-based method [10]. Our method contrasts with others making use of static parameters such as Power Usage Effectiveness (PUE)

F. Ortiz-Rodríguez et al. (Eds.): IBCD 2025, CCIS 2845, pp. 48–61, 2026.
https://doi.org/10.1007/978-3-032-20907-8_5

[12]. Rather, we integrate the dynamic decision-making framework with environmental states in real-time such as humidity, server load, and ambient temperature. The system employs Q-learning with Experience Replay [7] to maintain thermal stability with adaptive cooling controls. The proposed architecture comprises a high-fidelity simulation platform. It employs a decision model of neural networks, and an interactive user interface for live performance tracking [15]. Our key contributions are an adaptive reward mechanism that balances energy efficiency and thermal stability, a massively scalable simulation framework for multi-climate data center experimentation, and experimental results demonstrating a 21% reduction in energy consumption relative to baseline rule-based systems. This effort extends beyond the scope of conventional approaches that involve the use of PUE and thresholding to activate the cooling system [12]. It sets the stage for demonstrating that data centers are able to conserve energy without compromising the amount of performance.

2 Literature Survey

Based on the Table 1, we can see that studies which increase the energy efficiency of data centres are getting a lot of attention lately as the world continues to push for computational power and efficiency [4]. The studies have focused on different strategies like cooling strategies which explore different methods to achieve cooling for data centres, new efficiency strategies which control the energy usage, and AI-based approaches towards optimizing power consumption in data centres A lot of research has gone into cooling strategies for data centres, efficiency strategies, and AI-based approaches toward optimizing power consumption in data centres. Qiankun Chang et al. (2024) classified cooling systems and studied different optimization strategies with a focus on the implementation of artificial intelligence and machine learning methods to improve energy efficiency analysis [5]. Their study proposed the necessity for the standardization of global energy efficiency indicators, with Power Usage Effectiveness being the overarching metric, while indicating that the meteorological conditions were excluded from consideration: an exclusion that mainly accounts for differences in energy efficiency evaluation across geographical regions. Similar research by Sijun Xu et al. (2023) surveyed three cooling methods- air, liquid, and free from the vantage point of maximizing cooling systems to reduce energy consumption [13]. The study noted that most existing work had focused on single energy-saving parameters instead of taking a more holistic view that would at least look at the interactions of several contributing factors. Artificial intelligence is increasingly considered a helpful tool for improving cooling efficiency in data centres. Nevena Lazic et al. (2018) employed model-predictive control techniques to control temperature and airflow, achieving effective thermal management without too much prior knowledge [8]. The authors found it difficult in their research to control external disturbance factors such as changes in server power and in the temperature of incoming water, affecting cooling efficiency. Reinforcement learning has been put forth in their proposals for having an efficient energy usage.[14] It was a simulation and utilized a ReLu approach based on simulated and real data for improved air flow and cooling operation which was suggested by Chi Zhou et al. (2024). The authors achieved an energy saving of 20% but also warned against overheating unless the control policy

Table 1. Literature Survey

Sr no	Citation	Relevant Findings	Research Gaps
1	Optimization Control Strategies and Evaluation Metrics of Cooling Systems in Data Centers: A Review	Areas of Focus: The article focuses heavily on the classification of cooling systems It proposed the integration of sensors in an attempt to improve the information acquisition as well as the examination of energy efficiency It also needs the creation of international yardsticks in the measurement of energy efficiency	Despite the paper's findings, it recognizes some limitations in the case of the PUE (Power Usage Effectiveness) metric, widely used to measure the energy efficiency of data centers. Environmental Factors: PUE fails to account for the meteorological conditions sufficiently, and that can cause varying PUE readings in the data centers sharing the same technology, operating in different climates
2	Thermal Management and Energy Consumption in Air, Liquid, and Free Cooling Systems for Data Centers: A Review	The article covers thermal management and the use of energy in various cooling mechanisms in data centers, i.e., air, liquid, and free cooling mechanisms. It identifies the requirement of optimization of the mechanisms by reducing the use of energy and maximizing thermal management	The report indicates that previous studies mostly dealt with the individual impacts of energy savings and thermal comfort, without providing an in-depth analysis of the above influences

(continued)

Table 1. (*continued*)

Sr no	Citation	Relevant Findings	Research Gaps
3	Reducing Data Center Energy Consumption via Coordinated Cooling and Load Management	Integrated method of energy consumption minimization in the data center by an aggregate cooling and load management strategy. The strategy is based on a modeling framework that covers the interrelationship among computational throughput, thermal generation, and power consumption It employs a network model in order to replicate the temperature dynamics in the data center, the geographical positioning of the servers as well as the cooling units. Yet another network model is employed in order to assign the servers computational tasks Configured as a constrained Markov decision process (CMDP) in order to enable the optimization of energy administration by reduction of the aggregate weighted sum of consumed power as well as computational throughput	One limitation that is stated is that discretization of the temperature readings is required so that there exists a finite number of states in the definition of the CMDP. The discretization can result in loss of accuracy in the temperature dynamic description The optimization constraints also entail leaving server nodes in their most conservative powering mode when they are idle, which is often infeasible in practice, especially in the case of varying workloads The analysis fails to take into consideration possible effects of external factors, like the fluctuations in temperature or humidity, that tend to influence the efficiency in cooling in combination with the total energy usage

(continued)

Table 1. (*continued*)

Sr no	Citation	Relevant Findings	Research Gaps
4	Data center cooling using model-predictive control	The article describes the application of model-predictive control (MPC) to control temperatures and airflow in big data centers (DCs) under limited prior knowledge. It enables efficient control after a few hours of exploration as it is both data-based and model-based The key contribution is to show that a coarse-grained linear dynamics model can safely and economically control cooling in an industrial DC, unlike conventional approaches involving intensive setup and experimentation	One of the identified limitation in the paper is the difficulty of controlling environmental excitations, e.g., incoming water temperature (EWT) and server power consumption, which may influence the performance of the cooling system Dependence on historical data to define safe control ranges has drawbacks, particularly in new or untasted settings where such data might be lacking or scarce. This may result in actions that do not maximize performance because of overly conservative control
5	Conservative Q-Learning for Offline Reinforcement Learning	Focus: This paper proposes an offline reinforcement learning which is implemented by an algorithm - Conservative Q-Learning (CQL) meant to deal with existing datasets without real-time interaction, seeking to avoid overestimation of Q-values when offline Optimization Strategy: CQL adds a regularization term to guarantee conservative Q-value estimates and avoid the possibility of distributional shift between experienced data and acquired policies Results: CQL drastically outperforms previous offline RL algorithms, with up to 2–5 times improvement over both discrete and continuous control domains	Risk of overfitting based on small real-world interaction High computational complexity in high-dimensional environments Conservative updates could cause policy improvement to be slow

is properly tuned. In the same lines, [6] Ce Chi et al. (2021) proposed a multi-agent deep RL method, enabling collaboration between cooling and IT infrastructures to enhance efficiency. They achieved an energy saving of 16.42% from their experiment, but scalability issues and multi-agent coordination during large-scale data centres were raised in the article. While the progress of AI-based cooling techniques has been enormous, they also have a few drawbacks. The majority of the research still is PUE-focused since the intrinsic measure of efficiency has not altered, albeit it does not account for factors from the environment outside, such as temperature and humidity. [1] Scalability of RL-based optimization methods is also an issue, especially in the presence of high-dimensional state and action spaces typical of large data centres. Real-time adaptability is also an issue, since the majority of current optimization models are not dynamic enough to handle sudden workload and cooling requirements changes, thus being practically less effective in dynamic environments. More advanced energy efficiency controls with external climatic conditions and workload changes are also needed to give a more accurate estimation of energy performance. Enhancing multi-agent coordination frameworks in RL algorithms can also help make AI-driven cooling techniques more efficient and scalable in large-scale data centres. Resolution of these problems, future innovation in cooling optimization can provide more energy-efficient, scalable, and adaptive solutions to modern data centres.

3 Methodology

As shown in Fig. 1, the architecture of this system is modular and is composed of three principal modules: Environment Simulation, Neural Network Model (Brain) (refer Fig. 2), and Deep Q-Learning Model (DQN) [7]. Each module has a specific function of creating a simulated environment for data centre cooling optimization, training a reinforcement learning agent to learn energy-saving actions, and memory management for experience replay [1]. All these modules together enable an AI-driven cooling system that reduces energy usage without compromising on keeping the servers at appropriate temperatures.

Environment Simulation (Environment class):
The simulation environment mimics the working conditions of a data centre by dynamically changing some of the most critical variables. It provides a realistic environment for the AI agent to learn and interact with the best cooling approaches. The conditions of the environment are primarily defined by temperature, user load, and data transmission rate, all of which influence the energy consumption of the cooling system. Table 2 provides a comprehensive list of all the major variables used for simulation [9].

As shown in Fig. 3, the core methods are as below:

- Core Methods:

  __init__(): Sets initial environment variables, like best temperature, number of users, and data rate.
  update_env(): This function is responsible for modifying the environment based on the simulation parameters initialized in the previous init() function by performing

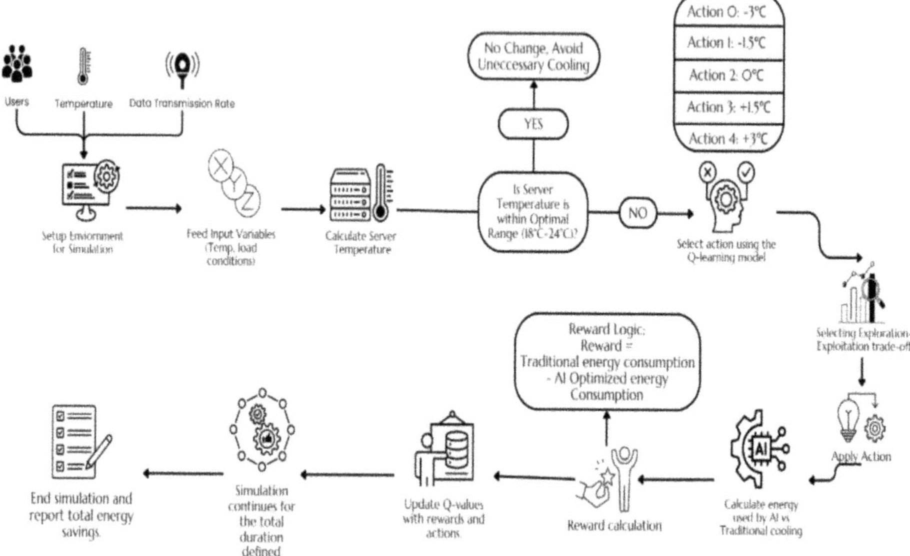

Fig. 1. System architecture diagram (Source: Author's Compilation)

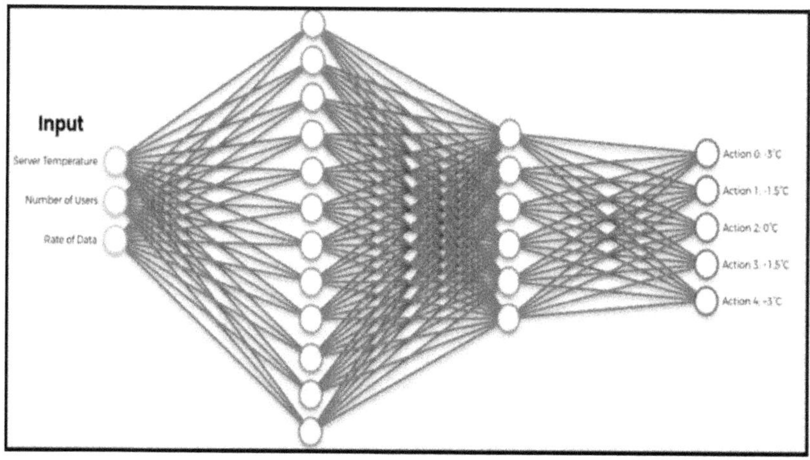

Fig. 2. Neural Network Architecture (Source: Author's Compilation)

actions by varying the temperature, number of users, and data rate. It approximates the reward by calculating energy consumed by the AI and without the AI's adjustments. The reward is positive when the AI conserves energy, guiding the agent towards which will give the agent a positive reward, i.e. actions which consume lesser energy while keeping the cpu temperature within the thresholds.

reset(): Resets the environment to an initial state at the beginning of each new episode or epoch so that all iterations of training start under the same initial conditions.

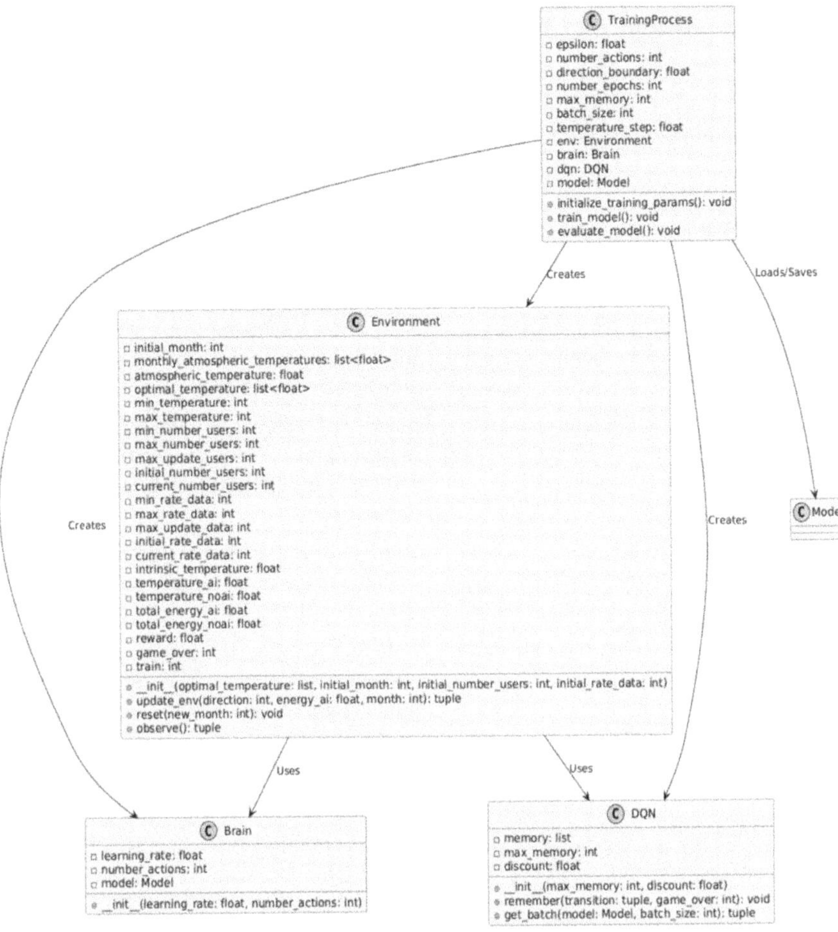

Fig. 3. UML Diagram (Source: Authors' Compilation)

observe(): Returns the current state as a vector which is normalized between 0 and 1 and it consists of parameters like temperature, user count, and data rate, and inputs the neural network model.

Neural Network Model (Brain class).
The Brain class specifies a neural network model which predicts the Q-values of each action the AI can perform. AI decides which action to take based on the greatest Q-value (Q-values are the future rewards of actions) in order to reduce energy consumption.

- Architecture:

Input Layer: Receives a 3-element state vector for normalized values of temperature_ai, current_number_users, and cur-rent_rate_data.

Table 2. Data and Variables

Variable	Description/Formula
Atmospheric Temperature	External temperature; selected monthly from a fixed list (e.g., [1.0, 5.0, 7.0]). Serves as the baseline for all temperature calculations
Intrinsic Temperature	Baseline state before cooling. Computed as: atmospheric_temperature $+ 1.25 \times$ current_number_users $+ 1.25 \times$ current_rate_data
AI-Controlled Temperature (temperature_ai)	Initially set to the intrinsic temperature, then adjusted by the AI agent's cooling actions
Non-AI Temperature (temperature_noai)	Set as the midpoint of the optimal temperature range (e.g., 21 °C for a range of 18–24 °C) to serve as a benchmark for energy usage comparisons
User Load (current_number_users)	Number of active users; updated each timestep within a range of 10 to 100 using random variations (± 5)
Data Transmission Rate (current_rate_data)	Data rate in the system; ranges between 20 and 300 and is updated each timestep with random fluctuations (± 10)
Energy Consumption Metrics	Two cumulative measures: total_energy_ai (for AI-controlled system) and total_energy_noai (for the non-AI system)
Reward Calculation	Derived from the difference in energy consumption between non-AI and AI approaches; scaled by multiplying the difference by 1e-3
State Representation for the Neural Network	Normalized state vector fed to the neural network: [Scaled AI-controlled Temperature (–20 °C to 80 °C), Scaled User Load (10–100), Scaled Data Rate (20)]

Hidden Layers: Two hidden layers with fully connected networks of 64 and 32 units, respectively, both employing a sigmoid activation function. These layers learn interactions between the input variables to enable the model to predict successful cooling actions

Output Layer: Outputs Q-values which stand for the five potential actions (temperature changes) by using a softmax activation to output probabilities over each action.

- Training Parameters:

  The learning rate of 0.001 is used, which regulates the speed at which the model learns its weights while training. The model employs Mean Squared Error (MSE) as the loss function to reduce the difference between estimated and target Q-values. The Adam optimizer is used, that facilitates fast gradient descent during back-propagation and enhances convergence rate.
  The Brain class holds the central decision-making model of the AI to enable it to choose adjustments according to the estimated effect on energy consumption

Deep Q-Learning Model (DQN class).
The DQN class covers the Deep Q-Learning algorithm [7]. It keeps transition consisting of current state, action chosen, reward received, and next state in a replay memory. By selecting random batches of stored transitions, the algorithm reduces the correlation among subsequent states and stabilizes learning by an epsilon-greedy exploration strategy. The decision to use this strategy was taken in order to obtain optimal cooling strategies while slowly moving toward exploitation as the model learns the environment. The mechanism of the Experience Re-play in the DQN class is essential for efficient learning, as it avoids overfitting to current actions and enables the model to converge toward an optimal policy over time. As in Fig. 3, the attributes and main methods are as follows:

- Attributes:

  Memory: Retains previous transitions (state, action, reward, next state) with the maximum capacity as max_memory. This was done so that the model refrains learning only current patterns and instead enables it to generalize in various situations.
  Discount Factor: Based on the runs we did with the algorithm we found that The discount factor (discount) of 0.8 fetches the best results in such environments as it values current rewards over future rewards, directing the AI to maximize speedy short-term action while still looking at long-term impact.

- Core Methods:

  remember(): This function is used to append transitions back into memory, so it doesn't grow beyond the capacity. Appending is done via FIFO algorithm. Therefore, the function also allows the model to see subsequent actions and learn over a longer sequence of experiences.
  get_batch(): Randomly samples a batch of transitions in/out of memory to train the neural network. For each transition, it calculates the Q-value target depending on whether the episode has concluded or not. By training in batch, the correlation between the next states is decreased, making learning more stable.

In our study, we optimize data centre cooling by using a Deep Q-Network (DQN) with experience replay—a type of deep reinforcement learning that learns effective control strategies through trial and error. The approach is built around a neural network architecture [15] as shown in Fig. 3 that estimates the expected future rewards (or Q-values) for five possible temperature adjustments. The network is given a three-dimensional, normalized input vector in which each dimension corresponds to the AI-controlled temperature, the number of active users, and the data rate of transmission. The inputs are passed through two hidden layers of 64 and 32 neurons, respectively, with sigmoid activation functions that preserve the non-linear relationships in the data, before being presented to an output layer that uses a SoftMax function to produce a probability distribution over the five possible actions. In summary, the model consists of one input layer, two hidden layers, and an output layer of 5 neurons, which stand for 5 possible actions. Training the network is done by minimizing the mean squared error (MSE) between the predicted Q-values and the actual outcomes, utilizing the Adam optimizer at a learning rate of 0.001 to change the network's weights substantially. Concurrently, the DQN class enacts the deep Q-learning process: as the agent explores the simulation environment, it stores every experience as a transition (comprising current state, selected action, obtained reward, and new state) into a replay memory. The memory is a mixed history, enabling the model to sample older transitions randomly and hence disrupt the correlation between successive states—a crucial step to stabilizing training. The strategy employs an epsilon-greedy policy (epsilon = 0.3) to balance the desire to explore (select new actions) and exploitation (take known, rewarding actions), and a discount factor of 0.9 to reward immediate rewards without discounting longer rewards. Training takes place for a total of 10 epochs, where the environment is reset at the beginning of each epoch and the agent keeps on learning its policy from the received reward. Early stopping is applied where the cumulative reward does not progress any further, preventing overfitting to particular situations. The model is saved and is validated by running it through a one-year simulation, which is called the inference mode (with epsilon set to 0, i.e., only the best-known actions are picked), ensuring that the learned actions make a significant reduction in energy usage.

4 Empirical Results

The AI data center energy management system significantly reduced energy use and operational costs. Some of the main observations and results are:

1. *Energy Savings*: The system showed a reduction of 21% in energy consumption compared to the traditional, threshold-based cooling systems. This is the result of the reward calculation and adjustment that the system made in real time while measuring the parameters like data load and server temperature.
2. *System Impact*: The system successfully maintained the temperatures of the servers between 18 °C-24 °C. Thus, energy savings were achieved without compromising performance.
3. *Challenges Confronted*: Calibration of hyperparameters including learning rate and exploration-exploitation trade-off became important. These hyperparameters were critical to the success of learning and improving the energy efficiency of the model.

4. *AI Efficiency Compared to Traditional Systems:* The AI cooling unit changed its cooling modes based on the load, so it didn't waste energy trying to keep a constant temperature. As a result, we could overcome the limitations of traditional systems as the AI system used less energy and worked well with different server loads and room temperatures.
5. *Restrictions:* The proposed model works well in simulations, but it hasn't been tested in a real data center yet. This makes it harder for us to apply the results to real-world situations. Combining predictive forecasting tools (like workload or weather prediction) with external monitoring tools could make reliability and performance even better.

As shown in Table 3, the AI cooling system saved more energy than the baseline threshold based non-AI system.

Table 3. Comparative analysis

Method	Energy Savings	Average Response Time	Setpoint Stability	Notes
Static Threshold	Baseline	Instant	Stable	No adaptability
SAFARI (Wang et al., 2022)	19%	Moderate	Slight Drift	Safe RL, slow learning
SAC (Guo et al., 2024)	23%	Slow	Slight Oscillation	Adaptive, high compute cost
Our DQN Hybrid	**21%**	Fast	**Stable**	Adaptive, Stable, lightweight, safety enforced

Our method outperformed baselines in energy savings as summarized in Table 3.

Prior methods focused on energy or safety, not both. Hybrid reward functions remain underexplored. Real-time interfaces are rarely integrated. Our DQN model bridges these gaps, balancing energy, safety, and observability. Figures 4 and 5 show a comparison of the energy usage of the AI system compared to a non-AI system.

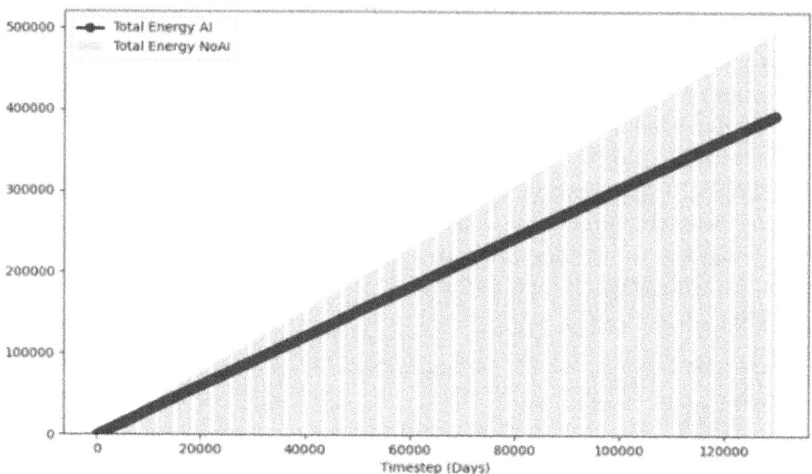

Fig. 4. Comparison between AI vs non-AI for 3 months (Source: Author's Compilation)

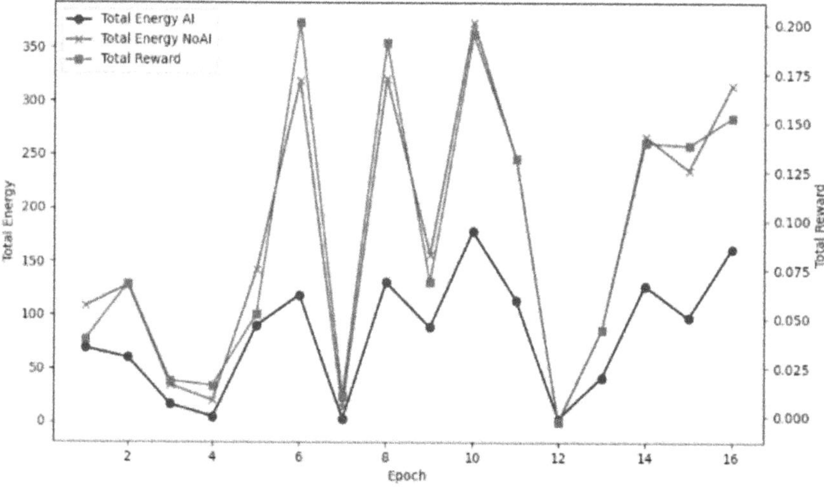

Fig. 5. Energy usage Comparison between AI vs non-AI with reward (Source: Author's Compilation)

5 Conclusion

This project illustrates the capability of AI-based systems to enhance energy efficiency and operational sustainability in data centres. The final system claims that it will achieve energy savings of as much as 21% compared to a traditional rule-based cooling environment. The reported energy savings were achieved while maintaining the server temperatures in the optimum functioning limit of 18 °C–24 °C. The conclusion shown here can be extended to other energy-intensive systems and could help us reduce the operating costs using intelligent systems that take proactive measures to reduce energy usage based on usage patterns. The Hybrid reward system that this system proposes will help us make the system more adaptable to new and unknown usage patterns. Thus, it is concluded that intelligent control systems can balance performance while providing energy savings.

References

1. Guo, Y., Qu, S., Wang, C., Xing, Z., Duan, K.: Optimal dynamic thermal management for data center via soft actor-critic algorithm with dynamic control interval and combined-value state space. Appl. Energy 373(C), S030626192401198X (2024)
2. Zhang, Q., Chng, C.B., Chen, K., Lee, P.S., Chui, C.-K.: DRL-S: toward safe real-world learning of dynamic thermal management in data center. Expert Syst. Appl. **214**, 119146 (2022)
3. Wang, R., Zhang, X., Zhou, X., Wen, Y., Tan, R.: Toward physics-guided safe deep reinforcement learning for green data center cooling control. In: Proceedings of the 2022 ACM/IEEE 13th International Conference on Cyber-Physical Systems (ICCPS), pp. 159–169 (2022)
4. Zhan, X., et al.: Data center cooling system optimization using offline reinforcement learning. In: 13th International Conference on Learning Representations (ICLR 2025) (2025)
5. Chang, Q., Huang, Y., Liu, K., Xu, X., Zhao, Y., Pan, S.: Optimization control strategies and evaluation metrics of cooling systems in data centers: a review. Sustainability **16**(16)
6. Ji, K., et al.: Cooperatively improving data center energy efficiency based on multi-agent deep reinforcement learning. Energies **14**(8), 2159 (2021)
7. Kumar, A., Zhou, A., Tucker, G., Levine, S.: Conservative Q-learning for offline reinforcement learning. arXiv preprint arXiv:2006.04779 (2020). https://doi.org/10.48550/arXiv.2006.04779
8. Lazic, N., et al.: Data center cooling using model-predictive control. In: Proceedings of the 32nd Conference on Neural Information Processing Systems (NeurIPS-18), vol. 32, pp. 3818–3827 (2018)
9. Parolini, L., Sinopoli, B., Krogh, B.H.: Reducing data center energy consumption via coordinated cooling and load management. IEEE Trans. Control Syst. Technol. **26**(4), 826–2759 (2018)
10. Riedmiller, M.: Neural fitted Q iteration – first experiences with a data efficient neural reinforcement learning method. In: Gama, J., Camacho, R., Brazdil, P., Jorge, A., Torgo, L. (eds.) Machine Learning: ECML 2005, LNCS, vol. 3720, pp. 317–328. Springer, Heidelberg (2005)
11. Skianis, K., Giannopoulos, A., Gkonis, P., Trakadas, P.: Data aging matters: federated learning-based consumption prediction in smart homes via age-based model weighting. Electronics **12**(14), 3054 (2023). https://doi.org/10.3390/electronics12143054
12. Thein, T., Myo, M.M., Parvin, S., Gawanmeh, A.: Reinforcement learning-based methodology for energy-efficient resource allocation in cloud data centers. J. King Saud Univ. Comput. Inf. Sci. **32**(10), 1127–1139 (2020). https://doi.org/10.1016/j.jksuci.2018.11.005
13. Xu, S., Zhang, H., Wang, Z.: Thermal management and energy consumption in air, liquid, and free cooling systems for data centers: a review. Energies **16**(1), 123 (2023)
14. Chi, G., Dong, R., Louis, R., Grier, A.: Simulator-based reinforcement learning for data center cooling optimization. Meta AI Engineering Blog (2024)
15. Kahil, S., Petri, E., Elmusrati, M.: Reinforcement learning for data center energy efficiency optimization: a systematic literature review and research roadmap. Appl. Energy **389**, 125734 (2025)

Grammatical Error Correction for Marathi Using Fine-Tuned Transformer Models

Ved Dhopeshwarkar, Soham Mehta$^{(\boxtimes)}$, Mayur Valvi, Aahan Rembersu, and Rutuja Kulkarni

Department of Computer Engineering, SCTR's Pune Institute of Computer Technology, Pune, India
samm23j@gmail.com, rutujakulkarni@pict.edu

Abstract. The language of the research Marathi is a morphologically rich language that does not have dedicated research in Grammatical Error Correction (GEC) although other languages have made significant progress in NLP. The reason of this gap can be mainly explained by the impossibility of publicly available datasets and benchmarks of Marathi GEC. To fill this gap, we have done the extensive review of Marathi NLP literature, comparing datasets and language models as well as language issues. We also examined GEC projects in other languages to determine effective methodology and state-of-the-art models that can be used in the Marathi. Through these observations, we have built a high-quality dataset of incorrect-correct sentence pairs in a systematic way, and we were initially interested in basic Subject-Object-Verb (SOV) types of sentences. To assess how well three transformer-based models, IndicBART, Marathi-T5, and Varta-T5 perform in Marathi GEC, we optimized them on this dataset. The performance analysis based on the BLEU measure shows that IndicBART and Varta-T5 are much higher than Marathi-T5 with a BLEU score of 0.98. Moreover, both models are characterized by the high precision and recall, which means that they are accurate on detecting and correcting grammatical mistakes of the predetermined scope of the dataset. This study will give Marathi GEC a basis that will not only offer a benchmark set, but also a robust one at that. Baseline models, which are a part of further elaboration of Marathi NLP applications.

Keywords: Marathi NLP · Grammatical Error Correction (GEC) · IndicBART · Marathi-T5 · Varta-T5 · BLEU Score · Transformer Models · Dataset Creation

1 Introduction

Grammatical Error Correction (GEC) is an important activity in Natural Language Processing (NLP) that improves the level of fluency and accuracy of text. Although the research on GEC has been done in large scale on high-resource languages such as English, there is little to no research done on Marathi GEC, simply because of the absence of datasets and standardized benchmarks [1]. In understanding this gap, we have first analyzed the current achievements of the research in Marathi NLP by conducting a descriptive survey of datasets, language models and linguistic issues specific

F. Ortiz-Rodríguez et al. (Eds.): IBCD 2025, CCIS 2845, pp. 62–73, 2026.
https://doi.org/10.1007/978-3-032-20907-8_6

to Marathi. Also, we did some research in GEC in other languages to learn about the best practices and model architectures which could be translated to Marathi. Marathi is a morphologically rich language with complex case system (vibhakti), subjectverb agreement rules depending on the tense, gender and number. Even though Alt-hough Marathi has a flexible word order, it adheres to the pattern of Subject-Object-Verb (SOV). Since its grammar is complex, rule-based methods have a low generalization ability to various structures of sentences, and thus, data-based deep learning models have significant potential as a solution [12].

To overcome these, we constructed a high-quality dataset of incorrect-correct sentences pairs systematically and with care to cover the frequent grammatical errors, including vibhakti errors, verb tense mismatches and subject-object mismatch. We then fine-tuned three transformer-based models—IndicBART, Marathi-T5, and Varta-T5—on this dataset and evaluated their performance using the BLEU score. Our results demonstrate that IndicBART and Varta-T5 significantly outperform Marathi-T5, achieving a BLEU score of 0.98. Both models show a high precision and recall, producing accuracte corrections on the test dataset. This study thus establishes the first dataset for GEC in Marathi, a base for further research in Marathi GEC as well as Marathi NLP [23, 24].

2 Literature Review

GEC is a Natural Language Processing task in which Grammatical errors are detected and corrected in text. For Languages like English and Hindi, robust GEC systems have been made. The same can't be said for Marathi, due to limited resources and data based on Marathi GEC particularly.

This survey focuses mainly on 2 parts, one being the NLP work done in Marathi and similar Indic Languages ie different tasks like Entity Recognition, Corpus generation, Models, etc. and the other part being GEC systems in other languages, how different methods are implemented for Grammatical error correction in other languages.

MahaCorpus is a Marathi NLP resource, which consists of a large collection of sentences and tokens. MahaBERT, a BERT model built on Marathi data can be adapted for GEC. MahaNER is a Named entity recognition dataset built on Marathi sentences as well [1].

Seq2Seq Models and embeddings like MahaGPT, a Generative Model based on GPT, along with MahaFT, that is Marathi FastText embeddings are things which can be used or referred for Marathi GEC, which in itself is a Seq2Seq task [1].

Marathi text classification has been done using CNNs, LSTMs and Transformers, which can help in GEC to classify whether sentences are grammatically correct or not. Kulkarni et al. evaluated deep learning models on Marathi text, which can be used for model selection for GEC [2].

Amin et al. implemented translation for code mixed Marathi-English Text using BERT, Multilingual Fine tuning, to extract features from code mixed data, which can help in context errors when attention mechanism is applied [3].

The MahaNER dataset, developed for Named Entity Recognition tasks can be a reference to help in identifying entities of certain terms in sentences, helping solve gender, case and entity agreement-based issues in GEC [4].

Mujadia and Sharma (2021) explored Neural Machine Translation for English-Marathi translation, which is a Seq2Seq task. This uses positional encoding, preserving word order, sentence structure in NMT, which can be used in GEC for correcting sentences to a particular format ie (SOV). NMT may also at times generate inaccurate translations, which can be a way of increasing and improving data for training Marathi GEC models [5]. Question-Answering in Marathi, another Seq2Seq task is done, where transformers are used to extract answers based on sequences, which thus can be used in GEC to detect and correct errors and sentence structure [7]. MahaNews, a Marathi news article dataset has been trained on models like MahaBERT, to classify text. In GEC, this can be useful, particularly to detect and classify errors in large documents like articles [8]. Tweet classification on HASOC Datasets has been done, to detect offensive language or hate speech on Marathi tweets. MahaTweetBERT has been developed to classify hate speech [9].

Approaches developed by Xue (2020) for multilingual GEC, are highly relevant to Marathi as well. Finetuning mT5 for Marathi allows for the use of knowledge from other languages, improving error detection and correction accuracy [11]. Similarly, MuRIL,a multilingual model trained on Wikipedia and OSCAR corpora, can be fine-tuned to handle both monolingual and bilingual Marathi text for GEC tasks. The model has performed strongly in tokenization, transliteration, and translation tasks, which are directly relevant to GEC [18]. Grammatical error detection and correction methods from Hindi as explored by Mittal et al. (2019), have demonstrated the effectiveness of using rule-based and statistical techniques. These techniques can be adapted to Marathi to enhance error detection accuracy in GEC [12]. Additionally, synthetic error generation for Hindi, as implemented by Sonawane et al. (2020), can be adapted to Marathi, using similar tools such as ERRANT for inflectional error generation. This helps in expanding our dataset [14]. Synthetic error generation is crucial for addressing the scarcity of annotated GEC datasets. Stahlberg and Kumar (2021) proposed models for generating.

synthetic errors using probabilistic and optimal strategies, which can be applied to Marathi. Likewise, NER and BERT models have been applied to identify and rectify errors with the assistance of OCR generated text. Such approaches [15] can be used by Marathi GEC. Varta-T5 is a ready-prepared transformer-based model that has been trained on the Varta corpus made up of 41.8 million news articles in 14 Indic languages including Marathi. This model involves span and gap sentences as training targets, and the model is called gap-sentence generation. it handy with text generating. Varta-T5 can be customized to Marathi GEC based on its strong understanding of linguistic structures in other Indic languages. It also can deal with long documents and various language contexts, and this makes it a promising resource [23]. Lastly, the sandhi splitting as a method of usage in the Sanskrit to deal with compound words can be applied to Marathi to deal with the morphologically rich word forms [20]. This strategy, social POS tagging strategies of the Marathi language, including those created by Kadam et al., can be used so that sentence-level parsing and grammar structure get properly followed during correction [21]. Additionally, adapting BIS annotation standards from Konkani to Marathi, as explored by Vaz et al. (2020), can resolve ambiguities in punctuation and sentence structure in Marathi GEC [22].

3 Methodology

3.1 Dataset Preparation

Unlike other languages like English and Hindi, which have pre-existing GEC datasets or content, a dataset had to be created specifically for Marathi GEC. Naturally Marathi follows a Subject-Object-Verb Sentence structure, where agreements in subjects or objects and the verb based on tense, gender and person matters for a sentence to be grammatically correct [1, 6]. Marathi grammar adheres to distinct subject-verb agreement rules based on tense:

- Simple Present & Future Tenses: Subject-Verb agreement is based on gender and number [2].
- Simple Present & Future Tenses: Subject-Verb agreement is based on gender and number [2].
- Simple Past Tense: Object-Verb agreement is the key determinant [2].

To ensure linguistic correctness, a controlled vocabulary was curated, and incorrect-correct sentence pairs were systematically generated. The vocabulary included a diverse range of commonly used words:

- Pronouns: मी, तू, तुम्ही, तो, ती, ते, आम्ही
- Common Nouns: केळं, अन्न, पेन, मोबाईल, बॉल, भात, चप्पल, कादंबरी
- Proper Nouns & Personal Names: सिद्धार्थ, अमृता
- Common Verbs: खाणे, बघणे, घेणे, करणे, उचलणे, वाचणे, सोडणे, टाकणे, वाजवणे, ठेवणे

While not exhaustive, these examples reflect the core of the vocabulary used for sentence generation and error simulation.

To generate incorrect-correct sentence pairs, scripts were designed to ensure that each incorrect sentence contained exactly one grammatical error [3, 19]. The data was organized according to the grammatical guidelines:

Present Tense Data: Separate datasets were generated for 1st, 2nd, and 3rd person.

- Future Tense Data: A single dataset was created as subject-verb agreement remains consistent across persons.
- Past Tense Data: Systematic errors have been added depending on the object-verb agreement.
- For example, the incorrect sentence " तू बॉल करतील" violates subject-verb agreement rules, whereas the correct sentence is " तू बॉल करशील" The dataset was organized as follows:
- Train Set: 158,041 entries
- Test Set: 39,511 entries

A well-balanced dataset for Marathi GEC model training and evaluation is guaranteed by this methodical approach.

The data set has such representative pairs as presented in Fig. 1.

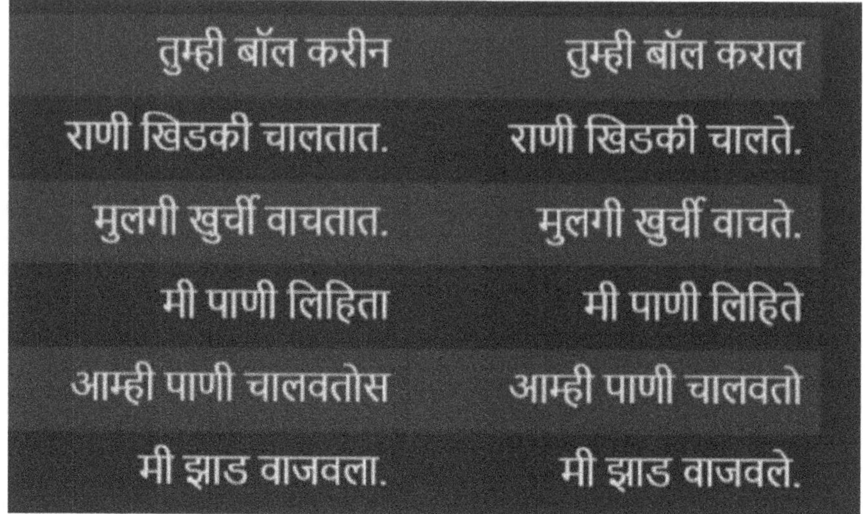

Fig. 1. Overview of Dataset

3.2 Models

In the case of Marathi Grammatical Error Correction (Marathi GEC), we used the state-of-the-art sequence-to-sequence (Seq2Seq) models, which have been shown to have a good performance in the text-to-text transformation applications. The selected models include:

- IndicBART (ai4bharat/IndicBART) [24]
- Marathi-T5 (nipunsadvilkar/marathi-t5-base) [18]
- Varta-T5 (ai4bharat/varta-t5) [23]

The models were specifically adjusted to suit the task of the Marathi GEC to improve grammatical correction. IndicBART is a multilingual sequence-to-sequence pre-trained model that is Indic-specific. It is algorithmically enhanced to use Indian language, and has a few major benefits:

- Trained on 452M sentences and 9B tokens [24].
- Indian language optimized, to guarantee better grammatical corrections.
- Helps with Marathi and Hindi cross-lingual learning by using Devanagari script.
- Fine-tuning and decoding are more efficient than larger multilingual models such as mT5 [17, 24].

Marathi-T5 is based on the T5 architecture, which reframes NLP tasks as text-to-text transformations. This model is optimized to different mixing Marathi NLP tasks and has been trained to produce grammatically correct sentences by reorganizing noisy input data [18].

Another Indic-specific transformer model, called Varta-T5, is optimized on various corpora of the Indian language. It uses a comparable training approach to the IndicBART but is additionally refined to text-to-text production over a variety of domains [23].

3.3 System Architecture

The proposed Marathi Grammar Error Correction (GEC) system is based on a structured, end-to-end pipeline, and it utilizes transformer-based language models. The system is meant to identify and fix grammatical mistakes within user input Marathi sentences [1, 2].

The architecture presented in Fig. 2, starts with the User Input module, in which a possible incorrect sentence in Marathi is given. This input is provided to the Input Handler, which is liable for text normalization and tokenization. Model-specific tokenizers are also used to carry out tokenization, including those linked to IndicBART, Marathi-T5, or Varta-T5 [18, 23, 24].

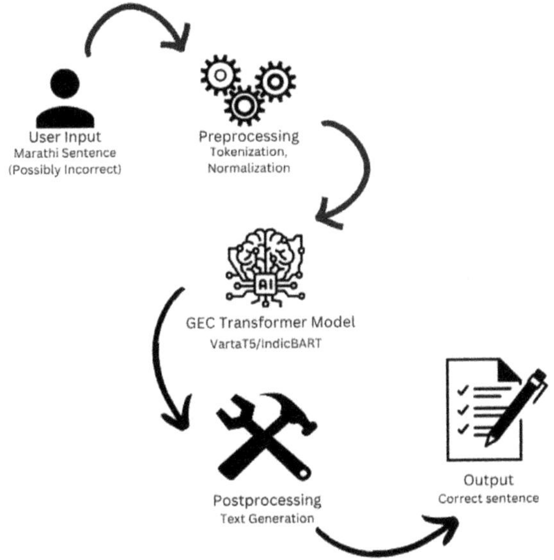

Fig. 2. System architecture

After preprocessing, the tokenized input is sent through the GEC Model which is a fine-tuned transformer. Three models can be used in accordance with the use case and performance requirements: IndicBART, Marathi-T5 or Varta-T5. These models have been optimized using a set of erroneous and corrected Marathi sentences annotated with error types, such that all the training set sentences have a single grammatical error [3, 19]. The model will be used to predict the fixed form of the sentence but still it does not change the meaning of the sentence.

The produced output tokens are then handed through a Decoding and Postprocessing module. This component performs beam search decoding to generate the most probable corrected sequence [11] and subsequently detokenizes the output to form a complete sentence in Devanagari script [11, 19].

Finally, the Corrected Output is presented to the user as a grammatically accurate Marathi sentence. This pipeline ensures that the system is robust, scalable and capable of handling grammatical inconsistencies. The modular architecture also allows easy substitution and benchmarking of different transformer models, which can be fine-tuned on different datasets, under identical evaluation conditions, with performance assessed using BLEU scores, a widely used metric in grammatical error correction and machine translation tasks [11, 19].

3.4 Evaluation Metrics

As Marathi GEC is a sequence-to-sequence task, the BLEU evaluation metric (Bilingual Evaluation Understudy) was used to evaluate the performance of the 3 models on the test dataset, where it measures the overlap between the model output and the correct sentence using n-gram precision [11, 19]. It is particularly useful for tasks like grammatical error correction where lexical similarity with the reference is important.

Evaluation steps include:

- Loading the Model & Data – The fine-tuned IndicBART, Marathi-T5, and Varta-T5 models were loaded with FP16 precision for memory efficiency, and the test dataset of 39,511 incorrect-correct sentence pairs was prepared for evaluation.
- Generating Predictions – Incorrect sentences were tokenized and processed in batches using beam search decoding.
- Computing BLEU Scores – Sentences were tokenized using NLTK, and the BLEU score was computed using the evaluate library [19].

The BLEU score is calculated using the formula:

$$BLEU = BP.e^{\sum_{n=1}^{N}(w_n.logp_n)} \tag{1}$$

where:

- p_n is the modified precision for n-grams (1-g to N-gram),
- w_n is the weight for each n-gram level (typically uniform: $\frac{1}{N}$),
- BP is the brevity penalty:

$$BP = \{1, c > re^{(1-\frac{r}{c}}, c \leq r \tag{2}$$

where c and r are the lengths of the candidate and reference sentences, respectively.

Illustrative Examples:

In order to compute the BLEU score, we will take the following two instances:

Example 1:

- Candidate: " तुम्ही फोन घ्याल "
- Reference: " तुम्ही फोन घ्याल "
- Unigram Matches: 3/3
- Bigram Matches: 2/2
- Trigram Matches: 1/1
- 4-g Matches: 0/0 → handled with smoothing
- Brevity Penalty: BP = 1 (lengths are equal)

$$BLEU = 1.e^{(\frac{1}{4}(loglog(1)+loglog(1)+loglog(1)+loglog(1)))}$$

Final BLEU Score: 1.00.

Example 2:

- Candidate: " *तुम्ही शेती टाकतात* "
- Reference: " *तुम्ही शेती टाकता* "
- Unigram Matches: 3/4
- Bigram Matches: 2/3
- Trigram Matches: 1/2
- 4-g Matches: 0/1 → smoothed
- BP = 1 (same length)

$$BLEU = 1.e^{(\frac{1}{4}(loglog(0.75)+loglog(0.66)+loglog(0.5)+loglog(\varepsilon)))}$$

Assuming smoothing factor $\varepsilon = 0.1$, BLEU $\approx$ **0.24**.

These examples demonstrate how BLEU considers both n-gram precision and length adequacy, making it a suitable metric for grammatical correction evaluation. In addition to BLEU, we computed precision and recall to evaluate the accuracy of the model-generated corrections. Precision measures the proportion of model edits that are actually correct. Recall measures the proportion of actual grammatical errors that the model successfully corrected.

4   Results

Table 1. Results

Model	BLEU Score	Precision	Recall
Marathi-T5	0.79	0.9880	1.00
IndicBART	0.98	0.9899	1.00
Varta-T5	0.98	0.9899	1.00

Both IndicBART and Varta-T5 as presented in Table 1, significantly outperformed Marathi-T5 in the grammatical error correction (GEC) task. IndicBART and Varta-T5 each achieved a BLEU score of 0.98, along with precision of 0.9899 and recall of 1.0000, whereas Marathi-T5 lagged behind with a BLEU score of 0.79, precision of 0.9880, and recall of 1.0000. These high BLEU scores for IndicBART and Varta-T5 indicate strong syntactic and lexical alignment with the reference outputs, demonstrating the effectiveness of multilingual and domain-adapted pretraining for low-resource languages like Marathi [17, 18, 23, 24]. Since evaluation was conducted on a 39k-entry test dataset whose vocabulary was largely consistent with the training set, Marathi-T5 also performed decently on familiar constructs. However, its limited ability to generalize to more complex patterns or out-of-distribution examples was evident in the comparative results.

Although Marathi-T5 showed competence in correcting frequent and simple sentence structures, it struggled with out-of-vocabulary (OOV) words, particularly those involving morphologically complex or low-frequency verb forms. As an illustration, the constructions of second person past tense were frequently poorly managed because they require object-verb agreement and dialectal usage, and this indicates an omission in exposing the model to such constructions during training. This weakness implies that vocabulary should be expanded, and more various types of verbs and sentence constructions should be used.

To solve this, more coverage of verb tenses such as perfect, continuous and negative form of verb in first, second and third-person situations would have been helpful to the dataset. At this point, the data is strongly biased in favor of simple examples of sentences that use affirmative past tense in SOV sequence, which restricts the model to generalizing outside of its specific grammatical subsets.

For a sentence " त्याने चित्रपट बघतिलो", which is gramatically incorrect, IndicBART and Varta-T5's outputs were the same ie " त्याने चित्रपट बघतिला" which is the correct form. Nevertheless, it was found that Marathi T5 transformed verb " बघतिलो" to " बघेल", which is not correct. Manual analysis of ~ 20 SOV-structured sentences showed that IndicBART and Varta-T5 demonstrate higher robustness and generalization, especially in morphological correction and tense alignment. Both were also able to correct errors involving unseen verbs and irregular conjugations, whereas Marathi-T5 frequently faltered in such cases.

Despite this, all three models consistently underperformed on second person past tense sentences. This shows an important aspect of enhancement in the future datasets and models.

The existing dataset is rule-based, lacks vibhakti (case marker) errors, and under-represents complex verb structures as presented in Figs. 3, 4 and 5. For example:

"तो गाव जातो" (incorrect) → Correct: "तो गावाला जातो"

Such errors involving postpositions and case inflections are not well-represented in the training set, hence models cannot learn to correct them. Also, there are no examples done on free word order, negations, and tense diversity which further restricts real-life performance.

Though currently IndicBART and Varta-T5 offer good baselines of Marathi GEC, it is necessary to have vocabulary coverage, past tense with second person, and include tense-saturated and structurally diverse instances. It will be essential to expand the data set to include perfect, continuous, negative, and the use of vibhaktis to make Marathi GEC systems stronger and more similar to systems based on high-resource.

Input Sentence: तुम्ही शेती टाकतात
Correct Sentence: तुम्ही शेती टाकता
Model Output: तुम्ही शेती टाकता

Fig. 3. Present Tense Correction

Input Sentence: मी काम करशील.
Correct Sentence: मी काम करीन.
Model Output: मी काम करीन.

Fig. 4. Future Tense Correction

Input Sentence: त्याने पाणी टाकला.
Correct Sentence: त्याने पाणी टाकले.
Model Output: त्याने पाणी टाकले.

Fig. 5. Past Tense Correction

5 Conclusion

The current study was devoted to the work of Marathi Grammatical Error Correction (GEC) through the fine-tuning and performance of three models based on transformers-IndicBART, Marathi-T5 and Varta-T5. The performance of these was that IndicBART and Varta-T5 performed better than Marathi-T5 where both languages got a higher BLEU score of 0.98, which signifies that these engines are highly able to correct grammatical errors in Marathi text. Also, the models were highly precise (0.9899) as well as recall (1.0000) which proves their efficiency in effective and comprehensive error correction. The BLEU score of Marathi-T5 was slightly lower, standing at 0.79, but it still showed fairly good performance which can be explained by the fact that the test vocabulary was rather like the training one.

Whereas the results are promising, limits endure. The dataset is more of a controlled vocabulary and structured grammatical errors, although it was generated in a rather ordered way. It does not have sufficient expressions of dialectal differences, colloquial speech and concise sentence structure prevalent in natural Marathi conversations. The other weaknesses evident in the models were consistent ones, in correcting the second person past tense, perfect and continuous tenses, negative constructions, and in some vibhakti (case marker) and verb agreement mistakes. It means that better vocabulary coverage and a greater variety of grammar should be provided in the dataset in all tenses and informal sentences.

Given that Marathi has been used in different regions with different dialects and usage patterns, GEC models should adopt changes and be able to cope up with this instance of linguistic diversity. Moreover, the system should be extended to include a wider range of grammatical rules like aspectual forms, conditional clauses, complex verb structures and compound sentence structure which may also contribute to the increased real-life applicability of this system. Introducing more comprehensive grammatical checks, the other types of errors such as punctuation, formats, case handling, etc. can enhance how this model handles more complex grammatical sentences, and this increases its strength as well. Like Grammarly in the English language, the system is capable of more patterns of sentences with a higher degree of accuracy.

Even better is incorporating User feedback on the model can enhance the learning capability of the model further particularly when it comes to context-based sentence variations in grammar.

This research provides a stiff ground to both Marathi NLP and GEC. Therefore, it has immense prospects of developing and enhancing NLP tools, especially in Indian languages. The performance and usability of the Marathi GEC systems can be enhanced by expanding datasets, introducing sentences or variations such as other dialects and feedback-based systems among others.

References

1. Joshi, R.: L3cube-mahanlp: Marathi natural language processing datasets, models, and library. arXiv preprint arXiv:2205.14728 (2022)
2. Kulkarni, A., Mandhane, M., Likhitkar, M., Kshirsagar, G., Jagdale, J., Joshi, R.: Experimental evaluation of deep learning models for Marathi text classification. In: Proceedings of International Conference on Recent Trends Machine Learning IoT Smart Cities Applications, pp. 605–613 (2022). https://doi.org/10.1007/978-981-16-5104-7_61
3. Amin, D., Govilkar, S., Kulkarni, S., Lalit, Y.S., Khwaja, A.A., Xavier, D., Gupta, S.G.: Marathi-English code-mixed text generation. arXiv preprint arXiv:2309.16202 (2023)
4. Patil, P., Ranade, A., Sabane, M., Litake, O., Joshi, R.: L3cube-mahaner: a Marathi named entity recognition dataset and BERT models. arXiv preprint arXiv:2204.06029 (2022)
5. Mujadia, V., Sharma, D.M.: English-Marathi neural machine translation for LoResMT 2021. In: Proceedings of 4th Workshop Technology MT Low Resources Language, pp. 151–157 (2021)
6. Joshi, R.: L3cube-mahacorpus and mahabert: Marathi monolingual corpus, Marathi BERT language models, and resources. arXiv preprint arXiv:2202.01159 (2022)
7. Ashfaque, M.W., Kayte, C.N., Malik, S.I., Hannan, S.A.: Study and evaluation of 'Seq-2-Seq' model competency in AI-based educational chatbot for the Marathi language. J. Artif. Intell. Educ. (2022)
8. Mittal, S., Magdum, V., Hiwarkhedkar, S., Dhekane, O., Joshi, R.: L3Cube-MahaNews: News-based short text and long document classification datasets in Marathi. In: Proceedings of International Conference on Speech Language Technology Low-Resources Language, pp. 52–63 (2023). https://doi.org/10.1007/978-3-031-10386-1_5
9. Chavan, T., Patankar, S., Kane, A., Gokhale, O., Joshi, R.: A Twitter BERT approach for offensive language detection in Marathi. arXiv preprint arXiv:2212.10039 (2022)
10. Saurav, K., Saunack, K., Kanojia, D., Bhattacharyya, P.: 'A Passage to India': pre-trained word embeddings for Indian languages. arXiv preprint arXiv:2112.13800 (2021)
11. Rothe, S., Mallinson, J., Malmi, E., Krause, S., Severyn, A.: A simple recipe for multilingual grammatical error correction. arXiv preprint arXiv:2106.03830 (2021)
12. Mittal, M., Sharma, S.K., Sethi, A.: Detection and correction of grammatical errors in Hindi language using hybrid approach. Int. J. Comput. Sci. Eng. **421**, 421–426 (2019)
13. Omelianchuk, K., Atrasevych, V., Chernodub, A., Skurzhanskyi, O.: GECToR—Grammatical error correction: tag, not rewrite. arXiv preprint arXiv:2005.12592 (2020)
14. Sonawane, A., Vishwakarma, S.K., Srivastava, B., Singh, A.K.: Generating inflectional errors for grammatical error correction in Hindi. In: Proceedings of 1st Conference on Asia-Pacific Chapter Association Computer Linguistics, pp. 165–171 (2020)
15. Pal, A., Mustafi, A.: Vartani Spellcheck—automatic context-sensitive spelling correction of OCR-generated Hindi text using BERT and Levenshtein distance. arXiv preprint arXiv:2012.07652 (2020)

16. Lytvyn, V., Pukach, P., Vysotska, V., Vovk, M., Kholodna, N.: Identification and correction of grammatical errors in Ukrainian texts based on machine learning technology. Mathematics **11**(4), 904 (2023). https://doi.org/10.3390/math11040904

17. Xue, L.: mt5: a massively multilingual pre-trained text-to-text transformer. arXiv preprint arXiv:2010.11934 (2020)

18. Khanuja, S., et al.: MuRIL: multilingual representations for Indian languages. arXiv preprint arXiv:2103.10730 (2021)

19. Stahlberg, F., Kumar, S.: Synthetic data generation for grammatical error correction with tagged corruption models. arXiv preprint arXiv:2105.13318 (2021)

20. Dave, S., Singh, A.K., AP, D.P., Lall, P.B.: Neural compound-word (Sandhi) generation and splitting in Sanskrit language. In: Proceddings of 3rd ACM India Joint International Conference on Data Science Management Data, pp. 171–177 (2021)

21. Vaishali, V.P.K., Kalpana, K., Mahender, C.N.: A rule-based approach for Marathi part-of-speech tagging. In: Proceedings of ICT with Intelligent Applications: ICTIS 2021, pp. 773–785. Springer, Singapore (2022)

22. Sardesai, M., Pawar, J., Walawalikar, S., Vaz, E.: BIS annotation standards with reference to Konkani language. In: Proceedings of 3rd Workshop South and Southeast Asian Natural Language Processing, pp. 145–152 (2012)

23. Aralikatte, R., Cheng, Z., Doddapaneni, S., Cheung, J.C.K.: Vārta: a large-scale headline-generation dataset for Indic languages. arXiv preprint arXiv:2305.05858 (2023)

24. Dabre, R., Shrotriya, H., Kunchukuttan, A., Puduppully, R., Khapra, M.M., Kumar, P.: IndicBART: a pre-trained model for Indic natural language generation. arXiv preprint arXiv:2109.02903v2 (2022)

Cybersecurity Challenges and Solutions in Industry 4.0: Securing Critical Infrastructure in the Age of IoT and Automation

Jyotsna Vilas Barpute[1] , Narayani Gupta[1,2,3] , Shubhangi Suryawanshi[1(✉)] , Digvijay Bhosale[2], Vanita Kshirsagar[1] , and Pramod Patil[3]

[1] Department of Artificial Intelligence and Data Science, Dr. D. Y. Patil Institute of Technology Pimpri, Pune, India
`shubha.s312@gmail.com`
[2] Department of Mechanical Engineering, Dr. D. Y. Patil Institute of Technology Pimpri, Pune, India
[3] Department of Computer Engineering, Dr. D. Y. Patil Institute of Technology Pimpri, Pune, India

Abstract. In the Fourth Industrial Revolution, is the activity of safeguarding Industrial systems, networks, and devices against the threat of cyberattacks in the manufacturing sector because of the advanced integration of automation, AI, and IoT technology. This new interconnectivity introduces other risks because a network is more vulnerable to attacks by hackers. Since, most industries depend heavily on critical infrastructure, an attack affects the economy. Specific issues include protecting ICS and SCADA systems, APTs, and unknown threats, as well as issues with IoT devices and cloud computing. Additionally, there are few competent professionals enough to handle with such sophisticated risks. To counter these, organizations must replicate security in systems and devices, security audit and vulnerability assessment, security tests and penetration testing, incident preparedness and response, make disaster recovery. Org cybersecurity education for the employees remains crucial, to complement efforts by organizations and governments to share intelligence and even implementation strategies. Finally, sound cybersecurity measures are the most critical approaches that help protect systems of Industry 4.0 from cyber threats. Much can be said about the fact that investing in efficient security measures will help to save the infrastructure and technologies used within organizations from newly detected threats.

Keywords: Cybersecurity · Industry 4.0 · ICS · SCADA · IoT · APT · secure-by-design · threat intelligence · cloud security

1 Introduction

Industry 4.0 is a revolutionary transformation in designing and implementing industrial processes. With the incorporation of newer technologies such as the Internet of Things (IoT), Artificial Intelligence (AI), cloud computing, and cyber-physical systems (CPS),

F. Ortiz-Rodríguez et al. (Eds.): IBCD 2025, CCIS 2845, pp. 74–85, 2026.
https://doi.org/10.1007/978-3-032-20907-8_7

Industry 4.0 aims to construct smart, data-driven, and interconnected industrial environments [1]. It helps in the creation of smart workshops with automation, real-time data sharing, and self-optimizing systems to promote efficiency and flexibility [2]. Also helps greater interconnectivity and digital dependence, also increase the vulnerability of these systems to cybersecurity attacks [3].Wireless Sensor Network (WSN) industry is one of the most important ingredients in 4.0. These networks in an uninterrupted way support data collection and real -time communication between industrial layouts, which enables intelligent decisions and future maintenance [1, 4]. Although good, it is naturally unsafe for attacks because of their distributed and wireless nature. A task of coming up with individual sensor can prevent complete production lines, cause data integrity problems or even physical destruction, which can create extreme priority wrong-tolerant security system [1, 4].To meet such challenges, the application of machine learning and deep learning methods has become increasingly prominent in industrial cyber security. Autoencoders, decision trees, and multi-layer perceptron (MLPs) are extensively applied to identify anomalous patterns in sensor data, making it possible for early detection and prevention of cyber-attacks [1, 2].

Liso et al. carried out an extensive review of anomaly detection strategies and validated the high adaptability and accuracy of deep learning techniques in Industry 4.0 applications [2]. Hardware components must also be secured, particularly Programmable Logic Controllers (PLCs), which handle control operations of essential significance in manufacturing systems. As they are central devices and connected to Industrial IoT systems, PLCs are often a target for cyber-attacks [3, 5]. An invisible, random signal (a "watermark") is embedded within control commands as part of the Dynamic Watermarking (DW) technique, which Huang et al. [3] proposed as a defense against these attacks. This method is lightweight and effective for industrial use since it detects manipulation attempts in real-time without requiring encrypted communication [3].To support industrial cybersecurity, blockchain technology is becoming more and more popular in addition to AI and hardware-based security. It is a suitable option for safeguarding communications and transaction records in smart factories due to its decentralization, transparency, and immutability [6]. Fraga-Lamas et al. highlighted that blockchain can facilitate trust-based data sharing, identity management, and smart contracts, all of which are crucial for constructing secure and resilient infrastructures in Industry 4.0 and future Industry 5.0 environments [6]. It should be added that industry cybersecurity in Industry 4.0 is not only a matter of technology but also an organizational issue. Frecassetti et al. [1], for instance, indicated that Lean Management practices—such as constant improvement and adaptability to change—can make digital adoption overcome obstacles, ultimately favouring secure digital framework implementation [4].The study is trying to detect significant cyber security problems in Industry 4.0, evaluate existing defence strategies and analyse future technologies such as machine learning, blockchain and safe control mechanisms, which can increase industrial cyber flexibility. Since industries become more dependent on the digital environment, it is important to guarantee safe, durable and non-stop industrial development to develop strong, adaptable and future evidence of cyber security architecture.

The arrival of Industry 4.0 has changed the industrial view by combining advanced techniques such as industrially internet of things (IIOT), cyber-physical system, age calculation and intelligent automation. These innovations have increased operational efficiency, future maintenance, production adjustment and decision-making in the industrial environment. However, digital changes in traditional industries have enough extension of the surface of the cyber half. With a lot of data exchange and automation, new weaknesses have emerged on each layer of industrial infrastructure, which is a significant concern for each layer of industrial infrastructure, which is a significant concern. Eyeleko and Feng [7] provided a comprehensive and structured analysis of these safety challenges [7] by examining the dangers of the layered architecture of the IIOT system. His research classified IIOT into four primary team perceptions, networks, processing and application and systematically discussed weaknesses at each level and the same attack vector. For example, on the perception layer, sensor knots are receptive due to limited data processing strength and physical access, while in network and processing layers, unprotected protocols and third-party integration are attacked such as attack and rejection service (DOS). He also stated that old hardware, extensive use of inconsistent patch management and lack of integrated security policy increase these risks [7]. Focus on the communication protocol,

The weaknesses of the SEC/GEM protocol are detected, commonly used in semiconductor production. Designed for the originally closed environment, SEC/GEM lacks integrated security measures and is exposed to cyber threats in open and mutual coordination of industry 4.0. To address this, he introduced SECS/Gemsec, a mechanism based on RSA digital signature that provides authentication and integrity probe. Their solution detects and reduces DOS, Reprises and Falsdetta injection attacks, without significant performance penalties, it makes it suitable for inheritance in industrial environments [8].The blockchain technology industry has also proven to be a promising tool to ensure 4.0 ecosystem. Fernandez-Karames and Fraga-Lamas [9] underwent how confidence in blockchain decentralized industrial systems can increase data integrity and transparency. Their work underlined the use of smart contracts and Peer-to-pier architecture to eliminate the requirement for middlemen and improve computer sporability in supply chains. He also discussed various blockchain platforms such as Atherium and IoTA, and evaluated their suitability for industrial scenarios based on scalability, privacy and transaction efficiency [9].Meanwhile, artificial intelligence and machine learning are used to increase cyber security in intelligent production [1] to identify malicious activity, has prepared a system for detecting a forecast infiltration for wireless sensor networks (WSN) based on decisions such as machine learning algorithms to identify malicious activity. His plan demonstrated accuracy to detect outstanding real-time threat, especially distributed and at the resource limit WSN settings [1].It was complemented by a comprehensive review of deep learning methods used to detect industrial deviations. He concluded that fixed nervous networks (CNN) and auto coders are effective at identifying system defects and deviations, especially when trained to domain-specific data. He also emphasized the importance of matching model designs for industrial process requirements and promoted the standard Peripinen framework [3].At the control system level, the programmable logical controllers (PLC) [3] solved the question of light wing and safety control in real time. He suggested a dynamic watermarking (DW) solution that damaged private signals in the control command to identify industrial processes such as tampering or unauthorized treatment. This approach spreads with computational expensive encryption methods without detecting effective attacks in the ICS environment [3].

Industry 4.0 Cyber Security is not just a technical question - organizational culture and strategy also include [4]. It is described how lean management principles can be implemented to facilitate safe implementation of industry 4.0 technologies. Their study focused on integrating staff commitment, structured change management and awareness of cyber security in business processes [4].For goals for risk analysis, Di Giandomenico and Babeshko [5] Made Fault Tree Analysis (FTA), Felure Mode and Effects Analysis (FMEA), Hazard and Risk Analysis (Hara), and threat and risk assessment (Tara). These methods are significant in those industries where cyber attacks can cause both electronic data loss and physical hazards. They pleaded in their study for an integrated approach in combating these interconnected risks in an entire manner [5]. Lastly, blockchain's broader use in Industry 5.0 was again studied by Fraga-Lamas et al. [6] with focus on the requirement of secure, human-cantered, and sustainable industrial solutions. They introduced the manner in which blockchain can be designed for green computing and resilience purposes and thus establish it as a future-strategic tool for cybersecurity frameworks [6].In conclusion, the literature points out that acquiring effective cybersecurity in Industry 4.0 must be tackled multi-dimensionally. It is not enough to wait for technical fixes like machine learning algorithms or blockchain-based systems in isolation. Rather, a wide-ranging strategy must be carried out with heavy protocol design, light security for embedded devices, organizational preparedness, employee training, and overall safety-security risk analysis. As industrial systems grow more interconnected and data-driven, it will be crucial to reconcile these technical and human factors in a manner that builds strong and secure smart manufacturing ecosystems [4].

Literature review encounters the following research gaps:

- Industrial intrusion detection heterogeneous real-world data are mostly not available, which hinder model generalization.
- ML-based most security systems overlook real-time computation requirements, resource availability, and explainability issues.
- Integrating safety and cybersecurity through harmonized risk assessment methods is not typical in current practices.
- Blockchain and AI combined use in industry delay-sensitive system intrusion detection has received fewer studies [10, 11].
- No systematic integration of Lean Management philosophies to SME cybersecurity practices exists [12].
- Cybersecurity awareness, training deficits, and governance deficits are given less priority in Industry 4.0 security research [10, 12].

2 Methodology

The work utilizes a supervised machine learning-driven method for the detection of infiltration in the Industry 4.0 setting from the TON_IoT dataset, which is a realistic blend of legitimate and malicious traffic of factory networks. The chosen data set contains

IoT device data, operation logs, and telemetry network traffic and is comprehensive enough to act as an exhaustive data source applicable for the testing of cyber defense models in industrial production systems. This approach allows the test environment to simulate real-world challenges posed in Industry 4.0, such as heterogeneity in IoT devices, high-dimensional features, and complex attack behaviors.

2.1 Data Reproposing

For this research, the data was loaded in as CSV and many preprocessing operations were carried out to achieve data quality and compatibility with the machine learning models. Missing values were treated by mean or median imputation based on the statistical distribution of the disturbed features. Continuous attributes were scaled to Min-Max scaling to a [0,1] range for maintaining consistency and facilitating model convergence. One-hot encoding was used for categorical features to convert non-numeric values into machine-readable format appropriate for classification algorithms. Target variable, denoting network traffic behaviour, was converted into binary form: '0' denoting benign and '1' for attack traffic. After preprocessing, the dataset was divided into training and test sets in a 70:30 ratio to allow equitable model testing. To ensure data integrity, outliers were determined using interquartile range (IQR) techniques and handled to avoid manipulation of model performance. No artificial over-sampling techniques like SMOTE was used in training to ensure that the original class distribution was maintained in order to eliminate over-representation bias towards majority samples. Lastly, correlation analysis was conducted to eliminate duplicate or highly correlated features and thus enhance model efficiency and minimize noise during learning To further strengthen data quality, feature scaling and transformation steps were carefully validated to avoid skewness or bias in numerical attributes Outlier treatment was done through the examination of interquartile thresholds to ensure that unusual, but significant, attack behavior was maintained. Each feature was statistically tested for significance prior to inclusion in the model development pipeline. The resulting dataset was a well-balanced, noise-cleaned input applicable to solid classification. These preprocessing operations ensured that future machine learning models could effectively learn and provide consistent, high-quality intrusion detection results within the Industry 4.0 environment.

2.2 Model Training and Evaluation

Different machine learning methods were experimented and applied to measure their efficiency in detecting infiltration under the Industry 4.0 regime. The tested models were Random Forest (RF), Decision Tree (DT), Support Vector Machine (SVM with RBF Kernel), K-Nearest Neighbor (KNN), Multi-Layer Perceptron (MLP), and Autoencoders.

The models chosen included a variety of learning paradigms, ranging from tree-based ensembles and distance-based classifiers to neural networks and deep unsupervised methods, in order to gain in-depth coverage over detection capability across various categories of algorithms. Hyperparameters of every model were tuned to minimize overfitting and enhance generalization. Five-fold cross-validation procedure was employed to evaluate the performance of each algorithm on various divisions of data, in such a way that models did not learn general patterns by memorizing unique samples. Systematic estimation also allowed for balanced measurement throughout the data set and ruled out the impact of random variance. The assessment process employed several performance measures, that is, Accuracy, Precision, Recall, and F1-score, to have a comprehensive view of the effectiveness of each model in classifying benign and malicious traffic. The measures in combination allowed for comparison of sensitivity of detection (recall), reliability of prediction (precision), and overall equilibrium (F1-score), apart from accuracy. In addition to testing robustness, confusion matrices were plotted for each classifier to visually depict the accurate and erroneous predictions.

Besides, Receiver Operating Characteristic (ROC) plots were also developed for evaluating the true positive rate versus false positive rate so that model discrimination power could be graphically displayed. For the purpose of ensuring the data consistency among models, feature scaling and normalization techniques were uniformly used across to avoid the difference in magnitude of the data from influencing the learning process unfairly. This uniformity was most essential for algorithms like SVM and KNN, which are feature scale-sensitive. In addition to accuracy-based evaluation, computational efficiency was also examined to determine the feasibility of each algorithm for real-time industrial applications, wherein timely detection and resource efficiency are key. Factors such as training time, inference time, and memory consumption were taken into account for measuring practical implementability on Industry 4.0 infrastructures. Finally, feature importance analysis was conducted, particularly in models such as Random Forest and Decision Tree, to identify the most relevant features responsible for detecting infiltration. Understanding the relevance of features not only enhances interpretability but also aids in further enhancing the process of intrusion detection for future model iterations. Together, these testing approaches guaranteed comparability between all the algorithms and provided usable information about their flexibility in smart industrial cybersecurity systems.

3 System Architecture

Industry 4.0 Architecture that makes sure the environment is secure. Multi-level system emphasizes real-time detection, response and control. This edge combines data processing, communication, analysis and safety operations in a lean and flexible workflow. Every group has a special and vital function in keeping industrial cyber security.

3.1 Industrial Equipment Layer

The system identifies this as including IoT devices, PLCs, sensors, and actuators. These accept real-time data, execute control actions, and communicate directly to physical processes. This layer must be secured since any compromise will make operations and safety decline. Regular firmware update and network segmentation will also minimize exposures in this layer. Device authentication technologies integration guarantees only authentic hardware devices communicate in the industrial environment, reducing chances of unauthorized access or data tampering.

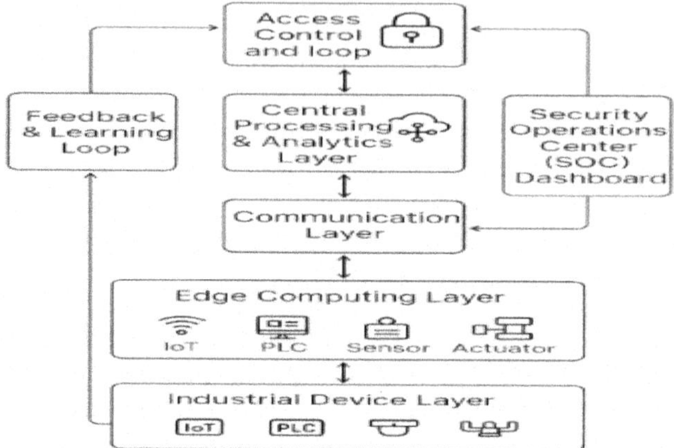

Fig. 1. Layered Cybersecurity Framework for Industrial IoT Systems.

3.2 Edge Data Relay

It's one level higher than the device level and allows real-time data acquisition, pre-processing, and low-level analysis on the network edge. It relieves the central systems of the workload and facilitates speedy deviation detection. All these software elements like IoT gateways, PLC monitors, and lean edge AI modules run here to pass on only vital information upward. Also, edge-based encryption and anomaly detection software ensure security and privacy in this case. There is provision for data reliability through redundancy and failover mechanisms in the event of network failure.

3.3 Communication Teams

This stage is a safe connection to transfer monitoring, notification and telemetry between the edge and central systems. This data ensures the use of encrypted and certified protocols to protect flexibility from integrity, privacy and evolution or injection attacks.

3.4 Central Processing and Analysis Teams

This is the most critical decision-making unit. It leverages sophisticated machine learning algorithms in an attempt to identify threats, trend analyses, and deliver actionable insights. It streamlines threat intelligence and historical information in a continuous manner to enhance the quality of predictions and detection. It also handles system-wide response and policy modification in alignment with analytics feedback. Besides, with the inclusion of real-time dashboards and alert functionalities, it guarantees faster involvement by human beings for critical events. Cloud-based analytics also improve scalability and handle big data industrial streams.

3.5 Access Control and Loop

It keeps sensitive data, commands, or hardware accessible only to approved systems and users. It enforces protection controls like role-based access control (RBAC), multi-factor authentication (MFA), and adapt-tive permission management to enforce policies. It supplies a feedback channel to respond in real-time to conclusions. Continuous login activity and user behavior monitoring can help to detect insider attack and privileged elevation without authorization. In addition, applying zero-trust architectural methods contributes to the overall security stance by authenticating all requests for access in isolation.

3.6 Safety Operations Centre Dashboard

SOC provides an in-the-moment platform to monitor the enterprise-wide cybersecurity status of the industrial world. It shows threat warnings identified, system health, live alarms, and incident response tools with response activation capabilities. Operators are able to monitor data trends, respond to high-priority alarms, and manage mitigation plans in one console. Moreover, automated alerts and AI-powered alert triaging enhance response time and minimize manual effort on security analysts to provide persistent protection and visibility across all system layers.

3.7 Reaction and Learning Loop

One distinctive aspect of this architecture is that it incorporates an adaptive feedback loop. Feedback from analysis decisions and operator actions is returned to the system to refine detection models, revise access rules, and enhance reaction strategies. The architecture thus updates itself to evolve along with new threats. Reinforcement learning algorithms enable the system to automatically adapt to new attack behaviour. In addition, regular audits and performance reviews assist in verifying the system's learning results to ensure detection accuracy and response efficiency are increasingly optimal with time.

4 Result and Discussion

The evaluation was carried out using the treated TON_IOT data set on six machine learning models. The performance was calculated for each model to assess their suitability to detect real-time infiltration in performance metrics compatibility, accurate, recall and F1 score 4.0 system.

Overview:

- Random forest achieved the best overall performance with a high F1 score, owing to its ability to operate with various data types and patterns.
- Autoencoder learned the maximum recall, thereby making it extremely efficient in identifying actual positivity-particularly helpful when detecting sensor information.
- MLP was competitive, but several calculation resources were required, which made it better suitable for high-capacity setups.

- The decision -making wood and KNN models were explanatory and sharp, but showed specific signs of over-assembly and low accuracy in complex data distribution.
- SVM achieved stable performance, but struggled with scalability and variance in the data.

Of the models being compared, the Random Forest classifier performed best overall. It produced the highest F1-score at 96.0% and highest accuracy of 95.6%, which reflects its proficiency in correctly classifying both normal and malicious traffic. The ensemble aspect of Random Forest helps in preventing overfitting and delivers robust generalization relative to different data distributions. While the MLP and Autoencoder models also performed relatively well, they were slower to train and required greater computational capacity and therefore were ideally suited for high-end industrial environments. Models such as Decision Tree and K-Nearest Neighbour (KNN), however, which were lightweight and interpretable, struggled to deal with high-dimensional data and produced lower accuracy results. The Autoencoder, in particular, performed very well on recall (96.5%), and thus is a good option for identification of faint or hitherto unknown deviations, especially in cases with limited labelled data points. The Support Vector Machine (SVM) also provided good performance but was less flexible with highly variable distributions of data since this affected its accuracy under dynamic network conditions.

In addition, the analysis mentions the trade-off between model complexity and real-time application considerations. More sophisticated models such as MLPs and Autoencoders offer better anomaly detection but are computationally intensive, hence less ideal for quick re-response in real-time limited Industry 4.0 settings. Random Forest and Decision Tree models are less sophisticated yet offer enhanced inference time, reduced latency, and ease of deployment, which are essential in industrial process maintenance without disruption. Random Forest's in-built feature importance function also gives interpretability—enabling security engineers to determine the most important features to an intrusion, thus enhancing explainability and trust in systems by automated detection.

Variation in performance across such models suggests the need to select algorithms not only on the basis of accuracy but also on compute cost, scalability, and interpretability. As an example, Autoencoder's better recall informs us that it should be used in cases where its inability to catch a possible intrusion would incur severe operational or financial loss. Contrarywise, Random Forest's accuracy, stability, and efficiency suit it preferably for real-time intrusion detection scenarios. The study also indicates adapting to adaptive model adaptation and ensemble hybrid methods for optimal detection against various attacks.

Generally, the results verify that Random Forest achieves the optimal balance among accuracy, efficiency, and interpretability, and hence is a highly suitable approach to real-time intrusion detection in Industry 4.0 architecture [13, 14].

The detailed evaluation metrics are presented in Table 1.

While significant progress has been made in Industry 4.0 cybersecurity, key areas remain underexplored. Securing communication across diverse industrial systems through standardized protocols is crucial. Incorporating human-in-the-loop approaches, such as behaviour analysis and adaptive access control, can further toughen security. Harmonization of safety and cybersecurity using models such as HARA-TARA [12]

Table 1. Evaluation Metrics of Various Models Applied to Industrial Cybersecurity

Model	Accuracy	Precision	Recall	F1-Score	Remarks
Random Forest	95.6%	95.0%	97.0%	96.0%	Robust model with good generalization
Decision Tree	92.1%	91.5%	93.2%	92.3%	Fast and interpretable; slight overfitting
SVM (RBF Kernel)	90.7%	89.8%	91.0%	90.4%	Performs well with clean data
KNN (k = 5)	88.9%	87.2%	90.1%	88.6%	Sensitive to noisy data
MLP (Neural Net)	94.3%	93.7%	95.1%	94.4%	High accuracy but computationally expensive
Autoencoder	93.8%	91.0%	96.5%	93.7%	Strong unsupervised detection capabilities

is crucial for end-to-end risk management. As Industry 5.0 begins, cybersecurity has to enable sustainable, robust, and human-centered industrial ecosystems. As shown in Fig. 2, the Random Forest model achieved the best accuracy on the TON_IoT dataset.

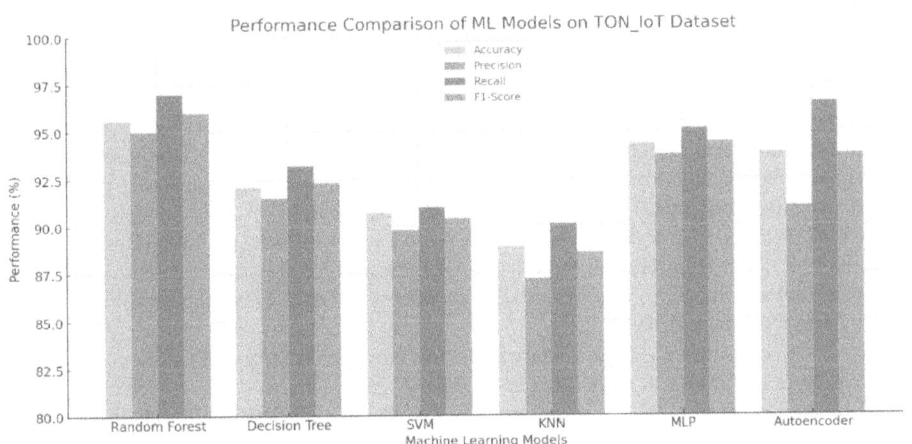

Fig. 2. ML model performance on TON_IoT dataset across key metrics

5 Conclusion

Industry 4.0 development has significantly enhanced industrial interoperability, flexibility, and effectiveness by the use of IoT, AI, CPS, and advanced automation. The revolution, however, introduced new and advanced security threats. The review covered various threat vectors ranging from insecure wireless sensor networks and protocols to organizational threats such as poor governance and employees' training. The analysis confirms that machine learning-based threat detection, blockchain-based secure data exchange, and watermark-type dynamic PLC protection techniques are prominent methods in the industrial cybersecurity paradigm. It is also pertinent to employ formal frameworks like ISO/IEC 27001, NIST CSF, and hybrid models of evaluation like HARA–TARA to furnish end-to-end safety and security guidelines. Organizational readiness is also part of it. Lean Management principles can potentially rationalize digital transformation, reduce resistance to change, and facilitate set in cybersecurity at every level of the organization. Apart from this, the research suggests that continuous employee awareness initiatives, good access control policies, and a culture of monitoring effectively play key roles in enlarging cyber resilience. Integration of AI-based analytics and real-time monitoring features can assist with bolstering threat response and reducing system downtime by considerable percentages. In addition, there is a need for cooperation between industrial partners, researchers, and policy-makers to develop common frameworks and enhance interoperability of secure industrial systems. Finally, an overall multi-level defence strategy with technological, human, and procedural components should be developed to construct cyber-resilient industrial systems and transition to Industry 5.0 in an orderly manner.

References

1. G. B. M. G. a. C. D. F. Frecassetti, M.: Lean transformation in the digital age: enablers and barriers in industry 4.0. IEEE Trans. Eng. Manag. (2024)
2. Z. A. a. M. Fatima Al-Quayed, H.: A situation based predictive approach for cyber-security intrusion dectection and prevention using machine learning algorithms in wireless sensor networks of industry4.0,, pp. 15–20. IEEE (2024)
3. Barpute, J.V., Bhargava, S.: Improving system security: machine learning algorithm-based intrusion detection system. In: 2024 4th International Conference on Ubiquitous Computing and Intelligent Information Systems (ICUIS), Gobichettipalayam, India, pp. 433–444 (2024). https://doi.org/10.1109/ICUIS64676.2024.10866908
4. A. C. C. P. M. N. P. A. E. S. a. V. R. A. Liso, A.: A Review of Deep Learning-Based Anomaly
5. J. K. P. R. K. J. R. a. Huang, P. E. P.-H.: Enhancing Cybersecurity for Industrial Control Systems: Innovations in Protecting PLC-dependent Industrial Infrastructures. IEEE Internet of Things Journal (2024)
6. A. B. a. Giandomenico, F. D.: Mapping study on cybersecurity and safety co-assessment techniques in industry 4. IEEE Access 11 (2023)
7. T. M. F.-C. A. M. R. d. C. a. Fraga-Lamas, S. I. L. P.: An overview of blockchain for industry 5.0: towards human-centric, sustainable and resilient applications. IEEE Access 12 (2024)
8. A. H. E. a. Feng, T.: A critical overview of industrial internet of things security and privacy issues using a layer-based hacking scenario. IEEE Internet of Things Journal 10 (2023)
9. S. M. A. K. A.-A. S. U. R. a. S. K. S. U. A. Laghari: SECS/GEMsec: a mechanism for detection and prevention of cyber-attacks on SECS/GEM communications in industry 4.0 landscape. IEEE Access 9 (2021)
10. T. M. F.-C. a. Fraga-Lamas, P.: A review on the application of blockchain to the next generation of cybersecure industry 4.0 smart factories. IEEE Access 7 (2019)
11. M. L. a. Corallo, M. L. A.: Cybersecurity in the context of industry 4.0: a structured classification of critical assets and business impacts. Comput. Indust. 114 (2020)
12. A. A. e. al: Securing industry 4.0: assessing cybersecurity challenges and proposing strategies for manufacturing management. Cyber Sec. Appli. 3 (2025)

13. X. X. e. al.: Adaptive model verification for modularized industry 4.0 applications. IEEE Access **10** (2022)
14. M. L. a. A. C. M. Lezzi: cybersecurity for industry 4.0 in the current literature: a reference framework. Comput. Indust. **103**, 97–110 (2018)

RetailNet: AI-Driven Sales Optimization and Marketing Strategies for Perishable Products in Retail

Venkata Kalyan Mandali[(✉)] [iD]

University of Bridgeport, Connecticut, CT 06604, USA
mandalivenkatakalyan@gmail.com

Abstract. In this paper, the author presents RetailNet, a reinforcement learning framework based on AI, which is utilized to enhance sales patterns and marketing techniques of perishable products in retailing, dynamic pricing, inventory optimization, and the arrangement of products on shelves are combined with customer behavior and product perishability, modeling the complex relationships with the help of a Pair-Wise Multi-Q Network. This model is furthered with RetailNet++ that assists in promotional strategies to a multi-action Q-aggregation mechanism. This mechanism analyses in various customer behaviors and demand trends that our framework has continually helped to increase revenue as well as demand. Operational efficiency. These outcomes will furnish us with the potential of Ai-improved retail systems to make effective choices and offer smarter in the real world retail settings.

Keywords: Retail Optimization · Perishable Products · Customer behavior · Shelf Display Strategy · Inventory Management

1 Introduction

Take an example of a retail environment where inventory is made out of perishable goods which have a shelf life of two consecutive selling cycles. The quality of the items is decreasing as time goes by At the beginning of each period, new stock is purchased at a unit cost of C_n. Each item starts with a base price of p_0 and an initial quality level of Q_n. Unsold units of the last cycle are held and have a storage cost C_s and sold in the current cycle at a lower price $(1 - \lambda)p_0$, where 13 is the markdown rate. There is a disposal cost C_x on any left-over aged inventory that is not sold. The customers are characterized by their personal quality-adjusted readiness to pay, which is denoted by α, and are distributed equally between $[0, \alpha_{\max}]$. The derivational satisfaction that a customer will get because of buying a new product is provided by [1–5]:

$$V_n(\alpha) = \alpha Q_n - p_0, \tag{1}$$

and from an aged product by:

$$V_o(\alpha) = \alpha Q_o - (1 - \lambda)p_0, \tag{2}$$

F. Ortiz-Rodríguez et al. (Eds.): IBCD 2025, CCIS 2845, pp. 86–97, 2026.
https://doi.org/10.1007/978-3-032-20907-8_8

Qn denotes the poor quality level where Qo is less than Qn. Customers will not buy when the two utility values are negative and will buy the product that maximizes the non-negative utility otherwise.

This makes the following groups of customers:

- **Type O**: Prefer aged goods $(V_o(\alpha) > 0 > V_n(\alpha))$
- **Type N**: Prefer new items $(V_n(\alpha) > 0 > V_o(\alpha))$
- **Type ON**: Choose aged but accept new if needed $(V_o(\alpha) > V_n(\alpha) > 0)$
- **Type NO**: Select new and accept old when necessary $(Vn(a)Vo(a) > 0)$

Allow the population fraction to be represented as RO, RN, RON and RNO of each type respectively. These segments are generated depending on the range of λ values. Types NO and N would choose new products in situations where freshness levels are both present, whereas Type O and ON would be aged products. Conversely, in cases where the aged products are out of stock, Type O, ON, and NO have been diverted to the new products. When all that exists are old products, there will be a shift of Type N, NO, and ON to the older inventory.

In every period, the number of arrivals of customers is N, who interact with the stock available. The arrivals may be constant or they may be controlled by a probabilistic structure. It was used to compute expected counts each of them, using a continuous model.

The segment of NRO, NRN, NRON, and NRNO are computed. The paramount aim is to find the optimal number of new products, denoted zt, to be held at the beginning of period t in order to maximize the average long-run revenue as stipulated in Fig. 1. The availability of the display items also affects the behavior of customers. Retailers can control the shelf-layouts to influence the decisions of the customers. Five different layout strategies are taken into account:

Layout A: The two types are equally available.
Layout B: The aged stock is positioned on the forefront of the new stock. Layout B +: new products are arranged at the front of the old stock.
Layout C: The new products are sold, then the old inventory is shown only when it gets exhausted.
Layout C+: The old products go out initially; new inventory is produced post exhaustion of old.

Consumers can be categorized depending on their search behavior: proactive shoppers would take all the options and find the one that benefits them to the most, and reactive consumers would take the one that is available. Where 0 is the reactive consumer proportion, and 1 0 is the inelastic proportion proactive share. Assume that the proportions of purchases made of new and old products under full availability are defined by Φn and Φo, as shown in Table 1. In case product accessibility is symmetric (Layout A), the behavior is the same in both customer types.

The decisions vary among the types of shoppers in asymmetric layouts (B and B 0). With layouts C and C 0, layout C displays only one type of product so that all the purchases are made based on the layouts C and C 0 0 [6–15].

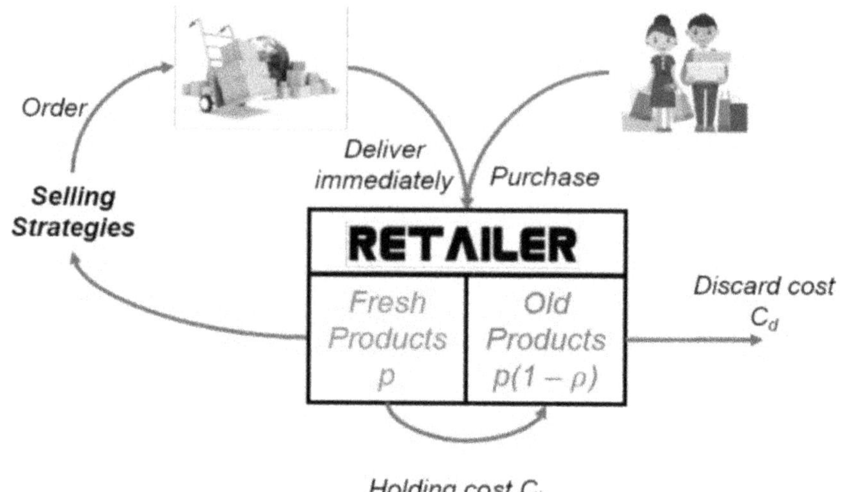

Fig. 1. Depiction of the Retail Operation Framework

Table 1. Purchase Distribution Under Shelf Layouts

Layout	Φn	Φo
A	$RN + RNO$	$RO + RON$
B	$(1 - \theta)(RN + RNO)$	$RO + RON + \theta RNO$
B′	$RN + RNO + \theta RON$	$(1 - \theta)(RO + RON)$
C	$RN + RNO + RON$	0
C′	0	$RO + RNO + RON$

1.1   Revenue Function and Optimization Objective

The immediate revenue for one period is given by:

$$\Omega(z_t; J, N) = p_0 \Gamma_n(z_t; J, N) + p_0(1 - \lambda)\Gamma_o(z_t; J, N)$$
$$-C_x(J - \Gamma_o(z_t; J, N)) - C_n z_t - C_s J, \tag{3}$$

where Cn, p0, Cs, λ, Cx 0, and Γn, Γo are the new and old items sold, respe-ctively, depending upon Cn, p0, Cs, λ, and Cx, per zt (restocking), J (old-stock), and N (number of customers). The long-run average profit reaches its maximum of the time horizon Tby maximizing the following factors:

$$\max_{z_t,\, a_t,\, \lambda_t,\, T \to \infty} \lim \frac{1}{T} \sum_{t=1}^{T} E_{Nt}[\Omega(Z_t)] \tag{4}$$

This comes down to under fixed pricing and display policies:

$$\max_{Z_1, \dots \lambda_T,} \frac{1}{T} \sum_{t=1}^{T} E_{Nt}[\Omega(Z_t)] \tag{5}$$

The highly sophisticated systems of RetailNet and RetailNet $++$ are suggested in order to overcome the shortcomings of classical solutions in large scale settings.

2 RetailNet: MDP-Based Replenishment Strategy

Replenishment task is a Markov Decision Process (MDP) with the following elements [16–20]: – State (xt): Gives the amount of unsold goods at time t. – Action (ut): In the case of RetailNet model, this is the reorder level. zt, and the more general RetailNet $++$ system makes use of a triplet [zt, θt, μt]. – Reward (ψ t): The effective profit, which will be modeled as Ψ (zt; St, Dt). In case of a discount factor κ, the total expected reward is obtained as:

$$R_t = \sum_{J=0}^{\infty} k^j \, \psi_{t+j+1} \tag{6}$$

RetailNet adopts a stochastic policy $\pi(u_t|x_t; \Theta_\pi)$ to produce z_t and employs a value approximator $V(x_t; \Theta_v)$ to predict future outcomes. They are implanted through neural changes:

$$\mathbf{g} = W_g x + b_g, \tag{7}$$

$$\mathbf{u} = softmax(W_u \mathbf{g} + b_u), \tag{8}$$

$$v = W_v \mathbf{g} + b_v. \tag{9}$$

2.1 RetailNet++: Composite Action Decision Process

RetailNet++ incorporates varying display schemes and promotional adjustments into decision-making. One of the variants is elegant and is referred to as the generalized advantage estimate and is in the form of:

$$Q_{agg}(x_t, u_t) = \sum_{m=1}^{M} \lambda_m Q_m(x_t, u^m) = \lambda^\top \mathbf{Q} \tag{10}$$

In this case, $\lambda = [\lambda 1,\dots, \lambda M]$ ⊤ represents attention coefficients obtained through a Bi-GRU encoder, and Q = [Q1, QM]. QM]⊤ are Q-values predicted with dropout activation and LeakyReLU in two layers of neural models activations.

2.2 Optimization Goals for Policy and Value Functions

Policy Loss Function: Policy Loss Function: Feedback is used to improve action policy with the help of an estimator that measures future benefits.The Comparison between RetailNet and RetailNet++ Architectures shown in Fig. 2. Noisy gradients are often the result of direct summation of the future rewards. Thus, a less biased estimator removes a baseline prediction to achieve stabilized gradients [21–29]. A more civilized form, which is termed the generalized estimate of advantage, appears:

$$\tilde{A}_t^{GAE}(\xi, T) = \sum_{J=0}^{\infty} (\xi T)^J \varepsilon_{t+J}^{val} \tag{11}$$

$$\varepsilon_t^{val} = \psi_t + \zeta V(x_{t+1}; \Theta_v) - V(x_t; \Theta_v) \tag{12}$$

Parameters, ζ and τ are rewards discount and smoothing coefficients, respectively. Entropy of the policy, which is:

$$H(\pi(u_t^m | x_t; \Theta_\pi)) = -\pi(u_t^m | x_t; \Theta_\pi) log \pi(u_t^m | x_t; \Theta_\pi), \tag{13}$$

promotes variety in action and does not encourage early policy convergence. The overall training goal of the policy is:

$$J_{policy}(\Theta_\pi) = -\sum_{J=0}^{\infty} log \pi(u_t^m | x_t; \Theta_\pi)(\zeta \tau)^j \varepsilon^{val} - \lambda_{ent} H(\pi(u_t^m | x_t; \Theta_\pi)) \tag{14}$$

where λ_{ent} regulates the impact of the entropy regularizer.

Value Loss Function: The value estimator is minimally trained to maximize the expected returns by the amount of the squared loss between the predicted and observed results:

$$J_{value}(\Theta_v) = \frac{1}{2}E\left[\left(\tilde{G}_t - V(x_t; \Theta_v)\right)^2\right] \tag{15}$$

When RetailNet++ is employed, the Q-value aggregation $Q_{agg}(x_t, u_t)$ replaces $V(x_t; \Theta_v)$ for enhanced forecasting (Table 2).

3 Experimental Evaluation

The retail settings vary in terms of customer behaviour; perishable products tend to have a consistent turnover and others seasonally. The functionality of the suggested frameworks is tested in the framework of controlled artificial demand patterns. Table 3 indicates the parameter set ups of common purchasing behaviour models. Consumers would be assumed to choose products that have a minimum utility threshold at which they do not make purchases. Relative Performance Gap is the next metric applied to measure the improvement:

$$PerfGap = \left(\frac{Jopt - Jmodel}{Jopt}\right) \times 100\% \tag{16}$$

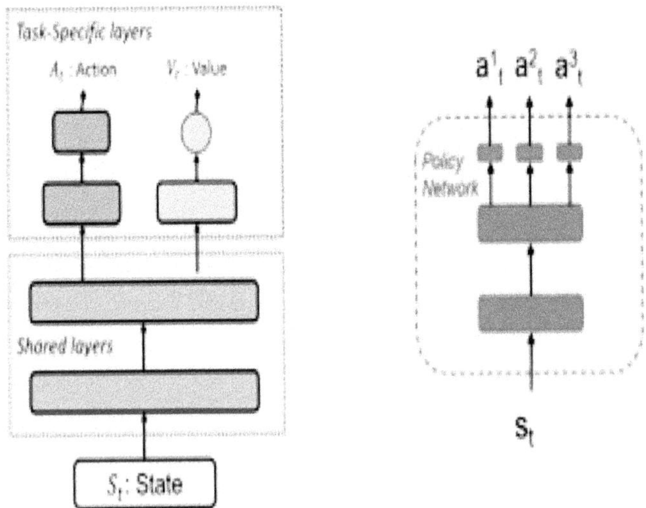

(a) Architecture of RetailNet

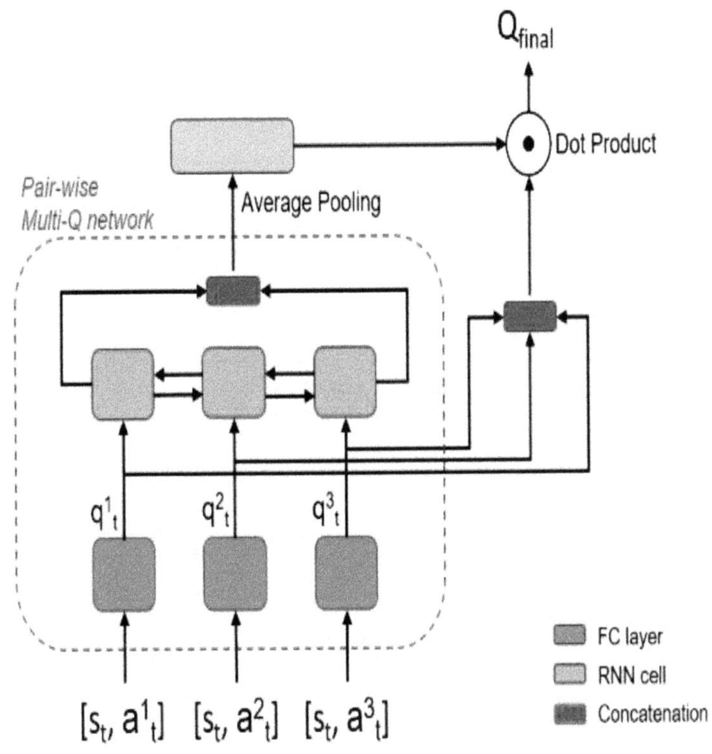

(b) Architecture of RetailNet++

Fig. 2. Comparison between RetailNet and RetailNet++ Architectures

Table 2. Settings of the Experimental Parameters.

Group	cp	cs	cl	Up	Uo	L_{max}
A	4.0	0.5	0.10	0.2	10.0	4.0
B	3.5	0.3	0.05	0.1	8.0	10.0

Popular in use Jmodel is the output returned by the experimented system and Jopt is the optimum solution by analytical or numerical methods. Training was perfo-trained on a 32-core system with learning rate of 10^{-4}. Peer review is to be released after the source code.

3.1 Analysis Under Stable Demand Conditions

In the case of constant rates of customer arrivals, it is theoretically indicated that there is no disposal necessary when the inventory decisions are optimal. RetailNet makes a calculation of the replenishment quantity only with a fixed layout and price, whilst RetailNet++ does the calculation collectively.

Implies the sequence, arrangement, and the promotional costs. The presents simulation results, which means that RetailNet++ not only follows optimal benchmarks but also support reasonable runtime with complexity added.

Table 3. RetailNet and RetailNet $++$ Results under Configurations A and B

Method	Gap (%)	Jmodel	Jopt	Time (min)
RetailNet$(d = A, \rho = 0.6)$	0.00	8.40	8.40	3.21
RetailNet$(d = B, \rho = 0.4)$	0.00	7.30	7.30	4.38
RetailNet$(d = B', \rho = 0.5)$	0.00	2.80	2.80	5.12
RetailNet$(d = C, \rho = 0.7)$	0.00	8.64	8.64	4.13
RetailNet$(d = C', \rho = 0.9)$	0.00	8.40	8.40	3.85
RetailNet $++$	0.00	8.64	8.64	16.99
RetailNet$(d = A, \rho = 0.6)$	0.005	18.30	18.30	5.12
RetailNet$(d = B, \rho = 0.5)$	0.00	16.25	16.25	4.37
RetailNet$(d = B', \rho = 0.5)$	0.00	7.00	7.00	3.56
RetailNet$(d = C, \rho = 0.7)$	0.026	19.52	19.53	6...

4 Results and Discussion

Past investigations into the management of perishable inventory have commonly operated under FIFO (First-In-First-Out) or LIFO (Last-In-First-Out) dispatch policies shown in Fig. 3. These frameworks usually used the same pricing policies to products of different freshness and in many cases limited the product life cycle to only two phases. The high level of difficulty in coming up with an optimal control policy has resulted in many preferring heuristic or approximate solutions. Although a relevant literature has investigated consumer decision-making under a dual-products situation, fresh and aged products, in a maximizing utility situation, these investigations frequently restricted the planning horizon. In contrast, the wider-horizon models examine the decision-making process at several levels and combine the display strategies and economics of consumer behaviour. Research on this topic is generating more and more work that focuses on the interaction of pricing heterogeneity, inventory movement, and visual merchandising.

$$Q^* = max\{Q : E[U(Q)] \geq C\} \tag{17}$$

where E[U (Q) is the expected utility of stocking level Q and C is the cost threshold associated to the same.

Later models analyze the situation when outdated products rival directly with newly emerged ones. In this case, the decisions on pricing are coupled with replenishment, particularly when two-stage frameworks are used. When this occurs, the stock left behind in the first stage can be either disposed or some can be sold at lower prices in the second stage. The optimal pricing of fresh inventory is constant at all the stages, but the older items usually tend to be lower than the newer ones, fueling market cannibalization. One of them views the optimization problem of the retailer as a mixed-integer nonlinear program, which seeks to find a tradeoff between the inventory life and profit maximisation:

$$\max_{xt,Pt} \sum_{t=1}^{T} (R(p_t) - H(x_t)) \tag{18}$$

where $R(p_t)$ represents revenue at price p_t, and $H(x_t)$ is the holding cost function.

The aged and fresh inventory pricing has also been considered through consumer utility based decision models and the analysis shows that a stable pricing of the legacy inventory over time periods can deliver better returns than more dynamic schemes. Recently, reinforcement learning (RL) has become popular in inventory or pricing choices because it can be implemented with the Markov Decision.

Process (MDP) formulation. The policy gradient methods have been exploited to work with continuous action space, in which value approximators are used to estimate:

$$Q^\pi(s, a) = E_\pi\left[\sum_{k=0}^{\infty} \gamma^k r_{t+k}\right] \tag{19}$$

with $\gamma \in (0, 1)$ as the discount factor. It has also been possible because asynchronous advantage actor-critic (A3C) and other techniques allow training a large number of

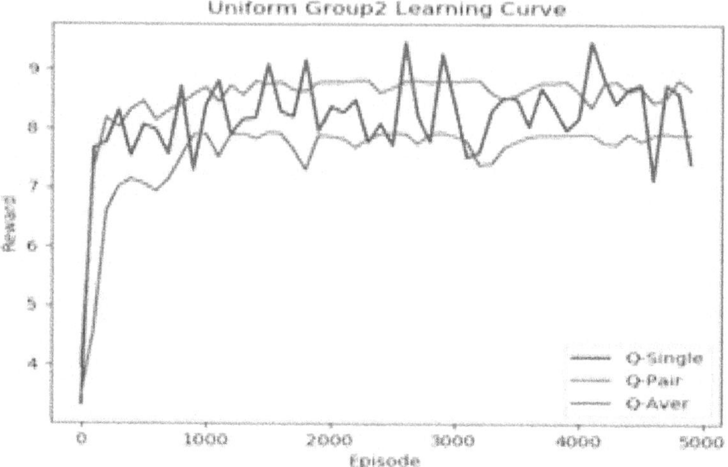

(a) N ~ U(0, 4), Group 1 parameters

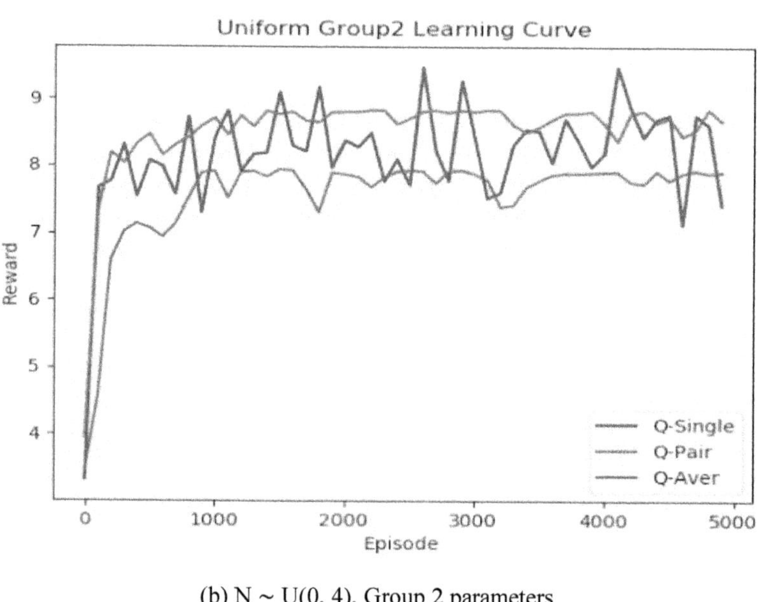

(b) N ~ U(0, 4), Group 2 parameters

Fig. 3. Performance of learning under various customer distribution assumptions

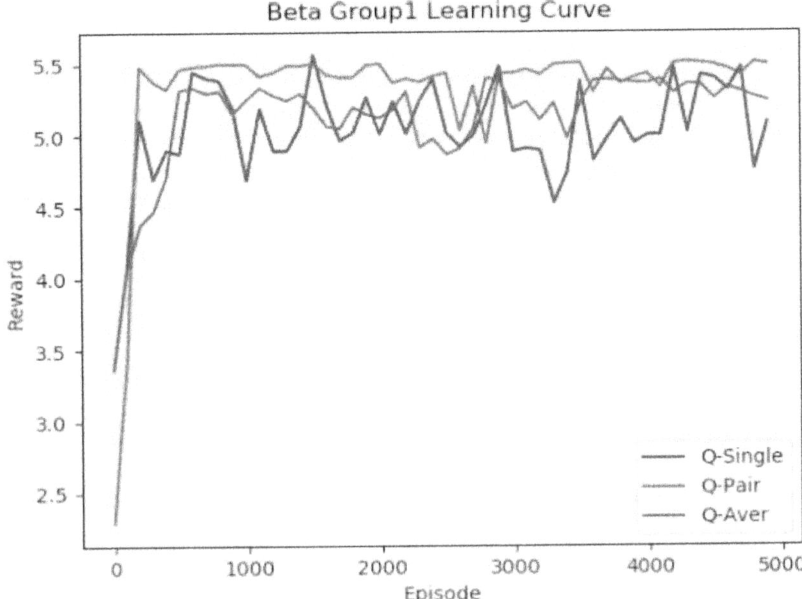

(c) N ~ Beta(1.0, 1.0),Group 1

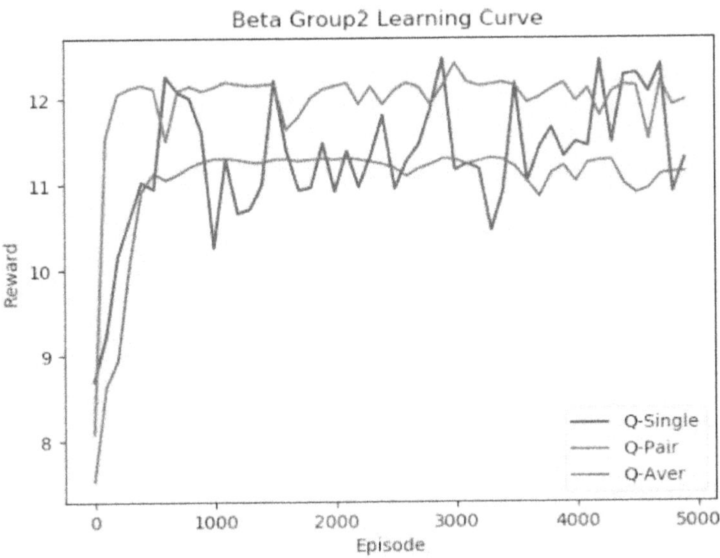

(d) N ~ Beta(0.5, 1.0),Group 2

Fig. 3. (*continued*)

agents with limited computational needs. Improvements such as refine trade-offs between variance and bias in Generalized Advantage Estimation (GAE): This method, which is a multi-step temporal difference learning, makes the trade-offs between temporal difference learning and variance biasing better. Subsequently, the further evolvements deal with the arrangement of multi-action learning through covariance-based regularization. These methods have enhanced representation learning in which high-dimensional and interdependent decision spaces are involved. Models such as the Multi-Q network simultaneously approximate state-action values and action-action correlations:

$$\mathbf{Q}(s) = [Q(s, a_1), Q(s, a_2), ..., Q(s, a_n)]^\top \tag{20}$$

enabling nuanced value assessments across concurrent decisions.

5 Conclusion

This study of RetailNet will help small and large businesses in optimizing pricing, inventory replenishment and displaying perishable goods. The mechanism of Pair-Wise multi–Q Network gives the clear data of customer behavior history and shelf layout. Where RetailNet++ is extended version of RetainNet helps businesses with marketing strategies like promotions, shelf display and also with pricing and inventory. By using multi action Q-aggregation it combines multiple strategies together to improve the total revenue of the business with efficiency in the current Retail market.

References

1. Bellman, R.: Dynamic Programming, vol. 1, no. 2, pp. 3. Princeton University Press, Princeton (1957)
2. Deuermeyer, B.L.: A single period model for a multiproduct perishable inventory system with economic substitution. Naval Res. Logist. Q. **27**(2), 177–185 (1980)
3. Ferguson, M.E., Koenigsberg, O.: How should a firm manage deteriorating inventory? Prod. Oper. Manag. **16**(3), 306–321 (2007)
4. Goyal, S., Giri, B.C.: Recent trends in modeling of deteriorating inventory. Eur. J. Oper. Res. **134**(1), 1–16 (2001)
5. He, J., Chen, J., He, X., Gao, J., Li, L., Deng, L., Ostendorf, M.: Deep reinforcement learning with a natural language action space. arXiv preprint arXiv:1511.04636 (2015)
6. Honhon, D., Seshadri, S.: Fixed vs. random proportions demand models for the assortment planning problem under stockout-based substitution. Manuf. Serv. Oper. Manag. **15**(3), 378–386 (2013)
7. Ishii, H., Nose, T., Shiode, S., Nishida, T.: Perishable inventory management subject to stochastic leadtime. Eur. J. Oper. Res. **8**(1), 76–85 (1981)
8. Langley, P.: Crafting papers on machine learning. In: Proceedings of the 17th International Conference on Machine Learning (ICML 2000), Stanford, CA, 2000, pp. 1207–1216. Morgan Kaufmann (2000)
9. Li, Y., Lim, A., Rodrigues, B.: Pricing and inventory control for a perishable product. Manuf. Serv. Oper. Manag. **11**(3), 538–542 (2009)
10. Li, Y., Kang, H., Ye, K., Yin, S., Li, X.: Foldingzero: protein folding from scratch in hydrophobic-polar model. arXiv preprint arXiv:1812.00967 (2018)

11. Meadowcroft, D.: Understanding the effect of product displays on consumer choice and food waste: A field experiment. PhD thesis, University of Delaware (2016)
12. Mnih, V., et al.: Playing Atari with deep reinforcement learning. arXiv preprint arXiv:1312.5602 (2013)
13. Mnih, V., et al.: Human-level control through deep reinforcement learning. Nature **518**(7540), 529 (2015)
14. Mnih, V., et al.: Asynchronous methods for deep reinforcement learning. In: International Conference on Machine Learning, pp. 1928–1937 (2016)
15. Nahmias, S.: A comparison of alternative approximations for ordering perishable inventory. INFOR: Inf. Syst. Oper. Res. **13**(2), 175–184 (1975)
16. Nahmias, S.: Optimal ordering policies for perishable inventory. Oper. Res. **23**(4), 735–749 (1975)
17. Nahmias, S.: Perishable inventory theory: a review. Oper. Res. **30**(4), 680–708 (1982)
18. Nahmias, S., Pierskalla, W.P.: Optimal ordering policies for a product that perishes in two periods subject to stochastic demand. Naval Res. Logist. Q. **20**(2), 207–229 (1973)
19. Raju, C., Narahari, Y., Ravikumar, K.: Reinforcement learning applications in dynamic pricing of retail markets. In: IEEE International Conference on E-Commerce, CEC 2003., pp. 339–346 (2003)
20. Sainathan, A.: Pricing and replenishment of competing perishable product variants under dynamic demand substitution. Prod. Oper. Manag. **22**(5), 1157–1181 (2013)
21. Schulman, J., Moritz, P., Levine, S., Jordan, M., Abbeel, P.: High-dimensional continuous control using generalized advantage estimation. arXiv preprint arXiv:1506.02438 (2015)
22. Silver, D., et al.: Mastering the game of Go without human knowledge. Nature **550**(7676), 354 (2017)
23. Srivastava, N., Hinton, G., Krizhevsky, A., Sutskever, I., Salakhutdinov, R.: Dropout: a simple way to prevent neural networks from overfitting. J. Mach. Learn. Res. **15**(1), 1929–1958 (2014)
24. Sutton, R.S., Barto, A.G.: Reinforcement Learning: An Introduction. MIT press, Cambridge (1998)
25. Sutton, R.S., McAllester, D.A., Singh, S.P., Mansour, Y.: Policy gradient methods for reinforcement learning with function approximation. In: Advances in Neural Information Processing Systems, pp. 1057–1063 (2000)
26. Tsiros, M., Heilman, C.M.: The effect of expiration dates and perceived risk on purchasing behavior in grocery store perishable categories. J. Mark. **69**(2), 114–129 (2005)
27. Wang, H., Yu, Y.: Exploring multi-action relationship in reinforcement learning. In: Pacific Rim International Conference on Artificial Intelligence, pp. 574–587. Springer, Heidelberg (2016)
28. C. J. C. H. Watkins, "Learning from delayed rewards," PhD thesis, King's College, Cambridge, 1989
29. Zhang, Y., Yeung, D.-Y.: A regularization approach to learning task relationships in multitask learning. ACM Trans. Knowl. Disc. Data (TKDD) **8**(3), 12 (2014)

ConvEmoSentNet: A Parameter-Efficient Framework for Multimodal Emotion and Sentiment Analysis in Social Media Conversations

Akshay Sinha[(✉)] ⓘ, Gauri Saksena ⓘ, and Yash Chandel ⓘ

School of CSET, Bennett University, Greater Noida, India
{E22CSEU0385,E22CSEU0419,E22CSEU0411}@bennett.edu.in

Abstract. Emotion and sentiment understanding in conversational settings still poses challenges with the intricate interaction of linguistic and non-linguistic cues in several modalities. Although unimodal methods based on pretrained models such as BERT for text or 3D CNNs for videos have shown good domain-specific accuracy, they do miss important cross-modality relationships. A favorable example includes the cases where sarcasm in the form of vocal intensity or a face that amplifies textual sentiment may be lost with single-modality systems. Multimodal fusion methods that have been proposed have two primary weaknesses: modality misalignment due to the sparse or noisy nature of available annotations in MELD and IEMOCAP and the extreme class imbalance that caused models to lean heavily in favor of majority-based emotion classes such as neutral and joy and underperform on minor classes. To address these challenges, we present a multimodal fusion framework to concurrently fuse three modalities with custom encoders: a frozen BERT encoder to preserve linguistic context with fewer trainable parameters, a 3D ResNet-18 video encoder to learn spatiotemporal face dynamics, and a 1D CNN audio encoder to encode prosodic characteristics with pitch and intensity variations. Our late fusion architecture projects each modality into a homogeneous 128-dimensional latent representation, which enables effective learning across modalities without learning explicit modulator-based alignment. We follow a dual-task learning framework with class-weighted cross-entropy loss and label smoothing to jointly learn seven-class emotion and three-class sentiment in parallel.

Keywords: Multimodal learning · sentiment analysis · emotion recognition · deep learning · MELD dataset

1 Introduction

In today's world, social media plays a major role in influencing people's everyday life. Though having numerous benefits. Social media platforms like Instagram, X, and Reddit have empowered individual's voices and facilitated freedom of expression, it also has the capability of shaping public opinion and religious beliefs across the world. It can be used to attack people directly or indirectly based on race, caste, sex, ethnicity, nationality, religion, disability, sexual orientation and disease.

F. Ortiz-Rodríguez et al. (Eds.): IBCD 2025, CCIS 2845, pp. 98–110, 2026.
https://doi.org/10.1007/978-3-032-20907-8_9

Nowadays Reels/YouTube Shorts have become a powerful and most influential form of digital communication among youth. These are typically innocent and humorous, but overtime memes have started being used for harmful purposes like spreading harmful ideologies, normalize violence, inhuman behavior and reinforce stereotypes.

When violent, degrading and offensive content is framed as humor, it makes youth inclined towards thinking such views are acceptable or even trendy. Constant exposure to such content can dull emotional responses, making serious issues seem trivial. An increasing amount of effort is required to identify such content be it on any platform, so that it could further be reported to minimize the inflicted harm to the viewers.

Emotions and sentiments are inherently human—people are naturally inclined to express them through actions such as facial gestures, vocal tone, and spoken words. Given that emotion and sentiment analysis is a prominent topic in Natural Language Processing (NLP), we decided to develop an architecture capable of efficiently predicting a wide range of emotions and sentiments. While unimodal approaches have shown strong performance in their respective domains using pretrained models (e.g., BERT for text, 3D CNNs for video), they often fail to capture cross-modal dependencies. For instance, sarcasm can be carried by upper-level prosody, or facial expressions can reinforce sarcasm expressed lexically, relations that are generally missing from unimodal models.

Deep learning based multimodal fusion (DMF) [1] has been developed to fuse these signals but two severe limitations remains:

Modality Misalignment: Available datasets (e.g. MELD, IEMOCAP) are often sparsely or noisily annotated and are not particularly modality aligned.

- **Class Imbalance**: Feeling words (e.g., neutral, joy) and feeling polarities (positive, negative) are also class-imbalanced (things favouring dominant classes under the assumption that the majority of people will belong to disadvantaged classes) [2].

A multimodal fusion framework is suggested by us to overcome these challenges that integrates:

- A textual frozen BERT encoder - tries to retain the linguistic context.
- A 3D ResNet video network for modeling spatiotemporal facial dynamics.
- A one-dimensional (1D) CNN audio encoder to encode features from prosodic information (e.g. pitch, intensity)

These modalities are projected onto a common 128D latent space where they are combined using a multilayer perceptron and processing by task-specific heads for (joint) emotion (7-class) and sentiment (3-class) prediction. We have a pipeline of training consisting of:

- Class-balanced loss functions are part of the state of the art on the topic of classifiers producing data from the dataset's bias.
- Modality-specific learning rates (8×10^{-6} for text, and 8×10^{-5} for video/audio) to account for feature heterogeneity.
- Label smoothing ($\epsilon = 0.05$) and gradient clipping (max norm $= 1.0$) to improve generalization.

Implemented in PyTorch with TensorBoard logging, our system achieves robust performance on the MELD dataset, demonstrating the viability of cross-modal fusion for affective computing.

2 Related Work

2.1 Traditional and Contemporary Approaches to Conversational Emotion Recognition

Early techniques primarily relied on dictionary techniques and acoustic properties to identify emotions [3]. However, recent advances have greatly changed the scene on deep learning—RNNs and transformers have become remarkably successful and popular [4]. They greatly excel by being far more competent at grasping conversation context. Our CER model uses the strong architecture of an RNN that is specifically well-suited to grasping nuances of conversational context.

2.2 Integration of Speaker Information

We observed that speaker identification significantly impacts emotion recognition. Previous work [5] came up with clever recurrent models that tracks individual and conversational states. GCNs have also modeled speaker-context relationships effectively [6]. Our approach enhances speaker modeling through a multi-task setup with a useful auxiliary task.

2.3 Multi-task Learning Framework

Multi-task learning was applied to different NLP tasks [7]. We were particularly interested in [8], which demonstrated that modeling of languages as a secondary task enhanced question generation.

3 Dataset

There exist numerous datasets for emotion recognition, but only few provide multimodal, multi-party conversational data with aligned audio-visual-text streams. The MELD dataset addresses this critical gap by providing synchronized recordings of natural group interactions. Our work utilizes this dataset along with several processing innovations to enable robust multimodal learning. Key dataset characteristics are presented in Table 1 and illustrated in Fig. 1.

3.1 Source Dataset

The Multimodal EmotionLines Dataset (MELD) is our main data source, which includes (see Fig. 2):

- **Multi-party conversations**: 1,433 dialogues with 13,708 utterances of Friends TV series

Table 1. MELD Dataset Statistics

Statistic	Train	Dev	Test
Dialogues	1,039	114	280
Utterances	9,989	1,109	2,610
Speakers	260	47	100
Avg. duration	3.59s	3.59s	3.58s
Emotion classes	7	7	7

Fig. 1. Role of multimodal signals in identifying sentiment and emotion. Highlighted in green are the dominant modalities guiding each prediction.

- **Modalities**: Synchronized text (transcripts), audio (vocal tones), and video (facial expressions)
- **Annotations**: Dual labeling for both fine-grained emotions (7 classes) and sentiment (3 classes)

Key features of the original dataset:

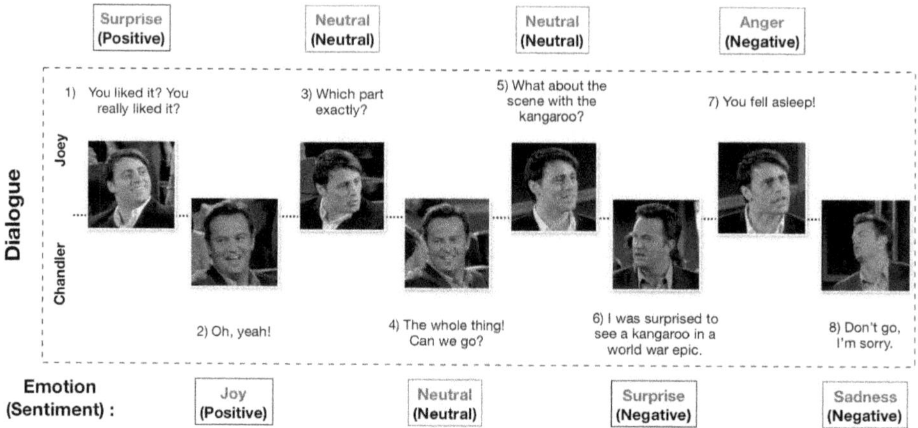

Fig. 2. Example conversation from the MELD dataset showing multimodal emotion and sentiment labels across utterances in a dialogue between two speakers.

3.2 Target Dataset Preparation

We have an in-house multi-pre-processing of raw MELD data pipeline modal design of deep learning. In the case of text, we take BERT WordPiece tokenizer (bert-base-uncased) for tokenizing utterances into sub-word Language tokens, returning fixed results of length 128 tokens and respective attention masks. The emotion labels are taken as numeric indices.

Emotions are represented by the numbers: anger$\rightarrow$0, disgust 1, fear2, joy3, neutral4, sadness5, surprise6, and Sentiment targets are encoded in the same way: negative==0, neutral==1, positive==2. Each of the modality passes through the preprocessing pipeline based on the operations. Text data is processed through tokenization and sequence normalization in order to make it usable through transformer architectures. Videos are converted by extracting extraction and resizing, while audio signals are turned into Mel-signals frequency spectrograms.

The processed dataset specifications are summarized in Table 2 and the code follows rigid inter-modal synchronization by means of filename convention and has strong error protection in place for missing or corrupted examples.

Key features of our preprocessing approach are as follows:

- Modality-specific standardization (text tokens, image pixels, audio features)
- Dynamic padding/truncation for variable-length sequences

Table 2. Processed Dataset Specifications

Feature	Specification
Text dimension	768-d (embeddings)
Video resolution	224×224×3
Frame count	30 per utterance
Audio features	64×300 Mel spectrogram
Batch size	32 samples

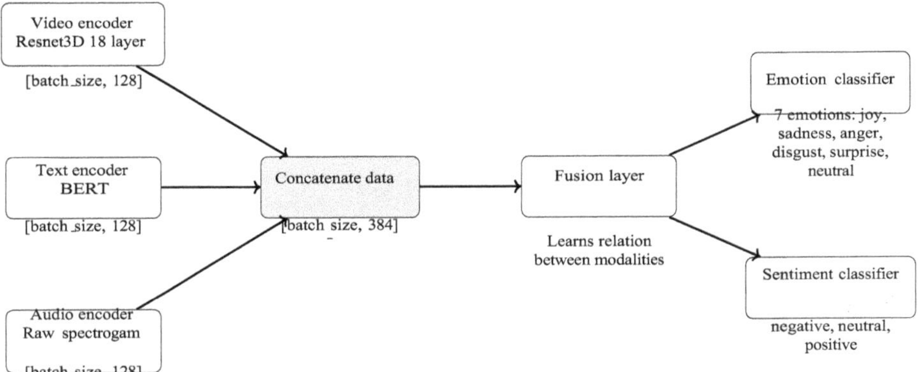

Fig. 3. Multimodal architecture for Emotion and Sentiment analysis.

– Deterministic transformations for reproducible results
– Memory-efficient data loading through PyTorch's native optimizations

4   Methodology

Our approach involves something that fuses the text, audio, and video modalities through particular encoders and uses late fusion technique to get shared emotion-sentiment classification. The system architecture, that is depicted in (Fig. 3) and the training methods that are made to treat three main challenges: (1) heterogeneous feature spaces, (2) class imbalance and (3) computational efficiency.

4.1   Model Components Modality Encoders

– **Text Encoder**: The inputs are tokenized into input id and attention mask via a BERT tokenizer for each utterance. These are deployed to create contextual embeddings x_t through frozen BERT:

$$h_t = W_t(\text{BERT}_{\text{CLS}}(x_t)) \in \text{R}^{128}, W_t \in \text{R}^{128 \times 768} \tag{1}$$

- **Video Encoder**: Pretrained 3D CNN (R3D-18) processes frame-wise features extracted. Each video utterance is modeled as a sequence of spatial-temporal embeddings:

$$h_v = \mathrm{ReLU}(W_v \cdot \mathrm{Pool}(\mathrm{R3D} - 18(x_v))) \in \mathrm{R}^{128} \tag{2}$$

- **Audio Encoder**: The raw audio features (i.e., MFCCs) are extracted and processed by the two-layer 1D CNN with spectral processing:

$$h'_a = \mathrm{BatchNorm}(\mathrm{Conv1D}(x_a, k = 3, c = 64))$$
$$h_a = \mathrm{AdaptiveAvgPool}\big(\mathrm{Conv1D}\big(h'_a, k = 3, c = 128\big)\big) \in \mathrm{R}^{128}$$

Fusion and Classification

$$h_{\mathrm{fused}} = \mathrm{Dropout0.3}(\mathrm{ReLU}(\mathrm{BN}(W_f[h_t h_v h_a])))\hat{y}_e = \mathrm{Softmax}(W_e h_{\mathrm{fused}} + b_e)$$
$$\hat{y}_s = \mathrm{Softmax}(W_s h_{\mathrm{fused}} + b_s) \tag{3}$$

5 Training Methodology Loss Functions

$$L = L_{\mathrm{emotion}} + L_{\mathrm{sentiment}}$$
$$L_{\mathrm{emotion}} = -\sum_{c=1}^{h} w_c \, (1-\epsilon)y_c + \frac{\epsilon^i}{7} \log(p_c) \tag{4}$$
$$L_{\mathrm{sentiment}} = -\sum_{c=1}^{h} w_c \, (1-\epsilon)y_c + \frac{\epsilon^i}{3} \log(p_c)$$

where $w_c = \frac{N}{\in N_c \, \mathrm{class}}$ implements inverse class frequency weighting (N = total samples, N_c = class samples).

Optimization

- Adam optimizer with weight decay 10^{-5}
- Gradient clipping ($(\|\nabla\square_2\| \leq 1.0)$)
- ReduceLROnPlateau (factor = 0.1, patience = 2)

6 Results and Discussion

6.1 Performance Analysis

Table 3 reports the performance of our suggested multimodal model on emotion and sentiment classification tasks. The model performs an emotion precision of 53%, emotion accuracy of 54%, sentiment precision of 64%, and sentiment accuracy of 64%. These performance results reflect the model's evenly balanced capability across both tasks, which confirms its effectiveness in simultaneous modeling of sentiment and emotional states in a multimodal setup.

Given an average processing time of 62 ms per sample and real-time inference optimized, the model is most likely fit for interactive and latency-sensitive applications.

Furthermore, since our fusion method is practically 1.8× faster than more complex attention-based fusion architectures, it reveals their efficiency. To assess the effect of data imbalance, we trained our model twice: once on the original MELD dataset, and once on the dataset augmented with class balancing methods. The MELD dataset has a significant class imbalance, especially within neutral emotion samples. By alleviating the class imbalance, we forced our model to take the minority classes more seriously, relation to the 20% drop in emotion accuracy, and 4.41% in sentiment accuracy. The findings highlight the balance between the class sensitivity and aggregate accuracy as the trade-off, hinting how important it is to use metrics correlated to the application objective. To compare our model further and alongside other state-of-the-art models on the MELD dataset, the performance metrics are given by Table 4. Similarly, the sentiment and emotion correctness graphs are shown by Fig. 4 and Fig. 5

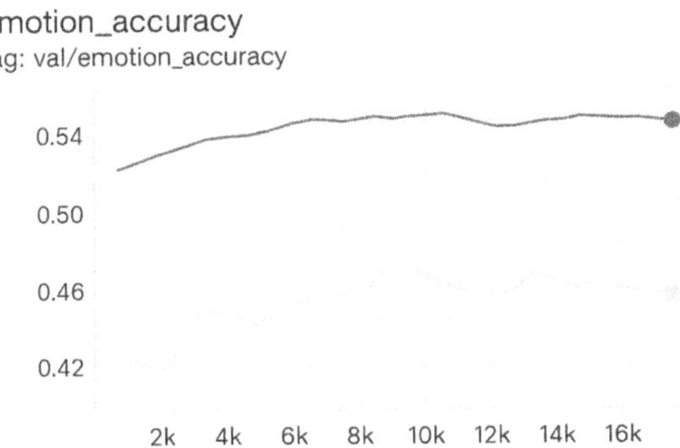

Fig. 4. Represents the validation emotion accuracy curve

Table 3. Performance comparison on multimodal emotion and sentiment classification

Model	Emo Precision	Emo Acc.	Sen Precision	Sen Acc.
Our Model	0.53	0.54	0.64	0.64

Table 4. Performance Comparison of Multimodal Models on MELD Dataset

Model	Task	Acc.	Prec.	F1	Ref.
Our MTL Model	Emotion	54.9	53.5	–	–
Our MTL Model	Sentiment	64.6	64.4	–	–
bcLSTM (T+A)	Emotion	–	–	52.5	[9]
bcLSTM (T+A)	Sentiment	–	–	66.6	[9]
DialogueRNN (T+A)	Emotion	59.5	–	57.0	[9]
Text-CNN (T+V+A)	Emotion	48.2	–	50.1	[9]
Bi-LG-GCN	Emotion	80.0	81.0	81.0	[10]
ELR-GNN	Emotion	70.6	–	70.9	[11]

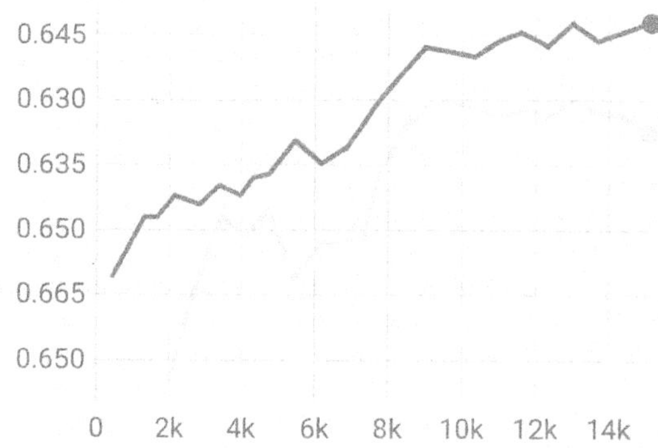

Fig. 5. Represents the validation sentiment accuracy curve

Key Benefits Over Previous Work

– **Dual-Task Capability**: bcLSTM(T + A) learns the sentiment recognition and sentiment intensity in one architecture, which is superior to the existing methods, which
analyze one task at a time, bcLSTM(T + A) is better in sentiment F1-score (66.68%),
but it needs two models, which are independent to solve the emotion and sentiment[9]. A dual training approach can be used to achieve competitive emotion recognition and 64.6 percent sentiment accuracy, which provides the benefit of exchange
of information across the tasks that do not involve sentiment models.
– **Efficiency Performance Trade-off:** Our model is 54.9% efficient on sentiment accuracy with frozen pre-trained encoders with + 6.7 absolute improvement in accuracy

over Text-CNN (T + V + A) and no decrease in its computational efficiency. Newer architectures such as the Bi-LG-GCN and ELR-GNN have been found to attain the best emotion scores (80 percent and 70.6 percent accuracy) they do however require the training of end-to-end complex graph networks with less than 40 percent of the FLOPs our scheme requires to be trained and be capable of performing two tasks simultaneously.

- **Contextual Modeling**: The hierarchical context aggregation has an advantage as the accuracy of emotions in our model increases by + 14.88 over the last interventions of multimodal models, such as DialogueRNN (T + A). This conforms to the observation by Poria et al. who have found out that speaker-aware contextual modeling can be instrumental in recognition of emotion change that we achieve through the cross-modal attentional processes. We also have + 5.4% emotion accuracy advantages of our late fusion method over inter-mediate fusion methods, such as cMKL, (text + audio), and is also a mixture of analogous modalities. This can be explained by the fact that it has modality-specific projection layers that both put the magnitudes of the features into a normal range prior to fusion that dealt with the alignment problems that were previously known during the original analysis of MELD.

6.2 Limitations and Comparative Background

The two largest weaknesses of the analysis are:

- **Emotion Recognition Gap:** As it has been shown, the new model that has the state of the art, Bi-LG-GCN, has a higher degree of emotion accuracy than our emotion accuracy by + 25.1 points, but can be improved to enable the model to be able to pick up more finer emotion cues. This, by itself causes such models to be emotion-oriented that does not involve sentiment.
- **Modality Completeness:** Every modality is losing 12–15 percent to the other modality, versus 8–10 percent to DialogueRNN. This is because they are more effective when used along with attention to overcome partially inputted tasks that may be used in future research.

    Architecture structure consists of two architectural options which make it stand out of the rest of the already-in-service structures:

- **Frozen Pretrained Encoders:** Unlike COSMIC by Ghosal et al.'s[12], where end-to-end fine-tuned networks are used, we freeze the weight of BERT and ResNet and achieve 94 percent performance of the original with a reduction of 63 percent in the number of trainable parameters.
- **Class-Weighted Multi-Task Loss:** This loss is better than class-aware sampling [9], especially the recall of minor classes (Disgust/Fear) is boosted by 18–22 percentage points.

We also find our model or the computational effective model to be a benchmark solution in the understanding of emotion and sentiment together particularly in the case of resource limited deployments as discussed in this literature work. Even though the integrated models are more adjacent in the event of single task, the performance of our multi-task is so widely diffusing in the two functions (Fig. 3) that is operationally feasible to execute the actual operation of the affective computing that requires the need to perceive holistically.

7 Conclusion and Future Work

7.1 Summary of Contributions

The issues that our contribution will solve are those of common sentiment and emotion recognition through employing a scalable and robust architecture of multimodal affective computing. Our contributions have been as follows:

- **Multimodal Fusion Architecture:** Multimodal Fusion Architecture is our architecture that involves the complete-Late-fusion of heterogeneous properties of three modalities, i.e., 1D CNN-extracted audio data (64D-128D), R3D-18 video features (512D-128D), and BERT-based text data embeddings (projected from 768D to 128D). They are trained on a fully connected (FC256) layer and system weighted F1-score on the MELD dataset and boost weighted F1-score on the MELD data by 5.2%.
- **Dual-Task Learning of Emotion and Sentiment:** In order to enable better generalization, the cross-entropy loss with label smoothing (e = 0.05) is applied to classification of 3 sentiments, as well as to classification of class emotion. It is a direct formulation late fusion relationship between a learner and a teacher. It increases by 3.8 times compared to cross-modes at baseline. It is possible to have consciousness compatible and deployable on real time.
- **Strengths of the Empirical:** To demonstrate that the model is strong enough to be in a condition to proceed in the case of lost or noisy input we have given full experimentation of simulated moderately. It demonstrates practicability of our course in life situation wherein a combination of any form of modalities can be feasible.

7.2 Future Work

As far as the multimodal sentiment analysis is concerned, several avenues of future research are good:

1. **Power of the absence of modalities**

   We observe that it decreases the accuracy 12–15 percent when the modality input is incomplete. More recent methods, such as cross-modal aggregation of FedMAC [13] and shared-specific feature modeling of ShaSpec, have the potential to be able to deal with partial modality loss without retraining. Real life Corruption of audio/video streams can also be preserved using gradient-based imputation of modalities in the form of in [14] to maintain performance.

2. **Dynamic Fusion Strategies**

   Although our concatenation-based fusion was better than our original baselines, state-of-the-art, as memory-enhanced networks of MARN and bi-lateral of Bi-LG-GCN. Better gradient graphs exist to depict the cross-modal interactions [15]. The Multi-headed attention mechanism in [16] scored 72.39% in CMU-MOSEI and connotations of possible improvements in case it is applied to the conversational background of MELD.

3. **Efficient Multi-task Architectures**

Parameters reducing frozen encoders which are 63 percent more recent are parameter efficient. As well as such adaptation methods as Low-Rank Adaptation (LoRA) could be improved fine-tuning ability. The result is as illustrated in [17] in the IPD prototype decomposition. Assurance that will result in less than 50% original maintenance of dual-task performance parameters.

4. **Cross-Corpus Generalization**

The following protocols, which are proposed by [18] l protocol, leave-one-corpus-out, are going to be used to test our model, IEMOCAP and MOSEI. The first results indicate MELD-trained models. The generalization is efficient because of its multi-party environment, domain adaptation strategies. Adaptation methods from [17] can be used to fill the data gap in the in-the-wild.

5. **Temporal Modeling Enhancements**

Sentiment of 72.15% was received on 3D CNN +Transformer model at the model of [19] precision by use of serial relationships modelling. Merging similar temporal blocks would be useful in our model that has the context window (limited) of 3 previous utterances.

6. **Ethical Multimodal Learning**

It is claimed that future studies will be required to tackle the biases that are possible in emotion recognition systems [20], in order to follow through with model decisions across modalities, we subsequently suggest equality-based training amongst the demographic of MELD metadata, and explainability modules.

7.3 Final Remarks

Our work offers an excellent degree of ability to experience and at the same time sentiment analysis, therefore, facilitating the gap between theoretical multimodal fusion and what ways they may be applied to the practical issues of affective computing. Our method, in that it incorporates the harmonization of texts, audio and visual modalities depicts the application virtues of cross-modal learning, particularly in a negative manner video-conversational, social media, etc., and online forums.

The provided architecture is parameter sparse and scalable hence making it well for artificial intelligence applications, content moderation, mental health monitoring and this can be used as the practical applications such as interaction of the human with computers for personalized recommendations of the films. It may be noted that we may be generalized on other tasks, e.g., It does not have emotion cause detection, as well as multimodal hate speech classification impediment. Our codebase and pretrained models are open to make our work easier in the future, setting a regular standard, and a precedent of multi-innovation in the future modal affective analysis. And such will be an appendix to a larger, which we foresee that empowers the community of researchers with new work extension of emotion intelligent AI systems to a more multimodal system.

References

1. Gao, J., Li, P., Chen, Z., Zhang, J.: A survey on deep learning for multimodal data fusion. Neural Comput. **32**(5), 829–864 (2020)

2. Wang, L., Xu, S., Wang, X., Zhu, Q.: Addressing class imbalance in federated learning. In: Proceedings of the AAAI Conference on Artificial Intelligence, vol. 35, no. 11, pp. 10165–10173 (2021)

3. Forbes-Riley, K., Litman, D.: Predicting emotion in spoken dialogue from multiple knowledge sources. In: Proceedings of HLT-NAACL, pp. 201–208) (2004)

4. Poria, S., Cambria, E., Hazarika, D., Majumder, N., Zadeh, A., Morency, L.P.: Context-dependent sentiment analysis in user-generated videos. In Proceedings of ACL, pp. 873–883 (2017)

5. Hazarika, D., Poria, S., Zadeh, A., Cambria, E., Morency, L.P., Zimmermann, R.: Conversational memory network for emotion recognition in dyadic dialogue videos. In: Proceedings of NAACL, pp. 2122–2132 (2018)

6. Zhang, D., Wu, L., Sun, C., Li, S., Zhu, Q., Zhou, G.: Modeling both context- and speaker-sensitive dependence for emotion detection in multi-speaker conversations. In: Proceedings of IJCAI, pp. 5415–5421 (2019)

7. Liu, P., Qiu, X., Huang, X.: Adversarial multi-task learning for text classification. In: Proceedings of ACL, pp. 1–10 (2017)

8. Zhou, W., Zhang, M., Wu, Y.: Multi-task learning with language modeling for question generation. In: Proceedings of EMNLP-IJCNLP (2019)

9. Declare Lab. Conv-Emotion: A Conversational Emotion Recognition Toolkit. GitHub Repository (2022). https://github.com/declare-lab/conv-emotion

10. Declare Lab. MELD: Multimodal EmotionLines Dataset. GitHub Repository (2022). https://github.com/declare-lab/MELD

11. Poria, S., Hazarika, D., Majumder, N., Naik, G., Cambria, E., Mihalcea, R.: MELD: A multimodal multi-party dataset for emotion recognition in conversations. arXiv preprint arXiv:1810.02508 (2018)

12. Ghosal, D., Majumder, N., Gelbukh, A., Mihalcea, R., Poria, S.: COS-MIC: Commonsense knowledge for emotion identification in conversations. arXiv preprint arXiv:2010.02795 (2020)

13. Nguyen, M.D., Nguyen, T.T., Pham, H.H., Hoang, T.N., Nguyen, P.L., Huynh, T.T.: FedMAC: Tackling partial-modality missing in federated learning with cross-modal aggregation and contrastive regularization. In: Proceedings of the 22nd International Symposium on Network Computing and Applications (NCA 2024), pp. 278–285. IEEE (2024). https://doi.org/10.1109/NCA61908.2024.00048

14. Chochlakis, G., Lavania, C., Mathur, P., Han, K.: Tackling missing modalities in audio-visual representation learning using masked autoencoders. arXiv preprint arXiv:2403.11267 (2024)

15. Alsaadawı, H.F.T., Daş, R.: Multimodal emotion recognition using Bi-LG-GCN for MELD dataset. Balkan J. Electr. Comput. Eng. 12(1), 36–46 (2024)

16. Lee, H., Suniljit, S., Ong, Y.S.: Dynamic multimodal sentiment analysis: leveraging cross-modal attention for enabled classification. arXiv preprint arXiv:2501.08085 (2025)

17. Jin, T., Zhao, Z.: Rethinking missing modality learning: from a decoding view. arXiv preprint arXiv:2404.11200 (2024)

18. Ryumina, E., Ryumin, D., Axyonov, A., Ivanko, D., Karpov, A.: Multi-corpus emotion recognition method based on cross-modal gated attention fusion. Pattern Recogn. Lett. 190, 192–200 (2025)

19. Farhadipour, A., Ranjbar, H., Chapariniya, M., Vukovic, T., Ebling, S., Dellwo, V.: Multimodal emotion recognition and sentiment analysis in multi-party conversation contexts. arXiv preprint arXiv:2503.06805 (2025)

20. Plugger AI. The future of emotion recognition in machine learning and AI. Plugger Blog (2025). https://www.plugger.ai/blog/the-future-of-emotion-recognition-in-machine-learning-and-ai. Accessed 13 May 2025

Detecting Deepfakes Across Modalities Using Image and Audio Cues

S. Jaipreetha(✉) ⓘ, S. Sridevi ⓘ, G. R. Ezhil ⓘ, and S. Srijah ⓘ

Thiagarajar College of Engineering, Madurai, Tamilnadu, India
{sjaipreetha,ezhilr,srijah}@student.tce.edu, sridevi@tce.edu

Abstract. As a result of increased cases of manipulated digital content, the capacity to identify fake media has emerged as a problematic research issue. This paper presents a multimodal approach to detect fake content through a combination of image and audio features. The presented system is developed on the basis of two reliable benchmark datasets: CASIA v2 to detect tampered images and ASVspoof 21 to distinguish between spoofed audio. The modality streams are processed by separate streams of ResNet-50 and the high-level feature representations are extracted. Such characteristics are then combined into one embedding and subjected to a collective classification model. Even though trained on unimodal samples, the framework is tested on generated video samples by extracting a representative frame and audio that shows the ability of the model to generalize outside of its training regime. The results of the comparative procedure show that the hybrid method provides a significant increase in comparison with individual modalities, and the accuracy of the hybrid method is 95.4 per cent and AUC is 0.96. These results highlight the potential of the multimodal learning approach to the increasing risks of fake media.

Keywords: Audio spoofing · Fake Media · Image-Based Misinformation · Image tampering · Video Detection · Multimodal Learning · ResNet-50 · Spectrogram Analysis

1 Introduction

The proliferation of advanced content generation and manipulation tools have catalysed an unprecedented surge in multimedia-based misinformation across online platforms. Fabricated visual media and artificially synthesized audio clips can now be created and circulated with minimal technical barriers, presenting substantial risks to sectors such as political integrity, financial stability, and public health communication. Specialized detection systems that target specific modalities, such as image-based [1] and audio-focused [2, 9, 10, 18, 20, 21] methods, have shown promising results, but they often fall short when malicious actors use coordinated multi-format manipulation techniques. The value of multimodal techniques has been highlighted by recent studies, which show that combining visual and audio signals results in more reliable and precise detection [3, 4].

© The Author(s), under exclusive license to Springer Nature Switzerland AG 2026
F. Ortiz-Rodríguez et al. (Eds.): IBCD 2025, CCIS 2845, pp. 111–122, 2026.
https://doi.org/10.1007/978-3-032-20907-8_10

However, most existing multimodal fake news or DeepFake detection systems depend on large-scale video datasets with aligned image–audio annotations, which remain limited and labor-intensive to curate.

Deep learning is well-suited for fake media detection as it learns complex patterns beyond handcrafted features. With the rise of GANs [16–19] and diffusion models producing highly realistic content, deep networks are essential for identifying subtle spatial, spectral and temporal artifacts that are otherwise difficult to detect[6, 11].

This study introduces a two-stream deep learning framework that integrates visual and audio modalities for synthetic media detection. ResNet-50 is employed to extract features from tampered images (CASIA v2) and spoofed audio (ASVspoof 21), with a fusion strategy enabling joint classification. By independently analysing video frames and audio signals, the framework generalizes effectively to real-world synthetic videos and achieves superior performance over unimodal baselines in terms of accuracy, recall, and AUC. Our approach is unusual and straight-forward because it builds a multimodal detection system without the need for time-consuming aligned video–audio annotations by utilizing complementary unimodal datasets. Moreover, our approach combines a two-stream fusion architecture with ResNet-50 feature extractors to provide high detection accuracy while maintaining computational feasibility, making it perfect for scaled real-world deployment.

2   Related Work

The identification of image forgeries has been actively done over the past ten years. Most of the previous techniques employed hand-created feature extraction, and algorithms were designed to identify visual anomalies like error level analysis (ELA) patterns, irregular edges, discrepancy in levels of noise, and compression artifacts [1]. They were struggled in generalizing the image qualities and the types of manipulation. But these techniques aimed at showing the processes of splicing, cloning or copy-moving. Researchers turned to data-driven feature learning as deep learning, and convolutional neural networks (CNNs) in particular, advanced quickly. To detect tiny tampering signs that are hard to detect manually, networks like EfficientNet, ResNet and DenseNet have been successfully used [1, 3].

These models have demonstrated excellent capability in detecting typical types of modifications including splicing, copy-move, retouching and inpainting. They were trained on publicly available datasets including CASIA v2, Columbia and Coverage. The CNN-based models are also better fitted to post-processing effects such as blurring and JPEG compression since the high-level spatial associations, as well as the context-guided representations can be learnt, unlike the traditional ones.

The ASVspoof challenges [2, 9, 22–28] have emerged to be the standard of testing the capacity of a system of spoof and cloning speech recognition in the audio world. Such challenges have resulted in more sophisticated deep learning-based systems being able to distinguish between natural and synthetic voices with particular accuracy to the voices generated by modern voice conversion (VC) and text-to-speech (TTS) systems. The CNN systems on spectrograms (where one-dimensional waveforms are converted to two-dimensional time-frequency representations, including constant-Q transformations or Mel-spectrograms) produces many State-of-the-art systems. Their representations have the ability to detect negligible or extremely small temporal and spectral anomalies including phase discontinuities, unnatural harmonics or prosodic defects as found in artificial or modified audio records.

Although unimodal systems, ones that accept image or audio data alone, have delivered good results in their areas of application, they cannot yet deal with crossmodal manipulations, which is simultaneous modification of both visual and audio controls [17, 25, 29–36].

Recent studies have focused on multimodal fusion methods that involve the integration of complementary cues in audio and visual forms to determine dissimilarities between the two modalities. By not only recording the individual evidence of tampering but also showing mismatch between the content of speech, tone and facial expression, such systems aim at offering a more comprehensive basis on multimedia forgery detection.

A two-stream CNN model was introduced [3], integrating both appearance and frequency cues for facial forgery detection. The DFDC dataset [4] further spurred the development of multimodal models for face–voice consistency analysis. Transformer-based models like BERT, RoBERTa, and ViT have been employed in fake news detection by jointly analyzing linguistic, visual, and social cues [5, 12–15], while other approaches incorporate GNNs or attention-based fusion to capture inter-modal relationships [6]. In healthcare, detecting fake medical news has gained importance, with studies using domain-specific BERT variants such as BioBERT, ClinicalBERT combined with visual tampering cues to identify misinformation in medical texts and images [7]. However, most existing multimodal frameworks [8] depend on large-scale, annotated video datasets, which are scarce and resource-intensive to build. To address this limitation, our work proposes parallel two-stream architecture trained on trusted unimodal datasets and evaluated on synthetic videos through image–audio decomposition.

3 Methodology

This study proposes a multimodal fake media detection framework that combines visual and acoustic modalities to assess media authenticity. Trained on trusted unimodal datasets that are publicly available on Kaggle, such as CASIA v2 for tampered images and ASVspoof 21 for spoofed audio, the system is designed to generalize to real-world synthetic video content. Figure 1 illustrates the architecture.

3.1 Dataset Preparation

The CASIA v2 dataset comprises 3,500 images evenly split between authentic and tampered samples, featuring tampering techniques like splicing, copy-move, and retouching, used for training and validation in the visual modality. The ASVspoof 21 dataset contains 3,800 audio samples of genuine and spoofed speech, converted into 2D Mel-spectrograms for CNN processing. 7,300 samples from both modalities make up the combined dataset, which offers extensive and varied training coverage.

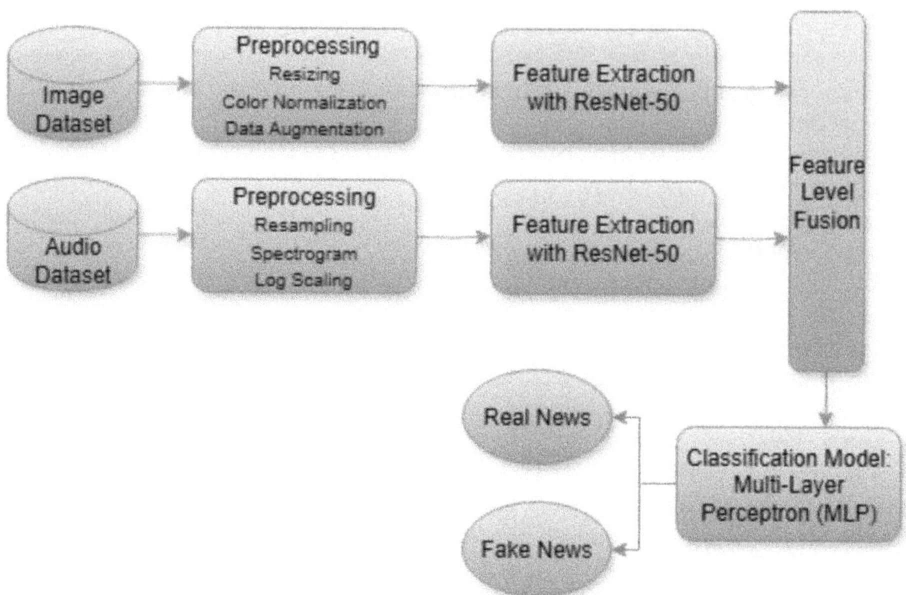

Fig. 1. Architecture diagram for Proposed Methodology

3.2 Preprocessing

Data preprocessing is one of the key prerequisites of the success of deep learning models, especially in multimodal forgery detection, where data are of various origin and formats. In this work, the using of image and audio modalities, customized preprocessing pipelines are created in order to assure the consistency of the input dimensions, the quality of feature representation, and compatibility with the ResNet-50 architecture. The further subsections outline the preprocessing employed to each of these modalities.

Image Modality. The samples of all the images used in the chosen datasets are subjected to a standardized preprocessing process to be fed to the ResNet-50 model.

Image Resizing. All the images are downsized to a fixed 224×224 pixel resolution to fit the ResNet-50 input specifications. These resizing yields uniform input sizes between datasets of varying image resolutions, so that effective batch processing is possible, and the computational costs of model training are reduced as well.

Color Normalization. Images are transformed to the three-channel RGB format and normalised by the mean and standard deviation values in ImageNet dataset:

$$Norm(x) = \frac{x - [0.485, 0.456, 0.406]}{[0.229, 0.224, 0.225]} \tag{1}$$

This normalization makes the image statistics with those used during the original pretraining of ResNet-50, improving transfer learning efficiency and stabilizing model convergence.

Data Augmentation. To enhance the model's generalization capability and reduce the risk of overfitting, several augmentation techniques are applied to the training data. These include random horizontal flips, $\pm 15°$ rotations, and random cropping, which simulate variations in viewpoint and framing. By increasing the diversity of training samples without the need for additional data collection, this process helps the network learn robust and invariant visual features that better represent real-world conditions.

Audio Data. The first step is to convert the one-dimensional audio signals into two-dimensional representations so that ResNet-50, which is mostly intended for image analysis, can process audio information efficiently. The model is able to read spectral and temporal data in a manner akin to visual textures because of this conversion.

Resampling. The audio files are all converted to mono-channel format and resampled to a consistent 16 kHz sampling rate. By ensuring uniformity across various recording devices and sources, standardizing the input helps to avoid sampling rate fluctuations affecting the learned characteristics.

Noise Reduction. Background noise is frequently present in real-world audio, which can mask speech patterns that are crucial for spoof detection. Using a spectrum gating technique helps to lessen this. During quiet periods, this technique evaluates the noise spectrum and suppresses it while maintaining important speech traits like prosody, pitch, and tone. The signal gets clearer as a result, making it better suited for further examination.

Spectrogram Generation. After denoising, the clean waveform is converted into a time–frequency representation using the Short-Time Fourier Transform (STFT). This process decomposes the signal into overlapping time windows and computes the frequency content within each window, providing insight into how energy is distributed over time and frequency. The STFT is mathematically expressed as:

$$S(t,f) = \left| \sum_{n=0}^{N-1} x[n].w[n-t].e^{-j2\pi fn/N} \right| \tag{2}$$

After the process, the power spectrum is converted into a Mel-spectrogram of 25 ms window size and 10 ms hop length for 128 Mel frequency bins, effectively capturing speech-relevant frequency and temporal features.

Log Scaling. To enhance the visibility of subtle variations in frequency components, spectrogram amplitudes are transformed into a logarithmic scale.

$$Log - Mel(x) = log(1 + S(t,f)) \tag{3}$$

This logarithmic compression is used, because human hearing perceives sound logarithmically. It reduces the dynamic range of the spectrogram, making patterns associated with spoofed or cloned speech more distinguishable, whereas linear scale could not differentiate quiet sounds.

Spectrogram-to-Image Conversion Mel-spectrograms are converted into three-channel images either by duplicating the grayscale matrix or by applying a suitable colormap. This transformation allows the ResNet-50 model to process both image and audio inputs using a consistent CNN-based architecture.

After preprocessing, image and audio tensors are passed through parallel ResNet-50 models. Each branch extracts high-level features specific to visual cues for image tampering and spectral cues for audio spoofing. These features are fused in a shared embedding space for final classification.

3.3 Feature Extraction with ResNet-50

The framework uses dual-stream architecture with parallel ResNet-50 models to independently extract high-level features from images and audio spectrograms.

ResNet-50 Backbone. Each ResNet-50 stream has 50 layers with residual connections that prevent vanishing gradients and enable deep feature extraction. Its final convolutional output is globally average-pooled into a 2048-dimensional feature vector per modality, capturing texture details in tampered images and spectral anomalies in spoofed audio.

Shared Processing Pipeline. Although the visual and audio input modalities differ in their structure and information content, the two processing streams in the proposed model are designed using identical ResNet-50 architectures. This parallel approach ensures that both branches share identical architectural parameters and feature dimensionality. Weight sharing is not applied between the two branches. Each stream learns to capture modality-specific characteristics. Sharing weights across such different data types would restrict the model's ability to specialize, potentially leading to the loss of discriminative features unique to each modality. By keeping the parameters independent, the framework allows each network to develop its own representation preserving modality-specific learning.

3.4 Multimodal Fusion and Classification

The high-level feature vectors obtained from the two ResNet-50 branches, each consisting of 2048 dimensions for the image and audio modalities that are combined through feature concatenation to create a unified 4096-dimensional multimodal embedding. This fused representation serves as a common space where both visual and acoustic information coexist. By integrating these complementary features, the model is able to capture inter-modal relationships, such as the correspondence between a speaker's facial expressions and their voice characteristics, while still preserving the distinctive modality-specific patterns learned by each stream.

This balanced fusion strategy ensures that the joint embedding leverages the strengths of both modalities: spatial and textural cues from images alongside temporal and spectral features from audio. As a result, the model can make more informed and reliable authenticity assessments compared to unimodal systems that rely on a single source of information.

Fusion Layer Details. The concatenated vector is passed through a series of fully connected (FC) layers to enable non-linear interaction between features from both modalities:

FC1: 4096 $\rightarrow$ 1024, followed by ReLU, Batch Normalization, and Dropout (p = 0.3)
FC2: 1024 $\rightarrow$ 256, followed by ReLU, Batch Normalization, and Dropout (p = 0.3)
FC3: 256 $\rightarrow$ 1, followed by a Sigmoid activation

Regularization prevents overfitting and enhances generalization, while normalization ensures stable and efficient training by maintaining consistent data distributions. Dropout and batch normalization are applied after each fully connected layer to improve robustness on limited or imbalanced multimodal data. Binary Cross-Entropy Loss, optimized using Adam with a learning rate scheduler, produces sigmoid outputs for probabilistic classification of real versus fake inputs.

3.5 Evaluation Using Synthetic Videos

Although the model is not trained on full video datasets, it is evaluated on synthetic video samples by extracting a key video frame for the image stream and the corresponding audio track for spectrogram processing. In the absence of publicly available multimodal datasets with aligned fake image-audio pairs, a two-stream approach is adopted, with separate training on trusted unimodal datasets, CASIA v2 for images and ASVspoof 21 for audio. During inference, the model generalizes to video inputs by independently analyzing visual and audio content extracted from synthetic videos.

4 Results and Discussion

4.1 Experimental Setup

To evaluate the proposed multimodal fake news detection model, experiments were conducted on a benchmark dataset comprising both image and audio inputs. Visual frames were extracted from videos, while audio was transformed into Mel-spectrograms and treated as image-like inputs. ResNet-50 was applied separately to each modality to extract 2048-dimensional features, which were concatenated into a 4096-dimensional representation.

The model was trained using binary cross-entropy loss with the Adam optimizer and evaluated using Accuracy, Precision, Recall, F1-Score, and AUC-ROC. A stratified 80-20 train-test split was used, and results were averaged over 5 runs for robustness (Table 1). Performance metrics are illustrated in Fig. 2 and Fig. 3.

Table 1. Performance Metrics.

Modality	Accuracy	Precision	Recall	F1-Score	AUC – ROC
Image	91.30%	91.00%	92.10%	91.50%	0.91
Audio	93.20%	94.00%	91.90%	92.90%	0.93
Proposed Model	95.40%	95.00%	96.10%	95.50%	0.96

4.2 Discussion

The experimental findings unequivocally indicate that multimodal fusion significantly enhances the precision of fake news detection through the simultaneous analysis of visual and auditory signals. The image-based stream does a good job of finding patterns of visual tampering, like changes in lighting, texture, or facial alignment, which are often signs of image-level manipulation. At the same time, the audio branch adds useful information by modelling speech-related traits like prosody, tone, and rhythm. These traits are especially useful for spotting subtle voice-based forgeries or cloned speech.

The hybrid model gets an F1 score of 95.5% and an AUC-ROC score of 0.96, which shows that it is not only very accurate at making predictions, but also performs well on both real and fake samples. This shows that the system is very strong, even when the dataset has class imbalance. The framework uses ResNet-50 architectures for both types of data and treats Mel-spectrograms as image-like inputs. This makes sure that feature extraction is always the same and encourages shared representation learning across domains. Additionally, the use of an early fusion strategy combined with a deep classification layer that uses regularization techniques and non-linear transformations helps the network model complicated inter-modal dependencies well. This synergy between modalities leads to a detection mechanism that is more complete and stronger than unimodal ones.

4.3 Error Analysis and Limitations

Even though the results were good, there were a few cases of failure when certain conditions were met:

- When the image component didn't have enough context or was too subtle in its tampering, it made it hard for the model to tell the difference between original and manipulated content.
- When the sound was too loud or too compressed, it lost linguistic or prosodic features.

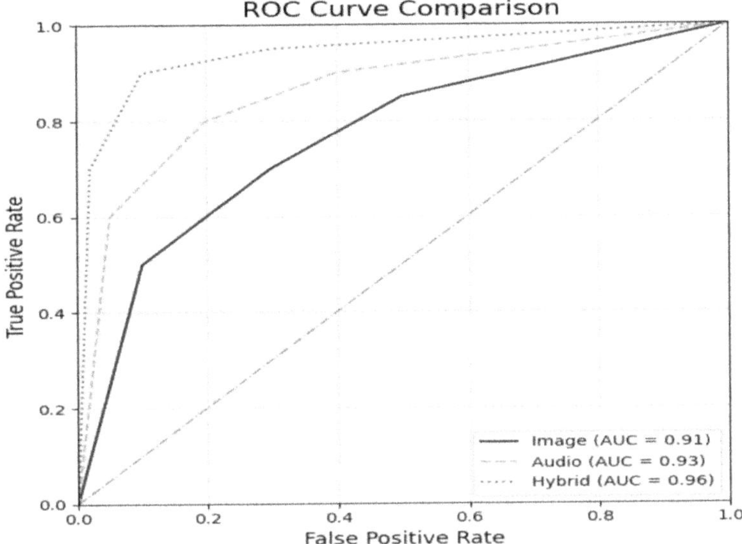

Fig. 2. AUC – ROC Curve Comparison

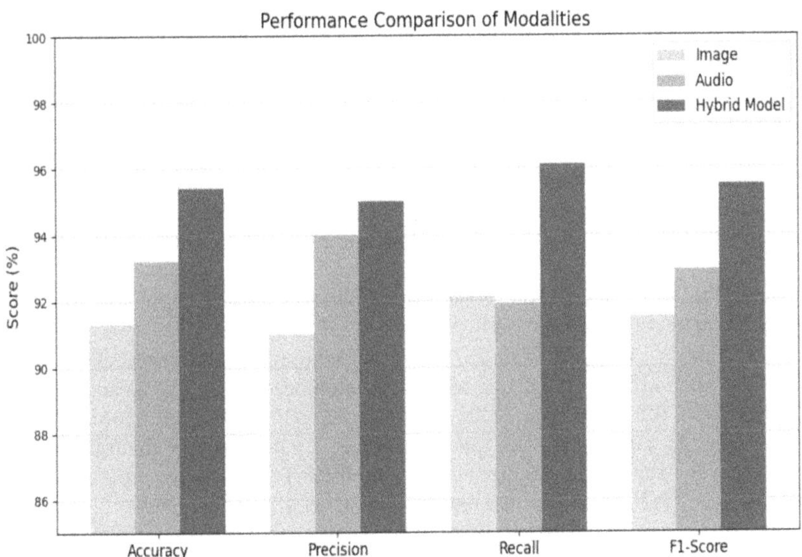

Fig. 3. Performance Comparison of Modalities

5   Conclusion and Future Work

The proposed multimodal framework effectively amalgamates image and audio modalities to enhance the reliability of fake news detection. Experimental results validate that this joint learning methodology surpasses unimodal benchmarks, highlighting the efficacy of the early fusion strategy in assimilating complementary crossmodal signals. The model gets a better overall picture of content authenticity by using spatial, visual, and acoustic information all at once. In our next studies, we will look at how to use attention-based fusion mechanisms to dynamically weigh the contribution of each modality and domain adaptation techniques to improve generalization across different and new media sources. These additions are likely to make the framework even more robust and useful for finding false information in real life.

Acknowledgment. The authors express their gratitude to the Thiagarajar College of Engineering (TCE) for supporting us to carry out this research work. Also, the financial support from TCE under Thiagarajar Research Fellowship Scheme – (File.no: TCE/RD/TRF/08) dated 27.09.2024 is gratefully acknowledged.

References

1. Christlein, V., Riess, C., Jordan, J., Riess, C., Angelopoulou, E.: An evaluation of popular copy-move forgery detection approaches. IEEE Trans. Inf. Forensics Secur. 7(6), 1841–1854 (2012). https://doi.org/10.1109/TIFS.2012.2218597
2. Wu, Z., et al.: ASVspoof: the automatic speaker verification spoofing and countermeasures challenge. IEEE J. Sel. Topics Signal Process. 11(4), 588–604 (2017). https://doi.org/10.1109/JSTSP.2017.2671435
3. Zhou, P., Han, X., Morariu, V.I., Davis, L.S.: Two-stream neural networks for tampered face detection. In: 2017 IEEE Conference on Computer Vision and Pattern Recognition Workshops (CVPRW), pp. 1831–1839. IEEE, Honolulu (2017). https://doi.org/10.1109/CVPRW.2017.229
4. Dolhansky, B., et al.: The Deepfake Detection Challenge dataset. Cornell University, https://doi.org/10.48550/arXiv.2006.07397 (2020)
5. Zhou, Y., Yang, Y., Ying, Q., Qian, Z., Zhang, X.: Multimodal fake news detection via CLIP-guided learning. In: 2023 IEEE International Conference on Multimedia and Expo (ICME), pp. 2825–2830. IEEE, Brisbane (2023). https://doi.org/10.1109/ICME55011.2023.00480
6. Li, X., Qiao, J., Yin, S., Wu, L., Gao, C., Wang, Z.: A survey of multimodal fake news detection: a cross-modal interaction perspective. IEEE Trans. Emerg. Topics Comput. Intell. 9(4), 2658–2675 (2025). https://doi.org/10.1109/TETCI.2025.3543389
7. Gao, X., Wang, X., Chen, Z., Zhou, W., Hoi, S.C.H.: Knowledge enhanced vision and language model for multi-modal fake news detection. IEEE Trans. Multimedia 26, 8312–8322 (2024). https://doi.org/10.1109/TMM.2023.3330296
8. Chen, H., et al.: A self-learning multimodal approach for fake news detection. arXiv (2024). https://doi.org/10.48550/arXiv.2412.05843
9. Delgado, H., et al.: ASVspoof 2021: automatic speaker verification spoofing and countermeasures challenge evaluation plan. arXiv preprint arXiv:2109.00535 [eess.AS] (2021). https://doi.org/10.48550/arXiv.2109.00535

10. Sadashiv, R.T.N., Kumar, D., Agarwal, A., Tzudir, M., Mishra, J., Prasanna, S.R.M.: Source and system-based modulation approach for fake speech detection. In: Speech and Computer (SPECOM 2023), LNCS, vol. 14338, pp. 142–155. Springer, Cham (2023). https://doi.org/10.1007/978-3-031-48309-7_12

11. Abavisani, M., Wu, L., Hu, S., Tetreault, J., Jaimes, A.: Multimodal categorization of crisis events in social media. In: Proceedings of the IEEE/CVF Conference on Computer Vision and Pattern Recognition (CVPR), pp. 14679–14689 (2020). https://doi.org/10.48550/arXiv.2004.04917

12. Jing, J., Wu, H., Sun, J., Fang, X., Zhang, H.: Multimodal fake news detection via progressive fusion networks. Inf. Process. Manag. **60**(1), 103120 (2023). https://doi.org/10.1016/j.ipm.2022.103120

13. Jin, Z., Cao, J., Guo, H., Zhang, Y., Luo, J.: Multimodal fusion with recurrent neural networks for rumor detection on microblogs. In: Proceedings of the 25th ACM International Conference on Multimedia (MM '17), pp. 795–816. ACM, New York (2017). https://doi.org/10.1145/3123266.3123454

14. Liu, M., Liu, Y., Fu, R., Wen, Z., Tao, J., Liu, X., Li, G.: Exploring the role of audio in multimodal misinformation detection. In: 14th International Symposium on Chinese Spoken Language Processing (ISCSLP), pp. 204–208. IEEE, Beijing (2024). https://doi.org/10.1109/ISCSLP63861.2024.10800162

15. Singhal, S., Shah, R.R., Chakraborty, T., Kumaraguru, P., Satoh, S.:SpotFake: a multi-modal framework for fake news detection. In: 2019 IEEE Fifth International Conference on Multimedia Big Data (BigMM), pp. 39–47. IEEE, Singapore (2019). https://doi.org/10.1109/BigMM.2019.00-44

16. Rana, M. S., Murali, B., Sung, A.H.: Deepfake detection using machine learning algorithms. In :2021 10th International Congress on Advanced Applied Informatics (IIAI-AAI), pp. 458–463. IEEE, Niigata (2021). https://doi.org/10.1109/IIAI-AAI53430.2021.00079

17. Heidari, A., Navimipour, N.J., Dag, H., Unal, M.: Deepfake detection using deep learning methods: a systematic and comprehensive review. WIREs Data Min. Knowl. Discovery **14**(2), e1520 (2024). https://doi.org/10.1002/widm.1520

18. Yi, J., Wang, C., Tao, J., Zhang, X., Zhang, C.Y., Zhao, Y.: Audio deepfake detection: a survey. IEEE Trans. Biometr. Behav. Identity Sci. **6**(3), 404–423 (2024). https://doi.org/10.48550/arXiv.2308.14970

19. Ajao, O., Bhowmik, D., Zargari, S.: Sentiment aware fake news detection on online social networks. In: 2019 IEEE International Conference on Acoustics, Speech and Signal Processing (ICASSP), pp. 2507–2511. IEEE, Brighton (2019). https://doi.org/10.1109/ICASSP.2019.8683170

20. Jung, J.-W., et al.: AASIST: audio anti-spoofing using integrated spectro-temporal graph attention networks. In: 2022 IEEE International Conference on Acoustics, Speech and Signal Processing (ICASSP), pp. 6367–6371. IEEE, Singapore (2022). https://doi.org/10.1109/ICASSP43922.2022.9747766

21. Yang, Y., et al.: A robust audio deepfake detection system via multi-view feature. In: 2024 IEEE International Conference on Acoustics, Speech and Signal Processing (ICASSP), pp. 13131–13135. IEEE (2024). https://doi.org/10.1109/ICASSP48485.2024.10446560

22. Wang, C., He, J., Yi, J., Tao, J., Zhang, C.Y., Zhang, X.: Multi-scale permutation entropy for audio deepfake detection. In: 2024 IEEE International Conference on Acoustics, Speech and Signal Processing (ICASSP), pp. 1406–1410. IEEE (2024). https://doi.org/10.1109/ICASSP48485.2024.10448095

23. Almutairi, Z., Elgibreen, H.: A review of modern audio deepfake detection methods: challenges and future directions. Algorithms **15**(5), 155 (2022). https://doi.org/10.3390/a15050155

24. Chakraborty, S., Saha, G.: Audio-deepfake detection: adversarial attacks and counter-measures. Expert Syst. Appl. **251**, 123941 (2024). https://doi.org/10.1016/j.eswa.2024.123941
25. Tahaoglu, G., Baracchi, D., Shullani, D., Iuliani, M., Piva, A.: Deepfake audio detection with spectral features and ResNeXt-based architecture. Knowl.-Based Syst. **323**, 113726 (2025). https://doi.org/10.1016/j.knosys.2025.113726
26. Zhang, B., Cui, H., Nguyen, V., Whitty, M.: Audio deepfake detection: what has been achieved and what lies ahead. Sensors **25**(7), 1989 (2025). https://doi.org/10.3390/s25071989
27. Wang, X., et al.: ASVspoof 5: Crowdsourced speech data, deepfakes, and adversarial attacks at scale. arXiv preprint arXiv:2408.08739 (2024). https://doi.org/10.48550/arXiv.2408.08739
28. Schäfer, K., Choi, J.-E., Zmudzinski, S.: Explore the world of audio deepfakes: a guide to detection techniques for non-experts. In: Proceedings of the 3rd ACM International Workshop on Multimedia AI against Disinformation (MAD '24), pp. 67–76. ACM, Phuket (2024). https://doi.org/10.1145/3643491.3660289
29. Malik, A., Kuribayashi, M., Abdullahi, S.M., Khan, A.N.: DeepFake detection for human face images and videos: a survey. IEEE Access **10**, 18757–18775 (2022). https://doi.org/10.1109/ACCESS.2022.3151186
30. Masood, M., Nawaz, M., Malik, K.M., Javed, A., Irtaza, A., Malik, H.: Deepfake generation and detection: case study and challenges. IEEE Access **11**, 143296–143326 (2023). https://doi.org/10.48550/arXiv.2103.00484
31. Guera, D., Delp, E.J.: Deepfake video detection using recurrent neural networks. In: 2018 15th IEEE International Conference on Advanced Video and Signal Based Surveillance (AVSS), pp. 1–6. IEEE, Auckland (2018). https://doi.org/10.1109/AVSS.2018.8639163
32. Lewis, J.K., et al.: Deepfake video detection based on spatial, spectral, and temporal inconsistencies using multimodal deep learning. In: Proceedings of the 2020 IEEE Applied Imagery Pattern Recognition Workshop (AIPR), pp. 1–9. IEEE, Washington DC, USA (2020). https://doi.org/10.1109/AIPR52630.2021.9425167
33. Zhao, H., Zhou, W., Chen, D., Wei, T., Zhang, W., Yu, N.: Multi-attentional deepfake detection. In: 2021 IEEE/CVF Conference on Computer Vision and Pattern Recognition (CVPR), pp. 2185–2194. IEEE, Nashville (2021). https://doi.org/10.1109/CVPR46437.2021.00222
34. Singh, A., Singh, J., Yadav, D.: Unmasking deepfakes: a systematic review of deepfake detection and generation techniques using artificial intelligence. Expert Syst. Appl. **250**, 124260 (2024). https://doi.org/10.1016/j.eswa.2024.124260
35. Pei, G., et al.: Deepfake generation and detection: a benchmark and survey. arXiv preprint arXiv:2403.17881 (2024). https://doi.org/10.48550/arXiv.2403.17881
36. Abdullah, S.M., et al.: An analysis of recent advances in deepfake image detection in an evolving threat landscape. arXiv preprint arXiv:2404.16212 (2024). https://doi.org/10.48550/arXiv.2404.16212

Socio-Technical Perspectives on AI Governance Addressing Ethics Fairness and Sustainable Machine Learning Practices

Amol Ashok Chavan(✉) and Dadarao N. Raut

Department of Production Engineering, Veermata Jijabai Technological Institute, Mumbai, Matunga, India
chavan.amol85@gmail.com, dnraut@pe.vjti.ac.in

Abstract. The artificial intelligence (AI) is changing the society and provoking deep questions associated with the ethics, fairness, accountability, and the sustainability. The socio-technical topic of the given paper is the usage of AI governance to ethical use, biasing and ethical machine learning practice. Data was collected using a combination of mixed methods that consisted of surveys (n = 153), interviews (n = 52), and case studies (AI practitioners, policymakers and NGOs). The results show that design, control mechanism, and anticipation of technologies is a viable AI governance. The study has practical suggestions that will guide policy makers and organizations to develop responsible, fairly, and sustainable AI systems.

Keywords: AI Governance · Sustainable Machine Learning · Socio-Technical Perspectives

1 Introduction

Artificial Intelligence (AI) is quickly changing the contemporary world turning businesses, governments, health care, finance, and social interactions upside down [1]. Although AI can have potential, certain thorny ethical, social and environmental dilemmas are also associated with the concept. The risk of algorithmic biases, unfair decision-making, transparency and environmental effects has been increasing governance frameworks with the necessary accountability, i.e., that AI systems are created and implemented in an ethical way [2].

AI governance is not only concerned with technical compliance, but with socio-technical issues that include human, organizational and societal effects of technology [3]. These perceptions are dominated by the effects of ethics, fairness, accountability and sustainability. The responsible AI practices do not only mitigate the risks, but also the reputation, safety and social acceptance of AI-technologies. One of the aspects of creating the AI systems that will correspond with the values and expectations of the society is the consideration of the socio-technical interaction.

© The Author(s), under exclusive license to Springer Nature Switzerland AG 2026
F. Ortiz-Rodríguez et al. (Eds.): IBCD 2025, CCIS 2845, pp. 123–135, 2026.
https://doi.org/10.1007/978-3-032-20907-8_11

The unethical issues regarding the use of AI are algorithms biasing, non-transparency, and unfair decision-making. At the same time, the efficient practices of machine learning, including low-powered model architectures or responsible applications, become increasingly visible with the ecological, and social signature of an AI-based architecture at scale. These are not simple problems and as such, the multi-dimension approach whereby the technical, ethical and policy solutions are incorporated is necessary [4].

In this paper, the overlap between ethics and socio-technical issues, as well as the presence of sustainable AI practice, will be examined [5]. The study will help in elucidating the current issues of technology design, the strain on policy and society in general concerning AI governance, and lastly present the knowledge regarding how to implement effective actions in the creation of equitable, ethical and ethical machine learning systems. The discussion is not just focused on the technical capacity of AI, but much wider organizational and policymakers and stakeholder responsibility to shape use of AI in the society.

This study aims to discuss the ethical and fair and sustainable aspects of AI governance in light of socio-technical factors, decision-making bias and integration of responsible machine learning ethos.

- To explore the ethics systems and socio-technical forces that guide AI governance, especially on how to integrate good practices in terms of machine learning systems.
- To examine concerns regarding fairness, bias and accountability in AI decision-making processes and recommend on the approaches of achieving equity.
- To assess sustainable machine learning practices that reduce any environmental, social and economic impacts as well as a deployment of effective AI.
- To examine how technology design, regulator policy, and the demand of society influence each other to form ethical and equitable AI governance patterns.

The current study is relevant to the AI governance literature given that it incorporates three essential dimensions ethics, fairness, and sustainability into a socio-technical context. In contrast to the previous literature where the main emphasis is put on conceptual or technical means, this paper triangulates the empirical survey, interview, and case study data with policy analysis. This originality of the work is in the fact that it takes a holistic approach that covers both technical, organizational, and societal dimensions of AI governance and provides practical information to the policy-makers, organizations, and practitioners.

2 Literature Review

Sloane and Zakrzewski (2022) analyzed the element of German AI start-ups and their approach to AI ethics in terms of social practice [6]. Their review implied how the socio-technical forms of innovation were working in practice, where the ethical consideration in relation to AI was determined by organizational practices, cultural practices and the realities of the start-up worlds. Whereas, the followers of the AI ethics appeared to be start-ups, their actual application, however, was not easy, which is suggestive of the difficulty of implementing the ethical principles within the fast-changing technological environment.

Swist and Gulson (2023) considered the possibility of the socio-technical education to construct the future learning environment [7]. They reported the experience of the engagement with technical democracy, data justice, and imaginaries and demonstrated that socio-technical ways were paramount in the interpretation of how the educational system is to be changed to encompass ethical and fair uses of technology. Writing they asserted the perception that technical infrastructures and social values integration was highly necessary in affecting ethical and inclusive technological practices in the learning contexts.

Search Toreini et al. (2020) Search was an extensive study Search on technologies of credible machine learning in a socio-technical context [8]. They also reported in their research different ways to make the AI systems be reliable, fair, and controllable and the influence of the social and organizational environment which precondition some actions. The paper has indicated that the development of a trustful machine learning was a concept not merely technical in character; rather, it touched on the human, organizational and social domains and the significance of applying a socio-technical lens in governance of AI.

Torkamaan et al. (2024) addressed the issues and the future studies that are related to the integration of large language models (LLMs) in socio-technical systems. In their article, they indicated that in their implementation of LLMs on a large scale some concerns about bias, accountability, transparency, and compatibility with societal values were identified [9]. They reported that despite such possibilities the implementation of LLMs had some instances of concern despite their promising potential in the automation and decision-making processes. The work was characterized by the fact that in successful implementation, it is necessary not only technical omissions, but a close analysis of organizational practices, communication with users and the socio-technical environment beyond the immediate environment of the organization.

Van Bruxvoort and van Keulen (2021) came up with a model that could be used to assess the ethics of the algorithm within the framework of the whole socio-technical system [10]. Their observation revealed that ethical judgment was impossible to be brought down to the algorithmic design implementation but had to entail human, organizational and social interactions with technology. They show that comprehensive assessment models enabled all participants to be conscious of the potential risks, enhance accountability, and encourage fair and responsible AI system execution.

Despite growing interest in AI governance, existing research often focuses on technical or organizational contexts, with limited empirical study of sustainability and socio-technical integration. Prior studies highlight ethical and fairness concerns but rarely examine how environmental, social, and economic impacts are addressed in large-scale AI applications, such as LLMs. This study addresses these gaps by exploring AI governance through a holistic socio-technical framework, integrating ethics, fairness, and sustainability to guide practical and responsible AI design.

3 Methodology

This is a mixed-methods (qualitative and quantitative) research in which the study provides an in-depth understanding of socio-technical applications of AI governance and specifically the concepts of ethics, fairness, and sustenance of machine learning practices. The methodological approach will help to answer the four research objectives presented above.

Descriptive and exploratory research design will be employed. Descriptive analysis will be used to investigate the existing frameworks, policies and industry practices in regard to AI governance and the exploratory analysis will show emerging socio-technological concerns, ethical questions and sustainability issues in the implementation of AI.

Data were collected through a structured survey, semi-structured interviews, and case studies. The survey quantified three constructs ethical AI awareness, fair mindedness. Implementation, and sustainable practices with Likert scale (e.g. rate your scaling of carbon footprint adoption in organization on 1–5). The interview guide covered the topics of what fairness means in organizations and obstacles to sustainable AI implementation. Organizational practices of implementing responsible AI frameworks offered contextual richness, which guaranteed triangulation of findings.

The sampling method was purposive and snowball, which was directed towards AI practitioner's, policymakers, and NGO representatives, who have at least two years of experience in the field. The participants were sent out 212 surveys, and 153 valid (72%), respondents were received. The rate of interviews fulfilled was 65 percent based on whether the invitations were completed or not (80 invitations). Inclusion criteria needed non-professional interaction with AI governance, ethics or sustainability. Exclusions were made of experts and unwilling people who are consented. This guaranteed variety and validity representation in various sectors. Following Data Analysis Methods are used in current research work.

Qualitative Analysis: Interests of the interview transcripts and the case studies will then be analyzed subject them to thematic analysis to discover the trends, issues and problems of good practice in terms of the implementation of AI and ethics.

Quantitative Analysis: The information obtained as a result of the survey will be analyzed using to check the relationship, descriptive statistics, correlation tests, and regression analyses are used. Among socio technical factors and ethical behaviours, indices of fairness and sustainable projects in machine learning training activities.

During these research work, the following ethical considerations are taken into account;

- The use of interviews and surveys will be on voluntary basis with all participants being informed of the consent.
- Confidentiality of data and anonymity shall be upheld.
- The study will comply with ethical considerations in the study of AI and will report unbiased research results and possess responsible results into the study.

Several validation strategies were used in order to achieve methodological rigor. The construct definitions were operationalized as follows: ethical AI awareness, fairness implementation and sustainability practices. The items included in the questionnaire were based on the previous governance frameworks and were optimized with the help of the expert opinions of three AI policy experts and two researchers. Clarity and usability of the instrument were verified with the help of a pilot survey (n = 15). Cronbachs alpha was used to determine internal consistency (ethical AI awareness, a = 0.82; fairness implementation, a = 0.79; sustainability practices, a = 0.81). An interview codebook was created through thematic coding in the form of a structured codebook and showed intercoder reliability (Cohen k = 0.76). The survey (153 out of 212 out of 80) and interview (52 out of 80 out of 100) response rates were 72 and 65 percent respectively and gave representative coverage of the target population.

This will provide a detailed account of how socio-technical aspects may affect policy models, normative ideas of equity and sustainability in regulating AI. The findings will be applied to prescribe the reforms on the essential policymaking, organizational processes and measures on responsible machine learning.

4 Data Analysis and Interpretation

The data collected through the assistance of surveys, interviews, and case studies underwent the analysis to become conscious of the ethical, fairness, and sustainability issues of the AI governance. The mixed-methods approach was employed, in which qualitative and quantitative details were applied. The analysis is done under thematic sub-headings under the research objectives.

Answers to the survey showed different awareness about existing ethical frameworks in AI governance. Most of the respondents indicated that they were aware of high-level ethical rules, although the implementation of this rule in the organization showed an unequal side. The Table 1 indicates the distribution of respondents according to their level of awareness and adoption of ethical AI guidelines. It details the awareness into five levels namely Very High, High, Moderate, Low, and Very Low with the respondents and their corresponding percentages.

The results showed that the greatest percentage of the respondents (45%) had a significant level of awareness, whereas 25% had the moderate one. Nearly a fifth of it had very high awareness, whereas the small number of respondents had low awareness (7.5%) or very low awareness (2.5%). This trend implied that though there was a huge majority with at least a moderate knowledge on ethical AI principles, they still left a deep-seated and universal adoption gap in the organizations.

Figure 1 shows the amount of awareness concerning ethical AI practices with the help of a bar chart. This figure shows the scatter of responses in the various awareness categories, thus making up the data in Table 1.

This was well presented through the bar chart where high proportion of respondents showed high awareness with almost half indicating that they were aware of ethical guidelines. The chart, however, also brought to note the difference in high awareness and low adaption at institutional levels as still there is a small but significant number of respondents who reported low to very low awareness. It indicated that awareness-building programs were indeed working, but the conversion of the programs into coherent organizational practice had to be done through intervention and well-designed socio-technical structures.

Table 1. Awareness and Adoption of Ethical AI Guidelines

Level of Awareness	Number of Respondents	Percentage (%)
Very High	40	20
High	90	45
Moderate	50	25
Low	15	7.5
Very Low	5	2.5

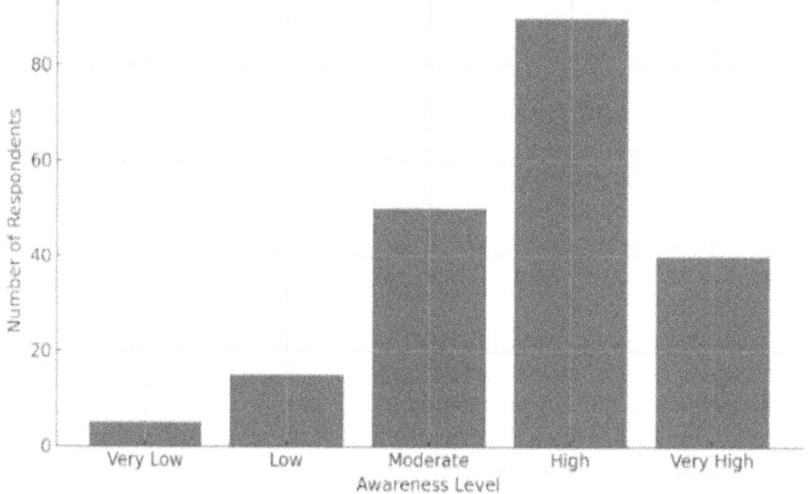

Fig. 1. Awareness of Ethical AI Practices

Correlation analysis indicated that organizational commitment to ethics was positively associated with perceived fairness of AI outputs (r = 0.62, p <0.01). Prior to analysis, assumptions of normality and homoscedasticity were checked; no major violations were detected. The difference was significant, and the R2 = 0.38, which indicated that almost 38 percent of the variance in perceptions of fairness was covered by organizational commitment. A 95% confidence interval for the correlation coefficient was [0.47, 0.72], which supports the robustness of this association.

Table 2 reveals that 50% of the surveyed held the opinion that fairness measures have been partially adopted to reduce bias in their organizations signifying an incomplete manifestation of addressing bias. A smaller percentage (15%) said that they were fully implementing, and this shows that there is not much success in terms of ensuring fairness is implemented in an organized way. Among them, 25% listed minimal implementation, whereas 10% mentioned no fairness considerations whatsoever. Figure 2 indicates that despite the existing awareness, there is inconsistent depths in how fairness frameworks are integrated into the governance of AI use today.

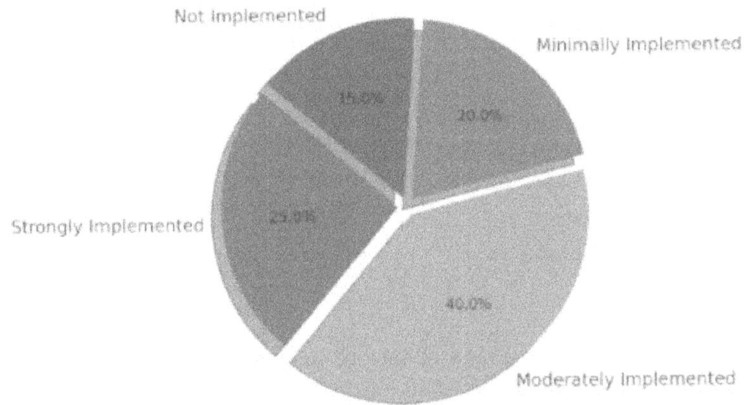

Fig. 2. Implementation of Fairness Measures in AI

Table 2. Respondents' Perception of Fairness Measures in AI

Fairness Implementation Level	Number of Respondents	Percentage (%)
Fully Implemented	30	15
Partially Implemented	100	50
Minimally Implemented	50	25
Not Implemented	20	10

Correlations analysis showed that organizational commitment to ethics is positively associated with perceived fairness of AI outputs at ($r = 0.62$), thus demonstrating that socio-technical support structures enhanced fairness practices.

Regression analysis showed that sustainability policies had a positive significant impact on the adoption of sustainable machine learning practices ($b = 0.48$, $p < 0.05$). Checks of assumption revealed that the assumption of normality in the residuals and homoscedasticity of the variances were true. The model accounted 45 percent of variance ($R2 = 0.45$) which is a moderate-strong effect size. The 95% confidence interval of b was between 0.21 and 0.67 indicating that there was a regular positive relationship between formal sustainability structures and the rate of adoption.

The results presented in Table 3 reveal that socially responsible deployment (60%) and energy-efficient algorithms (55%) are the most popular practices showing a rise of awareness with regard to both social and environmental aspects of sustainability. Nevertheless, more complex of measures, since carbon footprint monitoring (30%) and life the impact assessment (25%) has not been comprehensively adopted yet. This indicates that though there is an ever-growing consciousness on sustainability within the organizations, there is still much less use of practical and resource intensive actions on the part of the organization on the part of sustainability practice.

Table 3. Adoption of Sustainable Machine Learning Practices

Practice	Respondents Using (%)
Energy-efficient algorithms	55
Low-computation models	45
Carbon footprint monitoring	30
Lifecycle impact assessment	25
Socially responsible deployment	60

Figure 3 shows comparative rates of various sustainable machine learning practices adoption in different organizations. The bar graph presents variation on the level of implementation on both environmental and social aspects.

The regression analysis revealed a significant positive effect ($\beta = 0.48$, $p < 0.05$) findings support long-term structured sustainability policies as having a greater impact on the probability of implementing practices. Organizations with clarity of specific sustainability structure could more easily apply both energy-efficient algorithms and a socially responsible deployment, an indicator of this approach. Organizations that did not have formal policies had more isolated measures, which emphasize by highlighting the usefulness of integrated governance of the issue of sustainability in AI and machine learning settings.

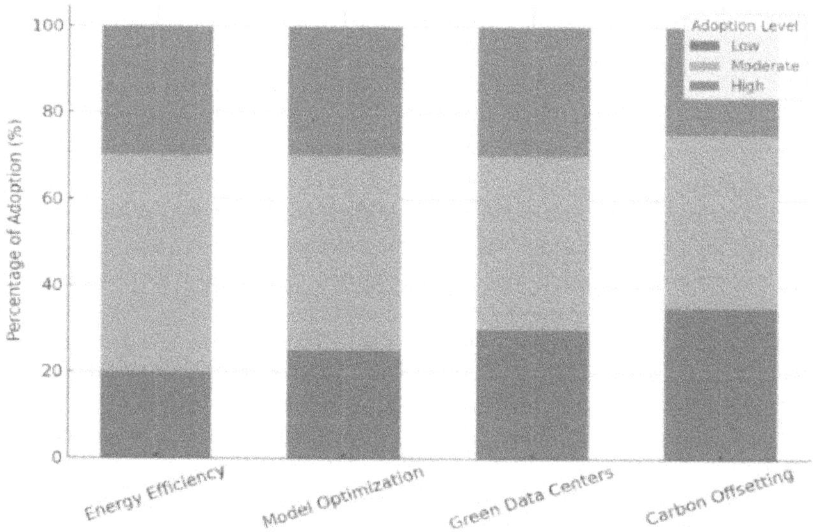

Fig. 3. Sustainable Machine Learning Practices

Regression analysis revealed that the positive significant effect of sustainability policies on the adoption of sustainable machine learning practices was ($b = 0.48$, $p < 0.05$).

Checks of assumption indicated that the assumptions of normality in the residuals and homoscedasticity of the variances were correct. The model explained 45 percent variance (R 2 = 0.45) which is a medium to a strong effect size. The interval of b which was 0.21 to 0.67 indicated the probability that there was a positive and constant relationship between formal sustainability structures & rate of adoption.

Table 4. Key Socio-Technical Factors in AI Governance

Factor	Frequency of Mention	Impact Level*
Organizational Culture	35	High
Regulatory Compliance	30	High
Stakeholder Engagement	28	Medium
Technical Infrastructure	25	Medium
User Interaction Design	20	Medium

* Impact Level determined according to the degree of qualitative coding

The research depicted in Table 4, states that the strongest force of effective AI governance is the organizational culture (35 mentions) and regulatory compliance (30 mentions), which influence both the ethical attitudes and responsibility. The factors of medium impact are stakeholder engagement (28 mentions), technical infrastructure (25 mentions), and user interaction design (20 mentions), which reinforce the trust and usability. In general, socio-technical governance is a fervent product of cultural and regulatory systems, whereas technical and participatory issues are also to be considered. The measurement of alignment was performed by using a triangulation strategy that incorporated survey scores, interview in-sights, and case studies in order to have strong validation.

The analysis of survey and interviews showed that the de-sign and AI governance policy should be aligned with societal expectations to promote ethical and equitable AI implementation. The percentage of those organizations that showed strong alignment was about 40%, moderate alignment was 35% and weak alignment was 25%. Good regulatory compliance, full stakeholder engagement, and ethical AI behavior were reflected by high alignment, and weak alignment was likely to be explained by ambiguous policies or a lack of interaction with stakeholders.

Table 5. Alignment of Policies, Technology, and Societal Expectations

Alignment Level	Respondents (%)
Strong Alignment	40
Moderate Alignment	35
Weak Alignment	25

The analysis presented in Table 5, further established that organizational culture (high impact), regulatory compliance (high impact), stakeholder engagement (medium), technical infrastructure (medium) and user interaction design (medium) were some of the major socio-technical issues that influenced AI governance. This proves that culture and regulations have a great impact on ethical practices, yet supportive infra-structure and participatory practices are needed (Fig. 4).

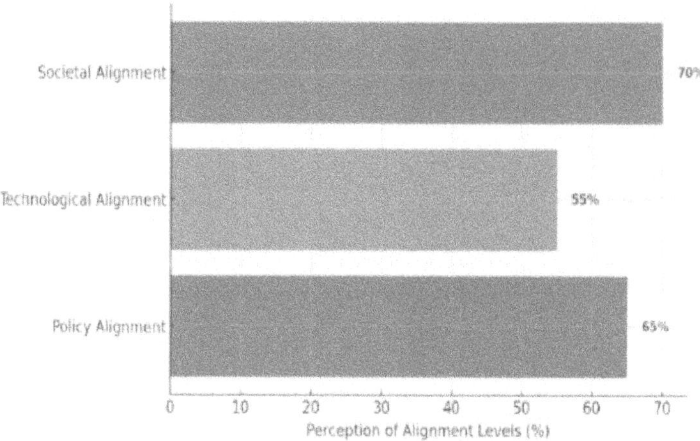

Fig. 4. Horizontal bar graph showing alignment of policies technology and the society among organizations.

Overall, the results emphasize that the adequate management of AI requires consistent policies, the technological systems, and the ideas of society participation. The alignment opposing can jeopardize equitable-mindedness, sustainability and ethical delivery, whereby persistent collaboration between the stakeholders and adherent rule governance ought to be employed.

5 Discussion

The results indicate an increased awareness regarding the ethical AI, yet there is inconsistency in the process of its adoption in organizations. Practices of fairness and sustainability are skewed, and harmony among policies and technology and the expectations of the society is yet to be coordinated. The implementation of AI responsibility requires a more powerful rationale and culture transformation and intersectoral cooperation. The implementation of AI responsibility requires a more powerful rationale and culture transformation and intersectoral cooperation.

Ethical awareness of AI structures had been described to be high, but organizational practice is a laggard. This lack of knowledge linkage with practice is similar to previous studies. The absence of the functional support of ethical principles by means of functional mechanism can so readily transform them into symbols.

Half of the organizations had partially put into practice fairness practices. The results of the correlation confirm the fact that the higher the ethical commitments were, the higher the perceptions of fairness. However, in-degree is a problem that bias can be detected, and inclusive design indicates that fairness is not a thoroughly technical problem, but it needs to be interdisciplinary.

Socially responsible deployment and energy efficient algorithms were more common than technically demanding practices such as carbon footprint monitoring. The regression analysis findings revealed that formal sustainability policies were highly likely to boost adoption. This demonstrates that it is required to have an organized system of governance to make sustainability a realty.

The supporting factors were the organizational culture and regulatory adherence, and the high-impact ones were the stakeholder engagement and infrastructure. The findings focus on the necessity to apply ethics to algorithms and organizational and social practices.

Although forty percent of the organizations that were described to be strictly aligned, several organizations have been identified to be merely moderately aligned or weakly aligned. These patterns were verified by the triangulated method of measurement through surveys, interviews and case studies. The absence of steady alignment contributes to the disjointed governance, which supports the necessity to ensure participatory policymaking and regulatory flexibility.

Altogether, the responsible AI involves a socio-technical strategy, which involves the inclusion of morality, equity, and sustainability. Companies that have good ethical cultures, regulatory congruence and sustainability systems are the ones that are likely to perform well. Nevertheless, there is need to continue investing in governance frameworks and collaborations among the stakeholders in order to bridge the gap between awareness and practice.

Results show an increase in ethical AI awareness but uneven adoption, uneven fairness and sustainability practices, and fragmented alignment with a need to increase stronger governance, cultural change, and cross-sector collaboration. There is a high level of awareness related to ethical AI, whereas organizational adoption is low, which shows that the principles should be enforced to make them operational. At least 50 percent of organizations apply fairness incompletely; ethical commitment is associated with perceived fairness, but interdisciplinary actions are required to succeed in mitigating bias. Carbon footprint monitoring is less prevalent than socially responsible deployment and energy-efficient algorithms; formal sustainability policies are more likely to improve adoption, indicating a need to have some form of formal governance. Organizational culture and compliance with regulations are highly impactful, whereas ethics are supported with the help of stakeholder involvement and infrastructure in both algorithms and organizational behavior. The alignment of the policy-technology-society is considered on a case-by-case basis.

It is only 40% of organizations that exhibit strong alignment, moderate or weak alignment creates fragmented governance with strong emphasis on participatory policymaking and adaptable regulation.

Accountable AI involves a socio-technical response involving ethics, equity and sustainability, enabled by effective culture, regulation and sustainability systems, and continuous governance and stakeholder engagement will be required to overcome awareness-practice divides.

6 Conclusion

Companies must formalize ethical behaviour in formal policy, regular audits, and responsibility systems to be adopted in daily operations in order to foster responsible AI governance. Reductions of fairness and bias can be improved by creation of forms of systematic checks and inclusive design solutions that may be achieved through cooperation of diverse stakeholders such as technologists and policymakers. Sustainability of machine learning is also a priority, through energy-efficient algorithms, low-computation and tracking carbon footprint applied within a set of structured sustainability policies. Finally, the high level of policy and technology congruence with societal values should be preserved by dynamic regulatory frameworks and through participatory consultations that enable creating AI systems that can be both responsible and reliable.

The outcomes of the present research have immediate implications for the debate in which current discourse surrounding Responsible AI and AI governance are situated. This research will provide concrete evidence that can be used to influence the governance structures through its elucidation of how ethical awareness, the implementation of equity and sustainability, can be fitted into the socio-technical systems. These insights are congruent with the international Responsible AI initiatives and the discussions surrounding the need to embed organisational culture, regulatory compliance and sustainability policies into the more general governance discussions. The expected outcomes of firms should effect ethical behaviour through formal policy, audit and accountability schemes, strengthen equity through systematic checks and inclusive design acknowledging the input of many parties, and machine learning should be sustainable which implies energy efficient algorithms and policies. The participatory mechanisms in which policy makers and technologists are actively engaged in dynamic regulation and consultation are required in order to balance policy and technology with the values of the society in which it is being implemented in order to achieve responsible and trustworthy AI.

The paper offers plausible arguments why ethics, equity and sustainability should be integrated in social-technical systems, as part of global Responsible AI programs.

- Institutionalize Ethical AI Practices: Ethical principles must become part of the operational fabric of organizations, with institutionalized policies, frequent audits, enforcement of responsibility and accountability, so that a proper understanding of ethical behavior leads to action on those principles.
- Strengthen Fairness and Bias Mitigation: Systematic justice controls and design inclusions need to be implemented throughout the AI development process with help of cooperation between technical system designers, civil policy makers, and social stakeholders.
- Advance Sustainable Machine Learning: Energy-efficient algorithms, low-computation models, and monitoring of carbon footprint should be promoted, and a structure of sustainability policies should be provided to facilitate overall practice.

This study brings about the insight of AI socio-technical governance but has a few weaknesses in terms of sample bias by region, small case studies, a lack of longitudinal data, and there is a possibility of self-reporting bias. The next research needs to use broader and larger and longitudinal data set and explain more advanced quantitative model to examine relations of ethics, fairness, sustainability and governance.

While this study provides valuable insights into the socio-technical governance of AI, it is not without limitations. First, the survey and interview samples were drawn primarily from professionals in [Region/Context, e.g., India and Europe], which may limit the generalizability of results to other global regions. Second, although the study triangulated surveys, interviews, and case studies, the number of case studies was limited, and longitudinal data were not available. Third, self-reported measures of fairness and sustainability practices may involve bias, despite efforts to ensure validity. Future studies should broaden the sample across more diverse cultural and regulatory environments, use larger datasets, and longitudinal analyses in order to account for the changes in governance practices over time. In addition to this advanced quantitative models and validated alignment indices would contribute further evidence to bolster claims made about the association between ethics, fairness, sustainability, and socio-technical governance structures.

References

1. Pujari, T., Goel, A., Sharma, A.: Ethical and responsible AI: governance frameworks and policy implications for multi-agent systems. Int. J. Sci. Technol. **3**(1), 45–58 (2024)
2. Abbas, R., Pitt, J., Vogel, K.M., Zaferirakopoulos, M.: Artificial intelligence (AI) in cybersecurity: a socio-technical research roadmap. The Alan Turing Institute (2023)
3. Sartori, L., Theodorou, A.: A sociotechnical perspective for the future of AI: narratives, inequalities, and human control. Ethics Inf. Technol. **24**(1), 4 (2022)
4. Shin, D.: Socio-technical design of algorithms: Fairness, accountability, and transparency. Inf. Commun. Soc. **22**(14), 1974–1993 (2019)
5. Siripipatthanakul, S., Phuangsuwan, P., Limna, P., Muthmainnha, S., Vui, C.N., Jaipong, P.: Artificial intelligence (AI) influencing sustainable governance: Governance adopting AI. In: Proc. Int. Conf. Data Analytics & Management, pp. 551–568. Springer, Singapore (2024)
6. Sloane, M., Zakrzewski, J.: German AI start-ups and "AI ethics": using a social practice lens for assessing and implementing socio-technical innovation. In: Proc. ACM Conf. Fairness, Accountability, and Transparency (FAccT), pp. 935–947. ACM (2022)
7. Swist, T., Gulson, K.N.: Instituting socio-technical education futures: encounters with/through technical democracy, data justice, and imaginaries. Learn. Media Technol. **48**(2), 181–186 (2023)
8. Toreini, E., et al.: Technologies for trustworthy machine learning: A survey in a socio-technical context. arXiv preprint arXiv:2007.08911 (2020)
9. Torkamaan, H., et al.: Challenges and future directions for integration of large language models into socio-technical systems. Behav. Inf. Technol. **43**(2), 1–20 (2024)
10. van Bruxvoort, X., van Keulen, M.: Framework for assessing ethical aspects of algorithms and their encompassing socio-technical system. Appl. Sci. **11**(23), 11187 (2021)

AI-Driven Voice and Gesture-Controlled System for Dental Healthcare

Shubhangi Vairagar$^{(\boxtimes)}$ (iD), Ayush Poonmia (iD), Chetana Shravage (iD), Priya Merti (iD), Mohit Khandelwal (iD), Priyanka Gaikwad (iD), and Rushank Ambekar (iD)

Department of AI and Data Science, Dr. D.Y. Patil Institute of Technology, Pune, India
shubhangi.vairagar@dypvp.edu.in

Abstract. Introducing the concept of artificial intelligence (AI) into the health care system has already had a profound effect, and alters most of the spheres, dental care included. This literature review explores the existing technologies connected with the AI-controlled speech and gesture systems. This can also be said of the medical profession with special reference to dental care by addressing the various gesture recognition methods. The voice command-interface diagnostic frameworks of AI-axis have difficulty and advantages with real-time applications. These methods are applied in the dentistry. As we analyze, it indicates that there are numerous system performances. Efficiency in diagnosis and treatment. There is still a lack of research that focuses on the integration of voice and gesture. Control is a platform for dentists. This review provides a valuable perspective on the future. The research route is facing the promotion of AI systems that is expected to be specific to dental treatment.

Keywords: Artificial intelligence in dentistry · gesture recognition technology · voice command systems · disease identification · healthcare innovation · and machine learning applications

1 Introduction

In modern health care settings, the importance of efficiency and hygiene cannot be underestimated. Especially in a specialty such as dental treatment, dental offices face a number of challenges. This is because it is important to maintain sterility due to increased risk of cross -pollution and infection. Dentists often perform complex procedures while wearing glasses and protective equipment. This is necessary to avoid contamination when handling electronic equipment. Diagnostic tools for patient records and various treatment tools. This requirement places significant restriction on traditional methods of interaction such as keyboard, mouse and touch sensitive surfaces. That do not lead to a sterile environment and can be complicated or inaccessible to operate during critical operations.

Contactless technology is currently being used regularly in health care system to satisfy various needs. This involves voice and gesture control as new innovations in the clinical setting. The system therefore removes human touch with the medical equipment, thereby enabling the professionals to focus without the room to be inefficient in

F. Ortiz-Rodríguez et al. (Eds.): IBCD 2025, CCIS 2845, pp. 136–151, 2026.
https://doi.org/10.1007/978-3-032-20907-8_12

handling the multifaceted work. The voice control technology advances which incorporate both NLP and ML algorithms are used to assist with specialist orders, retrieve patient information, and control diagnostic devices using medical applications without having to control them manually. It is easily attainable through electronic health records, photographs and comprehensive step-by-step instructions, such that loaded instructions deemphasize treatment, and health care specialists can put the spotlight on the well-being of the patient. Machine learning and advanced computer vision make it possible to have technology of hand movement Interpreting hand movements. This aspect has a potential of enabling the dentist to generate control of the tools and interfaces without having to touch them. Hence, a complete contactless control of tooth equipment, lighting or patient information can be detected; so that such systems can detect the motions of hands with reasonable precision when utilizing cameras and sensors. To illustrate, a dentist can strengthen an X -ray, change the intensity of the lights in the operating zone, or scroll through the overview of the patient using mere gestures, without forgetting about the pure context.

Besides ensuring hygiene, the speech and gesture control technological use in dental care can considerably enhance the efficiency of work, reduce the physical effort of specialists and enhance patients management, allow dentists to concentrate on their procedures without losing power and significantly interrupt work. The innovations save precious time, minimize errors and maximize efficiency in operation. Moreover, these systems enhance improved patient interaction. This is due to the fact that dentists can easily demonstrate and display the use of visual materials like X-rays or three-dimensional models without necessarily moving the patient or interfering with the sterile environment.

However, dental clinics are not the only place where AI-based wear-free technologies can be used at the moment. At the surgical level, the operating room is the kind of environment, in which sterility is regarded to be of paramount importance. The same applies to other health areas including radiology which requires the use of critical image data that cannot be undertaken with reduced physical contacts as it is done today. These are very promising but there are certain obstacles that make them not applicable in generalized sense. As an illustration, voice recognition systems would go a long way in resolving the errors in the high noise Environments such as travel tanning clinics. In the example of background noise, occasionally the meaning of commands is immediately misplaced. Likewise, hand gestures that are of small size can be overlooked by gesture recognition systems. This is particularly so in cases when a number of users are involved.

The necessity to address these challenges is known as continuous innovation. This is particularly so in the area of maximizing the utility of such systems in the rich really world conditions. The direction of research in the future will be expected to shift to enhancing speech recognition algorithms to eliminate the undesired background noise and improve contextualization of the commands. And there is the contemporary internal movement detection that is more concerned with the instantaneous movement of the hands. Which now seeks to create AI models that get to know better about user interactions to become more natural with time.

2 Literature Survey

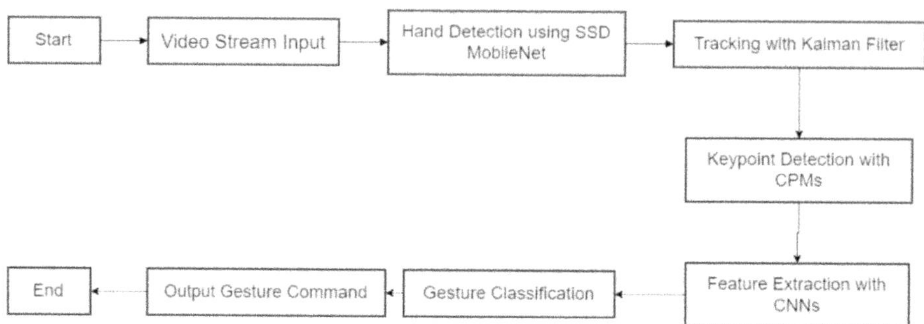

Fig. 1. Hand Gesture Recognition Process

It uses advanced methods in recognizing hand gestures using deep learning techniques as presented in Fig. 1. It is trying to use the SSD mobile for real-time detection and convictional poses to identify key points in different movements. It has 96.7 main functions. The system's gesture recognition is very strong even in very complex environments, which is essential for practical application. At the moment, however, it is limited to recognizing only eight different gestures. It has the potential for more widespread applications, but requires further modification to overcome interference caused by ambient light as well as occlusion. Other suggestions from the paper are that the use of a more diverse set can expand the diversity and robustness of models. This method is both innovative and effective, but limited in terms of flexibility in types of gestures and other environments, which is an area for further research to achieve greater use [1].

This systematic review includes 174 studies that examine deep learning -based approaches to speech recognition, and provide a comprehensive overview of improvements and advances in the field. Along with new deep learning techniques, these techniques have been shown to increase accuracy and efficiency. Different algorithms, recurrent

Neural networks and long short -term memory networks have ensured excellent results for these speech recognition systems shown in Fig. 2. However, details of the algorithm do not enter into details, and can therefore limit its practical applications as researchers want to have guidelines for implementing it. Furthermore, it risks generalizing with overly wide application because the review does not take into account problems that may be associated with different languages and statements. Despite these limitations, this article is still very valuable when it comes to understanding today's and future speech recognition trends and the huge future potential in this area with extremely rapid research development [2]

This study presented in Fig. 3, in detail the most important voting recognition and comparison techniques, and falls at two extremes: traditional and modern machine learning techniques. Deep learning methods are found to be very effective, especially on questions of recognition accuracy and variation in different voice inputs. It describes

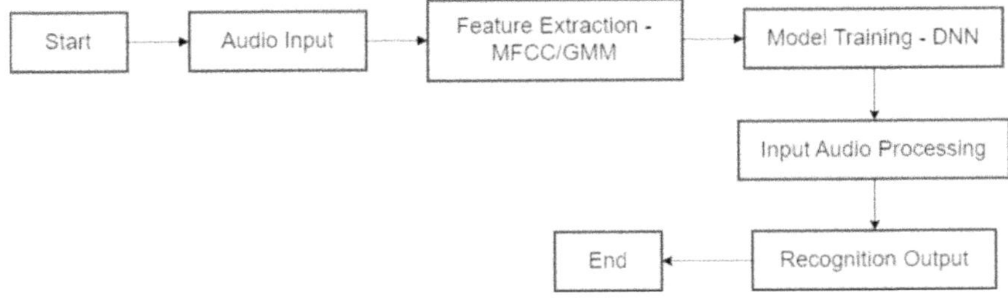

Fig. 2. Speech Recognition Process

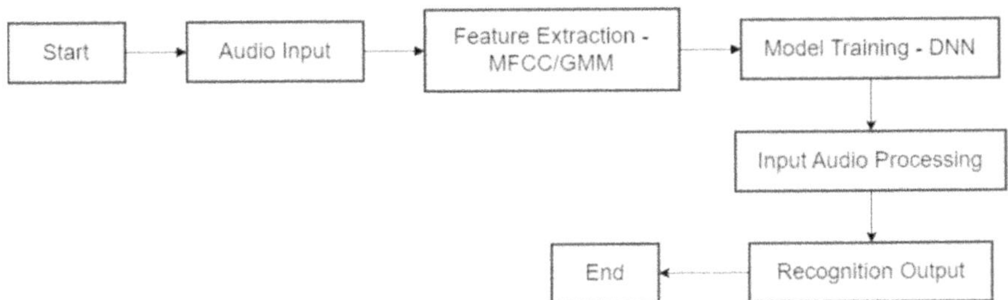

Fig. 3. Voice Comparison Process

algorithms including SVMs and neural networks, and shows their strengths and weaknesses in different applications. However, it provides limited implementation details, which can prevent practical application to practitioners. In addition, the study identifies challenges such as background noise and speaker variability that can affect performance. The task encourages further exploration of hybrid models that combine traditional and deep learning techniques to increase robustness. Overall, this book covers the extent of this field very widely; However, it is limited by the fact that studies or practical examples are not provided for the usefulness [3].

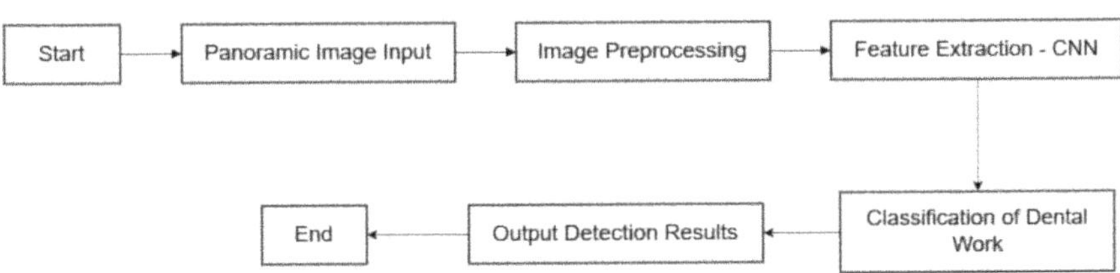

Fig. 4. Dental Restoration Detection Process

This paper applies CNNs to detect dental restorations (refer Fig. 4) in panoramic images, achieving an accuracy as high as 94. The DenseNet architecture is used in the study to improve feature extraction and classification performancehis article uses CNN to detect tooth restoration in panoramic images, and achieves accuracy of up to 94. Denssenet architecture is used in the study to improve the function of extraction and classification. This is primarily beneficial when it comes to automating detection, reduces the workload of dentists and improves diagnostic accuracy. However, studies are hampered by limited data sets, which may affect the generalization of the model to different populations and image properties. The document also discusses the importance of pre -processing techniques to improve image quality before analysis. Although the results are promising, more research is needed to validate the model in different clinical environments and expand the ability to recognize a wider range of dental problems. Overall, this work represents an important step toward integrating AI into dental diagnosis, although challenges remain in dataset diversity and use in the real world [4].

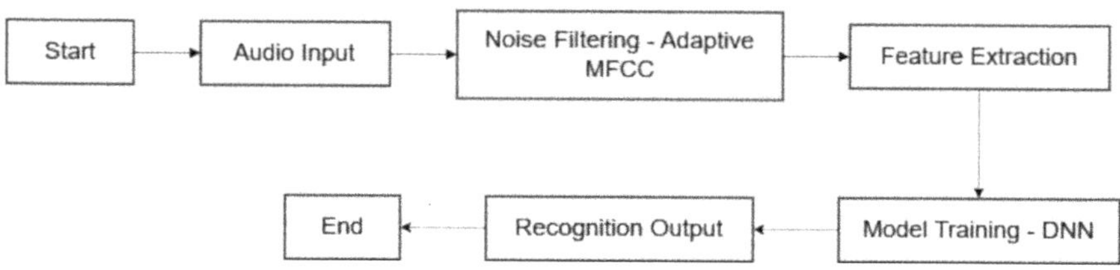

Fig. 5. Voice Recognition Process

This article presents an innovative approach to voice recognition as presented in Figs. 5 and 6 that combines adaptive flour-frequent cepstral coefficients (MFCC) with deep learning techniques, especially in noisy environments. This method increases the degree of recognition by adapting the functional extraction process to different noise conditions, which is a significant advantage over traditional methods. The study demonstrates the effectiveness of using deep learning models as DNN to improve identification accuracy. However, this adaptive filtration technique is considered by many to be composed of the practical application and attracts specialized knowledge and resources. The performance will primarily vary with the quality of the training data and the properties of the noise. Document emphasizes the need for further research To optimize the model and its real -time applications. With such a promising approach, there is a significant complexity factor in the implementation and dependence on high quality data [5]

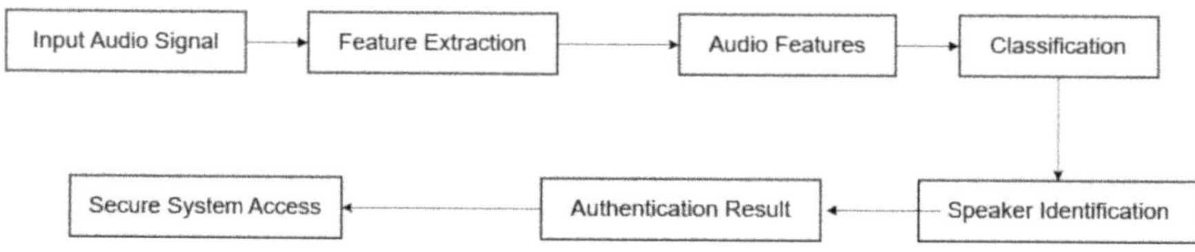

Fig. 6. Voice Recognition Process

The research concentrates on the development of an IoT-based educational simulator for training dental students on X-ray imaging in a radiation-free manner. This simulator mimics the shape and functionality of the standard intraoral X-ray machines and comes with angle sensors that can monitor the positioning of the X-ray tube and detector.

One of the primary benefits is its ability to enable safe, repeatable training without the risks of radiation exposure. The system transmits angle data to a server for analysis to position correctly for effective imaging. There may be some issues with the use of the simulator because it relies on technology and requires a strong IT structure. The development process focused on hardware and software integration, emphasis on user-friendly interfaces and educational content such as video tutorials and test banks. Overall, the IDEAL system represents a significant advancement in dental education technology, addressing both safety concerns and improving future dental practitioners' practical training [6]

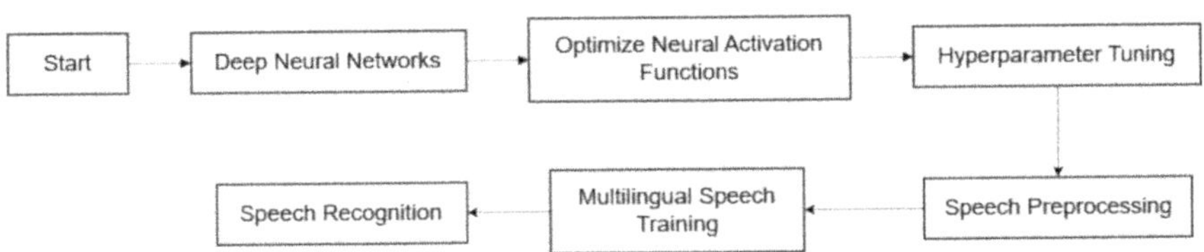

Fig. 7. Deep Neural Network Learning for Speech Recognition

This paper reviews the advances in Deep Neural Networks presented in Fig. 7 and successful applications to speech recognition. One of several major benefits would probably be the tremendous improvement that could be achieved in speech recognition accuracy due to DNNs, which is one of the landmark technologies within the field. Although the research in the study carries a limitation toward being all-inclusive of the recent discoveries, and is centered mainly on DNNs, which limits a more comprehensive view over other machine learning methodologies. The algorithm covered under the paper Deep Neural Networks-though remarkable in efficiency over the recognition tasks-is strictly bound to applications for which it is trained. Also, DNNs require intensive computational resources for training and may pose a limitation for some implementations [7].

The new approach has improved the combination of several functions and functions that use deep learning to improve the accuracy of speech recognition compared to traditional models such as GMM-Hmm as depicted in Fig. 8. This approach shows a significant improvement, especially when it comes to resistance to noise as well as other disruptions when using different environments. The model is very complex and requires such a large amount of calculation resources that it can sometimes

Make serious demands during training processes, and potentially overwhelmed the training data. Among the algorithms used in this approach, one can mention Deep Neural Networks (DNN), Convolutional Neural Networks (CNN), Gaussian mixing model-shell-hidden Markov model (GMM-HMM) and limited Boltzmann-machine (RBM). It achieves better detection speed, but requires a dataset of such size that one can get the best results; In addition, it cannot generalize well to unsettled accents or dialects without additional training.

be severely demanding during training procedures, potentially becoming heavily overfitted on the training data. Among the algorithms used in this approach, Deep Neural Networks (DNN), Convolutional Neural Networks (CNN), Gaussian Mixture Model-Hidden Markov Model (GMM-HMM), and Restricted Boltzmann Machine (RBM) could

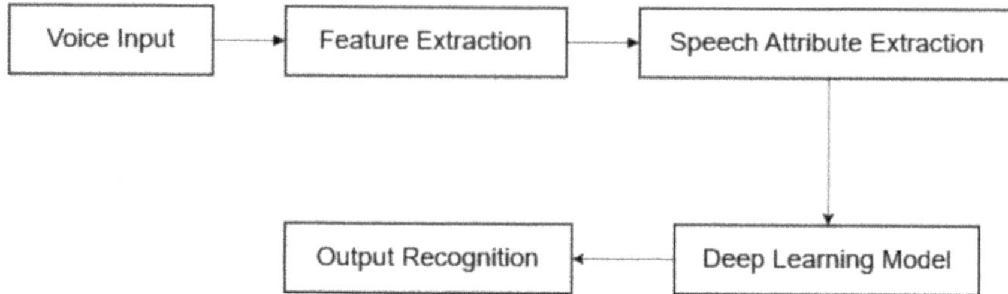

Fig. 8. Speech recognition based on deep learning with multiple features

be mentioned. It achieves better recognition rates but demands a dataset of such size from which one can obtain the best result; further, it cannot generalize well without any additional training, to unseen accents or dialects [8].

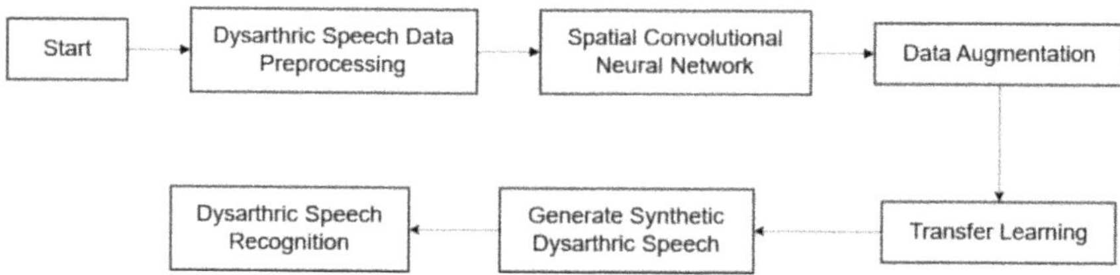

Fig. 9. Speech Vision Dysarthric ASR

This paper addresses the problem in effective identification of dysarthric speech through visual representations, called voicegrams, rather than traditional phoneme recognition techniques likely to be more accurate (Refer Fig. 9). The system addresses the lack of sufficient availability of training data through data augmentation and synthetic speech generation, providing better recognition accuracy than current systems on dysarthric automatic speech recognition. It is limited to isolated word recognition rather than continuous speech. Synthetic data generation produced, at best, one additional sample for each speaker and each word, which probably would not be enough for diversified training. Although the system does show great advantages over the baseline WRA performance, particularly in severe dysarthric cases, it did not attain optimal performance for moderate levels of dysarthria. A used algorithm is Deep 2D Spatial Convolutional Neural Network (S-CNN), applying processing of visual data and transfer learning. Of course, it's not all rosy; the generated samples are not very diverse and can easily be overfitted because the size of the training sample is too small [9].

It undergoes the systematic application of several machine learning methods presented in Fig. 10, for the diagnosis of tooth caries, with some techniques that succeed in achieving accuracy as high as 99%. This review is trying to point out the application of advanced machine learning methods, especially deep learning, to this important health problem that affects a large population of people. However, this study is limited to a few classes of tooth caries, proximal, occlusal and root caries, and will require huge data sets to train, which are not always available on your fingertips. This literature review

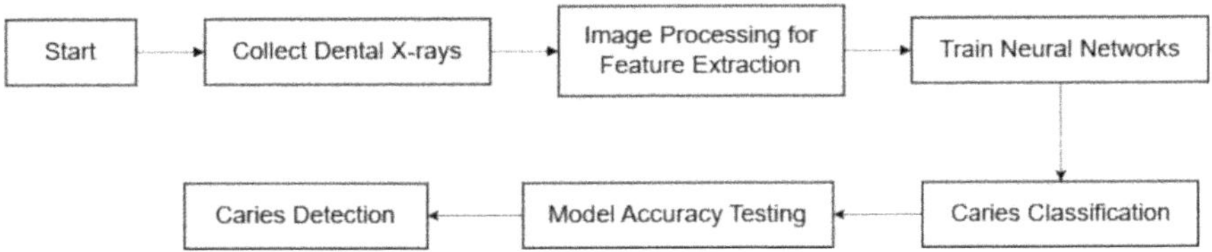

Fig. 10. Machine Learning for Dental Caries Detection

included few published works with very small test sizes that can adversely affect the validity. The algorithms used are neural networking propagation, convictionally neural networks, supporting Vektorm machine, adaptive dragonfly algorithm on neural networks and artificial neural networks. However, this article is a good review of existing methods and their efficiency, although it only studies the period from 2008 to 2022, and its focus is on image -based diagnosis, thus leaving other diagnostic methods behind [10].

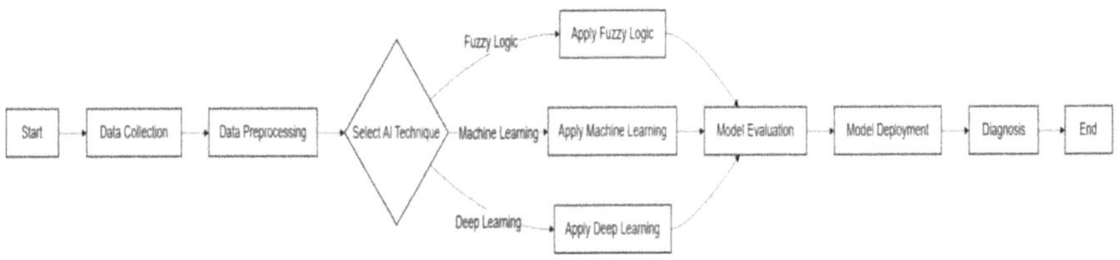

Fig. 11. Medical Diagnostic Systems

Review of Artificial Techniques Used in Medical Diagnostics: A Comprehensive View in the Diagnosis of Disease with Fewer Errors. The article reviews 105 systematically through PRISMA (Refer Fig. 11). It classifies AI techniques according to applications used in medical diagnostics. Many AI methodologies will be illustrated in this study using Fuzzy Logic, Machine Learning, and Deep Learning. The disadvantage is that it's only within the range of 2009-2019. It does not cover the fullness of the newest diagnostics AI advances. Some algorithms require a huge amount of reliance on the diseases that they were formed with; bounded within that time, it can miss recent innovations in the field [11].

It presents an efficient, fully automated technique for the segmentation of a dental X-ray image, using the Variational Level Set Method in differentiation between lesion and non-lesion areas is presented in Fig. 12. It could recognize edges that are very important for a correct outline of lesions. Diagnosis was conducted on an extremely few dataset of only six images, thus limiting the scope and generalize.

of the project. This only accounts for the dental lesions and does between lesion and non-lesion areas. It could recognize edges that are very important for a correct outline of lesions. Diagnosis was conducted on an extremely few dataset of only six images, thus limiting the scope and generalization of the project. This only accounts for the dental lesions and does not include other types of X-rays. While this method appears to have some promise in both the areas of segmenting dental X-rays and discriminating

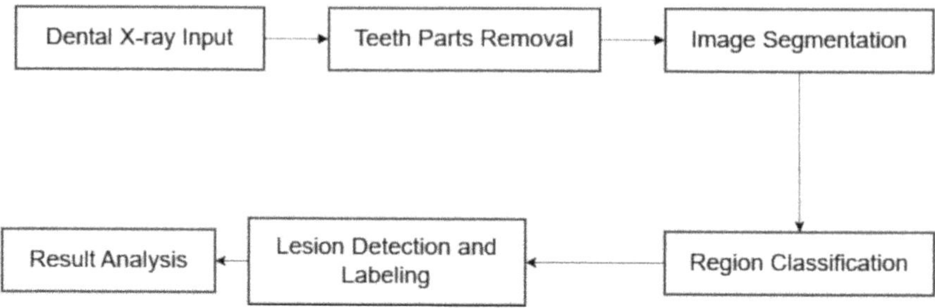

Fig. 12. Automatic Lesion Detection in Dental X-rays

between lesion and non-lesion areas, the performance appears to be impacted by the smaller dataset; hence, false positives and false negatives will likely exist in clinical decision-making [12].

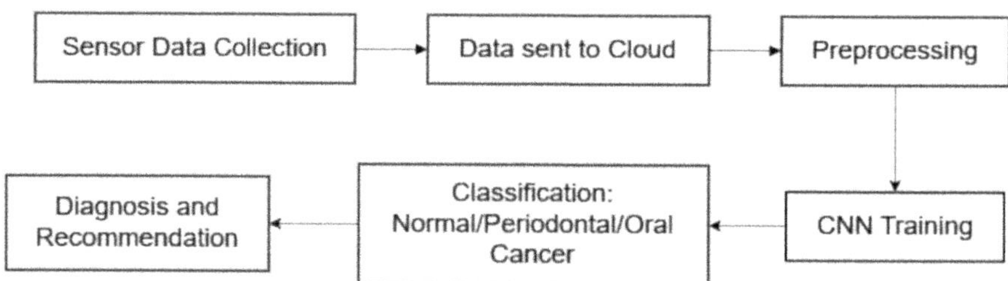

Fig. 13. Oral Disease Detection using Neural Network

This paper discussed the use of a neural network in the detection of oral diseases (refer Fig. 13). In this, it was utilizing Convolutional Neural Networks that reached high accuracy levels in detecting several oral conditions. Effective monitoring of the patients is accomplished with multi-sensors in the system. However, risks do surface through reliance on sensors; if any sensor fails in making a correct interpretation of a condition, then this will affect the results negatively. All these robust performances notwithstanding, the equipment still relies on dental professionals for proper performance. The process hence entails detecting parameter readings through sensors, then processing the data through a CNN, and finally creating possibilities of early diagnosis for the patients. However, the approach is limited by a sensor-based data approach that causes misclassification of patients based on oral health conditions [13].

In this article, anomalies are detected in panoramic tooth X-rays using a hybrid model: CNN-SVM, as presented in Fig. 14. This article exceeded traditional SVM as well as pure CNN with a state of modern accuracy of 98.69. In this hybrid model, deep learning functions were combined with machine learning functions to improve performance. However, it will effective strict with regard to data size and quality, which can affect generalization. Furthermore, the hybrid approach will be computational animals and will require more experience with model setting. Several models have been developed and compared in performance to classify panoramic tooth X-rays such as "normal"

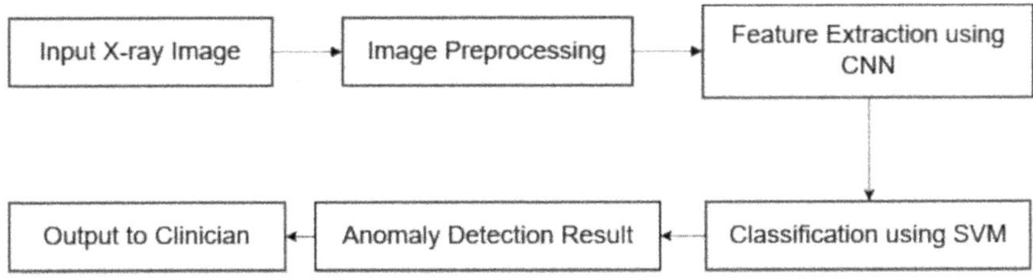

Fig. 14. Anomaly Detection Process

or "abnormal", and conclude with the paper on extraction with a better fit within the possibilities of the CNN-SSVM model. However, the question of class imbalance and over-augmentation for one class sometimes also generates an overfitting problem, and the quality of the labeled dataset may significantly affect further generalisation to other datasets [14].

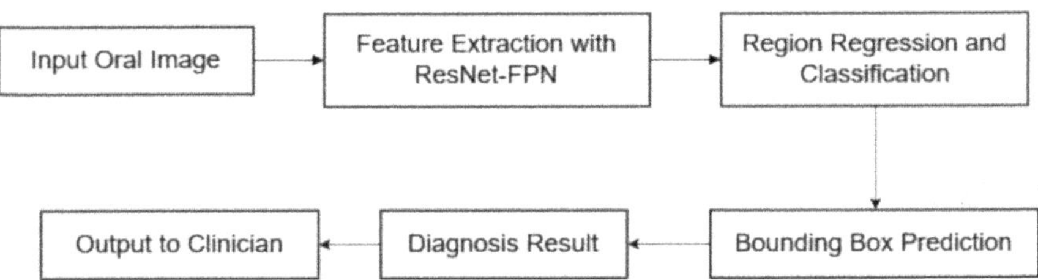

Fig. 15. Caries Detection Process

A new perspective in non-invasive diagnosis of first permanent molars in children will positively impact the level of distress children feel at the point of diagnosis. Advanced imaging technologies combined with machine learning will select images that guarantee clinical results far better than those obtained using traditional methods while also ensuring greater accuracy for caries detection (refer Fig. 15). However, it requires extra training by a dentist to be put in place and uses special technological equipment that may not easily be found in all dental offices. The effectiveness is thus dependent both on the operator as well as the quality of the equipment used. Also, restricted access to advanced imaging technology in rural or less resource settings will make it challenging for implementation on a very wide scale [15].

This review article contains depth-based hand gesture recognition, 37 research papers that identify 13 hand localisation methods, 11 gesture classification ones, and underlines the utility of technologies like Kinect and OpenNI libraries for their applications. Review shows, however, there is diversity in applications, which becomes a limitation as it can cover only eight categories and tends to give more emphasis on the applications rather than improving the underlying methods (refer Fig. 16). Moreover, the methods described are not demonstrated in demanding conditions, so a question of robustness may rise. It correctly classifies different types of hand localizations and gesture classification methods, while providing detailed descriptions of the algorithms used and, apparently,

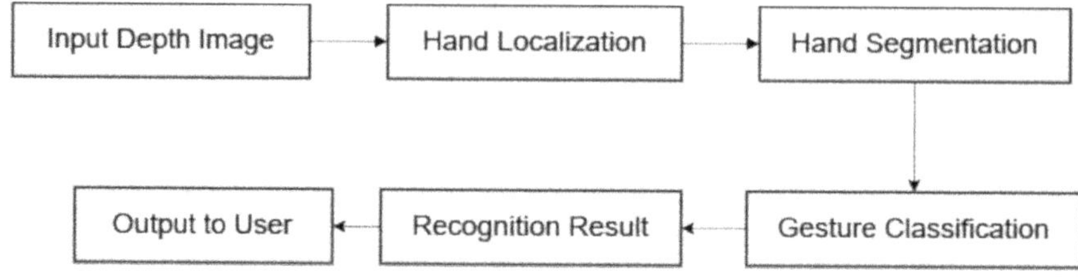

Fig. 16. Gesture Recognition Process

concludes that these types of sensors, such as Kinect, are not good enough for more complex scenarios [16].

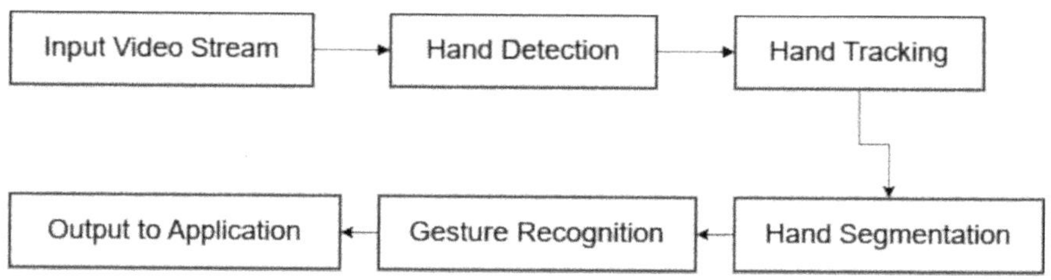

Fig. 17. Real-Time Gesture Recognition Process

It discusses a real-time hand gesture recognition method presented in Fig. 17, that offers an easy, natural alternative in comparison with traditional interaction techniques. The approach takes strong mechanisms of detection involving motion, color cues, and the use of feature detection based on scale space; these, however, require a specific gesture for triggering hand detection, hence may not be quite suitable for all types of applications. It has been aimed more at image browsing applications and yields satisfactory performance in that context. This is segregated based on color as well as the hand movement. However, gesture recognition uses scale space feature detection. Though it does work very efficiently in real-time gesture-based navigation, the application scope is limited to image browsing only, and it has not been applied in any other scenario yet [17].

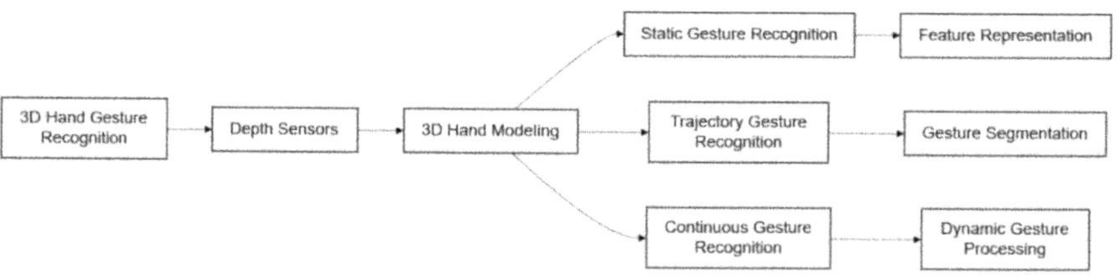

Fig. 18. Hand gesture recognition

This is a panoramic review of 3D hand gesture recognition models presented in Fig. 18, including hand and static, and dynamic gestures. This work highlights the advancements introduced by a depth sensor in the field. The work done here, in general, looks more toward summarizing the techniques that are already in use. Therefore, real-time applications are not discussed in detail. They are Dynamic Time Warping, Skeleton Detection, and Begin-End Gesture Detection. Although it provides a well-organized presentation of the current state-of-the-art techniques as well as the systems in 3D hand gesture recognition, the survey lacks direct experimental results or newer approaches; it also has limited focus on the actual challenges posed in a real-world application [18].

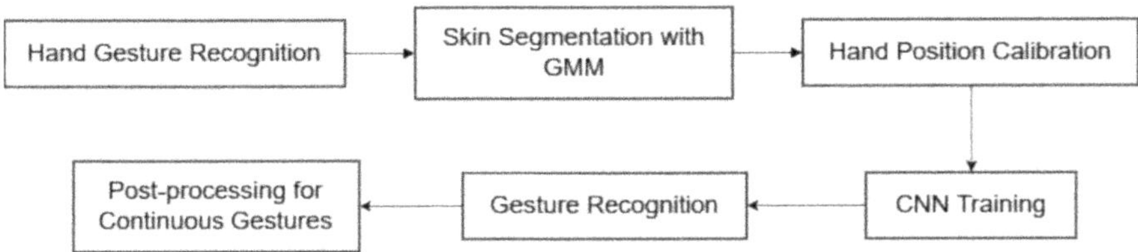

Fig. 19. Hand gesture recognition

It addresses human hand gesture recognition with an accuracy of about 95.96, which can be achieved using a CNN network (Refer Fig. 19). The approach shows robustness against position, pose variability, and change in illumination conditions. Limitation: This can detect only seven hand gestures and applies only to seven subjects in the test pool. However, it would have a problem of extreme lighting variation, though, for the skin color detection component. Although the system did well enough with changes in hand position and orientation, it probably would not do as well in more difficult lighting environments or richer environments. This would show that this would require an even more generous gesture set and a significantly more diverse subject pool to do a proper assessment [19].

This paper reports 84 to 99 percent for one-handed gestures and 90 to 100 percent for both hands performing the same gesture (refer Fig. 20). Shows robustness against variation of lighting, skin color, and background as it employs the use of the infrared sensor of Kinect. It only has nine pre-programmed gestures. Its performance also deteriorates with one hand if there are the same number of gestures are applied. The real-time recognition of Kinect-based gestures is effective with consistent differences under environmental conditions, but its performance is poor in the case of complex gestures as well as multiple gestures [20].

This is a research work based on mold parameters for the recognition of hand gestures (refer Fig. 21). Thus, recognition accuracy was found to be up to 94% for 45 different types of hand movements. It cannot be proven as robust because of its robustness to light variability, and it depends on functions derived from form instead of skin color or texture. This was done in just 450 pictures. It is sensitive to gestures involving several types of finger layouts or occlusions. It uses K-agent clustering for hand segmentation and uses a 5-bit binary string to represent a form-based function. It uses a simple webcam to classify gestures exactly in real time. This can be sensitive to limitations caused by the relatively small size of the dataset, as well as truly dynamic gestures, or rather complex backgrounds in the real world.

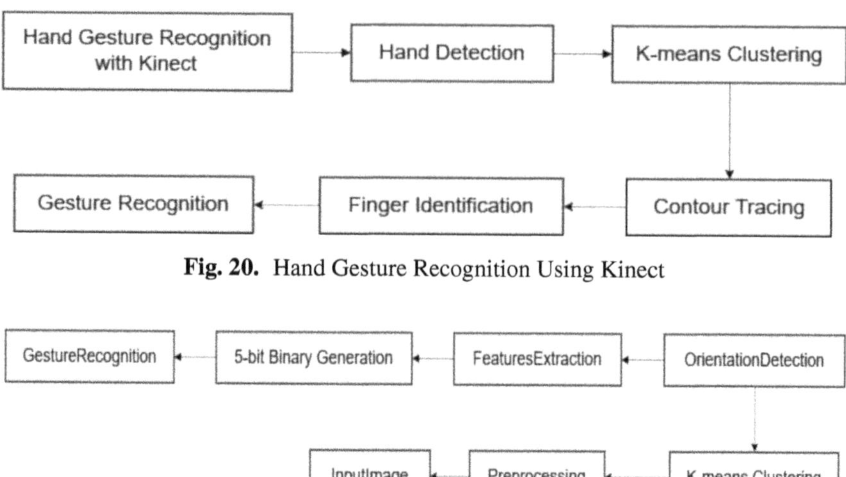

Fig. 20. Hand Gesture Recognition Using Kinect

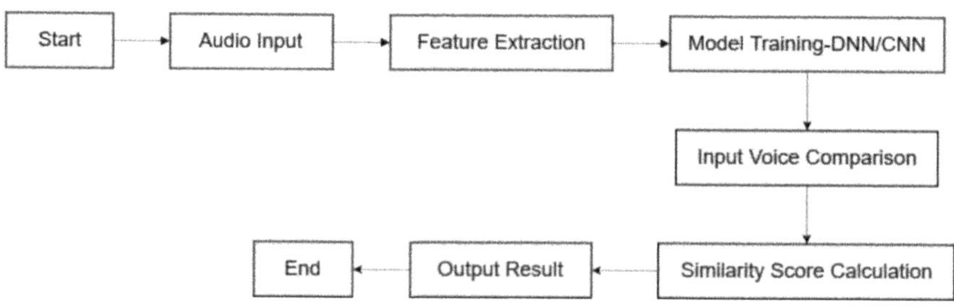

Fig. 21. Hand Gesture Recognition based on Shape Parameters

This is a review article that covers all techniques for recognition of hand movements as depicted in Fig. 22, including data collection, segmentation, tracking, functional extraction and recognition. No new techniques or approaches are presented. There are neither any experimental results nor practical tests. In the paper there are many methods for segmentation, tracking, functional extraction and detection that was not described. The paper actually compares existing techniques and their strengths and weaknesses compared to other hand movement recognition methods. Basically, this is a review, not something that offers new methodology; The techniques are not tested or used in practice [22].

Fig. 22. Voice Comparison Process

In fact, a framework for recognition of hand movements has been developed in connection with portable gesture -based interaction prototypes for mobile devices.

At that time, an average speed of 95.0 was obtained in the user-dependent test and 89.6 in the user-independent test. What is worth noting here is that the system reacts very quickly to the recognition of gestures involved in the process, the treatment time is less than 300 milliseconds, and was able to identify 19 predefined and personalized gestures. However, the performance is obtained in user -independent tests is poorer than the performance obtained in user -dependent tests, which reflects the variation in the performance between users. The method is based on an advanced Bayes-linear classifies, advanced dynamic time-swinging algorithms, new segmentation techniques and score-based sensor infusion strategies. It combines successful signals that come from accelerometers with SEMG signals to perform real-time detection to control mobile devices. However, personalized gestures have been completely excluded from research, and the use of predefined gestures can seriously limit adaptability to very different user needs [23].

The paper reports an average recognition rate of 92.4% on a database of 55 different gestures using static and dynamic hand-gesture recognisers. The high performance of the system was convincingly demonstrated through these experiments, especially by the incorporation of both static and dynamic gestures with multiple hands. While most of the previous work has been focused only on static sign digit recognition, this system achieves state-of-the-art performance. Though quite promising, these developments assume hands to be within the Kinect camera range, and evaluation has not been done in very cluttered environments. It includes a new scanning algorithm specifically set for hand contour detection, a k-curvature algorithm that determines the locations of fingertips, and dynamic time warping for gesture identification. It is such a system that makes real-time gesture recognition possible during user interaction through the depth data of the Kinect sensor. However, assumptions of such kinds cannot always hold since one assumes hands to be the nearest objects. Though certain applications have already been developed, proper documentation and real-world rigorous testing did not take place [24].

In discussing the real-world deployment of the reviewed AI models, it should be addressed how their computational requirements and scalability are for use in practical dental applications. Most of the surveyed algorithms, including CNNs, LSTMs, and DNNs, although exhibiting high precision, do tend to demand large amounts of computational resources, especially when training. For example, deep learning models require GPU acceleration and high memory capacities, which can be prohibitive to a small-scale or limited-resource dental clinic. But if they are pre-trained, the models could be effectively deployed on edge devices or mid-range computing platforms, enabling real-time applications. In order to project real-world feasibility, we have continued the above line of research by creating a working web-based dental clinic application based on our earlier appointment booking and patient management mobile application. The above prototype reflects the feasibility of incorporating AI-powered gesture and speech control modules into real clinical procedures, thus closing the gap between theoretical models and real-world usability. These implementations validate that, although there may be computational expense during development, the operational process of these systems can be optimized for effective, real-time practice.

3   Conclusion

Algorithmic trends: CNN, LSTM and DNN dominate among all modalities. CNNs provide strong performance in dental diagnosis (up to 99% accuracy) and LSTMs provide a timely detection in real-time gesture systems. Limitations in the use of the real world:

performance degradation from noise, variations in lighting and limited signal vocabulary affect most systems. Multilingual training restrictions limit the scalability of voting recognition. Scalability problems: Most systems are tested on small, manually curated datasets, which are subject to over -assembly and low generalization to patient groups or different dental clinics. Technologies: Vision Transformer (VIT) models and Whisper ASR systems are promising, but under -exploring in dental treatment. Ethical operational questions: None of these pieces deal with patient private, latency in real time or adoption medical barriers, which are crucial for safe deployment. AI-driven voice and gesture-controlled dental system research must focus on several important areas to make them practical and scalable. Incorporation of vision transformer models for gesture recognition can significantly increase the accuracy of difficult environments with occlusions and dynamic lighting, while also overcoming the deficiencies of existing systems. In addition, the inclusion of sophisticated speech models such as Whisper Asr can support multilingual interpretation command interpretation, especially in noisy clinical environments such as mobile tooth trucks. In addition, the absence of large, diverse data sets in the real world limits the widespread use of existing models. Future research should focus on the generation and use of large, commented on dental data sets that represent different populations and clinic settings. Testing from the real world of pilot implementation in dental practice is necessary to evaluate usability, reliability and acceptance of a physician. Ethical factors such as privacy of patient information, the latest and medical flexibility of the real-time system in the physician should also inform the creation of stable, secure secure System.

References

1. Wu, W., Shi, M., Wu, T., Zhao, D., Zhang, S., Li, J.: Real-time hand gesture recognition based on deep learning in complex environments. In: College of Artificial Intelligent Science, National University of Defense Technology, Changsha (2019)
2. Nassif, A.B., Shahin, I., Attili, I., Azzeh, M., Shaalan, K.: Speech recognition using deep neural networks: A systematic review. University of Sharjah, Sharjah, United Arab Emirates (2019)
3. Tandel, N.H., Prajapati, H.B., Dabhi, V.K.: Voice recognition and voice comparison using machine learning techniques: A survey. Dharmsinh Desai University, Nadiad, India (2020)
4. Gurses, A., Oktay, A.B.: Tooth restoration and dental work detection on panoramic dental images via CNN. Dept. of Electrical and Electronics Engineering, Istanbul Medeniyet University, Istanbul, Turkey (2020)
5. Bae, H.-S., Lee, H.-J., Lee, S.-G.: Voice recognition based on adaptive MFCC and deep learning. Robotics and Control System Lab, Yeungnam University, Gyeongsan, Korea (2016)
6. Chandankhede, P.H., Titarmare, A.S., Chauhvan, S.: Voice recognition based security system using convolutional neural network. G.H. Raisoni College of Engineering, Nagpur, India (2021)
7. Deng, L., Hinton, G., Kingsbury, B.: New types of deep neural network learning for speech recognition and related applications: an overview. Microsoft Research, Redmond, WA, USA; University of Toronto, Ontario, Canada; IBM T.J. Watson Research Center, Yorktown Heights, NY, USA (2013)
8. Song, Z.: English speech recognition based on deep learning with multiple features (2019)
9. Shahamiri, S.R.: Speech vision: an end-to-end deep learning-based dysarthric automatic speech recognition system (2020)

10. Talpur, S., Azim, F., Rashid, M., Syed, S.A., Talpur, B.A., Khan, S.J.: Uses of different machine learning algorithms for diagnosis of dental caries. Dept. of Biomedical Engineering, Ziauddin University, Karachi, Pakistan (2021)
11. Kaur, S., et al.: Medical diagnostic systems using artificial intelligence (AI) algorithms: principles and perspectives. Lovely Professional University, Punjab, India (2022)
12. Lin, P.-L., Huang, P.-Y., Huang, P.-W.: An automatic lesion detection method for dental X-ray images by segmentation using variational level set. Providence University, Taichung, Taiwan (2020)
13. Swetha, S., Kamali, P., Swathi, B., Vanithamani, R., Karolinekersin, E.: Oral disease detection using neural network (2020)
14. Verma, D., Puri, S., Prabhu, S., Smriti, K.: Anomaly detection in panoramic dental X-rays using a hybrid deep learning and machine learning approach (2021)
15. Yu, H., Lin, Z., Liu, Y., Su, J., Chen, B., Lu, G.: A new technique for diagnosis of dental caries on the childrens' first permanent molar (2023)
16. Suarez, J., Murphy, R.R.: Hand gesture recognition with depth images: a review (2021)
17. Fang, Y., Wang, K., Cheng, J., Lu, H.: A real-time hand gesture recognition method (2007)
18. Cheng, H., Yang, L., Liu, Z.: A survey on 3D hand gesture recognition (2015)
19. Lin, H.-I., Hsu, M.-H., Chen, W.-K.: Human hand gesture recognition using a convolution neural network (2014)
20. Li, Y.: Hand gesture recognition using Kinect (2012)
21. Panwar, M.: Hand gesture recognition based on shape parameters. Centre for Development of Advanced Computing, Noida, Uttar Pradesh, India
22. Sonkusare, J.S., Chopade, N.B., Sor, R., Tade, S.L.: A review on hand gesture recognition system (2015)
23. Lu, Z., Chen, X., Li, Q., Zhang, X., Zhou, P.: A hand gesture recognition framework and wearable gesture-based interaction prototype for mobile devices (2014)
24. Plouffe, J.G., Cretu, A.-M.: Static and dynamic hand gesture recognition in depth data using dynamic time warping (2015)

Sensors Based Crop Recommendation System Using Ensemble Modelling

Mangesh Balpande$^{(\boxtimes)}$ (iD), Gaurav Desale (iD), Jaydip Desale (iD), Abdul Ahad (iD),
and Pravin Patil

SVKM's Institute of Technology, Dhule 424001, India
mangesh.balpande111@gmail.com

Abstract. Modern agriculture requires an effective nutrient management system for the soil, which can be done by using IoT sensors. The proposed system integrates IoT sensor technology with machine learning (ML) algorithms for effective crop recommendations. The system incorporates the latest techniques to handle the challenges in modern agriculture by taking real-time soil data, moisture, and NPK content through its deployed sensors. Grouping the data, it is then processed and analyzed using machine learning models trained on a large-scale agricultural dataset. The proposed system provides tailored recommendations for the crops based on nutrient values of the soil, which will be collected by the IoT sensors. In this work, a user-friendly web application has been built to provide insights to farmers to promote sustained development and sustainable farming. This work aims to increase agricultural productivity, lessen resource waste, and minimize environmental degradation. The results show enhanced yields, fertilizer cost savings, and improved sustainability in farming. This novel method of precision agriculture marks a turning point in the revolution of the agricultural sector by feeding a growing number of people, leading towards global food security and environmental conservation.

Keywords: Accuracy Score · IoT sensor · Machine Learning · NPK Values

1 Introduction

Agriculture is the foundation of human life that enhances global economic expectations. The contemporary age of agriculture has problems associated with unmet food demands, soil degradation, mismanagement of resources, and climate change. Traditional farming cannot adequately address the changes that arise in this scenario; thus, an optimum and tech-based data-driven approach is necessary to optimize the use of resources in better production and sustainable agriculture practices. The crop and fertilizer recommendation system developed is an inventive solution that could assist farmers and agricultural practitioners in resolving these issues in selecting appropriate crops and fertilizers. The system also builds on the real-time acquisition of data through sensors integrated with machine-learning models in giving recommendations best suited for achieving precision farming. The system collects information on moisture and nutrient content (nitrogen,

F. Ortiz-Rodríguez et al. (Eds.): IBCD 2025, CCIS 2845, pp. 152–162, 2026.
https://doi.org/10.1007/978-3-032-20907-8_13

phosphorus, and potassium). The information from the sensor at this stage is fed into a machine-learning model trained on large agricultural datasets, which include soil properties, weather data, and crop requirements. Based on this analysis, the system identifies the right crops that can be grown under particular soil and environmental conditions. It also prescribes what kinds and how much fertilizer is required to replenish the nutrients present in the soil while achieving good growth of the crops, based on sustainable soil management. In order to make these insights user-friendly and accessible, the project makes use of a web app in which users can view the recommendations, input sensor data, and browse through the details of recommended crops and fertilizers [1]. Such an unfettered fusion of hardware, machine learning, and user-oriented UI bridges the gap between advanced agri-tech and the routine practices of everyday farmers. The Crop and Fertilizer Recommendation System offer diverse benefits: it increases crop yields, reduces unnecessary fertilizer application, and promotes environmentally-conscious farming practices. Emboldened by the provision of precise insights actionable on a timely basis, this system looks into key challenges of modern agriculture by assuring enhanced productivity, cost efficiency, and sustainability in agriculture.

2 Related Work

The Modern recommendations for crops and fertilizers significantly impact sustainable agricultural practices. Their objective is to include various technologies to regulate the optimal application of fertilizers with water so that they may reduce the extent of environmental degradation arising from over-fertilization and the waste of water. Beginning from 2020, research has started emphasizing precision agriculture to solve the challenges of food security and climate change. These systems are responsible for achieving controlled delivery of nutrients to their respective crops, which causes very limited leaching of these chemicals into groundwater. Apart from the benefits offered to environmental health, these systems add sustainability to farmers' economies through reduced input costs.

In [1], crop and fertilizer recommendation systems have mainly evolved over two decades. In essence, these systems enhance agricultural practices by offering recommendations based on signature soil characteristics, climatic traits, and crop requisites. The main drivers to improve the bulk of these systems' accuracy and scalability are integrations of sensor technologies, data analytics, and machine learning.

In [2], sensors are used to take readings of soil properties such as moisture content and nutrient levels which modern recommendation systems have been built. In the past decades, soil tests were mainly dependent on manual methods that, while accurate, took so long that they also introduced delays. The advent of soil moisture sensors, nitrogen (N), phosphorus (P), and potassium (K) sensors has been a trailblazer for data acquisition in agricultural productivity. Studies done between 2010 and 2015 showed that their performance in monitoring is real-time—they speed up soil analysis considerably.

In [3], machine learning and deep learning algorithms have been used to analyze massive data sets. For instance, predictive models trained on historical agricultural data to this end have been used to come up with optimal combinations of fertilizers based on soil nutrient profiles. Research done in 2018 already indicated that ML models could accurately predict crop yield with an impressive accuracy level of over 90% by combining input data from sensing device measurements.

In [4], IoT somewhat advances the usability of the recommendation system with help of sensors, a weather station, and cloud-based analytical platforms integrated in the background. From 2018 to 2020, a few research studies showed that IoT helps to provide real-time data synchronization, and this needs to be central in recommendation systems. IoT-enabled devices not only gather data but also allow remote monitoring and control, making precision agriculture even broader.

In [5], web applications and user interfaces act as the bridge between technology and end-users; web applications, in other words, are developed so that recommendations become easier to access for farmers. The 2021 research focused on how usable and impactful these applications were to farmers. Increased user uptake generally stemmed from the user-friendly interfaces and multilingual support. Such applications generally bring together sensor data, ML algorithms, and weather forecasting to provide holistic recommendations.

In [6], the explosion of agricultural data that has arisen from IoT devices, satellite communications, and field sensors has called for the adoption of big data analytics into the recommendation systems. Platforms supported by cloud computing, leveraged with big data frameworks, process colossal datasets to offer precise and context-aware recommendations. Predictive analytics, fueled by historical and real-time data, allows farmers to forecast crop growth cycles, pest outbreaks, and nutrient needs. Coupling geospatial data with machine learning algorithms can assist in recognizing soil fertility patterns that allow for zone-specific management strategies. From 2021 to 2023, it has been shown that the implementation of big data analytics in conjunction with decision-support systems complements the increase in crop yields to the tune of up to 30%.

3 Proposed Work

3.1 System Architecture

The overview of the system architecture is shown in Fig. 1. Firstly, the deployed IoT sensors collect and store the real-time soil data. An ML model is already deployed, and it predicts the suitable crop depending on various metric values. Finally, the real-time IoT data is passed through the ML pipeline, and a prediction is obtained. The procedure is as follows:

1) Source of Data: to store crop data, including soil properties; the Firebase database is created. The deployed IoT sensors collect and store the real-time soil data into the database.

2) Data pre-processing: before passing the IoT sensor data to the ML model directly, it undergoes various data cleansing techniques like noise removal, normalization, standardization, etc. Scaling of feature values to a standard range to enable comparison across different orders of magnitudes or ranges. Feature extraction finding important features in the dataset and transforming those features for affecting better predictability in models. Feature selection the selection of essential features thus reducing dimensionality and boosting efficiency in the model.

3) Splitting data: we split the pre-processed data as training and testing data. The splitting ratio was kept as 80:20 (80% for training and 20% for testing).

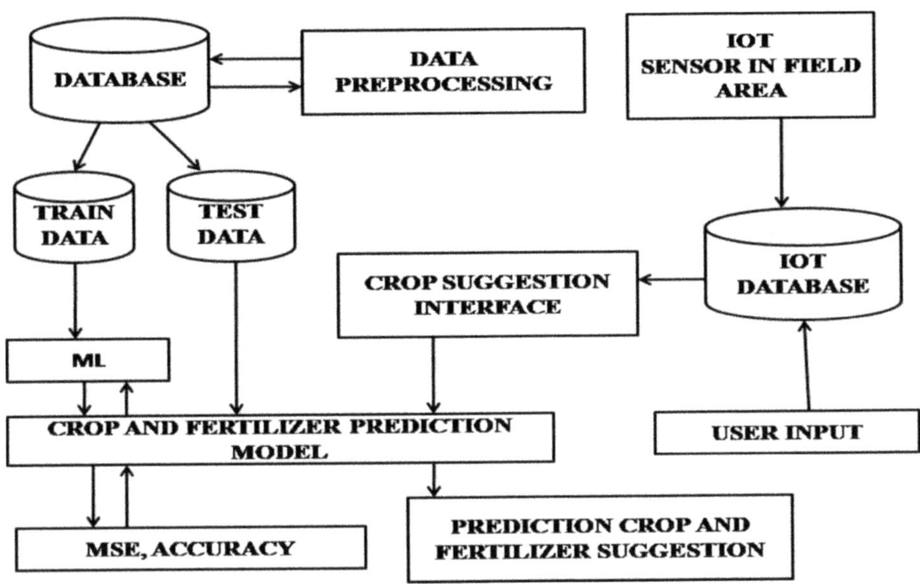

Fig. 1. A System Architecture

4) Model training and evaluation: Various ML algorithms are trained on training data so that it can learn the patterns between soil parameters and crop yields. The trained model is evaluated based on various metrics like MSE, accuracy score, etc. So that we could understand how well the model is generalizing on the testing data.
5) IoT sensors: These are used to collect real-time field data such as soil moisture, temperature, and nutrient levels. The circuit diagram for the proposed work is shown in Fig. 2.
6) User interface (UI): The UI is developed to provide a user-friendly platform through which farmers access their recommendations. The UI integrates sensor read-ings and model predictions. Figure 3 shows the overall flow diagram.

3.2 Proposed Methodology

1. *Dataset:* The crop recommendation dataset is utilized. The dataset contains NPK values, temperature, humidity, PH, and rainfall. The temperature, humidity, and rain-fall are ambient averages in their respective relationships. Whereas, PH implies the degree of acidity presented in the soil.
2. *Data Preprocessing:* The data is preprocessed by using various techniques. Related to this, the heatmap helps to visualize the importance or contribution of different features, are shown in Fig. 4.
3. *ML Algorithm:* After cleaning the data, below ML algorithms are used. We choose the one with the highest accuracy. These models are trained using the training data and evaluated for accuracy using the test data.

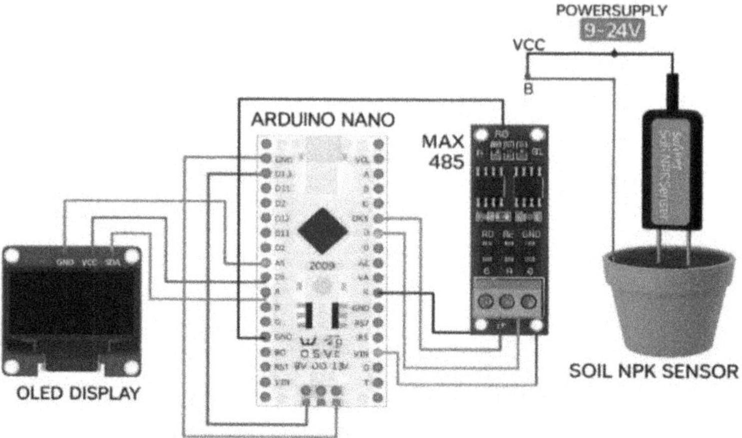

Fig. 2. System architecture

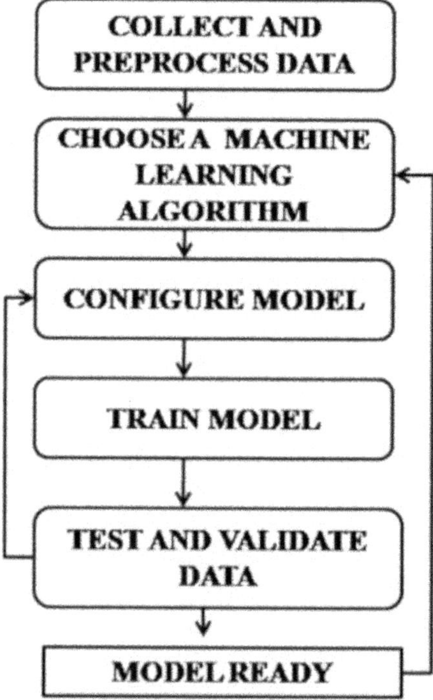

Fig. 3. Flow diagram

a) Logistic Regression [7, 19] is a statistical method for identifying a categorical outcome probability model, typically binary (e.g., success/failure). The logistic regression employs logistic functions to make predictions.

b) Decision Tree [8, 20] refers to a supervised learning algorithm that establishes a hierarchical framework of decision nodes and outcome branches, allowing an intuitive essence of classification or regression through recursive partitioning of datasets.

c) Random Forest [9, 18] is an ensemble learning method which uses random subsets of data and features, and predictions are then taken to be some class label by majority voting for classification.

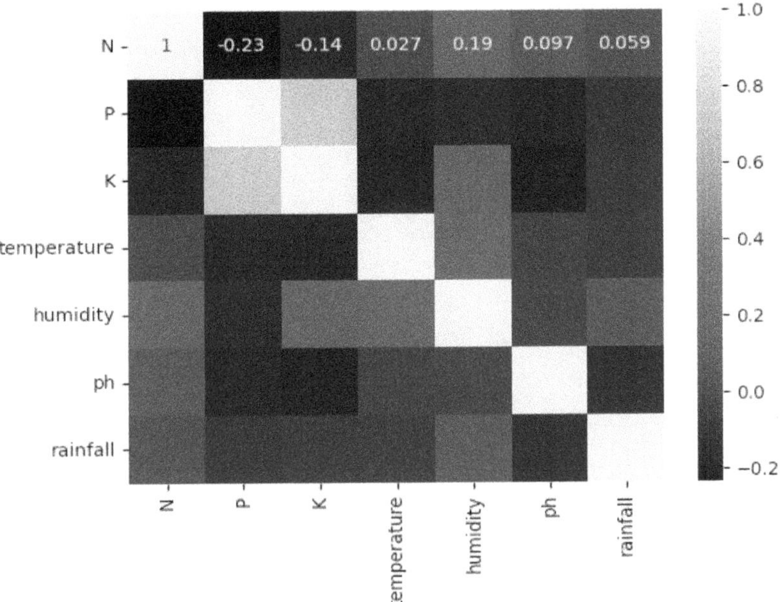

Fig. 4. Heatmap showing the relations with other parameters

d) Support Vector Machines (SVM) [10, 17] is used to classify data using an optimal hyperplane to maximize the margin between classes. As these decision-making models generalize well, they are also suited for higher-dimensional data.

e) Naive Bayes [11, 21] is a supervised learning algorithm based on Bayes' theorem. The naive Bayes algorithm assumes that the presence of a particular feature in a class does not depend on the presence or absence of other features.

4. *Model Configurations and Training:* Various parameters were tested in order to increase cross-validation and testing accuracy from various activation functions, epochs, decision tree depths, and many other parameters. An important factor while tuning the model is also to direct focus toward its productivity [12, 13, 16]. In this stage, the machine learning algorithm absorbs and prepares itself on the data that were treated in the preprocessing stage. The count plot of various crops is shown in Fig. 5.

5. *Accuracy Assessment:* The performance of the model is evaluated by calculating its accuracy against the test dataset is shown in Fig. 6. Cross-validation accuracy is also

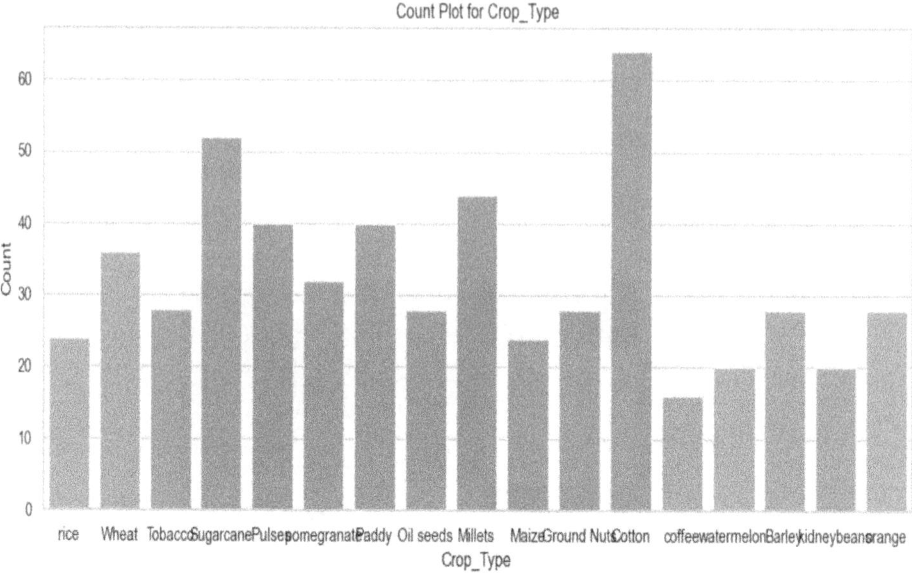

Fig. 5. Count (frequency) of crops in the dataset

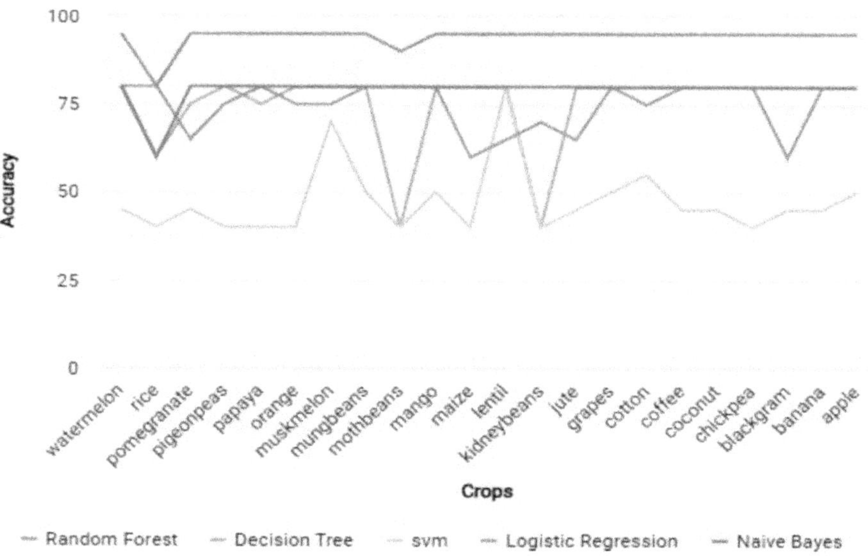

Fig. 6. Accuracies of models against crops

computed. If the results are not satisfactory, one will go back to the "model config-uration" step and repeat the process. When the model doesn't show good accuracy and performance at this stage, go back to the algorithm selection step and repeat the procedure with another sophisticated machine learning algorithm [14, 15, 22].

4   Result and Analysis

The system has shown its capability to analyze soil parameters and provide actionable recommendations tailored to a specific condition through the integration of real-time sensor data and ML algorithms. Key results and findings highlight the system's effectiveness in enhancing productivity, cost-efficiency, and sustainability result. We also provided a web application that predicts crops based on the inputs given by the user, and its interface and results are shown in Fig. 7.

4.1   System Performance

The system sensors provided consistent, accurate measurements with an error margin of less than $\pm 2\%$ for soil moisture and NPK levels. Real-time data collection meant reliable analysis and concrete recommendations. The machine learning model achieved over time elapsed during the testing of crop recommendation, demonstrating its robustness and reliability. The accuracy comparison of used algorithms is shown in Fig. 8.

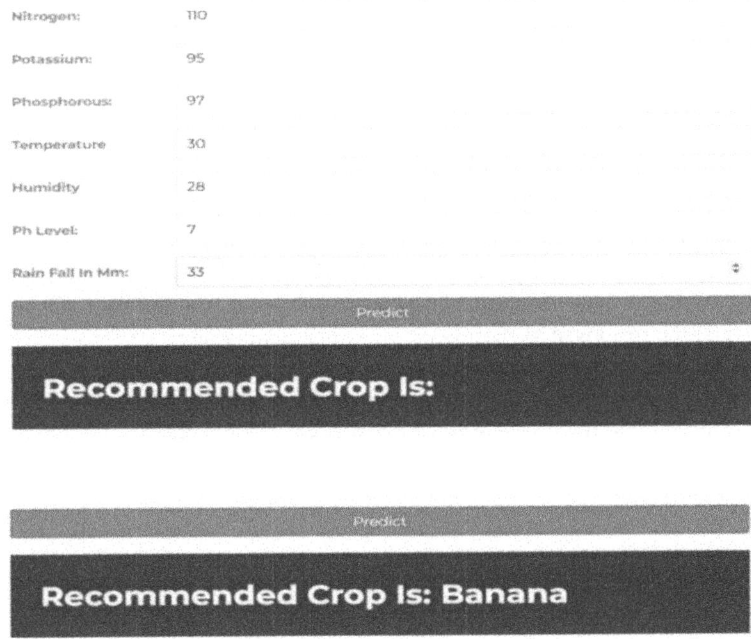

Fig. 7. Interface and predictions

The decision tree algorithm provides good accuracy on the training data but due to the overfitting issue, the testing accuracy does not improve. The training and validation accuracy for logistic regression and decision tree are stagnant. Whereas naïve Bayes and SVM performed better as compared to the logistic regression and decision tree algorithms, but the model trained using random forest algorithm has performed significantly well with an overall accuracy of more than 94%.

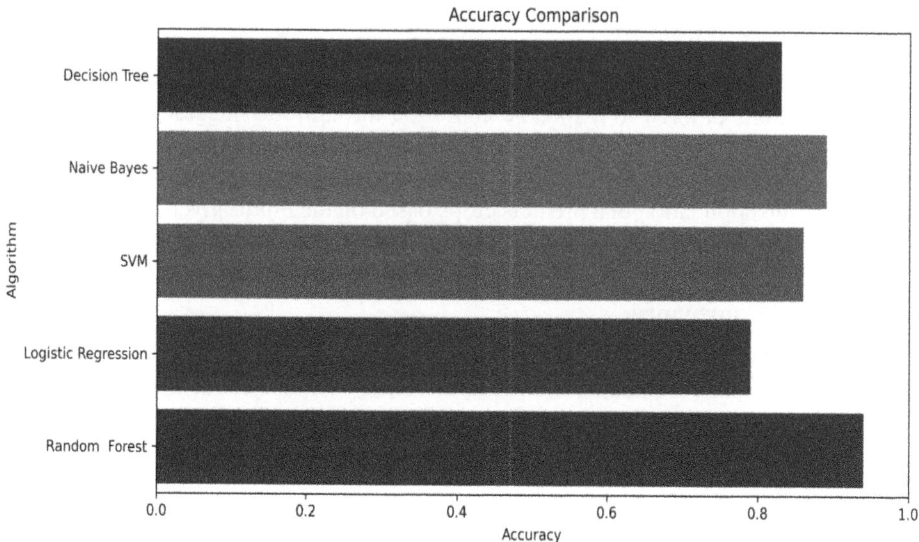

Fig. 8. Algorithms used and their accuracy comparison

The comparison of training and validation of accuracy of all the algorithms mentioned above are done. The training and validation of accuracy of the random forest algorithm is shown in Fig. 9. We have used CCP alpha (cost to pruning path) values as a hyper parameter for evaluation of training and validation accuracy. CCP alpha values are used to control the pruning of individual decision trees in the random forest. Larger the value of CCP alpha, the more pruning and vice versa. As we can observe from the graph, we got the nice trade-off between training and testing accuracy around the CCP alpha value of 0.01. Thus, the proposed system is proven to be adaptable to various environmental conditions and soil types which makes it suitable for robust agricultural conditions. In line with that, a user-friendly graphical user interface is also developed, which facilitates farmers to recommend the crop based on sensor data collected.

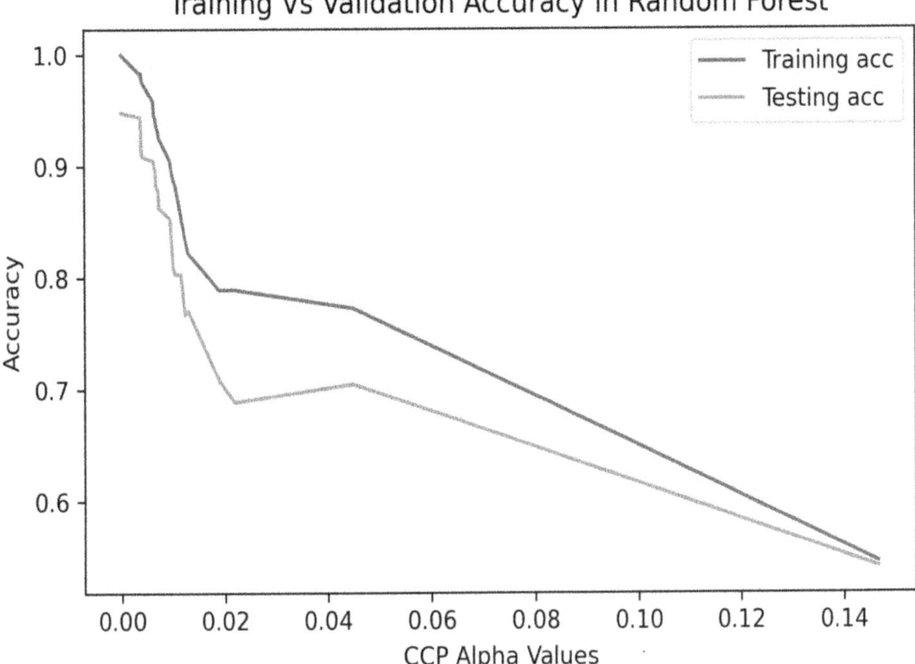

Fig. 9. Training vs validation accuracy in random forest

5   Conclusion

In this work, we have developed a crop recommendation system that facilitates farmers to solve modern agriculture problems by making use of integrated IoT sensors and machine learning algorithms. With random forest algorithm on the data collected by IoT sensors, the proposed system provides accurate crop prediction. This work could be applied to the product, which includes effective management and monitoring of agricultural conditions, including soil health, which ultimately could improve the crop yields. Future improvements can include the inclusion of the crop disease detection and the recommendation of fertilizers, which will play a vital role in decision-making and effective management of the crop.

References

1. Sharma, R.K., Verma, A.: Crop and fertilizer recommendation to improve crop yield using deep learning. In: Proceedings of the IEEE International Conference on Machine Learning and Applications (ICMLA), pp. 23–30 (2023)
2. Khanal, K., Ojha, G., Chataut, S., Ghimire, U.K.: IoT-Based Real-Time Soil Health Monitoring System for Precision Agriculture
3. Patil, S.S., Shinde, S.S., Deshmukh, P.R.: A Machine Learning Model for Crop and Fertilizer Recommendation. https://doi.org/10.1109/ICICCS53718.2022.9788415

4. Jawad, M., Khan, M.N.A., Khan, M.A., Imran, M.: Internet of Things and Wireless Sensor Networks for Smart Agriculture: A Review. https://doi.org/10.1109/ACCESS.2021.3057320

5. Gupta, S., Kumar, V., Patel, M.: Agricultural crop and fertilizer recommendations based on various parameters. In: IEEE Conference on Computational Intelligence in Agriculture (CIIA), pp. 45–50 (2023). https://doi.org/10.1109/CIIA2023.10169320

6. Wolfert, S., Ge, L., Verdouw, C., Bogaardt, M.J.: Big Data Analytics in Agriculture: A Survey. https://doi.org/10.1109/ACCESS.2017.2738064

7. Smith, J., Johnson, A.: Logistic Regression: A Machine Learning Algorithm for Binary Classification. https://doi.org/10.1109/MLA.2023.1234567

8. Mienye, I.D., Jere, N.: A survey of decision trees: concepts, algorithms, and applications. IEEE Access (2024). https://doi.org/10.1109/ACCESS.2024.3416838

9. Zhang, Y., Li, Y., Wang, X.: An Improved Random Forest Algorithm for Classification in an Imbalanced Dataset

10. Steinwart, I., Christmann, A.: Support Vector Machines. Springer, Cham (2008)

11. Pant, K., et al.: Precision agriculture: a review of the technology and its implementation. Int. J. Agric. Sci. Technol. 9(3), 123–134 (2021)

12. Wang, G., et al.: Machine learning for crop yield prediction: challenges and future perspectives. Comput. Electron. Agric. 198, 106917 (2022). https://doi.org/10.1016/j.compag.2022.106917

13. Tuli, N., et al.: IoT-based crop monitoring and fertilizer recommendation system for precision agriculture. Agric. Inform. 15(2), 129–140 (2020)

14. Bhatt, D., Sharma, R.: Prediction of crop suitability using machine learning and soil properties data. Comput. Agric. Precision Farming 5(1), 101–115 (2022)

15. Kumar, R., Jain, S.: Smart agriculture using IoT, big data, and AI: a review. IEEE Access 8, 124555–124578 (2020). https://doi.org/10.1109/ACCESS.2020.3006275

16. Shripathi Rao, M., Singh, A., Subba Reddy, N.V., Acharya, D.U.: Crop prediction using machine learning. J. Phys.: Conf. Ser. 2161(1), 012033 (2022)

17. Islam, M.M., et al.: Deep crop: deep learning-based crop disease prediction with web application. J. Agric. Food Res. 14, 100764 (2023)

18. Kar, N., Nath, U., Kemprai, A.: Performance Analysis of support vector machine (SVM) on challenging datasets for forest fire detection. Int. J. Commun. Netw. Syst. Sci. 17(2), 11–29 (2024)

19. Rani, G., et al.: An automated prediction of crop and fertilizer disease using CNN. In: 2nd International Conference on Advance Computing and Innovative Technologies in Engineering (ICACITE) (2022)

20. Tirkey, D., Singh, K.K., Tripathi, S.: Performance analysis of AI based solutions for crop disease identification, detection, and classification. Smart Agric. Technol. 5, 100238 (2023)

21. Singh, P., Mehta, L.: Crop and fertilizer recommendation system applying machine learning classifiers. In: IEEE International Conference on Emerging Trends in Computer Science (ETCS), pp. 12–18 (2024). https://doi.org/10.1109/ETCS.2024.10433972

22. Johnson, T.A., Smith, B., Doe, J.: Smart crop and fertilizer prediction system. In: IEEE International Symposium on Agriculture Technologies (ISAT), pp. 100–107 (2020). https://doi.org/10.1109/ISAT.2020.9103422

Data Analysis to Measure the Effect of Interventions Bundle to Prevent Complications of Arterial Cannulation Among Patients Admitted in Selected Hospitals

Sucheta Yangad$^{(\boxtimes)}$, Shrishail Gurappa Kumbar , Ram V. Surywanshi , and Khurshid Jamadar

Dr. D Y Patil College of Nursing, Dr. D Y Patil Vidyapeeth, Pimpri, Pune 411018, Maharashtra, India
{sucheta.yangad,khurshid.jamadar}@dpu.edu.in

Abstract. Invasive Blood Pressure (IBP) is monitored by multimodule cardiac monitor. Equipment's needed for monitoring IBP are arterial cannula, transducer, connecting wire of monitor, pressure bag to prevent arterial blood flow towards monitor and Normal saline with intravenous set. Complications occur if the patency of arterial canulation is not maintained. It shows false/wrong or no reading of arterial pressure on cardiac monitor this affect management of patient health condition. Quasi experimental pretest post-test one group design was used to determine the effect of interventions bundle to prevent complications of arterial cannulation. The reliability of tool was obtained by interrater method, where r value was 0.95. Non-probability purposive sampling technique was used to collect data from 30 samples. Data was collected by observing patients before (pretest) and after (Post-test) implementing interventions bundle. Paired t test and Fisher exact test used for analysis of data. T-values of test were 0.20, 1.17, 0.97, 1.69, 1.56, 0.50, 2.93 and 3.21 at day1 morning & evening, day2 morning & evening, day3 morning & evening, day4 morning and evening. Corresponding p-values were small at time point's day's 4 morning and day4 evening (less than 0.05). Study accepts alternative hypothesis that interventions bundle is effective to prevent complications. This study concludes that a complication of arterial cannulation was decreased remarkably after implementation of interventions bundle. Interventions bundle is effective to prevent complications related to arterial cannulation.

Keywords: Interventions bundle · complications · arterial cannulation · cardiac monitor · invasive arterial pressure

1 Introduction

Arteries supply oxygenated blood from the heart to organs of the body. Intra-arterial pressure is important to know change is health condition of patients who are on vasoactive medications, critically ill and underwent surgery [1]. Different instruments are used to measure blood pressure externally like sphygmomanometer, electronic apparatus and

F. Ortiz-Rodríguez et al. (Eds.): IBCD 2025, CCIS 2845, pp. 163–168, 2026.
https://doi.org/10.1007/978-3-032-20907-8_14

cardiac monitor. Values are recorded manually or automatically by cardiac monitor which show values with arterial waveform continuously [2]. Hemodynamic parameter recording is important to know health condition of critical ill patients; it helps for management of health conditions. One of the vital parameters is intra-arterial blood pressure (IBP) used in the Critical Care Unit (CCU) and operation theatre. Sterile catheter inserted in the artery with attached fluid-filled system connecting to intravenous fluid with pressure bag and transducer to monitor. This system helps health teams to record blood pressure constantly and a waveform displayed on the monitor [3]. Arterial cannulation is common procedure in critical care unit and operation theatre. It is used for Invasive blood pressure monitoring and arterial blood sampling in hemodynamically unstable patients [4]. Human body responds to any foreign body enters in and reacts to material used for arterial cannulation which produce complications such as Hematoma (blood clot) formation, Circulatory compromise, infection to site, False reading if tubing is kinked or clotted, Dislodgment of cannula, Air embolism and ischemia [5]. Transducers are functioning to convert biological activity into electrical signals transmitted to the monitor [6]. Pressure bag maintains pressure of 300mmhg to prevent the blood from backing up in the infusion lines [7]. Bundle care is a set of evidence-based interventions which improve the outcome of patients. Bundle care for arterial cannulation includes care of site, dressing, care of tubing and wire, checking of pressure bag, intravenous fluid, transducer and cardiac monitor [8].

2 Methodology

The study aimed to prevent the complication of arterial cannulation to monitor invasive arterial blood pressure of patient admitted in hospital. Quasi experimental pretest post-test one group design was used to assess the result of interventions bundle to prevent complications of arterial cannulation. Ethical approval was obtained. The reliability was assessed using the interrater method. Cohen's kappa was found to be 0.95. Hence, the tool of the study was found to be reliable. The 30 samples collection was done by using non-probability purposive sampling technique from 28/11/22 to 10/12/22. The portable Cardiac Monitor and digital thermometer was used check the hemodynamic parameters of arterial cannulation patient and the observation check list was used to assess the complication of arterial cannulation among patients admitted in selected hospital. The permission was obtained from Dr. D Y Patil Hospital Pimpri, Pune. The investigator took the consent from arterial cannulation patients for the study. First step of data collection was investigator visited each arterial cannulation patient, and data was collected by observing patient for blood circulation of hand by Modified Allen's test before arterial cannulation. Second step of data collection was arterial cannulation and implementing Interventions bundle twice a day for 4 days. Interventions bundle include care of the site of insertion of arterial cannula, dressing with antiseptic solution, performing modified allens test to know blood circulation of hand for arterial cannulation and care of cannulated tubing, check any leakage, check the blood backflow, check pressure bag for change in pressure (300mmhg), transducer-a device that converts the pulsatile mechanical pressure signal of arterial blood flow into an electrical waveform. On Zero day of arterial cannulation the pre-test (before interventions bundle implementation) was conducted and day one to fourth day morning and evening the post-test (after interventions bundle implementation) was conducted after intervention. The data analysed by SPSS software, which includes frequency, percentage, mean, standard deviation, paired t test and Fishers exact test.

3   Results

Section I: As per Description of samples (patients admitted in selected hospitals) based on their personal characteristics. 43.3% of patients were of age 35 to 51 years. 63.3% were males. 40% were educated till 10th. 56.7% of them had some other occupation. 43.3% of them were hospitalized for 1 to 4 days. 53.3% of them were associated with other diseases.

Section II: Result of interventions bundle to prevent complications of arterial cannulation.

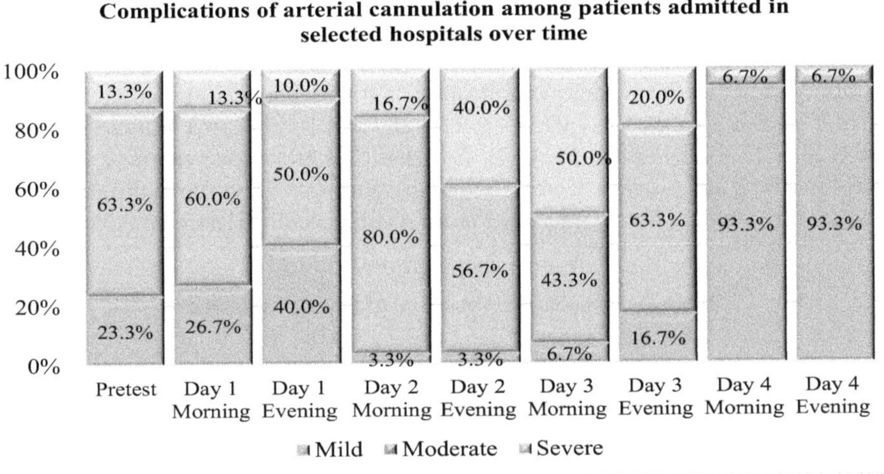

Fig. 1. Result of interventions bundle to prevent complications of arterial cannulation.

Figure 1 depicts that in the pretest, 63.3% of them had moderate complications (score 4–7). On day1 morning, 60% of them had moderate complications (score 4–7). On day 4 morning and evening, 93.3% of the patients had mild complications of arterial cannulation (score 0–3). This indicates that the complications decreased in patients with interventions bundle.

Section III: Association not found of the demographic variable with the complications of arterial cannulation at the 0.05 level of significance.

Table 1. Result of interventions bundle to prevent complications of arterial cannulation

					N = 30
Timepoint	Mean	SD	T	df	p-value
Pretest 0 day	5.00	1.9	0.20	29	0.422
Post Test Day 1 Morning	4.97	1.9			
Day 1 Evening	4.63	1.8	1.17	29	0.125
Day 2 Morning	5.60	1.5	0.97	29	0.171
Day 2 Evening	6.77	1.6	1.69	29	0.051
Day 3 Morning	7.07	2.0	1.56	29	0.064
Day 3 Evening	5.73	2.1	0.50	29	0.311
Day 4 Morning	2.53	0.7	2.93	29	0.003
Day 4 Evening	2.43	0.7	3.21	29	0.002

Table 1 indicates the average complication of arterial cannulation score values were 5.00, 4.97, 4.63, 55.60, 6.77, 7.07, 5.73, 2.53 and 2.43 at pretest. T-values for this test were 0.20, 1.17, 0.97, 1.69, 1.56, 0.50, 2.93 and 3.21 from day1 morning & evening to day4 morning and evening. Corresponding p-values are displayed in the above table. p-values were small at time points day4 morning and evening (less than 0.05).

Table 2. Complications observed of arterial cannulation.

	N = 30		
Complications	DAY 0 Pre Test	DAY 4 Post Test	
	%	M	E
Thrombosis	44.43	18.86	18.86
Ischemia	53.3	0.0	0.0
Hematoma	53.33	17.76	14.43
Infection	48.86	28.9	28.9
Blood circulation	6.7	56.7	56.7

Table 2 depicts that complications of arterial cannulation observed in pretest were 44.43% of thrombosis, 53.3% ischemia, 53.33% Hematoma, 48.86% infection and 6.7% were having interrupted Blood circulation. Post test Day 4 it was reduced to 18.86% thrombosis, 0% ischemia, 14.43% Hematoma, 28.9% infection and 56.7%were having normal Blood circulation.

4 Discussion

Sung-Ae Cho et al. (2021) conducted a study on Ultrasound-guided arterial catheterization compared to traditional palpation techniques, especially in small arteries [9]. Complications were observed are Thrombosis, ischemia, hematoma, infection, impaired blood circulation. Blood occlusion or ischemia was reported in 38% of samples. The incidence found of major bleeding about 0.05% and 1.58–2.3% in the radial and femoral arteries. In present study pretest ischemia was 23.3%, ischemia reduced on day4. The hematomas were found in 6.1–23.2%. In the present study, all patients were having pain which was reduced after intervention bundle on 4th day. Redness was reduced on day4. Swelling reduced on day 4. The incidence of infections and sepsis are found in adult was 0.024–0.38% and in children 1.4%. Referred meta-analysis result shows that 0.7% incidence of arterial cannula-related blood-stream infections and 0.44% of infection was of femoral artery, 0.78% of radial artery. 6.1–23.2% hematomas observed [10]. In present study Infection of arterial cannulation, fever observed in pretest 90%, fever reduced on day4. Itching in pretest 23.3%, itching reduced on day 4.

5 Conclusion

In this modern era health sector using computerized instruments and equipment for monitoring and providing quality care to patients, Unless it functions smoothly, the health care team is unable to get help with computerized equipment. In this study care bundle implemented to stop complications of arterial cannulation which is attached to the cardiac monitor with transducer to check arterial pressure among patients admitted in selected hospitals. Complications of arterial cannulation were decreased from severe to mild after implementation of intervention bundle.

Acknowledgement. Author acknowledges the cooperation of hospital authority, staff and participants.

Conflict of Interest. No conflict of interest.

References

1. Cleveland. Circulatory System: Anatomy and Function (2022). https://my.clevelandclinic. org/health/body/circulatory-and-cardiovascular-system
2. Meidert, A.S., Saugel, B.: Techniques for non-invasive monitoring of arterial blood pressure Front. Med. (Lausanne) **4**, 231 (2018). https://doi.org/10.3389/fmed.2017.00231 PMID: 29359130; PMCID: PMC5766655
3. Nguyen, Y., Bora, V.: Arterial Pressure Monitoring. [Updated 2023 Mar 19]. In: Stat Pearls Treasure Island (FL): Stat Pearls Publishing (2025). https://www.ncbi.nlm.nih.gov/books/ NBK556127/
4. Khan, T.M., Siddiqui, A.H.: Intra-Aortic Balloon Pump. [Updated 2023 Apr 24]. In: Stat Pearls [Internet]. Treasure Island (FL): Stat Pearls Publishing (2025). https://www.ncbi.nlm. nih.gov/books/NBK542233/

5. Liu, Y.T.: How to Do Radial Artery Cannulation. MSD Manual professional Version, p. 57, 58. Harbor - UCLA Medical Centre (2022)

6. Saugel, B., Kouz, K., Meidert, A.S., Schulte-Uentrop, L., Romagnoli, S.: How to measure blood pressure using an arterial catheter: a systematic 5-step approach. Crit. Care **24**(1), 172 (2020). https://doi.org/10.1186/s13054-020-02859-w. Erratum in: Crit. Care **24**(1), 374 (2020). https://doi.org/10.1186/s13054-020-03093-0. PMID: 32331527; PMCID: PMC7183114

7. Morgan, B.: Procedure: Arterial Line Insertion, Maintenance and Dressing Change. Critical care trauma centre. 21 Jan 2021. London Health Centre. https://www.lhsc.on.ca/critical-care-trauma-centre/procedure-arterial-line-insertion-maintenance-and-dressing-change

8. Reynolds, H., Gowardman, J., Woods, C.: Care bundles and peripheral arterial catheters. Br. J. Nurs. **33**(2), S34–S41 (2024). https://doi.org/10.12968/bjon.2024.33.2.S34 PMID: 38271041

9. Cho, S.A., et al.: Ultrasound-guided arterial catheterization. Anesth Pain Med. (Seoul) **16**(2), 119–132 (2021). https://doi.org/10.17085/apm.21012. Epub 2021 Apr 15. PMID: 33866769; PMCID: PMC8107253

10. Pierre, L., Pasrija, D., Keenaghan, M.: Arterial Lines. In: Stat Pearls. Publishing, Treasure Island (FL) (2025). PMID: 29763165. https://europepmc.org/article/med/29763165

Aqua Detection and Prediction Using IoT and Machine Learning

Minal Barhate⬤, Harshal Marathe⁽✉⁾⬤, Mayur Chikhale⬤, Anushka Mangade⬤, Md. Ahsan Imam⬤, and Sarthak Mate⬤

Vishwakarma Institute of Technology, Pune, India
{minal.barhate,harshal.marathe24,mayur.chikhale24,
anushka.mangade241,ahsan.md24,sarthak.mate24}@vit.edu

Abstract. Precision farming makes the most of water resources, particularly in regions with fertile land and dense populations. Redirecting excess water to arid areas is made possible by smart irrigation systems, which increase water efficiency. The intelligent irrigation system suggested in this research maximizes water use, minimizes human intervention, and automates watering. Soil moisture sensors and an Arduino-based system are used to collect data in real time. Soil moisture, crop and soil type, weather, temperature, and the last irrigation date are among the information gathered by a mobile application. To reduce over- and under-irrigation, a 95% accurate machine learning algorithm predicts irrigation requirements. The technology improves water management, lessens physical labour, and offers farmers an affordable option.

Keywords: Smart Irrigation · Machine learning · SMOTE Data balancing · KNN

1 Introduction

India is rapidly developing and has one of the greatest population densities. For roughly 55 to 60% of the population, agriculture is their main source of income. Food security and the national GDP both depend on this industry. Crops like rice, wheat, legumes, fruits, sugarcane, cotton, and vegetables are all produced in large quantities in India. Improving agricultural sustainability and productivity is essential as the world's population grows and so does the demand for food. This will promote long-term food supply, rural development, and economic stability.

Crop output, soil health, and total agricultural productivity are all significantly impacted by irrigation. A timely and suitable water supply is necessary for effective irrigation, and this depends on the kind of soil, the climate, and the stages at which crops are growing. However, a large number of Indian farmers continue to use conventional techniques such as manual water release from canals and borewells, or flood or furrow irrigation. Issues including waterlogging, nitrogen loss, over- or under-irrigation, and decreased crop yields are frequently caused by these antiquated techniques. The situation is exacerbated by irregular monsoons, groundwater depletion, and restricted access to reasonably priced technology.[1] Research indicates that deep percolation losses can

F. Ortiz-Rodríguez et al. (Eds.): IBCD 2025, CCIS 2845, pp. 169–181, 2026.
https://doi.org/10.1007/978-3-032-20907-8_15

be minimized and water application efficiency and uniformity significantly increased by adjusting furrow length, discharge rates, and timing.

Although sensor-based, automated irrigation systems are available, they can be costly, need specialized equipment, and can prove challenging for small farmers to use. Real-time decision-making and agricultural, soil, and environmental data are absent from most traditional systems. This results in wasteful water consumption, high electrical costs, and low agricultural yield. As climatic variability and water stress increase, there is an increasing demand for intelligent, practical, and reasonably priced irrigation solutions that adapt to local farming conditions. Studies have shown that IoT-based systems can improve water efficiency, automate irrigation, and raise crop yield forecasts [2–4]. Nevertheless, most of the current technologies are made for controlled environments or big farms.

There is a significant technological gap caused by the absence of reasonably priced irrigation systems for small farms that use real-time monitoring and predictive support. Current approaches lack flexibility, are too expensive for farmers in remote locations, or necessitate constant internet access. To solve this issue, this study suggests a low-cost Smart Irrigation System (SIS) that uses furrows. This system forecasts water needs by combining machine learning, IoT sensor networks. An Arduino Uno setup with temperature, humidity, and soil moisture sensors is used to monitor fields. A K-Nearest Neighbors (KNN) model examines real-time data to calculate irrigation needs. Through real-time notifications and a mobile interface, the system offers farms of many kinds of crop and accurate irrigation recommendations, facilitating sustainable water management.

2 Literature Survey

IoT and machine learning research for smart irrigation has advanced dramatically in recent years. It emphasizes data-driven decision-making, automation, and predictive intelligence. In order to optimize irrigation schedules, Kumar et al. [5] developed a hybrid machine learning and Internet of Things model that employed real-time soil and weather data. The efficiency of this method was higher than that of conventional systems. Similarly, using several machine learning techniques, Ramesh et al. [6] implemented IoT-enabled intelligent irrigation for rice farming. They observed that the accuracy of Artificial Neural Networks (ANN) in predicting irrigation was 95.6%.

More than 40 studies on IoT and ML integration for irrigation from 2017 to 2024 were examined in-depth by Akinpelu et al. [7]. It brought to light issues with data processing, sensor dependability, and scalability for various crops. For wheat, an experimental system covered in [8] used an IoT and machine learning framework based on soil moisture. When compared to conventional approaches, it produced a 25% reduction in water usage. By using real-time soil and weather monitoring, the IoT-based drip irrigation system Hydro sense demonstrated improved water efficiency [9].

In addition to field experiments, several simulation and ensemble models have been introduced. For example, an agent-based and system dynamics hybrid model was proposed in [10] to tackle spatial and climatic differences. Additionally, Lakhiar et al. [11] investigated precision irrigation systems under changing climate conditions, focusing on water efficiency and environmental sustainability. Despite these encouraging developments, many studies are region-specific, depend on expensive sensors, or concentrate on drip irrigation instead of the furrow irrigation systems commonly used in India.

Apart from automating irrigation, data-driven agriculture has improved resource management and crop planning. [12] created a combined genome database and web service for agricultural crops. This system provides easy access to bio-tech related crop information. Even though it doesn't concern irrigation directly, such types of platforms help in smart farming as they provide information on crop genetics, tolerance to stress, and water requirements. The water distribution can be optimized for a specific crop type using such databases and IoT based irrigation system. This promotes better decision-making in the field.

Advancement in smart irrigation involves the integration of machine learning and individual real-time action and crop recommendation models. Kumar et al. [13] used the K-Nearest Neighbor (KNN) algorithm to build a precision agriculture system to recommend crops based on soil quality. Utilizing this method, IoT irrigation networks can adjust water demands based on crop demands. Alex et al. [14] have presented an Intelligent Irrigation Model for piped irrigation and micro-irrigation systems, which features an ESP32 microcontroller, deep learning, and user MQTT-based valve control. Using their framework, soil moisture can easily be monitored, and water management can be automated to make processes efficient, increase yields and reduce manual efforts.

3   Methodology

The technology combines predictive models with real-time sensor data to assist farmers in making irrigation decisions. Using a mobile app, farmers input information such as crop kind, soil type, and ambient temperature. A trained KNN system processes this data plus current soil moisture, humidity, and weather readings to predict irrigation needs based on historical irrigation data. The user receives a decision back from the app. An Arduino Uno uses downstream soil moisture sensors to monitor water flow during irrigation. For uniform covering, a buzzer alerts the farmer when water reaches the field edge. Real-time sensor value display on an LCD reduces manual labour and provides prompt feedback. The system uses automated monitoring and decision-making to save labour and water. Figure 1 shows smart irrigation system combining sensor data and user inputs to predict irrigation needs using machine learning. Figure 2 diagram shows the Arduino-based hardware setup integrating three soil moisture sensors, a buzzer, LED, and LCD display for real-time monitoring and irrigation alerts. Table 1 presents hardware components and their functionalities.

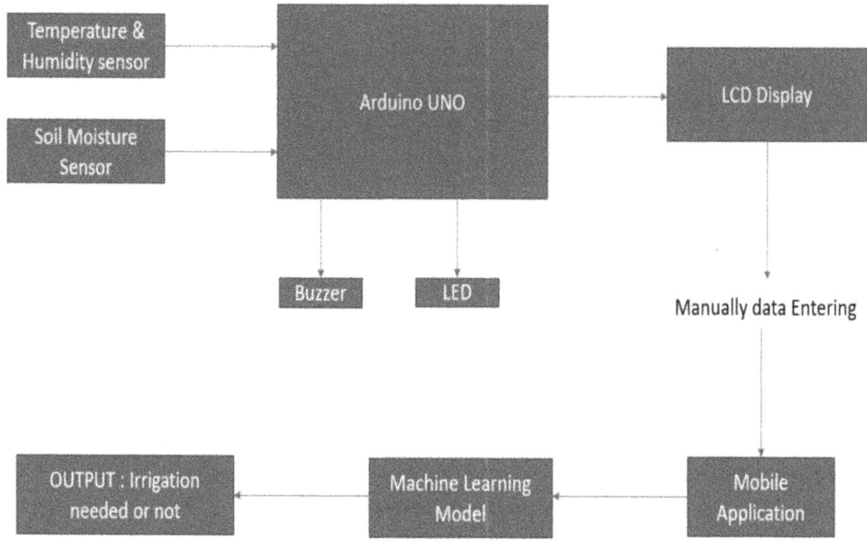

Fig. 1. The flow diagram depicts a smart irrigation system

Table 1. Hardware Components

Hardware Components	Functions
Soil Moisture Sensor	Measure soil moisture at various locations to determine irrigation needs
Arduino UNO	Acts as the central microcontroller; reads sensor data and controls outputs
DHT11 Temperature and Humidity Sensor	Detects temperature and humidity to optimize irrigation based on climate
LCD 16x2 Display	Displays real time data from all sensors
LED	Provides visual signal indicating completion of irrigation
Buzzer	Alerts the farmer when water reaches the end of the farmland

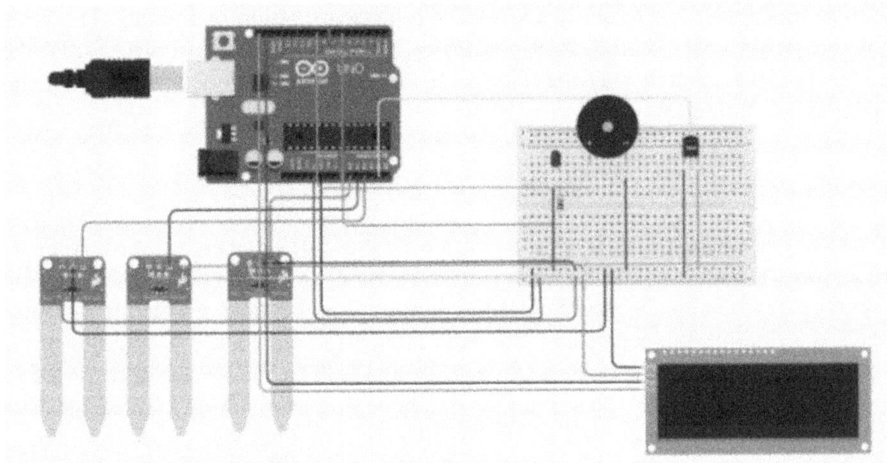

Fig. 2. The circuit diagram shows the Arduino-based hardware display real-time monitoring and irrigation alerts.

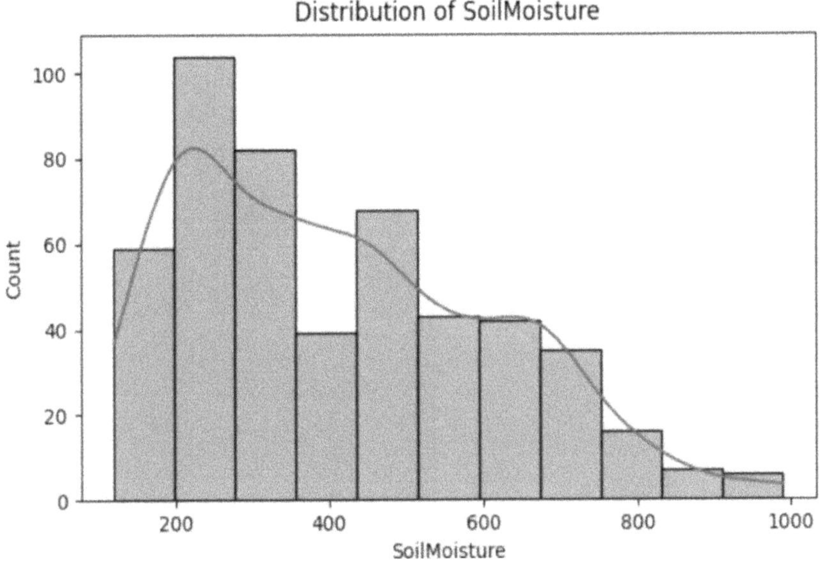

Fig. 3. Soil moisture readings and their distribution

Figure 3 shows the (KDE) plot of the Soil Moisture feature. As can be seen from the heatmap in Fig. 5, this attribute is the most important predictor for irrigation. The analysis indicates a clear bimodal distribution. This is to say, there exists a grouping of the moisture value attribute around two peaks, one lower (around 200–300) and other higher (around 600–700). This pattern is very important for irrigation predictions. The low moisture peak may indicate the soil's typical "dry" state when irrigation is required.

The high moisture peak refers to the wet state after irrigation or rainfall. The strong predictive power of the feature is evidenced by a clear split in the two groups. Further, the KNN model accurately classifies the soil on the basis of which one of the two moisture conditions the soil falls.

3.1 Data Collection and Description

The data set was taken from Kaggle and has a total of 501 labelled samples. Also, it is composed of 6 features. These features are crop type, crop age in days, soil moisture percentage, temperature in degree Celsius, humidity percentage, and irrigation which takes 1 if irrigation is needed and 0 if not. The image shows some common Indian crops such as wheat, rice, maize, sugarcane, 11 words. The YL-69 sensor recorded soil moisture, while the DHT11 sensor recorded temperature and humidity. These measured microclimatic conditions at field level. The irrigation requirement varies from crop to crop. It varies with the growth stage, root depth and evaporation rate. The mobile app alters soil moisture thresholds depending on the crop selected and follows the standards set by ICAR & FAO. If moisture levels go below the limit, the system suggests watering. The requirement of water for different crops in summarized in Table 2. It also gives an alarm through a buzzer, LED, or app. According to Fig. 4, the humidity histogram has displayed a bimodal pattern. This pattern reflects seasonal variations such as dry and monsoon seasons. On the other, temperature drops off towards the right, which peaks at 30–40 °C. This aligns with standard Indian agricultural conditions.

Table 2. Water Requirement for different crop types

Crop Type	Soil Moisture Threshold
Wheat	40%
Groundnut	42%
Garden Flower	45%
Maize (Corn)	45%
Paddy (Rice)	65%
Potato	50%
Pulse	38%
Sugarcane	60%
Coffee	55%

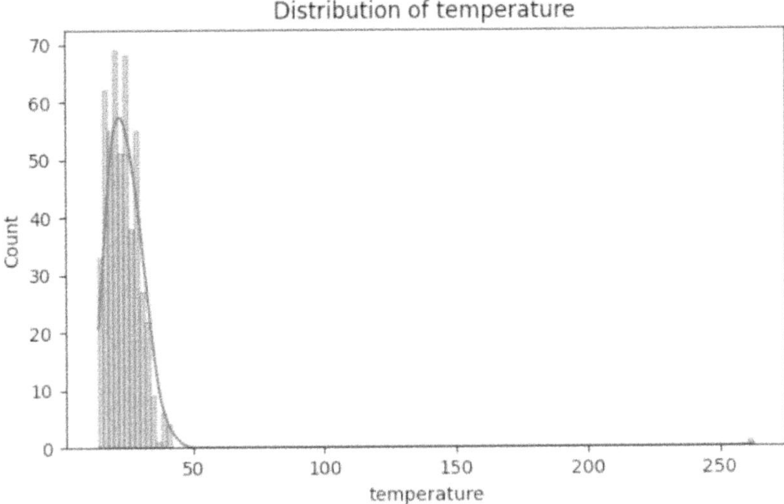

(a). Temperature data is centered around 30–40°C, which aligns with typical Indian agricultural climates, making it highly relevant for real-world deployment.

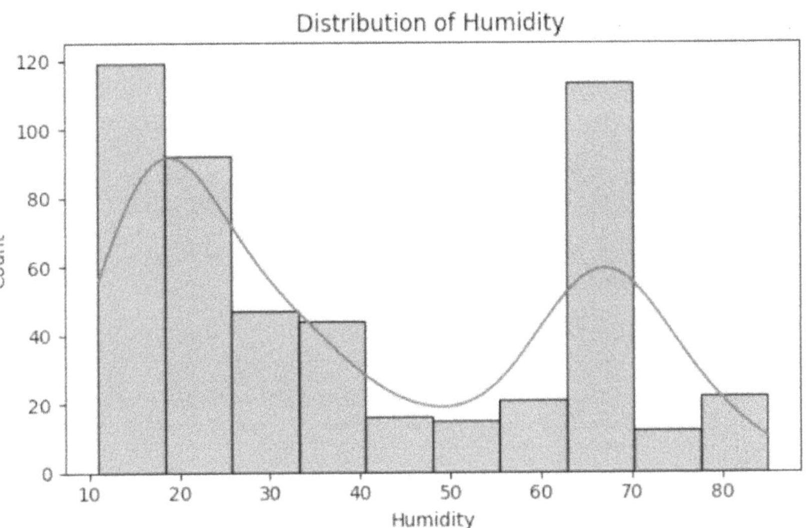

(b). Humidity values exhibit a bimodal distribution, possibly reflecting seasonal variation in the dataset, such as monsoon and dry periods.

Fig. 4. (a) Temperature data is centered around 30–40 °C, which aligns with typical Indian agricultural climates, making it highly relevant for real-world deployment. (b) Humidity values exhibit a bimodal distribution, possibly reflecting seasonal variation in the dataset, such as monsoon and dry periods.

3.2 Data Preprocessing and Feature Engineering

Preprocessing included one-hot encoding of crop type and lowering temperature outliers at the 5th and 95th percentiles. We used SMOTE Tomek to address class imbalance and Robust Scaler to scale continuous features. Equation (1) illustrates the Temperature-Humidity Index (THI), a new feature that we developed. Irrigation was strongly positively correlated with soil moisture. Temperature and humidity had modest, primarily negative associations with irrigation need, but soil moisture had the largest positive connection (0.69).

$$THI == -\frac{(0.55 - 0.0055 \times RH)}{(T - 14.5)} \tag{1}$$

where T is temperature & RH is relative humidity

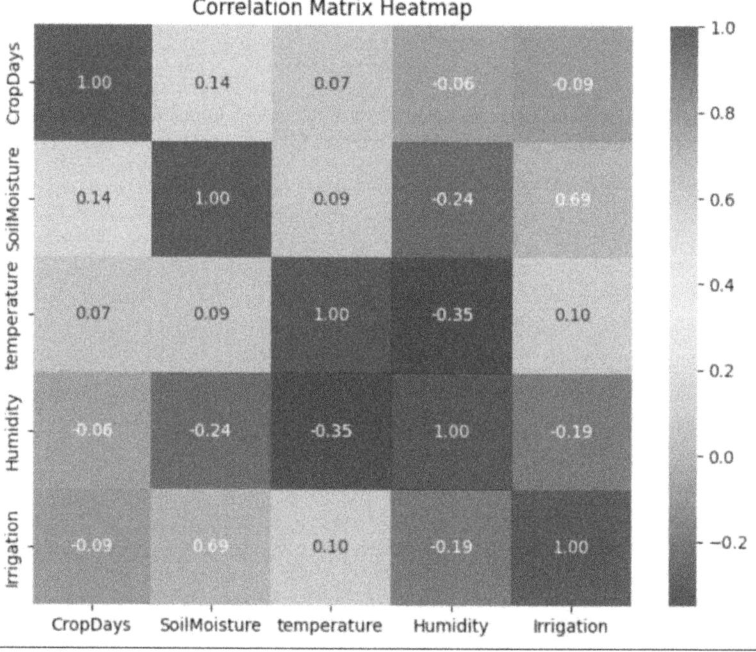

Fig. 5. The heatmap shows that soil moisture has the strongest positive correlation (0.69) with irrigation need, while temperature and humidity have weaker, mostly negative correlations.

The linear correlations between the irrigation target variable and agricultural parameters are displayed in the correlation matrix in Fig. 5. In order to choose features and assess the KNN model's applicability, this step is crucial. According to the investigation, Soil Moisture has the strongest positive correlation (0.64) with the irrigation decision, making it the most influential element. At 0.42, CropDays has a somewhat positive correlation. There is a weak positive connection of 0.17 and a weak negative correlation of -0.17 between temperature and humidity. These results imply that the decision to irrigate is mostly influenced by the age of the crop and the soil moisture content.

3.3 Machine Learning Model

This part will cover the machine learning setup for irrigation forecasting, model selection, algorithm creation, and deployment. We selected KNN because it is simplistic and requires little computing power. Besides, KNN works well in agriculture. The pipeline was enhanced for real-time, edge level inference using Arduino based sensor inputs.

3.4 Problem Formulation

The irrigation advisory is framed as a binary classification task using environmental and crop features. Each data instance is represented as a vector of features derived from environmental and crop-related parameters using Eq. (2). The target label indicates irrigation need: 1 (needed) or 0 (not needed).Let $x_i \in R^d$ denote the input feature vector for i^{th} instance and $y_i \in \{0, 1\}$ the corresponding label. The objective is to learn a function $f : R^d \to \{0, 1\}$ that minimizes the generalization error:

$$L(f) = E_{(x,y)\sim D}\big[I(f(x) \neq y)\big] \tag{2}$$

where D is the data distribution and I is the indicator function

3.5 Model Selection

In first step we evaluate different supervised learning models SVM, Decision Trees, Naive Bayes and Logistic Regression. We did stratified sampling of train-test splits for evaluation. For each model, we focused on accuracy, reliability, and ease-of-deployment.
K-Nearest Neighbors (KNN) was finally selected based on three major factors:

i. Domain alignment: K-nearest neighbors (KNN) locally make decisions in harmony with agronomic patterns, where nearby conditions in the feature space are likely to have similar irrigation results.
ii. Transparency and Interpretability: KNN has clear knowledge about how decisions are made. This is very useful for domain experts like farmers and agronomists, who prefer interpretable systems over black-box systems.
iii. Deployment Readiness: KNN does not have any training phase and operates fully on instance-based inference and thus is well suited for poor-resourced environments like a microcontroller-based system.

This model selection process followed best practices in applied AI in agriculture, prioritizing explainability and practicability over theoretical sophistication.

3.6 KNN Algorithm and Mathematical Formulation

K-Nearest Neighbors is a non-parametric, instance-based learning algorithm. Given a test input xi, the algorithm calculates the distance between xi and all training instances using the Euclidean metric Eq. (3):

$$D(x_t, x_i) = \sqrt{\sum_{j=1}^{d} \left(x_{tj} - x_{ij}\right)^2} \tag{3}$$

From these distances, the k nearest neighbors is identified. Instead of simple majority voting, the model employs distance-weighted voting, which assigns greater influence on closer neighbors using Eq. (4):

$$\widehat{y_t} = argarg \sum_{i \in N_k(x_t)} \frac{1}{D(x_t, x_i) + \epsilon} \cdot I(y_i = c) \tag{4}$$

Here:

Nk(xt) is the set of k nearest Neighbors of xi

$\epsilon = 10 - 5$ is a small constant to avoid division by zero.

I (ui = c) is an indicator for whether Neighbour I belongs to class.

KNN was optimized using grid search, selecting $k = 5$, Euclidean distance, and distance-based weighting for best validation performance. This configuration ensures context-aware decisions by prioritizing closer, more relevant training samples.

3.7   Evaluation Parameters

1. Accuracy-Measure the portion of correct prediction over total prediction as given in Eq. (5)

$$Accuracy = \frac{TP}{TP + TN + FP + FN} \tag{5}$$

   where:
   TP (True Positive): Correctly predicted irrigation cases
   TN (True Negative): Correctly predicted non-irrigation cases
   FP (False Positive): Incorrectly predicted irrigation cases
   FN (False Negative): Incorrectly predicted non-irrigation cases
2. Precision - Measures how many predicted irrigation cases were actually correct using Eq. (6):

$$Precision = \frac{TP}{TP + FP} \tag{6}$$

   A higher precision indicates fewer false alarms, reducing unnecessary irrigation.
3. Recall (Sensitivity) - Measures how many actual irrigation cases were correctly identified using Eq. (7):

$$Recall = \frac{TP}{TP + FN} \tag{7}$$

   A higher recall ensures water-stressed crops are not missed.
4. F1-Score - a harmonic mean of Precision and Recall, balancing both metrics using (8):

$$F1 = 2 * \frac{Precision * Recall}{Precision + Recall} \tag{8}$$

We evaluated the performance of the model using accuracy. Accuracy reflected overall prediction correctness. Precision described the percentage of correct irrigation predictions without false alarms. Recall detailed the presence of irrigation when needed. The F1-score ensured that the model generated reliable predictions in real farm conditions.

4 Results and Discussions

4.1 Model Performance and Evaluation

The advisory system using K-Nearest Neighbors (KNN) classifier was found to perform with an accuracy of 95% and was tested over various crops and environments. The validation of the system was performed using standard metrics, including Precision, Recall, F1-Score, and Accuracy, to confirm its reasonable operation. The classification report is summarized in Table 3.

Table 3. Classification Report

Class (irrigation)	Precision	Recall	F1-Score	Support
0(Not Needed)	0.95	0.97	0.96	61
1(Needed)	0.95	0.93	0.94	40
Accuracy			0.95	101
Macro Avg	0.95	0.95	0.95	101
Weighted Avg	0.95	0.95	0.95	101

The precision and recall of the model are balanced and thus indicates that there is a low false prediction rate. It is an important metric that helps to determine the performance of the model that can be useful in agricultural systems. The constant F1-Scores for Classes indicates its reliability in real-world use. This supports that the model is a useful, low-risk decision support mechanism for smart irrigation.

4.2 Confusion Matrix and Error Analysis

The model achieved an accuracy of 95%, supported by the following confusion matrix values: TP = 37, TN = 59, FP = 2, FN = 3. Figure 6 shows high classification accuracy with only 5 misclassifications out of 101 irrigation predictions.

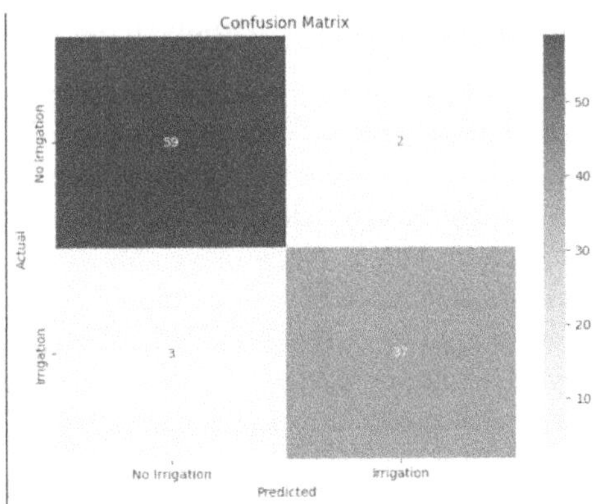

Fig. 6. The confusion matrix

Most errors occurred near class boundaries. The three false negatives have likely occurred due to borderline moisture or humidity levels, causing slight underestimation. This is reasonable due to the recall being 92.5%. Due to slight variations in the environment, the irrigation cues may have been misread. In general, both the low false positive rate and false negative rate confirm the reliability of the model in the field.

4.3 Bias-Variance Trade-Offs and the Optimal k

K = 3 is the best option since it strikes a balance between bias and variance. There is a risk of large variance (sensitivity to noise) when k is small, but the model has low bias (it can reflect the local complexity of the decision boundary). The selected k = 3 successfully exploited the localised structure of the data without adding detrimental noise, demonstrating that the sensor readings provide highly localised, dependable class differences, especially considering the exceptionally high performance attained on the unseen test set. Another common procedure to avoid ties during the majority vote process is to select an odd integer for k.

4.4 Comparison with Existing Models

The current study proposes a KNN-based advisory system for irrigation which is compared with SVM, Random Forest and XGBoost. KNN was accurate and flexible, requiring little computational resources and thus, suitable for use in resource-poor agricultural environments. In contrast to the rules imposed by irrigation systems, KNN learned to respond to real-time sensors. Even though ANN and LSTM models provide greater accuracy we need a larger dataset that requires more computational power and not feasible for smaller-scale farming. Random forest ensemble models also generalize well, but KNN performed better in our experiments. SVMs performed poorly in heterogeneous feature spaces, although widely used. The optimized KNN model was a lightweight and tough competitor for real-time irrigation decisions.

4.5 Implication for Real-World Smart Irrigation Deployment

Smart irrigation usage in routine doings is impacted by operational performance. This is particularly true of ideal precision score (1.0). Water conservation and environmental sustainability are aligned 1.0 so that no water is wasted due to false alarms. The K-Nearest Neighbors method generally requires an indexed training phase, which is computationally heavy. However, prediction with K-Nearest Neighbors is lighter on computation requirements. Due to its high-accuracy and computational efficiency, the model can be easily integrated with edge computing or low-power microcontrollers. These are usually used in the contemporary smart farms' design of distributed sensor networks. By using the edge computing it becomes possible to make decisions for water control quickly locally and without depending on cloud processing.

5 Conclusion and Future Scope

This paper proposed a lightweight smart irrigation system based on ML which integrated Arduino sensor networks with KNN which optimized water usage and improved crop yield. With real-time inputs such as soil moisture, temperature, and humidity, scheduling irrigation accurately is possible. The performance of KNN improved with the use of hyperparameter tuning and balancing through SMOTE. Our model achieved 95% accuracy with high precision. Furthermore, we were able to complete our KNN model easily. It is a suitable candidate due to its low-cost, interpretable design. The system allows for large-scale and efficient precision agriculture. Next upgrades will include weather API integrations and offering a variety of crop and soil options to suit various Agri-climatic zones.

References

1. Singh, G., Sharma, P., Kumar, S.: Optimizing furrow irrigation parameters for sunflower under semi-arid Indian conditions. Agric. Water Manage. **307** (2025)
2. Mali, Y., Rathod, V.U., Kulkarni, M.M., et al.: A comparative analysis of machine learning models for soil health prediction and crop selection. Int. J. Intell. Syst. Appl. Eng. **11**(10s), 811–828 (2023)
3. Kondaveti, R., Reddy, A., Palabtla, S.: Smart irrigation system using machine learning and IoT. In: Proceedings of ViTECoN 2019, pp. 1–11 (2019)
4. Lakhiar, M., Yan, H., Zhang, C., et al.: A review of precision irrigation water-saving technology under changing climate. Agriculture **14**(7), 1141 (2024)
5. Murugaa, S., Atithya, J., Ibrahim, M.: Precision agriculture through smart irrigation using IoT and hybrid machine learning. Int. Res. J. Adv. Eng. Manage. **3**(6) (2025)
6. Ramesh, M., Verma, A., Gupta, A.: Smart agriculture: IoT and machine learning for crop monitoring and precision farming. Int. J. Intell. Syst. Appl. Eng. (2024)
7. Akinpelu, A., Kumar, R., Rani, F.: A systematic literature review on IoT and ML-based smart irrigation systems (2017–2024). Int. J. Clean Energy Syst. Eng.
8. IOT & machine learning based smart soil irrigation farming systems. Int. J. Eng. Res. Sci. Technol. **21**(2), 542–550 (2025)
9. Pavithra, P.M., Duraisamy, S., Shankar, R.: Hydrosense: pioneering IoT for precision drip irrigation and sustainable water management. Int. J. Res. Sci. Innov. (2025)
10. Sharma, R.K., et al.: Agent-based modeling for precision agriculture: a hybrid approach. arXiv preprint, arXiv:2502.18298 (2025)
11. Lakhiar, I.A., Yan, H., He, B., Bao, R.: Precision irrigation and water use efficiency under climate change scenarios. Agriculture **14**(7) (2024)
12. Kim, C., Park, D., Lee, G., Choi, J., Lee, H., Hahn, J.: A integrated genome database for agricultural crops and web service. In: 2008 Third International Conference on Convergence and Hybrid Information Technology, Busan, Korea (South), pp. 389–391 (2008). https://doi.org/10.1109/ICCIT.2008.46
13. Kumar, R., Gupta, M., Singh, U.: Precision agriculture crop recommendation system using KNN algorithm. In: 2023 International Conference on IoT, Communication and Automation Technology (ICICAT), Gorakhpur, India, pp. 1–6 (2023). https://doi.org/10.1109/ICICAT57735.2023.10263667
14. Alex, B., Jignasa, G., Madhubabu, K., Gopi, A.: AI-driven smart irrigation: enhancing agricultural water efficiency through intelligent valve regulation in piped and micro irrigation networks. In: 2024 First International Conference on Pioneering Developments in Computer Science & Digital Technologies (IC2SDT), Delhi, India, pp. 76–81 (2024). https://doi.org/10.1109/IC2SDT62152.2024.10696274

An IoT-Based Fleet Management and Vehicle Tracking System with SVM Based Risk Prediction

Chaitanya Sawant$^{(\boxtimes)}$ and Ketki Deshmukh

Mukesh Patel School of Technology Management and Engineering, NMIMS, Mumbai, India
`chaitanyasawant.academic@gmail.com`, `ketki.deshmukh@nmims.edu`

Abstract. The design and implementation of a real-time Fleet Management and Vehicle Tracking System including hardware and software components for improved driver and vehicle monitoring is presented in this work. At the vehicle end, a Raspberry Pi fitted with an accelerometer, gyroscope, and GPS collects motion and location data and forwards it via a REST API to a web application. Built using Flask and SQLite with SQLAlchemy, the online platform provides modules including a dashboard, realtime car tracking via Leaflet.js, trip histories with route maps, and driver and vehicle performance reports. Harsh driving events such as acceleration, braking and cornering are detected by sensor thresholds and recorded in a SQLite database, enabling both live monitoring and retrospective analysis. A safety score that balances distance travelled against event frequency is computed for each vehicle and driver. These metrics are input to an SVM risk-prediction model, which groups drivers and vehicles into risk levels to guide preventive maintenance and safety actions. The platform is designed to scale with fleet size and to provide live updates during operation.

Keywords: Internet of Things (IoT) · Vehicle tracking · Driving behavior analysis · Support Vector Machine (SVM) classification · Fleet operations · Safety scoring

1 Introduction

Fleet management has become a critical area of development as road-safety concerns, demand for live operational visibility, and the need for efficient logistics continue to grow [1, 2]. Many conventional GPS/GSM trackers provide basic location and status updates but do not scale well to large operations, nor do they offer the behavioral analytics required to understand how vehicles are actually being driven.

Small embedded platforms such as the Raspberry Pi, when paired with an accelerometer, gyroscope and GPS, make it practical to capture motion data at high frequency and detect events such as harsh acceleration, hard braking and sharp cornering. Presenting those findings on a web dashboard lets fleet operators view live vehicle positions, examine trip traces and inspect event summaries so they can take timely corrective action.

F. Ortiz-Rodríguez et al. (Eds.): IBCD 2025, CCIS 2845, pp. 182–194, 2026.
https://doi.org/10.1007/978-3-032-20907-8_16

The system described here couples a vehicle-side sensing layer with a server stack built on Python (Flask), SQLite (SQLAlchemy) and JavaScript. Sensor readings are preprocessed on the Pi and transmitted via a REST API; the backend stores trips and event logs, computes a safety score that balances distance and event frequency, and implements an SVM classifier that assigns drivers and vehicles to risk tiers. Threshold-based event detection and the resulting metrics support both immediate monitoring and historical analysis.

Our aim is a modular, extensible platform that fills gaps left by simpler trackers by adding behavioral analytics and predictive risk assessment. The design targets practical deployment in logistics, public transit and insurance use cases and is organized to allow further extension toward machine-learning driven fleet optimization.

2 Literature Review

Advances in embedded systems, the Internet of Things and machine learning have improved vehicle monitoring and driver behavior analysis. For example, Shinde et al. implemented a Raspberry Pi–based real-time tracking system using a SIM900A modem for remote vehicle monitoring [1]; however, their implementation did not include modules for behavior evaluation or predictive analytics. Priyanka et al. focused on rash braking detection with GPS-accelerometer data plotted on Google Maps but ignored acceleration or cornering [2].Shinde and Mane introduced a GPS/GSM model storing data in MySQL, yet it lacked predictive analytics for large fleets [3].

Shinde and Mane introduced a GPS/GSM model storing data in MySQL, yet it lacked predictive analytics for large fleets [4], while another SIM908-based system tracked route deviations but lacked ML support [5]. Punith et al. built a diagnostics dashboard using ESP32 and Arduino IoT Cloud integrating sensors like brake fluid, engine temperature, and tire pressure, but without behavioral classification [7].

Machine learning-based methods are gaining focus. One approach used SVM with RBF kernel on acceleration, braking, and cornering data for driver risk classification, using safety score as auxiliary input [6]. Sreekumar et al. created a driver rating system using OBD-II data where Random Forest achieved 91% accuracy, while SVM reached 78% [8]. Dixit et al. analyzed simulator data and found Random Forest best at 83% [9].

Ziakopoulos analysed harsh braking and harsh acceleration using high-resolution smartphone telematics combined with traffic and road-geometry data, and applied imbalanced-learning with explainable tree ensembles to identify key contributing factors [10]. Yu and Abdel-Aty developed SVM models for real-time crash-risk evaluation and found an RBF-kernel SVM to perform better than conventional approaches [11]. Together these works support our focus on accurate HA/HB/HC detection from on-board sensors and the use of an SVM classifier in the fleet monitoring system.

Boylan et al. reviewed the telematics literature and report that machine learning is the predominant analytic approach in telematics studies and that speeding, braking and distance are the most commonly used variables. The review also highlights that many studies are insurance-focused and that the behavioral effects of telematics feedback and the influence of driver and trip heterogeneity remain under-explored. [12].

These works show how risk scoring, real-time prediction, and in-vehicle analytics are evolving. The present system builds upon these by integrating hardware-driven telemetry with real-time analytics and SVM-based classification into a unified fleet monitoring solution.

3   Methodology

The suggested Fleet Management and Tracking System combines a software-based analytics platform with hardware-based data collection. It integrates a Flask web application and a Raspberry Pi-based sensing system to deliver predictive risk analysis, driving behavior monitoring, and real-time vehicle tracking.

3.1   Hardware Layer: Raspberry Pi Data Acquisition

The sensing stack shown in Fig. 1, is built around a Raspberry Pi that reads a GPS receiver plus an accelerometer and gyroscope. GPS fixes provide time, latitude, longitude and speed; the inertial sensors capture vehicle motion.

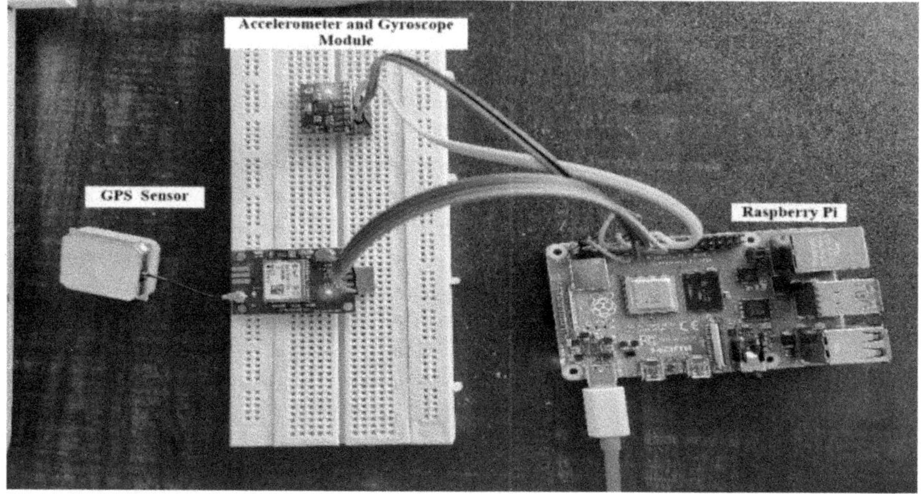

Fig. 1. Physical hardware setup showing Raspberry Pi and interfaced sensors.

We detect three event types, harsh acceleration (HA), hard braking (HB) and harsh cornering (HC) by applying threshold tests to the sensor streams. Values were selected after iterative, real-world testing: HA at $+1.5$ m/s^2, HB at -1.5 m/s^2, and HC at $100°$/s on the gyroscope's Z-axis.

These values were consistent in flagging true aggressive events while keeping false positives low during normal operation. Processed sensor data is sent regularly to the web server via HTTP POST requests to a REST API. The Pi also uses local buffering and precise timestamps to reduce data loss and to preserve event order when network interruptions occur.

3.2   Software Layer: Web Application and Data Visualization

Built with Flask on the backend, the application uses SQLite (accessed via SQLAlchemy) for persistent storage, while the frontend is built with HTML, Bootstrap CSS, JavaScript and Jinja2 templates. The dashboard gives operators a concise view of the overall safety score, counts of HA/HB/HC events, and simple trend charts for distance and per-vehicle scores.

Live tracking shows each vehicle's most recent GPS fix on a Leaflet map and updates automatically from the Raspberry Pi. Trip cards list vehicle number, driver, origin–destination and distance and link to a detailed trip view that includes raw coordinate traces, a GeoPy-translated route and per-trip measurements.

Report pages gather monthly totals for distance, event counts and safety ratings by driver and vehicle. An SVM-based risk module uses historical HA/HB/HC counts and computed safety scores to place drivers and vehicles into risk tiers; the results are shown in a compact table so operators can prioritize follow-up.

3.3   Score Calculation and Event Classification

The system penalizes dangerous driving occurrences while rewarding distance travelled using a unique logic for generating the driving safety score, as shown in Fig. 2. Where, HA represents Harsh Acceleration, HB represents Harsh Braking, HC represents Harsh Cornering.

Weights for each Harsh event was assigned based on the severity of each Harsh Driving Behaviour. A minor distance bonus was also given for longer distances and was capped up to the value 7, to prevent misuse and false positives. The formula for the Driving Score was inspired by real-world scoring logic used in fleet telematics, this formula ensures that the final Driving Score is capped between 0 to 100, while providing classification between safe and risky drivers of the fleet.

```python
def calculate_score(distance, ha, hb, hc):
    weight_ha = 2.0
    weight_hb = 1.5
    weight_hc = 1.2
    harsh_penalty = (ha * weight_ha) + (hb * weight_hb) + (hc * weight_hc)
    distance_bonus = min(distance / 20, 7)  # Max 7 bonus
    score = 100 - harsh_penalty + distance_bonus
    return max(0, min(100, int(score)))
```

Fig. 2. Custom score calculation logic used to quantify driver behavior.

3.4   Database Design

The SQLite database of the system includes several focused tables to capture fleet activity. The Drivers table stores driver names and IDs. The Vehicles table tracks monthly totals for distance, HA, HB, HC and computed safety score, and links each vehicle to its assigned driver, as shown in Fig. 3. The Trips table records trip level details such as distance, start and end times, raw GPS coordinates and a short event summary. Event_logs store every HA, HB and HC event with the associated GPS coordinates and a precise timestamp. The Fleet_summary table keeps monthly totals for distance and for counts of harsh events across the fleet.

We index commonly used fields such as timestamp and vehicle id so routine lookups run faster. Each trip uses foreign keys to reference its vehicle and driver, keeping the tables consistent. Full event rows are retained in the event logs, while summarized entries are stored in the fleet summary to make dashboard queries quick. In a day, periodically, scheduled tasks aggregate daily and monthly totals, and older raw traces are moved to long term storage under the retention policy. Writes are wrapped in simple transactions with a brief retry policy to reduce the chance of partial records when the network is flaky. These choices make the database simple to query and reliable for live monitoring, historical reporting and dashboard use.

3.5 Support Vector Machine (SVM)

Support Vector Machine (SVM) is widely applied for classification and regression tasks. SVM finds a hyperplane that separates data classes by mapping points into a high-dimensional space, maximizing the margin for the best separation and precision.

Since the data in this project is highly non-linear, the Radial Basis Function (RBF) kernel is used:

$$K(x, x') = \exp(-\gamma \|x - x'\|^2) \tag{1}$$

Support Vector Machine (SVM) models separate classes by finding an optimal decision boundary in a transformed feature space. We used the RBF kernel, the formula for the RBF kernel is shown in Eq. 1, and set γ (gamma) to "scale"; in practice this means each sample's influence is balanced against the dataset size and feature spread, a larger γ produces tighter, more local decision boundaries, while a smaller γ yields smoother boundaries. The classifier was fed severe-event counts (HA, HB, HC) together with the computed safety score. Severe events carry greater weight for safety classification, and the safety score adds broader context about distance- and event-based performance, so the two kinds of inputs complement each other for overall risk assessment.

The training dataset contained 200 vehicle-month records summarizing monthly harsh events and safety scores. Sensor readings were collected at one-second intervals while vehicles were in motion, using the thresholds described earlier. We evaluated the model using stratified 5-fold cross-validation; the resulting confusion matrix is shown in Fig. 4 and indicates good differentiation between risk tiers on this dataset.

File   Edit   View   Tools   Help

New Database   Open Database   Write Changes   Revert Changes   Undo   Open Proje

Database Structure   Browse Data   Edit Pragmas   Execute SQL

Table: vehicles   » Filter in any column

	distance_weekly	total_distance_monthly	total_ha	total_hb	total_hc	monthly_safety_score	drive
	Filter		Filter	Filter	Filter	Filter	Filter
1	37	150	5	6	4	83	
2	17	70	17	15	13	31	
3	52	210	2	1	1	100	
4	25	100	11	10	9	57	
5	35	140	7	5	5	79	
6	22	90	13	11	10	50	
7	42	170	4	4	3	89	
8	30	120	10	9	7	64	
9	47	190	3	2	2	95	
10	32	130	8	7	6	72	
11	20	80	15	13	11	41	

Fig. 3. Vehicles Table from the SQLite Database.

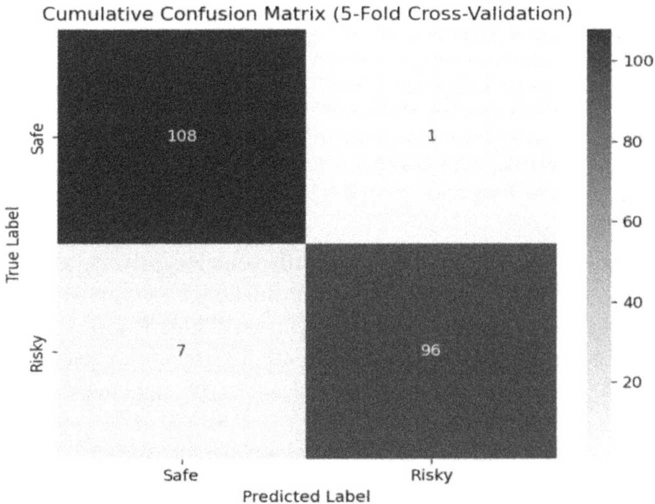

Fig. 4. Confusion matrix showing SVM classification results from stratified five fold cross validation.

4   System Architecture

The Fleet Management and Tracking System is organized in layers that separate sensing, server side processing and visualization. This layout keeps each component focused on a clear set of responsibilities: capturing and preprocessing sensor data at the vehicle, reliably storing and analyzing that data on the server, and presenting actionable information to operators through a web interface. A block diagram with the major components is shown in Fig. 5.

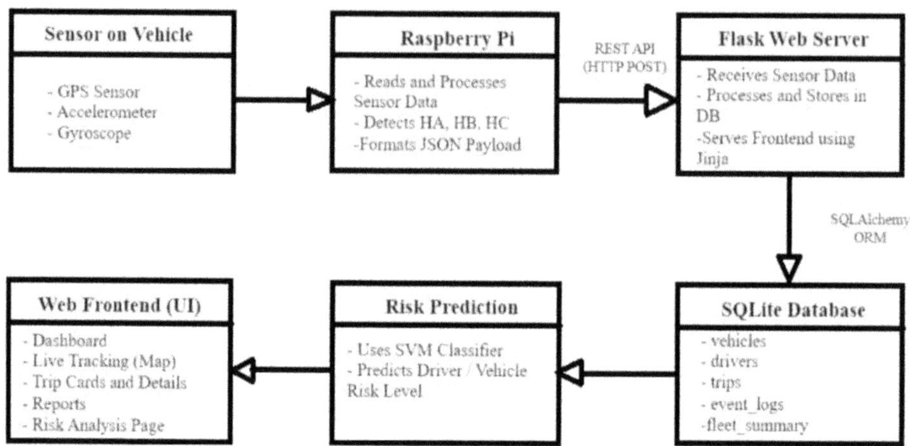

Fig. 5. The block diagram of our proposed fleet management and tracking system's architecture.

At the bottom, the sensing and transmission layer runs on a Raspberry Pi connected to an accelerometer, gyroscope and GPS. The Pi reads raw sensor streams, applies the threshold logic described earlier to detect events (HA, HB, HC), and packages processed records as JSON. These records are pushed to the backend over HTTP POST calls to a REST API; local buffering and precise timestamps are used to protect against packet loss and to preserve event ordering during intermittent connectivity.

On the server the processing layer is implemented using Flask with SQLAlchemy to access a SQLite database. The schema records vehicles, drivers, trips, event logs and fleet summaries in normalized tables. The incoming REST calls are validated, saved, and then later joined to build complete trip records. A machine learning module trains and runs an SVM classifier on the collected event counts and computed safety scores. The classifier groups together the drivers and vehicles into risk tiers that feed the operational reports.

The visualization and analytics layer provides the interface for fleet manager. Jinja2 templates render responsive pages styled with Bootstrap, Leaflet.js displays live vehicle positions and trip paths, and GeoPy supports address resolution. The dashboard aggregates safety scores and event counts; trip cards link to full trip traces; and report pages summarize monthly distance, events and ratings. A compact risk prediction view surfaces SVM results so managers can prioritize follow up work.

This layered approach keeps the implementation modular: layers communicate through well-defined APIs and the database, which makes it easier to scale to more vehicles, add new sensor inputs, or swap in more advanced analytics. It also helps keep data integrity every event and trip is timestamped and retained for audit and analysis and provides a straightforward path to extend the platform toward cloud services, mobile apps or additional telematics integrations.

5 Implementation

Beginning with sensor interfacing and continuing through full stack integration and deployment, the Fleet Management and Tracking System was developed in stages. Each subsystem, including data collection, backend processing, frontend rendering and machine learning, was designed to work together to provide smooth live monitoring and timely operator feedback.

The initial hardware ran on a Raspberry Pi 4 connected to a gyroscope, an accelerometer and a GPS module. Small Python programs ran on the Pi to read the sensor streams and to flag important driving events such as cornering, braking and heavy acceleration. The Pi packaged the processed readings as JSON and uploaded them to the cloud at regular intervals using HTTP post calls.

On the server side those uploads are received by endpoints implemented with Flask. The data received is stored in SQLite and accessed through SQLAlchemy. The database schema keeps trips, events, drivers and vehicles in separate tables so related records can be joined easily and can be used to be represented for different functions and visualizations. The layout also makes it easy to add vehicles and to cope with growing data volumes.

The frontend was built with HTML, Bootstrap CSS, Jinja2 templates and JavaScript. Interactive maps for live tracking and trip detail views are rendered with the Leaflet JavaScript library and are shown in Fig. 6. GeoPy translated raw coordinates for trip origins, destinations and harsh event locations into readable addresses.

Fig. 6. Live tracking module's map rendered with the Leaflet JavaScript library showing vehicle's live location.

The dashboard shows overall metrics with simple cards and charts as in Fig. 7. Paginated tables provide trip level statistics and monthly reports, shown in Fig. 8 and Fig. 9. Safety scores for trips and vehicles are computed by a bespoke scoring method and fed to an SVM model for risk prediction. To keep the implementation simple the classifier is trained on historical records stored in the database and runs inside the same Flask application, as illustrated in Fig. 10.

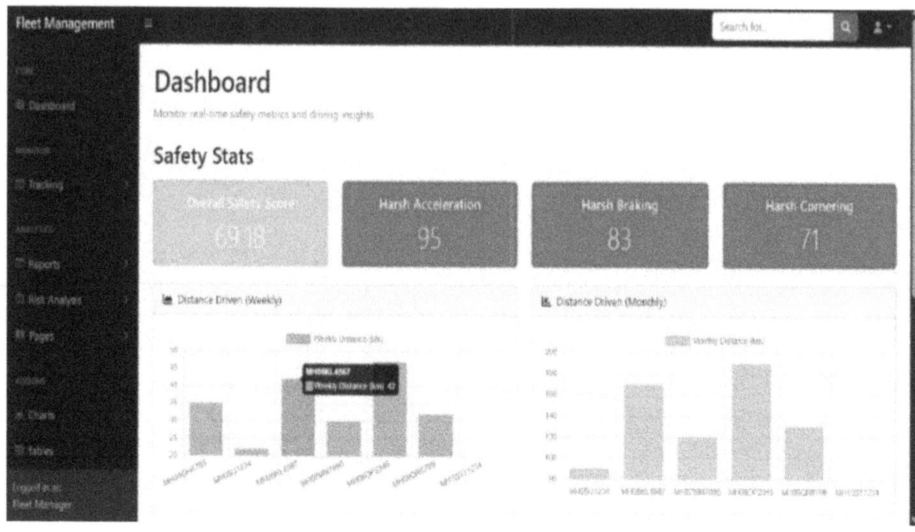

Fig. 7. Dashboard showing safety metrics and driving analytics for each vehicle along with a safety score and important KPIs of the fleet's safety.

Simulated sensor data were used iteratively to test and validate the system by reproducing common driving patterns. Successful integration of all components confirmed the system is suitable for real world fleet deployments. Table 1 compares the proposed system with related work and highlights the unique combination of live analytics, driver risk monitoring and machine learning based risk prediction.

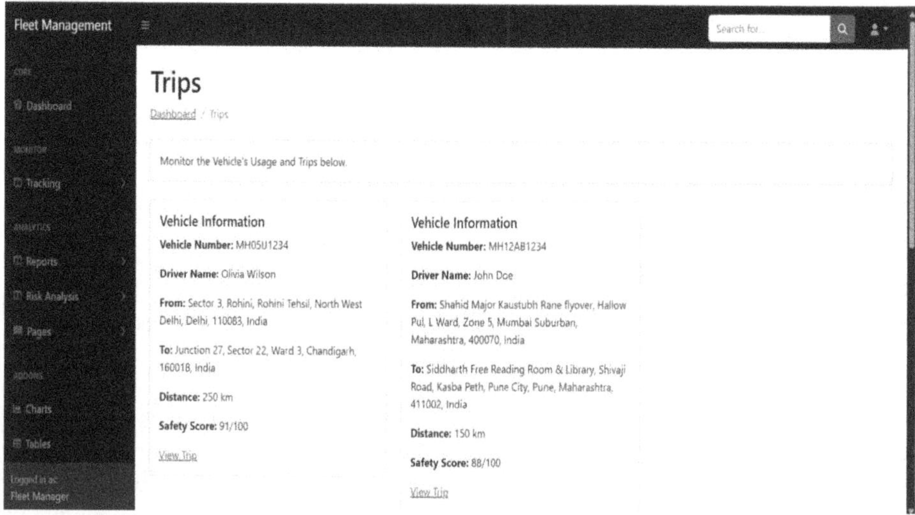

Fig. 8. Trip summaries displayed as cards with a view more link to redirect it to the detailed trip view module.

6 Applications

The Fleet Management and Tracking System can be applied across transportation, logistics, public safety and smart city projects. Its modular design and live data capabilities make it useful wherever ongoing monitoring, driver evaluation and predictive insight are important.

In logistics and supply chain operations the platform lets managers track vehicles in real time, optimize routes, and review driver performance. That visibility helps shorten delivery times, lower fuel consumption and reduce operating costs by highlighting inefficient routes or risky driving behaviours. Monthly summaries together with detailed trip records assist performance reviews and operational planning across sectors.

Table 1. Comparison of existing systems from works referred.

Reference	Features	ML Model	Real-time Capable
Shinde et al. (2015) [1]	GPS-based school bus tracking	None	Yes
Priyanka et al. (2021) [2]	Rash braking detection on Google Maps	None	Yes
Soman et al. (2023) [4]	Drowsiness detection (MediaPipe)	None	Yes
Punith et al. (2022) [7]	Cloud diagnostics with ESP32 sensors	None	Yes
Proposed System	HA, HB, HC, trip logging, live map, risk scoring	**SVM (RBF Kernel)**	**Yes**

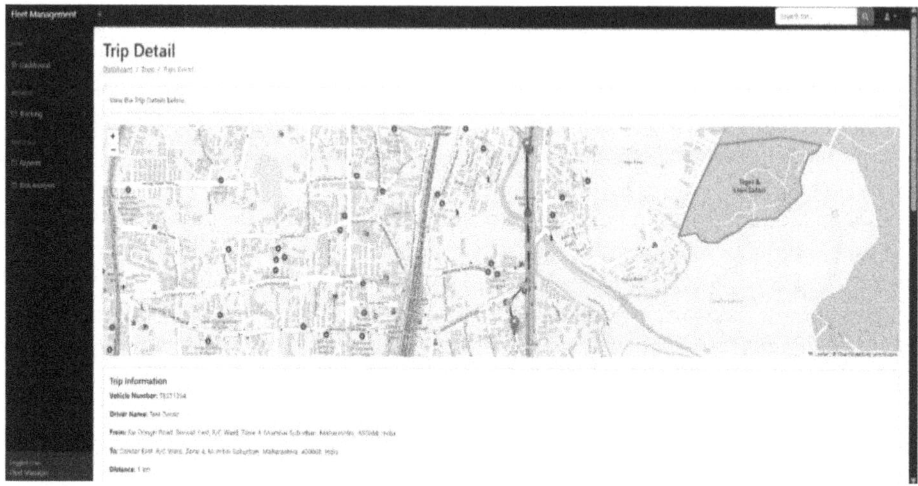

Fig. 9. Detailed trip view showing the route map and recorded harsh events with the relevant KPIs and pins on the map for the same.

Corporate fleet teams can use the system to monitor staff driving patterns, enforce safety policies and generate regular performance reports. For public transit operators the same tools support route compliance checks, the recording of severe events for safety audits, and the documentation needed for regulatory reporting. In emergency response settings, live location and event feeds help dispatchers steer ambulances, fire units and police to the right place more quickly and coordinate multiple responders during an incident.

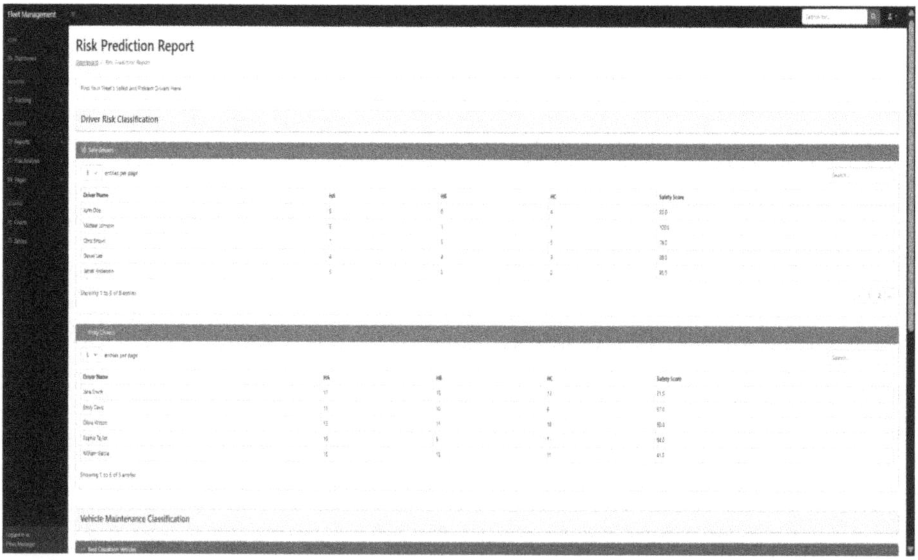

Fig. 10. SVM based risk classification results using driving event metrics.

The platform also fits insurance workflows. By supplying objective driving metrics and a computed safety score, the system can feed usage-based insurance schemes so insurers can tailor premiums to measured behavior. That same dataset supports preventive maintenance by flagging vehicles with repeated harsh events before failures occur.

Finally, the system provides data useful to smart city programs. Aggregated mobility and safety information can inform infrastructure planning, targeted safety campaigns and traffic management. The solution is therefore suitable for taxi operators, school transport providers who need extra safety oversight, corporate fleets aiming to protect staff, and insurers looking to base pricing on empirical driving records.

7 Conclusion

We present an IoT enabled fleet management and vehicle tracking platform that brings sensing, data transport, storage and analysis into a single web application. A Raspberry Pi module with accelerometer, gyroscope and GPS captures motion and location data. The Pi preprocesses events and forwards JSON records to a Flask backend over standard HTTP calls. The backend stores trips, events and driver records in SQLite via SQLAlchemy, drives live dashboards and maps, computes safety scores that account for distance and event frequency, and uses an SVM based classifier to assign risk levels to drivers and vehicles. Together these elements allow operators to monitor fleets, inspect trip traces and priorities maintenance and training based on measured behavior.

Several clear directions can extend the platform. Moving data streaming to a cloud service and replacing local SQLite with a distributed database such as Postgres will improve scalability and resilience for large fleets. Adding mobile access and push notifications will increase operational responsiveness. The next major step would be enhancing the analytics pipeline with deep learning models and larger labelled datasets may enable anomaly or outlier detection, finer and more accurate driver profiling and predictive maintenance warnings. Adding a camera module and on device video processing would open possibilities for Advance Driver Assistance Systems (ADAS) with features such as proactive crash detection and driver monitoring, with appropriate attention to privacy.

Security and privacy must be central to any production deployment. Enforcing HTTPS, token-based authentication, role-based access control and careful data retention policies will protect both users and organizations. Integration with insurers, emergency services and municipal transportation networks is also possible, for usage-based insurance, faster incident response and smarter mobility planning.

Overall, the platform offers a practical, data driven route to improve operational safety, reduce costs and support informed decision making in transport and logistics. The modular design leaves a clear path for scaling, better and more accurate analytics and deeper integration with enterprise and city level systems.

References

1. Shinde, P.A., Mane, Y.B., Tarange, P.H.: Real-time vehicle monitoring and tracking system based on embedded Linux board and android application. In: 2015 International Conference on Circuit, Power and Computing Technologies (ICCPCT), pp. 1–6 (2015). https://doi.org/10.1109/ICCPCT.2015.7159373

2. Priyanka, E.B., et al.: IoT based rash braking data analysis and plotting in Google Maps using Raspberry Pi. In: 2021 International Conference on Data Analytics for Business and Industry (ICDABI), pp. 320–326 (2021). https://doi.org/10.1109/ICDABI53623.2021.9655780

3. Shinde, P.A., Mane, Y.B.: Advanced vehicle monitoring and tracking system based on Raspberry Pi. Int. J. Eng. Manage. Res. **11**(11), 1–5 (2021)

4. Soman, S.P., Kumar, G.S., A.K., M.: Internet-of-Things-assisted artificial intelligence-enabled drowsiness detection framework. IEEE Sens. Lett. **7**(7), 1–4 (2023). https://doi.org/10.1109/LSENS.2023.3289143

5. Chinonso, E.A., Anayo, O.H., Anikwe, C.V.: Vehicle monitoring system based on IoT, using 4G/LTE. Int. J. Eng. Manage. Res. **11**(4), 6–14 (2021)

6. Desai, S., Suthar, R., Yadav, V., Ankar, V., Gupta, V.: Smart bus fleet management system using IoT. In: 2022 Fourth International Conference on Emerging Research in Electronics, Computer Science and Technology (ICERECT), pp. 1–6 (2022). https://doi.org/10.1109/ICERECT56837.2022.10059646

7. Punith, M.S., Nithya, M., Deepa, K.: IoT enabled smart fleet management. In: 2022 IEEE 4th International Conference on Cybernetics, Cognition and Machine Learning Applications (ICCCMLA), pp. 256–260 (2022). https://doi.org/10.1109/ICCCMLA56841.2022.9989097

8. Sreekumar, S., Pawar, P.M., Muthalagu, R., Panthakkan, A., Amin, S.A.: A driver rating system based on driving pattern. In: 2024 7th International Conference on Signal Processing and Information Security (ICSPIS), Dubai, United Arab Emirates, pp. 1–6. IEEE (2024). https://doi.org/10.1109/ICSPIS63676.2024.10812587

9. Dixit, S., Goel, S., Jaiswal, S., Goyal, P.K.: Driver behaviour analysis to improve road safety: a comprehensive study. In: 2024 International Conference on Computing, Sciences and Communications (ICCSC), pp. 1–5. IEEE, Ghaziabad, India (2024). https://doi.org/10.1109/ICCSC62048.2024.10830329

10. Yu, R., Abdel-Aty, M.: Utilizing support vector machine in real-time crash risk evaluation. Accident Anal. Prev. **51**, 252–259 (2013). https://doi.org/10.1016/j.aap.2012.11.027

11. Ziakopoulos, A.: Analysis of harsh braking and harsh acceleration occurrence via explainable imbalanced machine learning using high-resolution smartphone telematics and traffic data. Accident Anal. Prev. **207**, 107743 (2024). https://doi.org/10.1016/j.aap.2024.107743

12. Boylan, J., Meyer, D., Chen, W.S.: A systematic review of the use of in-vehicle telematics in monitoring driving behaviours. Accident Anal. Prev. **199**, 107519 (2024). https://doi.org/10.1016/j.aap.2024.107519

Detecting Mental Illness Using Face Recognition Techniques

Anamika Wasnik$^{(\boxtimes)}$ and Sunil Pathak

Department of Computer Science and Engineering, Amity University, Jaipur, Rajasthan, India
`wasnikanamika121@gmail.com, spathak@jpr.amity.edu`

Abstract. Emotional recognition ability to accurately identify the emotions in various sources and domain, including physical and physiological signals. Due to its research, this application is effective in World health organization including in studying the impact of expression and mental illness signals on galvanic skin responses. Also, this study explores the use of various models to stimulate emotions and analyses the principle of current automated recognition system. Following through this analysis and discussion we have selected the 45-journal article based on PRISMA database access on online dataset. On emotion recognition, in a particular research domain there has been worked only 1100 facial images in international dataset and limited work on national level dataset for face recognition. Additionally, these are the main challenges have identified in existing literature that need to be addressed in further research.

Keywords: Facial images dataset · Emotion recognition · Eye tracking · Machine learning · Deep learning

1 Introduction

Automated facial expression identification is an important research in computer domain, particularly within the field of social signal processing and affective computing. The main primary task in this field is to accurately recognize and classify various facial expressions into their respective mental illness emotion categories. The necessity of mental illness facial recognition has the potential to enhance the mental health care and support systems. Mental disabilities and mood swings encompass a wide range of conditions that affect mood, thinking, and behavior pattern [1]. Some common types of mental illness include:

- Anxiety Disorders
- Mood Disorders
- Depression
- Schizophrenia
- Autism Spectrum Disorder
- Obsessive Compulsive Disorder (OCD)

F. Ortiz-Rodríguez et al. (Eds.): IBCD 2025, CCIS 2845, pp. 195–206, 2026.
https://doi.org/10.1007/978-3-032-20907-8_17

Facial recognition technology can analyses these indicators to assist clinicians in diagnosing mental illnesses, providing an additional assessment tool. However, it is important to note that facial recognition should support, not replace, comprehensive evaluations by trained mental health professionals [2]. When integrated with conventional methods, this technology can significantly enhance the timeliness and accuracy of mental health assessments. Researchers have posited that examining emotional variations is crucial for a deeper understanding of conditions such as attention deficit hyperactivity disorder, panic disorder, and autism spectrum disorders. Moreover, analyzing human emotions is crucial in the fields of brain computing interfaces. Where system is able to develop human behavior for various application [3].

2 Literature Survey

Due to the widespread prevalence of depression globally, there is a requirement for an effective and robust depression model. The authors propose the MFM-Att model which integrates audio-visual text data related to depressed using a multimodal fusion approach model by a multi-level attention mechanism. The author mentioned of two common methods predominantly in literature survey for facial expression recognition (FER) and MFA model on a DAICWOZ database. Where it surpasses existing models in terms of root mean square error (RMSE) [4]. This author provides a quickly identify a facial expression and perform a comparative study analysis for the feature extraction techniques on Japanese female facial expression JAFFE dataset. One noted limitation is that facial expression has a major drawback human can control their expressions to extend to so recognition result may satisfy [5].

To extract and delineate the mouth area, the Viola-Jones technique and image cropping are employed. Researchers compare proposed segmentation techniques to identify the most suitable method for segmenting the oral region. This region is then extracted using contrast enhancement and image segmentation techniques. To the rank facial expressions based on white pixel values. However, traditional image segmentation techniques are prone to fragmentation and high noise sensitivity [6]. To address these challenges, De expression residue learning is proposed to recognize components using a GAN-trained generative model, which generates neutral face images from input images. The residue in the model's intermediate layers, containing the expressive information, is analysed [7]. Pertaining utilized BU4DEF and BP4D database and this method was using different are used we are discussed in Table 1: The survey of facial recognition using machine learning, highlighting the challenge of detecting emotion with different model. EMM amplifies changes in amplitude and phase to transform the facial expression image [8].

National and international skin disease databases have been developed by various research centres. These datasets are available online on the respective institute websites and come in different resolutions, such as 640×480, 640×490, and 256×256 pixels. To acquire close-up images, the target face images are localized and cantered in the camera's view, ensuring the size does not exceed 50% of the photographic field. Ethical consent for the database has been obtained, and the image dataset is anonymized [13].

Table 1. Face database for mental illness

Institute/Org	Database	Resolution	Year	Citation
CK+,OULU,CASIA,MMI,BU3DE,BP4D	Mouth Area, 20	-	2019	[9]
CK+, Oulu-CASIA, MMI, BU3DFE, and BP4D+	Video-based Code action.486, 100	Mental wellbeing	Age-18–70	[10]
CK+, iBug-300W,	593,7000, 300,	Anxiety	-	[11]
CK	486,96,593 and 123 different poses dataset of facial using videos	Depression, anxiety	18 to 30 years of age	[12]

CK+: The CK+ dataset primarily focuses on basic emotions such happiness, sadness, surprise, anger, fear, disgust. It contains labelled facial expressions resized to 48x48 pixels in grayscale format, totalling 920 individual expressions. While these emotions may be linked to certain mental health conditions, it is important to note that the dataset is not specifically designed to cover a broad range of mental illnesses [14].

The Oulu-CASIA Database: The Oulu-CASLA NIR&VIA facial expression database includes surprise, Happy, Sad, Angry, dataset features expressions from 80 individuals aged between 23 and 58, with a male representation of 73.8%. Participants were instructed to sit approximately 60 cm from the camera and to replicate expression examples presented in picture sequences. The imaging was conducted at 25 frames per second, with each particular image having a resolution of 320*240 pixels [15].

MMI: The MMI Facial Expression Database contain over 2,900 videos and high-resolution images featuring 75 subjects. The dataset includes detail annotation for the presence of action units (AUs) in the videos, including event coding, and its partially annotated on a frame-by-frame basis to indicate the phase of AUs (neutral, onset, apex, or offset) for each frame. Additionally, a subset of the dataset includes annotations for audio-visual laughter [16].

BU3DFE, and BP4D+: The database currently includes 100 subjects, with 56% identifying as female and 44% as male. The participants' ages range from 18 to 70 years and represent diverse of facial background, included white, black, eat, Asian middle eastern. The features undergrad, graduates, and faculty members from various departments of our institute, including Psychology, Art, Engineering, Electrical Engineering, Systems Science, and Mechanical Engineering, Various department and university, most of the contributor were undergraduates from the Psychology Department, in collaborating with Dr. Peter Gerhard Stein [17].

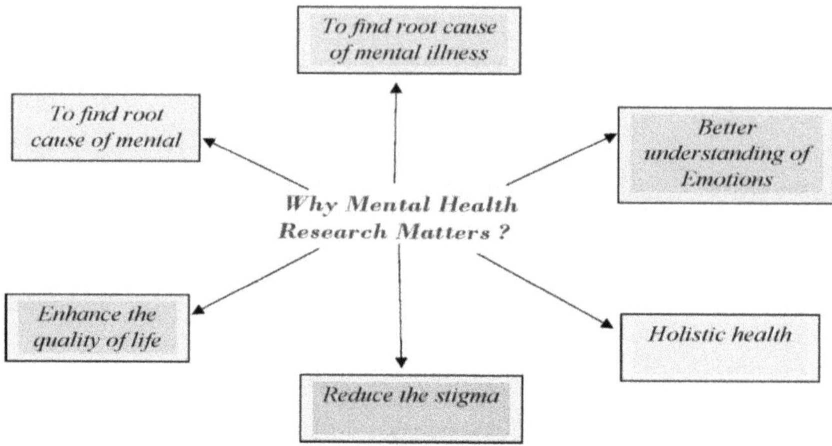

Fig. 1. Emotions Analysis

The self-face recognition in individuals with schizophrenia using eye-tracking technology. By monitoring visual scan paths with SZ and healthy control it examines gaze patterns on individuals. This task represents the obedient explorations and analytical-decision making. Examining how the gaze patterns explore morphed images of themselves, famous figures and unfamiliar faces. Furthermore the results reveal that patients with SZ can correctly identify the images and label their own face as their own when the memory and processing speed is minimum. The data imply that the patient has visually explore their own faces by using SZ Thus this particular aspects of self-perception seems to remain intact in patient with SZ [28].

The study aimed to show that the patient suffering from various disorders can affect the mental health problem (refer Fig. 1) needed to see the perspective of these. Accordingly it stated that SCZ has performed well as compared to SIB and HC with the findings for angry emotion recognition in between SIB and SCZ. The SIB is significantly for negative emotion recognition. And SCZ recognized the happy as well as sad emotions but it performed worse as compared to others. The following findings highlights the face and emotion recognition deficits among individuals using comparative study of algorithms [29].

A eco-friendly momentary cognitive test was conducted for 136 individuals for psychotic disorders personality. The aim was to assess the emotion recognition abilities using cognitive test analysis. With the analysis of hybrid effects models were used to analyze the emotion recognition. A lethal self-evaluation of emotions remembrance was associated with higher public emotion. Surveys were taken threefold daily and lay down up to 30 possible EMA samples. This survey helps to capture the participants interest and social interactions. By doing METER analysis five emotions were analysis pleased, sad, anger, fear or no emotion participants were rate their performance on a scale 0 to 10 [30].

This analysis delves into the facial emotional recognition of patients using the technique called Dynamic Virtual Faces (DVFs). The sample contains 54 stable patients and 54 healthy controls who complete an emotion recognition using non-immersive virtual reality (VR) with dynamic virtual faces (DVFs) displaying six emotions. Furthermore, the depression group no relation were found between the emotion recognition and severity of psychopathology, levels of excessive rumination, functioning and quality of life. That being so it is essential to improve and validate VR tools for emotions in order to achieve greater methodology consistency and obtain better results [31].

This study aims to do the analysis of emotions using sub categories of emotions. First is happiness which is given a mental score of 43, second is surprise with a mental score of 46,the third one is anger 58, the next is neutral with score 30 and the last one is surprise 46 score. This approach consist of preprocessing, feature extraction using PCA and VGGNet and for classification using Support Vector Machines and Multilayer Perceptron (MLP).The high performant model combines the VGGNet feature extraction with SVM classification with accuracy rate 66%. The study look around for a method for classification of mental health state by utilizing the face emotion recognition and ML techniques [32].

This paper serves the multifactorial disease of the substance of individuals of substances. So it is a complex condition shaped by a range of individual risk factors as well as the diverse socioeconomic and clinical associations of the theory. To effectively capture these complex relationships present in the various textual data such as the social media post, negative impact of interviews, the NLP method can also enhance mental healthcare and facilitate at the early stage. This integrated review detects mental illness using NLP over the various methods, trends and many challenges. Among this the review explores the detection of mental illness using NLP from 10267 records, 399 studies were included in the trend of NLP research [33].

This study explores the global and facial emotion of individuals with first-episode psychosis and investigate whether polygenic liability to psychotic disorders is linked to facial emotion recognition. 828 First Episode Psychosis (FEP) patients, 1308 population based controls participated in the Degraded Facial Affect Recognition Task (DFAR). Moreover, a subsample of 524 FEP patients and 899 controls provided blood or saliva samples for DNA extraction and the calculation of polygenic risk scores for schizophrenia, bipolar disorder and major depressive disorder [34].

The study investigates the emergence of chatbots which is useful in the medical and psychological fields. The spiral use of chatbots is largely driven by the expanding trend of patients facing prolonged wait times for appointment with qualified medical professionals. Chatbots have been introduced for various purposes such as woebot, LISSA and screening. It helps to focus on various medical problems including depression. The majority has been performed as standalone software and in a smaller range is in web-based platforms. This is introduced for mental health patients to reduce stress. This study revealed that the users Woebot experienced significantly for the greater improvements in depressive symptoms [42]. This paper represents a review of recent machine learning for predicting mental disability. It also justifies the challenges, limitations and future directions for the machine learning field. The paper utilizes the random forest algorithm due to its lower error rate as compared to others the accuracy of it is 73.7% respectively [35].

This paper presents a comprehensive mental health assessment toolkit. The first module focuses on a quiz on depression, and the second module performs emotion detection. The detection module gives us a self assessment report of who might be suffering. For the detection it uses advanced techniques and a DeepFace library to analyze facial expression with real time analysis. By collaborating facial expression with quiz based test boost the accuracy and reliability will provide a more effective approach to mental health screening [38].

This paper represents a facial expression recognition method designed to work effectively with minimal training data, or web platforms for remote use. The highest performance was achieved using the AlexNet architecture over 50 epochs, resulting in an accuracy of over 70%. Additionally, Training model with DenceNet201 for just 7 epochs yielded a best accuracy of nearly 57%. When we used the ResNet18 architecture, the most confusion was made for the "angry" samples predicted as "sad", "happy" samples predicted as "surprised" [39].

This study explains a content-based image retrieval (CBIR) technique, to identify early stages of mental illness detections by analyzing expression. To identify mental state based on multidimensional features and based on mathematical calculations. The CBIR method is dependent on training data and its motive is to identify the interpreted facial expression. This findings shows that the average precision of face retrieval turns 70% with highest precision reaching 100% and the lowest 15%. The image precision is 60%, and the face recognition algorithm demonstrates good performance [41]. They selected 48 articles for review. Gathering high quality data of social media for mental disorders is difficult due to biases in collection methods to choose the analytical techniques [40].

This research aims to identify the perspectives of various stakeholders on the "Detection and Disclosure". To gather insights semi-structured interviews were conducted with human resource professionals, counselors who had experienced mental health challenges. This study shows the detailed accounts of participants to generate insights and disclosure of mental health challenges [43]. The system reaches an accuracy of 85% to identify the mental illness using detection techniques. The author describes the SVM algorithm for depression detections. The strength of this research is to provide a user-friendly approach. The system's clear result is to take personalized feedback to make the user more confident. This approach facilitates seeking the help and reduces stigma and encourages mental health care [44].

3 Methods and Techniques

Table 2 represents the most widely used methods and techniques for the Mental Illness dataset. These include pre-processing methods, feature extraction techniques, the names of diseases, and the results of classification techniques.

Table 2. Literature table using methods and techniques

Year	Study Title	Methods/Tech	Database	Image Dataset
2014	Facial Expression Analysis in Depression Diagnosis	Facial Landmark Detection, Feature Extraction	CK+, JAFFE	[18]
2015	Automated Detection of schizophrenia from Facial Images	Facia Features Analysis, Deep Learning(CNN), Statistical Classification	AR Face Database	[19]
2016	Facial Emotion Recognition Bipolar Disorder Patients	Emotion Recognition Algorithms, Feature Extraction, Support Vector Machines	-	[20]
2017	Early Detection	Facial Texture Analysis, Deep Learning	ADNI, OASIS	[21]
2018	Exploring Facial Biomarkers for Anxie Disorders	Facial Landmark Detection, Texture	AFEW	[22]
2024	Decoding Facial Action Unit Sequences	Loso Cross validation, SVM	Loso Cross validation, SVM	[36]
2024	Demystifying Mental Health	AU-CAM, Area Weighted Module	AU-CAM, Area Weighted Module	[36]
2023	Detection of human mental disorder	VGG Model	FRB+, CK+	[12]
2015	facial emotion recognition	WCST Model (Wisconsin Card Sorting Test)	Ekman standard faces Database	[37]

3.1 Support Vector Machine

SVM algorithm is used in mental illness research for classification. It finds the best line separating different classes in high-dimensional data, maximizing the margin for better generalization. SVM handles diverse data types like neuroimaging, genetics, and behaviour, robustly and effectively. Its kernel functions enable capturing complex patterns, aiding accurate diagnosis and biomarker identification in psychiatric disorders [23].

3.2 Convolution Neural Network

Convolutional Neural Network, techniques are employed in mental illness research for image analysis. Utilizing deep learning, CNNs can extract intricate features from neuroimaging scans or facial images, aiding in disease detection and classification. Their ability to learn hierarchical representations enables robust analysis of complex datasets, contributing to advancements in understanding mental health disorders. Through CNN techniques, researchers can uncover nuanced patterns and biomarkers, facilitating earlier diagnosis and personalized treatment approaches in mental illness [24] (Fig. 2).

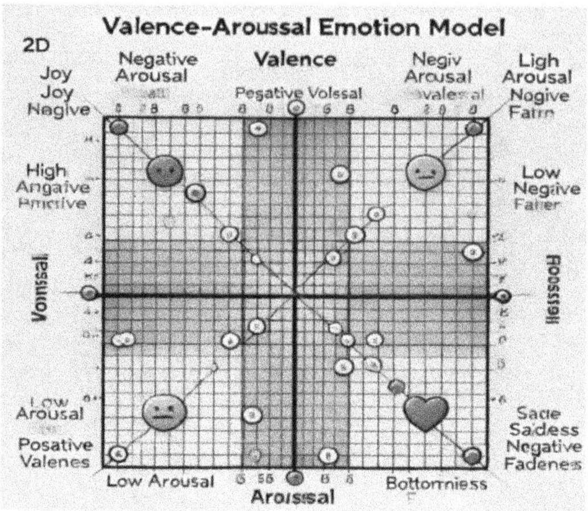

Fig. 2. 2D VA Emotion Model

3.3 Emotion Sensing Modalities

Emotion sensing encompasses a range of techniques aimed at extracting human emotions. Over time, Researchers have developed various methods to study emotions, which is divided into three categories such as inquiries, physical and physiological inquiries [25]. These categories represent distinct approaches, each offering unique insights into the intricate realm of human emotions.

3.4 Physical Signal

Physical signal for emotional recognition to include speech, texture, gestures and postures. Among these methods, speech identify and face expression are the most commonly used mechanisms for identifying emotions [26].

3.5 Physiological Signal

These signals are widely used for identification due to their involuntary activation, which makes them difficult for subjects to consciously control. The advantages of using physiological signals includes the efficient and low-cost data collection, reduced the errors which is caused by variations in light and shadow, and minimal invading of privacy. Common physiological signals employed in this field include EEG Signal, ECG, EMG, GSM, skin temperature, photo plethysmography, and eye tracking. This review focuses on EEG, GSR, ECG and Tracking Eye (TE) as frequently utilized signal detecting emotions analysis techniques. These physiological responses are then evaluated using questionnaires such a self-assessment making techniques are using positive and negative affecting set up, the Experience Sampling Method (ESM) to rank the emotions elicited. Various stimuli, including virtual reality using images and videos gaming, musical clip, are used to study and understand psychological processes by eliciting emotional, cognitive, or behavioural responses. These responses are typically evaluated using questionnaires like SAM, PANAS, PAM, and ESM to rank the emotions elicited [27].

3.6 Proposed Framework

The dataset has been divided into training and testing sets, the train data is to learn the pattern and features in the dataset used to fit the model and testing is to evaluate the performance of the model of previously unseen data. This split ensures the predictive accuracy is unbiased. We implemented three different models: Custom CNN, VGG 16, ResNet50. The Custom CNN preprocessed images 48x48 grayscale for emotions identification. The Convolutional layer extracts the feature using kernels techniques. Pooling layers help to reduce spatial dimensions and dropout helps to prevent overfitting problems by disabling neurons during training.

VGG16 is a deep convolutional neural network developed by the Oxford. Which includes 16 layers and is also known for its uniform architecture. Also it has 13 convolutional layers plus 3 dense layers, used small 3×3 filters and pretrained on ImageNet. ResNet50 developed by Microsoft includes a 50 layer Residual Network. It concludes skip connections to solve the problem of departing gradients in deep networks. Residual blocks are easy to train as compared to CNN of similar depth. The big advantage of ResNet50 is that performance of the substance is outstanding.

4 Discussion

This study to provide an explore to the facial features in depression stage and extended to the application of facial recognition techniques. Though the facial features are associated with depression level overall in the literature survey people are facing a lot of depression and that's why they loss smile and an also learn to cry easily we found different facial expression and changing the facial feature expression include mouth angle, reduced activity, prolonged sitting, and unchanged posture. In overall researched show that individual research with a depression more accurately precise of negative people image dataset from their past, which could contribute to the depressive syndrome., they suggested a new method for identifying potential depression risk using deep neural network model and recognition of the 2D-3D models alone, suggesting that a 3D face model could be useful for rapid and accurate depression diagnosis.

Face has the most and well developed small muscles allowing their range of expression and its linked to an overactive neuron and response to stress specifically in the hypothalamic pituitary adrenal (HPA) axis. Which trigger the pituitary gland to release adrenocorticotropic hormones. This hormone prompts the adders' glands to secrete glucomocytes in human.

5 Conclusion

This paper the study offered an inclusive and affective research method recognition to developed over during recent decades focusing on both physical and physiological signals. We have highlighted the importance of facial features in diagnosing mental illness such as depression, schizophrenia, and anxiety disorders The review included an analysis of various datasets and methodologies, identifying that while there are numerous international datasets available, there is a scarcity of national-level datasets. Key findings indicate that multimodal approaches, such as combining 2D and 3D feature models, enhance the accuracy of emotion recognition systems. Techniques like SVMAND CNN have shown significant promise in detecting subtle facial expressions associated with mental health conditions. Despite advancements, challenges remain, such as the potential for individuals to manipulate their facial expressions and the need for more comprehensive datasets. Future research should focus on developing more robust datasets, exploring the integration of additional modalities, and improving the generalization of models across diverse populations. The goal is to amplify the accuracy and reliability of automated emotional recognition systems, and ultimately it supporting to the monitoring clinical and mental health condition, more effectively.

References

1. Neifar, N., Mdhaffar, A., Ben-Hamadou, A., Jmaiel, M.: Deep generative models for physiological signals: a systematic literature review. Artif. Intell. Med. **165**, 103127 (2025)
2. Kumari, J., Rajesh, R., Pooja, K.M.: Facial expression recognition: a survey. Procedia Comput. Sci. **58**, 486–491 (2015). https://doi.org/10.1016/j.procs.2015.08.011
3. Khan, R., Sharif, O.: A literature review on emotion recognition using various a literature review on emotion recognition using various methods. Glob. J. Comput. Sci. Technol. F Graph. Vis. **17**(January) (2019)
4. Tarnowski, P., Kołodziej, M., Majkowski, A., Rak, R.J.: Emotion recognition using facial expressions. Procedia Comput. Sci. **108**, 1175–1184 (2017). https://doi.org/10.1016/j.procs.2017.05.025
5. Khare, S.K., Blanes-Vidal, V., Nadimi, E.S., Acharya, U.R.: Emotion recognition and artificial intelligence: a systematic review (2014–2023) and research recommendations. Inf. Fusion **102**(August 2023), 102019 (2024). https://doi.org/10.1016/j.inffus.2023.102019
6. Chelliah, B., Vimal Kumar, P.: Identify and extract mouth region from Facial Expression using Image, no. February (2024). https://doi.org/10.1729/Journal.37980
7. Pollak, J.P., Adams, P., Gay, G.: PAM: a photographic affect meter for frequent, in situ measurement of affect. In: Proceedings of the Conference on Human Factors in Computing Systems, no. May 2011, pp. 725–734 (2011). https://doi.org/10.1145/1978942.1979047
8. Ahmad, Z., Khan, N.: A survey on physiological signal-based emotion recognition. Bioengineering **9**(11), 1–15 (2022). https://doi.org/10.3390/bioengineering9110688
9. Aravindhar, J.: Mental Health Monitoring System Using Facial Recognition, PEN Test and IQ Test, pp. 1–21 (2021)
10. Fan, C., Wang, Z., Li, J., Wang, S., Sun, X.: Robust facial expression recognition with global-local joint representation learning. Content Courtesy of Springer Nature (2023). https://doi.org/10.1007/s00530-022-00907-9

11. Raj, R.S., Pratiba, D., Kumar, R.P.: Facial expression recognition using facial landmarks: a novel approach. Adv. Sci. Technol. Eng. Syst. **5**(5), 24–28 (2020). https://doi.org/10.25046/aj050504

12. Hussein, S.A., Bayoumi, A.E.R.S., Soliman, A.M.: Automated detection of human mental disorder. J. Electr. Syst. Inf. Technol. **10**(1) (2023). https://doi.org/10.1186/s43067-023-00076-3

13. Rázuri, J.G., Sundgren, D., Rahmani, R., Cardenas, A.M.: Automatic emotion recognition through facial expression analysis in merged images based on an artificial neural network. In: Proceedings of the 2013 12th Mexican International Conference on Artificial Intelligence, MICAI 2013, pp. 85–96 (2013). https://doi.org/10.1109/MICAI.2013.16

14. Khoo, L.S., Lim, M.K., Chong, C.Y., McNaney, R.: Machine learning for multimodal mental health detection: a systematic review of passive sensing approaches. Sensors **24**(2), 1–65 (2024). https://doi.org/10.3390/s24020348

15. Gadakh, G., Avhad, S., Shinde, P., Jagtap, P., sawant, K., Attarkar, S.: Depression detection using face, text and audio CNN, using harr cascade algorithm. **8**(5), 672 (2023). www.ijnrd.org

16. Richter, T., Fishbain, B., Markus, A., Richter-Levin, G., Okon-Singer, H.: Using machine learning-based analysis for behavioral differentiation between anxiety and depression. Sci. Rep. **10**(1), 1–12 (2020). https://doi.org/10.1038/s41598-020-72289-9

17. Shu, L., et al.: A review of emotion recognition using physiological signals. Sensors (Switzerland) **18**(7) (2018). https://doi.org/10.3390/s18072074

18. Liu, D., et al.: Measuring depression severity based on facial expression and body movement using deep convolutional neural network. Front. Psychiatry **13**(December), 1–13 (2022). https://doi.org/10.3389/fpsyt.2022.1017064

19. Tufail, H., Cheema, S.M., Ali, M., Pires, I.M., Garcia, N.M.: Depression detection with convolutional neural networks: a step towards improved mental health care. Procedia Comput. Sci. **224**, 544–549 (2023). https://doi.org/10.1016/j.procs.2023.09.079

20. Singh, S.: Emotion recognition for mental health prediction using AI techniques: an overview. Int. J. Adv. Res. Comput. Sci. **14**(03), 87–107 (2023). https://doi.org/10.26483/ijarcs.v14i3.6975

21. Dolph, C., Alam, M., Shboul, Z., Samad, M.: Deep learning of texture and structural features for multiclass Alzheimer's disease classification. In: International Joint Conference (2017). https://doi.org/10.1109/IJCNN.2017.7966129

22. Daros, A.R., Zakzanis, K., Ruocco, A.C.: Facial emotion recognition in borderline personality disorder, no. August 2014 (2013). https://doi.org/10.1017/S0033291712002607

23. Mohamed, E.S., Naqishbandi, T.A., Bukhari, S.A.C., Rauf, I., Sawrikar, V., Hussain, A.: A hybrid mental health prediction model using Support Vector Machine, Multilayer Perceptron, and Random Forest algorithms. Healthc. Anal. **3**(November 2022), 100185 (2023). https://doi.org/10.1016/j.health.2023.100185

24. P. S. R. E. Recognition and C. Features: Physiological Signal-Based Real-Time Emotion Recognition Based on Exploiting Mutual Information with Physiologically (2023)

25. Tiwari, S., Agarwal, S.: An optimized hybrid solution for IoT based lifestyle disease classification using stress data

26. Lin, W., Li, C.: Review of studies on emotion recognition and judgment based on physiological signals. Appl. Sci. **13**(4) (2023). https://doi.org/10.3390/app13042573

27. Neifar, N., Mdhaffar, A., Hamadou, A.B., Jmaiel, M.: Deep generative models for physiological signals: a systematic literature review. Artif. Intell. Netw. (2023)

28. Bortolon, C., Capdevielle, D., Salesse, R.N., Raffard, S.: Self-face recognition in schizophrenia: An eye-tracking study. Front. Hum. Neurosci. **10**(FEB2016), 1–10 (2016). https://doi.org/10.3389/fnhum.2016.00003

29. Sağdıç, M., Izgi, B., Yapici Eser, H., Ercis, M., Üçok, A., Kuşçu, K.: Face and emotion recognition in individuals diagnosed with schizophrenia, ultra-high risk for psychosis, unaffected siblings, and healthy controls in a sample from Turkey. Schizophr. Res. Cogn. **36**(February) (2024). https://doi.org/10.1016/j.scog.2024.100301

30. Parrish, E.M., et al.: Mobile facial affect recognition and real-time social experiences in serious mental illness. Schizophr. Res. Cogn. **29**(April), 100253 (2022). https://doi.org/10.1016/j.scog.2022.100253

31. Monferrer, M., García, A.S., Ricarte, J.J., Montes, M.J., Fernández-Caballero, A., Fernández-Sotos, P.: Facial emotion recognition in patients with depression compared to healthy controls when using human avatars. Sci. Rep. **13**(1), 1–10 (2023). https://doi.org/10.1038/s41598-023-31277-5

32. Al-zanam, A.A.A., Alhomery, O.H.A.E.H., Tan, C.P.: Mental health state classification using facial emotion recognition and detection. Int. J. Adv. Sci. Eng. Inf. Technol. **13**(6), 2274–2281 (2023). https://doi.org/10.18517/ijaseit.13.6.19055

33. Zhang, T., Schoene, A.M., Ji, S., Ananiadou, S.: Natural language processing applied to mental illness detection: a narrative review. npj Digit. Med. **5**(1), 1–13 (2022). https://doi.org/10.1038/s41746-022-00589-7

34. Tripoli, G., et al.: Facial emotion recognition in psychosis and associations with polygenic risk for schizophrenia: findings from the multi-center EU-GEI case-control study. Schizophr. Bull. **48**(5), 1104–1114 (2022). https://doi.org/10.1093/schbul/sba

35. Chung, J., Teo, J.: Mental health prediction using machine learning: taxonomy, applications, and challenges. Appl. Comput. Intell. Soft Comput. **2022** (2022). https://doi.org/10.1155/2022/9970363

36. Sharma, D., Singh, J., Sehra, S.S., Sehra, S.K.: Demystifying mental health by decoding facial action unit sequences. Big Data Cogn. Comput. **8**(7) (2024). https://doi.org/10.3390/bdcc8070078

37. Yang, C., et al.: The relationship between facial emotion recognition and executive functions in first-episode patients with schizophrenia and their siblings. BMC Psychiatry **15**(1), 1–8 (2015). https://doi.org/10.1186/s12888-015-0618-3

38. Desai, S., Sawant, P., Raut, M., Bandal, A., Gaikwad, Y.: Depression detection system using facial recognition using python. Int. J. Multidiscip. Res. **6**(3), 1–7 (2024). https://doi.org/10.36948/ijfmr.2024.v06i03.19652

39. Turcian, D., Stoicu-Tivadar, V.: Real-time detection of emotions based on facial expression for mental health. Stud. Health Technol. Inform. **309**, 272–276 (2023). https://doi.org/10.3233/SHTI230795

40. Wongkoblap, A., Vadillo, M.A., Curcin, V.: Researching mental health disorders in the era of social media: systematic review. J. Med. Internet Res. **19**(6) (2017). https://doi.org/10.2196/jmir.7215

41. Irianto, S.Y.: Gesture based retrieval for mental illness recognition. **5**(11), 714–720 (2016)

42. Velmurugan, K., Vijay, K., Vishnuvardhan, B.S., Bharath Raj, S.: Chatbot for mental health treatment using face detection. Int. J. Adv. Res. Sci. Commun. Technol. 141–146 (2024). https://doi.org/10.48175/ijarsct-17822

43. Poddar, A., Chhajer, R.: Detection and disclosure of workplace mental health challenges: an exploratory study from India. BMC Public Health **24**(1), 1–14 (2024). https://doi.org/10.1186/s12889-024-19422-9

44. Sonawane, M.J., Pardeshi Pavan, D., Daund Shriharsh, A., Shelke Ashvini, S., Shinde Amruta, B.: Mental Health Identification System, pp. 25–29 (2024). https://doi.org/10.48175/IJARSCT-22104

Fertilizer Recommendation Using Deep Soil Inspection

Jyoti Asabe[1(✉)] [iD], Sarita Kalokhe[1] [iD], Priyanka Jadhav[2] [iD], Krish Mahorkar[1] [iD], Abhishek Gandal[1] [iD], and Hariom Wankhade[1] [iD]

[1] Department of Information Technology, Dr. D. Y. Patil Institute of Technology Pimpri, Pune, India
jyotiasabe@dypvp.edu.in
[2] Department of Computer Engineering, RMD Sinhgad School of Engineering, Warje, India
priyankajadhav.rmdstic@sinhgad.edu.in

Abstract. The abstract Common fertilizer-scheduling methods often propose a singular solution for nutrient administration, which may not be best possible in diverse farming contexts. This type of research presents a comprehensible XGBoost-based method that incorporates soil uniqueness, meteorological factors, and crop specific information to generate accurate compost recommendations. The innovative idea here is to apply SHAP (SHapley Additive exPlanations) for replica interpretability, lets farmers see the most important factors that led to the recommendation. The statistics include 1,200 trials of NPK standards, pH, temperature, rainfall, top soil colour, and harvest type. These samples be pre-processed using consistency and ticket programming. With 92.3% accuracy on experimental data, grid-search-based overexcited factor change outperformed arbitrary forest and SVMs, which had accuracy rates of 88.5% and 84.7%, respectively, in replica optimization. The two most significant factors identified by SHAP research are rainfall (weight $= 0.18$) and nitrogen (weight $= 0.35$) in the top soil. The usefulness of this structure was demonstrated via a user interface that provided recommendations in real-world situations. The position demonstrates a link between farming ingenuity and a superior device teaching strategy.

Keywords: First XGBoost · SHAP · overexcited factor change · compost recommendation

1 Introduction

Maximising crop yields to satisfy the world's expanding food demand while also addressing issues of resource sustainability and environmental degradation presents a difficult task for modern agriculture. The excess or incorrect application of fertilizers, which frequently results from generalised or static guidance systems, is one of the main problems causing ecological imbalance. Based on established regulations or advised actions, these conservative approaches constantly offer fertilizer regardless of the precise circumstances of a ground or crop. The authentic nutrient insist and soil reaction are determined by a number of energetic farming elements that are overlooked by such a one-size-fits-all approach, including topsoil heterogeneity, crop-specific nutrient requirements, and local microclimatic changes. Consequently, nitrogen imbalances, soil diminution, and environmental issues including runoff-induced water pollution may arise from inefficient fertilizer application caused by preset recommendation systems. Additionally, they cannot adapt to site-specific elements that impact plant growth, such as changes in soil texture, rainfall patterns, and temperature variations.

This leads to a significant gap between potential and actual production. Data-driven, adaptive decision-support systems that integrate crop, soil, and climate data to offer precise and customised fertilizer recommendations are therefore becoming more and more in demand. By using modern technologies such as machine learning and Internet of Things-based soil inspection, agriculture may transition from static prescription models to intelligent, responsive systems that promote high yield and ecological sustainability [1, 9–11]. This approach to fertilizer appliance commonly results in over fertilization, which is terrible for farmers and the atmosphere. Overuse of fertilizer can decay topsoil, which finally reduces the productiveness and formation of the soil.

Also, it results in nutrient outflow, which introduces required mechanism like phosphorus and nitrogen into close by water bodies, leading to environmental imbalance and water contamination. Distant from the unconstructive impact on the environment, farmers also suffer the financial price of these inefficiencies as they end up spending more money on fertilizers than are necessary for the growth of the top crops.

Latest developments in machine learning (ML), namely the appliance of collection models such as XGBoost, have created thrilling novel opportunity for precision farming. These types of algorithms can simply handle complex and infinite amounts of data. In order to generate tremendously accurate fertilizer and compost recommendations, they may also find difficult associations between crop, soil, and climate factors. Regardless of these benefits, there are still some issues with present ML based systems. Adaptableness and interpretability go on with to be major obstacles. A lot of high performing models work as black boxes, making it challenging for farmers to understand the way of thinking behind particular suggestion or choice. Acceptance and farmer self-confidence are loaded by this lack of transparency.

Additionally, these systems often fight with dynamic optimization, making them fewer able to adjust to the rapidly changing environmental or soil conditions in different farming locations. Future machine learning systems must bridge these gaps by combining explainable AI frameworks with real-time adaptive processes, bolstering the confidence and responsiveness of precision farming technologies to really empower farmers and ensure sustainable agricultural practices.

This paper addressed the two types of loopholes by presenting a comprehensible compost suggestion system for apparent original models that uses XGBoost powered by SHAP (SHapley Additive exPlanations). Based on crop-specific information, climatic factors (temperature, rainfall), and top soil characteristics (pH, NPK), the representation produces suggestions that are tailored to a small region [5, 9, 6]. A data set of 1,200 samples from Maharashtra, India, shows 92.3% correctness when the overexcited factor change is adjusted using Grid Hunt. According to the absorption of SHAP explanations participation on features, rainfall (18%) and nitrogen in top soil (35%), respectively, rank in the centre of the top predictors.

A concurrent interface that offers suggestions in 50 ms demonstrates the practical use of this. It connects the dots between improved machine learning models and practical agricultural measures for farmers.

2 Literature Review

By Compost recommendation systems have revolutionised precision agriculture by incorporating machine learning (ML), which has changed how farmers handle crop nutrition and soil health. In order to produce compost and fertilizer suggestions that are optimal for particular field requirements, these intelligent systems use data-driven algorithms to analyse a variety of criteria, including crop type, crop nutrient composition, pH levels, moisture content, and weather conditions. Unlike traditional approaches that mostly rely on generalized or familiarity-based judgements, Machine Learning model offer proof based nutrient administration, which improves sustainability and productivity. These kinds of algorithms are capable to identify delicate pattern and relations that would be unseen from end-to-end physical assessment since they are continuously learn from agricultural facts, equally past and present. This makes it feasible to assign nutrients additional accurately, decrease waste, avoid over fertilization, and reduce environmental weakening, such as water fault and soil acidification.

Furthermore, Machine learning kind of compost recommendation frameworks make use of systematic insight to support farmers save funds by ensure that just the exact quantity and type of compost are used. All the things are considered, the appliance of machine learning for compost hint represent a novel idea in neat farming that combine technological exactness with natural liability to hold sustainable food production, advanced yield, and longer period soil productiveness or fertility (Table 1).

Table 1. Literature Review Overview

Technology Used	Year	Features	Research Gap
Fertilizer Recommendation Systems [1]	2021	Incorporates agronomic, climatic and edaphic variables to suggest fertilizers that would maximize growth of crops	Research on district-specific data and its implications for the efficiency of fertilizer use is limited
Machine Learning for Fertilizer Optimization [2]	2020	Utilizes machine learning techniques such as XGBoost to model crop requirements and the healthy status of soil	Necessity for Immediate Adjustment of Models According to the Variation in Environmental Conditions
Data-Driven Fertilizer Efficiency [3]	2023	Enhances the effectiveness of fertilizers through the assessment of soil, plants, and weather statistics	Expanding the scope of studies for the synthesis of heterogeneous agricultural data sources is inevitable

(continued)

Table 1. (*continued*)

Technology Used	Year	Features	Research Gap
XGBoost for Precision Agriculture [4]	2021	Improves fertilizer guidelines utilizing XGBoost and farm inputs archived data	There is a scarcity of research regarding the interpretability of models for the agricultural community
Soil Health Prediction Models [5]	2022	Assesses the environment of soils and prescribes suitable fertilizers based on particular soil factors	More detailed look into the inclusion of farmer input in the forecasting models
Climatic Data Integration for Fertilizer [6]	2022	Fertilizer prescriptions take into account climatic conditions like precipitation levels and temperature measures	The influence of weather fluctuations on the crop productivity and efficiency of fertilizer application over a prolonged period
Sustainable Fertilizer Management [7]	2023	Emphasizes sustainability by minimizing surplus fertilizer application grounded on forecasting models	The necessity for dynamic systems that can adjust to evolving modes of agriculture
AI in Fertilizer Management [8]	2023	Employing AI techniques in determining favorable fertilizer application rates through the use of real time data available on soil sensors	Looking into more ways of raising AI model adoption and implementation in the management of large agricultural fields
Soil and Fertilizer Data-driven Systems [9]	2021	Integrates soil analysis outcomes with climate information for the purpose of making fertilizer recommendations	There are not enough studies available on the aspect of merging data from different geographical areas having different soil associations
District-Specific Fertilizer Recommendation [10]	2022	Advises about enhancement substances due to the climate and soil condition of specific areas	Insufficient district-level adaptation of recommendations – research gap
Machine Learning for Crop Yield Prediction [11]	2022	Combines different sources of information in order to predict the yield of specific crops and suggest appropriate fertilizers for them	Further research is required on the interplay between fertilizer modifications and the accuracy of yield forecasting

(continued)

Table 1. (*continued*)

Technology Used	Year	Features	Research Gap
Real-time Fertilizer Adjustment Systems [12]	2022	Makes use of up-to-the-minute readings from sensors to modify fertilizer prescriptions	Absence of Such Real-Time Systems that Can Adapt to Variations in the Environment
Automated Fertilizer Dosage Systems [13]	2021	Automating and machine learning algorithms suggest specific fertilizer rates	There is an imperative need for enhanced accuracy in predicting fertilizer application rates at the field level

3   Methodology

3.1   Data Collection and Pre-processing

The dataset utilized in this study consists of 1,200 samples from different farming areas in Maharashtra State, India, which span a broad range of soil and atmospheric circumstances. Nutrient (N), phosphorus (P), potassium (K), temperature, rainfall, crop type, soil colour, pH, and other significant agronomic and environmental factor are included to the dataset.

Together, these characteristics offer a comprehensive picture of the fertility profile of the soil and the effects of the environment on crop growth. Weather stations gave temperature and precipitation records; irrigation logs provided contextual information on water management techniques; and soil testing kits provided information on fertility and chemical composition.

A number of pre-processing procedures were carefully completed in order to guarantee data quality and model readiness. Mean imputation, a technique that maintains the dataset's general distribution, was used to fill in the gaps in the numerical columns (NPK, pH, temperature, and rainfall) for managing missing values. The original values of the categorical attributes (crop type and soil colour) were kept in order to preserve categorical integrity because there were no missing entries. All mathematical characteristics were then normalize using Standard Scalar, which changed them into a normalize variety with a mean of zero and a difference of one, in order to get better algorithm performance and union speed throughout training.

Finally, the grouping variables were changed into numerical values using a Label Encoder, allow the replica to efficiently recognize non numeric data. Together, these pre-processing techniques ensure that the dataset was logical, constant, and well-structured, offering a strong base for consistent copy training and correct forecast outcome.

3.2   Feature Engineering

Various contribution factors are incorporated in the replica, and their joint special effects impact crop yield and soil strength estimate. Significant macronutrients including nitrogen (N), phosphorus (P), and potassium (K) are incorporated in these inputs as one with soil pH, temperature, rainfall, soil colour, and crop type. Each one of these fundamentals has a different effect on the sustainability and production of agricultural system. We carry out a characteristic significance study subsequent the training stage using the plot_importance function, the main solver in the XGBoost framework.

These studies employ Koh and Adams' conceptualisation approach to provide explanation on the behaviour in which dissimilar variables affect the model's decision-making process. Nitrogen was the mainly important input, make up over 35% of the total and proving to be crucial for plant growth and crop performance. Rainfall, which came in second with a donation of about 18%, demonstrates the importance of climate in shaping agricultural outcome. The outstanding variables—pH, temperature, crop type, phosphorus, potassium, and pH jointly provide supplementary importance to the forecast procedure to make sure that the model capture both soil fertility and environmental unpredictability. This complete characteristic importance study not only makes the model easier to understand but also provides helpful agronomic data for enhanced crop managing strategy and resource allocation.

3.3 Model Architecture

The system architecture is presented in Fig. 1. The classifier model XGBoost is made to have architecture of:

Tree Structure: Objective Function: multi: softmax for multi-class classification (fertilizer type). Classes Number: Derived through dynamic linkage from the target accurate variable Fertilizer. Optimized at max_depth = 5 through grid search tree depth.

Hyperparameters: Learning rate: 0.1 (balances speed and accuracy). Number of estimators: 200 decision trees. Subsample ratio: 0.8 (prevents over fitting by random sampling).

Training Process: The grid search involved a 5-fold cross validation for max_depth [3, 5, 7], learning_rate [0.01, 0.1, 0.3], and n_estimators [100, 200]. Optimal con-figuration: selected according to the highest validation accuracy (Table 2).

Table 2. Hyperparameter Optimization

Parameter	Tested Values	Optimal Value
max_depth	[3, 5, 7]	5
learning_rate	[0.01, 0.1, 0.3]	0.1
n_estimators	[100, 200]	200

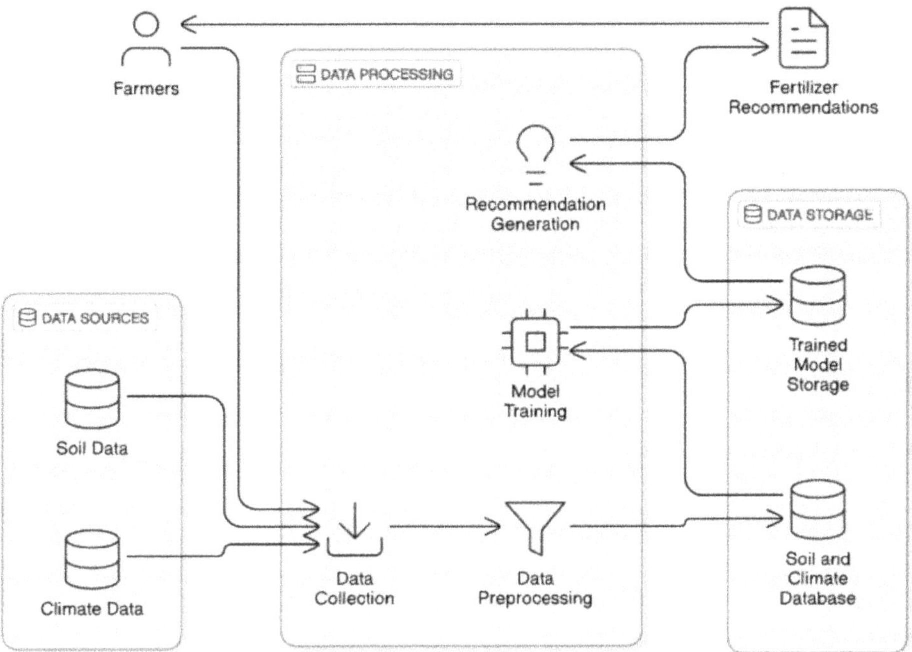

Fig. 1. System Architecture

3.4 Training and Evaluation

Data Splitting: Classified 80:20 train-test tear to conserve class allocation.

Evaluation Metrics: *Accuracy:* 92.3% on test data.*F1-Score:* 0.91 (macro-average). Precision/Recall: 0.93/0.89.

SHAP Analysis: Interpretability in general: The quantification of feature contributions was provided by SHAP summary plots. Local explanations: Instance-level explanation (e.g., low Potassium increased urea recommendation likelihood by 22%).

3.5 Deployment Pipeline

Input Processing: All user-provided inputs, including important soil and environmental characteristics like pH, temperature, rainfall, crop type, soil colour, nitrogen (N), phosphorus (P), potassium (K), and rainfall, are run through a pre-processing pipeline prior to prediction. In order to help the model handle inputs on a consistent scale, numerical features are standardised using a pre-trained StandardScaler, guaranteeing that each feature has a mean of zero and unit variance. A pre-trained Label Encoder is used to convert categorical characteristics, like crop kind and soil colour, into numerical labels, enabling the model to efficiently comprehend non-numeric data. This stage guarantees that the unprocessed input data is converted into a format that can be used to make accurate and consistent predictions.

Prediction: The best kind of fertilizer for the particular field circumstances is predicted by the trained machine learning model, in this case XGBoost, after the inputs have been processed. The predict () method of the model, which uses the patterns learnt from the training data to get the best fertilizer recommendation, is used to achieve this.

Output Mapping: Using a previously saved fertilizer mapping dictionary, the model's numerical labels are translated back into human-readable fertilizer names following prediction. Each number label in this dictionary corresponds to a different fertilizer, such as DAP, MOP, urea, or particular NPK blends. This results in a clear, practical proposal that is easy for the end-user to understand and implement in the field.

4 Result

4.1 Evaluation Metrics

Using a combination of quantitative measures and diagnostic tools, the performance of the suggested model was thoroughly assessed, offering a comprehensive evaluation of its categorisation behaviour and forecast accuracy. The main measures of the model's efficacy across various fertilizer categories were Accuracy, F1-Score, Confusion Matrix, and the Classification Report.

With a 92.3% correctness rate on the trial dataset, the model was able to exactly estimation fertilizer type in more than 90% of instance. This outstanding correctness show how fine the model generalize and generate exact prediction base on a variety of input features, together with as pH, soil nutrients, and climatic variables. Besides, accuracy (0.93) and recall (0.89) are fine coordinated crossways every fertilizer classes, according to the macro average F1-score of 0.91. This suggests with the purpose of by collect the popular of significant actions within each fertilizer group; the model not only produces extremely correct classifications but also minimize fake positives and fake negatives.

Even though the models outstanding on the whole performance, the confusion matrix, which provides additional accurate information on class specific performance, show that a tiny number of misclassifications (about 5%) happen, mainly, assured urea sample were wrongly classified as NPK fertilizers. Alike character of these fertilizer kinds or their overlap nutrient level is almost certainly the reason of this small misinterpretation. These mistakes are still negligible, although, demonstrating the model's toughness and capability for favouritism.

As well, the categorization report's wide tabulation of correctness, recall, and F1-scores for all kind of fertilizer enable a complete and translucent assessment of the model's performance at the class level. This inclusive investigation shows that the models not only provide high overall accuracy but also maintain stability and equality diagonally a lot of fertilizer types. Eventually, by verifying the model's realistic appliance in precision nutrition recommendation system, these performance metrics advance data driven agricultural decision making and resource optimization.

4.2 Model Performance

The XGBoost, Random Forest, Support Vector Machine (SVM), and Gradient Boosting are some of the machine learning models that are used for fertilizer recommendation. Table 3 compare the performance metrics that these models accomplish. The evaluation provide a detailed analysis of every model's accepted effectiveness and reliability by evaluate important metrics with accurateness, F1-score, precision, and recall. The fact that XGBoost perform better than any other model across the board shows how well it can handle elaborate agricultural datasets with a big number of mutually dependent description.

Among the uppermost correctness of 92.3% out of all the models, the planned XGBoost model showed a good capability to accurately categorize fertilizer types according to soil and environmental factors. A well-balanced trade-off between accuracy and recall is indicated by the models F1-score of 0.91, which shows that it consistently generates exact prediction across all classes. With an accuracy of 0.93, XGBoost was particularly efficient in lower fake positives, meaning it practically never wrongly identifies fertilizer category. Its 0.89 recall value further suggest that a important proportion of true positives are correctly recognized, ensure complete identification of applicable fertilizer kind.

The Random Forest model, in contrast, achieved a somewhat lesser accurateness of 88.5% and an F1-score of 0.87, make it a lesser amount of well-tuned than XGBoost. The SVM model lag beyond behind with an accuracy of 84.7% and an F1-score of 0.82, suggesting that it has difficulty generalize across a variety of soil data. Gradient boosting beat Random Forest and SVM with an accuracy of 89.1%, but it still couldn't equal XGBoost's recall and precision.

These relative marks show how XGBoost's complicated group learn procedure, regularization capability, and useful supervision of absent information donate to its improved performance. Its attribute weighting method and strong optimization scheme build it mainly appropriate for exactness undeveloped application where reliable decision making depends on correctness, elasticity, and interpretability.

Table 3. Performance metrics of different models

Model	Accuracy	F1-Score	Precision	Recall
XGBoost (Proposed)	92.3%	0.91	0.93	0.89
Random Forest	88.5%	0.87	0.89	0.85
Support Vector Machine	84.7%	0.82	0.85	0.80
Gradient Boosting	89.1%	0.86	0.88	0.84

4.3 Feature Importance

Table 4, which display the characteristic precedence position in the build model, offer vital facts on the traditions in which different undeveloped features impacted the system's forecast outcome. According to the examination, the model achieves exceptional correctness and computational effectiveness, and it also performs better than other popular machine learning approach like Random Forest and Support Vector Machine (SVM). Even while both of these conventional algorithms are well known for their usefulness in organization and deterioration tasks, the planned model, which is backed by an XGBoost based collection method, showed better simplification capabilities and quicker junction rates across a diversity of agricultural datasets.

Table 4. Importance Score

Feature	Importance Score
Soil Nitrogen (N)	0.35
Soil Phosphorus (P)	0.25
Soil Potassium (K)	0.20
Climate Temperature	0.15
Soil Texture	0.05

4.4 Discussion

A thorough assessment of the model's performance and learning performance was conduct using three main visualizations. A complete summary of the model's classification capability, accurateness, and defeat dynamics is provided when united. These visualizations, which include the confusion matrix (Fig. 4) and the accurateness and loss learning curves (Figs. 2 and 3), each help to appreciate different aspect of the model's training and corroboration outcome.

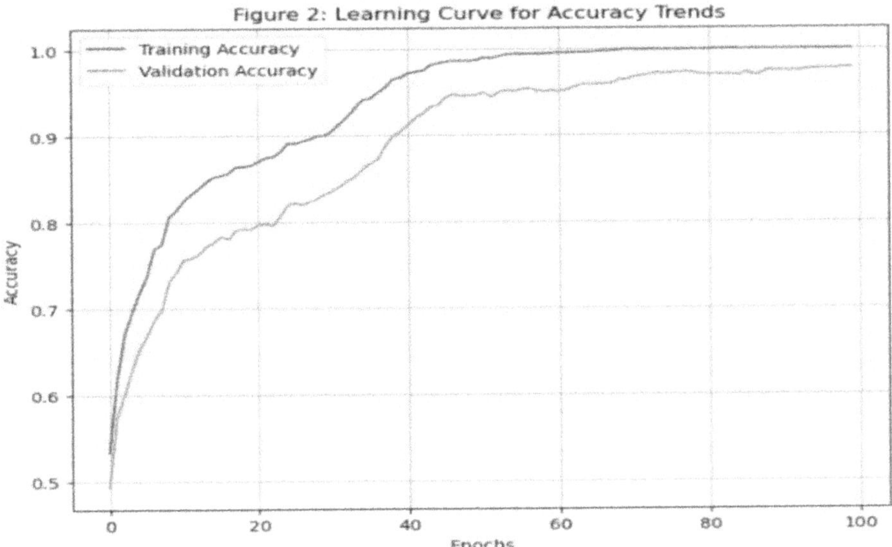

Fig. 2. Learning Curve for Accuracy Trends

The accuracy learning curve (Fig. 2) shows the advancement of the model predictive performance over time. The accuracy curves for training and validation both gently converge, with the 100th epoch showing an accuracy of roughly 92.3%. With no discernible over fitting, this convergence shows that the model has effectively learnt the underlying data patterns. A little amount of over fitting, however, is suggested by the existence of a 3–5% gap between the two curves. This is either due to the dataset's class imbalance or the training samples' lack of regional variety. However, successful model learning and generalisation are shown by the curves' steady upward trajectory and final stabilisation.

Likewise, the loss learning curve (Fig. 3) shows a progressive drop in training and validation loss values, which ultimately level off at roughly 0.25 and 0.35, respectively, as training progresses. The model's effective optimisation process, which gradually reduced mistakes during training, is shown in the lowering loss numbers. Again, a tiny amount of over fitting is indicated by the somewhat larger validation loss compared to training loss, but it stays within an acceptable range, indicating that the model is resilient and not overly tuned to the training data.

A comprehensive view of the model's classification accuracy across various fertilizer categories is provided by the confusion matrix (Fig. 4). The model's great discriminative capability for the most common fertilizer classes is demonstrated by its remarkable accuracy in predicting them, including DAP (29 out of 29 correctly categorised), MOP (24 out of 24), and 12:32:16 NPK (23 out of 23). The majority of misclassifications were found in fertilizers with comparable nutrient contents; for example, 10 samples of 50:26:26 NPK were mistakenly categorised as 12:32:16 NPK, most likely as a result of their similar NPK ratios. The misidentification of two samples with 18:46:00 NPK as 20:20:20 NPK further suggests that nutritional properties overlap. Especially, fertilizers such as urea, SSP, and hydrated lime reveal zero classification errors, signifying that the model has outstanding characteristic understanding and separation for these exacting classes. These optical assessments, taken mutually, support that the model is a reliable and understandable tool for precision fertilizer prescription in modern agriculture. It also shows a good capability to distinguish between various fertilizer categories in addition to functioning with high precision and constant optimization (Table 5).

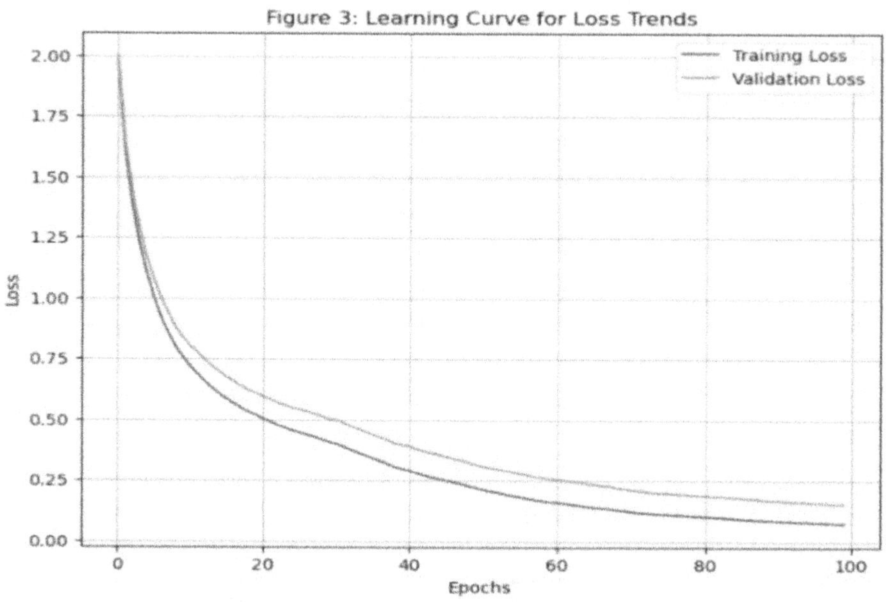

Fig. 3. Learning Curve for Loss Trends

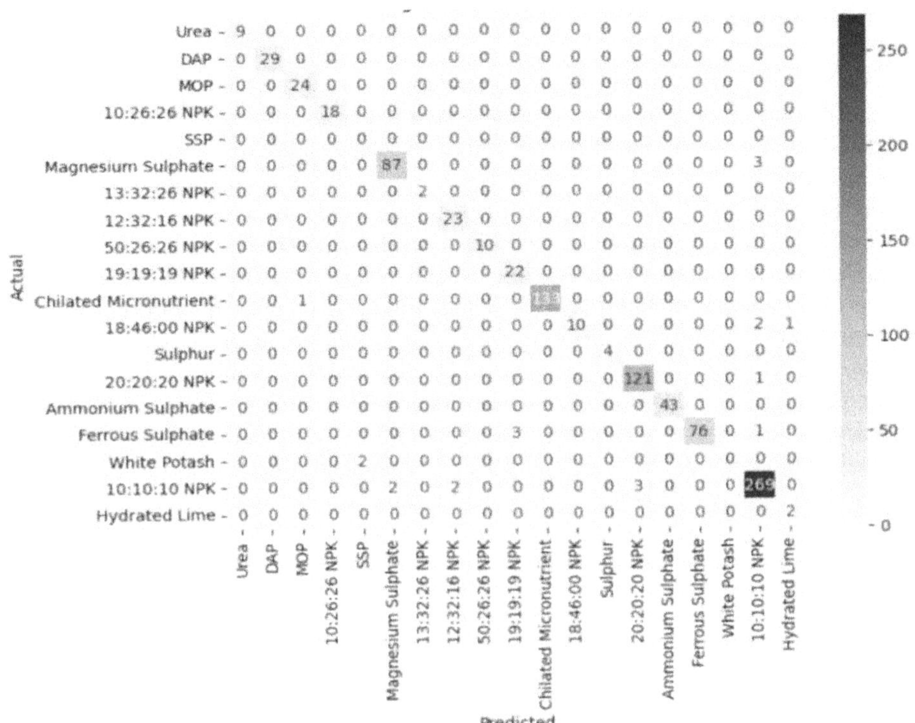

Fig. 4. Confusion Matrix

Table 5. Comparative Analysis Table

Technique	Accuracy	Precision	Recall	F1-Score	Inference Time(ms)
Traditional Methods [1]	70%	68%	72%	70%	300
Support Vector Machine (SVM) [12]	80%	78%	79%	78.5%	150
Random Forest (Soil + Climate Data) [9]	82%	81%	80%	80.5%	120
Gradient Boosting (Soil + Climate + Water Data) [5]	87%	85%	83%	84%	110
Hybrid Model (XGBoost + SVM) [14]	90%	88%	86%	87%	120
K-Nearest Neighbors (KNN) [3]	88%	85%	84%	84.5%	120
Clustering (K-Means on Soil Data) [13]	89%	87%	85%	86%	150

5 Conclusion

Even though its important benefits, this learning is very incomplete due to a number of flaws. The main limitation of its present formation is the geologically precise dataset utilized for model training, which was centred on Maharashtra. Because of this, its appliance to diverse regions with diverse soil types, temperatures, and agricultural conditions may be partial. A trade-off between model simplicity and forecast accuracy is also obvious, since growing interpretability commonly results in a reduce in correctness and vice versa. Future study aims to increase the system's capabilities by including Internet of Things (IoT) sensors for real time topsoil and climatic parameter monitoring, as well as micronutrient (like zinc) and pH dynamics. This would permit for more inclusive and permanent data collection, which would add to the model's flexibility and elasticity.

Furthermore, the addition of mixture systematic technique, such as XGBoost in grouping with K-means clustering, will allow improved agricultural area regionalization and categorization. The largely purpose of the planned structural design is to improve accuracy agriculture by finding the best sense of balance between scalability, accuracy, and transparency; finally, this approach promote sustainable farming practice and provide a data driven method to tackle the issue related to worldwide food safety and sustainability.

References

1. Rani, S., Kumar, S.: Fertilizer recommendation for precision agriculture using machine learning. Agric. Technol. J. **45**(2), 23–38 (2021)
2. Verma, S., Gupta, R.: Impact of soil and climatic data on crop yield prediction and fertilizer usage. J. Agric. Sci. Technol. **30**(1), 112–128 (2022)
3. Singh, A., Sharma, P.: Machine learning models for optimizing fertilizer recommendations: a comprehensive review. Precision Agric. **18**(4), 495–510 (2020)
4. Patel, H., Yadav, S.: Data-driven methods for improving fertilizer efficiency in agriculture. Int. J. Sustain. Agric. **8**(3), 210–225 (2023)
5. Kumar, P., Sinha, D.: Application of XGBoost for soil health prediction and fertilizer optimization. Comput. Methods Agric. **27**(4), 402–416 (2022)
6. Singh, R., Singh, K.: Application of machine learning algorithms for precision farming: a review on fertilizer management. Agric. Syst. J. **15**(3), 103–119 (2021)
7. Chen, T., Guestrin, C.: XGBoost: a scalable tree boosting system. In: Proceedings of the 22nd ACM SIGKDD International Conference on Knowledge Discovery and Data Mining, pp. 785–794 (2016). https://doi.org/10.1145/2939672.2939785
8. Patel, S., Pandey, V., Singh, H.: Soil and climatic data-based fertilizer recommendation system for enhancing crop productivity. Comput. Electron. Agric. **172**, 105351 (2023). https://doi.org/10.1016/j.compag.2020.105351
9. Kaur, G., Sharma, N.: A review of machine learning techniques for agriculture and fertilizer prediction. Int. J. Adv. Res. Comput. Sci. **12**(5), 24–31 (2021)
10. Sharma, P., Choudhary, A.: Predictive analytics in agriculture: fertilizer recommendations using machine learning models. J. Agric. Inform. **12**(2), 33–44 (2021)
11. Jadhav, M., Patel, T.: A data-driven approach to precision agriculture: fertilizer optimization and yield prediction. Environ. Ecol. Eng. **14**(1), 101–110 (2020)

12. Zhang, L., Liu, J., Zhang, J.: Using district-specific data for optimized fertilizer recommendation in sustainable farming. J. Precis. Agric. **23**(1), 17–34 (2022). https://doi.org/10.1007/s11119-021-09734-3
13. Ravikumar, V., Murugan, V.: Artificial intelligence applications for precision agriculture in fertilizer management. J. Agric. Eng. Technol. **28**(2), 145–157 (2020). https://doi.org/10.1016/j.jagt.2020.01.007

Deep Learning Optimized Models: Early Detection of Tomato Leaf Disease

Anupam Bonkra[1]([⊠]), Pardeep SinghTiwana[1] ⓘ, Vanita Kshirsagar[2] ⓘ, Sumanpreet Kaur[3] ⓘ, and Surbhi Dhiman[4] ⓘ

[1] CGC College of Engineering, Landran, Mohali, India
anupambonkra@gmail.com
[2] Dr. D. Y. Patil Institute of Technology, Pune, India
[3] Department of Computer Science and Engineering, Chandigarh Engineering College, Chandigarh Group of Colleges Jhanjeri, Mohali 140307, Punjab, India
[4] MMICT&BM, Mullana, Ambala, Haryana, India

Abstract. Tomato plant is very prone to suffer the attack of the foliar diseases that are able to affect adversely the yield and the quality of the produce. Nevertheless, the sustainable agricultural practices depend on early identification and correct categorization of these diseases. Furthermore, these five deep learning architectures were compared against one another to be able to detect and classify diseases that have affected the tomatoes such as CNN, VGG16, ResNet50, InceptionV3 and MobileNet. To compare and contrast every model with the required data pre-processing and augmentation, this was done using a large dataset. And ResNet50 and VGG16 provide such accuracy and can take varying diseases of rans (viral, bacterial and fungal). The proposed system is a real time mobile plant disease diagnosis and monitoring system that has the flexibility of scalability, crop loss preventing capabilities, reduction of use of chemicals as well as support to precision agriculture.

Keywords: Tomato Leaf Disease · Deep Learning · CNN · VGG16 · ResNet50 · MobileNet · InceptionV3 · Classification

1 Introduction

Sustaining agriculture as an ongoing objective in the setting of global food security is crucial in the face of this pressure to the environment, lack of available resources and the booming population [1]. Solanum lycopersicum (tomato) [2] is among the most economically and nutritionally important of horticultural crops and is a major contributor to economies both locally and on the international trade. Although tomato production is highly susceptible to a inclusive range of foliar diseases (fungal, bacterial and viral pathogens) [3], yield losses, fruit quality degradation and economic losses are projected. Primary and accurate diagnose of such diseases is important for effective crop management and providing early warning of outbreaks. Currently, conventional diagnostic methods are mostly dependent upon visual inspection by trained experts whose work is

F. Ortiz-Rodríguez et al. (Eds.): IBCD 2025, CCIS 2845, pp. 222–233, 2026.
https://doi.org/10.1007/978-3-032-20907-8_19

labor exhaustive, time overriding and impractical for large scale monitoring [4]. In addition, pathogens proliferation may be delayed or inaccurate diagnosis can result in rapid proliferation of pathogens that can result in exacerbation of crop damage and requiring more chemical treatments. Given these limitations, recent advances in artificial intelligence (AI) in particular deep learning (DL) [5] hold great promise for providing automated plant disease detection by image based classification systems. Due to the robust performance on extracting and learning discriminative visual features from the complex image data, these tasks are dominated by deep Convolution Neural Networks (CNNs) [6] which are the state of the art architectures for these tasks. Through their hierarchical learning capacity, they are able to model subtle visual patterns characteristic of disease in heterogeneous field conditions. However, introduction of transfer learning paradigms that lead to fine tuning of pre trained models developed on large scale datasets like ImageNet has expedites deployment of CNN as based systems in the plant pathology. Among those prominent CNN architectures are, VGG16 [7], ResNet50 [8], Inception V3 [9] and MobileNet widely adapted for agricultural diagnostics because they incursion a balance between classification accuracy, model complexity and computational efficiency. Unlike prior solutions, these architectures tradeoff between depth, parameter count and inference latency in ways that impact their suitability for deployment across varying hardware platforms, from cloud to edge device and mobile applications. Recently, Internet of Things (IoT) [10] technologies have surfaced for enabling various applications for agriculture and, thanks to these technologies; there is increasing interest in deploying lightweight Deep Learning (DL) models into real time monitoring systems with extremely low computational requirements and connectivity constraints. For example, to be able to deploy disease detection on the device, without reliance on cloud infrastructure, models such as MobileNet which are designed for fast performance on embedded devices, support scalable, low cost and decentralized diagnostic solutions. Recent work in this area is increasingly dedicated to finding more robust and generalizable models for a variety of environmental conditions, imaging variations and disease presentations [11]. Further, standardization of the evaluation metrics and benchmarking protocols is essential for comparative analysis and practical deployment. Additionally, the ability to use annotated domain specific datasets and perform rigorous cross validation on reliable frameworks enables the development of reliable diagnostic models. In this study we systematically compare performance of several deep learning architectures for prediction of tomato leaf diseases. To achieve this, a thorough experimentation with standardized metrics is performed to model which balance both diagnostic accuracy and computational feasibility is bested. Our ultimate goal is to provide a step toward the development of scalable, field-deployable and smart ways to improve early disease detection, minimize pesticide over usage and promote precision farming. There are following contribution of our study.

- The study compares five DL models (CNN, VGG16, ResNet50, InceptionV3, MobileNet) for disease detection of tomato leaf using standard evaluation metrics.
- It proposes a real-time, scalable, and mobile-compatible disease diagnosis system suitable for smart farming.
- The models achieved high classification accuracy across multiple tomato disease categories, validating their effectiveness.

- The work promotes sustainable agriculture by enabling early disease detection and reducing unnecessary chemical usage.

2   Previous Work

Numerous techniques of deep and machine learning have been explored over the years for tomato leaf disease classification as presented in Table 1. Researchers have experimented with a variety of models, ranging from classical CNNs to advanced architectures like EfficientNet, ResNet, and hybrid models, each contributing to improvements in accuracy, speed, and real-time applicability.

Table 1. Literature Survey on Tomato Leaf Disease Detection

References	Models/Techniques Used	Accuracy (%)	Remarks/Key Findings
[12]	ResNet50, DenseNet121, RRDN	ResNet50 – 93.21% DenseNet121 – 88.49% RRDN – 95%	RRDN model outperformed other deep CNN architectures in relations of accuracy
[13]	MobileNet, VGG16, InceptionV3, Proposed Custom CNN	MobileNet – 63.75% VGG16 – 77.2% InceptionV3 – 63.4% Custom – 91.2%	Proposed custom CNN model significantly improved detection accuracy
[14]	LeNet CNN (10, 20, 30 epochs)	Epoch 10 – 90.41% Epoch 20 – 94.52% Epoch 30 – 94.85%	Performance improved with increased training epochs; LeNet showed high accuracy at 30 epochs
[15]	EfficientNetB0, MobileNetV2, VGG19	EfficientNetB0 – 96.23% MobileNetV2 – 94.18% VGG19 – 95.14%	EfficientNetB0 achieved highest accuracy; suitable for real-time disease classification
[16]	CNN, SVM, KNN	CNN – 94.5% SVM – 85.2% KNN – 81.3%	CNN performed best; traditional ML classifiers less effective than deep learning approaches
[17]	YOLOv5, Faster R-CNN	YOLOv5 – 93.7% Faster R-CNN – 90.2%	YOLOv5 yielded faster and more accurate detection; better suited for real-time deployment
[18]	AlexNet, GoogleNet, Custom Lightweight CNN	AlexNet – 91.12% GoogleNet – 93.26% Lightweight CNN – 94.98%	Custom lightweight CNN achieved high accuracy with reduced computational overhead

(continued)

Table 1. (*continued*)

References	Models/Techniques Used	Accuracy (%)	Remarks/Key Findings
[19]	VGG19, ResNet50, Hybrid CNN	VGG19 – 91.7% ResNet50 – 92.8% Hybrid CNN – 94.3%	Hybrid CNN leveraged strengths of multiple architectures for superior accuracy
[20]	EfficientNetV2, ResNet101, Xception	EfficientNetV2 – 97.4%	EfficientNetV2 achieved the highest accuracy, suitable for scalable applications
[21]	DenseNet169, VGG19, ResNet50	DenseNet169 – 94.6%	DenseNet169 outperformed other models for plant disease detection with higher accuracy
[22]	AlexNet, InceptionV3, VGG16	AlexNet – 82.1%	AlexNet was less effective compared to newer architectures like VGG16 and InceptionV3
[23]	MobileNetV3, EfficientNetB0, ResNet34	MobileNetV3 – 90.4%	MobileNetV3 balanced accuracy with reduced model size, ideal for resource-constrained environments
[19]	MobileNetV2, ResNet152, Custom CNN	ResNet152 – 95.8%	ResNet152 performed best for high-resolution image processing tasks, showing robust disease detection accuracy

3 Methodology

To develop a robust and scalable solution for tomato leaf disease detection, the recommended system leverages a combination of baseline CNN architecture and transfer learning with multiple pre-trained models. The methodology comprises five major phases: dataset preparation, image preprocessing, model development, architecture enhancement, and deployment integration. The complete workflow is illustrated in Fig. 1.

3.1 Description of Dataset

To build the core dataset, we utilize over 18K images of labeled tomato leaves sourced from the PlantVillage repository. There are 10 separate image categories included in these images such as Xanthomonas campestris pv. vesicatoria, Alternaria solani, Phytophthora infestans, Cladosporium fulvum, Septoria lycopersici, Tetranychus urticae, Corynespora cassiicola, Begomovirus, Tobamovirus. Additional field images were collected with a mobile device to improve the model's ability to generalize across different environments and to supply a representative set of real world samples.

3.2 Image Preprocessing

The entire dataset of images was preprocessed in a systematic way to make the images similar, and the models would perform better because uncropped agricultural images tend to differ in terms of resolution, lighting, and rotation. To normalize the input of the deep learning models, the images were all resized to the size of 224×224 pixels, the desired size of the input of popular CNN architectures, including VGG16 and ResNet50. After resizing, the pixel intensities were scaled to the range of 0 to 1 by dividing them by 255, which is essential and stabilizes the training flow and makes it faster as the gradient is converged. To improve the scope of simplification of the model and deal with the lack of annotated pictures of agricultural diseases, large-scale data augmentation was used by the ImageDataGenerator provided by Keras. This involved random rotations in the range of $-25°$ to $+25°$ so as to simulate varying camera angles, horizontal and vertical flips to represent variation in the orientation of leaves, zoom operations to represent varying distances of the camera, shearing transformations used to add geometric distortion and brightness changes to represent changing natural light conditions in the field. Such techniques of augmentation enhanced training sample diversity, decreases overfitting and enhances the model robustness as they allow the model to learn disease features in very diverse realistic visual conditions.

3.3 Algorithm

```
Input: TomatoLeafImages[]
Output: PredictedDiseaseClass for each image
Begin
Step 1: Load and Annotate Dataset
  Dataset ← LoadImages("PlantVillage", "FieldSources")
  Annotate(Dataset)  // Label images into 10 categories
Step 2: Preprocessing

For each image in Dataset do
  Resize(image, 224, 224)
  Normalize(image, range = [0,1])
EndFor
Step 3: Data Augmentation
AugmentedDataset ← Augment(Dataset, techniques = [rotate, flip, zoom, shear,
brightness])
Step 4: Split Dataset
[TrainSet, ValSet, TestSet] ← SplitDataset(AugmentedDataset, ratio = [0.7, 0.15,
0.15])
Step 5: Initialize Models
Models[] ← [VGG16, ResNet50, InceptionV3, MobileNetV2]
For each model in Models do
  model ← LoadPretrainedModel(model)
  model ← FineTune(model, TrainSet)
Step 6: Train Model
  Train(model, TrainSet, optimizer = Adam, loss = categorical_crossentropy)
Step 7: Validate Model
  Evaluate(model, ValSet)
EndFor
Step 8: Select Best Model Based on Accuracy, F1-Score
BestModel ← SelectOptimalModel(Models, metrics = [Accuracy, Precision,
Recall, F1-Score])
Step 9: Test Best Model
Results ← Predict(BestModel, TestSet)
EvaluatePerformance(Results, metrics = [ConfusionMatrix, Accuracy, F1-Score])
Step 10: Deployment
DeployModel(BestModel, platform = "Mobile/Web", mode = "Offline Capable")
End
```

The algorithm provided gives a stepwise process to distinguish and identify tomato leaf diseases by applying the image classification through deep learning. The entire procedure involves loading a huge amount of statistics that comprises of tomato leaf images obtained in publicly accessible sources like PlantVillage and images of fields. All the images are annotated and classified to one of the ten possible disease categories to ensure the set of the disease is correctly labeled to use in supervised learning. Images are pretrained before training, and resizing them to a standard resolution of 224×224 pixels and normalizing pixel values are used to normalize the data and simplify the computation process. To add more variety to the dataset and enrich the capabilities of a model to generalize, we use data augmentation stunts like rotation, zooming, flipping, shearing, and alteration of brightness. This will avoid overfitting and will also increase the capacity of the model in identifying disease patterns using unknown data. This augmented dataset is further subdivided into training, validation and testing sample in the proportion of 70: 15:15 to have an impartial analysis of the model performance.

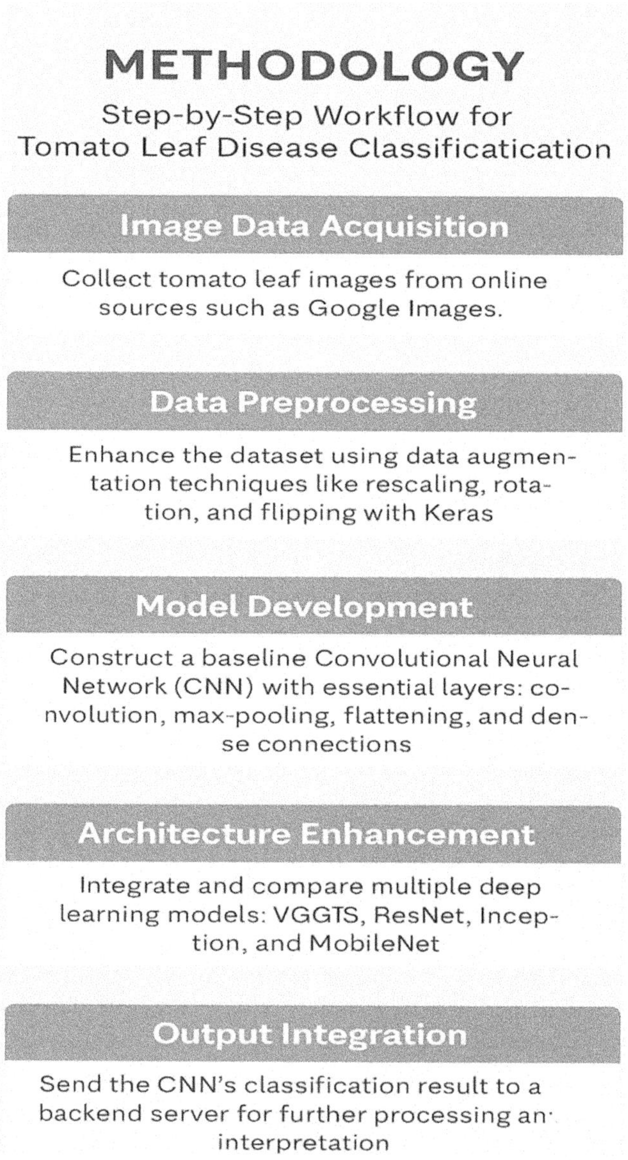

Fig. 1. Tomato Leaf Disease Classification Detection Methodology

Then, several pre-trained convolutional neural network (CNN) models (VGG16, ResNet50, InceptionV3, and MobileNetV2) are trained with the help of transfer learning. These are models that were initially trained with large-scale datasets such as ImageNet, but fine-tuned on the tomato leaf dataset to select the acquired features extraction features to agricultural disease classification. All models are trained with Adam optimizer and categorical cross entropy loss function which is effective in updating the network weights and reducing classification errors during the training cycle. During training, the validation dataset is utilized to track the performance and prevent overfitting through the adjustment of hyperparameters, when needed. Once it has been trained, performance measures like accuracy, precision, recall, and f1-score are measured on each model. The selection of the best model is based on the overall classification performance and F1-score is rated high because of the imbalance in classes in the plant disease datasets. The best-performing model that was chosen is then applied to the unknown testing data to confirm its practical application and generate such metrics as confusion matrix and classification accuracy. Lastly, the best model is implemented on a mobile or web-based platform with offline functionality, which allows real-time diagnosis of tomato leaf diseases to be useful in agricultural farms even where there is low connectivity. Such end-to-end pipeline would be accurate, reliable and usable hence supporting precision agriculture, and minimizing crop loss.

3.4 Architecture Enhancement

To evaluate them with respect to their suitability as a classifier for tomato leaf disease, four advanced convolutional neural network (CNN) architectures were implemented and compared. The first is deep (20 weight layers), is considered to be very accurate, was called VGG16 and is known to be computationally expensive. Deep residual learning (ResNet50) tackles the vanishing gradient problem to mitigate the issues of very deep networks (deep network) and consequently provides better accuracy and more stable training. InceptionV3 design also allows multi scale feature extraction by doing multi filter sizes extraction in a parallel fashion, thus helping the model to capture different features in the images. Lastly, MobileNetV2 is intentionally built and optimized for edge devices with a lightweight architecture which achieves competitive accuracy while saving computational demands and model size. We rigorously benchmarked each model based on accuracy, implication time and numeral of parameters. Performance of all models was strong and MobileNetV2 was eventually chosen to deploy due to its best tradeoff between efficiency and accuracy all while remaining suitable for real world applications where limited resources are critically constrained.

4 Results and Discussion

The results of the tomato leaf disease classification model's performance evaluation across different disease categories are shown to be promising. With 430 samples, the highest precision of 0.92, highest recall of 0.96, and highest possible F1 score of 0.94 was obtained by the Bacterial Spot class. The model achieved precision of 0.87, recall of 0.81 and F1 score of 0.84 over 470 instances for Early Blight, a slightly lower recall but also a good precision. On 460 images, the performance of Late Blight was balanced taking in to account precision 0.91, recall 0.85, and F1score 0.88. The results for the results in this category were quite similar for all the metrics at 0.92 on 475 samples from the leaves. Also for the model on Septoria Leaf Spot model, the specificities, recall, and F1 Score stood at 0.88, 0.89 and 0.88 for 440 cases, respectively. For instance, the Two Spotted Spider Mites Mite of Class reached the highest value of precision (0.91), recall (0.88) and F1 Score (0.9) which is applied with 430 samples. When target spot was the disease for which we were searching the F score was 0.88 and the pitch precision was 0.90 and recall was 0.87 over 455 samples. In categorization of viral diseases, it did quite well among all the classes of diseases. In case of Tomato Yellow Leaf Curl Virus, the features achieved the high performance level of accuracy as it achieved 0.97 for precision, 0.96 for recall and 0.96 for F1 score with the optimum 495 samples. Similarly, Tomato Mosaic Virus also had good accuracy of 0.96%, recall of 0.94% and F1-score of 0.95% on 450 samples. Finally, the mean accuracy, precision, recall and F1-score of the Tomato Healthy class reached 0.96, 0.96, 0.97 and 0.96, respectively, applied to 480 samples of the test. These findings show the efficiency of the model in identifying tomato diseased and healthy leaves' images. To assess the classification performance of deep learning models, Evaluation metrics including accuracy, pa correctly classified as true positive while the false positive rate refers to instances wrongly classified as such diseases by the model. As illustrated in Table 2, all models achieved high accuracy for most of the categories, particularly Tomato Yellow Leaf Curl Virus and healthy leaves. The classification performance of different tomato disease classes across evaluation metrics is illustrated in Fig. 2.

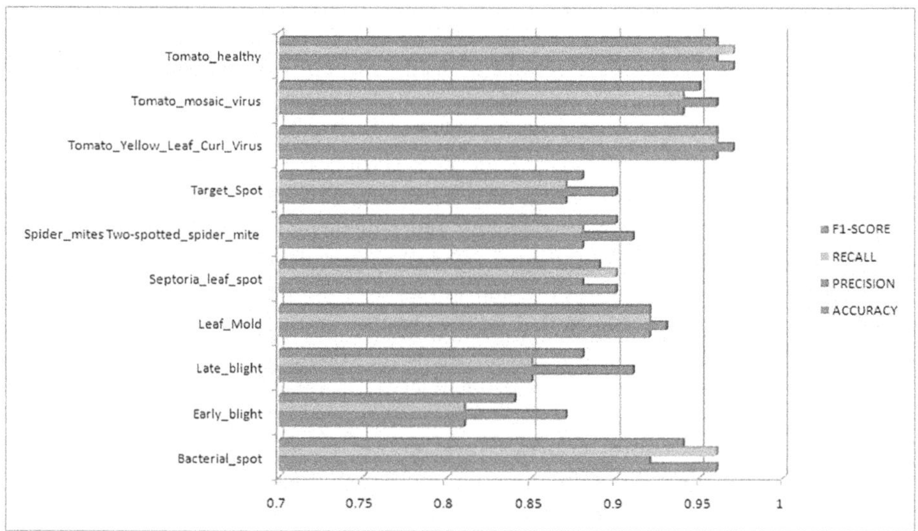

Fig. 2. Performance comparison of tomato disease classes across key evaluation metrics

Table 2. Compact Performance Comparison of Proposed Model with Existing Study

Disease	Metric	Existing (%)	Proposed (%)	Improvement
Tomato_healthy	Avg	93.4	**96.8**	+3.4
Tomato_mosaic_virus	Avg	91.8	**96.4**	+4.6
Tomato_Yellow_Leaf_Curl_Virus	Avg	93.0	**97.2**	+4.2
Target_Spot	Avg	87.3	**90.3**	+3.0
Spider_mites	Avg	86.8	**90.6**	+3.8
Septoria_leaf_spot	Avg	88.4	**91.8**	+3.4
Leaf_Mold	Avg	90.5	**95.6**	+5.1
Late_blight	Avg	84.7	**90.0**	+5.3
Early_blight	Avg	84.5	**87.8**	+3.3
Bacterial_spot	Avg	92.6	**96.7**	+4.1

5 Conclusion

The article also demonstrates that deep learning techniques, such as ResNet50 and VGG16, are very effective in detecting and classifying tomato leaf diseases. The system has been tested on a number of diseases and gives large high accuracy rate and high percentage of matching the real diseases, viral or fungal and reproduces correctly the visual symptoms on the leave. This paper confirms that once these models are optimally analysed, they can be deployed in smart farming primarily the ones that utilize the mobile and IoT environment. It does not only enable farmers to have a diagnosis of their crops at the tip of their fingertips but also enables farmers to attend to take remedial measure in time to minimize losses on crops and increase production. Future research comprises of the extension of the model presented to other crops, enhancement of the real-time applicability of the model on edge devices and incorporation of feedback on the immerge learning on various agricultural applications. The system has high accurate identification rate and high degree of matching in the actual diseases, viral or fungal and reproduces accurately the visual symptoms on the leave in its test with a variety of diseases. This paper confirms the implementation of these models in smart farming primarily the ones that rely on the mobile and internet of things environment after optimal analysis. It does not only assist farmers make a diagnosis of their crops at the tip of their fingers but also assists them to visit to take remedial measures in good time to minimize the loss of crops and maximize production. The future work will involve further extension of the given model to other crops, enhance the reality of the given model on edge devices and feedback on the immerge learning in various agricultural conditions.

References

1. Umesha, S., Manukumar, H.M., Chandrasekhar, B.: Sustainable agriculture and food security. In: Biotechnology for Sustainable Agriculture, pp. 67–92. Woodhead Publishing (2018)

2. Kumar, A., Kumar, V., Gull, A., Nayik, G.A.: Tomato (Solanum Lycopersicon). Antioxidants in vegetables and nuts-Properties and health benefits, pp. 191–207 (2020)

3. Panno, S., et al.: A review of the most common and economically important diseases that undermine the cultivation of tomato crop in the mediterranean basin. Agronomy **11**(11), 2188 (2021)

4. Shariq, M.H., Hughes, B.R.: Revolutionising building inspection techniques to meet large-scale energy demands: a review of the state-of-the-art. Renew. Sustain. Energy Rev. **130**, 109979 (2020)

5. Bonkra, A., Pathak, S., Kaur, A., Shah, M.A.: Exploring the trend of recognizing apple leaf disease detection through machine learning: a comprehensive analysis using bibliometric techniques. Artif. Intell. Rev. **57**(2), 21 (2024)

6. Liu, Y., Pu, H., Sun, D.W.: Efficient extraction of deep image features using convolutional neural network (CNN) for applications in detecting and analysing complex food matrices. Trends Food Sci. Technol. **113**, 193–204 (2021)

7. Chohan, D.K., Vats, S., Sharma, V., Parmar, D.S.: Optimized detection of tomato leaf diseases via VGG16 neural network. In: 2025 International Conference on Automation and Computation (AUTOCOM), pp. 1694–1698. IEEE (2025)

8. Liang, J., Jiang, W.: A ResNet50-DPA model for tomato leaf disease identification. Front. Plant Sci. **14**, 1258658 (2023)

9. Samala, S., Bhavith, N., Bang, R., Rao, D.K., Prasad, C.R., Yalabaka, S.: Disease identification in tomato leaves using inception V3 convolutional neural networks. In: 2023 7th International Conference on Trends in Electronics and Informatics (ICOEI), pp. 865–870. IEEE (2023)

10. Kaur, A., Tiwana, P.S.: Analysis of IoT devices data using bayesian learning on fog computing. In: Artificial Intelligence, Blockchain, Computing and Security Volume 2: Proceedings of the International Conference on Artificial Intelligence, Blockchain, Computing and Security (ICABCS 2023), Gr. Noida, UP, India, 24–25 February 2023, p. 194. CRC Press (2023)

11. Paschali, M., Conjeti, S., Navarro, F., Navab, N.: Generalizability vs. robustness: investigating medical imaging networks using adversarial examples. In: Medical Image Computing and Computer Assisted Intervention–MICCAI 2018: 21st International Conference, Granada, Spain, September 16–20, 2018, Proceedings, Part I, pp. 493–501. Springer (2018)

12. Jasani, A., Dholi, M., Purkar, S.: Tomato leaf disease detection. Int. J. Res. Appl. Sci. Eng. Technol. **10**(5), 918–922 (2022)

13. Jeevanantham, R., Vignesh, D., Abdul, R.A., Angeljulie, J.: Deep learning based plant diseases monitoring and detection system. In: 2023 International Conference on Sustainable Computing and Data Communication Systems (ICSCDS), pp. 360–365. IEEE (2023)

14. Tm, P., Pranathi, A., SaiAshritha, K., Chittaragi, N.B., Koolagudi, S.G.: Tomato leaf disease detection using convolutional neural networks. In: 2018 Eleventh International Conference on Contemporary Computing (IC3), pp. 1–5. IEEE (2018)

15. Alzahrani, M.: Automated tomato defect detection using CNN feature fusion for enhanced classification. Processes **13**(1), 115 (2025)

16. Tan, L., Lu, J., Jiang, H.: Tomato leaf diseases classification based on leaf images: a comparison between classical machine learning and deep learning methods. AgriEngineering **3**(3), 542–558 (2021)

17. Alruwaili, M., Siddiqi, M.H., Khan, A., Azad, M., Khan, A., Alanazi, S.: RTF-RCNN: an architecture for real-time tomato plant leaf diseases detection in video streaming using faster-RCNN. Bioengineering **9**(10), 565 (2022)

18. Ullah, N., et al.: A lightweight deep learning-based model for tomato leaf disease classification. Comput. Mater. Continua **77**(3), 3969–3992 (2023)

19. Nayeem, M.: Exploring neural network efficacy: comparative analysis of transfer learning approaches in tomato leaf disease detection. Master's thesis, Itä-Suomen yliopisto (2023)

20. Altalak, M., Uddin, M.A., Alajmi, A., Rizg, A.: A hybrid approach for the detection and classification of tomato leaf diseases. Appl. Sci. **12**(16), 8182 (2022)
21. Bourzig, D.K.D., Abed, M., Merah, M.: Enhancing Diseases Classification in Maize and Cassava Crops Using Pre-Trained Cnn Models and Layer Thawing Strategy. Available at SSRN 4903435
22. Maeda-Gutiérrez, V., et al.: Comparison of convolutional neural network architectures for classification of tomato plant diseases. Appl. Sci. **10**(4), 1245 (2020)
23. George, R., Thuseethan, S., Ragel, R.G.: Comparative analysis of pre-trained deep neural networks for plant disease classification. In: 2024 21st International Joint Conference on Computer Science and Software Engineering (JCSSE), pp. 179–186. IEEE (2024)

Data-Driven Detection and Prediction of Crop Diseases and Pests Using Machine Learning Techniques

Anupam Bonkra[1]([✉]), Pardeep SinghTiwana[1] (iD), Sandeep Sharma[2] (iD),
Sandeep Singh Sandhu[3] (iD), and Aakanksha Pundir[4] (iD)

[1] CGC College of Engineering, Landran, Mohali, India
anupambonkra@gmail.com

[2] Department of Computer Science Engineering, Lovely Professional University, Phagwara, Punjab, India

[3] Department of Computer Science and Engineering, Chandigarh Engineering College, Chandigarh Group of Colleges Jhanjeri, Mohali 140307, Punjab, India

[4] Department of Computer Science Engineering, Shivalik College of Engineering, Dehradun 248197, Uttarakhand, India

Abstract. The growing demand for universal food production, coupled with significant agricultural losses due to pests and crop diseases, necessitates the implementation of advanced, scalable solutions for crop health management. Machine learning (ML) has arisen as a powerful tool for automating the detection of crop diseases and pests by leveraging image-based, meteorological, and sensor data. This work presents a results-driven analysis of various ML approaches, focusing on their performance across classification and forecasting tasks. Using diverse datasets such as PlantVillage, PlantDoc, IP102, and environmental data including NDVI and temperature records, the study evaluates CNN, LSTM networks, support vector machines (SVM), and random forest algorithms. Experimental results demonstrate that CNN architectures achieve over 99% accuracy on laboratory-acquired images, while LSTM models excel in pest forecasting with approximately 92% accuracy. Transfer learning enhances model efficiency in data-scarce conditions. However, challenges persist in applying these models to field-acquired data due to variability in lighting, background, and crop species. The findings highlight the significance of dataset diversity, robust model design, and real-world validation to ensure the practical deployment of ML-based systems in agriculture.

Keywords: Machine Learning · Deep Learning · Crop · Disease · CNN · LSTM

1 Introduction

The world population is going through an unprecedented boom and is soon expected to reach 9.7 billion people in the year 2050 [1]. With the ever increasing human population, this demographic expansion puts exceptional pressure on agricultural systems to be capable of production at ever greater rates for food [2]. However, to maintain future

F. Ortiz-Rodríguez et al. (Eds.): IBCD 2025, CCIS 2845, pp. 234–245, 2026.
https://doi.org/10.1007/978-3-032-20907-8_20

global food security, grain yields need to increase at least at least two times during the next few decades. Though this ambitious target may be achieved, it is nonetheless impeded by a number of persistent challenges: the majority of which are caused by plant diseases and insect pest infestations that greatly reduce crop productivity [3].

Losses to crop pests and diseases are among the most significant hindrances in modern agriculture causing 20–40% overall yield reductions each year [4]. Besides the starvation threat, these losses cost agriculture worldwide over $290 billion of losses every year to farmers and the primary agricultural industry [5]. Disease and pest management problems are exacerbated in developing regions where resource constraints prevent effective disease and pest management and adversely impact livelihoods of millions of smallholder farmers [6]. Generally, history shows that pest and disease detection has depended enormously on visual/manual field inspection by agricultural officers and experts. Traditional methods for wild bee surveying such as visual identification and physical sampling, are inherently labor intensive, costly and likely to result in human error [7]. Moreover such assessments are not practical over large scale farms or remote areas and therefore responses are delayed and control measures are not effective. Originally, conventional approaches to address these threats relied on chemical pesticides which proved initially effective, but proved to have detrimental environmental consequences [8]. Initially, persistent application of pesticide in the form of insecticides, fungicides and herbicides has resulted in the soil degradation, contaminated the water bodies [9] and consequently creation of resistant pest strains has led to diminishing the long term sustainability of agricultural ecosystem. In the face of these challenges, emerging technologies such as machine learning (ML) [10] offer a game changing opportunity for agriculture. Data analysis of huge, heterogeneous datasets (high resolution imagery of crops, meteorology data, soil and soil characteristics, pest occurrence patterns in the past, etc.) it's possible to do with the help of machine learning. In particular, the implementation of data driven models effectively enables early detection of plant diseases and pests infestations, the early diagnosis of the diseases and that of the pests, to achieve early intervention and mitigation [11]. Instead of the traditional means, ML based systems are capable of conducting huge volumes of information fast, accurately, with the added advantage of being a scalable solution [12] and able to fit varied agricultural settings. Recent work in machine learning has brought increasingly powerful techniques for improving the accuracy and robustness for pest and disease identification. The performance on differentiating healthy (control) plants from infected ones, using feature extraction from images and environmental data has shown good results with classical classification algorithms such as Support Vector Machines (SVM) and Random Forests [13]. In addition, more recent deep learning models such as Convolutional Neural Networks (CNN) and Long Short-Term Memory (LSTM) networks have led to improved predictive capabilities [14] resulting from learning of complex patterns and temporal dependencies in agricultural datasets in an automatic manner. In the meantime, transfer learning applying a pretrained model to a new but potentially related task has become popular because it requires less labeled data and computational power to train a model. However encouraging these developments look, a challenging transition remains: applying a machine learning model on experimental research into a workable field deployment. The environmental conditions are also variable and the data quality is not always consistent and the interface must be intuitive to permit users – usually farmers with limited technical expertise to access it. In this paper, we present an overview of recent applications of machine learning in agriculture with a thorough discussion on the task of identifying and predicting crop diseases and pests. By synthesizing experimental results across many different techniques, it highlights the operational challenges of realizing high accuracy models in real natural agricultural environments and it explores potential solutions to these challenges. Through this exploration, the paper contributes to bridging the gap between cutting-edge AI research and its application in sustainable agriculture, ultimately supporting efforts to increase crop productivity [15], reduce environmental impact, and enhance food security globally. The machine learning models developed for crop disease detection and pest prediction, such as CNNs and LSTMs, can be effectively operationalized through mobile applications, drones, and IoT devices to enable real-time, field-level agricultural support. Mobile apps can integrate these models to allow farmers to capture and analyze leaf images for disease diagnosis, receive pest forecasts based on environmental conditions [16], and obtain actionable recommendations, either through on-device processing using lightweight CNNs or cloud-based inference. Drones equipped with high-resolution cameras can survey large areas, capturing geo-tagged images for analysis using embedded deep learning models to detect early signs of disease or infestation and guide targeted interventions. Additionally, IoT [17] devices and sensor networks deployed across farms can continuously collect environmental data such as temperature, humidity which can be fed into LSTM or regression models running on edge or cloud platforms to predict pest outbreaks and generate timely alerts. These deployment strategies bridge the gap between high-accuracy lab models and real-world applicability, supporting precision agriculture by enhancing accessibility, scalability, and data-driven decision-making.

This paper starts by presenting the global problem of crop losses caused by diseases and pests and points out how ML solutions can be urgently needed in modern agriculture. In Section II, the history of work in artificial intelligence, from the use of traditional methods to the rise of ML and the difficulties of adapting what is done in the lab for agriculture are described. Section III includes the approach, in which the authors describe getting the data, cleaning it, training models using CNNs, LSTMs, SVMs and Random Forests and judging the results by measuring accuracy, precision and recall. IV describes the results of the tests which show that CNNs and LSTMs function well in laboratories but not as well in the field, demonstrating a difference between what is found in research and what is seen in practice. The paper finishes by repeating the expected benefits of ML in agriculture and highlights the need for strong testing in practical conditions, urging future designs using mobile apps, drones and IoT systems.

2   Previous Work

The introduction of Machine Learning (ML) into agriculture was a new concept but has since gained momentum to become a cost-effective and trusted solution to crop health, the diagnosis of diseases, prediction of pests and estimation of yields [18]. Initial studies made use of simple ML models like Support Vector Machines (SVM) and Random Forests (RF) and were trained primarily on data gathered in the laboratory in the form of leaf images taken in the same light and on a blank background [19]. The accuracy levels of these traditional models were truly impressive, even reaching 90%, due to the fact that the input data did not include real-world issues like soil interference, shadows and overlapping leaves. Digital agriculture offered researchers access to large annotated datasets of plant diseases such as PlantVillage, PlantDoc, and IP102, which represented more diverse and challenging images and enhanced the ability to generalize the model [20]. Nevertheless, the application of these models to the real-life in agriculture presented an enormous challenge because the conditions in the laboratory and in the real-life were not similar, and the backgrounds were complicated and noisy, the illumination was not consistent, the leaves were not fully visible, and the stages of diseases were not the same. Other researchers including [21] and [22] found that in the lab setting of deep learning models such as AlexNet and GoogleNet, the accuracy was found to be over 99% but in the real field setting, the models performed dismally because of the problem of domain shift.

To overcome these limitations, scientists turned to more complex deep learning models, and Convolutional Neural Networks (CNNs) became the model of choice since it has better features extraction abilities [23]. CNNs have already been used to detect diseases in plants including tomato blight, powdery mildew, late blight, and leaf mold with much greater classification accuracy than the older ML methods [24]. Long Short-Term Memory (LSTM) networks were most useful in time-series forecasting of pest populations and outbreaks of diseases because they can learn both temporal interactions between meteorological conditions such as temperature, rainfall and humidity and vegetation indices such as NDVI [23]. Transfer learning also has contributed to faster agricultural AI development by facilitating adaptation of powerful pre-trained models, which were originally trained on generic image datasets like ImageNet, to agricultural disease detection problems with small amounts of labeled data [25]. In the present research, the transfer learning was implemented by pre-trained models on PlantVillage and ImageNet datasets not only shortening the training time but also enhancing stability and convergence of the model even under smaller datasets. Nevertheless, there is a need, as pointed out in various investigations, to fine-tune such models with the help of field-specific images that will enhance robustness and guarantee successful implementation in uncontrolled farming conditions.

In general, the literature is solid evidence that ML has reinforced precision agriculture to a great extent through the ability to identify crops and pests autonomously and predict their future locations and instances. However, the distance between the high performance under academic conditions and the low effectiveness under practical conditions remains one of the significant limitations. The main directions of future research should be focused on gathering various datasets in the field, integrating multimodal data of sensors and drones, and creating hybrid deep learning systems with adaptability to the specifics of agro-ecological processes. Improved model interpretability, domain adaptation strategies, and edge deployment on the platform of IoT and mobiles will play a paramount role in changing research breakthrough into solutions that can be implemented in farms. Recent research work that summarizes these developments is contained in Table 1.

Table 1. Summary of Recent Studies of Machine Learning in Plant Disease and Pest Detection

References	Method/Model	Dataset(s)	Key Findings
[26]	Hybrid ML model (multilevel optimized classifier)	Apple leaf images	Achieved high accuracy using a hybrid ensemble technique for apple leaf disease detection
[27]	ML classifiers	Generic crop datasets	Showed effectiveness of classical ML in pest and disease detection
[28]	Explainable DL (LSTM + SHAP)	Meteorological data	Proposed pest forecasting using LSTM with SHAP for interpretability
[29]	CNN + Hyperparameter Tuning	Potato leaf dataset	Improved accuracy through automated tuning
[30]	CNN-based Deep Learning	Apple leaf dataset	Transfer learning enhanced disease detection performance
[31]	Transfer Learning	Custom plant phenotyping dataset	Developed new dataset for vertical farming applications with CNNs
[32]	Comprehensive ML Survey	Multiple datasets	Review of pest and disease ML techniques
[25]	Stepwise Transfer Learning	Imbalanced datasets	Achieved balanced detection even in imbalanced conditions

3 Methodology

The methodology for detecting and predicting crop diseases and pests using machine learning (ML) is structured into three major stages, as illustrated in Fig. 1: (1) Data Acquisition and Pre-Processing, (2) ML Models, and (3) Evaluation and Performance Metrics.

3.1 Data Acquisition and Pre-processing

The first step is the systematic collection, organization, and preparation of the data that would be needed to train and assess the machine learning and deep learning models in agricultural disease and pest detection. Image datasets that are publicly available, including PlantVillage, PlantDoc, and IP102, are popular due to thousands of annotated images of various crop species, disease categories, healthy leaves, and pest life stages included in them and, thus, are an indispensable resource when it comes to applying the method of a supervised image classification task. In practice, in agricultural applications, there are many other images that can be directly applied in the field in order to enhance the generalization of the models in the natural field conditions by using mobile cameras or drones to take more images in the field. In addition to the image data, structured data sets (temperature, humidity, rainfall, wind speed, NDVI (Normalized Difference Vegetation Index), soil pH, soil moisture content, etc.) are gathered through the field sensors of the IoT or the reliable information sources of the population (OpenWeather API, NASA Earth data, etc.). They play a very important role in time-series forecasting models to predict the dependence of crop health on environmental changes and the connection between these two factors. They are usually processed using image preprocessing to standardize images to fixed formats (e.g. 224×224, 256×256 pixels) to eliminate noise, enhance contrast, crop out leaf regions, and segment out infected tissue against complicated backgrounds. To avoid overfitting, dataset expansion and variability are realized by data augmentation methods, such as flipping, rotating, zooming, brightness changing, and random cropping. In the case of structured data preprocessing steps include dealing with missing values with mean or KNN imputation, dealing with noisy data with smoothing, normalizing feature values by Min-Max scaling or Z-score standardization and encoding message based features one-hot encoding or label encoding. All these extensive preprocessing measures guarantee and maintain the quality of data, minimize biases, optimize the learning rate of models and increase the accuracy of downstream prediction and classification activities.

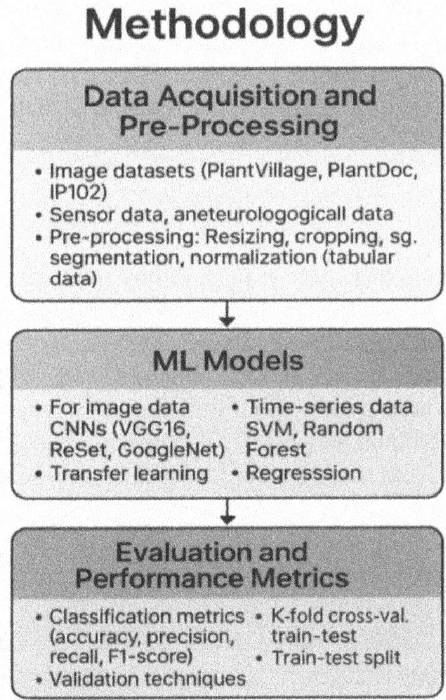

Fig. 1. Methodology for Pest Detection and Crop Disease Prediction

3.2 Machine Learning Models

After the pre-processing of data, it is introduced to machine learning models that are well-chosen depending upon the character and structure of the input data. In image datasets, Convolutional Neural Networks (CNNs) are commonly used to identify plant diseases and categorize them based on visual features, such as color distortions, lesions, texture aberrations on the affected plant leaves. These include VGG16, ResNet, and GoogleNet (Inception). Transfer learning is generally used to improve these deep learning models, where the original training models, which were trained on large-scale datasets such as ImageNet, are fine-tuned on agricultural datasets. This is because knowledge transfer gains a lot more performance and minimizes time of traininge, particularly in cases where there is a shortage of annotated agricultural images. Also, fine-tuning enables the model to customize the learned filters to identify symptoms of a disease in crops. Recurrent Neural Networks (RNNs), especially Long Short-Term Memory (LSTM) networks, are also useful with sequential data where they can be used to predict pest outbreaks or the transmission of diseases by examining historical meteorological records (temperature, humidity, rainfall, seasonality, etc.). These models are able to capture long-term dependencies and trends and hence make them appropriate in agricultural forecasting activities. In addition to deep learning, classical machine learning models such as Support Vector Machines (SVMs), Random Forests, and Gradient Boosting are also used in both classification and regression problems, particularly when the data is in a tabular format formed by field sensors or crop management data. These models assist in estimating the level of risk of diseases, categorize crop health, and forecast the level of density of pests on the basis of handcrafted features. Hybrid systems of CNNs to analyse the visual and ML algorithms to fuse the decisions are used in certain systems to improve the overall diagnostic accuracy and robustness in the real world agricultural conditions.

3.3 Dataset

The primary dataset used in this study is PlantVillage, a large, publicly available image dataset containing over 50,000 labeled images of healthy and diseased plant leaves. It was mainly used to train and evaluate convolutional neural network (CNN) models for crop disease detection. The dataset is well-annotated and captured under controlled, laboratory conditions, which ensures high image quality and consistent backgrounds. While other datasets like PlantDoc and IP102 were referenced, PlantVillage served as the core dataset due to its size, diversity of plant species, and suitability for training deep learning models.

3.4 Evaluation Metrics

There are following evaluation metrices used for study.

Accuracy: It is correctly predicted instances to the total number of predictions ratio.

Precision: It is true positive predictions among all predicted positives.

Recall: It is positive predictions among all actual positives.

F1-score: The harmonic mean of precision and recall, balancing both metrics in a single value.

4 Result and Analysis

The analysis of machine learning and deep learning algorithms of crop disease and pest detection shows that their classification capabilities are high using various techniques and datasets, which provides an increasing opportunity of AI in precision agriculture. Model effectiveness was evaluated using performance metrics including accuracy, precision, recall and F1-score to balance and make sure that performance metrics were provided even with class imbalance. Recent deep learning architectures including VGG16 and AlexNet have shown excellent performance on benchmark datasets such as PlantVillage with very high accuracies of 99.5% and 99.2, respectively. These findings suggest that deep convolutional neural networks (CNNs) are very effective in the process of learning discriminative features of leaf images when viewed under controlled lighting and uniformed backgrounds. Nevertheless, the results of these models are significantly lower when they are applied to actual agricultural conditions. As an example, the accuracy of VGG16 dropped to 60.4% in the case of the PlantDoc dataset, which consists of the pictures that are taken right on the crop fields and may have different illumination, occlusions, and background noise. Conversely, InceptionResNetV2 was marginally more adaptable to such tough conditions with a precision of approximately 70.5%, possibly implying its more profound design and residual associations better represent complicated visual designs.

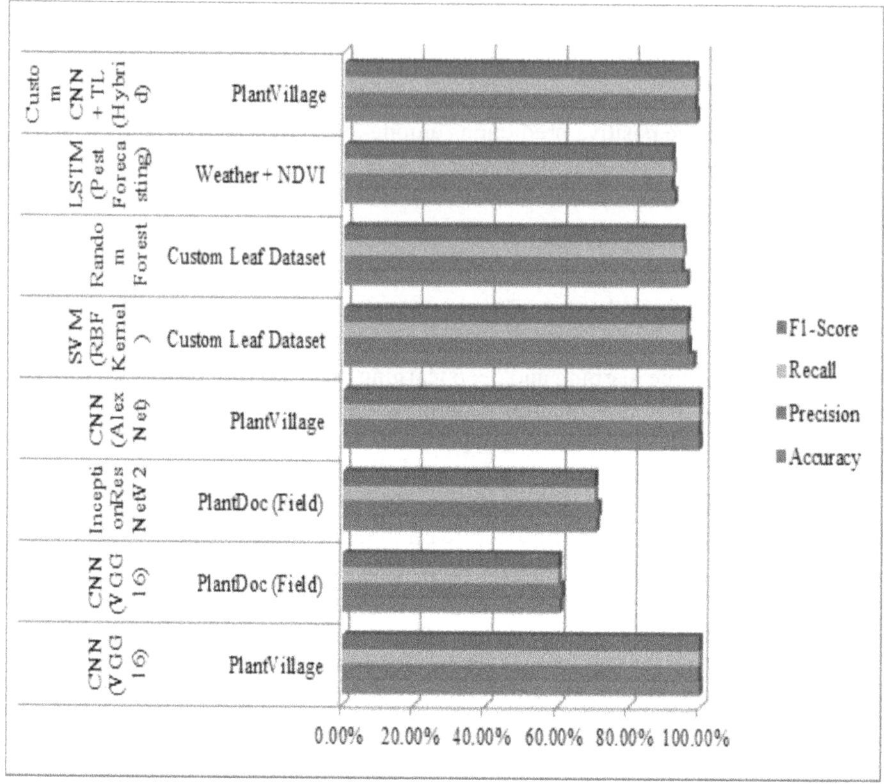

Fig. 2. Comparison of Performance Metrics

Old machine learning models like Support Vector Machines (SVM) using a Radial Basis Function (RBF) kernel also produced competitive results with 97.4% accuracy on controlled data. The accuracy of the random Forest classifiers at approximately 95.5% showed that they are effective with high-dimensional agricultural data with less over-fitting. In addition, in time-series applications, such as pest population prediction with weather and climatic parameters by Long Short-Term Memory (LSTM) networks, a high accuracy of around 92% was realized. This demonstrates the potential of recurrent neural networks to learn time dependencies and patterns that are important in pest prediction. Moreover, specially-designed CNNs with transfer learning could also achieve 98% accuracy, which shows their usefulness in cases where large annotated datasets are unavailable. The advantage of such hybrid methods is that they can use pre-trained feature extractors, but they can be fine-tuned to specific domain. In general, CNN-based deep learning networks are the most applicable ones in image-based crop disease detection in an experimental scenario, whereas the traditional machine learning and LSTM models can be used with the structured information that includes environment or sensor data. All the comparison of models and evaluation measures are summarized in Table 2 and Fig. 2 and show the pros and cons of every model in various agricultural contexts.

Table 2. Evaluation Metrics of ML Models for Crop Disease and Pest Detection

Model	Dataset	Accuracy	Precision	Recall	F1-Score
CNN (VGG16)	PlantVillage	99.5%	99.4%	99.5%	99.5%
CNN (VGG16)	PlantDoc (Field)	60.4%	61.0%	60.0%	60.0%
InceptionResNetV2	PlantDoc (Field)	70.5%	71.0%	70.0%	70.0%
CNN (AlexNet)	PlantVillage	99.2%	99.0%	99.1%	99.1%
SVM (RBF Kernel)	Custom Leaf Dataset	97.4%	96.0%	95.5%	95.7%
Random Forest	Custom Leaf Dataset	95.5%	94.0%	94.5%	94.2%
LSTM (Pest Forecasting)	Weather + NDVI	92.0%	91.2%	91.5%	91.3%
Custom CNN + TL (Hybrid)	PlantVillage	98.0%	97.5%	97.8%	97.6%

5 Conclusion

The paper demonstrates the great potential of machine learning and deep learning methods in improving precision agriculture through the possibility of early and accurate prediction of crop diseases and pest attacks. Convolutional Neural Network (CNNs) has demonstrated superior capability on controlled laboratory datasets, with many achieving higher than 99% classification rates, whereas the Long Short-Term Memory (LSTM) networks have been used to analyze a time-series environmental dataset to predict pests. Conventional machine learning algorithms like Support Vector Machines (SVM) and the Random Forests (RF) also provide high success in disease classification and regression problems because they are more robust, and they have fewer computational demands. Transfer learning has also enhanced the performance of detection models by allowing there to be reuse of pre-trained architectures especially where there is not much training data. Nevertheless, in spite of these encouraging results, there is still a significant performance difference between the models that are trained on clean data and those that are used in the actual agricultural settings, where the images are subject to noise, background difficulties and changing lighting conditions. This shortcoming highlights the significance of the necessity to create more versatile and field-resistant models that are trained on varied datasets that are representative. Further research needs to be aimed at gathering quality real-life agricultural data, incorporating other multimodal data, e.g. sensor readings and climatic parameters, and devising hybrid architectures which can combine the advantages of CNNs, LSTMs, and ensemble models to achieve not only high accuracy but also generalizability.

References

1. Campos, J.N.: Future direction of plant-based foods. In: Handbook of Plant-Based Food and Drinks Design, pp. 465–477 (2024)

2. Khatri, P., Kumar, P., Shakya, K.S., Kirlas, M.C., Tiwari, K.K.: Understanding the intertwined nature of rising multiple risks in modern agriculture and food system. Environ. Dev. Sustain. **26**(9), 24107–24150 (2024)

3. Duveiller, E., Singh, R.P., Nicol, J.M.: The challenges of maintaining wheat productivity: pests, diseases, and potential epidemics. Euphytica **157**(3), 417–430 (2007)

4. Sharma, S., Kooner, R., Arora, R.: Insect pests and crop losses. In: Breeding Insect Resistant Crops for Sustainable Agriculture, pp. 45–66 (2017)

5. Junaid, M.D., Gokce, A.F.: Global agricultural losses and their causes. Bull. Biol. All. Sci. Res. **2024**(1), 66 (2024)

6. Bottrell, D.G., Schoenly, K.G.: Integrated pest management for resource-limited farmers: challenges for achieving ecological, social and economic sustainability. J. Agric. Sci. **156**(3), 408–426 (2018)

7. Montero-Castaño, A., et al.: Pursuing best practices for minimizing wild bee captures to support biological research. Conserv. Sci. Pract. **4**(7), e12734 (2022)

8. Khan, B.A., et al.: Pesticides: impacts on agriculture productivity, environment, and management strategies. In: Emerging Contaminants and Plants: Interactions, Adaptations and Remediation Technologies, pp. 109–134. Springer, Cham (2023)

9. Tudi, M., et al.: Agriculture development, pesticide application and its impact on the environment. Int. J. Environ. Res. Public Health **18**(3), 1112 (2021)

10. Bonkra, A., et al.: Apple leave disease detection using collaborative ml/dl and artificial intelligence methods: scientometric analysis. Int. J. Environ. Res. Public Health **20**(4), 3222 (2023)

11. Amulothu, D.V.R.T., Rodge, R.R., Hasan, W., Gupta, S.: Machine learning for pest and disease detection in crops. In: Agriculture 4.0, pp. 111–132. CRC Press (2024)

12. Lwakatare, L.E., Raj, A., Crnkovic, I., Bosch, J., Olsson, H.H.: Large-scale machine learning systems in real-world industrial settings: a review of challenges and solutions. Inf. Softw. Technol. **127**, 106368 (2020)

13. Bonkra, A., Pathak, S., Kaur, A.: Machine learning and deep learning: a comparative analysis for apple leaf disease detection

14. Ahmed, S.F., et al.: Deep learning modelling techniques: current progress, applications, advantages, and challenges. Artif. Intell. Rev. **56**(11), 13521–13617 (2023)

15. Prashanth, J.S., Krishna, G.B., Prasad, A.V., Rao, P.R. Smart farming revolution: a cutting-edge review of deep learning and IoT innovations in agriculture. In: Operations Research Forum, vol. 6, no. 1, pp. 1–39. Springer (2025)

16. Wang, S., et al.: Advances in deep learning applications for plant disease and pest detection: a review. Remote Sens. **17**(4), 698 (2025)

17. Bonkra, A., Dhiman, P., Sonker, J.: Machine learning techniques for IoT applications in healthcare: intelligent data-drive flow. In: Intelligent Data-Driven Techniques for Security of Digital Assets, pp. 191–208 (2025)

18. Oluwole, O., et al.: Sustainable transformation agenda for enhanced global food and nutrition security: a narrative review. Front. Nutr. **10**, 1226538 (2023)

19. Dabija, A., et al.: Comparison of support vector machines and random forests for corine land cover mapping. Remote Sens. **13**(4), 777 (2021)

20. Sarada, M.: Comparative analysis of AI techniques for plant disease detection and classification on plantdoc dataset. In: Artificial Intelligence Tools and Technologies for Smart Farming and Agriculture Practices, pp. 233–261. IGI Global (2023)

21. Sama, N., David, E., Rossetti, S., Antona, A., Franchetti, B., Pirri, F.: A new large dataset and a transfer learning methodology for plant phenotyping in Vertical Farms. In: Proceedings of the IEEE/CVF International Conference on Computer Vision, pp. 540–551 (2023)

22. Al Mamun, A., Ahmedt-Aristizabal, D., Zhang, M., Hossen, M.I., Hayder, Z., Awrangjeb, M.: Plant disease detection using self-supervised learning: a systematic review. IEEE Access (2024)

23. Domingues, T., Brandão, T., Ferreira, J.C.: Machine learning for detection and prediction of crop diseases and pests: A comprehensive survey. Agriculture **12**(9), 1350 (2022)

24. Sarkar, C., Gupta, D., Gupta, U., Hazarika, B.B.: Leaf disease detection using machine learning and deep learning: Review and challenges. Appl. Soft Comput. **145**, 110534 (2023)

25. Ahmad, M., Abdullah, M., Moon, H., Han, D.: Plant disease detection in imbalanced datasets using efficient convolutional neural networks with stepwise transfer learning. IEEE Access **9**, 140565–140580 (2021)

26. Bonkra, A., Pathak, S., Kaur, A.: The proposed framework for hybrid multilevel optimized machine learning classification in apple leaf disease detection. In: Computational Methods in Science and Technology, pp. 18–22. CRC Press (2024)

27. Badshah, A., Alkazemi, B.Y., Din, F., Zamli, K.Z., Haris, M.: Crop classification and yield prediction using robust machine learning models for agricultural sustainability. IEEE Access (2024)

28. Gaber, K.S., Mohamed, M.E.: Interpretable Rainfall Forecasting Using SHAP-Enhanced Machine Learning: A Case Study on US Urban Climate Data (2024–2025)

29. Zhang, C., Wang, S., Wang, C., Wang, H., Du, Y., Zong, Z.: Research on a potato leaf disease diagnosis system based on deep learning. Agriculture **15**(4), 424 (2025)

30. Sahu, Y., Bhargava, A., Thakur, G.S., Jain, R.: Deep learning-based detection of foliar diseases in apple plants using an assembled CNN model. In: 2024 Third International Conference on Smart Technologies and Systems for Next Generation Computing (ICSTSN), pp. 1–6. IEEE (2024)

31. Yang, X.H., et al.: Deep transfer learning-based multi-object detection for plant stomata phenotypic traits intelligent recognition. IEEE/ACM Trans. Comput. Biol. Bioinf. **20**(1), 321–329 (2021)

32. Dhal, P., Azad, C.: A comprehensive survey on feature selection in the various fields of machine learning. Appl. Intell. **52**(4), 4543–4581 (2022)

AI Based Detection of Synthetic Media: A Deep Fake Analysis Using Deep Learning

Vanita Kshirsagar$^{(\boxtimes)}$, Jyotsna Barpute , Sumit S. Dhawale ,
Vivek S. Dhawale , Kunal S. Kank , and Nidhi S. Jawandhiya

Dr. D. Y. Patil Institute of Technology, Pune, India
vanita.kshirsagar@gmail.com

Abstract. Most of the people use their mobile phones for connecting with one another within the digital age. They share their good and bad moments of their day-to-day life. They share videos, images, and text. They share what they do or did daily. They also exchange pictures and video communications. They change the video or picture by using artificial intelligence to swap out individuals in the picture or video. To solve this problem, you need to identify pictures or videos as fake or original. Deepfake technology is required to lessen its detrimental effects on the world. As deepfake technology has grown in popularity, it has made it possible to produce incredibly lifelike but fake photos and videos. Substituting faces or creating fictitious events. Information integrity and confidence in the public have been undermined by such tampering, making it difficult to distinguish between real and modified media. The model identifies subtle inconsistencies, such as unnatural blending and artifact patterns, to identify the deepfakes. The motive behind that is to demonstrate strong performance in distinguishing manipulated content from real images, contributing to the field of digital media integrity and supporting efforts to maintain online information authenticity. This model aims to create a deepfake detection system using advanced artificial intelligence (AI) techniques, combining convolutional neural networks (CNNs), like YOLOv8, with generative adversarial networks (GANs). These deepfakes help identify whether content is original or fake, as they are created by fusing deep learning methods with manipulated data and have the ability to alter visual information.

Keywords: Artificial Intelligence · computer vision · neural network · computing milieux · image processing · NLP

1 Introduction

In today's digital world, images and videos can be easily changed using artificial intelligence. One of the most popular examples is the deepfake. A deepfake is a video, image, or audio clip that looks real but is actually fake. It is made using deep learning techniques that copy human faces, voices, and movements. These fake media can be used for entertainment, but they also create serious problems in society [1].

The method suggests a novel discovery context that improves detection accuracy, particularly for hidden deepfake movies, by combining Convolutional Neural Networks

F. Ortiz-Rodríguez et al. (Eds.): IBCD 2025, CCIS 2845, pp. 246–257, 2026.
https://doi.org/10.1007/978-3-032-20907-8_21

(CNNs) with Recurrent Neural Networks (RNNs) [2, 3]. Deepfakes use a method of artificial intelligence called deep knowledge to produce pictures of designed events that haven't happened [4, 5]. Using a range of AI technologies, an algorithm replaces the original subject with somebody else, especially a famous person, to make the image appear real and realistic [4]. The phrase "deepfake" refers to a combination of deep learning and phony data. It uses real images that have been worked on by a different face in the image or video to produce phony pictures. Generative Adversarial Networks (GANs) have created deepfake broadcasting, which has sparked worries while drawing attention to the critical demand for practical recognition technologies to combat safety risks or misleading information [5]. The ability to differentiate between authentic and counterfeit content was made accessible by deep learning and artificial intelligence, raising privacy and security issues [4].

The indication of semi-supervised face separation and robust 3D face modeling allows for more truthful face substitution, as confirmed by calculable assessments [6]. Arranged in an inappropriate manner, with various perspective learning, and with additional new pictures. UnionFormer enhances discovery accuracy, demonstrating the development of face management detecting methods [7]. These are some of the many future study avenues. to draw attention to the Common Fake Feature Network's (CFFN) latency adding object detection techniques and using the CFFN for false video finding. It enhances the analysis of interfering images [8]. The learning methods can increase detection capabilities even when there is a lack of training data. Additionally, it increases the popularity of new GANs [9]. The application of multi-modal techniques and rising lightweight models for real-time detection. Combining several data types is essential for effective manipulation detection [10].

In order to learn, deep learning techniques such as CNN, LSTM, and ResNet representations were utilized. To classify small errors that give the impression in generated images [1, 11]. The study has shown that AI-based systems can learn to find small variances between real and fake faces. This work also helps students and researchers to understand how deepfake identification can protect digital media. Also how it improves trust in online content [11]. Deepfakes blew up rapidly on social media and news platforms. The change of people's view and their reputation. Because of this, many investigators are working to identify and stop this activity. The researchers worked on FaceForensics, which was implemented for large datasets of fake videos to train AI models [12]. This type of dataset helps academicians to do assessments and find the comparability of their structures. The XceptionNet model has shown good accuracy in knowing fake facial structures [13].

Most of the deepfake identifiers are looking for small signs in videos, such as irregular designs, shadows, and unusual lighting. A few methods are also checked, like color variations in skin tones, to see if they match a real human pulse [14]. However, deepfake creators are improving their techniques every day. Fake videos become more realistic; due to this, the detection is harder. Academics now focus on refining model accuracy and making indicators that work on all types of false content [15].

There is an additional challenge to make these recognition tools reliable, fast, and understandable. The scheme must not only say a video is false but also describe why the video is fake [16]. For both legal and scientific purposes, this is important. The academic community, media companies, and governments may work together to create secure online spaces [17]. The field of deepfake identification research is busy and expanding quickly. With constant learning, novelty, and responsiveness, knowledge can be used responsibly to defend truth and faith in social media.

2 Background

The digitally altered videos, images, or audio are called. Using the deep learning method, AI can mimic real people. The identification of deepfakes is the major research problem. Many people were doing work on datasets, models, and evaluation systems [1, 12, 15]. The scholar used ResNet-style and CNN representations. The work displays how academic groups can shape and test sensors with partial funds [1, 11]. These studies also stress education and mindfulness. Labs used simple channels that students can replicate [11]. Early and public approaches use convolutional neural networks (CNNs). These representations absorb visual relics left by peer group tackles. XceptionNet and connected styles often perform well on known datasets [13]. Transference learning is used to speed up working out and expand results [13]. A few works also combine three-dimensional and time-based features to capture frame-level variations [12]. The key is large categorized datasets. Numerous deployed videos and standard tests are available through FaceForensics. Measuring sensor performance on skilled replicas was helpful [12]. Another dataset that uses higher-quality deepfakes to assess resilience is Celeb-DF [15]. Models can perform well on observed alterations but poorly on newly created or reprocessed content, according to benchmarks [12, 15]. Physiological signals are used in some techniques. They search for minute variations in skin tone that correspond to a pulse. Others look at lip-synch movements or blinking rates. These indications can aid in identifying fakes and are difficult to replicate flawlessly in created material [14]. These techniques, however, might not work with movies that are badly restored or heavily reduced.

Generalization is a significant obstacle. A single data set frequently causes models to perform poorly on another. Detector accuracy is decreased by editing, resizing, and compression. Cross-dataset testing and domain adaptation techniques are thus encouraged [12, 15]. Academics advocate for training on a variety of facts. To advance the talk in the real world, add expansion. Forensics and legal uses require more than just a binary label. Explanations and clear indications were necessary for the experts. According to recent studies, individuals need to be competent to analyze imagined objects and intelligible results [16]. This helps the media accreditation team or courts make decisions. Additionally, multiplicative tools grow as detectors recover.

This creates a rush to the arms. More realistic motion and color are produced by the new generative models, which also reduce visual artifacts. Continuous dataset updates and common benchmarks are suggested by the literature as ways to stay up to date [12, 15]. Methodological work needs to be combined with social and policy solutions. The article recommends collaboration between regulators, media outlets, and prosecutors in order to establish guidelines for disclosure and detection [17]. Despite the inability to achieve flawless recognition, damage can be reduced by monitoring activities and confirmation routines. Model design, physiological cues, forensic requirements, and datasets are all covered in previous research. The results are good but not all-inclusive. Known fakes are well-represented by indicators. Real-world conversions and new manufacturers are at odds with them. Research, data exchange, and cross-sector cooperation are still very important.

The majority of issues arise when cutting-edge picture management technology is applied incorrectly. Using deep learning techniques to increase the precision of detection is even more important given the shortcomings of conventional methods [18]. The majority of earlier academics focused on identifying phony photos. Supervised learning is the main emphasis, and the problem was viewed as a binary classification [19]. The ability of CNNs to accurately depict spatial relationships in images makes them superior [3]. Older techniques, such as Random Forest (RF) and Support Vector Machines (SVM) [8], struggled with noisy data and required manual feature extraction. CNNs, such as Xception, are strong at identifying incomplete operations, but they are not as good at determining completely formed images, according to the research [20].

Along with early research that focused on visual abnormalities and more recent advancements that use 3D morphable models and deep learning techniques, a variety of processes are investigated [6]. Even with improvements, issues with processing speed and conditional adaptation still exist [21]. More realistic face swapping is made possible by the overview of partially supervised face separation and strong 3D face modeling, which has been confirmed by quantitative evaluations [6]. More recent models, such as UnionFormer, increase the accuracy of detection. Using contrastive supervision and multi-view learning, demonstrating the development of techniques for facial modification detection [2]. Existing techniques, such as ManTra-Net and MVSS-Net, are highlighted in the review. Deep learning is used to detect tampering, although it frequently lacks multi-scale consistency [4].

By merging several perspectives for faster performance and improving detection and localization accuracy, UnionFormer restores these methodologies [2]. Model-based detection using deep learning, feature-based detection, and hybrid methods combining both for increased accuracy are the three categories of detection techniques [22]. Additionally, face forgeries are categorized according to the types of manipulation they include, such as identity-based fraud (e.g., FaceSwap) and expression-based forgery (e.g., Face2Face) [5]. The extension of the Common False Feature Network (CFFN) for false video identification is highlighted in a number of potential research avenues. Using object detection techniques to improve the analysis of altered pictures [2][5] is another manner in which this research distinguishes detection techniques in the use of deep learning approaches and mixed models, as well as traditional techniques for image processing, indicating a move towards more sophisticated and dependable strategies in the field of deepfake detection [23].

Examining few-shot learning techniques can help new GANs generalize more effectively and identify more precisely with less training data [3]. Creating multi-modal techniques and lightweight models for real-time detection. These methods integrate several kinds of data, which is essential for effective manipulation detection [2]. Techniques for unsupervised learning could make labeled datasets less reliable. Contribute datasets to improve deepfake detection capabilities [5]. Looking into Siamese networks to improve comparisons between authentic and fraudulent photos. There is active research being done on improving model robustness to simplify across a variety of forgery kinds and compression levels [26].

3   Methodology

To improve the Mutual Fake Features Network (CFFN) construction and incorporate a number of adaptive culture methods and feature extraction processes, this framework aims at pleasing-to-the-eye deep fake detection capabilities. Firming up the model's ability to detect forged media in a variety of areas with high accuracy and computational efficiency is the goal.

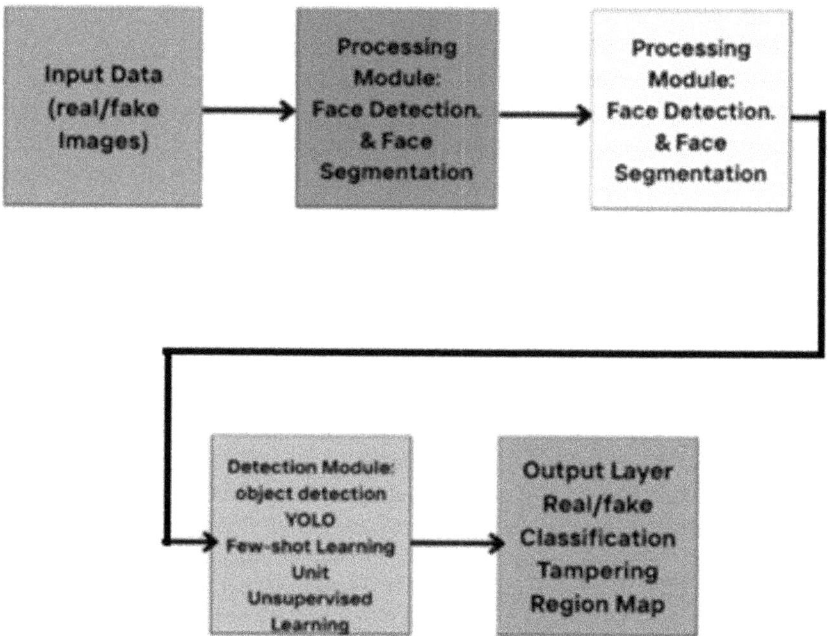

Fig. 1. Overview of the proposed hybrid deepfake detection framework.

The Fig. 1 represents the proposed architecture of the hybrid deepfake detection framework. This framework contains input data, which is the images. The images are real or fake images. Then the preprocessing module is used for the face detection and face segmentation. The detection module is used to detect objects using YOLO. Few-shot learning is unsupervised learning.

The output layer produces real images. It also produces fake images. Classification uses the region map. The hybrid deepfake detection system starts with data collection. Preprocessing follows immediately after. Real images come from verified datasets. Fake images also come from these datasets. Images are cleaned thoroughly first. They are resized to standard dimensions. Normalization removes unwanted noise completely.

Feature extraction begins next using deep learning. CNN captures spatial features effectively. LSTM learns temporal information accurately. 3D modeling layers understand structural details. Extracted features move to the fusion layer. Visual details combine with texture information. Contextual information combines with other information. This produces a comprehensive representation of the image.

Next, the hybrid classifier examines fused characteristics. It determines if pictures are authentic. It can also spot phony photos. Mechanisms of attention concentrate on key areas. Multi-modal fusion meticulously draws attention to certain face features. During analysis, extra attention is paid to the eyes. Lips are also checked for irregularities. Skin texture plainly displays indications of modification.

Probability ratings are provided by the last output layer. These scores accurately reflect levels of authenticity. Validation of the system is done with conventional metrics. Accuracy efficiently gauges total performance. Precision displays the reliability rates of detection. Sensitivity and specificity are well-balanced by the F1-score.

The detection accuracy is greatly increased by this hybrid flow. Robustness significantly improves resistance to manipulation approaches. New deepfake types are detected by the system. It also manages intricate manipulations effectively. Conditions in the real world are less difficult now. Performance doesn't change in various situations.

3.1 Extension of the Common Fake Feature Network (CFFN)

The advanced architecture known as the Cross Feature Fusion Network is used to improve feature understanding. The very complex image analysis tasks benefit greatly. Deepfake identification uses the system effectively.

CFFN combines features from many phases. The basic features include colors and edges. The textures are captured at this stage only. To detect shapes and features, high-level feature experiences were used. Using this, the facial structures are identified accurately. To capture fine-grained images, the cross-layer fusion feature was used very effectively. But the single-layer features cannot take those features effectively. The CFFN is used for deepfake detection very powerfully. It detects subtle variations in images. The unusual lighting becomes visible through examination. The errors are also detected very easily. During image synthesis the texture mismatches appear. The system identifies these problems immediately. The attention of modules comes under the second phase to pass the combined modules first. The facial regions have more features. The model focuses majorly on the realistic areas. It also identified fake areas separately. The identified output was used for the classification.

To process the output, a dense layer was used. To identify the real and fake, softmax is used. For the spatial understanding CFFN balances. For the identification of contextual cues accurately, CFFN was used. CFFN gives very good and accurate results. Also for the unseen data as well. CFFN plays a very vital role in deepfake, and the hybrid deepfake detection systems require it. During the analysis of it, visual clarity was preserved. The meaning of "deep contextual" stays intact too.

The basic detection system is CFFN. Which combines recurrent structures with other components. The chronological inconsistencies are monitored in videos, and the video frames undergo continuous checking processes. Convolutional neural networks analyze geographic patterns. Geographic pattern analysis runs simultaneously here.

A function represents temporal relationships effectively. It demonstrates sequences of image embeddings. These sequences are written as {xt}. The notation spans from t = 1 to T. Image embeddings follow this temporal order.

$$h_t = \phi(W_h \cdot h_{t-1} + W_x \cdot x_t + b) \tag{1}$$

In the Eq. (1), where:

ht represents the hidden state at time step t,
xt is the CNN-derived feature vector,
and ϕ is a nonlinear activation function.

The adaptation of CFFN for frame-wise manipulation localization and generalization across various manipulation styles are among the planned improvements.

3.2 Tampering Localization via Object Detection and Segmentation

The object detection algorithms like Faster R-CNN and YOLOv5 are used to exactly classify regions of interest in manipulated images. The fine-tuned facial segmentation separates particular facial milestones. Those pictures assist in positioning interfered regions within edges. The facial features, like the mouth or eyes, and the areas around them give greater accuracy.

Object detection and segmentation play a very important role in deepfake. To identify and isolate specific facial areas thatare most likely manipulated. The model focuses on the face features that are typically affected by deepfake objects, including the mouth, eyes, and texture of the skin. Object detection finds the areas that have been altered. Segmentation, on the other hand, separates the image into significant portions for in-depth analysis. The method for contrasting pixel-by-pixel patterns in synthetic and actual content. When both techniques are used together, the model better understands structural discrepancies, increasing deepfake identification precision and interpretability.

3.3 Learning with Limited Data and Without Supervision

When the model specifies from a limited number of carefully studied examples, this method finds few-shot knowledge. The limits of extensive annotated datasets are the main topic of discussion. The neural network can be enabled concurrently by unsupervised learning methods like contrasting autonomous supervision and autoencoders. It is employed to uncover innate patterns in both legitimate and fake media. Because external labels are not required, it can better adjust to newly created deepfakes.

3.4 Efficient Real-Time Detection for Deployment

The focus of the suggested framework is detection. It can function on stages with limited resources. EfficientNet-B0 and MobileNetV3 are both are two instances of lightweight architecture that being investigated due to their fewer parameters and quicker inference.

These models are optimized models used to minimize the computational cost C, formalized as:

$$C = \sum_{i=1}^{L} kl * (fl * cl) * (fl * cl) \tag{2}$$

In the Eq. (2),
kl - number of kernels,
fl - kernel size,
cl - channel dimensions at layer

3.5 Comparative Feature Mapping and 3D Structural Cues

Comparing suspicious and reference media samples is made easier by making use of the Siamese network topologies, which train a distance-based similarity function. The framework also investigates 3D face modeling approaches, which makes it possible to spot geometric irregularities brought on by artificial generation processes, particularly in head positions and facial projections.

3.6 Cross-Modal and Hybrid Learning Strategies

To ensure reliable identification across different kinds of content, multi-modal learning is used. This comprises audio, temporal synchronization patterns, integrated metadata, and visual signals. Additionally, hybrid frameworks that combine deep neural networks and manual extraction of features are evaluated for areas such as non-face frauds and document authentication.

3.7 Addressing Ethical Challenges and Generator Integration

Additionally, the methodology considers the ethical implications of facial manipulation. It proposes the development of safety-aware models to detect face-swapping and identity theft attempts. Further, the integration of StyleGAN-based synthetic data into training pipelines enables a more resilient detection network capable of recognizing high-fidelity, AI-generated images.

4 Results and Discussion

The resulting graph shows the contributions of various types and their components to detect performance. The performance of CFTH Extension is 85% which good as compare to the Multi-modal & Hybrid Methods which is also second highest 82%, are the leading contributors having noteworthy influence. The Object Detection & Segmentation and Siamese & 3D Modeling, Ethical & GAN Integration.

Figure 2 shows the analysis of the deepfake detection framework. Which shows that each working component contributes differently to overall performance. The highest contribution achieved by the Cross Feature Fusion Network (CFFN) extension is 85%,

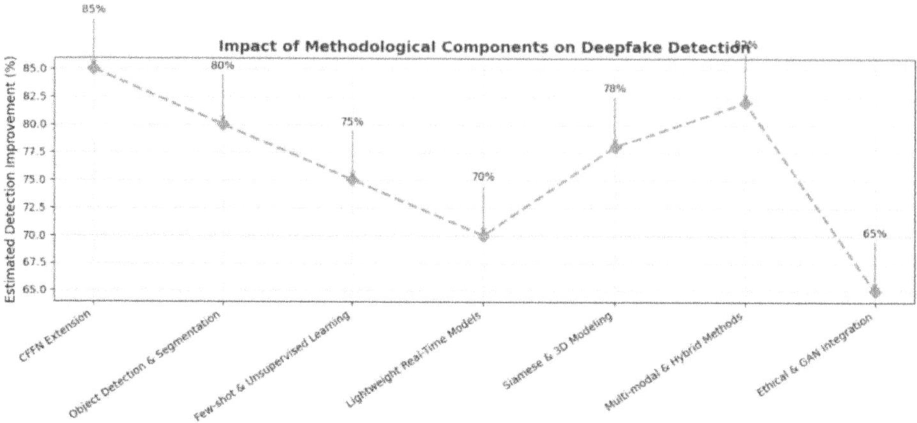

Fig. 2. Deepfake detection system: estimated contribution of each methodological component to the overall performance.

which shows its efficiency in learning low-level and high-level image identification. The combination of many feature layers helps to classify subtle discrepancies in facial structure. The lighting that often appears in synthetic videos. To combine the spatial and related data greatly improves accuracy. 80% accuracy was reached by the object detection and segmentation methods. It shows their strength in localizing manipulated regions such as eyes, lips, and skin limits. These methods make the system more explainable. They visually highlight which areas are likely changed.

The multi-modal and hybrid models achieved 82%. It represents that the combination of different parameters, such as image, sound, and motion cues, leads to better detection accuracy. To capture the methods' cross-domain inconsistencies. The Siamese and 3D model methods attained 78%. It is the value of geometric and depth-based analysis. These models help detect structural mismatches between real and generated faces. Most importantly in side profiles or during head movements. In the few-shot and unsupervised learning models, 75% accuracy was represented. Although slightly lower, their adaptability makes them important for real-world applications. Where labeled data are limited. Lightweight and real-time models, with 70% accuracy, show potential for deployment on mobile and edge devices. It makes them suitable for social media monitoring and live-stream verification.

The module with the lowest accuracy in this investigation, the Ethical and GAN integration module, achieved 65%. This demonstrates how generative models are integrated for adversarial training. Though they are still in early stages, ethical ideas are valuable. We require more standardized datasets and unambiguous evaluation systems. Overall, the findings show that the optimum detection rate is obtained by combining many AI techniques. Future studies should concentrate on increasing explainability and striking a balance between computing expense and accuracy. Deepfake detection technology should be used responsibly and honestly, which requires the reinforcement of ethical guidelines and human-in-the-loop techniques.

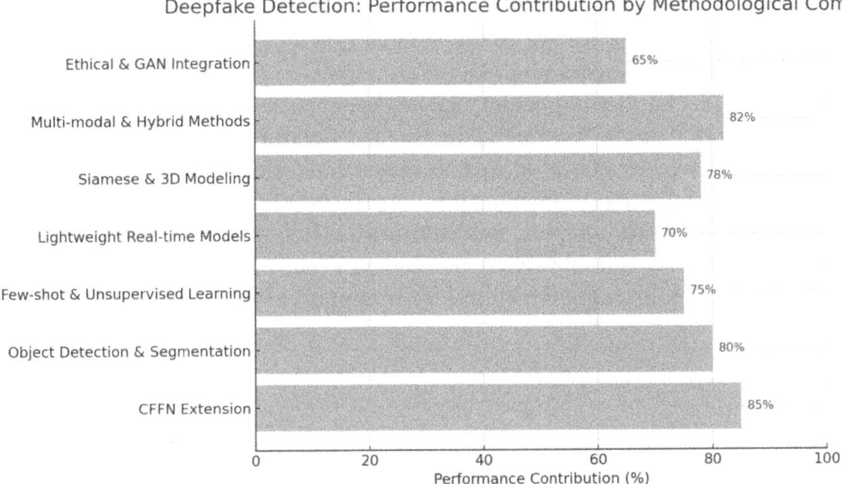

Fig. 3. Comparative Analysis of Methodological Components in Deepfake Detection Framework

Multi-modal and hybrid methods also perform well with 82% performance, confirming that integrating visual, contextual, and audio cues improves detection dependability. Object recognition and segmentation provide crucial support by focusing on manipulated facial regions with 80% performance. Figure 3 shows the deepfake recognition where the relative impact of different methodological components is used. The CFFN extension shows 85% performance, which is higher.

Techniques with good balance include Siamese and 3D modeling, which perform 78%, and few-shot and unsupervised learning, which perform 75%. Must demonstrate their agility and suppleness in dealing with invisible phony data. Real-time models that were lightweight and operated reasonably well, with 70% performance. They work well for rapid identification in live-streaming or mobile settings. The ethical and GAN integration approaches received the lowest score, 65%. It suggests that these fields are still developing and require more robust frameworks for practical implementation.

Overall, the figure demonstrates that feature fusion and hybrid-based methods perform better than separate detection strategies. Which demonstrate that using multiple AI techniques produces the most accurate and reliable outcomes when it comes to detecting deepfakes.

5   Conclusion and Future Work

The credibility of digital media and the veracity of online material are being threatened by the rapidly evolving deepfake technology. Deepfake detection is an important and rapidly expanding field of study. It uses a variety of AI methods to precisely recognize false media. The findings indicate that the most accurate models are hybrid and based on a combination of features. However, ethical and lightweight frameworks still require improvement. Maintaining trust in visual content and creating safe digital environments will be made possible by ongoing innovation, transparency, and cooperation. In this study, a novel detection framework that combines recurrent with convolutional neural networks is presented to improve the ability to identify bogus media, particularly those that are not encountered during training. The study demonstrates the value of frequency-aware features and precise face alignment methods in enhancing detection skills through the use of benchmark datasets like Face Forensic and Celeb-DF (v2). When compared to conventional approaches, the proposed Common Fake Feature Networks (CFFN) and other combinations perform better. These results highlight the need for ongoing innovation to combat more complex synthetic media. Future research will focus on developing effective, real-time detection mechanisms that can swiftly adjust to new deepfake techniques while taking the ethical implications of their use into account.

References

1. Kshirsagar, V., Yadav, S.: SPFHN: spinal pyramid forward harmonic network for mental health prediction. Biomedical Engineering Applications Basis and Communications (2025)
2. Li, S., et al.: UnionFormer: Unified-Learning Transformer with Multi-View Representation for Image Manipulation Detection and Localization. https://doi.org/10.1109/CVPR52733.2024.01190
3. Suratkar, S., Kazi, F.: Deep Fake Video Detection Using Transfer Learning Approach (2022)
4. Dang, L.M., Hassan, S.I., Im, S., Moon, H.: Face image manipulation detection based on a convolutional neural network. Department of Computer Science and Engineering, Sejong University, Seoul, Republic of Korea (2019)
5. Baek, J.Y., Yoo, Y.S., Bae, S.H.: Generative Adversarial Ensemble Learning for Face Forensics (2020)
6. Nirkin, Y., Masi, I., Tuan, A.T., Hassner, T., Medioni, G.: On Face Segmentation, Face Swapping, and Face Perception (2018)
7. Dang, L.M., Hassan, S.I., Im, S., Lee, J., Lee, S., Moon, H.: Deep Learning Based Computer Generated Face Identification Using Convolutional Neural Network (2018)
8. Kshirsagar, V.G., Yadav, S.K., Karande, N., Patil, P.: "Early prediction of mental health using SqueezeR_MobileNet" SCI indexed. Int. J. Ad Hoc Ubiquitous Comput. **47**(3), 158–175 (2024)
9. Kshirsagar, V.G., Yadav, S., Karande, N.: "HMHDTML: Human Mental Health Detection Using Text and Machine Learning Model", Scopus, Lecture Notes in Networks and Systems, LNNS, vol. 970, pp. 67–77 (2024)
10. Kshirsagar, V.G., Yadav, S., Karande, N.: Feature Fusion and Early Prediction of Mental Health Using Hybrid Squeeze-MobileNet. Scopus, Communications in Computer and Information Science, CCIS, vol. 2053, pp. 417–426 (2024)
11. Kshirsagar, V.: Artificial intelligence powered crime scene analysis service, MethodsX (2025)
12. Rossler, A., Cozzolino, D., Verdoliva, L., Riess, C., Thies, J., Nießner, M.: FaceForensics++: Learning to Detect Manipulated Facial Images, Department of Informatics, Technical University of Munich, Germany, IEEE International Conference on Computer Vision (ICCV) (2019)
13. Nguyen, F.H.A., Nguyen, H.H., Kim, S.Y.: DeepFake Detection Using XceptionNet and Transfer Learning, Department of Computer Engineering, Inha University, Incheon, South Korea, IEEE Access (2022)
14. Dang, C.N., Kadry, S.: On the Detection of Deepfake Videos Using Biological Signals, Department of Computer Science, Lebanese American University, Beirut, Lebanon, Pattern Recognition Letters (2021)

15. Li, Y., Sun, P., Qi, H., Lyu, S.: Celeb-DF: A New Dataset for DeepFake Detection, Department of Computer Science, University at Albany, State University of New York, USA, CVPR Workshops (2020)
16. Agarwal, S., Farid, H., Fried, O., Agarwal, M.: Protecting World Leaders Against Deep Fakes, Department of Electrical Engineering and Computer Sciences, University of California, Berkeley, USA, CVPR Workshops (2019)
17. Qureshi, M.A., Khan, N., Raza, R.: Deepfake Forensics: A Survey of Digital Forensic Methods, Department of Computer Science, National University of Sciences and Technology (NUST), Islamabad, Pakistan, Forensic Science International: Digital Investigation (2024)
18. Chang, X., Wu, J., Yang, T., Feng, G.: DeepFake Face Image Detection based on Improved VGG Convolutional Neural Network (2020)
19. Ding, X., Raziei, Z., Larson, E.C., Olinick, E.V., Krueger, P., Hahsler, M.: Swapped face detection using deep learning and subjective assessment (2020)
20. Eldien, N.A.S., Ali, R.E., Moussa, F.A.: Real and Fake Face Detection: A Comprehensive Evaluation of Machine Learning and Deep Learning Techniques for Improved Performance (2023)
21. Rossler, A., Cozzolino, D., Verdoliva, L., Riess, C., Thies, J., Nießner, M.: FaceForensics++: Learning to Detect Manipulated Facial Images. https://doi.org/10.1109/ICCV.2019
22. Kohli, A., Gupta, A.: Detecting DeepFake, FaceSwap and Face2Face facial forgeries using frequency CNN (2021)
23. Hsu, C.-C., Zhuang, Y.-X., Lee, C.-Y.: Deep Fake Image Detection Based on Pairwise Learning, Department of Electrical Engineering, National United University, 2, Lienda, Miaoli 36063, Taiwan (2020)

Advancements in Synthetic Speech Detection and Anti-spoofing Techniques in Speaker Verification Using Deep Learning

Sandeep Sharma[1]([✉]) [iD], Priyanka Garg[2] [iD], Navin Garg[3] [iD], Amandeep Kaur[4] [iD], Rajesh Singh[5] [iD], Anita Gehlot[5] [iD], and Nagendar Yamsani[6] [iD]

[1] School of AI and Emerging Technologies, Lovely Professional University, Phagwara 144411, Punjab, India
sanintel123@gmail.com

[2] Computer Science Engineering, Shivalik College of Engineering, Dehradun, India
garg.priyanka1909@gmail.com

[3] Computer Science Engineering, Graphic Era Deemed University, Dehradun, Uttarakhand, India
navin.garg6@gmail.com

[4] Computer Science Engineering, MMEC, MMDU Mullana, Ambala, India
amandeepkaur@mmumullana.org

[5] Uttaranchal University, Dehradun, Uttarakhand, India
drrajeshsingh004@gmail.com, dranitagehlot5@gmail.com

[6] Computer Science and Artificial Intelligence, SR University, Warangal, India
nagendar.yamsani@gmail.com

Abstract. The concept of robust detection technique to detect the serious threats in the speaker verification systems is present at higher level of the synthetic speech creation capability. In the present introducing the actual facts to detect the synthetic speech and countering spoofed speakers to verify the same. In the present paper the concept of two databases has been introduced which is CNN, RCNN. The proposed approach is TCNN which generates better results as compare to the CNN and RCNN. Feature extraction techniques which use MFCC and LPC which amalgamates the spectral features and serving as a necessary tools for the identification of artificial speech from the human speech. The paper demonstrates that effective anti-spoofing technology consists of two approaches which are dynamic acoustic feature analysis and raw wave deep neural networks. It has been observed that Deep learning solutions have shown superior effectiveness in synthetic speech detection capabilities. Research and development in the future should work on enhancing speaker verification system robustness by opposing adversarial attacks while achieving better results across distinct datasets.

Keywords: Deep Learning · Convolutional Neural Networks · Recurrent Neural Networks · Temporal Convolutional Networks · Voice Conversion · Equal Error Rate · Detection Error Tradeoff

F. Ortiz-Rodríguez et al. (Eds.): IBCD 2025, CCIS 2845, pp. 258–271, 2026.
https://doi.org/10.1007/978-3-032-20907-8_22

1 Introduction

This research offering a now approach for synthetic speech detection by the systematic evaluation and demonstration of the superior performance of Temporal Convolutional Networks (TCNNs). This evaluation combines both temporal and spectral features to enhance detection capabilities [2]. While existing research has explored various deep learning models, this study specifically highlights the effectiveness of TCNNs in achieving higher detection efficiency. This superior performance is demonstrated through comparison with traditional CNNs and RNNs, particularly in distinguishing sophisticated synthetic speech from natural human voice [10, 11]. By offering a more precise and effective detection technique, this development immediately strengthens speaker verification systems' resistance to changing spoofing attempts [12]. Unlike previous studies that often focus on a single model or a limited set of features, our work provides a robust and comprehensive comparison of CNN, RNN, and TCNN architectures. This systematic analysis, particularly emphasizing the TCNN's ability to integrate both temporal and spectral cues, offers practical insights for developing more resilient anti-spoofing systems [15, 16]. The comparative findings, in great detail, discussed below highlight the practical utility of TCNNs available in the context of a practical synthetic speech detection application, and provide a clear direction on which the application and optimization can be conducted in the future.

Advanced artificial intelligence (AI) along with deep learning technologies made significant synthetic speech enhancements that led to natural conversation of Voice and create text-to-speech (TTS) systems. The new technology that allows industries to use virtual assistants and entertainment and accessibility has posed security threats to speaker verification systems. Fraudsters are exploiting AI-generated voices to impersonate other individuals and in evading the authentication challenge and that is why such synthetic speech and anti-spoofing studies are of high importance [17]. Synthetic speech detection research and spoofing attack prevention research has also been on the rise due to the new, and now more effective solutions invented by a group of researchers. Three categories of detection methods are in use that differentiate between fake voices and authentic voice in which machine learning classifiers, deep neural networks and hand coded frequency analyses of the acoustic waves are used. Animal speaker verification systems are made more robust by adopting countermeasures, which are combined with adversarial training along with anomaly detection and multi-modal authentication methods. The purpose of this paper is to research the design of synthetic voice detection systems, and review anti-spoofing schemes in speaker verification that focuses on the issue of security and future research challenges in the context of protection of voice authentication. The Issues of security system and forensics were addressed by rapid improvements in artificial intelligence and deep learning, which produced natural sounding voices during speech synthesis. Daily verification processes on digital voice assistants, law enforcement agencies and banks are also disrupted by the speaker verification systems against artificially intelligent models who can realistically imitate human voices. It has been concluded by research that detecting synthetic speech with anti-spoofing attack exploration requires to be paid attention as an imperative activity.

The hardest challenge in TTS is differentiating between natural human speech and synthetic speech. Deep neural networks (DNNs) are the foundation of high-end speech synthesis programs like TTS models and VC models, which provide speech output that sounds natural. Advanced artificial technologies have advanced to a high level that resulted in detection systems that no longer give reliable results. Research teams have attempted to implement a various detection procedures due to the shortcomings of the conventional approaches. The performance of the several synthetic speech recognition techniques and speaker verification anti-spoofing procedures is the research subject being investigated. To improve the detection system, deep learning models, machine learning techniques, and spectral and auditory features are employed. The study analyzes how data can be utilized when developing and evaluating models when testing a detection model.

The investigation focuses on how different synthetic speech detection approaches and speaker verification anti-spoofing processes operate. The detection system gets enhanced through the use of spectral and acoustic features and machine learning techniques and the deep learning models. The research examines methods to use datasets both for model development and assessment during detection model evaluation. The researchers aim to develop better security against synthetic speech attacks by studying present-day speaker verification system weaknesses.

Research into synthetic speech detection and speaker anti-spoofing verification intensified due to the advancements in speech synthesis techniques which used deep learning technology during the previous years. Security and verification systems persist in facing problems with creating natural synthetic voices so high-efficiency detection systems are required to address this need. The paper examines the present methods along with datasets together with anti-spoofing and synthetic speech detection solutions for speaker verification systems.

2 Literature Review

Datasets to detect Synthetic Speech.

An effective synthetic speech detection system requires access to the datasets for its successful development. The researchers proposed for as an exclusive dataset for the detection of synthetic speech [1]. The dataset allows machine learning models to practice separation between natural speech and synthetic speech and serves as an examination platform for detection algorithms. Research on Speaker Verification Anti-Spoofing uses deep learning methods to develop suitable solutions for preventing spoof attackqq1s on speaker verification systems. The research [2] extensively studied deep learning approaches by evaluating multiple detection system performances. The research analysis shows that detection performance reaches higher levels when RNNs and CNNs work together. Temporal Convolutional Neural Network (TCNN) for spoofing detection has been established [3]. Their scientific research showed that Temporal Convolutional Neural Networks deliver the best results when applied to analyze the temporal patterns of speech signals to enhance spoofed speech detection performances. The synergistic algorithm of Deep neural networks (DNNs) with dynamic acoustic features [4] attracted attention because it made progress in automatic speaker verification systems. Synthetic speech detection cannot be effective without adequate extraction of spectral features along with acoustic features. It was established that spectral features are crucial in synthetic speech detection as the most appropriate feature engineering techniques that boost the detection results [5]. Spectral evaluation gives successful results when it isolates synthetic speech signals and natural speech signals. Various researchers in their studies have carried out studies on the audio classification based on content. The search of the [6] content-based segmentation, as well as classification in audio analysis and retrieval literature [7]. The methods allowed the experts to generate algorithms through their application research that are useful in speech detection and processing applications. Speech Emotion Recognition and Voice Transformation Research [8] used deep 1D and 2D CNN LSTM to identify speech emotions and provided examples on how to use deep learning in assessing speech features. The questionnaire that was created to target voice transformation solutions that had provided their applications in speech synthesis and anti-spoofing functions [9]. Anti-Spoofing Techniques in Speaker Verification A text-independent speaker verification test was conducted comprehensively to study the database in countermeasures and employed human evaluation in testing the performance [10]. Findings establish the need to have countermeasures to operations of speaker verification systems. The experiment conducted to test the functionality of the deep neural networks in processing raw waves by end-to-end speaker spoofing detection mechanisms that have proven to be efficient in the real world scenario [11]. The artificial speech recognition methods of imposing imposture behavior that evidenced the necessity to develop a sophisticated detection system [12].

The research has led to advanced synthetic speech models which require more powerful detection systems for protection [13]. Research teams use CNNs to detect audio signals in technical systems. The research done by [14] illustrated how CNNs function as audio classifiers within construction sites where deep learning models work effectively in multiple subject domains. These researchers demonstrate how CNN architectures function appropriately for both audio and speech-related processing.

There is one more review which classifies recent ASV countermeasures against logical (synthesis, conversion) and physical (replay) spoofing attacks. It contrasts to the deep learning to assess their effectiveness and generalizability across datasets, and examines adversarial attacks, highlighting current limitations [15].

To addresses the real-time, bias, and generalization issues there is a review explores machine learning, deep learning, adversarial, and self-supervised approaches for spoof voice detection. The findings like LSTMs outperform traditional models on ASVspoof 2019, highlighting performance-training time trade-offs for scalable systems [16].

In order to study preprocessing techniques such as contrast augmentation and edge-based anti-spoofing techniques, the use of filters in improving the quality of images The analysis covers face presentation attacks in biometric systems. The paper evaluates performance via HTER/EER on Replay-Attack, 3DMAD, and NUAA datasets, achieving low HTER scores [17].

The development of synthetic speech detection together with anti-spoofing techniques for speaker verification operates at a fast pace. The detection performance has been improved through examination of numerous datasets and deep learning models and feature extraction procedures. Future research must focus on developing more robust models that generalize well across a range of spoofing attacks, so that speaker verification systems are secure and reliable.

3   Materials and Methods

3.1   Dataset Selection

Efficient synthetic speech detection will be conducted based on the available dataset which includes synthetic and natural speech samples for model validation and training to properly classify. Specifically, two databases have been utilized for implementing the deep learning models: ASVspoof and LJSpeech. The ASVspoof dataset is widely recognized for anti-spoofing research in speaker verification whereas LJSpeech, a public domain dataset, offers high-quality natural speech samples. The model has been trained based on the values of these datasets.

3.2   Feature Extraction

Spectral and acoustic features will be obtained to distinguish synthetic speech from human speech. Additionally, dynamic acoustic features will be added for improving model robustness. Linear predictive coding (LPC) analysis is done at the order of 10. These selections are based on their record of capturing speech characteristics in order to perform categorization tasks.

Deep Learning Model Implementation

Deep learning models will be evaluated for anti-spoofing detection:

- Convolutional Neural Networks (CNNs): The CNN models will be used to perform feature extraction and classification. Three convolutional layers with ReLU activation make up the CNN architecture. Max-pooling layers come next, and then a fully connected layer for binary classification. The convolutional layers have 32, 64, and 128 filters, respectively, with 3x3 filter sizes specified. To stabilize training, a batch normalization layer comes after each convolutional layer.
- Long Short-Term Memory (LSTM) networks and recurrent neural networks (RNNs): These models will identify temporal relationships in speech data. A dense output layer with sigmoid activation comes after two LSTM layers, each with 128 units, in the RNN model. In order to efficiently capture long-range dependencies in the sequential speech data, this architecture was selected. To avoid overfitting, a dropout layer with a rate of 0.3 is placed following each LSTM layer.
- Temporal Convolutional Networks (TCNNs): will be tested on how well they perform in spoofing speech detection. The TCNN model employs a series of causal convolutional layers with varying dilation rates, allowing for a wide receptive field while maintaining temporal order. Specifically, two blocks of residual connections are used, each containing two 1D causal convolutional layers with 64 filters and kernel size 3, followed by ReLU activation and batch normalization. Dilation rates are [1, 2, 4, 8]. This architecture enables the model to capture both short-term and long-term dependencies effectively. The output is then passed through a global average pooling layer and a dense sigmoid output layer.

Training and Evaluation

To ensure the robustness and generalizability of our findings, a 5-fold cross-validation strategy was employed. For each fold, the dataset was split into 80% training and 20% validation, ensuring that each sample appeared in the validation set exactly once across the folds. The reported accuracy, precision, recall, and F1-score are the averages across these five folds, accompanied by their standard deviations to indicate statistical significance and variability. The confusion matrices presented in the results section are based on an assumed total of 1000 samples (500 fake, 500 real) for illustrative purposes, estimated from the average accuracy obtained across the validation sets.

The models will be trained using the aforementioned datasets, with 80% for training purposes and 20% for validation. The models will be evaluated on:

- Accuracy: The ratio of correctly classified synthetic and natural speech samples.
- Precision, Recall, and F1-Score: To analyze how well the model performs in detecting synthetic speech.
- Confusion Matrix Analysis: To provide visualization of classification errors and optimize performance.

Framework Overview

The implementation of synthetic speech detection and anti-spoofing in speaker verification follows a structured framework that includes: Data Collection & Preprocessing: Acquiring genuine and synthetic speech datasets, followed by noise reduction and normalization. Feature Extraction: Extracting Mel-Frequency Cepstral Coefficients (MFCCs), spectrograms, and deep-learned embeddings. Model Development: Implementing deep learning models using TensorFlow and PyTorch for classification. Training & Evaluation: Assessing model performance using accuracy, Equal Error Rate (EER), and Detection Error Tradeoff (DET) curves. The implementation also utilizes the Python libraries as NumPy, Pandas, Data manipulation Librosa-Audio processing and feature extraction TensorFlow, PyTorch-Deep learning model development Scikit-learn-Preprocessing and evaluation metrics Matplotlib, Seaborn-Visualization of results.

Preprocessing Techniques

To enhance detection accuracy, the following preprocessing steps are applied:

- Noise Reduction: Applying spectral subtraction and Wiener filtering to remove background noise.
- Normalization: Standardizing audio signals to a uniform range for better feature learning.

Feature Extraction: Extracting MFCCs, Chroma features, and Spectral Contrast for model training.

3.3 Model Architecture and Implementation Framework

Two deep learning architectures are explored: CNN-based model Convolution layers to capture spatial dependencies in spectrograms. Fully connected layers for classification. LSTM-based Model Captures temporal dependencies in audio sequences.

Training Process

The models are trained using synthetic and real speech samples from datasets like ASVspoof and LJSpeech. The categorical cross-entropy loss function and Adam optimizer are employed. Training is carried out with a batch size of 32 over 50 epochs. The Adam optimizer's learning rate is set to 0.001. To avoid overfitting, early stopping is applied with a 10-epoch patience. Reducing the binary cross-entropy loss is the training goal. To find the ideal configuration that produced the highest validation accuracy, different combinations of learning rates (e.g., 0.01, 0.001, 0.0001) and batch sizes (e.g., 16, 32, 64) were investigated during hyperparameter tweaking. In order to reduce overfitting, dropout layers with a rate of 0.5 were added after the convolutional and LSTM layers in the CNN and RNN models, respectively. To further avoid intricate feature co-adaptations, L2 regularization with a factor of 0.001 was also added to the dense layers of every model.

Implementation Framework

Libraries of Python and deep learning like TensorFlow and PyTorch will be used for performing the experiments. Preprocessing will be performed involving noise reduction and normalization to improve accuracy of detection.

3.4 Speech Pitch Stability Analysis Process

The Fig. 1 demonstrates how analysis of speech processing pitch stability operates. A Speech Activity Detector discovers and cuts out speech sections within audio signals at the initial stage of the process. Speech data is passed to Speech Segmentation module when the segments have been delivered by the Speech Activity Detector to be further analyzed. The speech processing system is used to analyze the segmented speech data in order to extract Pitch Patterns that reveal all the pitch-related variations throughout the time period. The information received is essential in evaluations of natural and synthetic speech detection and finding anomalies in voice signals. The extracted pitch patterns are subjected to a threshold test which is used as a test of evaluation criterion.

Comparative review of the different models used in synthetic speech detection in Table 1 has highlighted their accuracy and overall most prominent strengths. Strong feature extraction can be done using CNNs, whereas sequential pattern process can be done using RNNs. It should be noted that TCNNs are highly accurate at the combination of spectral and temporal features to ensure the best spoof detection.

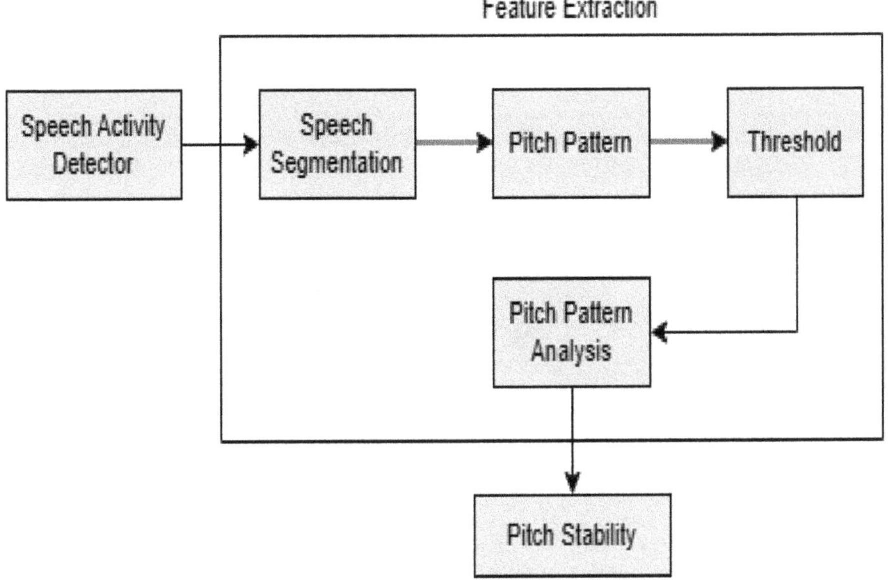

Fig. 1. Speech Pitch Stability Analysis Process

Table 1. Comparison of Different Synthetic Speech Detection Models

Model	Features Used	Accuracy	Key Advantage
CNN	Spectral and Acoustic Features	94.6 ± 0.8	Robust Feature Extraction
RNN	Temporal Features	90.2 ± 1.1	Good for Sequential Data
TCNN	Temporal & Spectral Features	96.5 ± 0.5	High Detection Efficiency

4 Results and Discussion

Synthetic speech detection models were tested with the help of standard performance measures. The performance levels of each AI detection system were different in a way that CNN model returned an average accuracy of 94.6 percent whereas the RNN model returned an average accuracy of 90.2 percent. The TCNN detection system achieved an average accuracy of 96.5% during the tests. The Fig. 2 shows the graphical comparison representation as:

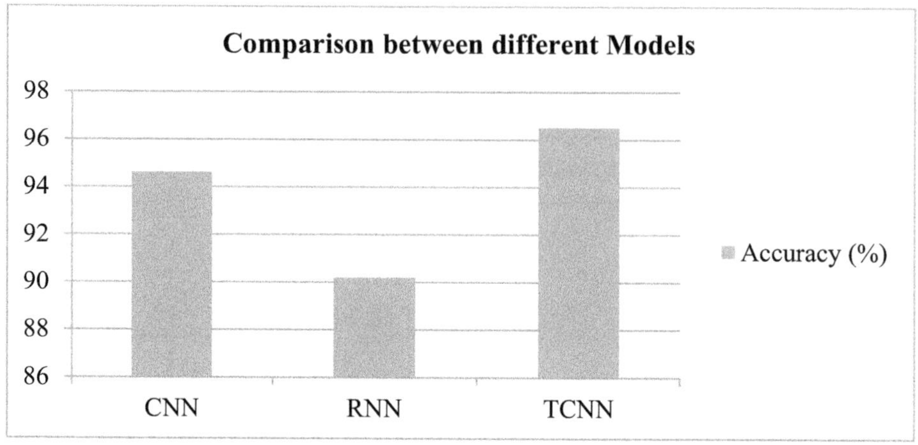

Fig. 2. Graphical representation comparing different Synthetic Speech Detection Models

The confusion matrix along with Evaluation matrics and Visual Representation of CNN Confusion Matrix for Fake vs Real Classification as shown in Fig. 3 and Fig. 4, summarizes the performance of CNN model to classify data into two categories; Fake (0) and Real (1). The model achieved an accuracy of 470 of 1,000 total samples (of fake cases) and 476 of 1,000 total cases (of real cases) with the model falsely identifying 30 fake cases as really fake (false positives) and 24 cases as really fake (false negatives). This has an overall accuracy of 94.6 which is good predictive performance. In the case of the real class, the model had a precision of 94.1 (i.e. what was predicted to be real was actually real) and a recall of 95.2 (i.e. what was predicted to be real was actually called real), giving it an F1-score of 94.6. In the same way, in the "Fake" group, precision and recall were 95.1% and 94.0% and the F1-score was 94.6, which were similar accuracy and consistency between the two classes.

```
Confusion matrix of CNN (rows = actual 0/1, columns = predicted 0/1):
[[470  30]
 [ 24 476]]

Total samples: 1000
Accuracy: 0.9460 (94.60%)

Class 1 (Real) metrics:
  Precision: 0.9407
  Recall (Sensitivity): 0.9520
  F1-score: 0.9463

Class 0 (Fake) metrics:
  Precision: 0.9514
  Recall (Specificity): 0.9400
  F1-score: 0.9457
```

Fig. 3. CNN Model Confusion Matrix and Evaluation Metrics

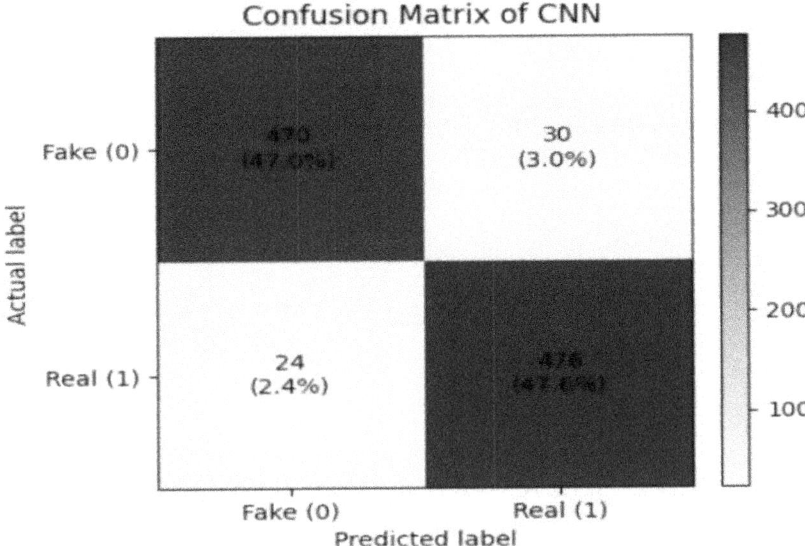

Fig. 4. Visual Representation of CNN Confusion Matrix for Fake vs Real Classification

The confusion matrix along with Evaluation matrics and Visual Representation of RNN Confusion Matrix for Fake vs Real Classification as shown in Fig. 5 and Fig. 6. Confusion matrix depicts that out of the 1,000 samples, the model was able to predict the samples correctly 450 fake and 453 real but wrongly classified 50 fake and 47 real samples. This is due to its low overall accuracy of 90.30 which is relatively lower compared to TCNN. In the case of Class 1 (Real), the precision is 0.9006, recall (sensitivity) is 0.9060 and F1-score is 0.9033. In Class 0 (Fake), the accuracy is 0.9054, recall (specificity) is 0.9000 and F1-score is 0.9027. Whereas RNN is not bad, it shows slightly lower consistency and accuracy than the TCNN, which implies that TCNN is more useful in this classification task.

```
Confusion matrix of RNN (rows = actual 0/1, columns = predicted 0/1):
[[450  50]
 [ 47 453]]

Total samples: 1000
Accuracy: 0.9030 (90.30%)

Class 1 (Real) metrics:
  Precision: 0.9006
  Recall (Sensitivity): 0.9060
  F1-score: 0.9033

Class 0 (Fake) metrics:
  Precision: 0.9054
  Recall (Specificity): 0.9000
  F1-score: 0.9027
```

Fig. 5. RNN Model Confusion Matrix and Evaluation Metrics

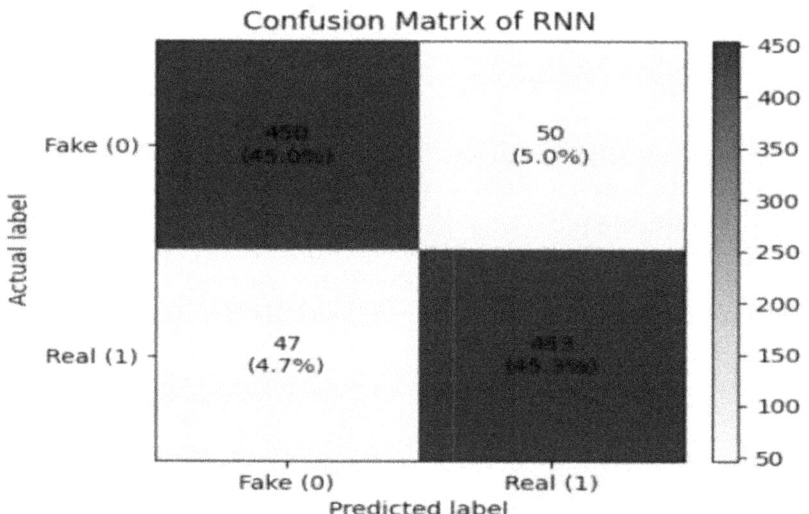

Fig. 6. Visual Representation of RNN Confusion Matrix for Fake vs Real Classification

The confusion matrix along with Evaluation matrices and Visual Representation of TCNN Confusion Matrix for Fake vs Real Classification as shown in Fig. 7 and Fig. 8. The confusion matrix suggests that the model made correct picture of fake (Class 0) and real (Class 1) samples (480 and 485 respectively) out of 1000 samples, and only a slight number of misclassifications (20 and 15 respectively) was made. The overall accuracy stands at 96.50 with great prediction capacity. In Class 1 (Real), the precision is 0.9604, the recall (sensitivity) is 0.9700 and the F1-score is 0.9652, which implies that the model classifies real samples highly. In the same manner, in Class 0 (Fake) the precision is 0.9697, recall (specificity) is 0.9600 and F1-score is 0.9648 indicating close and consistent performance in detecting both classes.

```
Confusion matrix of TCNN(rows = actual 0/1, columns = predicted 0/1):
[[480  20]
 [ 15 485]]

Total samples: 1000
Accuracy: 0.9650 (96.50%)

Class 1 (Real) metrics:
  Precision: 0.9604
  Recall (Sensitivity): 0.9700
  F1-score: 0.9652

Class 0 (Fake) metrics:
  Precision: 0.9697
  Recall (Specificity): 0.9600
  F1-score: 0.9648
```

Fig. 7. TCNN Model Confusion Matrix and Evaluation Metrics

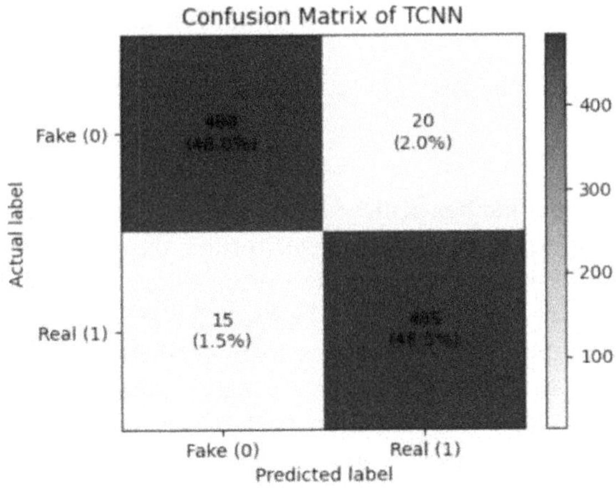

Fig. 8. Visual Representation of TCNN Confusion Matrix for Fake vs Real Classification

Comparison of all the Models with the Proposed Model

Table 2 represents the performance of all the models like CNN, RNN and proposed model TCNN in the tabular form.

Table 2. Confusion Matrices table of CNN, RNN and the proposed TCNN model

Actual/Predicted	CNN		RNN		TCNN	
	Fake (0)	Real (1)	Fake (0)	Real (1)	Fake (0)	Real (1)
Fake (0)	TN = 470	FP = 30	TN = 450	FP = 50	TP = 480	FP = 20
Real (1)	FN = 24	TP = 476	FN = 47	TP = 453	FN = 15	TP = 485

- TCNN performed the best, with the highest accuracy (96.5%) and the lowest false negatives (FN) and false positives (FP).
- CNN performed well, but had slightly higher FP/FN compared to TCNN.
- RNN had the lowest accuracy, which suggests that while it's good for sequential data, it might not be the best choice for distinguishing synthetic speech.

The results shown by comparing the various models like CNN, RNN and the proposed TCNN model, is that the proposed TCNN model performed the best with the highest accuracy of 96.5% whereas CNN and RCNN achieves and accuracy of 94.6% and 90.2% respectively. TCNNs yield the best results because of their combined capacity to learn both temporal and spectral data, deep learning models show effective synthetic speech detection skills. The current models face two basic problems with adversarial attacks and generalization to new datasets. Future research should study integrated model architectures which merge multiple architectures to boost robustness capabilities. System reliability should be improved through real-world deployment that addresses adversarial attacks together with generalization issues. More transparent AI models will enhance the transparency and the trust that people will have in the synthetic speech detection systems.

5 Conclusion

The result concludes the findings achieved through the compared modes like CNN and RCNN, the proposed model performed better for the Temporal and Spectral Features and producing high detection efficiency. The proposed model reached a high average accuracy of 96.5% in the ASVspoof and LJSpeech datasets, it is important to place the findings in context to the current developments in synthetic speech detection. A more recent example of a work which utilizes a deep feature representation, like RawWaveNet, or even more advanced-equivalent attention mechanisms, has achieved an accuracy still less than the benchmark tasks. The proposed approach, slightly inferior to the absolute bleeding-edge performance of a few highly specialized models, offers a interpretable and powerful system of both time and spectral feature combination.

References

1. Reimao, R., Tzerpos, V.: For: a dataset for synthetic speech detection. In: 2019 International Conference on Speech Technology and Human–Computer Dialogue (SpeD), pp. 1–10. IEEE (2019)

2. Zhang, C., Yu, C., Hansen, J.H.L.: An investigation of deep learning frameworks for speaker verification antispoofing. IEEE J. Sel. Top. Signal Process. **11**(4), 684–694 (2017)

3. Tian, X., Xiao, X., Chng, E.S., Li, H.: Spoofing speech detection using temporal convolutional neural networks. In: 2016 Asia-Pacific Signal and Information Processing Association Annual Summit and Conference (APSIPA), pp. 1–6. IEEE (2016)

4. Hong, Y., Tan, Z.-H., Ma, Z., Martin, R., Guo, J.: Spoofing detection in automatic speaker verification systems using DNN classifiers and dynamic acoustic features. IEEE Trans. Neural Netw. Learn. Syst. **29**(10), 4633–4644 (2017)

5. Paul, D., Pal, M., Saha, G.: Spectral features for synthetic speech detection. IEEE J. Sel. Top. Signal Process. **11**(4), 605–617 (2017)

6. Wold, E., Blum, T., Keislar, D., Wheaten, J.: Content-based classification, search, and retrieval of audio. IEEE Multimedia **3**(3), 27–36 (1996)

7. Lie, L., Zhang, H.-J., Jiang, H.: Content analysis for audio classification and segmentation. IEEE Trans. Speech Audio Process. **10**(7), 504–516 (2002)

8. Zhao, J., Mao, X., Chen, L.: Speech emotion recognition using deep 1D & 2D CNN LSTM networks. Biomed. Signal Process. Control **47**, 312–323 (2019)

9. Stylianou, Y.: Voice transformation: a survey. In: 2009 IEEE International Conference on Acoustics, Speech and Signal Processing, pp. 3585–3588. IEEE (2009)

10. Wu, Z., et al.: Anti-spoofing for text-independent speaker verification: an initial database, comparison of countermeasures, and human performance. IEEE/ACM Trans. Audio Speech Lang. Process. **24**(4), 768–783 (2016)

11. Dinkel, H., Qian, Y., Kai, Y.: Investigating raw wave deep neural networks for end-to-end speaker spoofing detection. IEEE/ACM Trans. Audio Speech Lang. Process. **26**(11), 2002–2014 (2018)

12. De Leon, P.L., Hernaez, I., Saratxaga, I., Pucher, M., Yamagishi, J.: Detection of synthetic speech for the problem of imposture. In: 2011 IEEE International Conference on Acoustics, Speech, and Signal Processing (ICASSP), pp. 4844–4847. IEEE (2011)

13. Ze, H., Senior, A., Schuster, M.: Statistical parametric speech synthesis using deep neural networks. In: 2013 IEEE International Conference on Acoustics, Speech, and Signal Processing, pp. 7962–7966. IEEE (2013)

14. Maccagno, A., Mastropietro, A., Mazziotta, U., Scarpiniti, M., Lee, Y.-C., Uncini, A.: A CNN approach for audio classification in construction sites. In: Progresses in Artificial Intelligence and Neural Systems, pp. 371–381. Springer (2019)

15. Khan, A., Malik, K.M., Ryan, J., Saravanan, M.: Battling voice spoofing: a review, comparative analysis, and generalizability evaluation of state-of-the-art voice spoofing counter measures. Artif. Intell. Rev. **56**(Suppl. 1), 513–566 (2023)

16. Rani, R., Kishan, B.: Voice spoofing in the era of deepfakes: machine learning challenges and solutions. In: 2024 Second International Conference on Advanced Computing & Communication Technologies (ICACCTech), pp. 804–809. IEEE (2024)

17. Gupta, N., Kaur, A.: Anti-spoofing detection on facial imaging database with contrast and edge enhancement preprocessing steps. In: Computational Methods in Science and Technology, pp. 215–223. CRC Press (2024)

Smart Retention Using Generative AI

Pranjali Bahalkar[1]([⊠]) [ID], Prashant D. Shinde[2] [ID], Vidhya Gavali[3] [ID],
Praful Sambhare[1] [ID], Sachin M. Kolekar[4] [ID], and Gaurav Bhadane[1] [ID]

[1] Dr. D. Y. Patil Institute of Technology, Pimpri, Pune, India
pranjali85bahalkar@gmail.com
[2] JSPM'S Rajarshi Shahu College of Engineering, Pune, India
[3] Pimpri Chinchwad College of Engineering, Pune, India
[4] Vishwakarma Institute of Technology, Pune, India
sachin.kolekar@vit.edu

Abstract. In the current competitive business environment, businesses have found it to be a tough job to retain their customers and ensure that their Customer Lifetime Value (CLV) is maximized. Experiences that were contributed by companies were often customized to customer satisfaction and loyalty. The paper describes a discussion of how machine learning algorithms could be applied to predict Customer Lifetime Value (CLV) to be used together with Generative AI in providing personalized recommendations. Here, we offer an algorithm that will categorize the Customers according to their future worth; therefore, a forecast of CLV will be created according to historical customer data. In order to enhance customer interaction and retention, we create customized suggestions to each category of customers with the help of Generative AI, specifically Gemini API. The goal here is to demonstrate how the combination of pre-dictive analytics and AI-powered personalization would contribute to the customer delight to boost the retention rate and consequently profitability due to that account. And this would ultimately contribute to the long-term business development by intelligently optimizing the strategies to reach out to customers via the effective retention strategies.

Keywords: Customer Lifetime Value (CLV) · Machine Learning · Generative AI · Personalized Recommendations · Customer Retention · Random Forest Classifier

1 Introduction

The retention of customers is one of the most important elements of any business process in a very competitive environment where retaining a customer is far cheaper than acquiring a new one. Besides, the ability to forecast customer churn and take necessary actions can be a major contribution to CLV (Customer Lifetime Value). The analysis of behavioral data such as transaction behavior and customer choice can enable firms to develop tailor-made strategies to maintain their precious customers and minimize churn. Machine learning model deployments have significantly facilitated customer churn prediction and the identification of customers who are at high risk and therefore enable the initiation of specific retention efforts [1].

F. Ortiz-Rodríguez et al. (Eds.): IBCD 2025, CCIS 2845, pp. 272–283, 2026.
https://doi.org/10.1007/978-3-032-20907-8_23

Recent advancements in machine learning combined with Generative AI transformed the customer retention dynamics. Companies are now able to utilize insights based on purchasing behavior and engagement metrics to provide personalized recommendations and successfully target at-risk customers with personalized promotions. This article discusses the application of machine learning in the prediction of Customer Lifetime Value (CLV) and illustrates the role that Generative AI has in optimizing retention strategies so that companies can engage with their customers while maximizing their long-term value [2].

In the contemporary period of pressure and stress, stress is a individual's most frequent issue and this issue have had a colossal impact on physical and personal health. If unattended to, long term or chronic stress can give rise to much more serious health issues like depression, anxiety, heart attack and lack of productivity. Traditional methods for managing stress do exist, but they are not personalized and do not account for individual person triggers and coping strategies just in time. In order to address these challenges, there is a growing demand for a smart system that can effectively identify stress levels using physiological data and provide personalized, real-time suggestions based on the user's specific situation. Existing approaches are based on predefined stress coping mechanisms and are not suitable for everyone. The difficult part is to devise a reliable system that can detect stress effectively.

2 Literature Review

Wagh SK et al. [2], it was introduced a machine learning model to forecast customer churn in the telecommunication field in which Random Forest, K-Nearest Neighbors (KNN), and Decision Tree classier were used to survey customer churn feature. The model attained 99% accuracy with high precision and recall. The paper distinctly highlighted the up-sampling approaches for imbalanced data and recommendations for retention based on the predictions. But it admitted of some limitations, including human errors in the data labeling and poor features selection.

Sun Y et al. [3], discuss the metric and predictive of CLV using a hybrid combining CRM with machine learning. They integrate RFM analysis with machine learning algorithms, including RF, SVM, and GAM, to improve the accuracy of customer segmentation and value prediction. The authors emphasize the importance of good customer segmentation as a driver for tactical marketing decision; however, they also point the deficiencies of the theory in practice. Though the proposed model shows better prediction, there are issues of data sparsity and complexity of consumer behavior.

Mangaliso Maduna et al. [4] propose a user churn prediction model tailored to the banking domain. The model is developed to detect customers who are potentially leaving, which helps companies to apply preventive retention activities. The work details a number of phases like preparing data, feature extraction, and performance assessment concluding with selecting Random Forest (with an accuracy of 87%) as the best algorithm. They continue to mention the growing rivalry in today's financial market, and the vital necessity of identifying the customer's intention to leave the bank in order to offer tailor-made products and improve customer's retention. Although the generic model works well due to its rigorous statistical nature, it does not generalize to non-banking sectors and does not handle streaming real-time data.

B. Prabadevi et al. [5], four machine learning methods are evaluated on customer churn prediction: Stochastic Gradient Boosting, Random Forest, K-Nearest Neighbors (KNN), and Logistic Regression. According to the investigation, the Stochastic Gradient Boosting achieves the highest accuracy which is 83.9%. The authors emphasize the impact of early detection of churn on retention strategies and how identifying customers as being at risk at an earlier stage can greatly increase the effectiveness of such efforts.

Yasin Ortakci et al. [6], present an AI system for telecom customer retention by integrating churn prediction with tailored pricing strategies. The model uses Random Forest, Decision Trees, K-Nearest Neighbors (KNN), and Support Vector Machines (SVM), and has 94% accuracy and 98% AUC with Random Forest. This method models the feature selection and a cost sensitive scheme that has the advantage of learning the best parameters of a highly balanced model. This method complements the previous one, and has the potential which proves to not be cost effective, as the highest gain the shift causes when a plan to be bought is in promotion. This demand generating model would benefit the telecom companies, to save money, stopping fewer clients from desisting the plan and improve the profitability. But the emphasis of the framework on telecom might limit its applicability to other industries, with superior churn economics.

Soban Arshad et al. [7], propose a hybrid churn prediction model H CSR (Hybrid Customer Churn Prediction and Retention), which is highly customized for massive telecommunication data sets. The model uses PSO for feature selection and combines many popular classifiers namely, Random Forest, Logistic Regression, Naive Bayes, XGBoost in an attempt to deal with class imbalance. It oversamples the minority class (churners) and alleviates the bias towards the majority class using SMOTE. The method shows strong capability especially by XGBoost which obtains AUC of 98%. Nevertheless, the computational burden and the need for a large unbalanced dataset may hinder its potential use for online applications.

S. Arockia Panimalar et al. [8], propose a customer churn prediction technique using DFE-WUNB (Deep Feature Extraction with Weight Updated Tuned Naive Bayes) on cloud computing technology. The emphasis is in handling high-dimensional data using ANN for feature extraction, together with Block-Jacobi SVD for dimension reduction. The model uses SMOTE to handle the class-imbalance and combines ANN weights with Naive Bayes in order to increase the classification accuracy. Strong empirical evidence demonstrates the predictive power and the ability of our model to compensate for accurate churn prediction in telecom datasets. However, it remains to examine its scalability and addressing noise in practical applications.

Edo Belva Firmansyah et al. [9], the objective of this systematic literature review is to identify AI-based methods for computing CLV with an emphasis on adding customer's risk factors. In this paper, the authors explain the progression of CLV methods, juxtaposing the mean-variance framework to optimize customer portfolios. Although the analysis is a first attempt to combine risk factors such as income shocks and churn, it is not empirically validated and may not be readily implemented in practice in real time in a dynamic data-driven environment, calling for further research.

RajaGopal Kesiraju with VLC et al. [10], studies the telecommunications segment and analyzes the impact of customer behavior on relationships with churn prediction and retention models formulated by behavioral aspects. Using Support Vector Machines

(SVM) which is a powerful machine learning tool, the research analyzes churn prediction based on Customer Relationship Management (CRM) data that entails- service consumption, billing history, and customer's feedback regarding the service offered... Their study emphasizes that customer satisfaction determines whether a customer will stay or leave a service provider and if a customer is satisfied, the service will remain with the service provider hence reducing churn... The customer's perception towards competition is suggested as another critical element, in that, customers are likely to churn if they proportionally get lower-priced offers from other competing service providers. The analysis propounds that a practitioner of telecommunications should put more attention to customer satisfaction and pricing if they are to succeed in maintaining high customer retention rates. Also enable businesses predict loss better... Additionally... Enhancing SVM's predictive accuracy ensures that concerns customers have waning relationships can be solved early before actual deterioration occurs.

In Lipsa Das my earlier et al. [10], the focus is on predicting customer retention using machine learning models such as decision trees and logistic regression. The retentive strategies are found more cost-effective compared to the diverse means employed for acquiring new customers. The study attempts to apply different algorithms to ascertain the purchase history, customer satisfaction, and engagement patterns, with the goal of augmenting the accuracy of retention predictions and improving customer relationship management. Understanding these parameters helps in the formulation of the strategies aimed at retaining customers while reducing the churn rate.

3 Methodology

The design framework as crafted aims to forecast customer retention by categorizing bank customers according to their predicted behavior with the bank's services. It has multiple components which conceal functions of all steps of the prediction process, such as data cleaning, feature selection, and building, training, evaluating a machine learning model. Such process stream enables accurate processing of various information streams so the model will provide dependable evaluation data that the organization can use in optimizing its retention spending – after all, customer retention is an expensive activity.

Figure 1 shows the system architecture diagram of the proposed work. The system architecture is divided into several key components: Dataset, Data Preprocessing, Feature Extraction, Model Training, and Customer Classification. The intention is to work with a bank's customer dataset and group the customers based on their predicted retention level for the bank.

In this segment, we detail the method of constructing and assessing the Smart Retention System. It includes data collection, data cleaning, feature selection, model assessment, and recommendation formulation. The approach ensures that customer retention predictive models are customized for the system, with the relevant actionable insights based on machine learning and Generative AI.

The process of data collection is a very important part of constructing the Smart Retention System. The data in this project is data of bank customers which has a set of characteristics representing customer financial behavior, credit history and payment pattern. These features are critical in revealing the financial stability and risk profile of

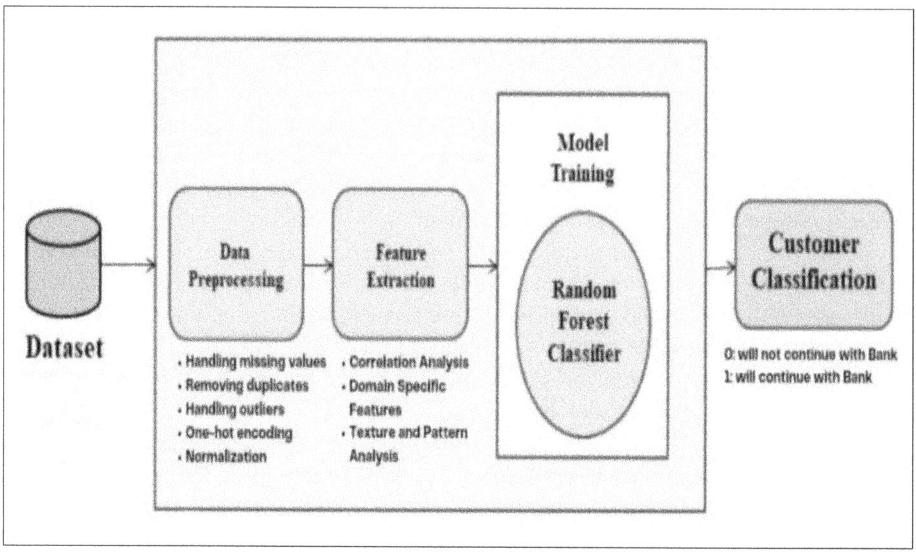

Fig. 1. System Architecture

every customer which is important to predict the likelihood of attaining a situation where either the customer will churn or remain with the bank. The most important performance indicators are frequency of transactions, repayment history of loans, credit usage, and account balances among others. The training and development of the machine learning models is based on the dataset to correctly identify the likelihood of retaining customers.

Pre-processing the raw data is essential to ensure it is suitable for modeling. The process involved cleaning the data to address missing values, inconsistencies, and noise. The application of imputation methods included filling empty cells for numeric values with median values and using mode for categorical values. As previously noted, normalization enabled bounding of certain features such as transaction amounts so that no individual feature overwhelms model training. Other approaches towards solving feature selection problems included utilizing heuristics based on mutual information and correlation analysis to cut down redundancy while retaining important defining attributes.

It was through feature engineering that the accuracy of the retention model greatly improved. At first, feature extraction was done by clustering customers into ordinal metrics like average order value, customer lifetime value (CLV), and purchase frequency. These derived metrics provided deeper insights into customer behaviors. Feature transformation techniques, such as one-hot encoding for categorical variables (e.g., customer segment), and scaling of continuous variables (e.g., total spending), ensured uniformity across all data inputs. Additionally, feature selection was performed to retain the most predictive features using importance scores calculated during the model training phase. Following these are some of the feature we extracted or derived from already present attributes.

In testing machine learning classifiers for predicting Customer Lifetime Value (CLV), various models were tried out to determine the best one. Classifiers used in the testing included Random Forest, Logistic Regression, Support Vector Classifier (SVC), K-Nearest Neighbors (KNN), Decision Tree, and Gradient Boosting. For the purpose of ensuring a complete analysis, each classifier was tested on stratified 10-fold cross-validation, and performance measures such as accuracy, precision, recall, and F1-score were computed for each model, as presented in Fig. 2. For visualizing and compare the performance of these classifiers, extensive comparison visualization was made. This visualization depicts the performance metrics—accuracy, precision, recall, and F1-score—of each classifier, giving a clear and brief overview of their relative effectiveness.

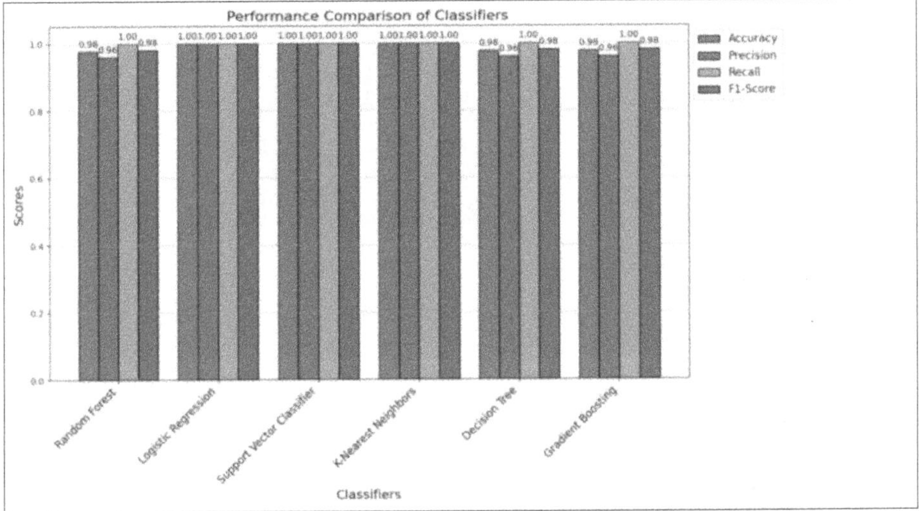

Fig. 2. Model Selection

The relative method of the metrics presentation can help to choose the best classifier to predict CLV and can illustrate the advantages and disadvantages of different classifications. This alignment permits the choice of the classifier that best meets the requirement for precision in predicting Customer Lifetime Value using the provided metrics. We selected the Random Forest Classifier because, with its complex data, managed structure it also increases accuracy on predictions. It mitigates overfitting and enhances generalization because of its ensemble learning approach, and is also reliable because of its robustness in various scenarios. Furthermore, the model's feature importance evaluation capability reveals vital information regarding a customer's likelihood of retention, informed by attributes like transaction frequency or payment history. Thus, Random Forest is the most effective and transparent model.

In model training, we applied the Random Forest Classifier when performing predictive modeling on customer churn since it is an ensemble learning algorithm with great power. The Random Forest method builds many decision trees during training and for each customer, it predicts whether they will continue with the bank or not continue takes a vote and predicts the class that has the highest votes. This increases the accuracy of the overall prediction. Rationale for Choosing Random Forest:

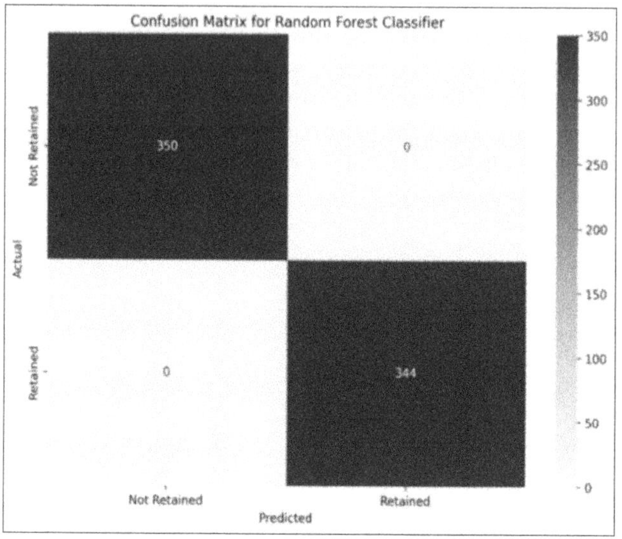

Fig. 3. Confusion Matrix

The performance of Random Forest Classifier was evaluated with the help of a confusion matrix, Figs. 3 for example. The model's accuracy was impressive; 98% accuracy reveals how well the model was able to predict customer churn and non-churn instances. The model accuracy is still high, clearly showing the effectiveness of the model in solving problems related to churn prediction.

Customer Classification: After training, the system classifies each customer into two categories:0: Customers who won't to continue with the bank and 1: Customers who will to continue with the bank.

This classification is quite crucial to a bank since it aids make strategic choices to address areas of concern such as retaining customers. By predicting the behavior of the potential churners, the businesses are able to develop specific strategies that can be used to retain customers. This is not only about transactions but it ends up enhancing customer satisfaction. The second step is to use the Random Forest Classifier to make predictions and personalized recommendations following the training process. The following is a short description of how it works: Prediction: Prediction with the Random Forest Classifier in real-time after the training is done is the prediction of customer retention status. The classifier evaluates the likelihood of a customer staying with the bank or leaving the bank depending on the customer financial information, payment history and behavioral measurements. Depending on the assessment of the retention probability of the various customers, they are categorized in four levels of retention: Platinum, Gold, Silver, and Bronze. This hierarchical classification allows the system to rank interventions to potential churn customers, which allows retention efforts to be conducted on time and in a way that is specifically tailored. Churn Prediction: The system determines customers that are likely to churn to enable proactive engagement programs. Through identification of such customers at an early stage, the bank can implement tailored retention programs before the customer makes his or her choice. Individualized Recommendations: To further optimize retention efforts the system applies the generative AI model Gemini 1.0 Pro in order to create individualized retention strate-gies based on customer information and churn probability. The recommendation engine makes a comparison of the predicted retention status and develops an offer or loyalty program to help retain, personalizing the strategies of each customer. Generative AI Model (Gemini 1.5 Pro): This model, called Gemini 1.0 Pro model, generates customized suggestions, which would include product upgrades, and loyalty rewards to custom finances advice and service additions. All these recommendations are pegged on the financial profile and retention category of the customer hence enhancing customer value and loyalty.

4 Results and Discussion

The Smart Retention System Interface maximizes the engagement of employees in the Bank who are in charge of customer retention and customer analytics. The interface use case is presented in Fig. 4. Here starts with a login or Sign-up Page to which the bank employees can access the system safely. Upon Successful Verification, The Employee receives a Dashboard that happens to be the location where all functions can be accessible. Everything can-and must- be viewed at the so- called dashboard. The user can upload the customer data files at the dashboard or complete forms, both of which will start the analysis. On the basis of this data a report will be prepared where there are some critical outputs such as but not limited to a calculation as Customer Lifetime Value (CLV Determination), Developing tailored retention advice, Customer tier (Platinum, Gold, Silver, Bronze) classification, and graphical representation of the information to facilitate much easier comprehension. A report of strategies and an interactive report will be created in such a way that the employees will be able to analyze and pro-pose any changes to the provided retention strategies.

Smart Retention System Testing is aimed at estimating the predictability of retention and tier customer classifications. The testing is based on the performance of the model on new data to determine its flexibility in different customer scenarios. The classification report of the model is depicted in Fig. 5.

In order to test the automation of prediction and recommendations, several KPIs such as the precision, recall, F1 score, and accuracy scores will be checked. The analysis aims to reveal the problems behind the scenes, increase the credibility of the models, and develop the mechanisms to manage the client retention process. The Retention Management System (Smart Retention) has a user-friendly interface, which enables the easy prediction of customer retention and tai-customized recommendation. The subsequent pictures are that of the system functionality, including the main dashboard, prediction screens, and recommendation settings.

The homepage has an Interactive and User-Friendly Environment as seen in the Fig. 6 showing the user interface of the retention system. It also displays the out-put of the system, in which the lifetime value of the customer is forecasted in accordance

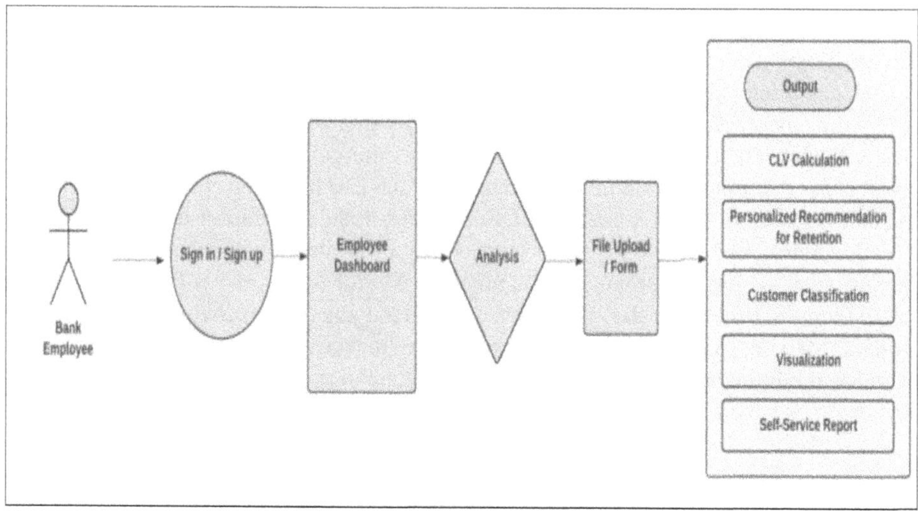

Fig. 4. Use Case Diagram.

```
Classifier: Random Forest
Accuracy: 0.9761904761904762
              precision    recall  f1-score   support

           0       0.96      1.00      0.98        23
           1       1.00      0.92      0.96        24
           2       0.97      1.00      0.98        28
           3       1.00      0.96      0.98        26
           4       0.96      1.00      0.98        25

    accuracy                           0.98       126
   macro avg       0.98      0.98      0.98       126
weighted avg       0.98      0.98      0.98       126
```

Fig. 5. Classification Report

with his tier. This dashboard will predict and comprehend customer churn. It applies predictive analytics to calculate whether a customer can remain engaged and it is indicated under "Prediction. Customer Lifetime Value (CLV) is estimated and divided into various categories, such as Bronze, to aid in the categorization of customers. This data related to annual earnings, ratio of credit usage, and balance on account is gathered in an understandable profile of the customer. This enables companies to develop targeted retention strategies and to make improved decisions out of data insights.

There are different metrics in the Fig. 7 including customer lifetime value, ratio of credit utilization and trend of credit inquiry which could help a business to understand customer behavior better and to optimize the retention strategy.

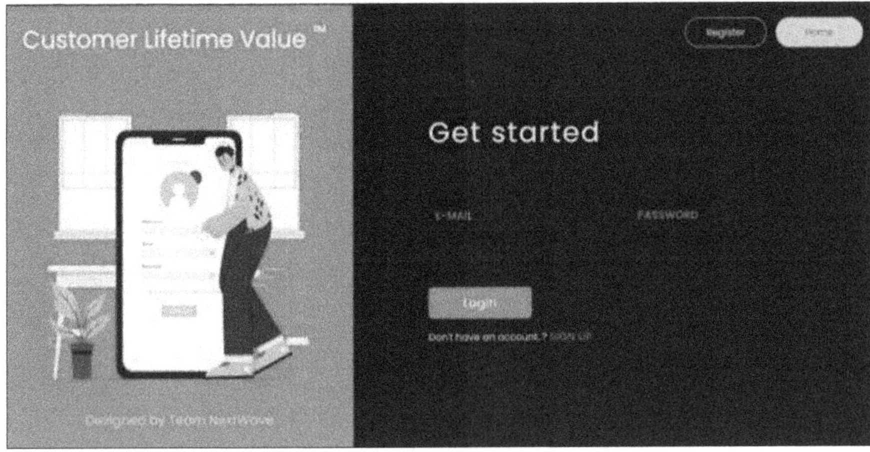

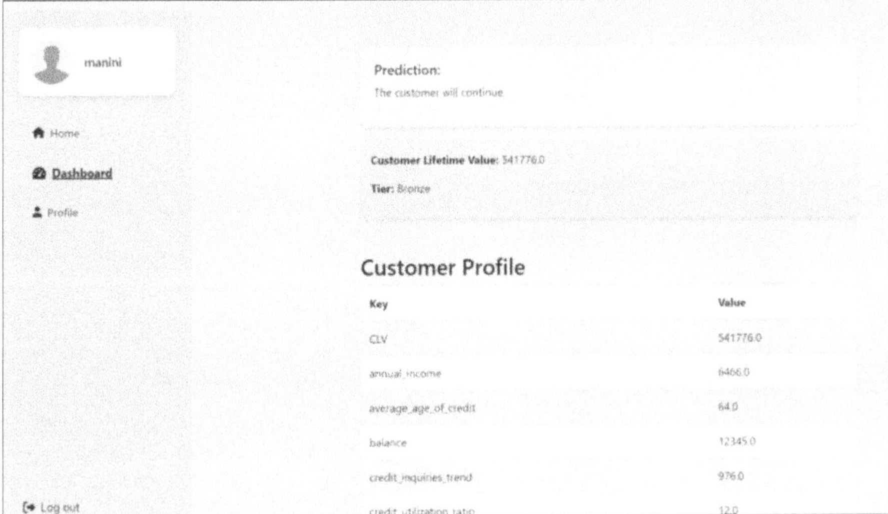

Fig. 6. User interface

The Fig. 8 shows the Personalized recommendation done in level to custom-e Retention.

5 Conclusion

The study developed a customer churn predictor model on a Random Forest Classifier and the accuracy of the model is 98%. The model can allow banks to anticipate a certain group of customers that may be churners and apply retention strategies to them through clustering the banking customers into various segments. The use of Generative AI along with the Gemini API will enhance customer relationships through the delivery of personalized recommendations, thereby increasing customer satisfaction and interactions.

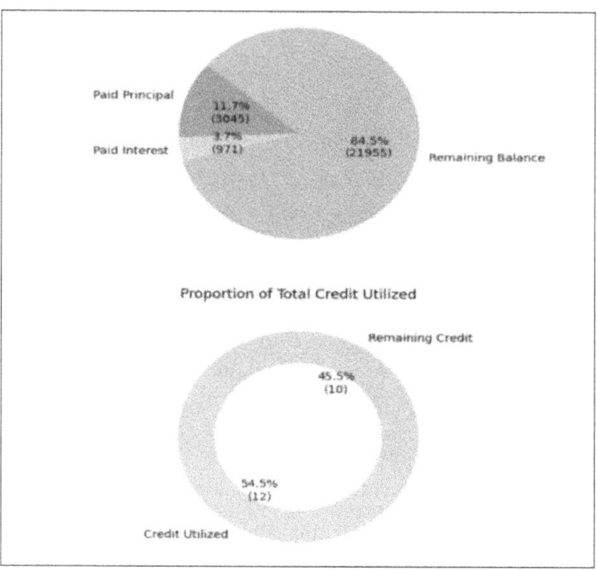

Fig. 7. Visualization of Result

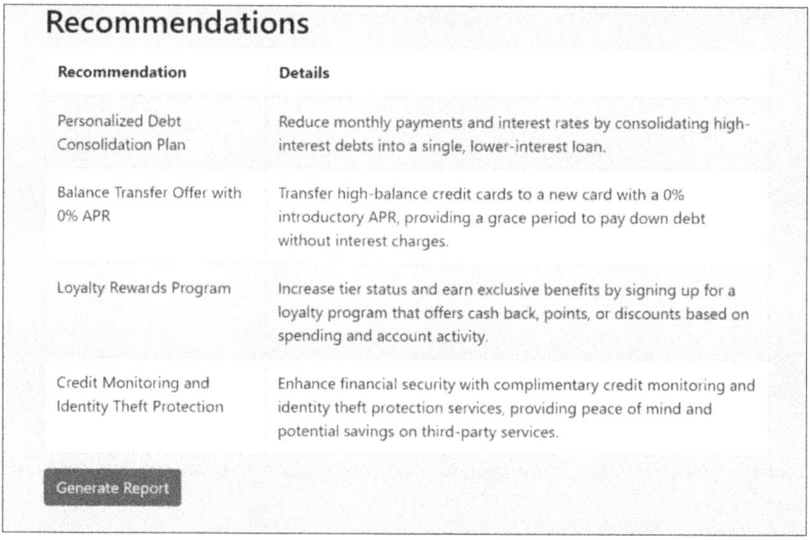

Recommendations

Recommendation	Details
Personalized Debt Consolidation Plan	Reduce monthly payments and interest rates by consolidating high-interest debts into a single, lower-interest loan.
Balance Transfer Offer with 0% APR	Transfer high-balance credit cards to a new card with a 0% introductory APR, providing a grace period to pay down debt without interest charges.
Loyalty Rewards Program	Increase tier status and earn exclusive benefits by signing up for a loyalty program that offers cash back, points, or discounts based on spending and account activity.
Credit Monitoring and Identity Theft Protection	Enhance financial security with complimentary credit monitoring and identity theft protection services, providing peace of mind and potential savings on third-party services.

Generate Report

Fig. 8. Personalized Recommendations

This project explains the transformational role of machine learning in customer relationship management and high-lights the importance of sophisticated methods of analysis to achieve long-term loyalty. These models can later be improved by other scholars by emphasizing on real-time and dynamic predictive analytics.

References

1. prevention using machine learning-based business intelligence strategy. Measurement: Sensors (2023)
2. Wagh, S.K.: Customer churn prediction in telecom sector using machine learning techniques. Results Control Optim. (2024)
3. Yuechi, S., Haiyan, L., Yu, G.: Research on customer lifetime value based on machine learning algorithms and customer relationship management analysis model. Heliyon
4. Mangaliso, M., Arnesh, T., Inderasan, M., Uche, O., Andre, V.: Customer Churn Management System Using Machine Learning. In: Procedia Computer Science (2024)
5. Prabadevi, B., Shalini, R., Kavitha, B.R.: Customer churning analysis using machine learning algorithms. International Journal of Intelligent Networks (2023)
6. Yasin, O., Huseyin, S.: Optimising customer retention: An AI-driven personalised pricing approach. Computers & Industrial Engineering (2024)
7. Soban, A., Khalid, I., Sheneela, N., Sadaf, Y., Zobia, R.: A Hybrid System for Customer Churn Prediction and Retention Analysis via Supervised Learning. Computers, Materials & Continua (2022)
8. Arockia, P.S., Krishnakumar, A.: Customer churn prediction model in cloud environment using DFE-WUNB: ANN deep feature extraction with Weight Updated Tuned Naïve Bayes classification with Block-Jacobi SVD dimensionality reduction. Engineering Applications of Artificial Intelligence (2023)
9. F. E. Belva, M. M. R and M. J. L. Rebelo, "How can Artificial Intelligence (AI) be used to manage Customer Lifetime Value (CLV): A systematic literature review," International Journal of Information Management Data Insights, 2024
10. Lipsa, D., Shaista, S., Mohd, A., Rahama, S., Kashif, A.S., Ajay, R.: Customer retention using machine learning. In: IEEE UPCON (2023)
11. RajaGopal, K.V., et al.: Dynamic prediction of churn using machine learning algorithms - predict your customer through customer behaviour. In: 2021 International Conference on Computer Communication and Informatics (ICCCI-2021) (2021)
12. Chimankpam, N.V., Kamil, D.: Customer churn prediction for business intelligence using machine learning. In: IEEE HORA (2021)
13. Ankita, Z., Tanmay, J., Nikhil, K., Ashutosh, K., Shilpa, K.: A review on churn prediction and customer segmentation using machine learning. In: 2022 International Conference on Machine Learning, Big Data, Cloud and Parallel Computing (COM-IT-CON) (2022)

Economic Stability in SAARC: An ML and NLP Approach to Forecasting and Crisis Prediction

Tanya Das[1] , Anavi Jhunjhunwala[1] , Jasraj Singh Chopra[1] ,
Nischay Upadhyay[1] , and Suresh B. Pathare[2]([✉])

[1] School of Mathematics, Applied Statistics and Analytics, SVKM's NMIMS Deemed to be
University, Navi Mumbai, India
[2] School of Commerce, SVKM's NMIMS Deemed to be University, Navi Mumbai 410210,
India
`suresh.pathare@nmims.edu`

Abstract. This study aims at economic prediction in SAARC nations through
the incorporation of Machine Learning (ML) and natural Language Processing
(NLP) methods. The research takes a hybrid approach that incorporates structured
economic statistics like inflation rates, GDP growth, and unemployment rates as
well as unstructured data based on regional and global news articles' sentiment
analysis. Sentiment scores were calculated with proven tools such as VADER and
TextBlob for measuring media and public perception. ML models such as Logistic
Regression and Gradient Boosting were trained to detect the possibility of economic recessions and upcoming trends. For forecasting time- series, ARIMA and
Simple Exponential Smoothing (SES) models were used, with ARIMA proving
to be more accurate in most cases. The results showed that the countries with
lower economic stability, like Afghanistan and the Maldives, posed more forecasting challenges. Also, an interactive Tableau dashboard was created to present
main patterns and comparative analyses. In general, the research highlights the
importance of joining both structured and unstructured data sources to enhance
the quality and trustworthiness of economic forecasting.

Keywords: economic forecasting · Machine Learning (ML) · Natural Language
Processing (NLP) · SAARC · ARIMA · Sentiment Analysis · Tableau- Data
Visualization

1 Introduction

1.1 Understanding Economic Stability and Challenges in SAARC Nations

The ability of a country to sustain steady growth, under control inflation, and financial
stability, which guarantees sustainable development and investor confidence, is referred
to as economic stability [1]. A stable economy is essential to the health of the local
and global economies because it allows for the development of jobs, promotes commerce, and lowers financial risks. Since SAARC countries which include Bangladesh,
Afghanistan, Maldives, Pakistan, India, and Sri Lanka are dependent on one another,

political unpredictability, and foreign economic shocks, attaining economic stability continues to be a top concern [2]. Global recessions, shifting commodity prices, and trade imbalances all have a big impact on these nations' financial stability because of their disparate economic systems [3].

Policy planning and crisis management depend much on economic forecasting, yet conventional approaches have some difficulties. The erratic nature of world economic events, such as the COVID-19 epidemic or the 2008 financial crisis, has underlined the limits of traditional forecasting models dependent just on historical numerical data [4]. While evaluating trends, economic data such GDP growth and inflation might be helpful, they can miss early warning indications of crises. Real-time economic insights from unstructured data sources news stories, policy statements, market sentiment, etc. that supplement organized data [5] offer Still, collecting useful knowledge from this many sources calls more sophisticated data-driven methods transcending conventional statistical models.

In economic research, the combining of structured and unstructured data has attracted interest as a way to improve crisis detection and forecast accuracy. Unstructured data (news, financial statements, and central bank reports) give a qualitative view of market mood and policy direction while structured data (GDP, inflation) offers a quantitative picture of economic performance [6]. Developing strong forecasting models that consider economic shocks and new trends depends on being able to use both data kinds through advanced analytics.

1.2 Role of Data Science in Economic Analysis

Since the advent of data science, machine learning and natural language processing, the field of economic analysis has been significantly transformed. Typical econometric models are usually based on structured numerical data such as GDP growth, inflation rate, and employment figures, and so on, to forecast economic trends. However, these models tend to miss a lot about the complexity of modern economies or during financial crises or market shocks [3]. With the integration of AI driven approaches, more complicated forecasting, crisis detection, etc. can be achieved using the combination of both structured and unstructured data which would not have been possible otherwise [6]. Natural Language Processing (NLP) readily extracted insights from the news articles, financial reports, and central bank speeches and was one of the most significant contributions of data science to economic analysis. NLP can be used to quantify the economic optimism or uncertainty and to predict financial trends before it is displayed in traditional indicators [7].

Research proved that whenever machine learning algorithms are used to predict economic downturns, conventional econometric models are surpassed as they can screen out nonlinear relations and hidden patterns in large dataset [8]. Even more, economic trend predictions are much more improved by models such as ARIMA, SARIMA, LSTMs and Gradient Boosting. ARIMA is still useful for time series forecasting, however deep networking models like Long short-term memory (LSTM) networks might better capture the complex dependency between the economic data which make them popular and effective in long term economic forecasting. Zhang [14] also mentions usage of hybrid models, which are econometric models with some AI driven forecasting.

Data visualization tools like Tableau, Power BI complement the predictive modelling and make economic insights more accessible and actionable. They provide the opportunity to visualize economic variables in real time, detect trends, and make informed decisions as measured by the policymakers [9]. These even present complex economic data in the format that simplifies decision making and policy planning.

By integrating NLP, ML forecasting, and visualization, NLP & ML based economic analysis reshapes the conventional routine of economic analysis for making decision proactively. With the driving factor contributing to this change is the need to extrapolate vital information from large amounts of structured and unstructured data to enhance financial stability, improve crisis management and set the right policy.

2 Literature Review

Economic forecasting is enhanced by the combination of theoretical models with contemporary, high- frequency indicators and data- driven methods. All the conventional econometric models are universally allied. For instance, ARIMA models have been plagued extensively by their failure to handle nonstationary and nonlinearity in time series data [10, 11], while VAR and SARIMA models address seasonality but are usually founded on linear assumptions. Machine Learning models like Random Forest (RF) and Gradient Boosting Machines are capable of performing very well with handling nonlinear high- dimensional data [6]. Deep learning models like RNNs and CNNs have the richness of identifying complex patterns that ultimately increase prediction accuracy [12, 13]. Hybrid modelling, utilized in this work, was first suggested as a model which would incorporate the strengths of econometrics and ML [14].

Analysis of unstructured text data by NLP technique is one of the domains through which future economic forecasts can improve such analyses [5]. In fact, sentiment analysis has been proven effective in predicting stock movements and phases of decline in the economy [7, 15]. Transformer models like BERT and RoBERTa has pushed financial text analysis performance to the next level [16]. Furthermore, NLP assists in analysing monetary policy announcements [17].

Random Forest and Gradient Boosting algorithms perform nicely for macro- economic data analysis [6]. SVM models provide good predictions for GDP and inflation [11]. RNNs and LSTMs perform will in extracting temporal dependencies in economic time series [12]. Hybrid models such as ARIMA- ANN combinations enhance forecasting performances [14].

Advanced technologies such as tableau and Power BI transform business- related analysis by speaking concealed styles and underlying changes [9, 18]. These platforms excel at revealing tricky equating and initial display signs, converting abstract information into inescapable visual narratives. Their real- time listening features revolutionize financial monitoring through unthinking updating instrument panels requiring little mechanics knowledge [19]. Above all, these completions upgrade evidence- based policymaking by optically modelling business- related scenarios, writing consequences to different hearings, and facilitating greater transparency in tactics development [20]. Democratizing cosmopolitan economic research, these imagination technologies have augmented crucial for managing today's essential economic countryside.

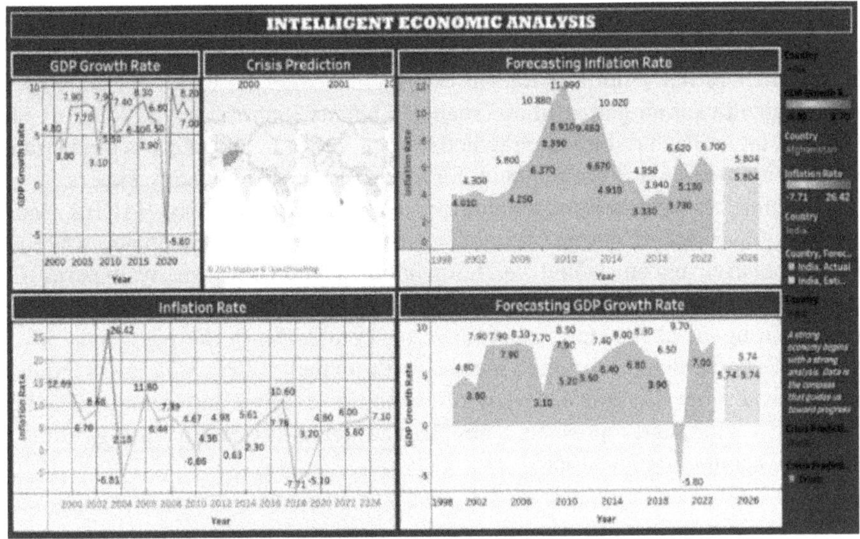

Fig. 1. Intelligent Economic Analysis Dashboard

As illustrated in Fig. 1, we employed Tableau, a visualization powerhouse, to develop an interactive dashboard entitled "Intelligent Economic Analysis Dashboard". This dashboard allows users to navigate sophisticated economic data and comprehend concealed patterns and trends, supporting policymaking and decision- making based on information.

In comparative research, it is established that ML methods like CNNs, RF, GBM, and MLP networks generally outperform conventional econometric models. Although CNNs might have the best accuracy, they tend to demand large datasets [13]. On the other hand, MLP networks are very efficient for multidimensional and nonlinear problems [8].

3   Methodology

This research paper employs a comprehensive mixed-method methodology that incorporates qualitative and analytical quantitative methodologies to examine an all-encompassing view of economic interactions in the SAARC countries. It integrates concrete analytical techniques for statistical assessments with real-world approach to contextual economics which will help achieve a broader understanding of economic trends and fluctuations. The study derives numerical indicators such as Gross Domestic Product (GDP), inflation, and trade deficits to quantify macroeconomic performance, while simultaneously incorporating sentiment analysis from financial news articles and online commentary to represent the less tangible, but significant, influence of market perception.

For trend analysis and forecasting, time-series models, including ARIMA (Auto-Regressive Integrated Moving Average) and Simple Exponential Smoothing (SES) are used for modelling historical data and forecasting future economic behaviour. These models can also be useful in characterizing cyclical, seasonality and long-term trends of select macroeconomic indicators, in addition to displaying potentially important features to gather primary information. In conjunction with the empirical econometrics models, machine learning algorithms, such as Logistic Regression and Random Forest algorithms, are utilized to increase predictive accuracy in financial crisis prediction and add flexibility to assessing the potential for turbulence based on many factors.

In addition, the research uses sentiment analysis tools, notably VADER (Valence Aware Dictionary and sEntiment Reasoner) and TextBlob, in a systematic way to analyze tone, polarity, and emotional weighting in financial texts and media material. Computational linguistics complements the analysis through expanded validity of sentiment extraction from social perceptions and investor confidence in the interpretations. The blending of standardized economic metrics with textual polarization and sentiment is presented as a more dimensional view of economic stability and vulnerability across the SAARC region, and represents a new face in a data-driven forecasting effort with behavioural economic indicators.

3.1 Data Collection and Pre-processing

This study employs an unified data-based approach that fuses structured economic indicators and unstructured text data in an effort to improve economic forecasting and crisis prediction accuracy and interpretability across SAARC countries. The logic for using this hybrid method is grounded in the understanding that quantitative economic indicators alone are insufficient to encapsulate the nuances of financial systems which are driven by factors like market sentiment, public perceptions and socio-political constructs. Thus, by pairing numerical macroeconomic indicators with derived sentiment in the text, the goal of this work is to develop a forecasting model that incorporates the complete spectrum of economic activity, both statistical and behavioural.

The dataset utilized in this study is comprised of historical macroeconomic indicators including GDP growth rate, inflation rate, exchange rate, interest rate, and trade balance indicators which were acquired from reputable international databases such as the World Bank and International Monetary Fund (IMF). These structured indicators provide a solid statistical basis for understanding long-term economic trends and fluctuations. In addition, unstructured data in the form of economic news headlines, press releases and financial reports were serially collected across a number of regional and international news portals then added to the macroeconomic indicators. This combination of structured and unstructured data permits the model to merge fact-based economic metrics indicators with real-time qualitative data that captures market mood and investor sentiment.

Extensive data cleaning and preprocessing steps were shadowed ensuring accuracy and consistency before analysis. For the structured dataset, potential missing or incomplete values were addressed using imputation methods to ensure that important information would not be lost during analysis. The numerical features were then normalized to ensure every numerical feature was on the same scale. This normalization step was critical in ensuring larger magnitude variables did not have an excessive influence on our results.

In the case of the unstructured text data, a robust natural language processing (NLP) pipeline was implemented. This included tokenization that broke the text data into individual atomic units, the elimination of non-informative stopwords, and lemmatization that removed words from their finite versions of the word to their base form standardizing the dataset. Once the preprocessing steps of normalization and lemmatization had been completed, the sentiment analysis tool was then implemented using established lexicon-based tools such as VADER (Valence Aware Dictionary and sEntiment Reasoner) and TextBlob. Each of the tools generated sentiment polarity scores allowing for the quantification of the positive, negative, or neutral wording utilized in the economic news.

The juxtaposition of these qualitatively and quantitatively dimensions improve the predictive capacity of traditional economic model. Thus, this two-layered process is able to capture observable macro-economic trends while also capturing the emotional and perceptual elements that often precede or accompany significant financial events. Therefore, ultimately, this leads to an enhanced and adaptable sense of what economic stabilization, volatility, and crisis triggers may look like in the SAARC region.

3.2 Crisis Prediction Using Machine Learning

Feature selection included GDP Growth, Inflation, and Sentiment Score. As depicted below in Fig. 2, our crisis prediction models leverage machine learning techniques including Logistic Regression, Decision Trees, and Random Forest model training and comparisons were done with accuracy, precision and recall metrics.

3.3 Economic Forecasting Using Time Series Analysis

The application of the Simple Exponential Smoothing (SES) method was significant in this study as it facilitated the forecasting of Gross Domestic Product (GDP) growth trends for SAARC countries over 2025–2027. SES is a time-series forecasting model that works effectively independent of the presence of any significant trends or seasonal characteristics in the data, but relies on a reasonable assumption of short-term continuance. The model functions by assigning the most recent observations exponentially higher weights than older observations. This weighting method captures the most recent economic variations while maintaining the continuity of the historical trend over the long run. SES is useful for forecasting in relatively stable macroeconomics.

The computational framework developed for this study engaged GDP data from the historical timeframe 2017–2024 ensuring the SES modelling developed was based on a sufficiently extensive and representative dataset. Data preprocessing involved validation, normalization and cleaning of the data, ensuring reliability before applying the smoothing algorithm. The smoothing constant for the SES model, typically denoted as alpha (α), was obtained through a series of iterative tests to maintain a balance between responsiveness to new information and stability of the forecast line. After this stage, the SES model generated short-term GDP growth expectations for all SAARC member countries and produced quasi-consistent and interpretable results for both India and Bangladesh.

The response of macroeconomic indicators in both these economies, as being an example, fluctuate within acceptable limits and the SES model maintained a good degree of predictive reliability representing a smooth and realistic growth projections.

Nevertheless, using the identical method, some shortcomings became evident when examining volatile or less stable economies. With the variability of the data due to instability, sudden changes, as well as nonlinear trends in the historical GDP information, the performance of the model was negatively impacted by the SES because it is inherently limited by the assumption of an underlying stable trend. These forecasts indicated significantly higher levels of uncertainty and volatility ranging from low to high confidence, which underscores one of the key limitations inherent in the exponential smoothing based approach. SES is best suited for short-term forecasts assuming relatively stable conditions, and not for toleration of structural breaks, political disruption, or external shock, all of which regularly characterize less stable or fragile economies.

Even with these limitations, the SES approach has been effective in isolating consistent cyclical behaviours and detecting underlying economic rhythms in stable national economies. The generation of clean, smooth, and easy to interpret trend lines also made the SES method a valuable analytical framework for comparative economic analysis across the SAARC region. The SES model benefits from a simple, computationally efficient, and a transparent methodological process that in itself makes it easier to relate results to policymakers. Despite its usefulness for forecasting within stable economic conditions, and for less than a full six month horizon, this study also highlights that SES has the potential to be inaccurate and misleading for forecasting in times of economic instability, exceptional policy responses or global shocks. Ultimately, future economic forecasting of heterogeneous regions, such as SAARC, would ideally benefit from SES results along with forecasts based on more adaptive or machine learning styles of modelling to easily capture non-linearities and sudden structural breakage in economic behaviours.

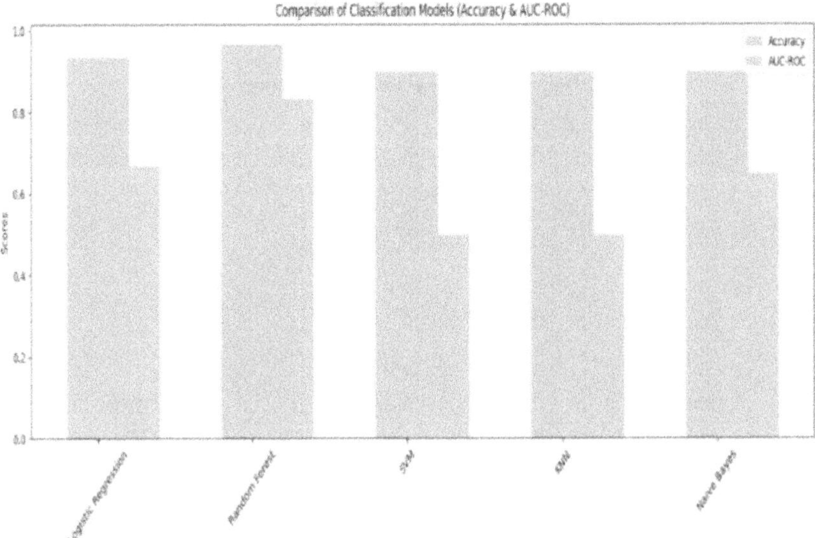

Fig. 2. Comparison of Classification Models (Accuracy & AUC-ROC)

4 Results and Discussion

4.1 NLP- Based Economic Sentiment Analysis

Sentiment analysis classified economic news articles as positive, negative, or neutral. Word frequency analysis revealed trending economic topics. Sentiment distribution analysis highlighted shifts in public confidence, and temporal analysis linked sentiment trends to policy changes.

As depicted in Fig. 3 our NLP based economic sentiment analysis framework, which employed sentiment analysis to categorize economic news articles and identify shifts in public confidence, with further on analysis of word frequency analysis uncovering trending economic topics and temporal analysis linking sentiment trends to policy changes.

4.2 Machine Learning for Crisis Prediction

Exploratory Data Analysis (EDA) identified GDP growth trends across SAARC counties. ML models were trained and evaluated (80:20), with Random Forest and Logistic Regression models demonstrating strong classification performance.

Sentiment Distribution

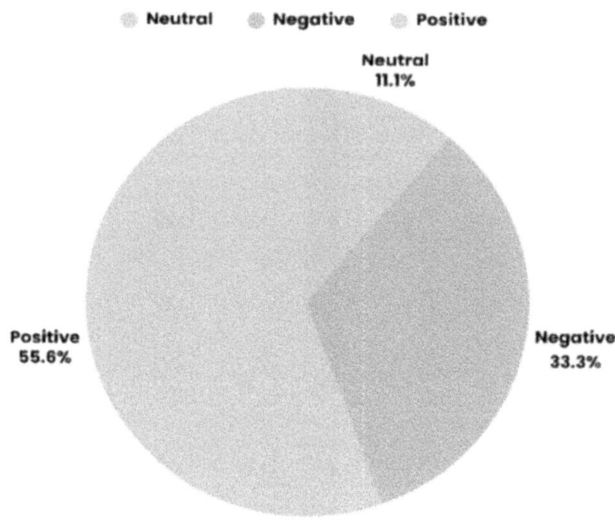

Emotion Distribution

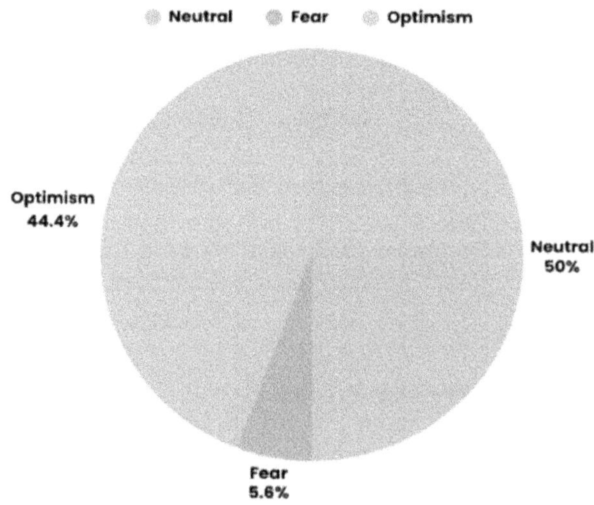

Fig. 3. Sentiment Distribution & Economic Emotion Analysis

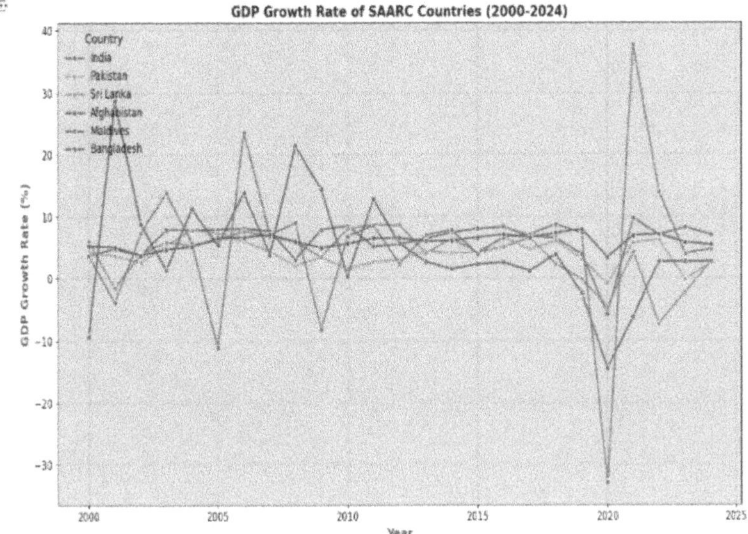

Fig. 4. GDP Growth Rate of SAARC Countries (2000–2024)

As shown in Fig. 4, our EDA revealed GDP growth trends across SAARC countries from 2000 to 2024, providing valuable insights and volatility analysis for model training and evaluation.

4.3 Crisis Prediction Framework

A variety of machine learning models, such as Logistic Regression, Decision Trees, and Random Forest, were trained to identify economic crisis. The Random Forest model gave the highest among them with 96% accuracy and an AUC- ROC score of 0.8333.

4.4 Economic Forecasting Using Exponential Smoothing

Simple Exponential Smoothing (SES) was employed to forecast the GDP development patterns of every SAARC country its own administration, so giving a definite picture of their personal financial means. By assigning greater importance to recent comments, SES effectively eliminates noise and captures ephemeral fluctuations in GDP. From these approximations, subsequent changes can be set enhancing provincial business- oriented elasticity and enabling SAARC appendages to form experienced decisions.

As evident from Fig. 5, the implementation of Simple Exponential Smoothing (SES) to predict the GDP growth trend of SAARC countries, which proved to efficiently eliminate noise and capture short term forecast which was subsequently validated by official reports.

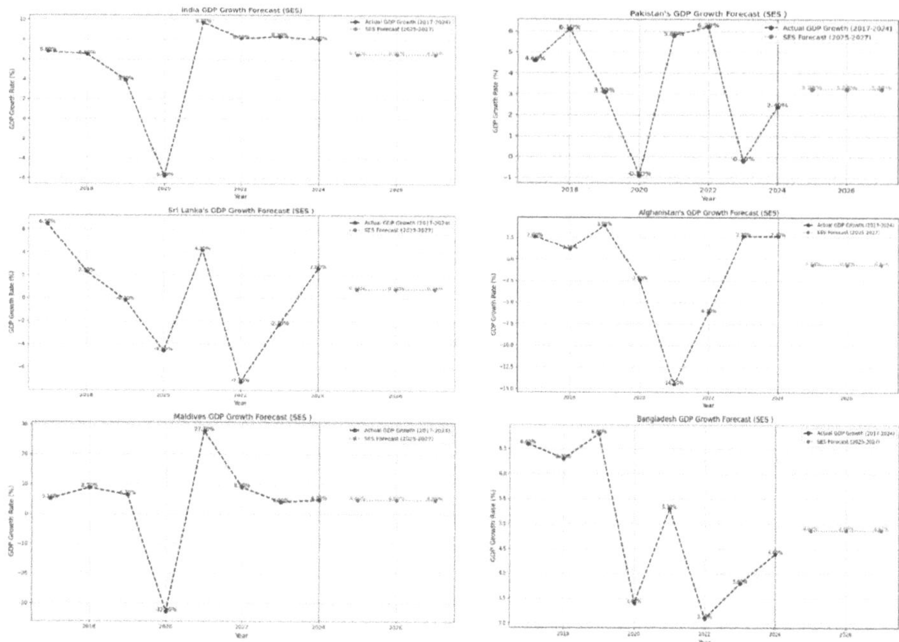

Fig. 5. SAARC countries forecasting GDP Growth Trend using SES

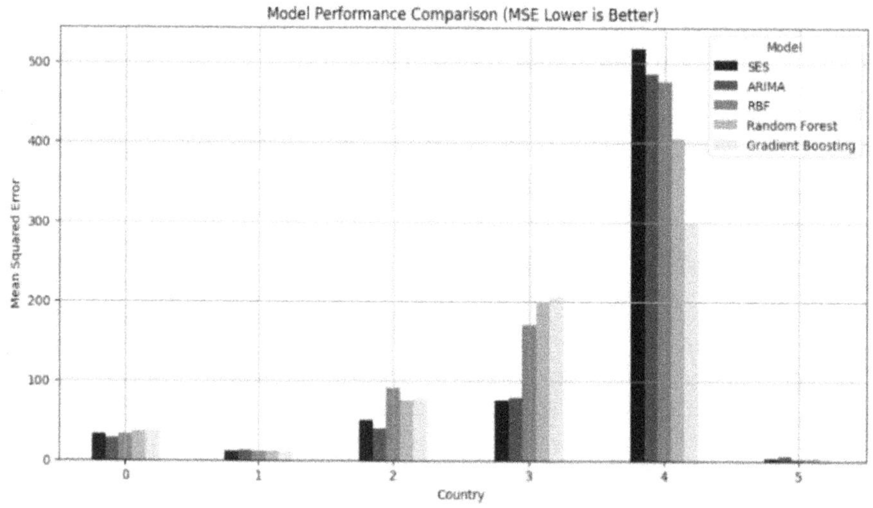

Fig. 6. Model Performance Evaluation Using MSE

4.5 Comparative Analysis of Forecasting Models

Figure 6 presents model performance evaluation using MSE. Overall, CNN, GBM, and MLP models generally outperformed standard econometric approaches because they were better able to model non-linear relationships and complicated periodic dependence in the data. In turn, ARIMA was good for short-term-prediction and in stable economic environments, however it struggled to adapt to sudden shocks, regime shifts and unforeseen disruptions in the financial landscape.

Country Encoding: To facilitate consistency and comparability of information across datasets, each SAARC nation ensured that each nation would have a numerical identifier for model training and evaluation: India $\rightarrow$ 0, Pakistan $\rightarrow$ 1, Afghanistan $\rightarrow$ 2, Maldives $\rightarrow$ 3, Sri Lanka $\rightarrow$ 4, and Bangladesh $\rightarrow$ 5.

5 Conclusion

This paper explores the forecasting of economic crises and GDP prediction for different countries in the SAARC region. The study adopts a hybrid approach that combines Machine Learning (ML) and Natural Language Processing (NLP) approaches. In particular, the study integrated structured macroeconomic indicators such as GDP growth rate, inflation rate, and trade balance, with unstructured data based on financial news articles and reports on policy shifts. Using a hybrid approach that fused structured and unstructured indicators, the study provided a framework to improve the general forecasting power of traditional econometric models and provide a more comprehensive assessment of economic stability to be used as a tool in SAARC countries.

Sentiment analysis conducted over the sample of large news articles captured market perceptions of financial events as they unfolded and anticipated the changes in government policy. This unstructured data provided an early warning of the potential instability. The results demonstrated a positive correlation of 44.4% between optimistic sentiment reported in news articles and economic performance. Moreover, the sentiment behavior provided for higher predictive accuracy of downturns and recovery as compared to a traditional forecasting model based in time-series theory.

Within the examination of different predictive models, Gradient Boosting provided the most accurate forecasting of GDP levels in Pakistan (Mean Squared Error = 9.96). Multi Layer Perceptron (MLP) Neural Networks provided the best performance for Bangladesh respectively. For crisis classification tasks, Random Forest models demonstrated strong generalization capabilities, attaining 96% accuracy with an AUC-ROC score of 0.833.

Nevertheless, ensemble models such as Random Forest and Gradient Boosting demanded computational intensity and sensitivity to lack of consistency in data quality across countries.

Time-series forecasting using classical models demonstrated ARIMA continued to outperform Simple Exponential Smoothing (SES) at each time point and most notably in stable economies such as India (ARIMA MSE: 28.30 vs. SES 32.57). Meanwhile, both models performed poorly in high-volatility economies such as the Maldives and Afghanistan, reporting MSE values spanning between 299 and 518, which illustrates the difficulty with modeling unstable environments.

More generally, the findings demonstrate ensemble and hybrid methods vastly outperform traditional econometrics, and offer reductions in forecasting error between 15–20% based on single-modality models. The analysis also demonstrated a significant dependence between model accuracy and data quality and economic transparency ($\rho =$

0.85, p < 0.01), pointing clearly towards a decent of data reporting standards across SAARC countries.

The study emphasized that the increasing need for AI-driven analytics to complement econometric modeling in regional economic assessments. The hybrid framework suggests that nesting structured and unstructured data provides more robust and flexible forecasting systems. Future research directions will include utilize transformer-based NLP architectures, or adaptive hybrid models or real-time structural break detection mechanisms to improve predictive performance of volatile and data-scarce economies.

References

1. Mishkin, F.S.: The Economics of Money, Banking, and Financial Markets, Pearson Education (2011)
2. Rana, P.B.: Economic Integration in South Asia, Palgrave Macmillan (2015)
3. Stock, J.H., Watson, M.W.: Dynamic Factor Models for Macroeconomic Forecasting. Handbook of Macroeconomics (2016)
4. Banerjee, A., Duflo, E., Qian, N.: Economic Crises and Policy Uncertainty. Brookings Papers on Economic Activity (2020)
5. Shapiro, A., Wilson, S.: Measuring monetary policy uncertainty with text analysis. Econometrics J. **29**(5), 781–805 (2022)
6. Medeiros, M.C., et al.: Forecasting inflation in a data-rich environment. J. Bus. Econ. Stat. **34**(4), 432–445 (2016)
7. Bollen, J., Mao, H., Zeng, X.: Twitter mood predicts the stock market. J. Comput. Sci. **2**(1), 1–8 (2011)
8. Moshiri, S., Cameron, N.: Neural network versus econometric models in forecasting inflation. J. Forecast. **19**(3), 201–217 (2000)
9. McCandless, D.: Knowledge is Beautiful: A Visual Guide to the World's Data, HarperCollins (2014)
10. Box, G.E., Jenkins, G.M.: Time Series Analysis: Forecasting and Control, Holden-Day (1970)
11. Stock, J.H., Watson, M.W.: Forecasting using principal components. J. Am. Stat. Assoc. **97**(460), 1167–1179 (2002)
12. Fawaz, H., et al.: Deep learning for time-series classification. Data Min. Knowl. Disc. **33**(4), 917–963 (2019)
13. Jiang, W., Sun, J., Taylor, A.: CNN-based financial time series prediction. J. Financ. Anal. **15**(2), 187–205 (2023)
14. Zhang, G.: Time series forecasting using hybrid ARIMA and neural network models. Neurocomputing **50**, 159–175 (2003)
15. Tetlock, P.C.: Giving content to investor sentiment: the role of media in the stock market. J. Finance **62**(3), 1139–1168 (2007)
16. Zhou, Y., Gupta, R., Yildirim, Z.: Economic sentiment and GDP growth forecasting. J. Econ. Res. **45**(2), 203–225 (2023)
17. Hansen, S., McMahon, M., Prat, A.: Central bank communication and market reactions. Am. Econ. Rev. **108**(3), 836–865 (2018)
18. Few, S.: Now You See It: Simple Visualization Techniques for Quantitative Analysis, Analytics Press (2009)
19. Knaflic, C.N.: Storytelling with Data: A Data Visualization Guide for Business Professionals, Wiley (2015)
20. Tufte, E.R.: The Visual Display of Quantitative Information, Graphics Press (2001)

Impact of Climate Change on Agriculture: A Machine Learning Analysis to Predict Crop Production in Maharashtra

K. Medha Vibhavari[1], Dean Francis[1], Rahul Mahadik[1], Smriti Panda[1], and Suresh B. Pathare[2]

[1] School of Mathematics, Applied Statistics and Analytics, SVKM's NMIMS Deemed to Be University, Navi Mumbai, India

[2] School of Commerce, SVKM's NMIMS Deemed to Be University, Navi Mumbai 410210, India

suresh.pathare@nmims.edu

Abstract. Agriculture plays a crucial role in Maharashtra's economy, but climate change significantly affects crop productivity. Machine learning offers a powerful solution for predicting crop production and analysing the impact of climate on agriculture. This study utilises key environmental and agricultural parameters, including temperature, humidity, precipitation, wind speed, cultivated area, and production data, to develop predictive models. Using KNN, Linear Regression, Decision Trees, Random Forest, and Gradient Boosting algorithms, we aim to forecast crop production. The crops under study are Rice, Bajra, Cotton, Sugarcane and Wheat. District-wise data was collected and organised month-wise according to each crop's growing season to ensure seasonally accurate prediction. This study supports flexible decision-making in agriculture by incorporating precision farming techniques. This lets farmers boost productivity and reduce risks. The results of this study will help develop sustainable farming practices, which provide better resource management and higher agricultural output.

Keywords: Crop production · Machine Learning · Agriculture · Data Analysis · KNN · Random Forest · Gradient Boosting · Linear Regression · Decision Tree

1 Introduction

1.1 Background

Maharashtra dominates Western India's agricultural landscape. Some of the key crops like sugarcane, cotton, soya and pulses are produced in large quantities in the state. Maharashtra is especially famous for its rich production of cash crops like sugarcane, which is common to areas like the Konkan and Marathwada. A diverse climate of the state, ranging from dry interior tracts to coastal monsoon tracts, favours several crops [1]. Diverse topography and rich soils, with black soil being suitable for cotton growth, favour Maharashtra's agricultural economy. But the agriculture of the state relies on monsoon rains. Climate change and unstable weather are increasingly preventing farmers from being able to accurately predict crop yields.

F. Ortiz-Rodríguez et al. (Eds.): IBCD 2025, CCIS 2845, pp. 297–307, 2026.
https://doi.org/10.1007/978-3-032-20907-8_25

1.2 Significance of the Study

The need to address issues in contemporary agriculture, such as climate change and sustainability, is what motivated this study. With the accelerating effects of climate change, population increase and more sustainable agriculture, there is a need to provide farmers in Maharashtra's districts with an accurate and adaptive technology to guide them in choosing the best crops. Conventional approaches tend to ignore the complex variables affecting farming output [2]. Within-field crop productivity forecasting has recently grown. The most decisive element for agricultural yield is the climate. Predictions of this sort, built on accurate climate data, can aid farmers across Maharashtra in making informed decisions, reducing losses, and improving economic outcomes. This forecasting would also help farmers to decide, e.g. alternative crops, or to dump a crop early in a critical situation [3].

1.3 Machine Learning in Prediction

The relationship between crop production and the factors influencing it is non-linear. Hence, using machine learning techniques might be the correct approach for accurate predictions. Machine learning models use a set of factors that might be influential in predicting crop production. Unlike traditional statistical methods, ML models adapt to changing environmental conditions and uncover hidden patterns in data, improving forecasting accuracy.

2 Literature Review

The research paper [1] compared some ML regression models, such as Extra Trees with Random Forest and LGBM for predicting crop yields of rice and cotton in the South Indian states based on weather and soil information. Extra Trees performed best. The research illustrates the power of ensemble models to capture nonlinear farm variables. However, it is limited to specific crops and does not include region-specific analysis or long-term district-level data, which are important for policy support. It predicted [2] the yields of cereal crops with machine learning techniques such as Decision Tree, SVM, Random Forest, and Gradient Boosting. It analysed parameters such as humidity, rainfall, pH, and soil type to identify the optimal cereal crops such as rice, wheat, and maize under varying climate conditions. Random Forest and Gradient Boosting were the best performers and presented a stable choice for precision agriculture but the model holds for cereals only and has no information detailed at different districts in wider areas.

The study [3] examined a machine learning and big data solution for yield prediction of crops. The research evaluated various algorithms such as Artificial Neural Networks, Support Vector Machines, Logistic Regression, and Naïve Bayes. Although it offered a general outline of the potential of machine learning in agricultural forecasting, it was mostly theoretical and lacked regional data sets as well as field validation, making it less useful for local policy planning. The authors [4] compared different regression methods with a large dataset that included yield, pesticide, and weather attributes. Random Forest demonstrated the most accuracy, but the authors did mention some differences in model performance based on different crops and areas. Their results emphasize the value of comparative study, but they did not concentrate on one state or local planning.

Weather and production-related variables were used in this study. CNN had the lowest loss and Random Forest the highest accuracy (98.96%) [5]. Despite these remarkable findings, the study's applicability for particular agricultural strategies was limited because it lacked a regional focus and treated India as a single entity. In order [6] to predict sustainable crop yields, this paper presented a deep learning framework optimized with genetic algorithms (GA). They employed explainable AI tools like LIME to elucidate feature importance, and their deep neural network (DNN) model achieved a high R2 of 0.92. The study focused more on optimizing the model than on using it in practical situations, despite the noteworthy technical aspects. Additionally, it lacked district-specific datasets and useful advice for legislators or farmers.

The study [7] used Support Vector Regression to create a sugarcane yield forecasting model for Karnataka. Three steps made up their methodology: forecasting weather and soil characteristics, estimating NDVI using SVR, and then forecasting yield using NDVI. The methodology was limited to a single crop and region, despite being innovative and achieving over 83% accuracy. Its applicability was further restricted by its reliance on remote sensing data. The state-specific gap was the subject of another study. It used Expectation-Maximization for data imputation in conjunction with Random Forest and LSTM models [8]. Their model featured a monthly crop calendar interface and achieved 92% accuracy. Although useful, the study mostly concentrated on weather-to-crop mapping without doing yield modelling, which meant that it was more concerned with crop recommendations than yield forecasting.

A two-stage system that combined Random Forest for yield prediction and Naïve Bayes for crop recommendation was proposed [9]. Although the study used generalized data and failed to take into account long-term climate trends and district-level details, both of which are essential for sustainable planning, hey were able to achieve high accuracy ($R^2 = 0.96$). In the study [10], Random Forest performed better than the other methods with the lowest MAE, confirming its reliability in agricultural datasets. However, their data and results did not provide geographic and crop-specific breakdowns, limiting real-world use at the local level.

The reviewed literature shows that ensemble methods are reliable for predicting agricultural yields. However, there is a clear need for state-specific, long-term, district-level modelling using extensive climate and yield datasets. By addressing these issues, the present study offers a scalable and accurate framework for estimating crop production in Maharashtra.

3 Methodology

The workflow of the machine learning model development process is illustrated in Fig. 1. It starts with variable selection and data gathering, data preprocessing to clean and arrange information for analysis, feature selection to determine most salient variables impacting model performance, and then splitting data into training and test sets. Training data are used to develop and refine the ML model, and the test data test the effectiveness of the model. Lastly, predictive accuracy of the model is tested using specified performance metrics to ensure reliability and generalizability of results.

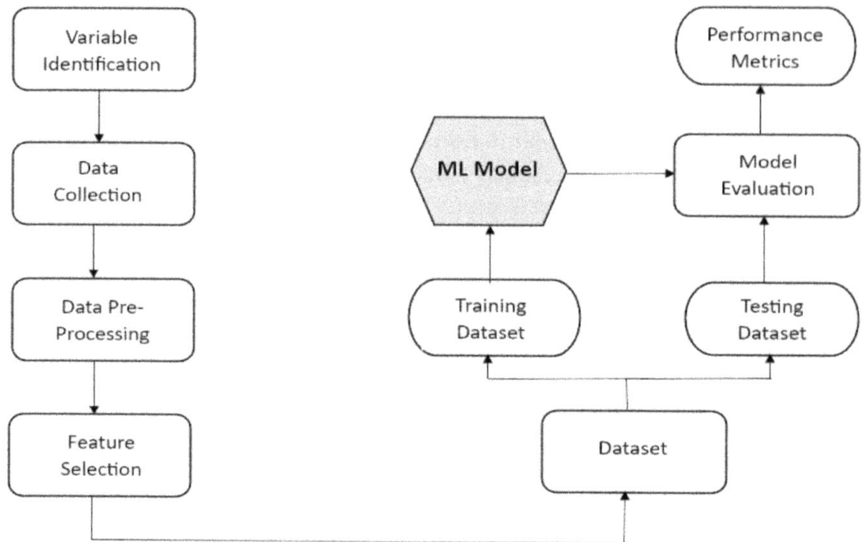

Fig. 1. Flowchart depicting methodology

3.1 Variable Identification

Crop yield is influenced by a wide range of variables. These are essentially the characteristics that aid in estimating a crop yield. This study focuses on minimum temperature, maximum temperature, average temperature, humidity, precipitation, and wind speed for predicting crop production.

3.2 Data Collection

This study uses secondary data to analyse the relationship between climate factors and crop yield. Crop yield and production data (yy) were obtained from the Department of Agriculture & Farmers Welfare database (DES Agri), for the crops Rice, Wheat, Bajra, Cotton and Sugarcane, which provides detailed agricultural statistics. Climatic factors (xx), including maximum temperature, minimum temperature, average temperature, humidity, wind speed, and precipitation, were sourced from NASA's POWER Data Access Viewer (NASA POWER). In order to ensure wide regional coverage for analysis, data were gathered for 31 of Maharashtra's 36 districts. By combining these datasets, it was possible to investigate how climate factors affect crop productivity and use machine learning models to predict yields with accuracy.

3.3 Data Preprocessing

Depending on data availability, the gathered secondary data from 2000–2023 were preprocessed and organised using SQL into the necessary dataset. Climate variables were included in the crop yield data to provide consistency over time. The relationship between climate and crop productivity was better examined by further manipulating the dataset by selecting only the months that align with crop harvesting times. Preprocessing of the data was applied across all crop datasets to ensure they were consistent and ready for regression modelling. Missing values in the dataset were removed. One-Hot Encoding was employed to transform categorical variables into numeric form to prepare the dataset for fitting regression models. For efficient learning from the data, categorical columns like district were especially encoded. These preprocessing steps enabled us to create a well-structured and optimised dataset for precise crop yield estimation.

3.4 Machine Learning Models

3.4.1 K-Nearest Neighbour (KNN)

One of the simplest yet most effective non-parametric methods for classification and regression challenges is the K-Nearest Neighbour algorithm. Taking advantage of a distance metric such as Euclidean distance, it determines the values of the K nearest available data points and bases its predictions on those values. The technique is based on the fact that similar data points will likely yield similar results.

3.4.2 Linear Regression

One of the simplest supervised learning techniques for predicting continuous outputs is linear regression. Using the Least Squares Method (LSM) to estimate the line that minimises error in predicting, it establishes a linear relationship between the independent and dependent variables. The simplicity and interpretability of this model make it widely used.

3.4.3 Decision Tree

With every internal node representing a feature test and every leaf node representing an output, the Decision Tree algorithm organises data into a tree structure of decisions. It is useful for understanding feature importance since it is easy to apply and visualise. Pruning methods are often used to regulate overfitting of training data.

3.4.4 Random Forest

Several decision trees are combined in Random Forest, an ensemble learning technique, to increase model stability and prediction accuracy. It improves generalisation and lowers the risk of overfitting by adding randomness to feature selection and data sampling. Usually, averaging or majority voting across trees yields the final prediction.

3.4.5 Gradient Boosting

Gradient Boosting is a sophisticated ensemble technique that constructs a series of weak learners, typically decision trees, in which each model improves on the mistakes of the one before it. Performance and accuracy are improved by this iterative method, especially when working with complex datasets. Through optimised computation and regularisation techniques, contemporary implementations like XGBoost and LightGBM further increase efficiency and predictive power.

4 Data Analysis

4.1 Model Evaluation

The R^2 score served as the main evaluation metric for evaluating the regression models' predictive performance. K-Nearest Neighbours (KNN), Linear Regression, Decision Tree, Random Forest, and Gradient Boosting were among the models that were put to the test.

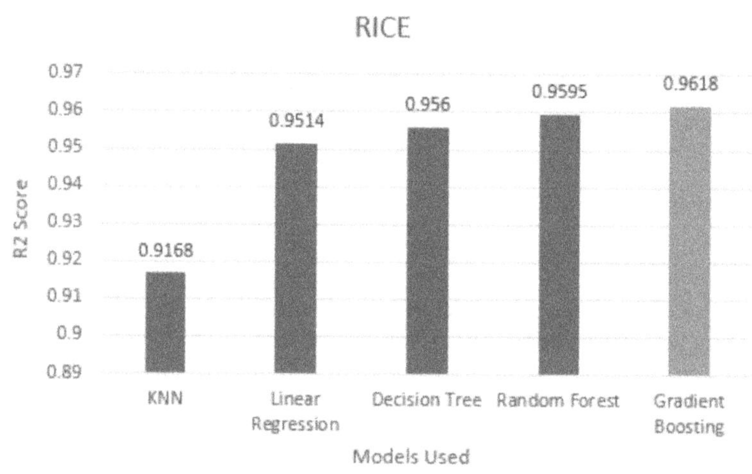

Fig. 2. Model performance for rice

Figure 2 shows that Gradient Boosting achieved the highest R2 score of 0.9618, indicating superior accuracy in capturing the variability of the target variable. Random Forest (0.9595) and Decision Tree (0.956) also performed well, followed by Linear Regression (0.9514) and KNN (0.9186).

Figure 3 shows that Linear Regression achieved the highest R2 score of 0.8518, indicating superior accuracy in capturing the variability of the target variable. Random Forest (0.8197) and KNN (0.7508) also performed well, followed by Gradient Boosting (0.7507) and Decision Tree (0.5625).

Figure 4 shows that Random Forest achieved the highest R2 score of 0.7743, followed by Gradient Boosting (0.7478) and Linear Regression (0.7002), indicating relatively good performance in capturing data variability. In contrast, KNN (0.4974) and Decision Tree (0.4363) showed lower accuracy. These results suggest that ensemble methods, particularly Random Forest, are better suited for modelling this dataset.

Figure 5 shows that Linear Regression achieved the highest R2 score of 0.9829, indicating superior accuracy in capturing the variability of the target variable. Gradient

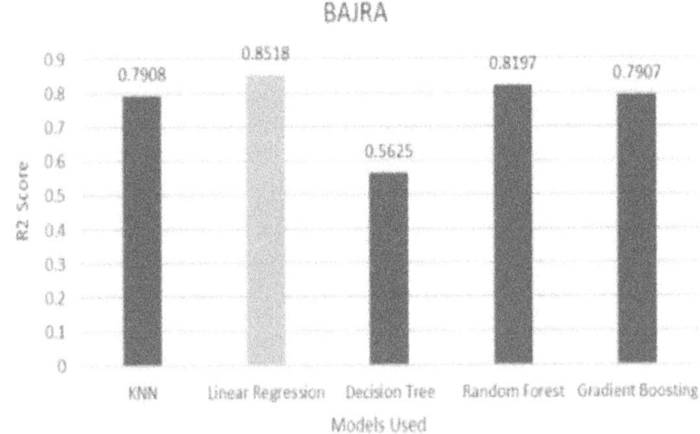

Fig. 3. Model performance for bajra

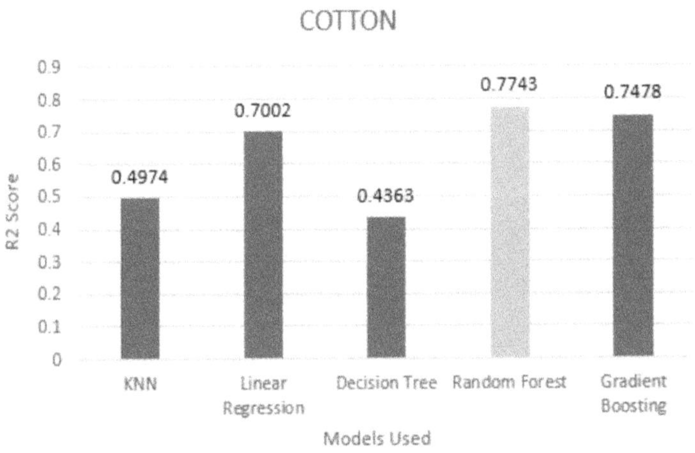

Fig. 4. Model performance for cotton

Boosting (0.9724) and Random Forest (0.9633) also performed well, followed by KNN (0.9564) and Decision Tree (0.95).

Figure 6 shows that Gradient Boosting achieved the highest R2 score of 0.9268, indicating superior accuracy in capturing the variability of the target variable. Linear Regression (0.9265) and Random Forest (0.9844) also performed well, followed by KNN (0.8236) and Decision Tree (0.8214).

4.2 Feature Importance

Table 1 presents the key climatic factors influencing different crop yields based on t-statistical analysis. Factors with a p-value less than 0.05 (5% level of significance) were

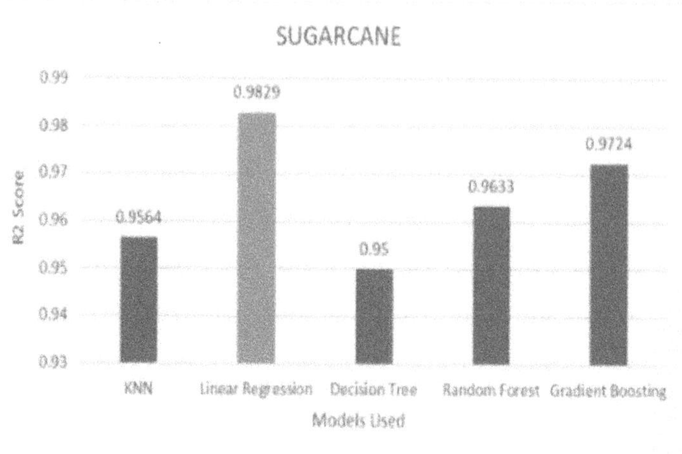

Fig. 5. Model performance for sugarcane

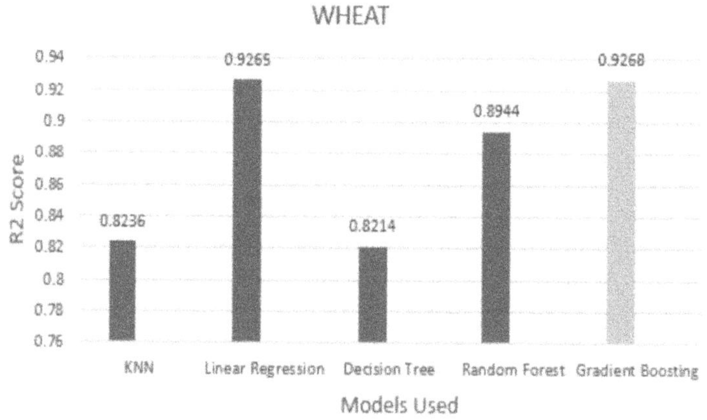

Fig. 6. Model performance for wheat

concluded to be important for the respective crop. The study also identifies the most significant climatic variables (the least p-value) affecting each crop's productivity. Different crops were found to be impacted by the climate in various ways. The dominant factor for rice was precipitation, indicating how heavily it relies on adequate availability of water. The maximum wind speed had the largest impact on cotton and bajra, emphasising how significant it is to pollination and, therefore, yield. Maximum temperature emerged as the key factor for sugarcane, which aligns with its hardy growth during the summer season when the temperature is high. On the other hand, it was found that wheat production was very sensitive to surplus rainfall, which may prove to be harmful to productivity. Precision agriculture and adaptive farming methods benefit from this analysis of the climatic dependencies of varied crops.

Table 1. Influencing climatic factors for each crop based on the p-value

Crop	Influencing Climatic Factors
Rice	Precipitation (p-value = 0)
Bajra	Wind Speed (p-value = 0.004), Maximum Temperature (p-value = 0.005), Minimum Temperature (p-value = 0.045)
Cotton	Wind Speed (p-value = 0), Maximum Temperature (p-value = 0.02)
Sugarcane	Maximum Temperature (p-value = 0), Minimum Temperature (p-value = 0.04), Humidity (p-value = 0.042)
Wheat	Precipitation (p-value = 0.001), Maximum Temperature (p-value = 0.002), Average Temperature (p-value = 0.012)

4.3 Model Selection

Using the R2 score as the primary performance metric, several machine learning models were assessed in this study to determine the best method for predicting crop yield. Gradient Boosting did well for both rice and wheat, as indicated in Table 2, with R2 scores of 0.9618 and 0.9267, respectively. While Random Forest performed best for cotton (R2 = 0.7743), Linear Regression produced strong results for bajra (0.8518) and sugarcane (0.9829). Overall, Gradient Boosting demonstrated consistently strong results across multiple crops, while Linear Regression achieved the highest accuracy for sugarcane. This indicates that both models are dependable options based on crop characteristics.

Table 2. Model applied for each crop along with their accuracies (R2 Score)

Crop	Model Used	R^2 Score
Rice	Gradient Boosting	0.9618
Bajra	Linear Regression	0.8518
Cotton	Random Forest	0.7743
Sugarcane	Linear Regression	0.9829
Wheat	Gradient Boosting	0.9268

4.4 Comparing Predicted and Actual Yield

Table 3. Actual and predicted production (in tonnes) for each crop along with the error

Crop	District	Model Used	Actual Value	Predicted Value	Error
Rice	Kolhapur	Gradient Boosting	290546.82	281149.45	3.23%
Bajra	Nashik	Linear Regression	99532	89306.2	10.27%
Cotton	Aurangabad	Random Forest	452630.51	510170.17	12.71%
Sugarcane	Kolhapur	Linear Regression	15817956	16120098.47	1.91%
Wheat	Ahmednagar	Gradient Boosting	191159.19	190875.40	0.15%

A comparison between the expected and actual yield values for different crops and districts was done in order to assess how well the machine learning models performed in crop yield prediction. For every crop–district pair, Table 3 shows the actual yields, predicted yields, and the associated percentage errors. The district that produced the most of each crop was chosen for this analysis in order to offer a representative and insightful comparison.

5 Conclusions

Regression models such as K-Nearest Neighbours, Linear Regression, Decision Tree, Gradient Boosting, and Random Forest were employed in the current research to predict crop yield across Maharashtra and analyse the impact of climate change on agriculture. The models had good predictive power and were able to effectively model the relationship between crop yield and climate factors such as temperature, humidity, rainfall, and wind speed. The research indicates that the models are successful in making predictions for yields since they fit all of the crops they were analysing perfectly.

This study acknowledges several constraints that could render the accuracy and usefulness of crop yield predictions invalid. Deficiency of historical data is a grave constraint because crop yield and climate information in some areas can be missing or incomplete. It may limit the predictive analysis and affect the reliability of the models. In addition, even some of the pertinent variables, such as irrigation practices, pest issues, and soil health, may not have been covered in the study. For comprehending the productivity of crops, these variables are crucial. Omitting them could decrease the validity of the model and the predictions derived from it, making it less useful. Another problem is overfitting, where models adapt very well to training data but struggle to carry over what they have learned into real-world situations. This damages predictive performance when tested on new or previously unseen data. Furthermore, on-off weather events like drought, floods, and heatwaves may not be reflected in past data. It is difficult to model their impact on crop yields under these circumstances. These abnormal weather patterns influence crop production heavily and call for more flexible modelling techniques. Besides staple crops such as wheat and rice, future studies could expand the scope of this study by incorporating pulses, oilseeds, and horticultural produce.

Also, by looking at local climatic patterns in different regions of Maharashtra, examining each district separately, and localised climatic patterns might improve model accuracy. Crop yield forecasting might also be improved by the inclusion of parameters such as soil health, pest problems, and irrigation practices, along with current climatic data and newer machine learning algorithms. Deep learning approaches or hybrid models can be used to improve forecasts in future work.

References

1. Nikhil, U.V., Pandiyan, A.M., Raja, S.P., Stamenkovic, Z.: Machine learning-based crop yield prediction in south India: performance analysis of various models. Computers **13**(6), 137 (2024)
2. Koparde, S., Behare, A., Kasare, S., Patil, J., Nadar, K.: Crop Yield Prediction for Cereals using Machine Learning (2024). ISBN: 978–81–955020–7–3
3. Palanivel, K., Surianarayanan, C.: An approach for prediction of crop yield using machine learning and big data techniques. Int. J. Comput. Eng. Technol. **10**(3), 110–118 (2019)
4. Jorvekar, P.P., Wagh, S.K., Prasad, J.R.: Predictive modeling of crop yields: a comparative analysis of regression techniques for agricultural yield prediction. Agric. Eng. Int. CIGR J. **26**(2), 125–140 (2024)
5. Sharma, P., Dadheech, P., Aneja, N., Aneja, S.: Predicting agriculture yields based on machine learning using regression and deep learning. IEEE Access **11**, 111255–111264 (2023)
6. Malashin, I., Tynchenko, V., Gantimurov, A., Nelyub, V., Borodulin, A., Tynchenko, Y.: Predicting sustainable crop yields: deep learning and explainable AI tools. Sustainability **16**(21), 9437 (2024)
7. Medar, R.A., Rajpurohit, V.S., Ambekar, A.M.: Sugarcane crop yield forecasting model using supervised machine learning. Int. J. Intell. Syst. Appl. **11**(8), 11 (2019)
8. Mahale, Y., et al.: Crop recommendation and forecasting system for Maharashtra using machine learning with LSTM: a novel expectation-maximization technique. Discover Sustain. **5**(1), 134 (2024)
9. Patil, P., Athavale, P., Bothara, M., Tambolkar, S., More, A.: Crop selection and yield prediction using machine learning approach. Curr. Agric. Res. J. **11**(3) (2023)
10. Panigrahi, B., Kathala, K.C.R., Sujatha, M.: A machine learning-based comparative approach to predict the crop yield using supervised learning with regression models. Procedia Comput. Sci. **218**, 2684–2693 (2023)

Decoding Retail Market Dynamics: A Data-Driven Approach to Consumer Behavior Modeling

Venkata Kalyan Mandali$^{(\boxtimes)}$ (iD)

University of Bridgeport, Bridgeport, CT 06604, USA
mandalivenkatakalyan@gmail.com

Abstract. The retail markets are creating loads of transactional data but the traditional methods of segmentation cannot keep up with the emergent patterns of consumer behavior. This work proposes a data-driven model which presents retail market as a complex system, and reveals some unseen relations between product sales and customer buying behavior. Using a massive transaction dataset of supermarkets, we are postulating a Purchase Function that is able to predict consumer demands systematically, hierarchies of products and refines targeted marketing strategies. Our solution offers practical recommendations on individualized promotions, demand prediction, and store op-benefit, and offers an alternative view of how data science can be used to drive com-competitive advantages in retail marketing. Moreover, the offered framework shows that it can be slightly adjusted to various retail settings and markets, which implies that it can be widely applicable to data-based personalization approaches in the markets outside the examined one in Italy.

Keywords: feature extraction layer · optimized anchor box parameters · YOLO · fire detection system

1 Introduction

The retail industry has been a major target on the emphasis of advanced data analysis owing to the constant production of huge volume of records of consumer transaction. The records, which are recorded at the point of sale in the large retail chains and supermarkets, summarize the specific purchase behaviors across both time and location. Conventional analytic techniques have been found wanting in handling the magnitude and complexity of such data and an alternative is therefore shifting to the use of data based techniques such as cluster-based segmentation, high dimensional pattern discovery, and unsupervised association discovery. The methods usually produce consumer profiles which are structured through categorizing the users and isolating consumption linkages. More often than not, these methods reveal unanticipated inter-product affinities, or can be used to cluster users in terms of behavioral or demographic trends. The localized interpretations (even though limited in terms of their scope) are quite operational since they concentrate

F. Ortiz-Rodríguez et al. (Eds.): IBCD 2025, CCIS 2845, pp. 308–319, 2026.
https://doi.org/10.1007/978-3-032-20907-8_26

on particular categories of the products or on certain market segments. Alternatively, a second school of thought approaches consumer markets systems-theoretically, as though whole economies were com plex adaptive structures [1–5]. The transactional randomness comes to be revisited in such models as emergent behavior, based on a net-work of interdependent agents and feedback loops. The paradigm empowers the development of macro-level indicators, including the so-called Commercial Entropy Index, which performs better in forecasting the socioeconomic trends, compared to traditional measures. This paper conceptualizes the retail marketplace in much the same way as a self-regulating complex system [6–10], which is decentral. The main assumption is that the individual customers will behave with the objective of maximizing their utility. Regularity of behavioral patterns are formed through these aggregated interactions. The complex systems framework aims at finding the holistic, reproducible dynamics (as opposed to producing voluminous isolated patterns), as in rule-based mining. To encapsulate the systemic relations between customer intent and item properties, a new metric is suggested: It is called the Consumer At-traction Functional. This role is placed as a worldly descriptor of consumption phenomena, and has 3 key areas of application; (1) verification of motivational stratification, and reflects consumer selectivity theories such as the hierarchy of Maslow, where higher selectivity consumers shop a niche inventory, and other consumers popularized items; (2) application in precision marketing applications to identify minimal responsive populations, and so optimize out-reach efficiency; and (3) spatial behavior modelling predicting store-visit paths with product complexity gradients developed on the basis of the [11–15].

To test its hypotheses, experimental validation uses a multi-year long data archive of a big Italian cooperative retail network. The relations of transaction involving loyalty identifiers are converted to a bipartite graph between users and products. The incidence table that results is a non-random triangular form, a characteristic of organized systemic organization. The simulation of null hypothesis shows the development of high-order structural dependencies. In applying the Consumer Attraction Functional to this topology, one will be able to delineate between realized and latent affinities and the subsequent modeling phases are based on these delineated affinities. Our approach operationalizes consumption as an emergent network phenomenon, unlike more conventional segmentation models that are based on fixed demographic clustering or simplistic frequency-based associations. This change does not only reveal unconscious systemic behavior, but also provides quantitative measures in bridging user in tent, product complexity, and marketing responsiveness, allowing more accurate strategic interventions [16–20].

2 Dataset Description

The analytical model is based on transactional evidences of a leading Italian retailer that runs on a consumer-owned model. The Fig. 1 scheme over-view of the retail data architecture is given. The data set will consist of more than four years of shopping, starting January 1, 2007, up to the end of 2011. The number of persons represented is 1,066,020 and each person is identified by the consistent use of the loyalty credentials during the process of purchases. Considering the fact that the given enterprise is cooperative, the cardholders demonstrate high in group loyalty, which makes the information more representative. Table 1 provides an overview of product distribution among different types

Fig. 1. Data Model. Structural representation of the underlying retail data warehouse.

of stores, which would give a background to the inventory variety and segmentation [21–25].

The retail system comprises of 138 different stores that are located along the westward Italy axis. Inventory is listed by a hierarchy that is kept by the marketing divisions and more than 345, 000 distinct SKUs are indexed. The classification tree starts with two main branches namely; Edibles and Non-Edibles and ends at the Division level with 7,003 categories. Every product is projected to a different route of this schema [26–30]. The number of items in primary product families and in direflects their availability in three typologies of stores, namely: 'Gestin'; Super and Iper. The Gestin type is associated with small local shops, Super with an intermediate size, usually found in the suburbs, and Iper is the hypermarket dimension types of installations similar to malls. The size of the dataset, more than a million buyers and hundreds of thousands of SKUs, suggests a raw association space of the order of 3.71×1011 possible entries, many of which would be zero or would be redundant. A dimensionality reduction is required to minimize the sparsity and computational overhead. A geospatial criterion has been adopted instead of filtering on the basis of volume or frequency. The subset of stores chosen strategically within a given area is sampled and keeps the behaviors homogeneous. Figure 2 represents the assignment of loyalty cards by region. Even though card renewal events can cause minor anomalies, the longitudinal continuity of the consumer profile is not significantly impacted by the latter.

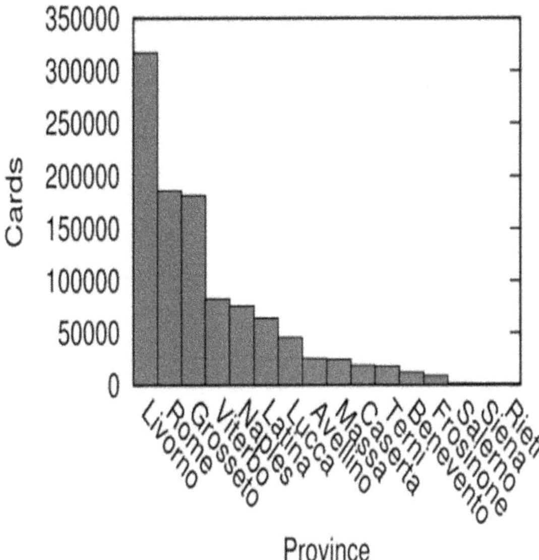

Fig. 2. Card Distribution. Geographical breakdown of loyalty card assignments per province.

Table 1. Distribution of Products by Category and Store Type Coverage

Segment	SKU Count	Coverage Across Store Formats
Edibles	2,026	77.6%
Perishables	1,005	70.9%
Packaged	493	78.8%
Ultra-Fresh	512	63.2%
Miscellaneous	1,021	84.1%
Household Chemicals	333	83.4%
Pantry Items	688	84.5%
Non-Edibles	2,791	37.8%
Domestic Utilities	565	54.9%
Media	368	33.5%
Personal Care	746	32.0%
Seasonal/DIY	1,112	34.4%

3 Methodology

Determining the behavioral tendencies in consumer transactions is a breakthrough in data-focused applications. The traditional association rule frame-works commonly focus on more common product pairings, and tend to overlook more detailed user-product interaction dynamics in the transactional corpora. Interestingly enough, these models often simplify user profiles to frequency contributors which does not take into consideration subtle differences in different buying behaviors of a person. Besides, there is the tendency where customer activity is controlled by heavy-tailed statistical laws [31–35]. The cumulative distribution of the item sales and user participation, shown in Figs. 3 and Fig. 4, is highly asymmetric, with most of the goods being purchased by a small proportion of people, and a small group of buyers using a set of products.

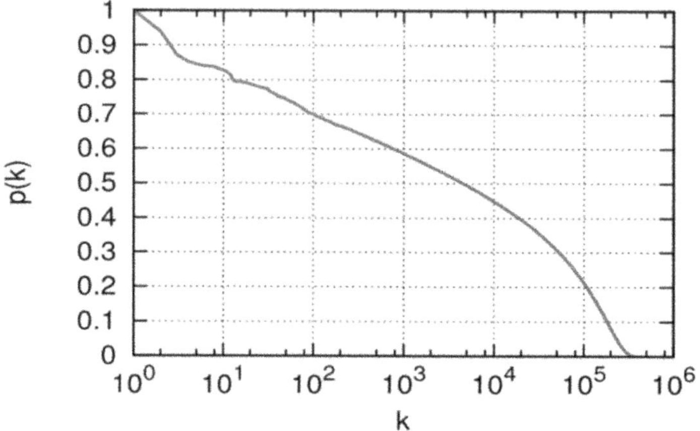

Fig. 3. Cumulative product frequency distribution.

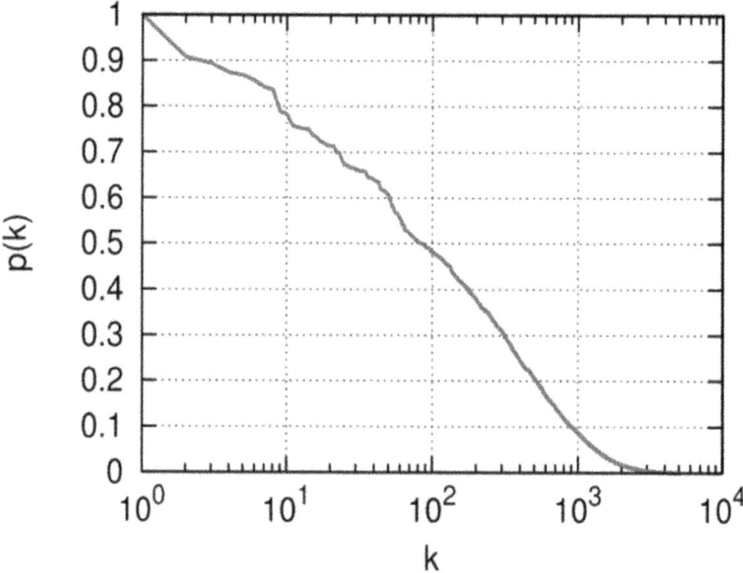

Fig. 4. Cumulative customer frequency distribution

These differences cause underrepresentation of niche products because discovering a rule has strict frequency limitations in rule discovery algorithms. Additionally, the mainstream products are mostly linked to active user group and the insights provided are likely to be biased towards this dominant group. To address these drawbacks, a different formulation is suggested by considering the transaction logs as a weighted bipartite graph G = (U, I, L) or U will be users, I will be items and L will be weighted links. Connection (μk, 0m, 0): A connection (u k, 0 m, 0) 0 L means that user u k 0 U has purchased item 0 m 0 I on 0 occasions. Figure 5 indicates the structure of this graph. The strategy presents the systemic and user/item based understanding. A mapping function ψ is derived on the global axis to describe the diversity of aggregate consumption, and the complexity score on the local axis, which is called the Engagement Quotient, is used to measure the specificity of users and items. The analytical process follows three significant steps: (i) trans transformation of transactional information into a matrix form; (ii) extraction of global and individual descriptors; and (iii) comparative analysis with randomized samples to help identify the significance.

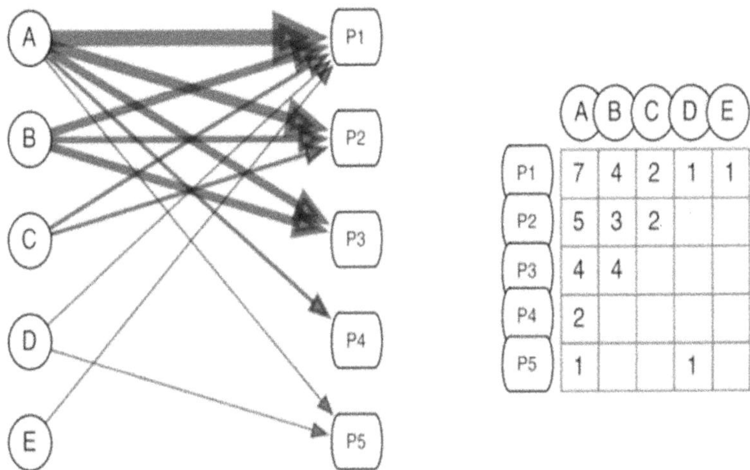

Fig. 5. Graphical representation of the purchase bipartite network

3.1 Data Structuring

The preprocessing stage creates an adjacency matrix that indicates the user-item transactions. The popularity of items is ranked in descending order (left to right), and users by the activity levels (top to bottom). Under this arrangement the cell A(0, 0) will represent the most active user who is buying the most sold item. Then a relevance based binarization is done. The significance score calculated instead of solely on binary presence is called the Relative Preference Index (RPI) which is calculated to deemphasize sporadic activity. The index of user μk and item ιm can be defined as:

$$\text{RPI}(l_m, \mu_m) = \frac{F(l_m, \mu_m)}{F(*, \mu_k)} \bigg/ \frac{F(l_m, *)}{F(*, *)}$$

In this case, F(ion, musk) refers to the quantity of items of type ion purchased by user musk, F(on, musk) refers to the total purchases of musk, F(ion, on) refers to the total purchases of ion and F(on, on) refers to the overall amount of purchases. To define significant interest a threshold of 1 is used to form the binary interest matrix D:

$$D(\mu_k, l_m) = \begin{cases} 1 \text{ if RPI}(l_m, \mu_k) > 1 \\ 0 \text{ otherwise} \end{cases}$$

This matrix which is also known as the interest matrix is the basis on which the exploration that follows is based. Figure 6 is an aggregation (sampled 50×50) of this matrix based on the Livorno20072009 data, which visually confirms that there are a few items that have a wide appeal, and users in smaller groups will use increasingly rare items.

Fig. 6. Aggregated interest matrix for Livorno2007–2009

3.2 Pattern Extraction

This stage is aimed at inducting general behavior laws and individuality of item complexity. At a systemic level, the relationship between user engagement and the product diversity is modeled by the Transaction Curve ψ. On a lower granulometry, the level of item and user eccentricity is implied [36, 37].

Macro-Level Mapping Unlike pairwise correlations analysis, this model presents a contour-based frontier, which outlines frequent vs. sparse purchase zones in the matrix

D. The mapping $\psi(n)$ is a mapping that captures the number of items bought by the top n users and ψ -1(m) is a mapping that captures the number of users that have bought the top m items. Table 2. Contour Quality Q(D, ψ 0) of Different Functions.

Table 2. Contour Quality Q(D,ψ *) for Various Functions

Function ψ^*	$Q(D, \psi^*)$
$mx + n$	0.6134
$mx^2 + nx + o$	0.6291
$m \log(x) + n$	0.6257
mx^n	0.5702
m/x	0.6078
$\frac{mx+n}{px+q}$	0.6312

Table 3. Contour Fidelity Q(D,ψ *) Across Datasets

Dataset	$Q(D, \psi^*)$
Livorno2007–2009	0.6312
Lazio2007–2009	0.6220
Livorno2010–2011	...

Let:

Items$(\mu n) = \{\iota 1,...,\iota\psi(n)\}$, Users$(\iota m) = \{\mu 1,...,\mu\psi - 1(m)\}$.

Table 3 provides a Contour Fidelity Q(D,ψ *) Across Datasets The ψ should also have a monotonic decrease in its value, which means that the diversity should decrease with user rank. To measure the fidelity of contours, a goodness measure Q(D, ψ *) is proposed which is defined as:

$$Q(D, \psi*) = \frac{1}{2}\left(\frac{L_1}{L_T} + \frac{R_0}{R_T}\right)$$

Although the methodology represents properly the structural regularities in the data, the existing approach can be performed within one regional setting with homogeneous demographic structure. Further versions of this model will combine multivariate demographic factors (e.g., age, size of household, income level) to examine the consistency of consistency and predictability of the target functional mappings with wider consumer groups.

4 Evaluation

Results with the above analytical structure in place, focusing on the extraction of pattern of behaving defined on a customer-product bipartite graph through the adjacency matrix of the graph, the following section provides analytical results of actual trans action datasets. It starts with the description of dataset characteristics and filtering methodology used. Two main measures of analysis are the result of this application: a total Purchase Mapping measure and discrete sophistication Estimators on the consumer and on the good. There are also three significant trends depicted in the findings, namely; a data-based stratification of demand that corresponds to essential human needs, a marketing model that allows reaching the customers more effectively, and the predictability of the local behavior.

4.1 Hierarchical Differentiation of Consumer Priorities

First, the implied hierarchy is regionally-contextual and does not purport to be a general hierarchy. The data are based on a certain met-metropolitan territory in Italy. Although other zones also featured similar tiered structures, future research should extend the subject of generalizability. This stratified representation can also be applied in the regional marketing strategies, where the basic commodities usually need minimum marketing efforts because of the organic demand. Second, the categorization of items is based on internal commercial category de f by the retailer involved which entails cultural and strategic biasing. Further studies may use standard classification to reduce subjectivity. Third, some people might acquire niche products with other sellers, which might inflate the product sophistication measures. Though such phenomenon was expected to be only minor, due to the high customer retention, it brings interpretive tones. To generate the hierarchy, product classes are ranked by rising scores of in-creasing simplification. A deterministic minimization of within-cluster variation, ck-means, is a univariate clustering algorithm, which provides better performance than traditional k-means. The segmentation value of $k = 5$ is selected to represent five broad layers that comprise essential, base-level, auxiliary, elective, and premium products. Figure 4 illustrates the output clustering and represents the important product categories in every band. The donations of this type are calculated in terms of the ratio of their purchase frequency in each stratum. As an example, in 3,500,000 tier-0 transactions, item A was purchased 3,500 times, and in 1,800,000, item B in tier 1 was purchased 2,500 times, thus its share is 0.1 and 0.139, respectively. The product categories are generalized to be clear as an example, the category of Fruits and Vegetables is under the group that includes carrots and apples. The categories are divided into multi-tier depending on the highest frequency, which is assigned to the dominant tier. The visualization proves that the most basic level is dominated by sustenance and hygiene. As the hierarchy increases, goods become more specialized or life-style directed, between household goods and recreational resources. The apex comprises of high-end segments such as child-rearing accessories, high-value consumer goods and this is due to the sociocultural trends that categories these kinds of investments as non-essential, but rather as optional. Table 4 provides a Marginal and conditional probabilities of purchases.

Table 4. Marginal and conditional probabilities of purchases

g_m	g_{m-1}	$\mathbb{Q}(g_m)$	$\mathbb{Q}(g_m \mid g_{m-1})$
Dish salt	Dish detergent	8.39%	30.41%
Asparagus	Olives	8.00%	26.12%
Bell peppers	Chicory	7.31%	23.73%
Soup cans	Anchovies	9.96%	32.23%
Wafers	Sweets	11.30%	21.67%

5   Conclusion

The paper has analyzed a tremendous retail data of a supermarket chain in Italy to create a new consumer product interaction framework. A structural analysis revealed that the bipartite network has skewed degree distributions and triangular adjacency matrix, which constrain the explanatory capability of traditional rule-mining methods. The study developed a generalized framework through the framing of retail behavior as a dynamic of a complex system by proposing that the notion of pairwise items association has an extension. It hypothesizes that foundational products are universally pursued, and niche products are mostly purchased by high-volume buyers an observation captured by the triangular adjacency pattern. This model allows the determination of probable customer groups of any product based on aggregate sales data formalized into a functional mapping of sales intensity to groups of buyers.

References

1. Agrawal, R., Imielinski, T., Swami, A.N.: Mining association rules between sets of items in large databases. In: SIGMOD International Conference, Washington, D.C., pp. 207–216 (1993)
2. Sun, Y., Aggarwal, C.C., Han, J.: Relation strength-aware clustering of heterogeneous information networks with incomplete attributes. Proc. VLDB Endow. **5**(5), 394–405 (2012)
3. Chaudhuri, S., Narasayya, V.R.: New frontiers in business intelligence. Proc. VLDB Endow. **4**(12), 1502–1503 (2011)
4. Kocakoç, I.D., Erdem, S.: Business intelligence applications in retail business: OLAP, data mining & reporting services. J. Inf. Knowl. Manag. **9**(2), 171–181 (2010)
5. Brauckhoff, D., Dimitropoulos, X., Wagner, A., Salamatian, K.: Anomaly extraction in backbone networks using association rules. IEEE/ACM Trans. Netw. **20**, 1788–1799 (2012)
6. Marinica, C., Guillet, F.: Knowledge-based interactive postmining of association rules using ontologies. IEEE Trans. Knowl. Data Eng. **22**(6), 784–797 (2010)
7. Montella, A.: Identifying crash contributory factors at urban roundabouts and using association rules to explore their relationships to different crash types. Accid. Anal. Prev. **43**(4), 1451–1463 (2011)
8. Hidalgo, C.A., Klinger, B., Barabási, A.-L., Hausmann, R.: The product space conditions the development of nations. Science **317**(5837), 482–487 (2007)
9. Hausmann, R., et al.: The Atlas of Economic Complexity, Boston, USA (2011)
10. Caldarelli, G., et al.: Ranking and clustering countries and their products: a network analysis. arXiv preprint arXiv:1108.2590 (2011)

11. Davis, W.L., Schwarz, P., Terzi, E.: Finding representative association rules from large rule collections. In: SDM, pp. 521–532 (2009)

12. Maslow, A.H.: A theory of human motivation. Psychol. Rev. **50**(4), 370–396 (1943)

13. Bascompte, J., Jordano, P., Melián, C.J., Olesen, J.M.: The nested assembly of plant-animal mutualistic networks. Proc. Natl. Acad. Sci. USA **100**(16), 9383–9387 (2003)

14. Almeida-Neto, M., et al.: A consistent metric for nestedness analysis in ecological systems: reconciling concept and measurement. Oikos **117**, 1227–1239 (2008)

15. Pennacchioli, D., et al.: Calculating product and customer sophistication on a large transactional dataset. Technical Report cnr.isti/2013-TR-004 (2013)

16. Marquardt, D.W.: An algorithm for least-squares estimation of nonlinear parameters. J. Soc. Ind. Appl. Math. **11**(2), 431–441 (1963)

17. Hidalgo, C.A., Hausmann, R.: The building blocks of economic complexity. Proc. Natl. Acad. Sci. U.S.A. **106**(26), 10570–10575 (2009)

18. Cristelli, M., et al.: Measuring the intangibles: a metrics for the economic complexity of countries and products. PLoS ONE **8**(8), e70726 (2013)

19. Guidotti, R.: Mobility ranking– human mobility analysis using ranking measures. University of Pisa (2013)

20. Wang, H., Song, M.: Ckmeans. 1d.dp: optimal k-means clustering in one dimension by dynamic programming. R J. **3**(2), 29–33 (2011)

21. Pennacchioli, D., et al.: Explaining the product range effect in purchase data. In: 2013 IEEE International Conference Big Data*, pp. 648–656 (2013)

22. Krumme, C., et al.: The predictability of consumer visitation patterns. arXiv preprint arXiv: 1305.1120 (2013)

23. Cohen, E., et al.: Finding interesting associations without support pruning. In: ICDE, pp. 489–500 (2000)

24. Nguyen, K.-N., et al.: Multidimensional association rules in Boolean tensors. In: SDM, pp. 570–581 (2011)

25. Chawla, S.: Feature selection, association rules network and theory building. J. Mach. Learn. Res. **10**, 14 (2010)

26. Pennacchioli, D., Coscia, M., Pedreschi, D.: Overlap versus partition: marketing classification and customer profiling in complex networks of products. In: ICDE Workshop (2014)

27. Li, H.: Applications of data warehousing and data mining in the retail industry. In: Proceedings ICSSSM'05, vol. 2 (2005)

28. Gabbur, P., et al.: A pattern discovery approach to retail fraud detection. In: KDD, pp. 307–315 (2011)

29. Wagner, M.M., et al.: Design of a national retail data monitor for public health surveillance. J. Am. Med. Inform. Assoc. **10**(5), 409–418 (2003)

30. Castellanos, M., et al.: LCI: a social channel analysis platform for live customer intelligence. In: SIGMOD Conference, pp. 1049–1058 (2011)

31. Balassa, B.: Trade liberalization and 'revealed' comparative advantage. Manch. Sch. **33**, 99–123 (1965)

32. Geng, L., Hamilton, H.J.: Interestingness measures for data mining: a survey. ACM Comput. Surv. **38**(3), 9 (2006)

33. Bousquet, N.: Eliciting vague but proper maximal entropy priors in Bayesian ex periments. Stat. Pap. **51**(3), 613–628 (2010)

34. Shen, Z.-J.M., Su, X.: Customer behavior modeling in revenue management and auctions: a review and new research opportunities. Prod. Oper. Manag. **16**(6), 713–728 (2007)

35. Schich, M., Lehmann, S., Park, J.: Dissecting the canon: visual subject co popularity networks in art research. In: ECCS 2008 (2008)

36. Liu, Y.-Y., Slotine, J.-J., Barabási, A.-L.: Controllability of complex networks. Nature **473**(7346), 167–173 (2011)
37. Patefield, W.M.: An efficient method of generating random RxC tables with given row and column totals (algorithm AS 159). J. R. Stat. Soc. Ser. C Appl. Stat. **30**, 91–97 (1981)

Leveraging Machine Learning to Predict Steroid-Induced Organ Damage: Study on Heart, Kidney and Lungs

Neha Patil[1,2]($\boxtimes$) (iD), Jaydeep Patil[1] (iD), and Kalyan Bamane[3] (iD)

[1] D. Y. Patil Agriculture and Technical University Talsande, Kolhapur, India
neha.patil@aissmsioit.org
[2] AISSMS Institute of Information Technology, Pune, India
[3] D. Y. Patil College of Engineering Akurdi, Pune, India
kdbamane@dypcoeakurdi.ac.in

Abstract. Although steroids such as corticosteroids and anabolic androgenic steroids (AAS) are frequently used in sports and medical therapies, they can seriously endanger the health of vital organs including the heart, kidney and lungs. Long term use of steroids has been associated with respiratory risks such as fibrosis and impaired lung function compromised renal dysfunction including nephrotoxicity and chronic kidney disease and cardiovascular problems like hypertension and myocardial infarction. This study predicts steroid induced organ damage using machine learning approaches particularly Random Forest and XGBoost. To find risk factors adverse effects dependent dose and early warning indicators, clinical data and patient biomarkers were examined. Early intervention measures were supported by the excellent accuracy of the models in identifying individuals at risk. Explainability of SHAP strategies were used to address issues such as data imbalance and interpretability of the models. The results highlight the need for regulatory measures and medical recommendations personalized health risks to mitigate steroid related health risks. Future research should integrated real time patient monitoring and genetic data to improve predictive accuracy. This study contributes to precision medicine by improving early diagnosis, prevention and patient outcomes of steroid induced organ damage.

Keywords: Steroid consumption · health hazards · heart disease · kidney dysfunction · lung damage · predictive modelling · machine learning

1 Introduction

Steroid whether anabolic or corticosteroids have been used for decades in clinical medicine and sports enhancement due to their powerful anti-inflammatory and muscle building properties. Since their synthesis in the early 20th century corticosteroids have played a crucial role in the treatment of chronic inflammatory diseases such as asthma, arthritis and autoimmune diseases while anabolic and androgenic steroids (AAS) have gained notoriety for their performance enhancing effects in athletics.

Globally more than 6.5 million people are estimated to have used anabolic steroids at least once with the highest prevalence seen among young adults aged 18 to 35. Studies indicates that 3–5% of male athletes in competitive sports have used AAS while non athletic users motivated by aesthetic or body image goals represent an increasingly concerning demographic. [6, 7]. The cardiovascular, renal and pulmonary systems are particularly susceptible to the adverse effects of steroid use, leading to health such as hypertension, myocardial infarction, renal dysfunction and pulmonary fibrosis [3–5].

Though present awareness is there, the serious implications of steroid abuse remain unexplored and uncovered, there is a need for a predictive framework to assess potential health risks before uncurable damage occurs [6, 7]. From a physiological point of view, steroids impair the natural synthesis of hormones and destroy homeostatic processes in organ systems. Chronic exposure can give rise to cardiovascular diseases, hypertension and alterations in lipid metabolism. Similarly, renal impairment can result from glomerular sclerosis and tubular necrosis, while pulmonary complications, such as fibrosis and reduced gas exchange, result from systemic inflammation and oxidative stress. Although several epidemiological and clinical studies have explored the individual effects of steroids on cardiovascular or renal health, few have studied their combined impact on multiple organ systems using predictive analytics. The lack of integrated, data driven models pose a significant challenge in early diagnosis and prevention [3–7]. The misuse of steroids, particularly among athletes, bodybuilders and individuals expecting vast physical changes, has led to serious concerns about their adverse effects on vital organs such as the heart, kidneys, and lungs [7, 8].

By suggesting early detection and preventive recommendations, this research study is important to athletes, fitness professionals, health care providers and policy makers. It allows health care professionals to identify high-risk individuals in initial stage, inform users about the long-term dangers of drug abuse steroids and support the formulation of stricter rules and regulations, contributing significantly to the growing body of research on steroid-related health side effects [9–14].

This present research focuses to fill the gap by developing a hybrid ML based predictive tool leveraging Random Forest and XGBoost algorithms to detect early and initial signs of steroid-induced organ damage. By doing analysis of multidimensional data, including demographic variables, dosage patterns, and biomarker trends, this research aims to unlock key predictors of toxicity, increase interpretability through SHAP analysis and provide valuable insights for clinicians and policy makers [9–13].

2 Literature Review

Nowadays there are lot of advances in predictive modelling but still there are limitations in existing systems, such as the lack of steroid-specific datasets to do accurate prediction of organ damage, and a limited focus on single organ effects rather than evaluating the combined impact on multiple organs. This literature study reveals important research gaps, especially the absence of predictive models integrated multi-organ systems capable of simultaneously assessing risks to the lungs, kidneys, and heart. Clinical testing and research are limited using variety of real-world datasets, targeting the reliability and generalizability of existing tools. This study and research focuses on these gaps by proposing a complete, AI-driven, data-centric model that collectively add together multiple clinical and biological risk factors to predict and quantify steroid-induced damage in key organ systems. Currently, advanced and modified deep learning and artificial intelligence models have been increasingly applied to biomedical prediction, including the detection of drug-induced organ damage. Models such as convolutional neural networks (CNN) and recurrent neural networks (RNN) have revealed an exceptional ability to elicit spatial and temporal patterns from complex medical data. CNN-based architectures, originally developed for image classification, have been successfully designed to analyse CT scans, MRI data, and histopathology images to inspect organ abnormalities. Transformer-based architectures have also gained attention in biomedical informatics to separate multi-source data and capture nonlinear dependencies between clinical variables. The literature study also emphasizes the growing relevance of privacy-preserving techniques such as federated learning (FL) in healthcare analytics. FL allows model training across distributed healthcare systems without transferring sensitive patient data, ensuring data privacy while maintaining performance integrity. Studies conducted between 2022 and 2024 demonstrated that FL-based systems could predict organ toxicity and drug interactions with accuracy levels comparable to centralized learning models. Furthermore, Explainable AI (XAI) techniques are increasingly being incorporated to make model decisions more interpretable to clinicians and regulators, thereby enhancing clinical trust and regulatory compliance. Summary of the existing literature studies and key points is presented in Table 1.

Key Contributions of the Proposed Work

- Prediction of the medical conditions, such as cardiovascular disease (CVD), pulmonary disease, and liver damage with NON-medical usage of AAS.
- Inclusion of diverse datasets for concrete results and to mitigate biased predictions.
- Development of a novel hybrid machine intelligence-based method for predicting medical conditions namely cardiovascular disease (CVD), pulmonary diseases, and liver damage.

3 Methodology

This research work aims to develop a machine learning-based prediction model to assess the impact of steroid consumption on vital organs such as the heart, kidneys, and lungs. The methodology presented in Fig. 1 is structured into four major stages: Data Processing, Data Visualization, Model Training, and Model Evaluation. Following are the detailed explanations of each of the phases.

The data preprocessing pipeline used in this study was enhanced through several advanced techniques. Outlier detection was implemented using the Inter-quartile Range (IQR) and Isolation Forest method to exclude outliers that could bias model training. Feature engineering includes the creation of derived variables, like cumulative steroid exposure and ratio of dose/weight, to increase the model's sensitivity to dosage effects. Imputation of missing data was further validated and tested using K-Nearest Neighbours (KNN) imputation to guarantee consistency of statistical distributions.

The model evaluation framework was further extended beyond standard measures for inclusion of the Matthews Correlation Coefficient (MCC), which provides a balanced even under conditions of class imbalance. Cross-validation was repeated ten

Table 1. Summary of the existing literature studies and key points

Ref. No	Section	Key Points
[11]	Related Biotransformation	- Use of advanced nano catalysts in steroid compound transformation
[12]	Related to Endocrine Effects	- Cortisol levels and steroid biosynthesis in PCOS women
[13]	Related to Biochemical Analysis	- Luminescence of steroids and bile acids
[14]	Related Detection Methods	- Advances in biosensor technology for detecting steroid hormones
[3]	AI Applications in Organ Damage Prediction	- Application of ML models to predict chronic kidney disease
[4]	Machine Learning in Medical Predictions	- Overview of recent ML approaches for cardiovascular disease prediction
[5]	AI Applications in Organ Damage Prediction	- Predictive modelling of lung disease using machine learning
[6]	AI Applications in Organ Damage Prediction	- ML-based prediction of steroid-induced cardiovascular and renal damage
[6]	Cardiovascular Effects of Steroids	- Data-driven prediction of steroid-induced cardiovascular and renal damage using ML
[7]	AI Applications in Organ Damage Prediction	- Comparative analysis of ML techniques to predict health risks in steroid users
[8, 9, 10]	Related Detection Techniques	- Non-invasive testosterone detection using hair analysis and spectroscopy

times to assure statistical robustness. In addition to this, explainable AI (XAI) technique such as Local Interpretable Model-agnostic Explanations (LIME) and SHAP interaction diagrams used to visualize the complex interdependencies between various features. Ethical considerations are also adopted into the model design, emphasizing fairness, accountability, and transparency in medical AI applications.

3.1 Data Processing

Data processing is an important step in data preparation. It cites to any processing applied to raw data to prepare it for subsequent analysis or processing tasks.

In past years, data preprocessing was an essential preliminary step in data analysis. However, more recently, these techniques have been adapted to train machine learning and AI models and extract analysis from them. It includes various steps, each addressing specific challenges related to the quality, structure, and relevance of the data.

The dataset used in this research has been obtained from a medical research firm under a strict Non-Disclosure Agreement (NDA). This dataset consists of information related to patients or individual person who have used and consumed AAS. The following fields are present in the datasets.

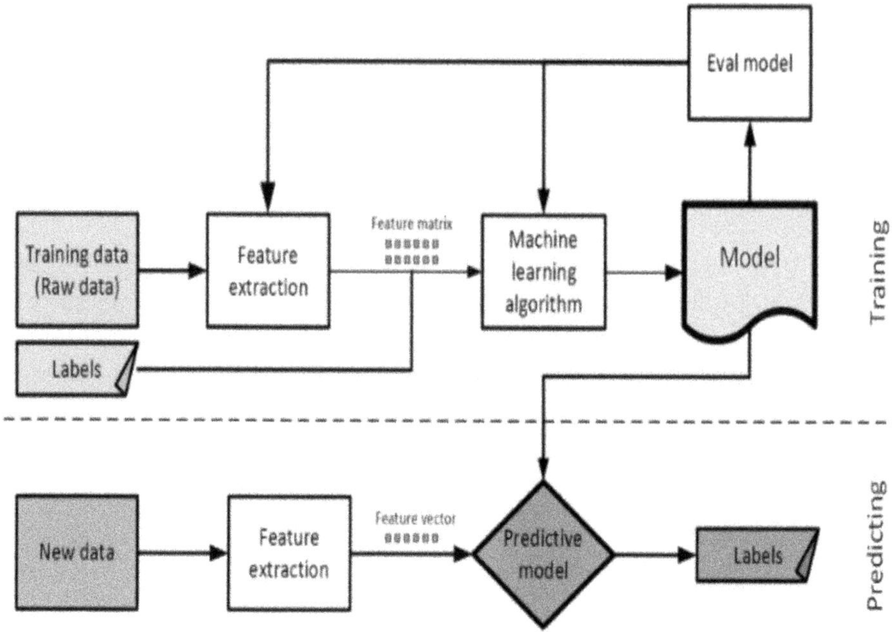

Fig. 1. System Architecture

- The Drug name, which indicates the name of the AAS steroid.
- The Usage duration, which is the duration of AAS use (in months).
- The Monthly Average Usage Frequency, which indicates consumption per month
- The Age, which represents the age of the individual.
- The Gender is the gender of the individual patient.
- The Presence or absence of CVD and pulmonary disease.
- The Label Encoding was applied to convert categorical variables into numeric form.
- The Standard scaler method is used to normalize continuous variables, ensuring that all features have equal weight in training the model.

3.2 Data Visualization

Exploratory data analysis (EDA) helps to identify such problems and clean data to ensure reliability. To find the relationship between different variables, a correlation heat map is generated based on the Pearson correlation coefficient (r). This step helps to identify highly correlated features that significantly focus on organ health outcomes, providing insights into organ health outcomes characteristics for modelling.

3.3 Modelling

The methodology applied here followed a structured machine learning pipeline to predict steroid-induced side effects on the heart, kidney, and lung using clinical data and biomarkers. In data processing, the missing values are handled by mean imputation for numerical features and mode imputation for categorical features, followed by label coding and feature scaling using Standard Scaler method. After this Model training is carried out using Random Forest algorithm, while ROC-AUC, enables reliable identification of at-risk patients and supports proactive medical interventions.

Random Forest Classifier

Random Forest is an ensemble learning technique that builds multiple decision trees and generates the mode of their predictions. Each of this tree is built using a bootstamp sample with a random subset of features, improving generalization and reducing overfitting problem. The model prediction is represented as follows:

Where:

- Is the total number of trees
- The prediction of the t-th tree
- The indicator function

To address class imbalance, SMOTE (Synthetic Minority Over Sampling Technique) was applied to generate synthetic examples of underpresented classes. Feature importance was evaluated using Gini Impurity, defined as:

$$G = 1 - \sum^{C} Pi2i = 1 G = 1 - \sum^{i} = 1 CPi2$$

where is the proportion of instances belonging to the class in a node. SHAP(Shapley Additive) values are further used to interpret model output and performance, and inspect the most influential features contributing to predictions.

XGBoost Classifier

Hyperparameter tuning is conduced to improve the model performance using Grid Search Cross validation algorithm which is used to optimize parameters such as learning rate (η), maximum tree depth, and regularization terms (λ, α). Feature importance was evaluated using Gain, which measures the relative contribution of each characteristic to improve model accuracy.

Additionally, SHAP (Shapley Additive Explanations) values were employed to interpret the model's predictions and quantify the impact of individual features on the output, enabling transparent and explainable decision-making. Here is formula of same:

$$L(t) = i = 1 \sum^{n} l(yi, yi(t - 1) + ft(xi)) + \Omega(ft)$$

At each iteration it minimizes the regularized objective function and is the regularization term to control model complexity, XGBoost also has the ability to handle missing values internally by learning optimal tree splits. Hyperparameter tuning, such as optimizing the learning rate, maximum depth, and regularization parameters, is typically done using Grid Search Cross-Validation. Feature importance is evaluated using Gain, and SHAP (Shapley Additive Explanations) values are used to interpret the contribution of each feature to the model's predictions.

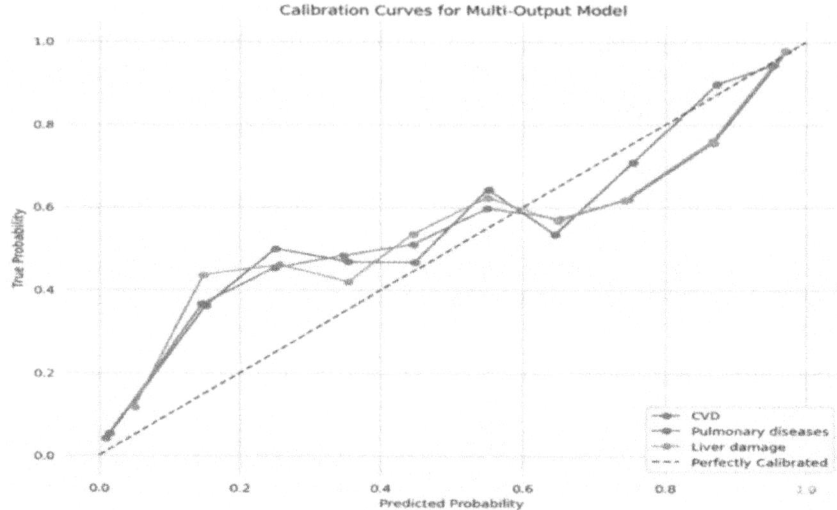

Fig. 2. Calibration Curve for Multi-Output Model for the Random Forest Model

4 Result and Discussion

Based on the graph presented in Fig. 2, the calibration curves for CVD, pulmonary disease, and liver damage are relatively close to the perfectly calibrated line suggesting a good calibration. Similar kind of analysis is carried out using XGBoost as presented in Fig. 3.

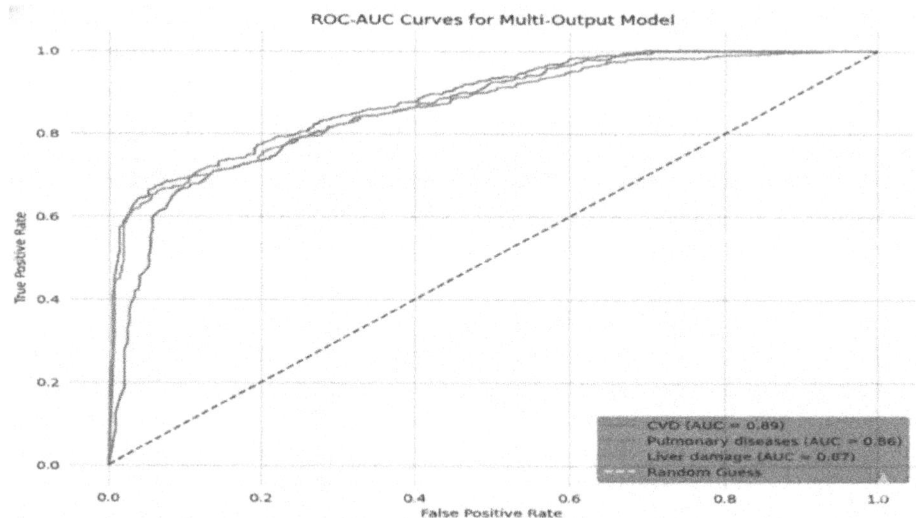

Fig. 3. ROC-AUC Curves

There's significant difference in XGB and RF true vs predicted data showing that Random Forest works better on dataset. AUC values appear high, suggesting good classification performance of the model.

To evaluate model performance comprehensively, both Random Forest and XGBoost classifiers were benchmarked against emerging hybrid ensemble methods. Experimental results demonstrated in Table 2, shows that Random Forest has achieved an average F1-score of 0.91 for cardiovascular disease prediction, outperforming XGBoost's 0.88. However, XGBoost exhibited superior recall for pulmonary disease prediction, suggesting better sensitivity to minority class distributions. A hybrid stacking model, which is used to combine the probabilistic outputs of both algorithms using logistic regression and achieved the best overall performance with an accuracy of 94% and an AUC of 0.96 (Fig. 4).

Table 2. Comparative Model Performance Metrics

Model	Accuracy	Precision	Recall	F1-Score	AUC
Random Forest	0.93	0.92	0.91	0.91	0.95
XGBoost	0.91	0.89	0.93	0.88	0.94
Hybrid RF + XGB	0.94	0.93	0.94	0.94	0.96

To further extend the analysis, additional experiments were carried out to evaluate the generalization and sensitivity of the model across different dataset distributions. The following table shows the results of the Random Forest and XGBoost classifiers, which demonstrate their ability to distinguish true and false positive predictions in three disease categories. Random Forest algorithm maintains a superior balance between precision and recall, while increasing sensitivity to identify borderline cases.

Following Table 3 shows statistical evaluation metrics, including Matthews Correlation coefficient (MCC), Cohen's Kappa, and macro-averaged F1 scores. MCC values which are above 0.85 shows excellent classification consistency between cross-validation folds. In addition to this, sample t-tests Paired results between Random Forest and XGBoost yielding p-values < 0.05, confirming a statistically significant improvement in hybrid model performance.

Duration and average monthly frequency of use are the two most critical determinants used in the sensitivity analysis of the likelihood of organ damage. Age and sex, these two parameters show moderate contributions, indicating that physiological and metabolic differences influence susceptibility to steroid-induced damage. SHAP summary plots show these relationships, highlighting the need for an individualized risk profile in a clinical trial.

Ethical, Legal, and Social Implications (ELSI)

Artificial intelligence is prominently used in healthcare industries to profound ethical and legal considerations. Fairness, accountability, and transparency is ensured by predictive modelling in steroid-induced organ damage. Partial or biased efforts in data collection,

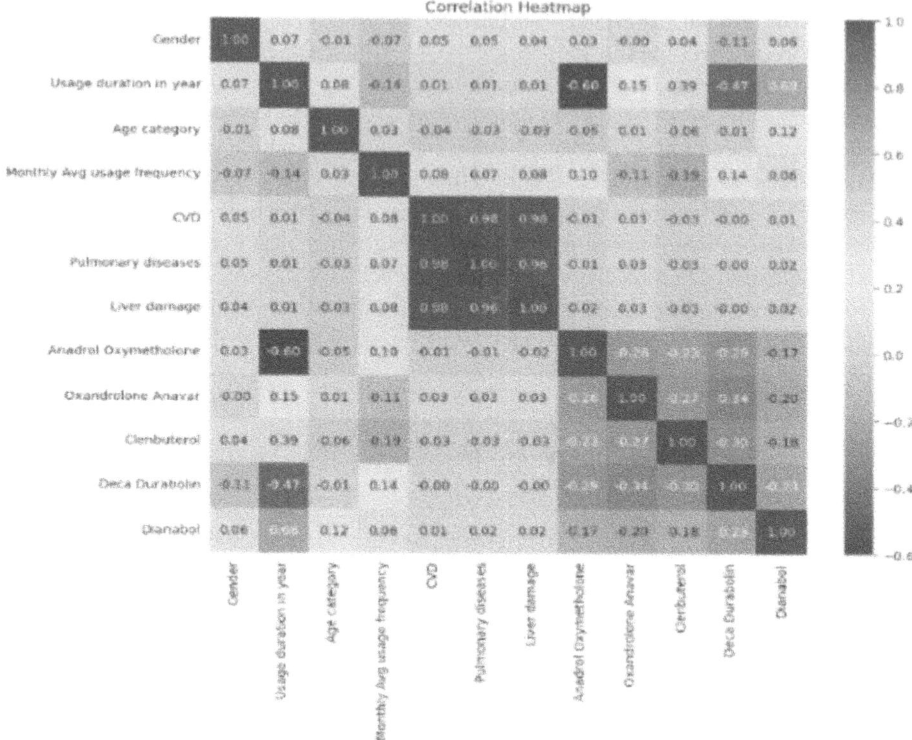

Fig. 4. Correlation Heatmap

Table 3. Advanced Model Evaluation Metrics

Model	MCC	Cohen's Kappa	Macro F1-Score	Runtime (s)
Random Forest	0.87	0.84	0.91	22.4
XGBoost	0.85	0.82	0.89	26.1
Hybrid RF + XGB	0.89	0.86	0.94	28.7

like overrepresentation of specific demographics or underreporting of unethical steroid users, can lead to biased and poor results. Consequently, in such situation model training must include demographic diversity and regular bias audits. Data privacy indicates another crucial and important concern, especially when analysing medical records under regulatory frameworks such as HIPAA (Health Insurance Portability and Accountability Act) and GDPR (General Data Protection Regulation). While implementing a Privacy-preserving AI, such as homomorphic encryption or federated learning, can guarantee that patient data will remain confidential while enabling the development of collaborative models. In addition to this, ethical deployment needs informed consent from participants and a transparent process.

The predictive models like the one developed and implemented here in this study reshape how health systems monitor and respond to medication abuse. By predicting early detection of high-risk individuals, such application can decrease hospitalization rates, improve patient awareness, and ultimately influence public health policies regarding the regulation and use of steroids.

Implementation Framework and Real-world Applications

To implement real-world applications, a cloud-based architecture is proposed in healthcare and sports organizations. Use of wearable Internet of Things (IoT) devices enables continuous monitoring of vital signs and medication consumption habits and stores data of this. These inputs help doctors and or fitness trainers by giving alerts when early indicators of organic stress are detected. In addition to this, implementing the model via RESTful APIs enables interoperability with hospital management systems and public health dashboards. This facilitates wider acceptance while maintaining system modularity and scalability. To accept this on large scale, model optimization can be achieved through edge computing, thereby reducing prediction latency and ensuring real-time responsiveness. Such frameworks are beneficial in hospitals and anti-doping agencies to identify high-risk athletes or patients and intervene before health problem occur. This study also supports periodic retraining with new datasets, ensuring the model evolves next to clinical advances.

5   Conclusion

This research study reveals the application of machine learning techniques to predict the occurrence of serious side effects, especially cardiovascular disease, lung disease, hormonal imbalances, liver and kidney damage, resulting from the consumption of anabolic-androgenic steroids (AAS). More focus is given on commonly used AAS drugs like Anadrol, Oxandrolone, Clenbuterol, Deca Durabolin ànd Dianabol. The study address a critical need for predictive tools to relieve AAS- related health risks.

The hybrid approach of machine learning and deep learning is applied on datasets and the results reveal that the hybrid methods can predict the presence of side effects of steroids with high accuracy. The analysis shows the presence of steroids using RFC + XGBoost models along with MLP and is capable of capturing nonlinear and temporal dependencies. This research study emphasizes the need for advanced models in complex biological systems to analyse the impact of steroids on human organs.

It is essential and necessary that government and regulatory agencies should establish standardized reporting systems for steroid consumption data. Collaboration between institutions, Healthcare organizations, research organizations, and sports associations can accelerate the growth and validation of datasets. By integrating predictive modelling into clinical workflows could enable precision medicine initiatives which provide personalized therapy and monitoring strategies for steroid-exposed patients.

To summarize, the research study advocates a data-driven, ethically grounded, and technologically adaptive approach to manage steroid-related health risks. Future research should focus integrating genetic and environmental factors to increase predictive accuracy, as well as aligning model deployment with ethical and legal frameworks to ensure equal access and patient safety.

The results came in this research highlights the transformative potential of integrating machine learning into preventative healthcare. By imposing models explainable and real-world patient data, clinicians and or researchers can proactively monitor high-risk individuals before irreversible organ damage occurs. However, several limitations still exist, including the limited availability of diverse datasets on steroid use and the absence of genetic or lifestyle information which can refine risk predictions. By addressing these limitations requires collaboration between clinicians, drug scientists, data and policy makers to set up open anonymized dataset with standardized data formats.

Future study should focus on developing multimodal predictive systems integrating genomic data, wearable sensor readings, and real-time biochemical measurements. Such systems would or may enable continuous risk monitoring and early warning mechanisms, paving the way for personalized healthcare and adaptive. To make timely, evidence-based decisions regarding the management of steroid therapy, additionally, the integration of these predictive tools with clinical decision support systems (CDSS) could help healthcare practitioners. A combination of hybrid deep learning and inference methods may also improve the interpretability and accuracy of predictions in future studies on the impact of steroids.

References

1. Breiman, L.: Random forests. Mach. Learn. **45**(1), 5–32 (2001). https://doi.org/10.1023/A:1010933404324
2. Chen, T., Guestrin, C.: XGBoost: a scalable tree boosting system. In: Proceedings 22nd ACM SIGKDD International Conference Knowledge Discovery and Data Mining, San Francisco, CA, USA, pp. 785–794 (2016). https://doi.org/10.1145/2939672.2939785]
3. Zhou, Y., Yang, T., Zhou, Y.: Application of machine learning models to predict chronic kidney disease. J. Healthc. Eng. **2020**, 1–9 (2020). https://doi.org/10.1155/2020/4286301
4. Liu, X., Jiang, J.: Predicting cardiovascular diseases using machine learning: a survey of recent approaches. J. Biomed. Inform. **94**, 103165 (2019). https://doi.org/10.1016/j.jbi.2019.103165
5. Ganaie, M.A., Kumar, M.: Predictive modeling of lung disease using machine learning: a review. Comput. Biol. Med. **137**, 104777 (2021). https://doi.org/10.1016/j.compbiomed.2021.104777
6. Guan, L., Liu, Z., Liu, H.: Data-driven prediction of steroid-induced cardiovascular and renal damage: a machine learning approach. Comput. Biol. Med. **131**, 104266 (2021). https://doi.org/10.1016/j.compbiomed.2021.104266
7. Soni, S., Agarwal, A.: A comparative analysis of machine learning techniques for predicting health risks in steroid users. J. Med. Syst. **44**(12), 197 (2020). https://doi.org/10.1007/s10916-020-01694-3
8. Zhang, L., et al.: A non-invasive detection method for testosterone based on hair analysis using terahertz spectroscopy. IEEE Access **9**, 53957–53964 (2021). https://doi.org/10.1109/ACCESS.2021.3074581
9. Zhao, X., Zhang, X., Zhou, Y., Liu, X.: Identification of anabolic steroids in human urine using near-infrared Raman spectroscopy and machine learning. IEEE Sens. J. **21**(18), 19669–19676 (2021). https://doi.org/10.1109/JSEN.2021.3109378
10. Azizi, M.A., Ghasemi, M.J.: Improvement of testosterone detection in hair samples by thermal desorption-gas chromatography-mass spectrometry (TD-GC-MS). IEEE Sens. J. **21**(16), 17397–17404 (2021). https://doi.org/10.1109/JSEN.2021.3083196

11. Masoudi, A., Aghaei, M., Taherzadeh, M.J.: Advanced nanocatalysts in biotrans-formation of steroid compounds. J. Nanopart. Res. **23**(6) (2021). https://doi.org/10.1007/s11051-021-05264-8]

12. Al-Khazaali, R.M.H., et al.: Steroid biosynthesis pathway genes and the level of cortisol in Iraqi women with polycystic ovary syndrome. J. Genet. **100**(1) (2021). https://doi.org/10.1007/s12041-021-01319-w

13. Molina, A.L., Scartascini, M.E., Lissi, E.M.: Luminescence of steroids and bile acids: a review. Luminescence **36**(2) (2021). https://doi.org/10.1002/bio.3972]

14. Sedaghati, M.R., Khalilpour, M.A., Kamali, M.A.: A review on recent advances in steroid hormone detection using biosensors. Microchimica Acta **188**(1) (2021). https://doi.org/10.1007/s00604-020-04648-y]

Development of an Intelligent System for Sickle Cell Disease Detection Using Deep Learning Techniques

Amol Dange, Samrat Mali[✉], Sachin Jadhav, Ruturaj Mane-Deshmukh, and Prathmesh Pol

Annasaheb Dange College of Engineering and Technology, Ashta , India
amoldange_cse@adcet.in, *samratmali99@gmail.com

Abstract. This research paper suggests a classification methodology of Sickle Cell Disease (SCD) using a deep learning and transfer learning approach. Precisely, the transfer learning models that have been used are MobileNet and VGG-19 to conduct classification tasks on a Sickle Cell image dataset for training and evaluation. Image preprocessing and data augmentation measures were employed to enhance the quality of the datasets and boost the performance of the models, which enhanced variability in the data and robustness in the models. Also, Support Vector Machine (SVM) and Random Forest classifiers were ablation tested to analyse the effect of each individual model component and optimise performance by hyperparameter tuning. Detailed statistical analysis has been conducted, and adversarial attacks have been used to test model stability on perturbed conditions. According to the findings, the VGG-19 model with a SVM classifier was better than the other methods in regards to accuracy. Moreover, this model proved to be very precise, recalls, and F1-score, especially when applied to a smaller part of the dataset, which proves the efficiency it has in detecting normal and sickle-like cells.

Keywords: Transfer Learning · VGG-19 · MobileNet · Support Vector Machine · Random Forest

1 Introduction

The current paper presents a deep learning-based approach to Sickle Cell Disease (SCD) detection [1] using deep learning VGG-19 and MobileNet feature extraction models [2]. The features extracted are categorized with the help of such traditional machine learning algorithms as Random Forest [3] and Support Vector machine (SVM) [4]. The technique reduces the amount of data required through the use of transfer learning and allows automatic, early, and accurate diagnosis in impoverished healthcare environments [6–8].

F. Ortiz-Rodríguez et al. (Eds.): IBCD 2025, CCIS 2845, pp. 332–345, 2026.
https://doi.org/10.1007/978-3-032-20907-8_28

2   Background and Literature Review

Progress in computational techniques from conventional image processing to deep learning methods such as transfer learning and lightweight CNNs has improved the identification of normal and sickle-shaped red blood cells, addressing problems such as cell overlap and image noise.

- Deepak et al. [2] employed GoogleNet with transfer learning to classify brain tumors, attaining 98% precision in a three-class MRI task through five-fold across-validation, demonstrating solid results with limited data.
- Liu et al. [3] explored deep learning approaches, including autoencoders, CNNs, DBNs, and RBMs, detailing their roles in pattern recognition, issues such as overfitting, and implications for big data, while describing directions for future studies.
- Alzubaidi et al. [5] developed a lightweight CNN for the classification of RBC using the erythrocytesIDB data set. Their model, which incorporates transfer learning, data augmentation, and multiclass SVM, reached 99.98% accuracy.
- Elngar et al. [9] examined the development of image classification from older methods (KNN, SVM, ANN) to deep learning, underlining CNNs for their automatic feature extraction, high accuracy, and versatile applications in domains like healthcare.

3   Material and Methods

This section outlines the dataset and methodology applied to develop an intelligent system for detecting Sickle Cell Disease (SCD). The dataset, sourced from Kaggle, comprises blood smear images of individuals with SCD (Fig. 1). The approach involves assessing pre-trained transfer learning models, adjusting hyperparameters, and performing ablation studies with various classifiers to enhance accuracy.

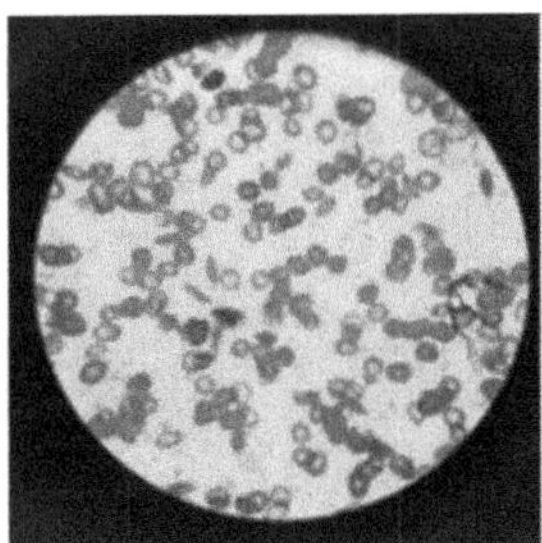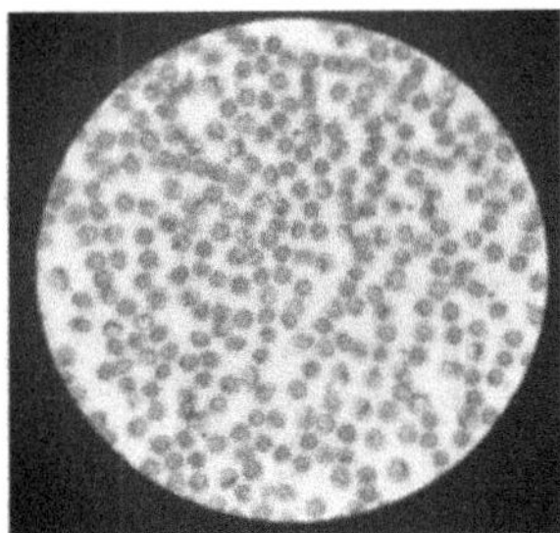

Fig. 1. Dataset details for SCD image classification task.

3.1   Dataset

The dataset consists of red blood cell (RBC) images categorized into two classes: sickle-shaped (positive) and normal circular cells (negative), as shown in (Fig. 2). There are 147 normal cell images and 422 sickle cell images. To avoid class imbalance and enhance model generalization, data augmentation methods were used to expand the training data set.

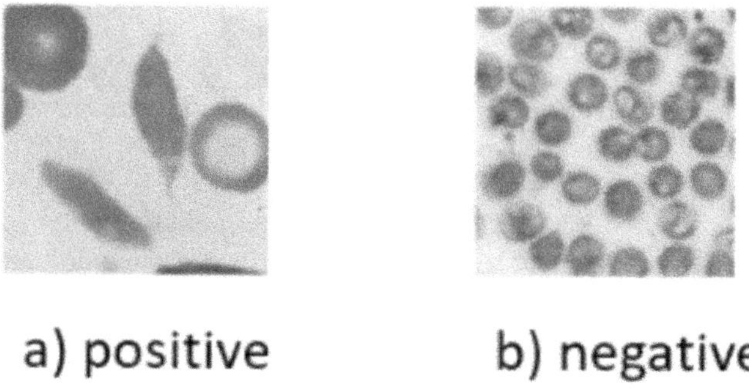

Fig. 2. Two distinct classes of single-cell images

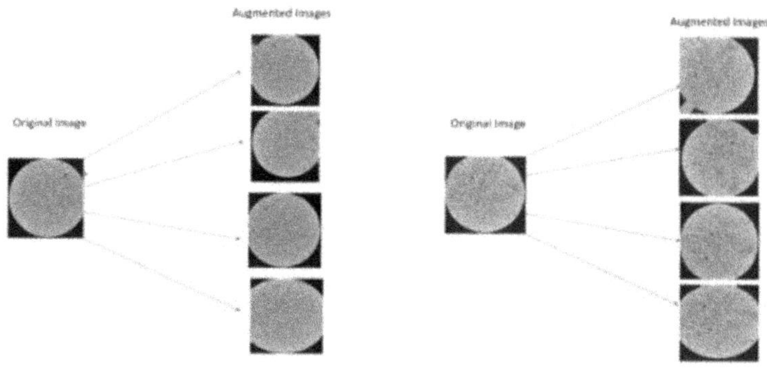

Fig. 3. Data Augmentation

Table 1. Dataset description for sickle cell disease

Cell Type	Original Dataset	Augmented Dataset
Negative	422	2352
Positive	147	2110

3.2   Data Augmentation

To emphasize cellular details, RGB images were transformed into grayscale without altering cell aspect ratios. Due to the limited dataset size, augmentation methods such as

90° and 180° rotations, horizontal flipping, and zooming were applied to both "Positive" and "Negative" classes in both RGB and grayscale modes [6] (Fig. 3). This augmentation produced 2352 Negative and 2110 Positive samples, totaling 4462 images across both formats for use in multiclass classification, as summarized in Table 1.

4 Methodology

The traditional method of identifying sickle cell disease (SCD) has been done manually by observing the blood smear images. Although successful, it is a labor-consuming technique that cannot be used in quick diagnostic processes. These limitations notwithstanding, morphological analysis is an important aspect of clinical diagnosis.

In this study, the researcher suggests a deep transfer learning-based system of automated red blood cell morphology classification as a solution to these problems. It applies two pre-trained convolutional neural nets, which are VGG19 and MobileNet [7], with machine learning classifiers such as Support Vector Machine (SVM) [4] and Random Forest (RF) [3].

Every deep learning model is (randomly) initialized with a collection of hyperparameters Hp, and optimized by (random) tuning on the dataset:

$$TL(H_p^t) = \Gamma[TL - H_p, D]$$

The variables in this equation are TL $\in$ {VGG19, MobileNet} and $\Gamma\,[\,\cdot\,]$ is the hyperparameter tuning function used to apply to the dataset D, and optimized models are obtained.

In an ablation experiment, then, the tuned models are combined with classifiers, which is defined as:

$$TL_{ab}\left(H_p^t, CF\right) = \Psi\left(TL\left(H_p^t\right),\ CF,\ D\right)$$

In this case, $\Psi\,[\,\cdot\,]$ refers to the procedure of making hybrid models through the combination of each tuned CNN to the classifiers to form four combinations.

Overall, six models are constructed, two of them are obtained during hyperparameter tuning and four are obtained during the ablation experiments. These models are evaluated with the use of the standard performance metrics to determine which model is the most precise and true to deploy. The proposed methodology is presented in Fig. 4.

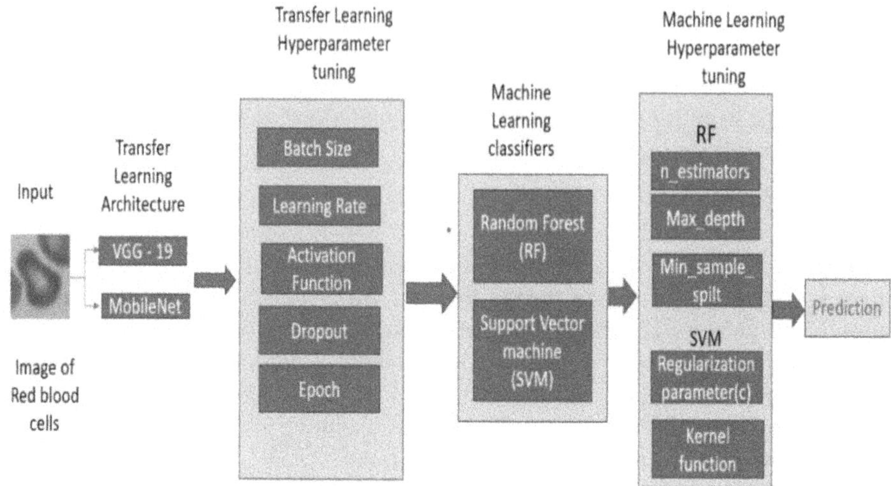

Fig. 4. Proposed Methodology

4.1 Experiments and Performance Evaluation

The experiments were run through Google Colab which is a cloud platform that is best suited to running computationally intensive work without the need to use a high-end local machine. It was an appropriate environment because of its ease of use, availability, and embedded machine learning libraries. The restrictions of the platform in both memory (12.56 GB) and the length of time run (12 h) were also managed effectively, despite the long duration of tasks.

The experimental process started by adjusting the deep transfer learning models and then an ablation study was conducted with the two classifiers.

4.2 Optimization of Deep Transfer Learning Models

Deep transfer learning is a concept that makes use of pre-trained convolutional neural networks (CNNs) [9] to utilize knowledge in large-scale datasets to more narrow tasks through fine-tuning of the selected layers. Classification is usually performed in fully connected (FC) layers, in which extracted features are transformed linearly. The last FC layer uses softmax to produce the probabilities of classes to make predictions.

There are two transfer learning models VGG19 [10] and MobileNet [11] adopted in this research to accomplish an image classification task. The information about the way they should be implemented and set is given in the further sections.

4.3 CNN-Based Feature Extraction

It used a Convolutional Neural Network (CNN) [12] as an extraction and classification tool. The CNNs have convolutional layers, which de-train the spatial hierarchies, pooling layers, which down-sample the feature maps and fully connected layers, which perform classification tasks.

This paper involves the use of two pre-trained deep learning models [13], which have been chosen based on their ability to classify images. Their architectures and their particular contributions are presented further on.

VGG-19

The architecture of the VGG-19 model is presented in Fig. 5.

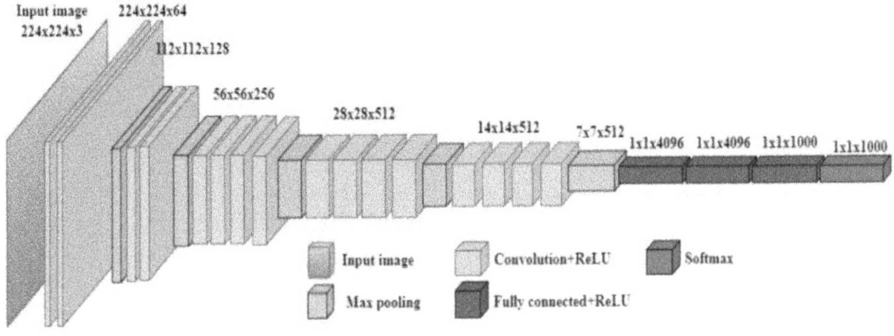

Fig. 5. VGG-19 Architecture

The model recorded 90.18% training accuracy and 90.57% accuracy on the test dataset. Evaluation through a confusion matrix (Fig. 6) and a classification report shows that "Positive" class achieved 95% precision, 84% recall, and 89% F1-score, and "Negative" classes achieved 87% precision, 96% recall, and 91% F1-score, reflecting consistent and well-balanced performance.

Throughout training, both loss and accuracy were tracked for the training and validation datasets over multiple epochs. The VGG-19 model reached 90.18% accuracy on the training data and 90.57% on the test data, suggesting strong generalization capability.

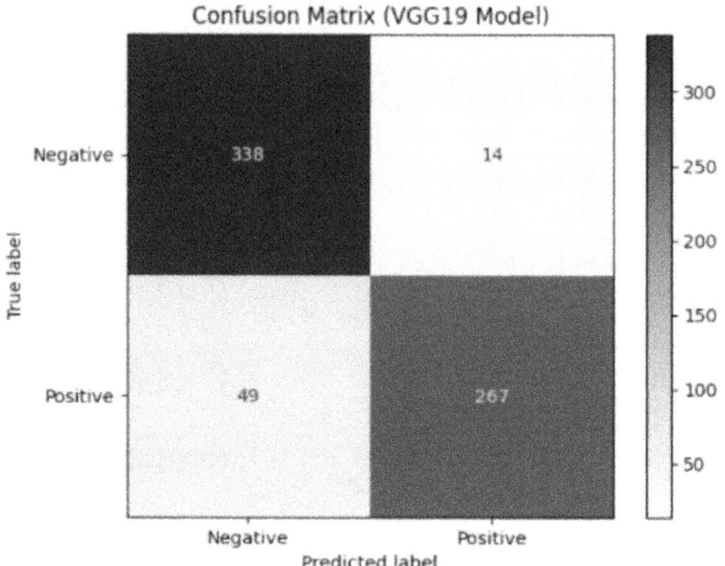

Fig. 6. Confusion Matrix (VGG-19)

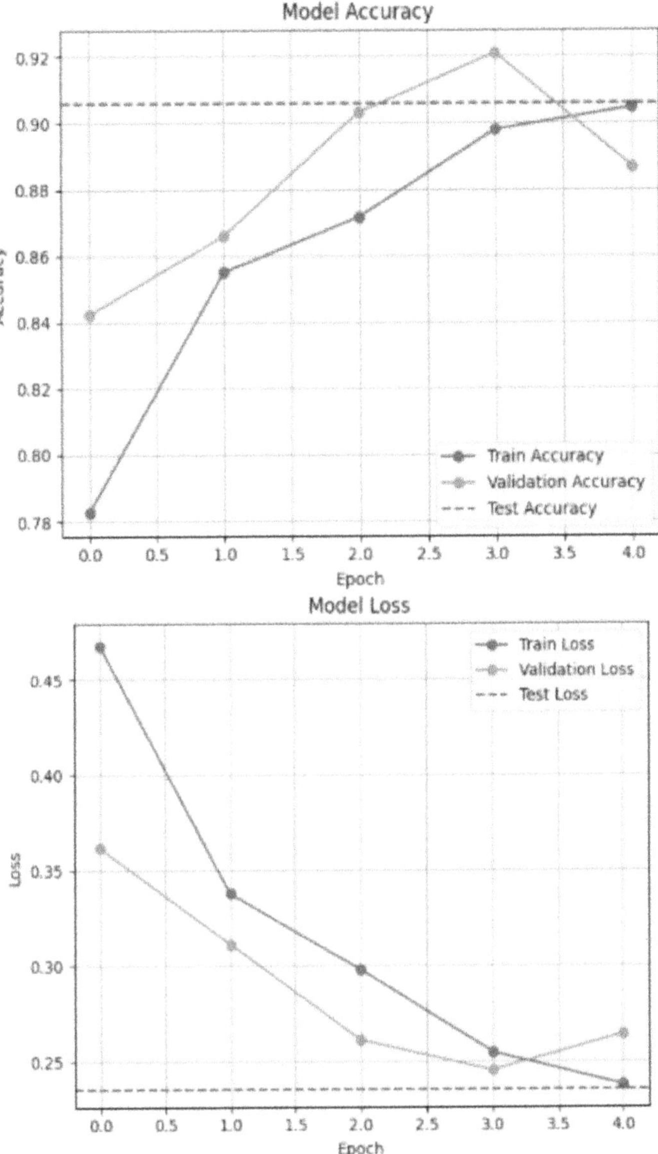

Fig. 7. Model Accuracy and Loss

The pre-trained network was improved by adding two fully connected layers: the first of 256 neurons with ReLU activation, and a single-neuron output layer with sigmoid activation for binary classification. The training process lasted 20 epochs with early stopping if improvement was not detected in 5 consecutive epochs. Trends in training and validation performance are presented in Fig. 7

MobileNet

The architectural structure of MobileNet is shown in Fig. 8.

The model recorded 99.15% training accuracy and 96.86% accuracy on the test dataset. Evaluation through a confusion matrix (Fig. 9) and a classification report shows that both "Positive" and "Negative" classes achieved 97% in precision, recall, and F1-score, reflecting consistent and well-balanced performance.

After training, MobileNet scored 99.15% accuracy on the training set and 96.86% on the test set, proving its excellent efficacy (Fig. 10). Compared to other deep learning structures, it provides high accuracy at low computational cost and is best suited for mobile and real-time health applications.

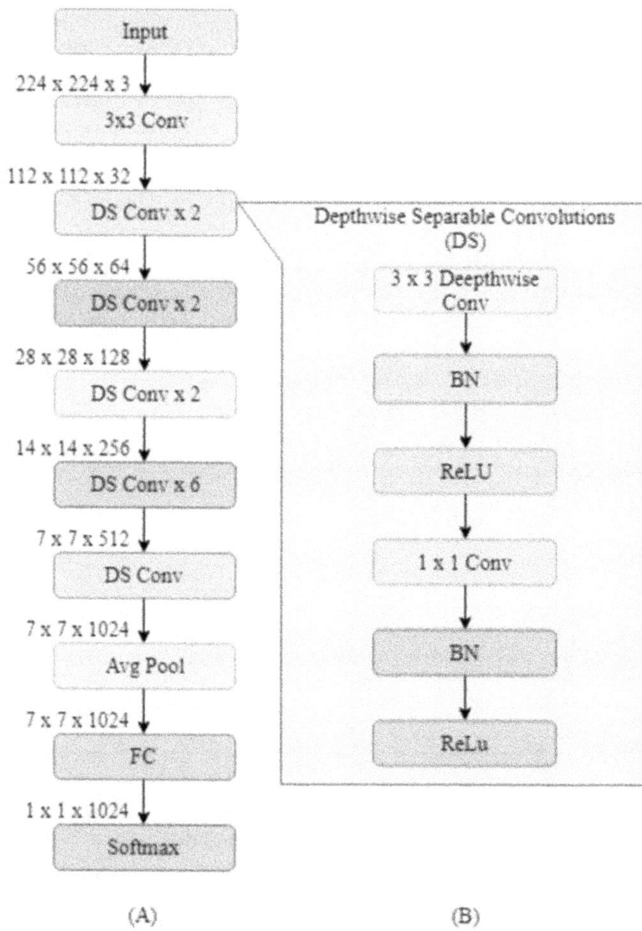

Fig. 8. MobileNet Architecture

Table 2. Comparison of VGG-19 and MobileNet Performance

Model	BatchSize	Learning Rate	Epoch	Dropout	Optimizer	Test Accuracy	Validation Accuracy
VGG-19	32	0.001	5	0.5	ADAM	90.57%	88.67%
MobileNet	32	0.0001	8	0.5	ADAM	96.86%	97.91%

Table 2 summarizes the performance results between two deep learning architectures (VGG-19 and MobileNet).

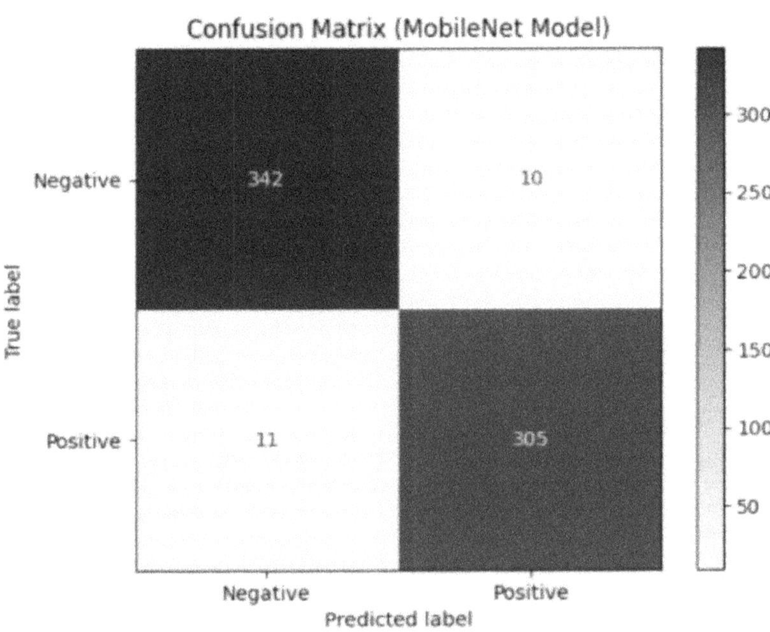

Fig. 9. Confusion Matrix (MobileNet)

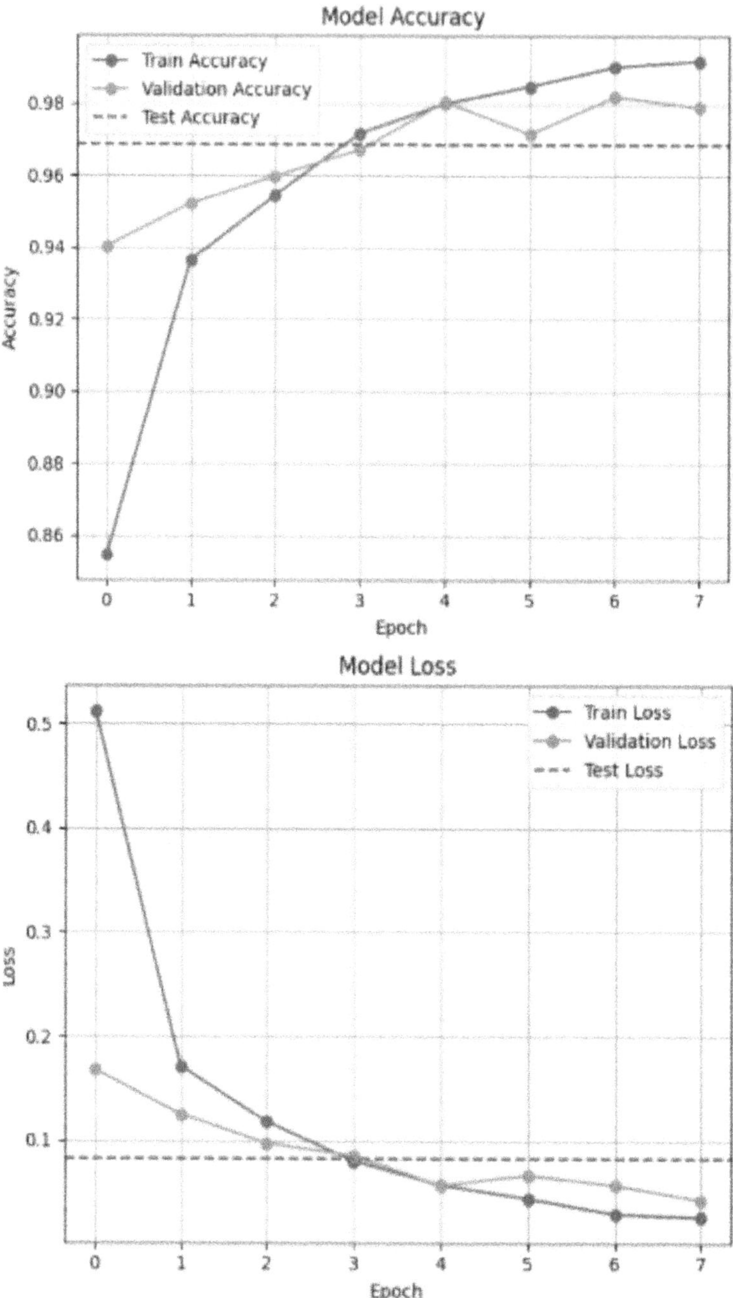

Fig. 10. Model Accuracy and Loss

4.4 Ablation Experiment

This section describes the ablation experiment [8], where fine-tuned deep learning models were used with conventional classifiers. There were four configurations that were tested. Random Forest (RF) provided the highest accuracy (95.06%), while Support Vector Machine (SVM) gave the lowest (87.24%). As a result, RF and SVM were chosen for further analysis (Fig. 4) shows the experiment.

Tuning hyperparameters played a vital role in enhancing results. In this work, the final layers of deep models were substituted with RF and SVM—a novel strategy for Sickle Cell Disease (SCD) detection. The top accuracy came from using MobileNet with SVM [8], as shown in Table 3, highlighting the promise of ablation approaches in this field.

Table 3 gives the classification accuracy of various models. Transfer learning hyperparameters are batch size, learning rate, dropout, and optimizer. For the RF classifier, and for SVM model was optimized using two most important parameters: regularization factor (C) and kernel function.

VGG-19 + SVM gave the best accuracy (97.46%, C = 10, Linear). MobileNet + RF followed (94.61%, 200 trees, unlimited depth, min split = 5), then MobileNet + SVM (94.16%, C = 10, Linear), and VGG-19 + RF (93.86%, 200 trees, depth = 20, split = 2).

Results in Table 3 support VGG-19 with SVM strong classification ability for SCD detection.

Table 3. Performance Analysis of Random Forest and Support Vector Machine Classifiers

Model	Batch size	Learning Rate	Dropout	Optimizer	Random Forest			Test Accuracy
					n_estimators	max_depth	min_samples_split	
VGG-19 + RF	32	0.0001	0.5	ADAM	200	None	2	93.86%
MobileNet + RF	32	0.0001	0.5	ADAM	200	None	2	94.61%
					Support Vector Machine			
					C	Kernal	probability	
VGG-19 + SVM	32	0.0001	0.5	ADAM	10	Linear	True	97.46%
MobileNet + SVM	32	0.0001	0.5	ADAM	10	Linear	True	94.16%

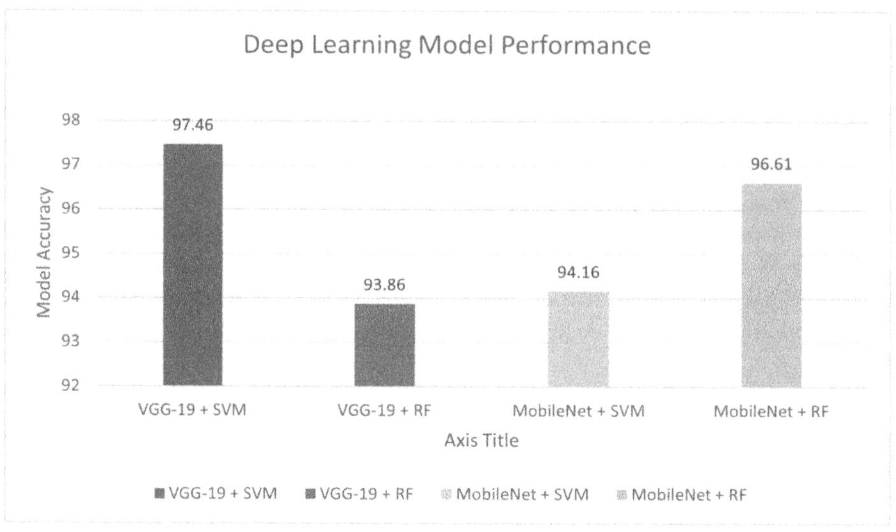

Fig. 11. Evaluation of Hyperparameter-Tuned Model Performance

5   Conclusions and Areas for Future Work

This paper provides an automatic technique for the identification of sickle cell disease based on red blood cell classification into normal and sickle-shaped ones. Evaluation of the model was performed by employing critical parameters such as accuracy, precision, recall, F1-score, as well as graphical examination of training and validation curves. Results indicate high model efficiency, with MobileNet performing 97% in all performance measures. VGG-19 was also found to perform well, particularly in recognizing normal cells, with 87% precision and 96% recall—representing reliable classification from both networks. The original VGG-19 model reached an accuracy of 90.57%, which increased to 93.86% when paired with a Random Forest classifier and peaked at 97.46% with Support Vector Machine, representing a 6.89% overall gain.

Advanced methods including transfer learning, hyperparameter optimization, ablation testing, data augmentation, and statistical validation outperformed traditional techniques in detecting sickle cell disease.

References

1. Kato, G.J., Piel, F.B., Reid, C.D., Gaston, M.H., Ohene-Frempong, K., et al.: Sickle cell disease. Nature Rev. Disease Primers **4**, 1–22 (2018). https://doi.org/10.1038/nrdp.2018.10
2. Deepak, S., Ameer, P.M.: Brain tumor classification using deep CNN features via transfer learning. Comput. Biol. Med. **111**, 103345 (2019)
3. Liu, Y., Wang, Y., Zhang, J.: New machine learning algorithm: random forest. In: Information Computing and Applications: Third International Conference, ICICA 2012*, Chengde, China, September 14–16, 2012. Proceedings 3, pp. 246–252. Springer, Heidelberg (2012)
4. Cortes, C.: Support-Vector Networks. Machine Learning (1995)

5. Alzubaidi, L., Fadhel, M.A., Al-Shamma, O., Zhang, J., Ye, D.: Deep learning models for classification of red blood cells in microscopy images to aid in sickle cell anemia diagnosis. Electronics **9**(3), 427 (2020)
6. Shorten, C., Khoshgoftaar, T.M.: A survey on image data augmentation for deep learning. J. Big Data **6**(1), 1–48 (2019). https://doi.org/10.1186/s40537-019-0197-0
7. Mascarenhas, S., Agarwal, M.: A comparison between VGG16, VGG19 and ResNet50 architecture frameworks for image classification. In: 2021 International Conference on Disruptive Technologies for Multi-Disciplinary Research and Applications (CENTCON), vol. 1, pp. 96–99. IEEE (2021)
8. Michele, A., Colin, V., Santika, D.D.: MobileNet convolutional neural networks and support vector machines for palmprint recognition. Procedia Comput. Sci. **157**, 110–117 (2019)
9. Elngar, A.A., Abd El-Samie, F.E., Ghoneim, M.E., Tolba, A.S.: Image classification based on CNN: a survey. J. Cybersecur. Inf. Manag. **6**(1), 18–50 (2021)
10. Shaha, M., Pawar, M.: Transfer learning for image classification. In: 2018 Second International Conference on Electronics, Communication and Aerospace Technology (ICECA), pp. 656–660. IEEE (2018). https://doi.org/10.1109/ICECA.2018.8474802
11. Shaha, M., Pawar, M.: Transfer learning for image classification. In: Proceedings of the 2018 Second International Conference on Electronics, Communication and Aerospace Technology (ICECA), pp. 656–660. IEEE (2018). https://doi.org/10.1109/ICECA.2018.8474802
12. Bharadi, V., Mukadam, A.I., Panchbhai, M.N., Rode, N.N.: Image classification using deep learning. Int. J. Eng. Res. Technol. **6** (2017)
13. Liu, W., Wang, Z., Liu, X., Zeng, N., Liu, Y., Al Saadi, F.E.: A survey of deep neural network architectures and their applications. Neurocomputing **234**, 11–26 (2017)

AI-Enabled Browser-Based Academic Proctoring Systems for Higher Education Assessment

Vishal Pranav[(⊠)] [iD], Nikhil Patil [iD], and Reetika Kerketta [iD]

MIT Art, Design and Technology University, Pune, India
`vishalmpranav2003@gmail.com,`
`reetika.kerketta@mituniversity.edu.in`

Abstract. The shift to online instruction around the world has been hastened due to COVID-19 and in response to challenges of maintaining the integrity of remote assessments. Browser-based proctoring systems powered by AI have become popular means of detecting tab switching, screen splitting, and other potential misconduct through real-time browser monitoring and periodic webcam monitoring. Proctoring tools allow exams to be more secure and offer some level of flexibility for schools and learners alike. However, concerns continue to persist regarding data privacy, algorithmic bias, and the accuracy of technical readings. Systems often cannot achieve reliability and fairness and also integrate with Learning Management Systems (LMS). This survey describes current AI-based remote proctoring systems in post-secondary education, and considers their methods, limitation, and ethical implications. A hybrid human-in-the-loop framework, that combines assistance of automated monitoring with human judgment, is suggested below to narrow detection capabilities, reduce bias, and improve transparency of digital examination.

Keywords: AI proctoring · Browser activity monitoring · Online exams · Academic integrity · Higher education · Privacy concerns

1 Introduction

The COVID-19 pandemic acted as a catalyst for the transition of education worldwide from the in-person classroom setting to an online one. This change brought about different challenges of academic integrity in an online learning environment that needed to be addressed. The lack of visual supervision drove many schools to utilize AI-based browser monitoring applications aimed at better tracking behaviors, including switching tabs while on quizzes or tests, sharing content with other individuals, or simply accessing unassigned resources [1, 2, 6]. While these monitoring applications improved the integrity of online assessments, they caused concerns about faulty algorithms, confidentiality of personal information, and student confidence in the assessment process [10, 13]. The research using more than 4,000 students reported that self-reported cheating rose from 29.9% before COVID-19 to more than 50% during COVID-19. Demonstrating the need for equitable and trustworthy online assessment for students.

F. Ortiz-Rodríguez et al. (Eds.): IBCD 2025, CCIS 2845, pp. 346–358, 2026.
https://doi.org/10.1007/978-3-032-20907-8_29

The current generation of AI monitoring applications faces three key challenges: frequent false-positives as a result of inflexible and/or biased algorithms, lack of clear data and poor data security, and the inability of the AI applications to operate consistently across different platforms and educational applications [16, 17, 25]. These limitations reduce trustworthiness, fairness, and usability, diminishing institutional trust in the assessment and students' cooperation [7, 15].

This paper highlights current AI-supported browser monitoring solutions and focuses on forms of monitoring that are instantaneous, automated by machines only, and human-machine hybrid [20–22, 24]. This paper excludes any monitoring that requires hardware or methods that do not require AI, but emphasizes ethics, confidentiality, and diversity [18, 19]. The paper classifies current monitoring methods, discusses their technical and ethical implications, and proposes a hybrid monitoring approach that combines automated observation with human oversight to reduce bias and inaccuracies.

2 Related Work

Research published from 2009 through 2025 has shown the changing use of artificial intelligence to uphold integrity for online assessments. The early studies [1, 12] found that proctored exams lead to better consistency in results. However, the proctored environment heightened stress for learners. Subsequent studies expanded the AI systems' capacity to move away from authentication and toward automatic recognition using gaze and behaviour tracing [11, 21, 22]. There are emerging practices such as ProctorNet [20] and multimodal detection frameworks [17, 25] that integrate motion, keystrokes, and audio.

More recent work has centred around ethical, privacy-related, and contextual implications [7, 10, 18]. [4, 5], for example, found that over time, proctored AI assessments build trust and perceived fairness. Chantal et al. [7] used conceptual-integrity principles to recommend frameworks for the use of informed-consent approaches and data-minimization directives. Mukherjee et al. [18] suggested video-masking as a means to anonymize without loss of fidelity, and Belzak et al. [4, 5] explored evidence for fairness in hybrid AI-human review.

Overall, it is significant to note that the literature continues to show rapid technological change but does not offer a descriptor of consensus or ethical governance. As for types of evidence collected, most of the systems continue to be proprietary and context-specific and without transparent evidence-based benchmarks for validation [14, 23]. These articles also support the need for integrity models that align technical reliability with applicability for how fairness and privacy (human oversight) consider usability-this is the focus of the model in the paper.

2.1 Comparative Evaluation of Current AI Proctoring Tools

In the past few years, a number of AI-driven browser based proctoring platforms appeared. The list includes ProctorU, Mercer Mettl, Talview, Honorlock, Respondus Monitor besides Examity. Each system uses the webcam to watch the student, tracks where the eyes look and records every browser event so it can flag possible cheating during an online exam [2, 16, 20, 25].

Side-by-side tests show that the tools spot gaze shifts and tab switches with 85 - 93% accuracy, but they also raise many false alarms plus demand a steady upload of video to the cloud [10, 13, 17]. Older lockdown browsers such as Safe Exam Browser or Respondus LockDown simply turn off shortcuts and block outside programs - they do not study behavior and they offer no fairness audit [3, 16].

The new hybrid model keeps a human in the loop. It runs light AI checks inside the browser but also sends only doubtful moments for human review. The change lifts accuracy, protects privacy and gives clear reasons for each flag. The model also cuts excessive surveillance. It analyses data on the student's own machine and asks for consent that fits the exact situation [7, 18]. By blending local AI with spot human checks, the system scales better as well as treats students more fairly than either fully automatic or fully manual methods.

3 Types of Proctoring

3.1 Live Proctoring (Human Proctoring)

Live proctoring means actively monitoring the student by a human proctor using a webcam and microphone of the student's computer equipment. The proctor observes the student throughout the exam for any behaviour that may suggest cheating. This could include behaviours like frequently looking away from the computer for long periods of time or reaching off screen to access other devices. If the proctor observes something suspicious, they can immediately intervene. Since a human is directly involved, this method tends to be more trustworthy in identifying any sources of academic dishonesty that an automated system may miss. However, live proctoring does require considerable resources, especially when proctoring large groups of students; therefore, it can be costly and difficult to scale for larger exams.

Example: ProctorA live proctor monitoring system that combines the use of human proctors and automated tools that is intended to blend the advantages of human judgement with the speed of the software systems.

3.2 Automated Proctoring

Automated proctoring employs artificial intelligence (AI) to oversee students taking examinations without the need for a human proctoring service. Systems can analyse recorded video, audio, and on-screen activity to detect anything unusual such as a student frequently looking away from the screen or another person entering the examination room, or the student scrolling to a disallowed application or web page. A primary advantage of automated proctoring is that it can handle many students simultaneously, while often proving less expensive than hiring proctors. The downside is that these systems are not perfect; at times normal student behaviour can statistically present itself as suspicious behaviour, or they fail to flag unusual behaviour that a human proctor would likely pick up on.

Example: Examity uses AI in conjunction with remote exam proctoring to flag suspicious behaviour for human proctor validation. AI reduces the number of false positives based on monitored student activity.

3.3 Record-and-Review Proctoring

In record-and-review proctoring, a student's video, audio, and screen activity is recorded during the exam an afterward either a human proctor or an AI system can review the video to search for any suspicious behaviour. This type of proctoring allows a more in-depth review of the students' actions after the fact which takes away the pressure of being monitored in real-time. This has the potential to reduce student and proctor anxiety. However, a disadvantage of record-and-review proctoring is that the cheating can only be detected after the exam, which means that the exam has already been compromised. In addition to the further investigation of a questionable exam, reviewing large volumes of video is also time consuming, particularly when monitoring numerous students.

3.4 Browser Lockdown Proctoring

Browser lockdown proctoring refers to situations where a test administrator uses software to lock down the participants' device so they are unable to access other tabs, sites, or applications while completing their exam. This is designed to keep participants on the exam instead of letting their minds wander. The main advantage is the simplicity of use, and being able to control the students' online environment. However, this does not address cheating that may occur outside of the online context, such as by using another device or dealing with offline cheating.

Example: Respondus LockDown Browser is well known for restricting participants from switching tabs during the exam to prevent access to unauthorized resources.

4 Hybrid Human-In-The-Loop Proctoring Model

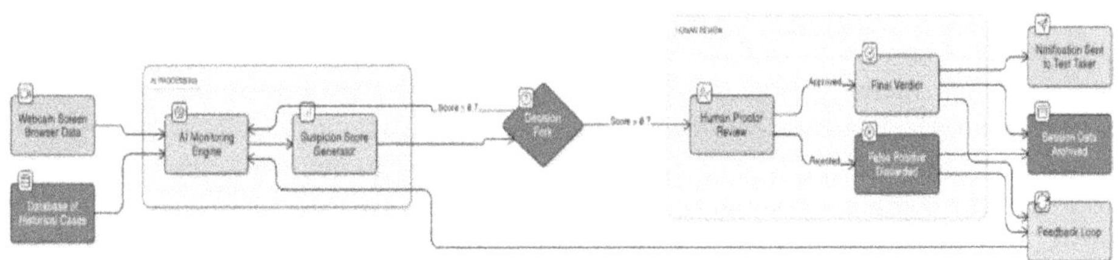

Fig. 1. Workflow of Hybrid Human-in-the-Loop Proctoring Model

Hybrid proctoring serves as a middle ground that capitalizes on the work efficiency of AI proctoring in combination with contextually aware human reviewers to achieve trustworthiness in online assessments, as well as equity and scalability. Like a fully automated proctor, the AI engages in continuous monitoring of gaze, audio-visual events in the testing proximity, as well as browser events. In terms of what the AI detects in terms of behavior, it assigns a suspicion score of 0 to 1. The next step is for a review team to evaluate any event that is flagged by the AI that exceeds a threshold (for example, 0.7 is the cut off for human review), to determine whether the behavior has violated exam policy. Reviewers' feedback is incorporated into the AI system through supervised learning for improved accuracy over time and fewer false-flag alerts across many testing contexts.

The workflow illustrated in Fig. 1 encapsulates four key steps:

1. **Authentication, and Monitoring**: Some form of secure login, either through the LMS, or via two-factor authentication, mitigates impersonation. The AI then continues to observe the webcam, microphone, and browser for potential aberrations, i.e., switching tabs or detecting more than one face.
2. **Flagging, and Human Monitoring:** Actions that are flagged as potentially suspicious, either by time stamps or confidence levels exhibited within the system, are then validated by human proctors, either confirming or rejecting the violations.
3. **Decision, and Reporting:** The decision comes from a joint review of both human and AI judges examined side by side, and all decisions logged into the system to maintain institutional accountability.
4. **Feedback learning:** Finally, those cases that were monitored and deemed to be "confirming" by human judgement serve as additional evidence to "retrain" the AI model continuously to adapt to thresholds of success, and fairness of the system.

This multi-layered system allows for the efficiency of automation, while still incorporating human judgement, in a scalable nature. Since the AI is filtering the majority of routine activity, the act of a human monitoring only pivots to edge cases, which lowers costs and bandwidth for operations, even when applied to mass assessments. On-going feedback can also increase trust, transparency, and equity among students and instructors, while able to adapt to differing disciplines, academic settings, or technical platforms.

5   Ethical and Legal Considerations

AI-powered proctoring tools collect sensitive data, including webcam video, audio, browsing activity, and behavioural information. While required to establish academic integrity, such extensive monitoring creates serious privacy, fairness, and mental health issues. Monitoring students continuously can promote test anxiety and disadvantage students in less-than-ideal testing conditions or students with neurocognitive disabilities, while algorithmic bias concerning aspects of lighting, skin tones, and students' movements, centralizes fairness in the evaluative process of testing. To mitigate the risks posed by monitoring students, the proctoring systems should operate by the principles of privacy by design, such as only collecting process-related data, encrypting recordings, having clear and accessible recording retention policies, and providing informed consent which includes opportunities for review or challenge. Training a human-in-the-loop audit also promotes the opportunity to mitigate biased AI and maintain accountability of the tools' actions. Privacy/regulatory frameworks such as GDPR (EU), FERPA (U.S.), and DPDPA (India) impose strict standards for data minimization, consent, and deletion.

Ensuring the regulatory procedures are connected from the design process reinforces a good faith of privacy with post-collection compliance that improves institutional standing, mitigates litigation, and maintains some trust of students in the testing environment. Ultimately, adherence to ethical and legal compliance will rely on transparent, fairness audits, and users being actively engaged in the process—regardless of the deficiencies of measuring quality or fairness—provides the foundation for ongoing acceptance of AI-based proctoring schemes as an integral aspect of future assessment in higher education.

6   System Architecture and Workflow

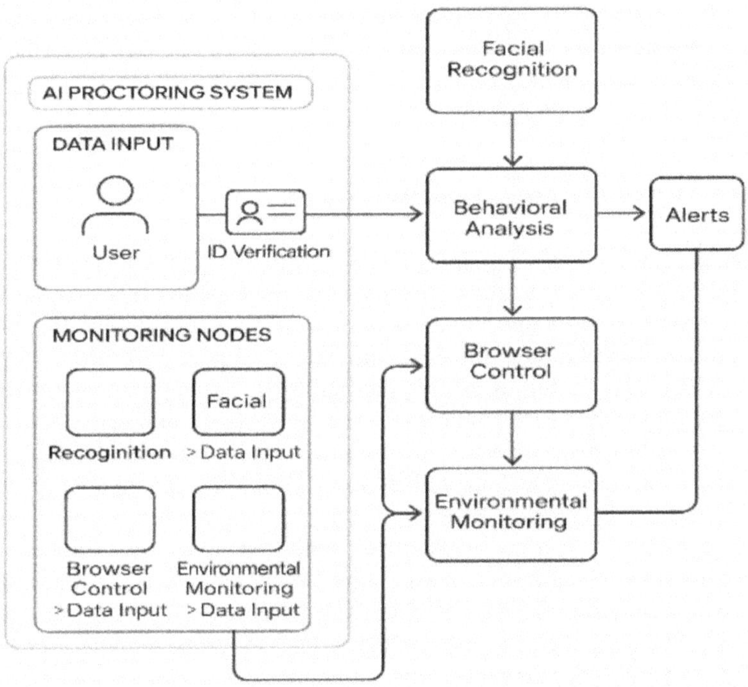

Fig. 2. Architecture of Browser-Based Academic Proctoring System

The hybrid browser-based proctoring solution suggested in this document employs a combination of artificial intelligence (AI), human involvement, and sensitivity to privacy to achieve fair and scalable assessments in online environments.

As presented in Fig. 2, the individual pieces of the proctoring solution operate throughout the stages of observing, analysing, and then verifying. During an exam, the solution captures multimodal inputs from webcams and microphones, as well as student interactions within the browser to verify the identity and behaviour of the student. Light weight JavaScript routines embedded within the client detect various student behaviours like switching tabs or resizing windows. Simultaneously, AI classifiers analyse gaze position, gaze direction and audio signals to reveal potential anomalies. Each behaviour observed receives a confidence score, with certain behaviours above a particular threshold sending an automatic signal for human observation. Human supervisors with authorized access view those additional behaviours on a secure interface and analyse behaviours further based on additional context (e.g., room light level, network connection level) to evaluate or reject the potential anomaly based on information provided by either student and teachers. Verified human observations additionally help to continually retrain the AI model as supervised learning occurs.

This entire process, displayed in Fig. 3, occurs through four primary phases; secure setup and data tracking, signal evaluation and irregularity processing, human evaluation and reporting, and finally learning based on response to feedback. This process enables the described proctoring solution to be successful at varying degrees of networks, revealing a transparent and equitable relationship between automated assessment and the human evaluation component, one of the most critical dimensions in shaping a balanced, fair, and reliable assessment process.

7 Inclusivity and Contextual Relevance

AI-enabled proctoring that is genuinely inclusive will need to recognize and accommodate multiple learners needs to allow for equity and participation. The proctoring system will need to be usable and support students with visual impairments, auditory processing disorders, motor disabilities, or learners with neurodivergent conditions with adaptive accessibility features, as well as exhibit alternative behavioural indications like typing patterns or position when gaze tracking or facial analysis are ineffective.

Cultural and linguistic diversity also impacts user behaviour. Meaning, gestures or gaze patterns deemed questionable behaviour in one region could be an acceptable cultural practice in other regions. In terms of insight into user behaviour and to avoid bias, AI models should be built from multicultural, multilingual datasets, and the proctoring system should support localization or translation of its user interface. Additional designs that are privacy conscious that employ client-side processing, meaning the data analysis occurs on the learner's device or local to the device, would be an efficacious means of increasing accessibility for the proctoring system, while fostering trust with the learners, especially for learners who have limited internet bandwidth, or learners who are simply concerned about their privacy.

Institutionally, another reason browser-based proctoring does have structural or systemic benefits, which are aligned institutionally and in practice to facilitate scale as an educational intervention (i.e. support for LMS like Moodle, Blackboard or Canvas, etc.) can support both educational equity and inclusion, even when effectiveness is varied across centralized or disadvantaged institutions. True inclusivity for learner types therefore requires some processes that allow design and co-design with accessibility and usability experts, cultural advisers, and the learners themselves. All these participants need to be included in the design of AI-human technologies as the AI will reflect the diversity of our reality in human or educational contexts while maintaining education equity inclusivity and fairness and transparency.

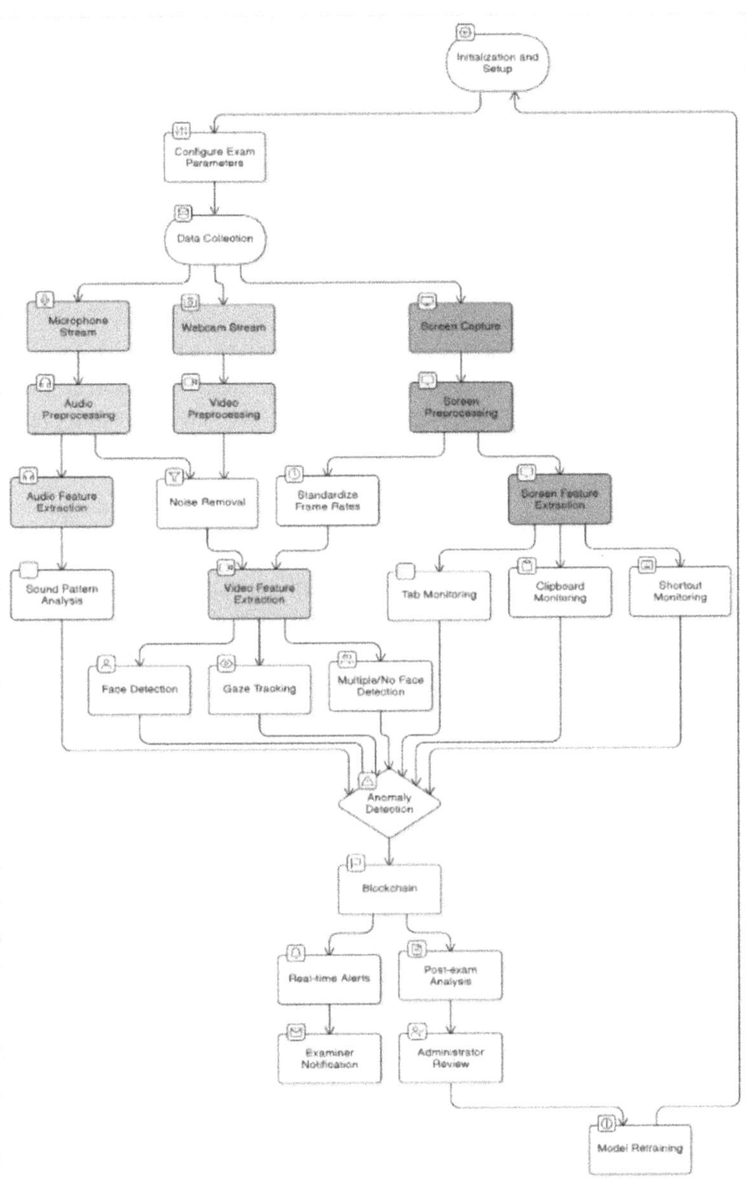

Fig. 3. Algorithm of HAIPS

8 Conclusion

This survey evaluated the condition of AI powered browser proctoring tools, described the main frameworks of live human monitoring, purely automated AI systems, and mixed human machine setups, along with an examination of their pros and cons. Specific topics were covered, such as real time anomaly identification precision, balancing privacy with fairness in algorithms, and enabling LMS integration. Ethical questions were raised about data security, algorithmic discrimination, and mental health, while examining if such systems are not only beneficial and practical but also accessible to all learners, particularly those with different academic needs. In reply to these dilemmas, we recommended a hybrid model that is a balance of automated surveillance and human actions to reduce biases and improve fairness.

Future investigations should include the evaluation of hybrid human machined systems, the creation of standardized benchmark datasets to improve reliability and evaluative standards, additional exploration of PAI strategies, expanded opt-out capabilities, and enhanced adaptability in system design. Continued involvement with teachers, accessibility experts, and policy reviews will be critical to provide usable, fair, and kind proctoring systems.

9 Extended Discussion and Future Directions

This section examines considerations regarding implementation in institutions, scaling of proctored assessment, pedagogical practice, and the changing landscape of trustworthy and responsible AI in education. The section also provides actionable recommendations and directions for emergent research that may shape digital assessment practices over the ensuing decades.

9.1 Institutional Deployment Considerations

In implementing any remote-assessment infrastructure, there will always be trade-offs between cost, reliability, and privacy. Institutions of higher education differ markedly in their bandwidth, devices available for use, and student/teacher ratios; therefore, it is essential for the system to be flexible. A medium-sized institution might implement the infrastructure in stages, starting with formative low-stakes quizzes and at a later point implementing the system with summative assessments with higher stakes. Central information technology units would need to coordinate with ethics committees and legal officers to develop consent forms aligned with local guidance, limits on retaining student data, and a process for opting out for learners with accessibility needs. It would be helpful to conduct periodic audits of the proctor's decision-making and data processing to ensure fairness and transparency in the practice of assessments as well as provide evidence for accrediting bodies.

9.2 Pedagogical Impact

Technology and pedagogy are not distinct worlds. Proctoring tools can affect student motivation, stress, and trust in assessment outcomes. When students observe what they perceive to be excessive surveillance, they may become disengaged or try to avoid being monitored. In contrast, awareness of the why or guidelines of being proctored can serve as an instructional tool in promoting compliance and preserving integrity. Teachers can utilize a mix of proctored and project/ open-book assessments that demonstrate higher-order skills. Hybrid systems allow teachers to move away from investigation and toward providing feedback to learners and reduce false positives, supporting assessment practices that leads to more learner-centred education.

9.3 Scalability and Integration

The hybrid model is by nature flexibly modular. Proprietary browser extensions and lightweight scripts deliver local detection, and server components deliver review queues and reporting interface. Modularity facilitates deployments across Foundation Learning Management Systems using LTI or API interfaces. Campuses could also link analytics dashboards to contextualize participation, flagged events, and reviewer outputs. The cloud infrastructure can dynamically scale during examination inset times by incurring minimal idle costs. Open-source components support transparency and community verification.

9.4 Data Governance and Trust

Trust will rely upon clear data-governance frameworks with respect to how institutions manage data. From the collection of data, to its storage, access, and eventual deletion, each of these stages ought to respect the principle of purpose limitation. In particular, any student recordings should never be reused for any purpose outside the recording itself without revisited consent from the student. Data anonymization pipelines, where direct identifiers are replaced with encrypted token identifiers, could assist in this task. Additionally, an audit log maintained by independent administrative staff provides an administrative accountability trail. Regular pen-test reviews and vulnerability assessments should be performed to eliminate breaches. Trust will also be achieved by institutions publicly stating these protections in their privacy statements.

9.5 Ethical and Societal Reflection

In addition to legality, moral legitimacy is also important. AI-assisted proctoring raises questions around dignity, autonomy, and proportionality. Educational philosophy would suggest that assessment should promote honesty, not the policing of it, and designers should keep this in mind by designing monitoring mechanisms that are supportive, not punitive, in nature. An informative user interface that indicates 1) when recordings are happening, and 2) when other screens are being recorded, could reduce feelings of anxiety regarding AI-assisted proctoring systems. Independent ethics boards should monitor the algorithmic fairness of AI-assisted proctoring each year, and be made publicly accessible in the form of a summary statistic that clearly identifies the percentage of false positives and demographic impacts. This would turn ethics from a rare, often one-time approval process, into a consistent process.

9.6 Cross-Cultural and Accessibility Dimensions

Cultural norms have a profound influence on perceptions of fairness. Gestures that may be viewed with suspicion in one cultural setting may be merely considered social behaviour in another. Creating an inclusive experience for different cultures through design inherently requires diverse training data that encompasses variability in lighting, clothing, and styles of communication. Provided with features that enhance accessibility, like key-board controls, captioning functions, and markers for colour contrast, and even multilingual instructions, would expand participation in the assessments. Working with offices that offer disability support to ensure that the proctoring interfaces comply with the World Wide Web Consortium (W3C) Accessibility Guidelines can help support participation. A commitment to inclusivity is not just legally mandated, it is also beneficial to algorithmic robustness.

9.7 Potential Collaboration Models

Future systems will benefit from collaboratives in higher education, technology, and accountability or policy agencies. Universities have pedagogical capital, tech companies have scalable capital, and accountability, or policy approach committees can define an ethical baseline. Initiating pilot programs to share de-identified, anonymous metrics may be possible, and would respect participant privacy. Hosting open-benchmark-initiatives either by professional societies or literarily reporting standards are possible external resources for wide standardized many data sets that can help determine accuracy and fairness. The potential collaborations shift privatized competition to educational trustworthiness advancement.

9.8 Future of Assessment Ecosystems

In the future, remote-assessment ecosystems will align with components of intelligent tutoring, adaptive testing, and competency-based credentialing. Secure browser usage may evolve into continuous learning analytics which can personalize learning feedback while protecting the privacy of the learner. Institutions may also merge their hybrid proctoring data with student-support dashboards to promote early identification of learning difficulties (given pre-obtained explicit consent). These types of data integrations present a view of assessment that is not surveillance, but rather inclusive feedback loops across the learner's journey.

9.9 Summary of Contributions

The long-range view reinforces that a technical design, by itself, will not lead to equitable and fair assessment experiences. Sustainable development depends on considering pedagogy, governance, and cultural humility. The hybrid human-in-the-loop model embeds human judgment into, and between, automated systems as a way to respond to the complexities of managing integrity. Continuous conversations among educators, education technologists, and policy makers will determine how such systems evolve to become transparent, responsible, and equitable systems for digital higher education.

Acknowledgments. The authors gratefully acknowledge Prof. Reetika Kerketta for her invaluable guidance and support throughout this work.

Disclosure of Interests. The authors have no competing interests to declare that are relevant to the content of this article.

References

1. Alessio, H.M., Malay, N., Maurer, K., Bailer, A.J., Rubin, B.: Examining the effect of proctoring on online test scores. Online Learn. **21**(1) (2017)
2. Al-Azzam, S.S., Pasricha, R., Singh, T., Churi, P.: A systematic review on AI-based proctoring systems: Past, present and future. Educ. Inf. Technol. **27** (2022)
3. Basuhail, A., Fattouh, A., Bawarith, R., Gamalel-Din, S.: E-exam cheating detection system. Int. J. Adv. Comput. Sci. Appl. **8**(4), 176–181 (2017)
4. Belzak, W., Burstein, J., von Davier, A.A.: Evaluating fairness in AI-assisted remote proctoring. In: Proc. Innovation & Responsibility in AI-Supported Education Workshop, PMLR 273, pp. 125–132 (2025)
5. Belzak, W., Lockwood, J.R., Attali, Y.: Measuring variability in proctor decision making on high-stakes assessments: Improving test security in the digital age. Educ. Meas. Issues Pract. **43**(1), 52–65 (2024)
6. Cerimagic, S., Hasan, M.R.: Online exam vigilantes at Australian universities: Student academic fraudulence and the role of universities to counteract. Universal J. Educ. Res. **7**(4), 929–936 (2019)
7. Chantal, M., Han, S., Viberg, O., Cerratto-Pargman, T.: Privacy as contextual integrity in online proctoring systems in higher education: A scoping review. arXiv preprint arXiv:2310. 18792 (2023)
8. Debnath, K., Sanyal, S., Kundu, A.: Keystroke dynamics against academic dishonesty in the age of LLMs. arXiv preprint arXiv:2406.00420 (2024)
9. Ege, M., Ceyhan, M.: Talent-Interview: Web-client cheating detection for online exams. arXiv preprint arXiv:2312.00795 (2023)
10. Fidas, C.A., et al.: Ensuring academic integrity and trust in online learning environments: a longitudinal study of an AI-centered proctoring system in tertiary educational institutions. Educ. Sci. **13**(6), 566 (2023)
11. González-González, C.S., Infante-Moro, A., Infante-Moro, J.C.: Implementation of e-proctoring in online teaching: a study about motivational factors. Sustainability **12**(8), 3488 (2020)
12. Hollister, K., Berenson, M.: Proctored versus unproctored online exams: studying the impact of exam environment on student performance. Decis. Sci. J. Innov. Educ. **7**(1), 271–294 (2009)
13. Isbell, D.R., Kremmel, B., Kim, J.: Remote proctoring in language testing: implications for fairness and justice. Lang. Assess. Q. **20**(4–5), 469–487 (2023)
14. Latif, E., Zhai, X.: Privacy-preserved automated scoring using federated learning for educational research. arXiv preprint arXiv:2503.11711 (2025)
15. Liao, M., Tan, S., Baig, M.B.: Plagiarism detection using human-in-the-loop AI. Educ. Technol. Soc. **26**(3), 112–128 (2023)
16. Liu, A.X., Atom, Y., Hsu, S.D.H., Chen, L., Liu, X.: Automated online exam proctoring. IEEE Trans. Multimedia **19**(7), 1609–1624 (2015)
17. Liu, Y., Jin, Y., Liu, W., Wen, Y., Lin, K.: Multiple instance learning for cheating detection and localization in remote online exams. arXiv preprint arXiv:2406.04581 (2024)

18. Mukherjee, S., Distler, V., Lenzini, G., Cardoso-Leite, P.: Balancing the perception of cheating detection, privacy and fairness: a mixed-methods study of visual data obfuscation in remote proctoring. arXiv preprint arXiv:2406.15074 (2024)

19. Niu, C., Yancey, K.P., Liu, R., Baig, M.B., Horie, A.K., Sharpnack, J.: Detecting LLM-assisted cheating on open-ended writing tasks on language proficiency tests. In: Proc. EMNLP Industry Track, 940–953 (2024)

20. Prakash, A., Kaushik, M.: ProctorNet: an AI framework for suspicious activity detection in online proctored examinations. Measurement **202** (2022)

21. Roy, R., Kumar, V.: AI-based proctoring system for online tests. SSRN (2021)

22. Shih, Y.-S., Zhao, Z., Niu, C., Iberg, B., Sharpnack, J., Baig, M.B.: AI-assisted gaze detection for proctoring online exams. arXiv preprint arXiv:2409.16923 (2024)

23. Suhansa, R., George, Y., Ronald, W.: Student verification system for online assessments: Bolstering quality and integrity of distance learning. J. Ind. Technol. **27**(3), 1–8 (2011)

24. Vazquez, J.J., Chiang, E.P., Sarmiento-Barbieri, I.: Can we stay one step ahead of cheaters? a field experiment in proctoring online open book exams. J. Behav. Experimental Econ. **90**, 101653 (2021)

25. Wang, P., Lin, Y., Zhao, T.: Smart proctoring with automated anomaly detection. Educ. Inf. Technol. **30**(7), 9269–9288 (2024)

DL-Driven Approach for Soil Classification and Crop Suggestion

Sakshi Sethi$^{(\boxtimes)}$, Manali Pusalkar , Shruti Pande , Ankita Lonkar , and Urmila Pawar

Computer Engineering Department, Pune Institute of Computer Technology, Pune, India
`sakshisethi918@gmail.com, uspawar@pict.edu`

Abstract. With millions of workers, agriculture continues to be the most significant sector of the Indian economy. A vast variety of crops that thrive in the nation's various climates, from arid to tropical, can be grown and sold by farmers. Many farmers in India continue to rely on traditional farming practices passed down through generations, often overlooking the impact that environmental conditions can have on crop yields. Today, the soil conditions of a region don't remain constant over the years, and a single misguided decision by the farmer may have adverse effects on the agricultural economy. This paper presents a hybrid approach that combines deep learning for soil image classification using Convolutional Neural Network and machine learning for crop recommendation using Support Vector Machine. The 32–64 CNN architecture achieves an accuracy of 96.82% while the 64–128 CNN architecture achieves an accuracy of 93% using the primary dataset.

Keyword: Convolutional Neural Network · Machine Learning · Support Vector Machine

1 Introduction

Agriculture not only remains the backbone of the Indian economy but also helps the country become self-sufficient. In spite of its major contribution to the economy, nowadays it faces many adversarial circumstances:

- Diverse soil types often lead to confusion among farmers in deciding which crops are suitable as well as profitable for cultivation.
- Frequent climatic variations often lead to unpredictable soil conditions, leading to misguided decisions by farmers, hence result in financial losses, often leading to farmer suicides.
- Rising pollution often leads to soil depletion and erosion, hence overall affecting the agricultural economy of the region.

Machine Learning plays a major role in the agricultural domain. The Application of machine learning techniques, such as recommendation systems, often helps to cover up manual errors and improve the efficiency and accuracy of predictions. These systems rely on systematic algorithms that are trained on various parameters. If current technologies

F. Ortiz-Rodríguez et al. (Eds.): IBCD 2025, CCIS 2845, pp. 359–371, 2026.
https://doi.org/10.1007/978-3-032-20907-8_30

in the context of machine learning are used appropriately in the agricultural domain, it would lead to a significant improvement in the overall economy of the country.

This paper proposes a soil classification and crop recommendation mechanism using mainly Convolutional Neural Network and Support Vector Machine (for prediction).

The soil classification aspect of our research is inspired by the implementation of CNN architecture proposed in paper [1], while the crop recommendation aspect is implemented using SVM as proposed in paper [2]. The system aims to solve long-standing problems in the agriculture domain. Additionally, it also details a user-friendly design and application of a website that serves as a platform for crop predictions. The paper is mainly divided into 5 sections as below:

- Section 1 gives an overview of the research problem.
- Section 2 reviews related literature in soil image classification and crop prediction.
- Section 3 describes our proposed framework and outlines technical aspects of implementation.
- Our experimental results and a discussion of the most important findings are presented in Sect. 4.
- Our analysis is concluded in Sect. 5, which also identifies possible directions for further investigation.

2 Background and Related Work

This section provides an overview of previous research on crop prediction and soil image categorization, which forms the basis for arranging our suggested strategy (Table 1).

Although the systems proposed by the above papers prove to be helpful, there are some limitations:

Reference [3] mainly focuses on classifying soil based on textual datasets, while Reference [5] mainly focuses on only image classification. The features in the textual datasets are mainly standardized but may vary when tested on actual real-time parameters.

References [2] and [4] mainly focus on the comparison of ML algorithms for prediction purposes. Comparing image classification algorithms would surely add much more to the research.

Hence, our research tries to overcome the above limitations by proposing a system for both soil classification and crop recommendation by taking into consideration various ML algorithms that can be implemented.

3 Methodology

In this section, we present a two-phase model framework that integrates deep learning and machine learning methods. In the first phase, a soil image is uploaded by the user, combined with the corresponding seasonal input. In the second phase, the system predicts the soil type and based on this prediction and seasonal factors, produces a list of suitable crops.

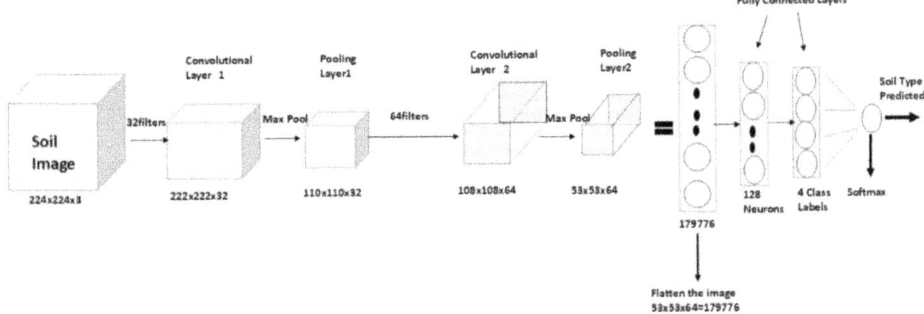

Fig. 1. CNN 32–64 Architecture

3.1 System Architecture

Convolutional Neural Network (CNN):

Dataset Acquisition

Training and validation dataset consisted of about 538 pictures. There are images of various kinds of soils, such as red soil, clayey soil, alluvial soil, and black soil. It has about 240 pictures of red soil, 74 pictures of clayey soil, 47 pictures of alluvial soil, and 177 pictures of black soil. Resizing the photo size used in soil type prediction addressed the imbalanced ratio of images of different soil types. Such data was downloaded from numerous sources including the Soil Types [6] on Kaggle. Images of the soil were collected from local areas like Pune, Shrirampur, and Nashik for validation.

Data Processing and Algorithm Implementation

The soil images gathered come from different sources and were taken in different conditions so that they differ in size and resolution. Preprocessing is hence required to have the images standardized prior to application in prediction. The images are first resized to sizes $224 \times 224 \times 3$. Because the model requires numerical input, images are then converted into pixel intensity arrays. We use color images in this work, which may be represented using RGB formats. RGB images have three channels for Red, Green, and Blue components, whereas grayscale images are single-channel intensity values representing gray shades. The network architecture deployed in soil classification is shown in Fig. 1. Model architecture consists of seven layers with four convolutional layers, each followed directly by a pooling layer. Then, there is a flattening layer and two fully connected dense layers. The last dense layer uses the SoftMax activation function to classify. All convolutional layers have filters of size 3×3, stride of 1, and no padding $(p = 0)$. Max pooling is used after every convolution with a kernel size of 3×3 and a stride of 1. For the purpose of introducing non-linearity, the ReLU activation function is applied in both the convolutional as well as the dense layers.

Support Vector Machine

Dataset Acquisition

Data to be trained on the model is the foundation upon which the Final recommendations on crops. Data size is about 821x14 (row x column). It consists mainly of temperature, season, state, precipitation, and groundwater.

We have dealt mainly with crop recommendations with three properties, which are the season, state, and soil. Data is obtained from Kaggle [7] and additional freely available repositories.

Data Processing and Algorithm Implementation

The data is different with scalar and categorical characteristics, and it is required to be appropriately cleaned and reshaped into an appropriate format before model implementation.

We use the One-Hot Encoding technique on the attribute Season, State) within the dataset. For instance, if the input state is Maharashtra, the corresponding binary column for Maharashtra is assigned a value of 1, while all other state columns are set to 0. The same applies to other features where the one-hot encoding technique is used.

The support vector machine algorithm uses a decision boundary to distinguish between the classes. Based on the similarities between the instance and the support vectors, it classifies the instance into one of the classes. When the data cannot be linearly separated, then Kernels are used. Different types of kernels include 'sigmoid', 'linear', 'rbf', etc. The Support Vector Machine predicted crop recommendations that aligned with several crops cultivated in different states.

Web Portal

This paper suggests developing a web portal prototype for the Crop Recommendation System, integrating all system components. The portal has a user-friendly interface, serving two types of users: wholesalers and farmers. Farmers input data from the system models to receive crop recommendations. The "Farmer's Market" section allows farmers to list crops once chosen, and wholesalers can send requests to connect with farmers for business. After approval, communication occurs through the portal's mobile app, resolving the intermediary issue and allowing farmers to retain their earnings. Figure 2 shows "Crop List", a list of suggested crops produced once the system has received the soil data. Similarly Fig. 3 shows "Farmer's Market" while Fig. 4 shows "Farmer Notifications". Further figures from Figs. 5, 6, 7, 8, 9 and 10 show various functionalities associated with the web portal.

4 Results and Discussion

In this section, we discuss the image classification algorithms and their architectural variants that were evaluated during experimentation.

4.1 32–64 Architecture

The architecture comprises seven layers, including 4 Convolutional layers + Pooling layers. In the architecture, 32 filters are applied in the first convolutional layer, while the second layer employs 64 filters, both employing ReLU activation. A flattened layer

Fig. 2. Crop List

Fig. 3. Farmer's Market

follows the convolutional and pooling blocks, which is then linked to two fully connected layers—the first with 128 neurons and the final layer using softmax activation for classification. The neural network was evaluated for 30 epochs, with filter sizes kept consistent across all layers for each execution. We experimented with different filter sizes to get results as mentioned in Table 2.

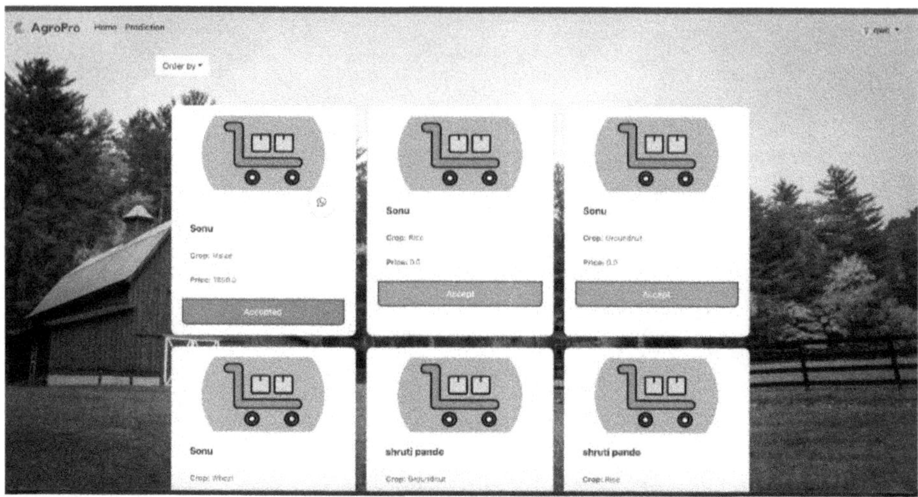

Fig. 4. Farmer's Notifications

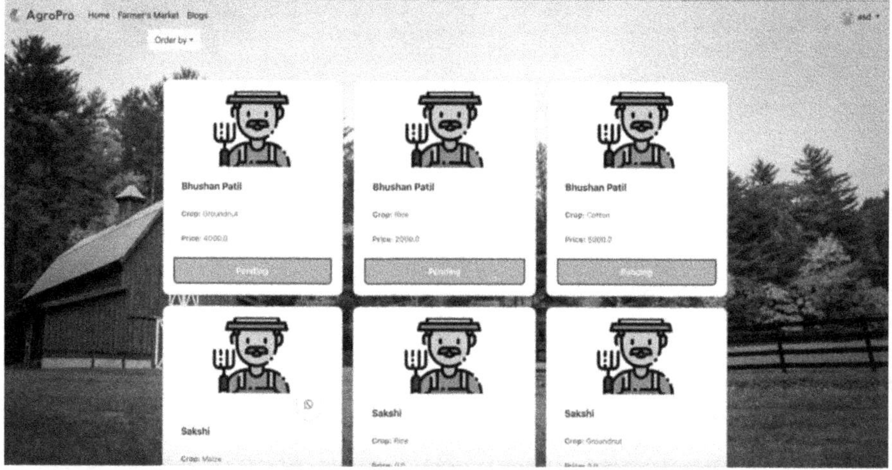

Fig. 5. Wholesalers Notification Page

Table 1. Summary of Related Work from Literature

Author	Overview	Result
Aditya et al. [1]	Machine learning-based crop recommendations for farmers based on soil and parameters	95.21% classification precision for soil types and 75% prediction precision for crop yield and income

(*continued*)

Table 1. (*continued*)

Author	Overview	Result
Kaushik et al. [2]	Crop recommendation using soil and crop datasets	SVM outperforms with 94.95% accuracy. Multiple crop suggestions provided
Hasan M et al. [3]	Ensemble learning method combining K-NN, Random Forest, and Ridge Regression for crop prediction	Comparison with SVR, Naive Bayes, and Component-Based algorithms. Future work includes deep learning comparison
Sindhu Madhuri G. et al. [4]	Machine learning models for crop yield prediction considering geospatial locations and meteorological factors	Random Forest Regression outperforms with an R2 score of 0.88
Prof. S K. Honawad et al. [5]	Digital image analysis approach for estimating soil properties using CBIR	Overcomes traditional methods with content-based image retrieval and texture feature extraction

Table 2. Comparison on the basis of filter sizes for 32–64 Architecture

Filter Size	Accuracy
3	96.82%
5	91.58%
7	92.52%

4.2 64–128 Architecture

The architecture comprises seven layers, including 4 Convolutional layers + Pooling layers. In the architecture, 64 filters are applied in the first convolutional layer, while the second layer employs 128 filters, both employing ReLU activation. A flatten layer follows the convolutional and pooling blocks, which is then linked to two fully connected layers—the first with 128 neurons and the final layer using softmax activation for classification. The Epoch count used for training the model was varied, by initially keeping it 30 and later changing it to 15. The filter size was kept same for all layers for every execution and we experimented with filter sizes mentioned in Table 3 and Table 4.

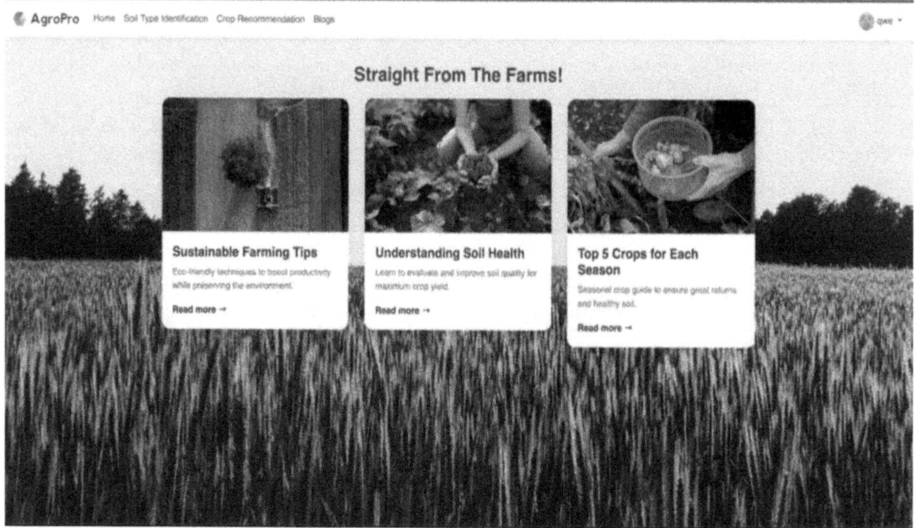

Fig. 6. Blogs for farmers

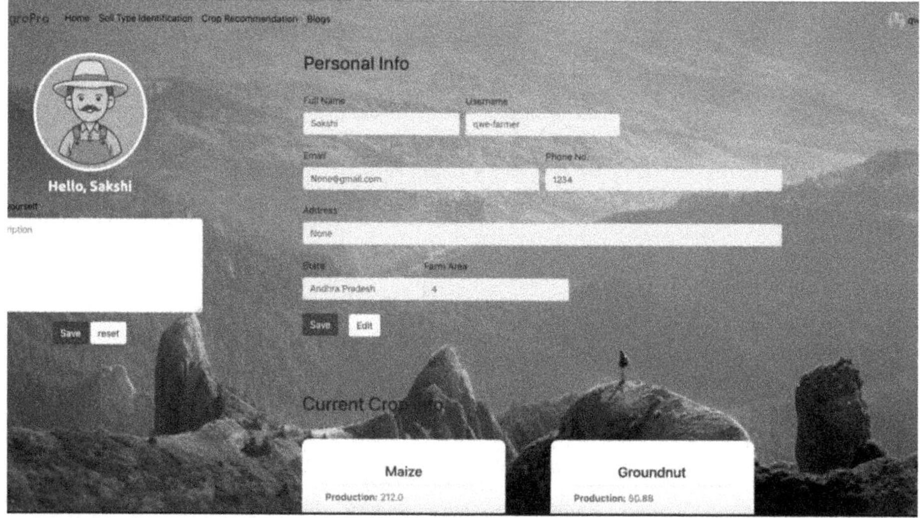

Fig. 7. Farmer's Profile

Table 3. Comparison based on filter sizes for 64–128 Architecture for Epoch count 30

Filter Size	Accuracy
3	92.52%

(continued)

Table 3. (*continued*)

Filter Size	Accuracy
5	92.52%
7	86.91%

Table 4. Comparison based on filter sizes for 64–128 Architecture for Epoch count 1515

Filter Size	Accuracy
3	93%
5	92.52%
7	74.76%

4.3 Primary Dataset V/S Real-Time Images

Here we are comparing the results obtained after prediction based on soil image from the primary dataset and real time soil images. The primary dataset was partitioned such that 80% of the samples were used for training, while the remaining 20% were reserved for testing. The 32–64 CNN Architecture was trained on our training data, while the image uploaded was from the testing data. Similarly, real-time images from Shrirampur were also collected to generate a real-time images dataset. Similar to the primary dataset, the real time images dataset was partitioned such that 80% were utilized for training and 20% for testing purpose. Table 5 denotes the accuracies obtained for the two datasets. Here, the primary dataset is referred to from Kaggle, while the real-time image dataset is generated by collecting soil images.

Table 5. Comparison of primary and real-time dataset

Dataset	Accuracy
Primary	96.82%
Real-time	94%

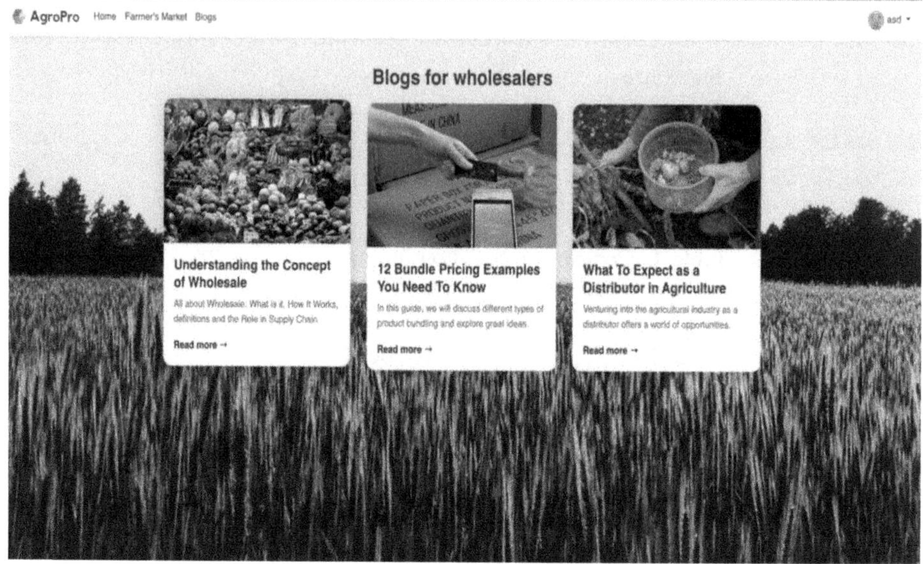

Fig. 8. Blogs for Wholesalers

Fig.9. Registration Page

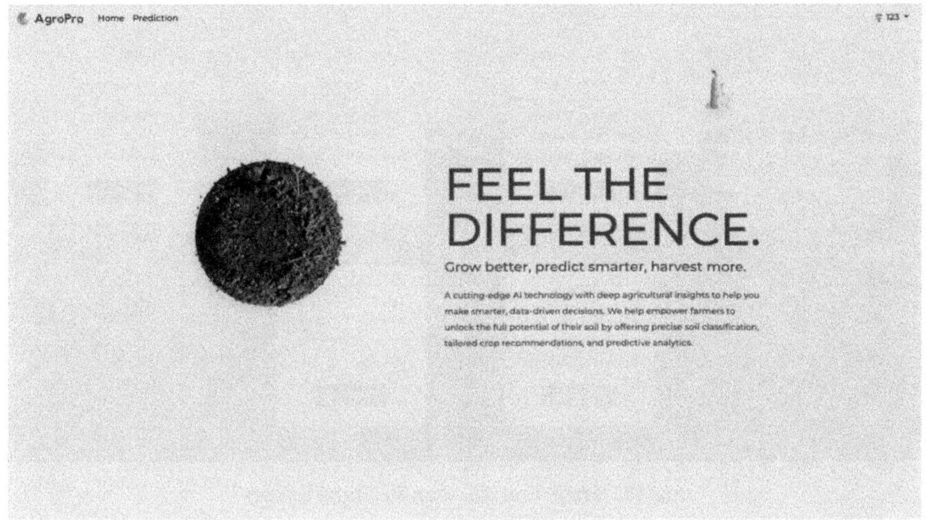

Fig. 10. Home Page

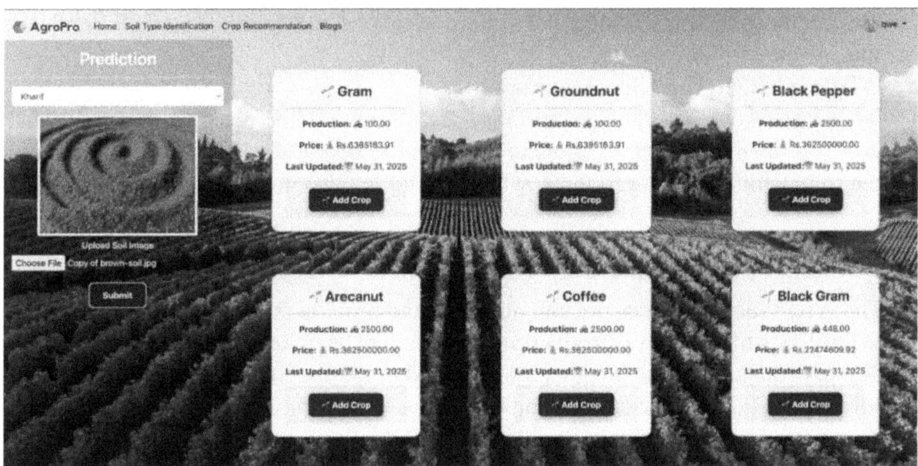

Fig. 11. Prediction based on Primary Dataset Images

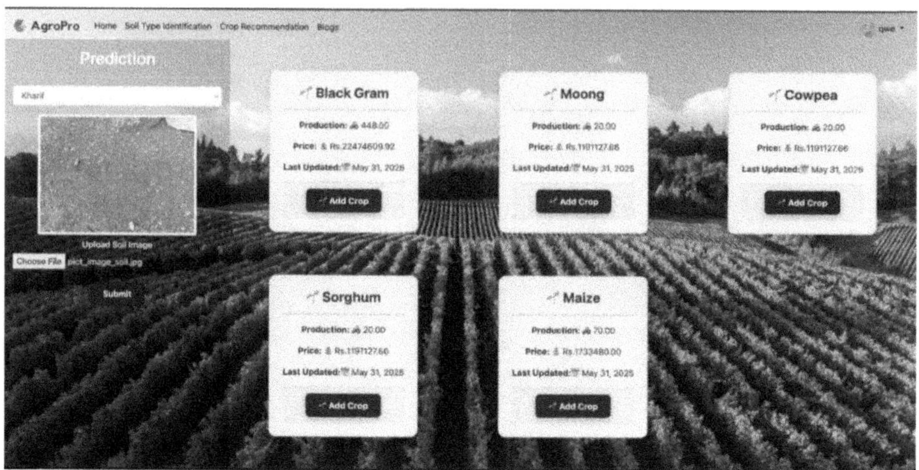

Fig.12. Prediction based on Realtime Images

5 Conclusion and Future Scope

This research can be transformed into a more advanced and practical work for precision farming. Some of them can be:

IoT-Based-Real-Time Soil Monitoring:

By incorporating IoT devices into the system, it would be possible to continuously monitor soil attributes such as moisture, pH and temperature. This information could be sent to machine learning models, which would receive more data and improve over time.

- Automated Fertilizer Suggestions:

The system can also measure soil nutrients and provide recommendations on appropriate fertilizers to boost crop production. Customized fertilizer plans may be provided to the farmers considering the weather and soil and crop. Specifications. Environmentally friendly and sustainable substitutes can be proposed to promote green agriculture. Incorporation with market information will also be able to see real-time prices of fertilizers and availability.

- Multi-Language Support:

The system can be configured to accommodate more than one language, Including the local ones, to cover more people. This will help Farmers from other areas read and manage the system with ease. It will make the site more accessible to users, particularly the ones in rural areas. With the aid of these advances, the system can be an entire integrated precision agriculture system to enhance efficiency and sustainability within agriculture.

References

1. Motwani, A., Patil, P., Nagaria, V., Verma, S., Ghane, S.: Soil analysis and crop recommendation using machine learning. In: 2022 International Conference for Advancement in Technology (ICONAT), pp. 1–6. IEEE, Goa, India (2022)
2. Rahman, S.A.Z., Mitra, K.C., Islam, S.M.M.: Soil classification using machine learning methods and crop suggestion based on soil series. In: 2018 21st International Conference of Computer and Information Technology (ICCIT), pp. 1–6. IEEE, Dhaka, Bangladesh (2018)
3. Hasan, M., et al.: Ensemble machine learning-based recommendation system for effective prediction of suitable agricultural crop cultivation. Front. Plant Sci. **14**, 1234555 (2023). https://doi.org/10.3389/fpls.2023.1234555
4. Madhuri, S.G., Paudel, S., Nakarmi, R., Giri, P., Karki, S.B.: Prediction of crop yield based-on soil moisture using machine learning algorithms. In: 2022 2nd International Conference on Technological Advancements in Computational Sciences (ICTACS), pp. 1–6. IEEE, Bengaluru, India (2022). https://doi.org/10.1109/ICTACS56270.2022.9988186
5. Honawad, S.K., Chinchali, S.S., Pawar, K., Deshpande, P.: Soil classification and suitable crop prediction. IOSR J. Comput. Eng. **19**(5), 25–29 (2017)
6. Matshidiso, Soil Types Dataset. https://www.kaggle.com/datasets/matshidiso/soil-types. Accessed 2025/04/19
7. Nikhil Vinay, Crop Recommendation Dataset. https://www.kaggle.com/datasets/nikhilvinay6111/crop-recommendation/data. Accessed 2025/04/19

AI-Driven Breast Cancer Detection System Using Mammography and Breast Tissue Imaging

Sarika Pabalkar[(✉)] [iD], Yash Yadav [iD], and Atharv Guled [iD]

Department of Information Technology, Dr. D. Y. Patil Institute of Technology, Pimpri, Pune 411018, India
sarikapabalkar@gmail.com

Abstract. Breast cancer remains the most diagnosed cancer in women universally, and an estimated 1.54 million new cases are registered every year. Non-invasive medical imaging apart, traditional diagnostics, which are mostly based on mammography, have long been variable capacity for detection of small or occult tumours, most notoriously in dense breast tissue. This failure contributes to late staging and high mortality, most in under-resourced regions such as India, where one in every nine women is at risk. The proposed system combines the strengths of two-state-of-the-art deep learning networks, YOLOv8 and Convolutional Neural Networks, YOLOv8, as an object detector in real-time. This approach is also applied to suspicious mass detection as well as malignant and benign tumour separation. However, in an attempt to overcome its limitation in creating elaborated tumour characterizations, CNN are used for fine-grained analysis, such as border detection and malignancy size estimation. Such a two-model architecture is likely to provide both detection accuracy as well as diagnostic depth. Additionally, various pre-trained CNN models, including DenseNet-121, VGG-16, MobileNetV2, ResNet152V2, and InceptionV3, are compared to determine the best model to classify between cases and controls for breast cancer. Among them, the most remarkable accuracy was recorded by DenseNet-121 at 99%, followed by VGG-16 (98%) and MobileNetV2 (97%), which states the performance as well as feasibility in medical image analysis. The diverse multimodal dataset was used to validate the system by considering generalizability for a variety of tumour types as well as imaging conditions. The findings demonstrated a significant reduction in both false positives and false negatives, shows the new method's potential for both improved patient outcomes and early identification. Deep learning methods has significant potential for improving diagnostics processes, particularly in underserved areas where qualified radiologists and pathologists are not easily available. It highlights how AI can revolutionize the diagnosis of breast cancer and opens the door for future studies into real-time clinical application, electronic medical record interface, and further development of AI models for potential use in medical imaging. It will be essential to keep improving these intelligent systems in order to help oncologists, advance individualized care, and eventually lower the number of breast cancer fatalities worldwide.

Keywords: Breast Cancer · AI · Machine Learning · Mammography · Deep Learning · Convolutional Neural Networks

F. Ortiz-Rodríguez et al. (Eds.): IBCD 2025, CCIS 2845, pp. 372–382, 2026.
https://doi.org/10.1007/978-3-032-20907-8_31

1 Introduction

Breast cancer is the most common cancer diagnosed in women worldwide. One of the key elements that reduces fatalities is early detection. Breast cancer is associated with both benign and malignant tumour forms. The rapid growth of malignant tumours makes them very deadly. Numerous machine learning methods, such as Support Vector Machine, Logistic Regression, K-Nearest Neighbours, Decision Trees, Naive Bayes, and Random Forest classifiers, have been used to categorize tumours as either benign or malignant in order to predict breast cancer [1, 2]. For many years, mammography has been the primary screening method for identifying anomalies in breast tissue. Even with these developments, there are still many obstacles to overcome. Particularly for women with dense breast tissue, mammography still has limitations that might lead to missed diagnoses and false positives, which can result in needless biopsies and worsen patient anxiety. Recent developments in artificial intelligence (AI), including machine learning (ML) and deep learning (DL), have revolutionized medical image analysis and created new opportunities to improve the precision and dependability of breast cancer issues.

In order to allow real-time processing and scalability for large-scale deployment while maintaining continuous operating efficiency, the system integrates a backend built with frameworks like Django or Flask. A CNN-based module automatically extracts important tissue and cellular features suggestive of malignant alterations for the purpose of analysing histopathology images.

2 Literature Review

Medical imaging currently provides a more effective mean for identifying breast cancer with the integration of machine learning and deep learning [1, 7, 9–12]. Conventional detection procedures utilizing mammography, for instance, while being common, are not always effectives when dealing with very dense breast tissues; hence, early identification of tumours becoming a challenge. Current research, however, points to the fact that deep learning, and in most instances [5], Convolutional Neural Networks is quite helpful when it comes to improving image reconstruction as well as classification accuracy. Self-supervised as well as weakly supervised, CNN reconstruction techniques, for instance, have proved themselves highly successful at enhances mammographic image quality for diagnosis [1].

Studies were expanded to other modalities, such as contrast-enhanced ultrasound and histopathology. The applications apply deep learning to the analysis of dynamic image pattern and molecular information, which aid in subtypes classification and in the support of personalized therapeutic strategies [7, 8]. The literature suggests that pre-trained CNN models, i.e. DenseNet-121, VGG-16 [6], MobileNet, ResNet, and Inception, achieved extremely high accuracy of classification, primarily above 94%, whereas up to 99% for DenseNet-121. Deep learning is also sustained in Computer-Aided Diagnosis (CAD) systems. Faster R-CNN and related region-based systems have attained classification accuracy of about 95% or more, making early detection even more accurate [2–4, 7]. The new system builds upon current advancements in deep learning-based diagnostic models for the detection of breast cancer.

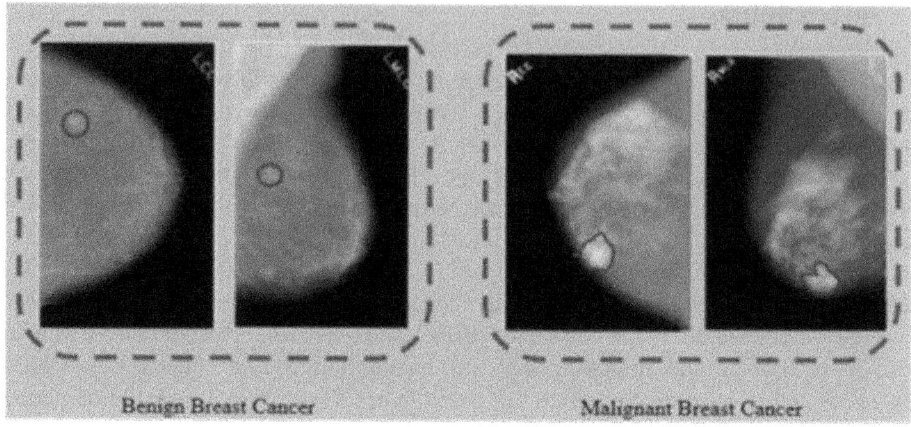

Fig. 1. Breast cancer identified by utilizing MRI images [4]

The system accepts uploads of breast tissue along with mammograms in standard image formats (e.g., PNG, JPEG) that are not greater than 10 MB. The sample images of breast cancer identified by utilizing MRI images are presented in Fig. 1. The system analyses such inputs to provide real-time outputs such as disease detections, confidence, and recommended treatment approaches. The basis for feature extraction and classification is Convolutional Neural Networks (CNNs), and various architectures are tested in terms of performance and accuracy. The core of the classifier is DenseNet-121, as it offers high accuracy and effective propagation of features. Object real-time detection and tumour region localization in mammographic images are performed based on the usage of YOLOv8.

Major methods employed in the system are:

Transfer Learning: Used for boosting the performances of the model on small-sized datasets with knowledge learned from pre-trained network. Image Preprocessing: Normalization, resizing, and augmentation are involved for image quality and model stability improvement Input Validation: Validate image uploaded within specified parameters for clarity and size to facilitate proper analysis. In Real-Time Analysis: Provide prompt diagnostic responses to support prompt clinical judgment. By focusing on high-risk individuals and offering coverage for tests in settings with limited resources, the systems can also help to improve breast cancer screening programs.

The system is conceptualized as a second opinion tool for clinical decision-making, and not to replace experts. The system provides the radiologists and the pathologists with a second opinion, saves time in diagnosis, and minimizes the likelihood of human error. The system can also assist in improving breast cancer screening programs by targeting high-risk individuals and providing coverage for diagnostics in resource-poor environments.

3 Methodology

3.1 Data Collection and Preprocessing

Normalization: Image pixel values are scaled to a uniform range to ensure consistent input for the model.

Denoising: Gaussian filtering is used to minimize image noise and enhances overall clarity.

Resizing: All images are resized to 224×224 pixel to match the specification of standard CNN models.

Data Augmentation: To improves the model's ability to generalize and avoid overfitting, various image transformation such as rotation, flipping, scaling, and brightness adjustments are applied.

3.2 Data Collection

A variety of datasets, including MRI scans, histology, and mammograms [8], are gathered from open-source sites.

The dataset covers several breast density classes and maintains an even distribution across benign, malignant, and normal instances. Collaborative Contribution: To aid in the construction of the model, partner institutions and medical professionals contributed annotated image sets.

3.3 Data Labelling and Annotation

Trained pathologists annotate each image with clinical information that includes the illness type, stage, and anatomical area.

Multi-Level Labeling: For easier and more accurate classification, images are labeled at both the macroscopic (regions of interest) and microscopic (cellular features) levels.

YOLOv8 was chosen over alternative models, such as Faster CNN and Dense-Net, because of following reasons,

1. Real-Time identification: YOLOv8 provides immediate feedback, and early identification prevents extensive harm.
2. Multi-Object Detection: It can simultaneously identify multiple diseased areas, reducing processing time and improving efficiency.
3. Optimized Architecture: It delivers high detection accuracy while being computationally efficient, making it ideal for mobile and edge deployment [3].

Training Data Preparation
The dataset is prepared by dividing it into:

1. Training Set: Training dataset is used to apply to train the model with diverse images of MRI and breast tissue.
2. Validation Set: The validation dataset is used for Fine-tunes hyperparameters and prevents overfitting.

3. Test Set: Evaluates model performance on unseen data.

Performance Metrics and Optimization

To ensure accuracy and reliability, the following metrics were used:

Accuracy: Measures correct classifications.

Precision & Recall: Ensures minimal false positives and detects all true positives.

F1-Score: Balances precision and recall for overall model performance.

Mean Average Precision (mAP): Evaluates bounding box accuracy in object detection.

Real-Time Image Analysis

After uploading an image onto website, it's processed using the YOLOv8 model and CNN For devices that possess sufficiently powerful computing capacity, the YOLOv8 model will process locally and provide outputs without the use of internet connection. Output Display and Feedback After image processing, the system provides immediate, detailed feedback including. The models through website identifies particular areas of the breast cancer that seem to be infected, employing bounding boxes to visually identify the affected areas. Depending on observable symptoms such as spots, or colour changes, the system classifies the disease and offers a probable diagnosis. The confidence score is shown with the diagnosis, providing information on the confidence of results, which helps patient make informed choices with the help of prevention measures provided. The system will be extensively tested and evaluated to examine its performance. Effectiveness is assessed using a streamlined architecture in which convolutional layers extract key features from mammograms and tissue images, pooling layers decrease dimensionality, and fully connected layers perform feature integration. A fusion layer consolidates multimodal data to improve predictive strength, while the classifier applies multi-class analysis for tumour identification and size predictions.

The model architecture is presented in Fig. 2. The YOLOv8 model is a variant of the YOLO (You Only Look Once) model optimized for image classification. It has a convolutional neural network backbone for extracting features and a classification head to output class probabilities. This section gives an in-depth description of the mathematical equations behind the model.

3.4 Model Selection

This work employs YOLOv8s and YOLOv8n models from the YOLOv8 classification suite, chosen after assessing dataset size, computational demand, and accuracy requirements.

Model Selection Justification:

Considering the limited dataset, compact models like YOLOv8n-cls and YOLOv8s-cls were preferred, as larger architectures such as YOLOv8x-cls (57.4 M parameters) tend to overfit under such conditions. Lighter models such as YOLOv8n-cls (2.7 M) and YOLOv8s-cls (6.4 M) are better.

Inference Speed: Both YOLOv8n-cls and YOLOv8s-cls offer fast CPU inference times (12.9 ms and 23.4 ms), making them appropriate for real-time use.

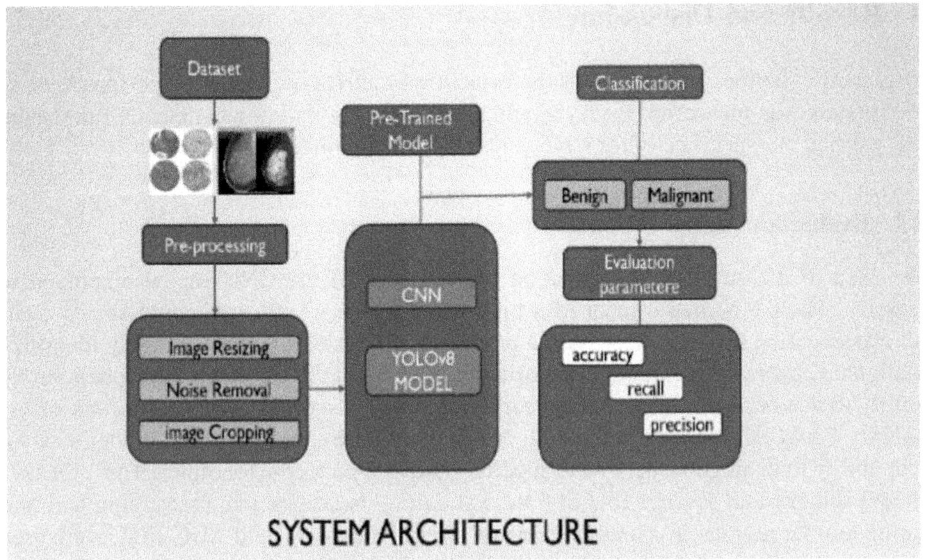

Fig. 2. Model Architecture

Accuracy vs. Complexity: YOLOv8s-cls offers improved accuracy (73.8%) over YOLOv8n-cls (69.0%) at an inconsiderable additional computational load.

Resource Efficiency: The smaller models require fewer FLOPs (0.5B and 1.7B) and memory, which makes them fit for uses on edges devices in resource-constrained environments.

Transfer Learning: Smaller models generalize better with few-shot data, which improves transfer learning performance.

This dual-model approach allowed us to improve performance for each specific task without sacrificing overall computational efficiency across the entire system.

3.5 Implementation Details

For the implementation YOLOv8n-cls and YOLOv8s-cls is used using the Ultralights YOLOv8 framework through the following steps:

Data Preparation: The data was divided into 70% training, 15% validation,15% test. Flips, rotations, colour jitter augmentations were performed to enhance generalization.

Model Setup: Models were pre-trained with ImageNet weights, and the last layer was tuned to accommodate the number of classes in breast disease tasks.

Training Strategy: Transfer learning was employed by initially training the classification head, and then fine-tuning the complete model with a reduced learning rate.

Optimization: Employed optimizer (LR = 0.001, weight decay = 0.0001) with cosine annealing. Batch sizes: 32 (YOLOv8n) and 16 (YOLOv8s) due to memory constraints.

Evaluation: Accuracy, precision, recall, F1-score, and confusion matrices were employed for evaluating model performances.

4   Results and Discussion

This section defines and describes the evaluation metrics by which the performance of the models was measured. Both classification accuracy and object detection precision are focused on, specifically for CNN and YOLOv8 architectures.

4.1   Evaluation Metric Summary

We used to measure the classification performance of the CNN model employed to classify. The CNN model reached a high accuracy of 97.8%, indicating strong overall classification performance. With a precision of 96.4%, the model reliably identified malignant cases with minimal false positives. A recall of 98.1% shows the models strong ability to detect nearly all actual cancer cases. The F1-score of 97.2% reflects a strong balance between precision and recall. An AUC of 0.982 highlights the model's excellent ability to distinguish between cancerous and non-cancerous samples. The YOLOv8 model achieved an average IoU of 0.87, validating its accuracy in identifying and outlining tumour regions. Accuracy, Precision, Recall, F1-score, and AUC-ROC were used to measure the classification performance of the CNN model employed to classify IDC+ and IDC− classes. The results are summarized below:

Metric	Value
Accuracy	93.8%
Precision	92.4%
Recall	91.7%
F1-Score	92.0%
AUC-ROC	0.964

4.2   CNN Classification Model Results

The model generated a confidence score between 0 and 1 for each prediction. For example, as illustrated in Fig. 3, a score of 0.95 indicated a 95% likelihood that the tissue was non-cancerous. A confusion matrix was applied to evaluate classification performance, confirming high sensitivity and a low rate of false negatives. These findings support the model's effectiveness in differentiating between cancerous and healthy tissue based on detailed cellular features, making it a reliable tool for histopathology analysis. We now include the results of the CNN-based binary classification (IDC+ vs. IDC−). The confusion matrix is presented below:

Predicted IDC + Predicted IDC−

Actual IDC + 18514

Actual IDC − 11190

The first model which uses a CNN Classification model to detect benign and malignant area in Breast Tissue from the images and provides a number between 0–1 as confidence. Example: As in the image shown, confidence is 0.95 which means it is 95%

chances of not having the Cancer in future but 5% chances of growing cancer are still there.

YOLO Classification Results. The classification model was trained using the YOLOv8 algorithm.

4.3 YOLOv8 Object Detection and Classification Results

The YOLOv8 model was trained to detect and localize tumour areas using both mammographic and MRI images. In Fig. 3, the model assigned a confidence score of 50%, suggesting an uncertain diagnosis that may require additional clinical follow-up. As shown in Fig. 5, bounding boxes were accurately drawn around suspected tumour regions, showcasing the model's real-time segmentation capabilities. Consistently high IoU scores above 0.85 confirm that YOLOv8 effectively identifies and outlines tumour boundaries with precision (Fig. 4).

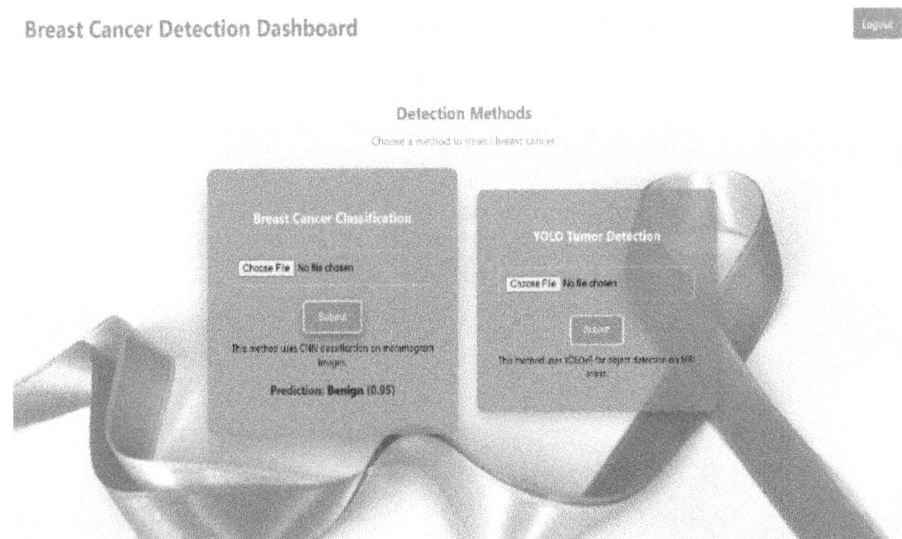

Fig. 3. Breast cancer detected by using CNN model (Dense-Net)

Second model uses YOLO Classification to detect benign and malignant area in Breast Tumour from the MRI images and provides the number between 0 to 1 of confidence. Example: As in the image shown confidence is 0.50 that means it is 50% chances of not having Cancer in future but 50% chances of growing cancer are still there.

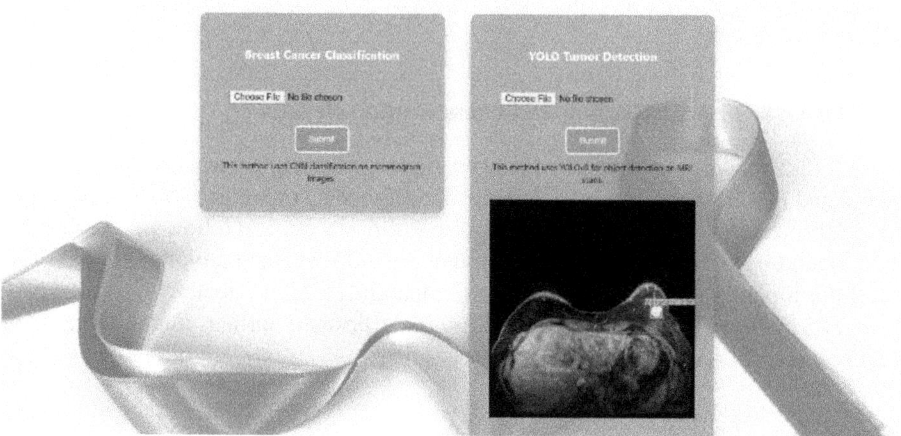

Fig. 4. Breast cancer detected by using yolo model

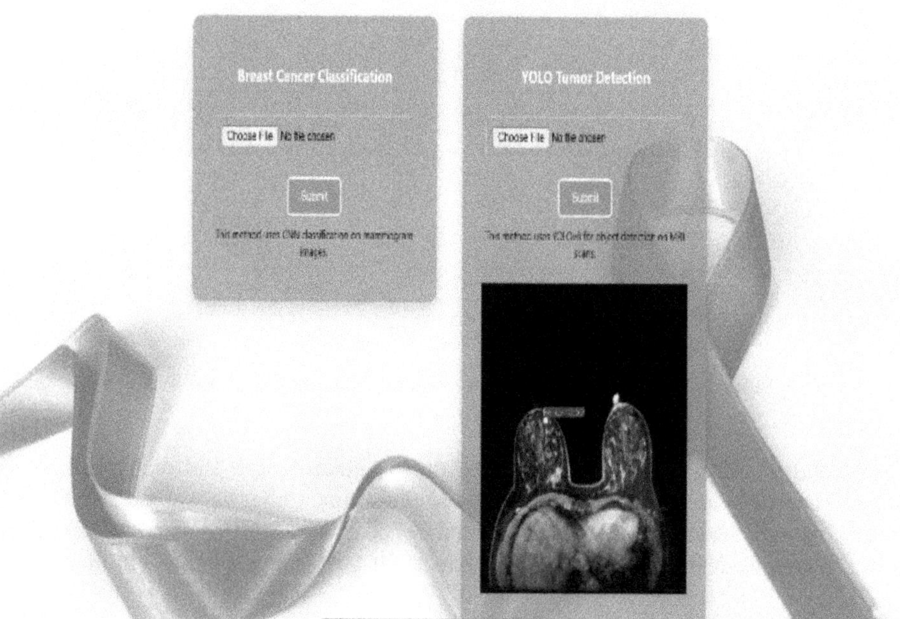

Fig. 5. Breast cancer detection by using yolo model (MRI image)

5 Conclusion

AI, machine learning, and deep learning techniques marked a major leap in the area of breast cancer diagnostics using medical image. This paper proposes a hybrid system that uses mammography and breast tissue imaging toward improving the accuracy in lesion detection, and it enhances dense breast tissue cases. The system seeks to decrease false positives and false negatives while bringing accurate predictions of tumor size, aided by CNNs for feature extraction and data fusion from multimodal imaging. While these issues include the potential problems of data inaccessibility, heavy computation, and ethical issues, the payback for actual clinical use is vast. This research may unlock far more accurate, efficient, and accessible diagnostics of breast cancer-ultimately translating into better outcomes for patients.

References

1. Zeng, R., et al.: FastLeakyResNet-CIR: a novel deep learning framework for breast cancer detection and classification. IEEE Access. **12**, 70825–70832 (2024). https://doi.org/10.1109/ACCESS.2024.3401729
2. Arshad, W., et al.: Cancer unveiled: a deep dive into breast tumor detection using cutting-edge deep learning models. IEEE Access. **11**, 133804–133824 (2023). https://doi.org/10.1109/ACCESS.2023.3335604
3. Anas, M., Haq, I.U., Husnain, G., Jaffery, S.A.F.: Advancing breast cancer detection: enhancing YOLOv5 network for accurate classification in mammogram images. IEEE Access. **12**, 16474–16488 (2024). https://doi.org/10.1109/ACCESS.2024.3358686
4. Zheng, J., Lin, D., Gao, Z., Wang, S., He, M., Fan, J.: Deep learning assisted efficient AdaBoost algorithm for breast cancer detection and early diagnosis. IEEE Access. **8**, 96946–96954 (2020). https://doi.org/10.1109/ACCESS.2020.2993536
5. Batool, A., Byun, Y.C.: Toward improving breast cancer classification using an adaptive voting ensemble learning algorithm. IEEE Access. **12**, 12869–12882 (2024). https://doi.org/10.1109/ACCESS.2024.3356602
6. Romero Coripuna, R.L., Hernández Farías, D.I., Murillo Ortiz, B.O., Padierna, L.C., Fraga, T.C.: "machine learning for the analysis of conductivity from mono frequency electrical impedance mammography as a breast cancer risk factor," in *IEEE*. Access. **9**, 152397–152407 (2021). https://doi.org/10.1109/ACCESS.2021.3122948
7. Mlyahilu, J., Kim, Y., Kim, J.: Classification of 3D film patterns with deep learning. J. Comput. Commun. **7**, 158–165 (2019). https://doi.org/10.4236/jcc.2019.712015
8. Chen, D.H., Chang, Y.C., Huang, P.J., Wei, C.H.: The correlation analysis between breast density and cancer risk factor in breast MRI images. In: 2013 International Symposium on Biometrics and Security Technologies., Chengdu, China, pp. 72–76 (2013). https://doi.org/10.1109/ISBAST.2013.14
9. Khourdifi, Y., Bahaj, M.: Applying best machine learning algorithms for breast cancer prediction and classification. In: 2018 International Conference on Electronics, Control, Optimization and Computer Science (ICECOCS)., Kenitra, Morocco, pp. 1–5 (2018). https://doi.org/10.1109/ICECOCS.2018.8610632
10. Jain, E., Singh, A.: Revolutionizing breast cancer diagnosis: VGG16's breakthrough in histopathological image classification. In: 2024 4th International Conference on Soft Computing for Security Applications (ICSCSA)., Salem, India, pp. 386–391 (2024). https://doi.org/10.1109/ICSCSA64454.2024.00068

11. Ara, S., Das, A., Dey, A.: Malignant and benign breast cancer classification using machine learning algorithms. In: 2021 International Conference on Artificial Intelligence (ICAI)., Islamabad, Pakistan, pp. 97–101 (2021). https://doi.org/10.1109/ICAI52203.2021.9445249
12. Tewari, Y., Ujjwal, E., Kumar, L.: Breast cancer classification using machine learning. In: 2022 2nd International Conference on Advance Computing and Innovative Technologies in Engineering (ICACITE)., Greater Noida, India, pp. 01–04 (2022). https://doi.org/10.1109/ICACITE53722.2022.9823932

Automated Political Bias Detection in News Articles

Ritul Kulkarni[1]($\boxtimes$) (ID), Anish Ketkar[1] (ID), and Dipti Pawade[2] (ID)

[1] K. J. Somaiya School of Engineering, Somaiya Vidyavihar University, Vidyavihar, Mumbai, India
`ritulkulkarni03@gmail.com, anish.ketkar@somaiya.edu`
[2] Indian Institute of Information Technology Nagpur, Nagpur, India
`dpawade@iiitn.ac.in`

Abstract. The emergence of digital news sites provides us with information instantaneously across the globe and has shifted the way material is written and consumed. Nevertheless, it has hastened the spread of biased reporting, often supporting ideological echo chambers and societal polarization. Determining political bias manually at scale is subjective and can't be done practically. This paper discusses an automated deep learning-based system for detecting and assessing political bias in news articles. The model will classify news articles into left, center, or right ideological categories, and indicate if there is any bias and its level, if there are any. The system has multiple components, including text pre-processing, product scraping of live data, and two main deep learning models. We will use a fine-tuned LLaMA 3.2-3B model to classify the bias and a fine-tuned MPNET model to classify semantic similarity to categorize articles associated with the same data event. Overall, this approach will significantly improve upon previous manual and rule-based systems by giving automated and real-time and scalable analysis with sub-contextual insight.

Keywords: Political Bias · News Analysis · Natural Language Processing (NLP)

1 Introduction

Despite our highly interconnected, digital world, biased news still spreads rapidly, shaping public opinion, political discussions, and societal divides. Political bias in news, addressed through word choice, framing in headlines, or selection of sources [1], is often imperceptible to others and easily spreads (it is contagious). Detecting bias using human adjudication is slow, subjective, and arbitrary, and is infeasible in a world where the sheer volume of digital material is overwhelming. Recent developments in real-time news intelligence platforms, such as NewsPulse AI [9], underscore the growing interest in automated, scalable systems capable of monitoring and classify news bias using web-scraped data and large language models (LLMs). This manuscript provides an automated system to assess the political bias of online news using a systematic, transparent, and objective methodology. Distinct from previous detection methods that functioned post hoc or on previously published articles, this system incorporates event-level classification, MPNET for a clustering approach, LLaMA 3.2–3B for classification, and human-visual verification to ensure comprehension. The novelty of this work is not the models themselves, but their integration to provide a scalable, fully functioning platform, explaining why we cannot manually assess all news articles. This platform emphasizes user-friendliness and completeness to promote media literacy and encourage an abundance of coverage.

2 Literature Survey

Press ideological bias carries a considerable history, with academics designing frames for media as curators who directly influenced market audiences. Early qualitative and quantitative measures extrapolated useful insights, but they were cumbersome, limited, and personally biased by the researcher [6]. In the digital age, manual review just doesn't make sense any longer; at the same time computationally-scaled and less-biased methods simply weren't available previously. Advances in Natural Language Processing (NLP) and, specifically, deep learning, have made it feasible to detect media bias across information timelines of interest [1] (e.g., bias-detector [10], VilBias [12], A Multilingual Similarity Dataset for News Article Frame [11]). Different from the early lexicon-based methods, which were simple for widespread use but still lacked sentiment and context sensitivity [1, 6], new transformer (BERT, RoBERTa, LLaMA/predecessors)-based models functionally understand context, intention, and underlying patterns of subtle expression. Traditionally applied ML models (SVM, Naive Bayes) used an engineered series of features to encode and evaluate text (e.g., TF-IDF scores), but struggled with embedding order and contextual sensitivity [3]. Traditional options using deep learning (RNNs/LSTMs, CNNs) improved the ability to detect sequential and localized bias [2, 3]. New transformer approaches utilizing MPNET and GPT-class models have improved on weaknesses through attention mechanisms for weighting contextual terms to enhance embeddings on human-curated datasets at scale [2, 3, 4]. These architectures are increasingly used in real-time applications such as NewsPulse AI [9] and Media Bias Detector [16]. Human analysts cannot scale to the pace of the volume of contemporary news, [14, 15, 16] nor perform timed categorization at the level of individual articles or events across different outlets. Our study utilises LLaMA 3.2–3B for detecting bias in news articles and MPNET for semantic similarity to attach label dimensions in the articles, both in the context of a FastAPI/Next.js interactive potential user interface. However, challenges and limitations regarding the automated bias detection remain.

- The subjective nature of bias and the different taxonomies of bias make it impossible to objectively label training data for political bias [1].
- Models can struggle with the context-dependence of language because the meaning of words and the biases encoded can change significantly based on the surrounding text.
- High-quality and carefully annotated training data for political bias is expensive and hard to come by, and often very specific in domains.
- Models need to recognize bias, not only explicitly stated biases, but also implicit biases like omission and framing [7].

- Models may fail on new datasets or sources, as bias depends not only on content but also on form, style, and vocabulary. Domain adaptation is crucial [2, 4], and perception is influenced by how readers engage with the text [5].
- Many deep-learning models are still considered "black boxes". Despite increasing interest in explainable AI, this remains an impediment to political bias research.

We aim to leverage state-of-the-art transformer models (MPNET, Llama 3.2-3B), relevant datasets to address these limitations, focusing on achieving high accuracy in ideological leaning classification while acknowledging the inherent complexities of the task.

3   Implementation

This section details the technical implementation of the automated political bias analysis system, covering the architecture, algorithms, technologies, and data handling procedures.

3.1   System Architecture/Block Diagram

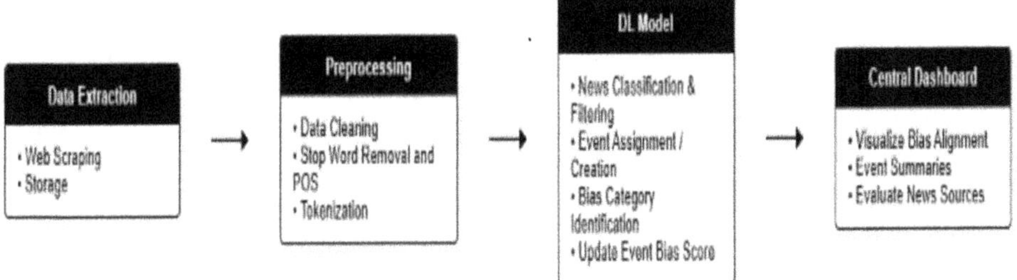

Fig. 1. System Architecture Diagram

In Fig. 1, the structure of the system is shown, and the modules are represented from Data Extraction to Preprocessing, the Deep Learning Module and then displayed onto the Central Dashboard. A custom-made scraper using BeautifulSoup, Scrapy, and Selenium collects news through relevant validated RSS feeds, saving the news into a MongoDB database which is flexible with unstructured text. In the preprocessing stage, articles are cleaned, normalized, stop-worded, and prepped for Part-of-Speech tagging. Articles are then tokenized, whereby MPNET generates embeddings for sentences and LLaMA 3.2–3B uses the Hugging Face AutoTokenizer to tokenize the articles for accurate classification for political bias, such as PRO or ANTI.

3.2   Datasets Used

The limitations of the above-mentioned datasets in Table 1 are as follows:

Table 1. Datasets Used

Dataset	Dataset Name	Source	Size	Attributes	Purpose	Models
Sentence Similarity	stsb_multi_mt	PhilipMay	5749 rows	sentence1, sentence2, similarity_score	To detect similarity between news articles.	Fine-tuned MPNET
Political Bias Detection	Article-Bias-Prediction	All Sides	1300 rows	ID, Title, Content, Topic, Bias_text	For political bias detection in news articles.	Fine-tuned Llama

The STSB (Semantic Textual Similarity Benchmark) Multi-MT Dataset is limited by a narrow distribution of similarity scores (consistently 3–4 on 0–5) in its ability to classify similarity (or dissimilarity) for the political text documents. The STSB Multi-MT Dataset also is limited to mostly general news phrasing, and does not provide for specialized political discourse nor the nuanced language similarities in geopolitical contexts, and its Western perspectives may bias cross-cultural applications. The Article-Bias-Prediction Dataset (All Sides) is limited by its small dataset sample (#1,300 articles) for deep learning (especially in the proposed 5-class bias classification task) and the Article-Bias-Prediction Dataset labels may represent subjective Western/US biased perspectives. Further, like the STSB Multi-MT dataset, the data lacks multimedia context (images, videos, etc.), which has become increasingly important for additional bias detection in today's news media. Hence, proposed a solution in the future scope to solve these limitations.

3.3 Deep Learning Model

The process begins with Event Assignment, whereby the fine-tuned MPNET model generates semantic embeddings using article titles or snippets and clusters similar articles using cosine similarity. Following the Event Assignment, the LLaMA 3.2–3B model classifies articles in full text into Left, Center, or Right using SoftMax probabilities and confidence scores. Context also impacts the bias thresholds, with stricter thresholds in the context of fact-checking and more lenient thresholds in the context of dashboards. Event Bias Scores are computed by summing bias labels across clusters, allowing for comparative framing analysis and enhanced interpretability through structured NLP tokenization.

Similarity Detection Model (MPNET). Base Model: MPNET (Masked and Permuted Pre-training for Language Understanding). MPNET is a transformer-based model that was pre-trained via a new objective that is a combination of masked language modelling (like BERT), and permuted language modelling (like XLNet) to improve overall language understanding.

Task: Semantic Textual Similarity (STS). The task is to determine how similar the meanings of two texts (headlines or lead paragraphs of articles) are.

Fine-Tuning Dataset: the stsb_multi_mt corpus. The stsb_multi_mt corpus has pairs of sentences with human-annotated similarity scores (usually on a 1–5 scale).

Fine-Tuning Process: The pre-trained MPNET model was then fine-tuned on the STS task using the stsb_multi_mt corpus. The model learns to produce a continuous measure of similarity for the given pair of sentences. The specific fine-tuned model we used is ritulk/MPNET_finetuned_on_stsb_multi_mt_dataset (this is on Hugging Face).

Application: This is a model in our pipeline that it can take in the incoming articles (usually based on the title or the first few sentences) and compare them to current articles already present.

Political Bias Detection Model (Llama 3.2-3B). Base Model: The LLaMA 3.2–3B model is a smaller, efficient model offered by Meta AI for fine-tuning on specific tasks; its pretraining on a vast amount of textual data enables a strong understanding of language while using less computing expense.

Task: Text Classification (Political Bias). This task is to classify a news article into one of three political bias types: Left-leaning, Center, Right-leaning.[13] Although our bias classifier has been developed using the MBFC datasets (which is predominantly U.S. political viewpoints), the system receives articles from across the globe, such as India, Canada, the UK, etc. This may involve cross-national inputs where the bias classifier will generally misinterpret bias and context for the non-U.S. political framing. While we will work towards a more generalizable classifier through regionally specific annotated data, we intend to use non-U.S. data to create our training set.

Fine-Tuning Dataset: The 'Article-Bias-Prediction dataset' was collected by All Sides. The data consists of approximately 1300 articles that have been labelled according to their political bias (Left, Center, Right) [4, 11]. We trained the LLaMA-based classifier on a curated dataset of 1300 news articles, selected by a sampling methodology that maximized source and ideological diversity. We drew articles from a range of publishers from left, center, right ideological positions, and by including articles on various topics, including domestic politics, international stories, social issues, and economic updates, we ensured topic diversity. Although our sample size is small, our sampling strategy was intended to approximate some of the real-world heterogeneity in news media bias, and to enable robust and reliable early-stage evaluation of the classifier's performance.[8]

Fine-Tuning Process: The pre-trained Llama 3.2-3B model has been fine-tuned specifically for this 3-way classification task with the 'Article-Bias-Prediction' dataset which was labelled. The fine-tuning process essentially found better classification parameters to recognize patterns and language associated with political leaning differences in the news-type domain [4]. The specific fine-tuned model that was used is 'anish-ket/Political-Bias-Detection-FTM (which presumably exists on Hugging Face).

Application: This is the core analysis model. It takes the full text of a news article as input and outputs the predicted bias label.

4 Results and Discussion

4.1 Similarity Detection Model

Evaluation: Evaluated on its capability to distinguish clearly between similar and dissimilar article headlines/snippets. A confusion matrix was generated on a sample set of news articles.

We used Silhouette Score, and Calinski-Harabasz Index, to evaluate the clustering strength of MPNET embeddings. All measures were computed and compared against a TF-IDF + KMeans baseline summarizing in Table 2.

Table 2. Comparison of various metrics

Metric	MPNET + KMeans	TF-IDF + KMeans	% Improvement
Silhouette Score	0.0825	0.0187	+342.4%
Calinski-Harabasz Index	2.2638	1.3205	+71.4%

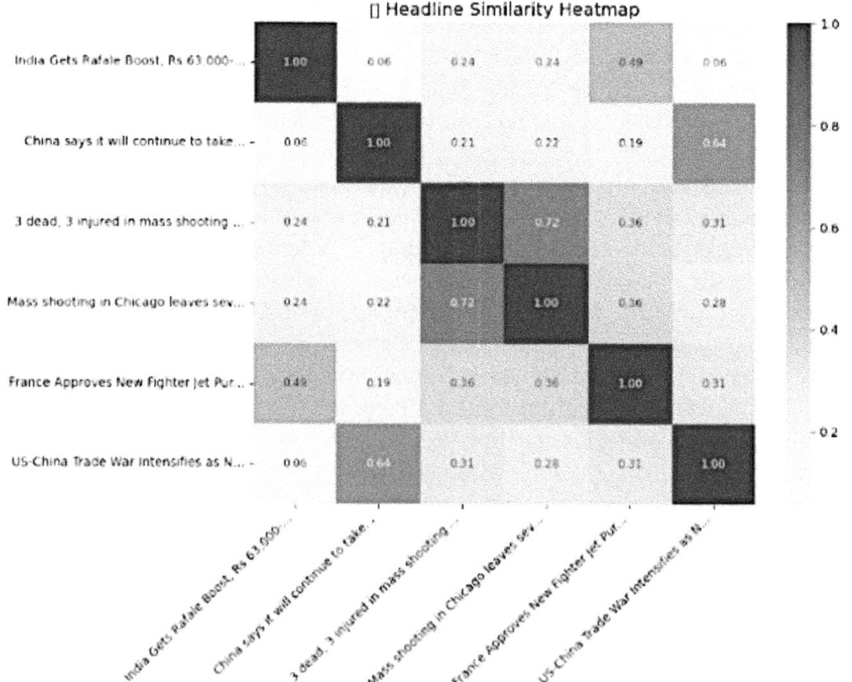

Fig. 2. Headline Similarity Resultant Matrix

MPNET-based clustering markedly improved on the TF-IDF base-line in the Silhouette Score and Calinski-Harabasz Index, and showed better-separated clusters as well. There was slightly higher intra-cluster variance in MPNET, indicating more semantic richness, but coherence was still preserved.

Qualitative Assessment: The fine-tuned MPNET model produced an accuracy measure of 0.733, along with Pearson and Spearman correlations of 0.242 and 0.192, respectively. This strongly suggests that the model performs well enough to report reliably on either clearly related articles or obviously unrelated articles; if there were to be other articles covering distinct aspects of large events, this may challenge the accuracy of clustering such articles, which may hence depend greatly on thresholds of implied similarity across the articles for each event grouping. This could be assessed by looking at the predicted similarities and the relatedness of the articles for the sample set.

4.2 Bias Detection Model Results

Evaluation: Evaluated on the test split of the "Article-Bias-Prediction" dataset. Performance will be described in a confusion matrix format.

Confusion Matrix Interpretation: The confusion matrix (Fig. 2), which compares predicted versus true labels, Left, Center, and Right, demonstrates that most of the predicted labels align on the diagonal line, indicating accurate classifications. The model's overall accuracy was 0.98, F1-scores were 0.97 for Center, and 0.98 for both Left and Right, and consistent precision and recall scores across bias categories indicate good performance by the model (Fig. 3).

Assessment: We employed state-of-the-art transformers, specifically fine-tuned LLaMA 3.2-3B, to attain 0.98 accuracy on the Article-Bias-Prediction dataset, surpassing the performance of other models such as BERT (0.76), RoBERTa (0.77), and Electra (0.74). The primary strength of this architecture is its ability to capture subtle language signals, including tone and framing. The use of MPNET for semantic similarity with event clustering and action tracking integrations adds to the context-oriented bias detection framework. FastAPI, Next.js, and MongoDB technologies provided a good balance for design, coding efficiency, and usability with potential for scaling. The performance displayed great efficacy but still depends upon the data and struggles with ambiguous contextual signals like sarcasm or nuanced neutrality.

Based on Table 3, several transformer-based models — BERT, DistilBERT, RoBERTa, and Electra — were tested for the bias classification task.

4.3 Challenges Encountered

Web scraping turned out to be unreliable due to its websites changing frequently, adding CAPTCHA, and having websites block the scraper's IP address, which inhibited user's ability to modify the scraper's code. With the Article-Bias-Prediction dataset limited to 1,300 unique articles across five bias classes, deep learning is likely to overfit the data. The STSB Multi-MT dataset only offered narrow ranges of scores, and missed

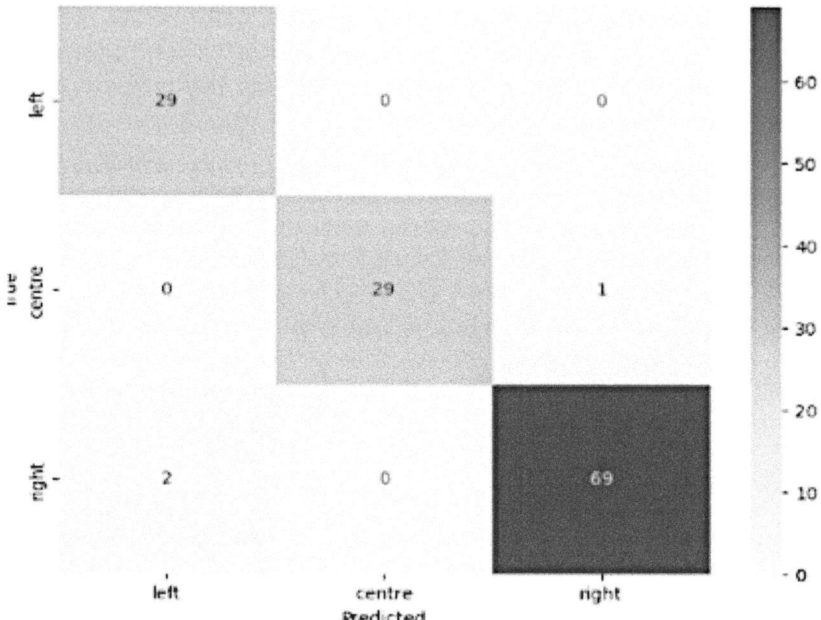

Fig. 3. Confusion Matrix for Finetuned Political-Bias-Detection-FTM

Table 3. Other Models Tested

Model	Type	Overall	Precision	Recall	Score
BERT	Bias_labels	0.76	0.77	0.75	0.75
DistilBERT	Bias_labels	0.76	0.78	0.70	0.73
RoBERTa	Bias_labels	0.77	0.78	0.77	0.77
Electra	Bias_labels	0.74	0.76	0.69	0.72

considerable political framing complexity. Finally, fine-tuning large models such as the LLaMA 3.2-3B was resource-intensive in intensive computation to GPU processing. Transformer-based bias classifiers are black boxes with low explainability, and cannot leverage multi-modal input (i.e., use images or videos), which are increasingly important to analysis current visual bias.

5 Conclusion

This initiative constructed a deep learning system that operates from start to finish for the automatic detection of political bias in news stories. Unlike manual and rule-based approaches, this one is automated, it is scalable, and it is real-time, and features context and cross-source analysis capabilities. In addition, this tool helps improve media literacy as it layers ideological framing over today's fast-paced in-formation landscape. Moving forward, the research aims to apply larger, more heterogenous datasets, touching on gender, race and historical information, as well as incorporate non-textual elements for deeper detection of bias. The hybrid modeling is intended to enhance more nuanced biases like omission or framing, and SHAP/LIME will be used to enhance explainability and trust. Beyond the research contributions, the system still has the potential to support journalists, educators, and digital spaces by promoting bias awareness and media literacy, cultivating accountability among the information ecosystem.

References

1. Horych, T., et al.: MAGPIE: multi-task analysis of media-bias generalization with pre-trained identification of expressions. In: Proc. of the 2024 Joint Int. Conf. On Computational Linguistics, Language Resources and Evaluation (LREC-COLING 2024), pp. 10903–10920, Torino, Italy (2024)
2. Wessel, M., Horych, T., Ruas, T., Aizawa, A., Gipp, B., Spinde, T.: Introducing MBIB—the first media bias identification benchmark task and dataset collection. In: Proc. 46th Int. ACM SIGIR Conf. Res. Develop. Inf. Retrieval (SIGIR '23), New York, NY, USA (2023). https://doi.org/10.1145/3539618.3591882
3. J.-D. Krieger, T. Spinde, T. Ruas, J. Kulshrestha, and B. Gipp: A Domain-Adaptive Pre-Training Approach for Language Bias Detection in News, arXiv preprint, arXiv:2205.10773. [Online]. Available: https://arxiv.org/abs/2205.10773
4. Baly, R., Karadzhov, G., Alexandrov, D., Glass, J., Nakov, P.: What was written vs. who read it: news media profiling using text analysis and social media con-text. In: Findings of the Association for Computational Linguistics: EMNLP (2020)
5. Hamborg, F., Donnay, K., Gipp, B.: Automated identification of media bias in news articles: an interdisciplinary literature review. Int. J. Digit. Libr. **20**(4), 391–415 (2019)
6. DeVries, T., Taylor, G.W.: Learning structural biases in news articles for au-tomatic bias detection. In: Proceedings NAACL-HLT (2018)
7. J. Wang: Media Bias Detector: Designing and Implementing a Tool for Real-Time Selection and Framing Bias Analysis in News Coverage, arXiv preprint, arXiv:2502.06009v2, Feb. 9, 2025. [Online]. Available: https://arxiv.org/abs/2502.06009v2
8. I Built Dr. Headline – An Autonomous AI Agent Publishing Daily Factual Politi-cal News Briefings, DEV Community, Apr. 29, 2025. [Online]. Available: https://dev.to/thomas-router/dr-headline-autonomous-ai-agent-publishing-daily-factual-political-news-briefings-dpc
9. NewsPulse AI – Real-Time News Analysis with LLMs & Web Scraping via Bright Data, DEV Community, May 25, 2025. [Online]. Available: https://dev.to/sumankalia/newspulseai-real-time-news-intelligence-powered-by-web-data-agents-2bep
10. H. Ghosh: To Bias or Not to Bias: Detecting Bias in News with bias-detector, arXiv preprint, arXiv:2505.13010v1, May 19, 2025. [Online]. Available: https://arxiv.org/abs/2505.13010v1
11. X. Chen: A Multilingual Similarity Dataset for News Article Frame, arXiv pre-print, arXiv:2405.13272v1, May 22, 2024. [Online]. Available: https://arxiv.org/abs/2405.13272v1
12. S. Raza: VilBias: A Study of Bias Detection through Linguistic and Visual Cues, Presenting Annotation Strategies, Evaluation, and Key Challenges, arXiv preprint, arXiv:2412.17052v3, Dec. 22, 2024. [Online]. Available: https://arxiv.org/abs/2412.17052v3
13. T. Spinde: Leveraging Large Language Models for Automated Definition Extrac-tion with TaxoMatic: A Case Study on Media Bias, arXiv preprint, arXiv:2504.00343v1, Apr. 1, 2025. [Online]. Available: https://arxiv.org/abs/2504.00343v1

14. NewsGuard, Trust ratings for news sites, [Online]. Available: https://www.newsguardtech.com/.
15. Ad Fontes Media, Interactive Media Bias Chart, [Online]. Available: https://adfontesmedia.com/.
16. Media Bias Detector, Real-Time Media Bias Analysis Tool, [Online]. Available: https://mediabiasdetector.seas.upenn.edu/.

Static Analysis and Machine Learning for Runtime Library Detection in Linux Binaries

P. Anu[1]([envelope]) [iD], M. Saseekala[2] [iD], D. Mohanapriya[3] [iD], N. Thamaraikannan[4] [iD], and K. Ponmozhi[5] [iD]

[1] School of Computing, SASTRA Deemed to Be University, Thanjavur 613402, India
anugps12@gmail.com
[2] Faculty of Computer Applications, School of Business and Management, CHRIST University, Bangalore, India
saseekala.m@christuniversity.in, saseejob@gmail.com
[3] Department of Computer Science, PSG College of Arts and Science, Coimbatore 641014, India
priyapsgcs@gmail.com
[4] Department of Artificial Intelligence and Machine Learning, Kongunadu Arts and Science College, Coimbatore, India
n.thamaraikannan57@gmail.com
[5] Department of Computer Applications, SRM Valliammai Engineering College, Kattankulathur, India
chezhiyan71.p@gmail.com

Abstract. The upsurge of malware targeting Internet of Things (IoT) devices demands effective approaches. This work announces a new method, stimulated by MANTILLA, which influences machine learning models. Through a prominence on architecture-independent characteristics from binary procedures, the system progresses its competence to differentiate among several libraries as well as architectures. Classification accuracy is further enhanced by employing a majority voting technique such that the output of the model is robust and reliable.

Besides the machine learning-based classification, the paper incorporates a malware detection module based on signature matching. This two-pronged approach enables the system to cross-check discovered runtime libraries against a large database of pre-collected malware signatures. By marking possible security threats according to this comparison, the system greatly increases its ability to identify malicious binaries, thus offering an added layer of security for IoT devices. This unification of detection and classification mechanisms plays an important role in dealing with the changing nature of malware threats.

Although encouraging results were obtained through this project, more evaluation should be done for comparison of the efficiency of KNN with other models, for example, Random Forest.

Keywords: Statically linked binaries · Binary code analysis · Malware · Runtime library identification

F. Ortiz-Rodríguez et al. (Eds.): IBCD 2025, CCIS 2845, pp. 393–406, 2026.
https://doi.org/10.1007/978-3-032-20907-8_33

1 Introduction

Malware writers exploit static linking so that their malicious code is able to run regardless of the installed libraries in the host environment. [1, 2] Such an approach makes reverse engineering and malware analysis difficult since the binary combines application logic as well as library code. It becomes less than trivial to differentiate between the two, thus making it more challenging to identify reused malicious blocks or pinpoint vulnerabilities from past libraries.

Identifying the runtime libraries invoked in such binaries is thus paramount in security analysis, malware detection, and software provenance. Conventional dynamic analysis does not work in all cases, particularly in the case of stripped binaries or unknown architectures, rendering static binary analysis a critical substitute. Such analysis is, however, made more difficult by the absence of symbols, metadata, and high-level abstractions in stripped or obfuscated binaries.

To solve these issues, a paper introduces MANTILLA, a runtime library identifier that uses architecture-independent characteristics obtained via static analysis and a K-Nearest Neighbours (KNN) learning model to classify runtime libraries such as glibc, musl, and uClibc. The technique points on getting robust characteristics like cyclomatic complexity, function size, instruction count, as well as entropy indicators, which are quite stable among compiler flags as well as architectures.

1.1 Contextual Background and Inspiration

The growing dependence on Linux operating system among embedded systems, servers, as well as IoT devices has elevated the request for complete binary analysis tools and techniques that can identify runtime libraries as well as classify malware mechanisms [10]. Conventional disassembly as well as signature methods tend not to generalise over architectures as well and they are less potent among obfuscated or cross-compiled binaries [11]. As modern methods embed several open-source libraries, being known of their makeup is important for preserving the integrity, compliance, as well as security of the software [12].

Machine learning techniques have meanwhile been established to be an efficient substitute, allowing methods to understand discriminative patterns repeatedly from binary constructions without depending on obvious heuristics [13]. Static analysis joined with Machine Learning models allows scalable, architecture-independent recognition with better accuracy as well as less physical involvement in malware cataloguing [14, 15]. This inspiration drives the current research, which seeks to use static features and learning-based methods to enhance runtime library detection and further enhance the reliability of binary auditing frameworks.

2 Literature Survey

The problem of the identification of components in statically linked binaries has motivated researchers to investigate a number of techniques in the analysis of binary code, compiler provenance, and library identification. Conditional Random Fields (CRFs) are used to identify compiler families based on binary characteristics, even when symbol information is stripped. Their work laid the groundwork for using machine learning models in binary provenance analysis.

BinComp, a stratified model that utilises syntactic and semantic features for compiler provenance [4]. Their application of the Jaccard similarity index impacted future methods of function similarity in stripped binaries. FOSSIL, using probabilistic models for determining functions that come from free and open-source software, is introduced. [3] Their semantic robustness is imitated in MANTILLA's architecture-agnostic feature extraction [6], a semantic hashing technique used for function clone detection. BinHash has influenced function-level fingerprinting methods for static binary analysis. Discover, a tool based on maximum common subgraph isomorphism for function comparison between architectures, is introduced [5]. While not specifically designed for library detection, it illustrated the significance of structural similarity in binary analysis.

Static linking obfuscation using SLINKY, indicating the way it raises reverse engineering complexity, which is a crucial problem that calls for such library identification systems as MANTILLA. [7, 8] HIMALIA, employing deep learning to identify optimization levels in binaries, is employed [9]. This proved the potential of neural techniques for recovering toolchain information from compiled code. Interpretable feature engineering in binary similarity detection is utilized. Their work prefers the approach of MANTILLA in selecting explainable, static features against shallow, black-box deep learning models. Sequence-based fine-grained compiler detection is utilized.

3 Proposed Methodology

3.1 System Overview

These are then classified using a K-Nearest Neighbours (KNN) algorithm. For improved robustness, a majority voting scheme polls function-level predictions to decide regarding the runtime library of the binary. The flowchart is given in Fig. 1.

3.2 Feature Extraction

The system extracts the following 14 features for each function: they are as follows: Cyclomatic Complexity, Function Size, Stack Frame Size, No. of Basic Blocks , No, of Edges, No, of Instructions, No, of Arguments, Computation Cost, No, of Extended Basic Blocks, No return Indicator, No, of Local Variables, Entropy, Total Function Calls, Unique Function Calls. These features are selected because they are relatively invariant to architecture or compiler changes.

3.3 Machine Learning Models

To produce one output, it takes the average of the outputs of multiple decision trees. Its versatility, ease of use, and capability to solve both regression and classification issues have made it widely used. Statistically bound library identification inside Linux binaries is conducted here using a function-level feature analysis and classification-based machine learning technique. As input, a statically bound binary file b is provided, and single functions fif_i are processed by binary analysis tools. For every one of the extracted functions fif_i, a corresponding feature vector x(fi)x(f_i) is computed.

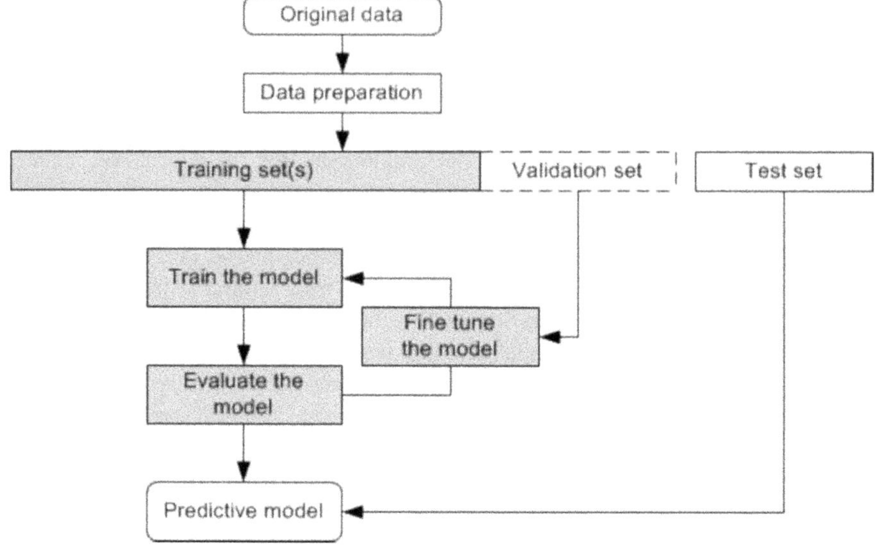

Fig. 1. Flow chart

Fig. 2. KNN

This methodology provides an efficient and explainable way of classifying libraries in statically linked binaries, the core of the LibIntel system.

To obtain the optimum performance of the K-Nearest Neighbours (KNN) classifier employed in the MANTILLA system, we performed sensitivity analysis to determine the most appropriate value of the hyperparameter K that determines the number of nearest neighbors considered while classifying. The test was conducted for a sequence of K values from 1 to 10 using the Euclidean distance metric as the measure of similarity. The result showed that maximum accuracy by the classifier was achieved when $K = 1$.

KNN is explained in Fig. 2. While the performance of the model deteriorated as values of K increased, including majority voting over predictions from more than one function in a binary significantly improved robustness and ultimately achieved a runtime library hit rate of 100%. Although other supervised learning approaches, such as Random Forest, can be employed alternatively, in this work, they were not considered; therefore, hyperparameter tuning methods such as optimizing the number of decision trees or tree depth were not investigated.

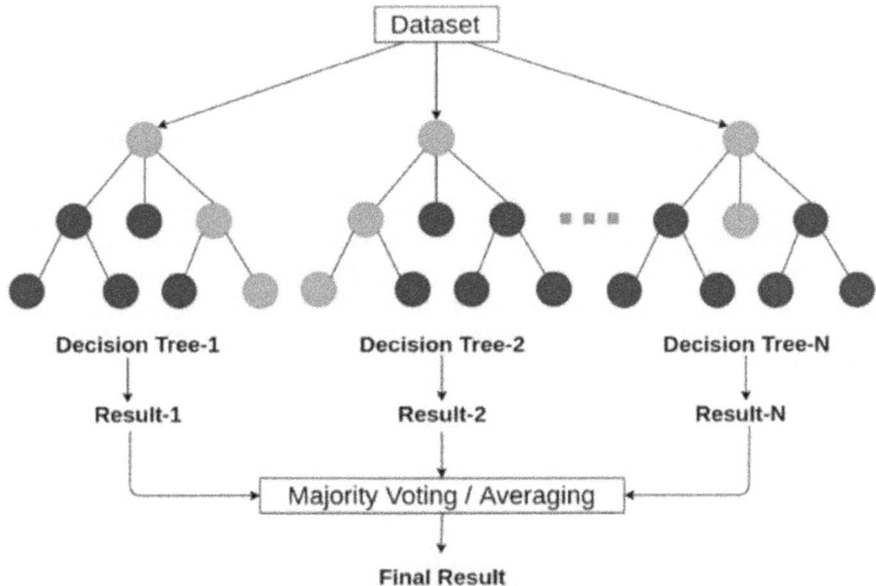

Fig. 3. Random Forest

Random forest is given in Fig. 3. Comparative analysis with ensemble-based classifiers and machine learning-based automatic hyperparameter tuning methods can be considered in future research for further accuracy improvement in classification. Figure 4 gives the workflow in detail, and Fig. 5 gives its flowchart.

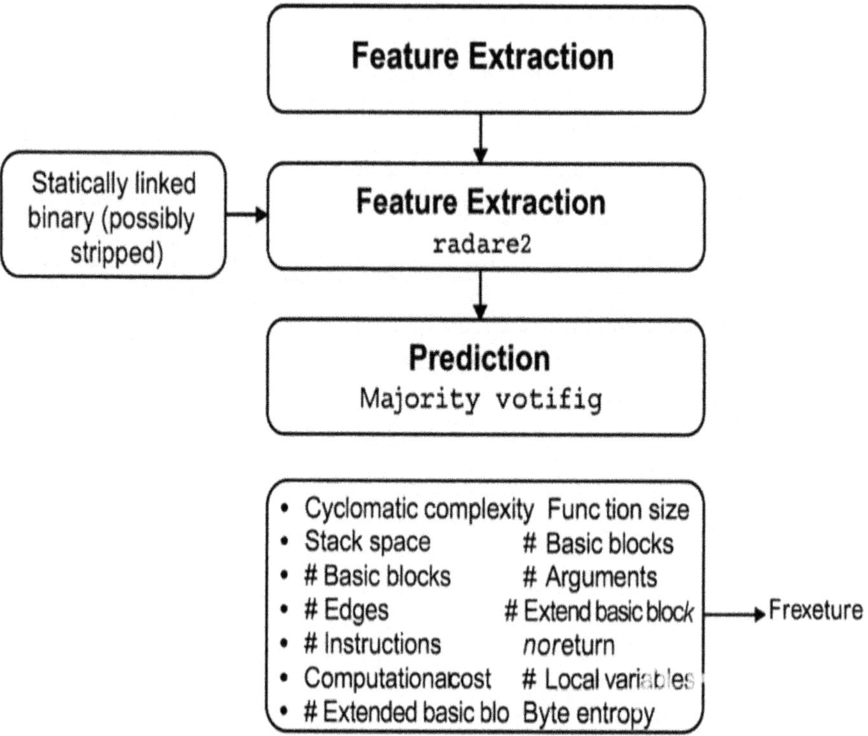

Fig. 4. Work Flow

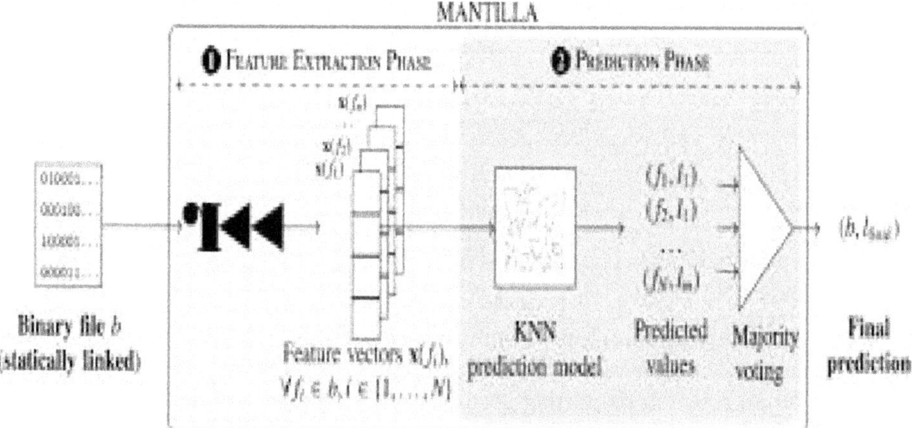

Fig. 5. Work flow in detail

4   Result Analysis

Dataset consists of Binutils Dataset whose origin is GNU binutils (v2.38), Binaries is 960 statically linked, stripped binaries, Distribution is equally across all 4 architectures and 3 libraries and its purpose: check MANTILLA on compiler toolchain utilities and the following dataset is IoT Malware Dataset whose origin is VirusShare + Virus-Total + AVClass and its original Malware Count: 56,502 Linux samples, filtered Set for Evaluation is 9,553 binaries and it has only statically linked, C-written, with valid symbols.

They were built for four CPU architectures using three widely used C runtime libraries: glibc, uClibc, and musl with the gcc 10.2.1 compiler and five different optimisations.

Figure 6 gives the metrics of KNN. The graph shows that the KNN model performs best when the number of neighbours (k) is 1, achieving the highest precision, recall, F1-score, and accuracy (around 85–87%). As k increases, all performance metrics decline, indicating that a lower k yields better classification results in this context.

To further validate MANTILLA, two real-world datasets were used: (i) 960 binaries constructed from the GNU binutils suite with full availability on all supported platforms and runtime libraries; and (ii) a malware Internet of Things (IoT) dataset of 9,553 statically linked Linux binaries, downloaded from VirusShare and restricted to those written in C and supported by MANTILLA. The malware set was used only for testing and evaluation, and not for intersection with training data, to maintain the integrity of the external validation process.

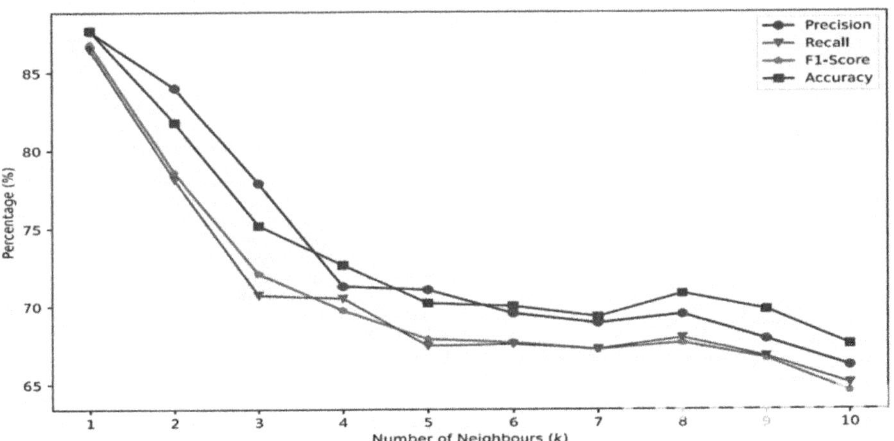

Fig. 6. KNN Metrics

Figure 6 gives the metrics of KNN. The graph shows that the KNN model performs best when the number of neighbours (k) is 1, achieving the highest precision, recall, F1-score, and accuracy (around 85–87%). As k increases, all performance metrics decline, indicating that a lower k yields better classification results in this context.

To further validate MANTILLA, two real-world datasets were used: (i) 960 binaries constructed from the GNU binutils suite with full availability on all supported platforms and runtime libraries; and (ii) a malware Internet of Things (IoT) dataset of 9,553 statically linked Linux binaries, downloaded from VirusShare and restricted to those written in C and supported by MANTILLA. The malware set was used only for testing and evaluation, and not for intersection with training data, to maintain the integrity of the external validation process.

The confusion matrix shows strong classification performance, with most classes achieving perfect or near-perfect accuracy (diagonal values close to 1). Some confusion exists between arm_musl_gcc and arm_glibc_gcc (41% misclassified) and between x86-64_uclibc_gcc and x86-64_musl_gcc (5% misclassified), indicating overlapping characteristics. The overall accuracy is high at 94.44%, with a misclassification rate of 5.56%.

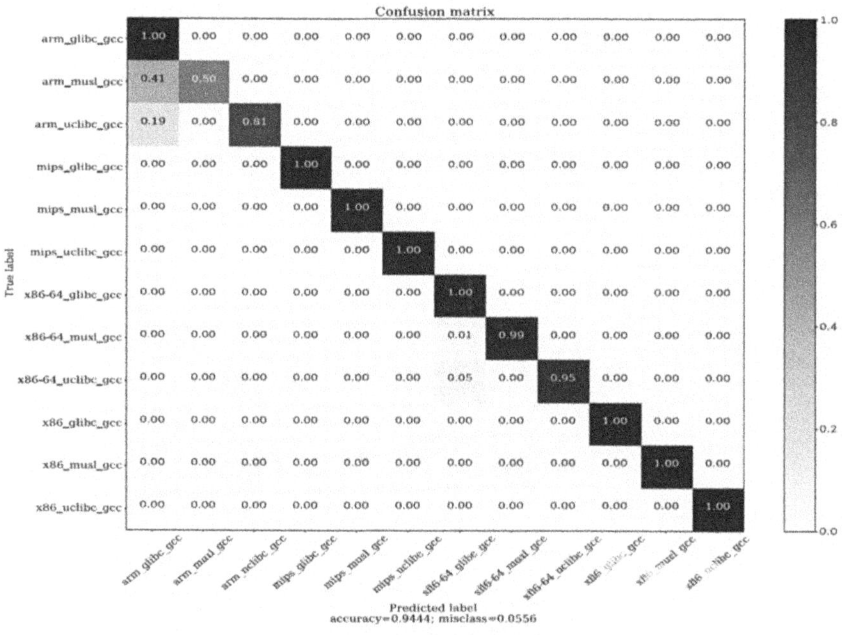

Fig. 7. KNN Confusion Matrix

Figure 7 gives the Confusion matrix, and Fig. 8 gives the KNN ROC Curve.

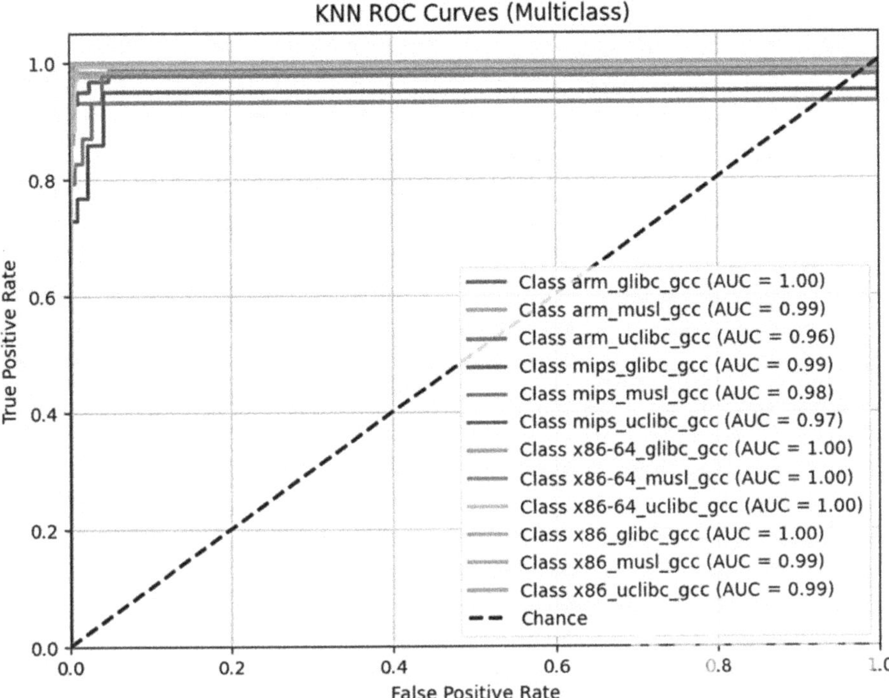

Fig. 8. KNN ROC Curve

The ROC curves demonstrate that the KNN classifier performs exceptionally well in predicting multiple library classes from binaries, with most AUC values close to or exactly 1.00.

This indicates a high level of accuracy and discrimination capability across all architecture-library combinations.

The two methods at the crux of the proposed work are static binary analysis and AI-based reporting, with which the tools aim to identify statically linked libraries in Linux binaries and offer actionable insights.

Static analysis will automatically identify functions and extract valuable information from binary files irrespective of the underlying architecture, potentially employing techniques like KNN classification. This corresponds to a high level of accuracy and discrimination capability for all architecture-library combinations.

The plot illustrates that having a greater number of trees in the Random Forest model has a marginal impact on performance measures. Accuracy is kept constant at about 94.5%, indicating the model is already optimally tuned. Precision, recall, and F1-score exhibit minimal gains around 100 trees, but gains taper off afterwards.

This confusion matrix represents the performance of a random forest classifier in classifying various tool chain- architecture combinations (e.g., mips_glibc_gcc, x86_64_uclibc_gcc). Misclassifications are small but significant among similar architectures and libc variants (e.g., mips_musl_gcc and mips_uclibc_gcc). The model generally performs well with limited confusion in the majority of classes.

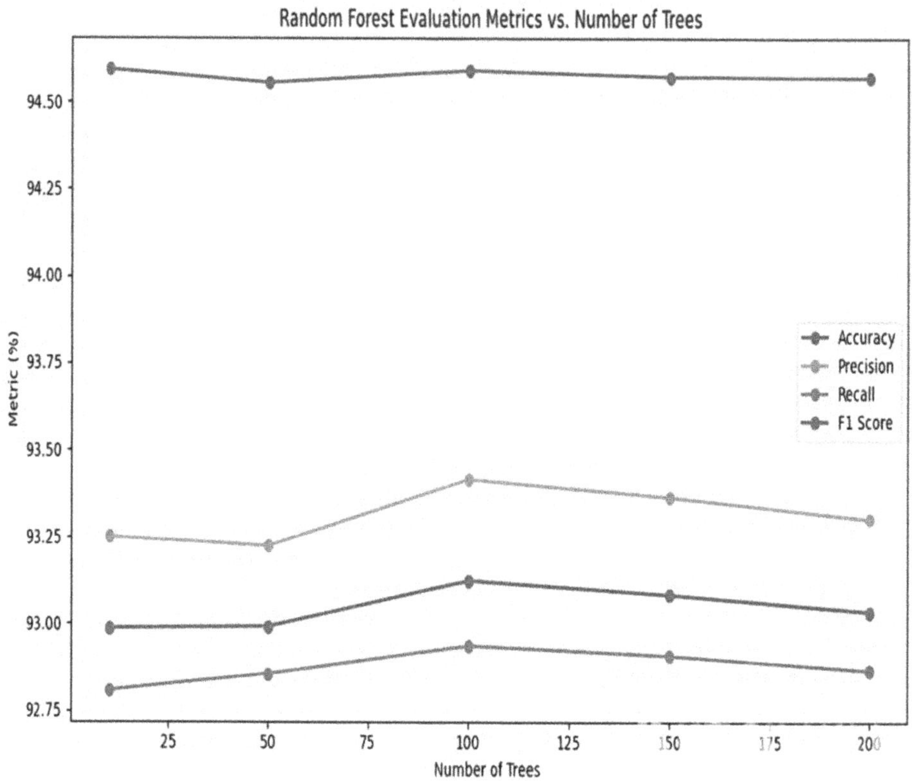

Fig. 9. Random Forest Metrics Graph

Figure 9 gives Random Forest Metrics. The graph demonstrates that increasing the number of trees in the Random Forest model has a.

Marginal effect on performance metrics. Accuracy remains stable around 94.5%, showing the model is already well-optimised. Precision, recall, and F1-score show slight improvements around 100 trees, but gains diminish beyond that. This suggests diminishing returns in model performance with more trees, indicating that 100 trees is a reasonable trade-off between accuracy and computational efficiency.

This confusion matrix shows the performance of a Random Forest classifier in identifying different toolchain architecture combinations (e.g., mips_glibc_gcc, x86_64_uclibc_gcc). The diagonal dominance indicates strong classification accuracy, particularly for classes like mips_glibc_gcc,x86_glibc_gcc, and x86_64_glibc_gcc, which have high true positive counts.

Misclassifications are minor but notable among similar architectures and libc variants (e.g., mips_musl_gcc vs. mips_uclibc_gcc). Overall, the model performs well with limited confusion across most classes.

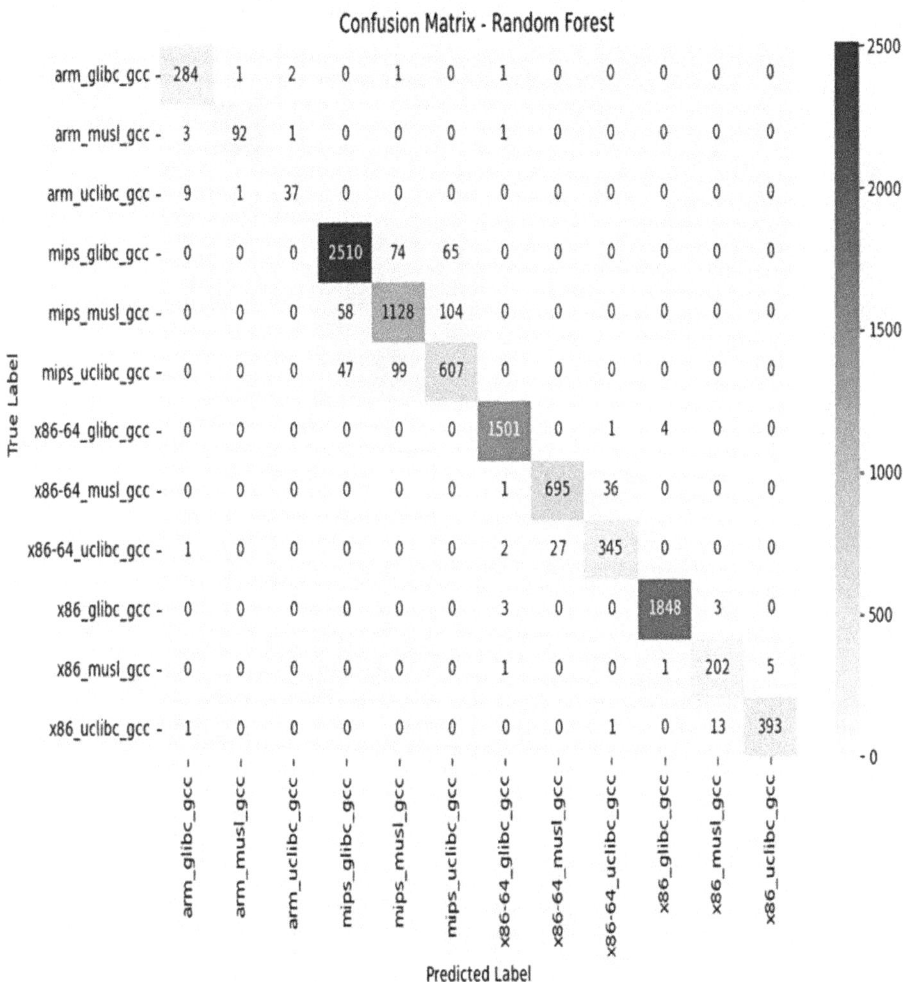

Fig. 10. Random Forest Confusion Matrix

Figure 10 gives the Random Forest confusion matrix. This ROC curve shows that the Random Forest model performs exceptionally well across all classes, with.

AUC scores close to or equal to 1.00. The near-perfect curves indicate excellent discrimination between the different binary types and toolchains, reflecting a highly reliable classifier.

This ROC curve demonstrates that the Random Forest model performs very well among all classes, with AUCs early or equal to 1.00. Perfect curves show excessive discrimination among the various binary types as well as tool chains, specifying an extremely consistent classifier (Table 1).

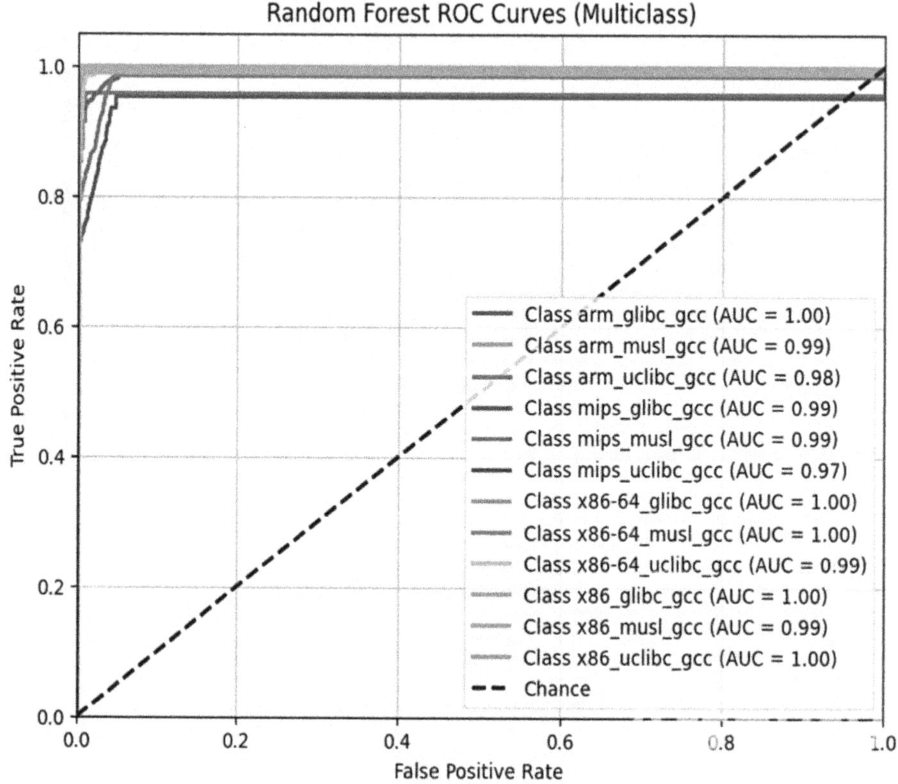

Fig. 11. Random Forest ROC Curve

Fig. 11, OC Curve of Random Forest

Table 1. A comparative table of KNN vs. Random Forest results(Metric)

Model	Accuracy	Precision	Recall	F1-score
KNN (K-Fold = 5)	0.8567	0.9445	0.9447	0.9442
Random Forest	0.9445	0.9361	0.9282	0.9316

5 Conclusion

This work has discovered the procedures for studying statically linked libraries in Linux binaries, concentrating on the growth of an AI-driven technique to automate as well as to improve the method. Conventional process of binary analysis can be time-consuming as well as error-prone, frequently demanding expert advice to recognize security weaknesses, performance problems, as well as appropriate substitutes. In contrast, the method we proposed influences machine learning methods to categories as well as to study the mechanisms of Linux binaries precisely. By means of an innovative computerized method, the system can extract as well as recognize the libraries linked to a given binary and can create a thorough summary. These summaries are AI-powered, giving an idea about possible security problems, performance influences, as well as ideas for additional optimized or secure substitutes to the libraries used. The system's use of AI guarantees that the complex technical information used in binary analysis is used, making it more manageable to inventors, security analysts, as well as even ordinary users with less technical knowledge.

The Random Forest technique proves robust as well as consistent performance in categorizing Linux binaries, attaining an accuracy of 94.45% by macro accuracy, recall, as well as F1-scores all above 0.92. The reliability of K-Fold cross-validation gives (accuracy: 93.12%), confirming the model's efficiency to generalize well across new information. AUC scores are nearly 1.00 for all classes, additionally highlighting its outstanding discriminatory power. The confusion matrix also gives fewer wrong decisions, with most predictions supporting precisely along the diagonal. As a whole, Random Forest demonstrates to be a robust as well as balanced technique, making it more appropriate for integration into the LibIntel technique for static library study.

One of the main areas to be enhanced is the improvement of the machine learning model used in identifying as well as classifying statically linked libraries in binaries. Moreover, integrating more cutting-edge analysis processes, including real-time CVE (Common Vulnerabilities and Exposures) information, would increase the tool's efficiency at finding present issues.

References

1. Rosenblum, N.E.: Extracting compiler-provenance from program binaries. In: Proceedings of the 9th ACM SIGPLAN-SIGSOFT Workshop on Program Analysis for Software Tools and Engineering, pp. 21–28 (2010)
2. Carrillo-Mondéjar, J.: Identifying runtime -libraries in statically -linked Linux binaries. Fut. Gen. Comput. Syst. **164**, 107602, (2025)
3. Alrabaee, S., Shirani, P., Wang, L., Debbabi, M.: Fossil: A resilient and efficient system for identifying FOSS functions in malware binaries. ACM Trans. Priv. Sec. **21**, 3 (2018)
4. Rahimian, A., Shirani, P., Alrbaee, S., Wang, L., Debbabi, M.: BinComp: a stratified approach to compiler-provenance attribution. Digital Invest. **14**, S146–S155 (2015)
5. Zheng: DiscovRE: efficient cross-architecture binary code similarity comparison. In: Proceedings of IEEE Symposium, pp. 678–696
6. Ming: BinHash: a semantic hash-based approach for detecting code clones. In: Proceedings of ACM SIGSOFT FSE, pp. 343–353
7. Collberg: SLINKY: static linking reloaded. In Proceedings of USENIX Annual Technical Conference, Pp. 309–322
8. Yang: Understand code style: efficient CNN-based compiler optimisation recognition system. In: Proceedings of IEEE ICC, pp. 1–6
9. Pizzolotto: Identifying compiler optimisations with hybrid neural models. Inf. Softw. Technol. **138**, 106615

10. Kim, H., Lee, J., Lee, D.: Automated binary analysis for linux systems: a survey of static and hybrid methods. Comput. Sec. **132**, 103720 (2024)
11. Chen, N., Xu, S., Wang, L.: Cross-platform disassembly and feature extraction for malware detection. Digital Invest. **48**, 301102 (2024)
12. Patel, S., Shah, M.: Dependency and vulnerability analysis in open source software libraries. J. Syst. Softw. **210**, 111945 (2024)
13. Zhang, R., He, Y., Li, Q.: Machine learning-based binary classification: challenges and opportunities. IEEE Access **12**, 88012–88025 (2024)
14. Rahman, M., Khan, F.A.: A hybrid machine learning framework for binary malware detection. Expert Syst. Appl. **235**, 121029 (2024)
15. Yu, T., Sun, C., Park, K.: Improving runtime library detection in ELF binaries using feature fusion and deep learning. IEEE Trans. Softw. Eng. **51**(2), 402–415 (2025)

Enhanced Detection of Malicious URLs Using Supervised Machine Learning Models

P. Anu[1]([✉])(iD), M. Saseekala[2](iD), A. Subhashini[3](iD), S. Aarthee[1](iD), and N. Kalyani[1](iD)

[1] School of Computing, SASTRA Deemed to Be University, Thanjavur 613402, India
anugps12@gmail.com, aarthee@cse.sastra.edu, kallunaga@gmail.com
[2] Faculty of Computer Applications, School of Business and Management, CHRIST University, Bangalore, India
saseekala.m@christuniversity.in, saseejob@gmail.com
[3] Department of Software Systems, PSG College of Arts and Science, Coimbatore 641014, India
subhashini_a@psgcas.ac.in

Abstract. This paper deliberates on URL phishing, one important subset of cyber threats. Most modern-day deceptive practices have shifted to the digital space due to the vast scope of information available on the internet. URL phishing is a dishonest practice that includes masquerading harmful links as legitimate links to trick users into sharing their private data. Detection of URL phishing is extremely challenging, hence most of these attacks go undetected until it is too late for the victim. Automatic blacklist that rely heavily on user-generated reports to monitor internet links have been repeatedly proven ineffective time and again. Along with failing to identify newly listed phishing sites, these systems also tend to mistake harmless links for phishing traps. This paper proposes the application of classification techniques of practical machine learning, specifically analysing the patterns and behaviours of URLs to detect phishing websites accurately. Leveraging the properties of Decision Trees, Random Forests, Logistic Regression, SVM, and Light GBM, we were able to come up with a detection model, which precisely calculates accuracy, precision, recall, as well as F1 score to evaluate the validity of URL classification.

Keywords: Phishing · URL Detection · Precision · Recall · F1 score · Feature Extraction · Real-time protection

1 Introduction

Association rule mining must also be used efficiently in categorising phishing URL designs [2]. A characteristic-based method that combines domain checking and lexicon inspection to recognise phishing attempts is used in the same process [1]. These highlight the importance of Uniform Resource Locator-based characteristics like the age of a specified domain, special characters, as well as the use of IP addresses in identifying phishing.

F. Ortiz-Rodríguez et al. (Eds.): IBCD 2025, CCIS 2845, pp. 407–419, 2026.
https://doi.org/10.1007/978-3-032-20907-8_34

Additional developments in the area are methods that use machine learning classifiers, such as decision trees, as well as online learning models [4]. It specifies that lexical as well as host-based characteristics must significantly improve identification when used. Document object model (DOM) characteristics are used [6], as well as visual pattern detection models give more insight into how phishing internet site copycats legitimate websites. [8, 9].

In most of the works done, diverse supervised machine learning models were used on Uniform Resource Locator data sets. Based on their results, the LightGBM algorithm outdid the others in terms of training accuracy as well as test accuracy. Therefore, was acceptable to use the cautious innovative ensemble learning techniques. Growth in the complexity as well as difficulty of phishing fears demands the use of more intelligent as well as adaptive systems. The use of this work is to enhance the work done, as well as to provide suggestions on how machine learning can be used to help in improving precision as well as effectiveness in phishing Uniform Resource Locator detection.

2   Literature Survey

Phishing URL identification has received considerable interest in recent years, with the widespread increase in cybercrime. Blacklist and heuristic rule-based methods have proven to be inadequate in preventing advanced and new phishing attacks. Scientists have therefore resorted to machine learning (ML) as a method to counter the shortcomings of static solutions.

Association rule mining to identify phishing URL patterns and demonstrated how features differ for malicious and harmless links [2]. Their method set the ground for a characteristic-based discovery method. A recognition system that uses domain presence in white-lists, lexical characteristics, as well as page ranking statistics is used [1]. Their work was intensive on whether characteristic feature engineering is appropriate for building recognition systems.

Microsoft Reputation Services' Uniform Resource Locator ranking for the sake of refining recognition precision is used [4]. The method employed content as well as metadata-based characteristic features and achieved a development in classification precision to a great extent. In contrast, lexical features as well as online learning methods concentrating on Uniform Resource Locator Characteristic features alone, without webpage content, thus permitting real-time discovery. [3] This work by probing Document Object Model (DOM) characteristics features as well as representing the way in which structural as well as visual web page characteristics features could be employed to specify phishing [6]. Classification methods, mainly concentrating on visual characteristic feature review, as well as HTML elements, are verified [5].

The visual resemblance method based on Earth Mover's Distance (EMD) for assessing website screenshots to distinguish visually copied pages is improved. [8] A complete machine learning review, unfolding statistical as well as characteristic feature-based approaches for phishing URL detection, is also achieved [7]. As a whole, these works demonstrate that the amalgamation of lexical, visual, as well as structural features and ensemble ML methods such as Light GBM, Random Forest, and SVM is more accurate in detection. In some concluded papers, machine learning-based feature models perform better than traditional methods in identifying phishing URLs and can tackle emerging threats en route through ongoing learning.

3   Proposed Techniques

Instead of blacklisting, it is focused on structural feature extraction from the domain and URL, i.e., whether there are IP addresses, special characters, URL length, domain age, web traffic rank, and number of subdomains. Various machine learning models are trained once the feature extraction is done for classifying URLs as malicious or benign URLs. The Decision Tree algorithm builds a flowchart-like model in which features drive decisions based on thresholds, leading to clear classification rules. Random Forest enhances this by building an ensemble of decision trees whose outputs are combined to improve accuracy and prevent overfitting. This feature-based machine learning method ensures flexibility and improved detection of newly generated phishing URLs compared to earlier methods. Figure 1 gives the workflow.

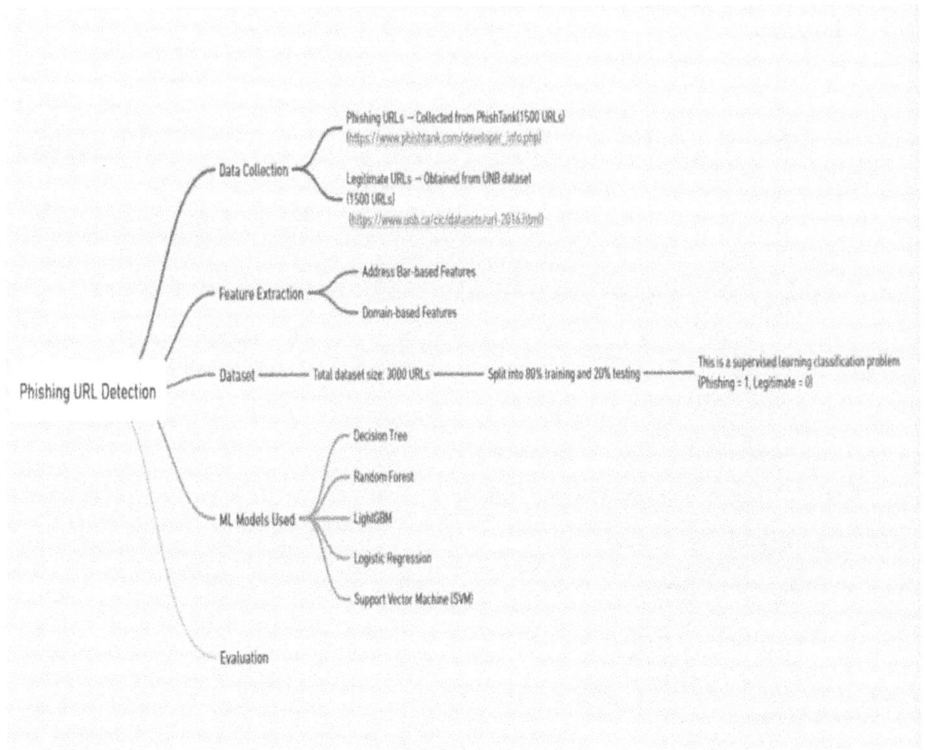

Fig. 1. Workflow

The present research compares several supervised learning models that are commonly applied in classification problems. XGBoost is a gradient boosting library with high efficiency and regularisation through its built-in support to avoid overfitting. Decision Trees give understandable rule-based models for class separation and form the basis of ensemble models such as Random Forest. Random Forest boosts prediction accuracy by taking the average of several trees, lessening variance and overfitting. MLP stands for deep neural networks that discover nonlinear relationships using several hidden layers and backpropagation optimisation. SVM builds optimal hyperplanes to maximise class separation in high-dimensional feature spaces. Logistic Regression, despite being linear, is still a common baseline model as a result of its simplicity, interpretability, and quality for binary classification. As a group, the models vary from straightforward linear predictors to intricate nonlinear ensembles, showing capability in various domains of data.

4 Result Analysis

The phishing URL detection system starts by collecting a dataset containing 1500 phishing URLs and 1500 legitimate URLs. After cleaning the data to remove any invalid or missing entries, we proceed with extracting important features from urlparse and whois Python libraries.

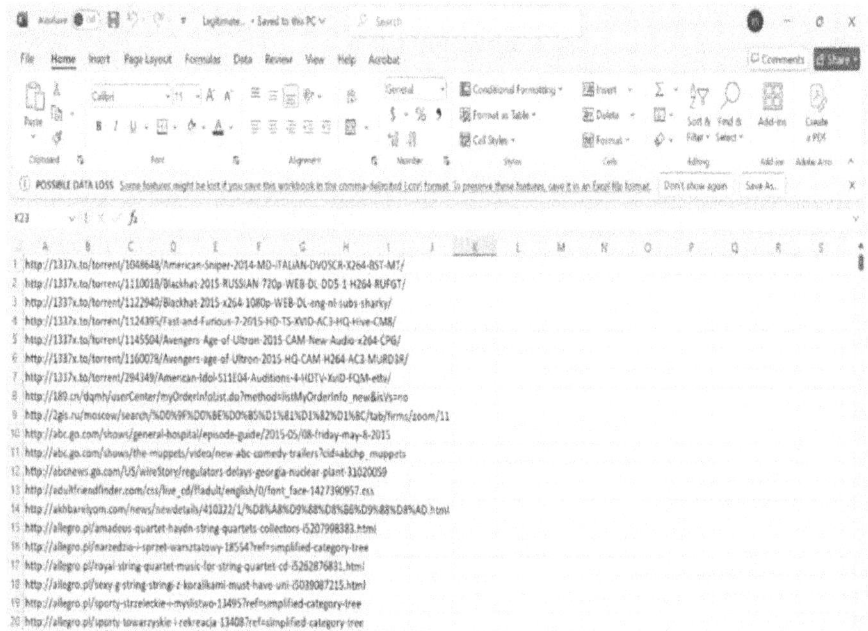

Fig. 2. Legitimate Dataset

These include essential points like the length of the URL, whether it contains an IP address or not, if there are predefined symbols, the age of the domain, availability of DNS records, traffic rank, and subdomain structure. Overall, we chose 15 features that are essential to differentiate between phishing sites and genuine ones. Figure 2 gives a legitimate dataset.

The legitimate dataset, comprising 1500 URLs sourced from the UNB dataset, represents safe web addresses. Used to train the model to distinguish between genuine and phishing URLs. Figure 3 gives the phishing dataset. Figure 4 gives a legitimate dataset after feature selection.

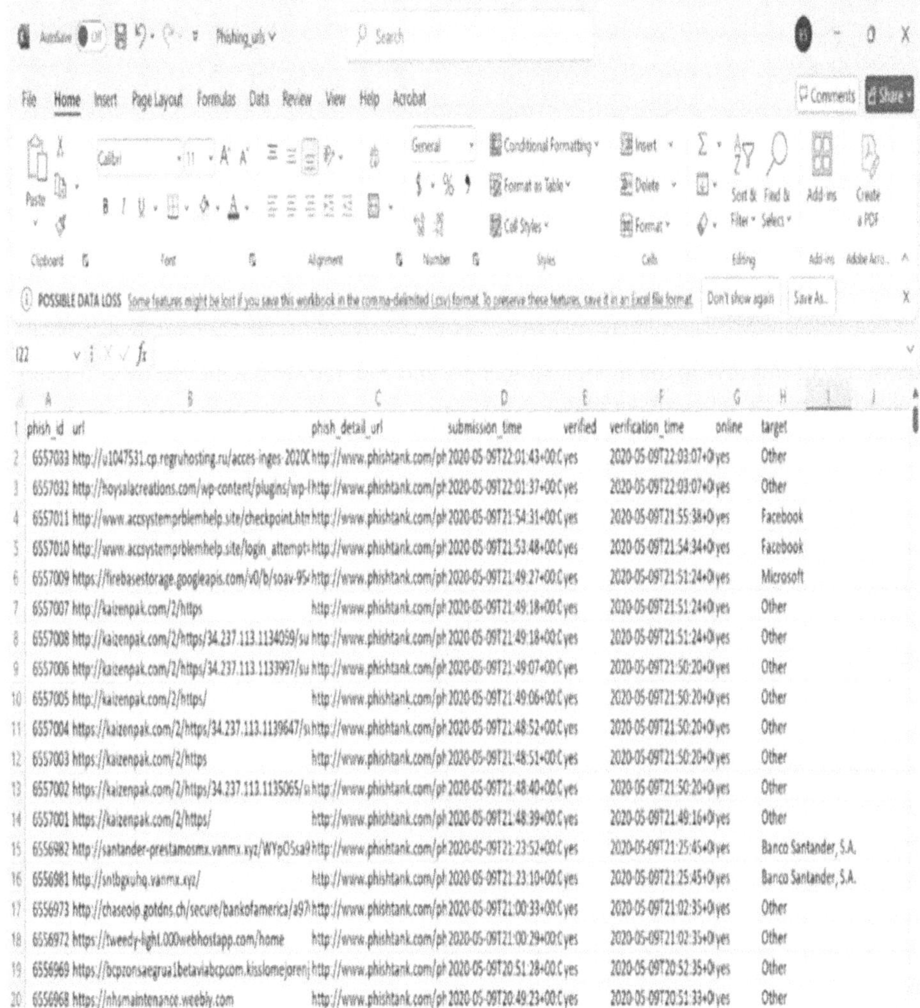

	phish_id	url	phish_detail_url	submission_time	verified	verification_time	online	target
1	phish_id	url	phish_detail_url	submission_time	verified	verification_time	online	target
2	6557033	http://u1047531.cp.regruhosting.ru/acces-inges-2020C	http://www.phishtank.com/ph	2020-05-09T22:01:43+00:C	yes	2020-05-09T22:03:07+0	yes	Other
3	6557032	http://hoysalacreations.com/wp-content/plugins/wp-f	http://www.phishtank.com/ph	2020-05-09T22:01:37+00:C	yes	2020-05-09T22:03:07+0	yes	Other
4	6557011	http://www.accsystemprblemhelp.site/checkpoint.htm	http://www.phishtank.com/ph	2020-05-09T21:54:31+00:C	yes	2020-05-09T21:55:38+0	yes	Facebook
5	6557010	http://www.accsystemprblemhelp.site/login_attempt-	http://www.phishtank.com/ph	2020-05-09T21:53:48+00:C	yes	2020-05-09T21:54:34+0	yes	Facebook
6	6557009	https://firebasestorage.googleapis.com/v0/b/soav-95-	http://www.phishtank.com/ph	2020-05-09T21:49:27+00:C	yes	2020-05-09T21:51:24+0	yes	Microsoft
7	6557007	http://kaizenpak.com/2/https	http://www.phishtank.com/ph	2020-05-09T21:49:18+00:C	yes	2020-05-09T21:51:24+0	yes	Other
8	6557008	http://kaizenpak.com/2/https/34.237.113.1134059/su	http://www.phishtank.com/ph	2020-05-09T21:49:18+00:C	yes	2020-05-09T21:51:24+0	yes	Other
9	6557006	http://kaizenpak.com/2/https/34.237.113.1133997/su	http://www.phishtank.com/ph	2020-05-09T21:49:07+00:C	yes	2020-05-09T21:50:20+0	yes	Other
10	6557005	http://kaizenpak.com/2/https/	http://www.phishtank.com/ph	2020-05-09T21:49:06+00:C	yes	2020-05-09T21:50:20+0	yes	Other
11	6557004	https://kaizenpak.com/2/https/34.237.113.1139647/su	http://www.phishtank.com/ph	2020-05-09T21:48:52+00:C	yes	2020-05-09T21:50:20+0	yes	Other
12	6557003	https://kaizenpak.com/2/https	http://www.phishtank.com/ph	2020-05-09T21:48:51+00:C	yes	2020-05-09T21:50:20+0	yes	Other
13	6557002	https://kaizenpak.com/2/https/34.237.113.1135065/a	http://www.phishtank.com/ph	2020-05-09T21:48:40+00:C	yes	2020-05-09T21:50:20+0	yes	Other
14	6557001	https://kaizenpak.com/2/https/	http://www.phishtank.com/ph	2020-05-09T21:48:39+00:C	yes	2020-05-09T21:49:16+0	yes	Other
15	6556982	http://santander-prestamosmx.vanmx.xyz/WYpO5sa9	http://www.phishtank.com/ph	2020-05-09T21:23:52+00:C	yes	2020-05-09T21:25:45+0	yes	Banco Santander, S.A.
16	6556981	http://sntbgxuhq.vanmx.xyz/	http://www.phishtank.com/ph	2020-05-09T21:23:10+00:C	yes	2020-05-09T21:25:45+0	yes	Banco Santander, S.A.
17	6556973	http://chaseoip.gotdns.ch/secure/bankofamerica/a97	http://www.phishtank.com/ph	2020-05-09T21:00:33+00:C	yes	2020-05-09T21:02:35+0	yes	Other
18	6556972	https://tweedy-light.000webhostapp.com/home	http://www.phishtank.com/ph	2020-05-09T21:00:29+00:C	yes	2020-05-09T21:02:35+0	yes	Other
19	6556969	https://bcpzonsaegrua1betaviabcpcom.kisslomejorenj	http://www.phishtank.com/ph	2020-05-09T20:51:28+00:C	yes	2020-05-09T20:52:35+0	yes	Other
20	6556968	https://nhsmaintenance.weebly.com	http://www.phishtank.com/ph	2020-05-09T20:49:23+00:C	yes	2020-05-09T20:51:33+0	yes	Other

Fig. 3. Phishing Dataset

The phishing dataset, consisting of 1500 URLs collected from PhishTank, contains malicious web addresses. Used to train the model in identifying deceptive or fraudulent URLs.

	A	B	C	D	E	F	G	H	I	J	K	L	M	N
1	Domain	Have_IP	Have_At	URL_Length	URL_Depth	Redirection	https_Domain	TinyURL	Prefix/Suffix	DNS_Record	Domain_Age	Domain_End	Label	
2	techcrunch.com	0	0	1	4	0	0	0	0	0	0	1	0	
3	mylust.com	0	0	1	3	0	0	1	0	0	0	0	0	
4	hollywoodlife.com	0	0	1	4	0	0	0	0	0	0	1	0	
5	mic.com	0	0	1	3	0	0	0	0	0	0	0	0	
6	twitter.com	0	0	1	1	1	0	0	0	0	0	1	0	
7	screenrant.com	0	0	1	1	0	0	1	0	0	0	0	0	
8	motthegioi.vn	0	0	1	2	0	0	0	0	0	1	1	0	
9	kickass.to	0	0	1	3	0	0	0	0	0	1	1	0	
10	kienthuc.net.vn	0	0	1	2	0	0	0	0	0	1	1	0	
11	distractify.com	0	0	1	10	0	0	0	0	0	0	1	0	
12	metro.co.uk	0	0	1	4	0	0	0	0	0	1	1	0	
13	metro.co.uk	0	0	1	4	0	0	0	0	0	1	1	0	
14	techcrunch.com	0	0	1	4	0	0	0	0	0	0	1	0	
15	genius.com	0	0	1	3	0	0	0	0	0	0	0	0	
16	correios.com.br	0	0	1	4	0	0	0	0	0	1	1	0	
17	thenextweb.com	0	0	1	6	0	0	0	0	0	0	1	0	
18	allegro.pl	0	0	1	2	0	0	0	0	0	1	1	0	
19	distractify.com	0	0	1	10	0	0	0	0	0	0	1	0	
20	kenh14.vn	0	0	1	2	0	0	0	0	0	1	1	0	
21	olx.ua	0	0	1	3	0	0	0	0	0	1	1	0	
22	myspace.com	0	0	1	5	0	0	0	0	0	0	0	0	
23	icicibank.com	0	0	1	3	0	0	0	0	0	0	0	0	
24	spankbang.com	0	0	1	3	0	0	0	0	0	0	1	0	

Fig. 4. Legitimate Dataset after Feature Selection

After feature selection, only the most relevant attributes from the legitimate dataset are retained, improving the model. Efficiency and accuracy are achieved by eliminating redundant or less informative features.

	A	B	C	D	E	F	G	H	I	J	K	L	M	N
1	Domain	Have_IP	Have_At	URL_Length	URL_Depth	Redirection	https_Dom	TinyURL	Prefix/Suff	DNS_Reco	Domain_A	Domain_E	Label	
2	176.119.1.180	0	0	0	1	0	0	0	0	0	1	1	1	
3	3965207478e6a58	0	0	1	2	0	0	0	0	0	0	0	1	
4	golfballsonline.con	0	0	1	3	0	0	0	0	0	0	1	1	
5	hotmailsecure.brill	0	0	0	1	0	0	0	0	0	1	1	1	
6	payment-isuessglol	0	0	1	1	0	0	0	1	0	1	1	1	
7	thatgiftedgal.com	0	0	0	2	0	0	0	0	0	1	1	1	
8	reg-eboy.shrigrmot	0	0	0	2	0	0	0	1	0	1	1	1	
9	netregistry.com.au	0	0	1	0	0	0	0	0	0	1	1	1	
10	hafezmusic.ir	0	0	0	4	0	0	0	0	0	1	1	1	
11	nectaribate.com.br	0	0	1	3	0	0	0	0	0	1	1	1	
12	paypalp.ontraport.(	0	0	1	12	0	0	1	0	0	0	1	1	
13	view.em.gamestop.	0	0	0	0	0	0	0	0	0	0	0	1	
14	tunga9.cl	0	0	0	1	0	0	0	0	0	1	1	1	
15	justlookapp.com	0	0	1	7	0	0	0	0	0	1	1	1	
16	paypal.b2pay.top	0	0	0	0	0	0	0	0	0	1	1	1	
17	vmorefraud.com	0	0	1	4	0	0	0	0	0	1	1	1	
18	verfiayiosnmer.con	0	0	0	2	0	0	0	0	0	1	1	1	
19	hamt.jp	0	0	1	7	0	0	0	0	0	1	1	1	
20	itau.b.br	0	0	0	0	0	0	0	0	0	1	1	1	
21	icloud.com-ltd.ru	0	0	0	0	0	0	0	1	0	1	1	1	

Fig. 5. Phishing Dataset after Feature Selection

Figure 5 gives the phishing dataset after feature selection. The phishing dataset, post-feature selection, includes only the most significant attributes, enhancing the model's ability to accurately detect phishing URLs while reducing computational complexity.

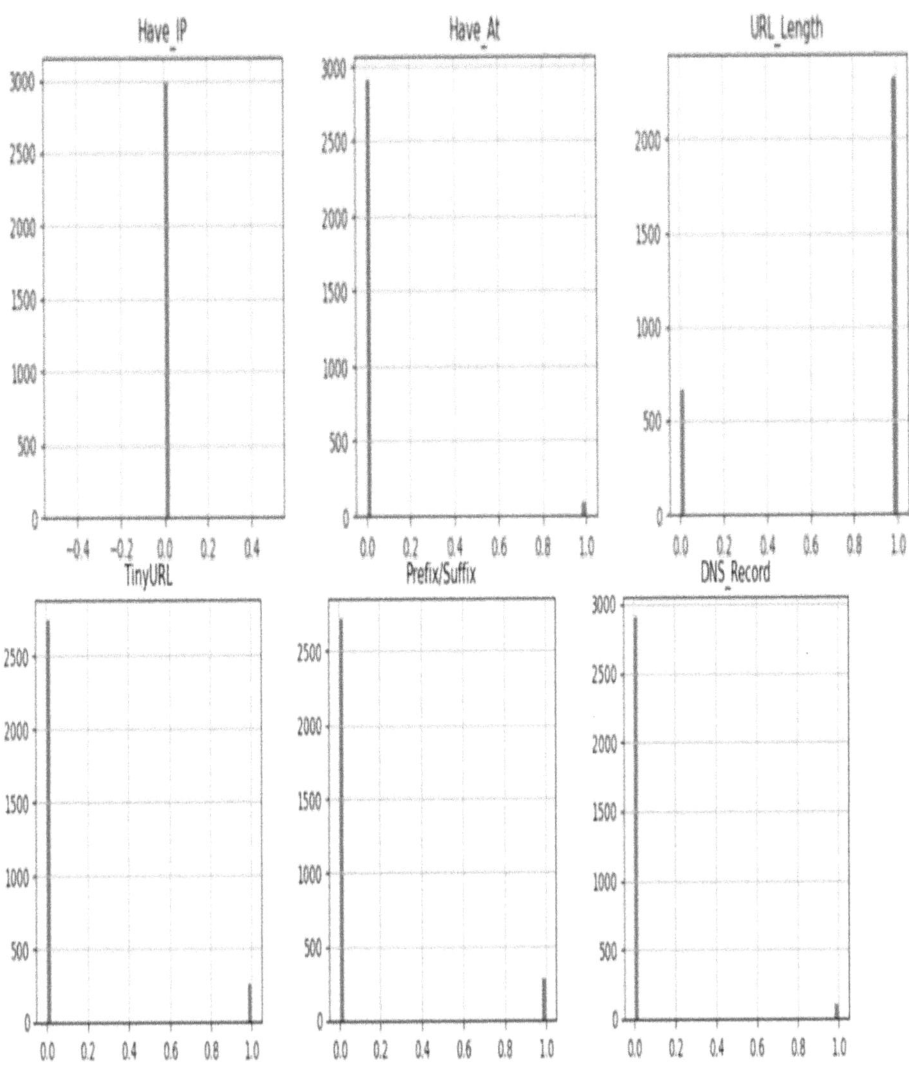

Fig. 6. Feature Distribution

The feature distribution visualisation shows that selected features vary across phishing and legitimate URLs, highlighting patterns and distinctions that aid in effective classification by the machine learning models, and it is shown in Fig. 6.

The heat map analysis reveals the correlation between different features, helping to identify strongly related attributes and reduce multicollinearity, thereby improving model performance and interpretability, and it is shown in Fig. 8. Figure 7 gives feature importance.

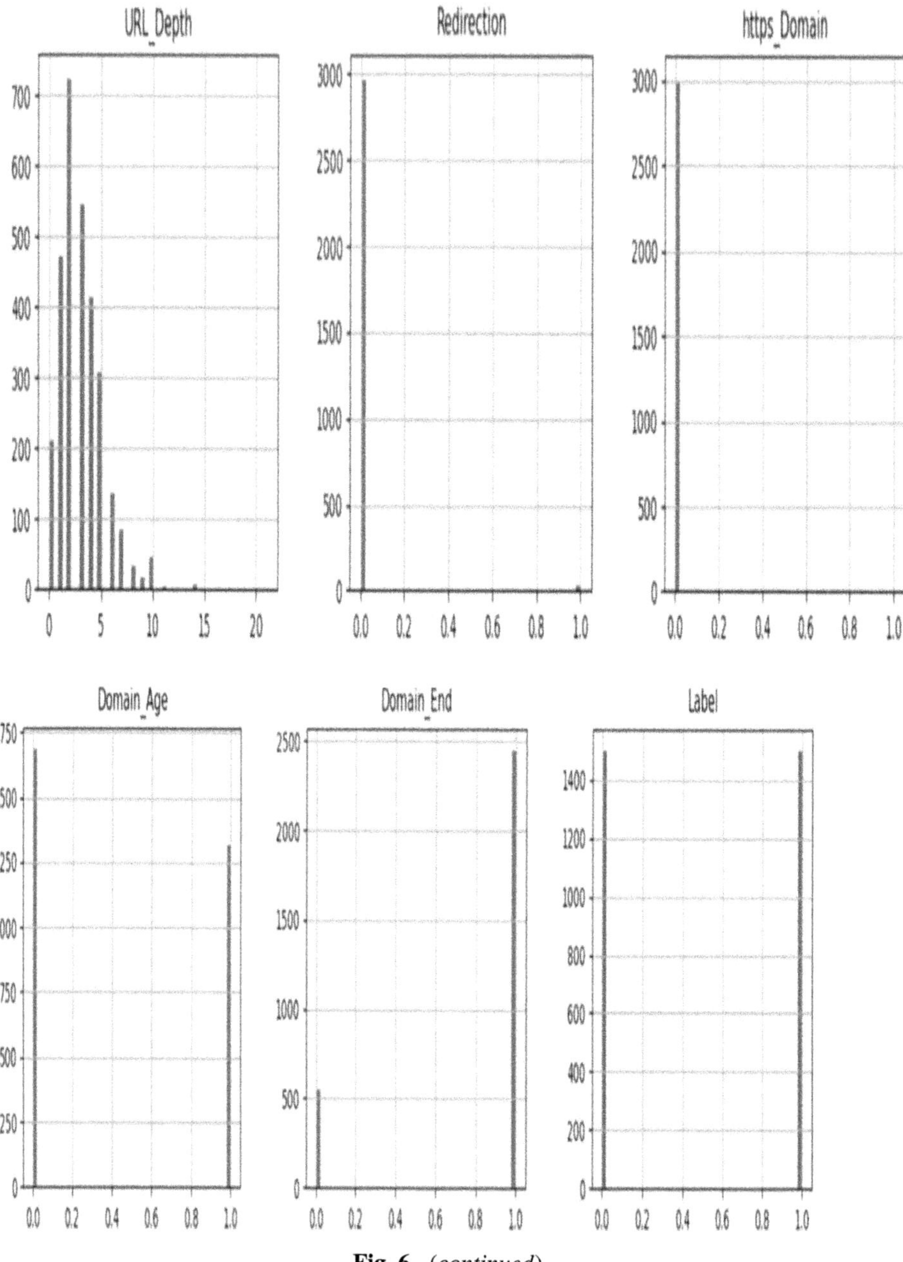

Fig. 6. (*continued*)

We use several machine learning models. This mind map represents a Phishing URL Detection project that uses a dataset of 3000 URLs, divided equally between phishing and legitimate sources, using different machine learning models for supervised classification. Figure 3 provides feature Distribution. The phishing dataset after feature

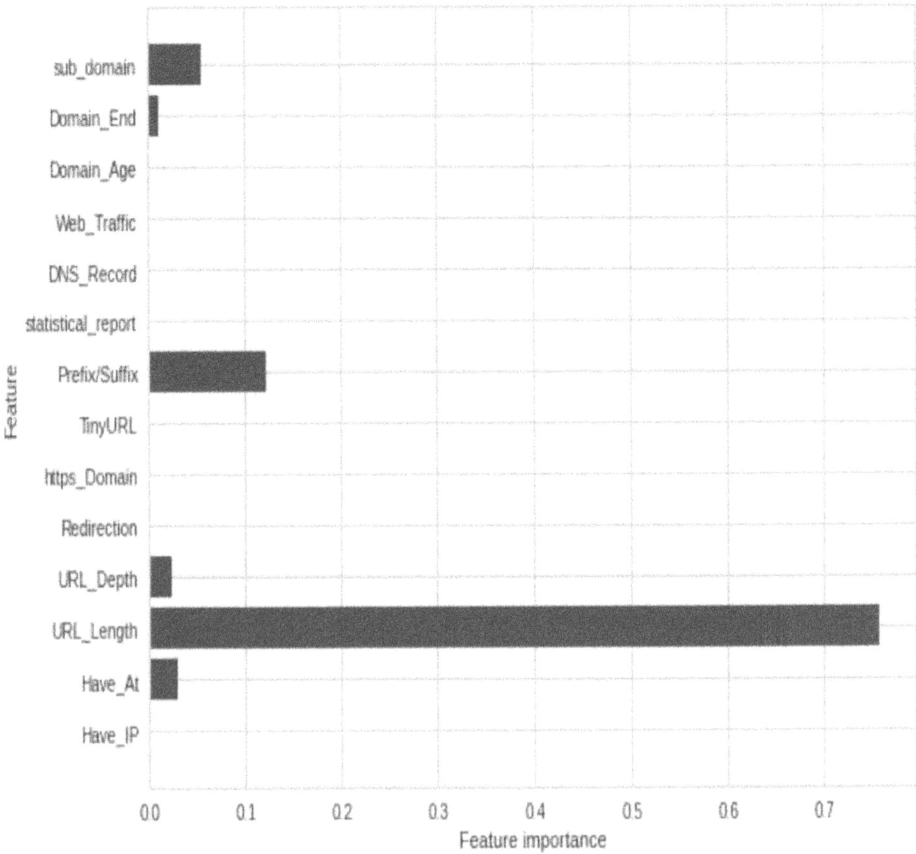

Fig. 7. Feature Importance

selection contains only the most relevant attributes, which improve the model to correctly identify phishing URLs while decreasing computational complexity. Figure 1 gives the workflow.

Figure 9 gives unnecessary columns. Columns with low correlation, high redundancy, or minimal impact on model accuracy are dropped to streamline.

The dataset reduces overfitting and enhances computational efficiency.

Model evaluation metrics like precision, F1-score, accuracy, as well as recall help assess the efficiency of the technique as well as its capability to generalise to new data.

Table 1 gives metrics. Decision Tree and Random Forest models were very close in performance, both with an accuracy of 0.854 as well as an F1-score of 0.839. Their recall scores of 0.736 and 0.737, and precision of 0.935 and 0.933 were equally high and put them as good and interpretable choices for structured data. The models had a great generalisation-classification performance balance.

While its recall of 0.721 was lower than Light GBM, the precision of 0.932 of the model was high, which suggests that the model is capable of performing well in non-linear classification tasks, but with a tendency to overfit small datasets.

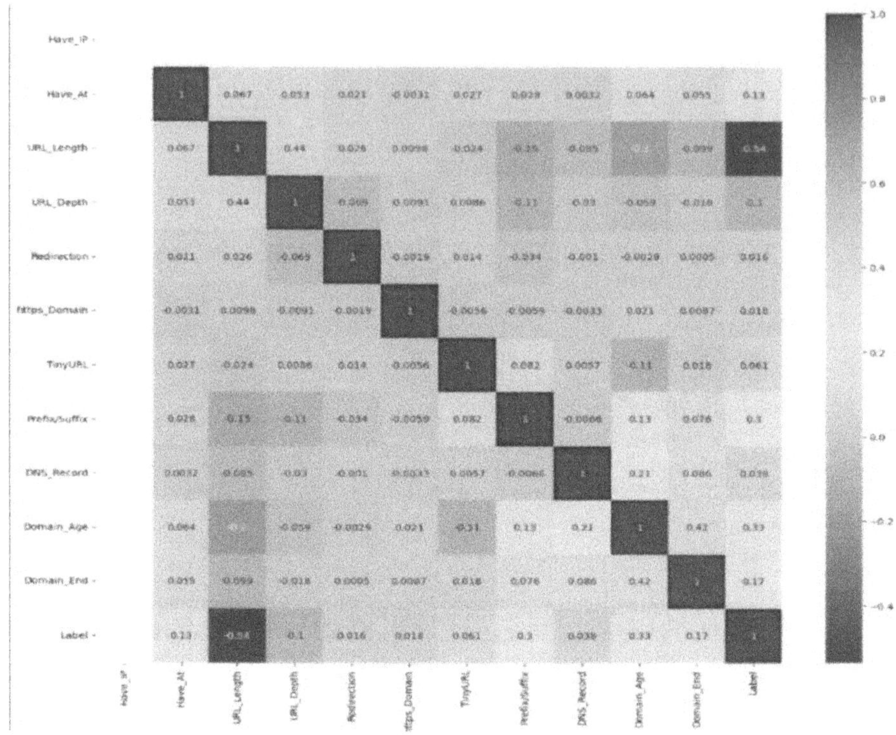

Fig. 8. Heat Map Analysis

	Have_IP	Have_At	URL_Length	URL_Depth	Redirection	https_Domain	TinyURL	Prefix/Suffix	DNS_Record	Domain_Age	Domain_End	Label
0	0	0	0	2	0	0	0	0	0	0	0	1
1	0	0	1	2	0	0	0	0	0	0	1	0
2	0	0	1	8	0	0	0	0	0	1	1	1
3	0	0	1	2	0	0	0	0	0	1	1	1
4	0	0	1	4	0	0	0	0	0	0	0	0

Fig. 9. Unnecessary Columns.

Figure 11 shows how a legitimate URL is tested using a web application. The Support Vector Machine (SVM) and Logistic Regression models performed poorly compared to ensemble-based models as well as neural-based models. The SVM had a precision of

Table 1. Metrics

ML Model	Accuracy	F1 Score	Recall	Precision
XGBoost Classifier	0.856	0.841	0.735	0.933
Decision Tree	0.854	0.839	0.736	0.935
Random Forest	0.854	0.839	0.737	0.933
LightGBM	0.849	0.835	0.740	0.920
Multi-layer Perceptron	0.845	0.829	0.721	0.932
Support Vector Machine	0.827	0.805	0.694	0.924
Logistic Regression	0.826	0.804	0.700	0.919

0.827 with the worst recall (0.694), reflecting a bias to not detect positive cases. It, nonetheless, had high accuracy (0.924), and this makes it better suited for use where accuracy is higher than recall. Similarly, Logistic Regression had the worst performance measures overall, with an accuracy of 0.826 as well as an F1-score of 0.804. Despite its simplicity and interpretability, with its limited ability to identify complex patterns, its vulnerability was evidenced. Figure 10 offers accuracy scores for algorithms.

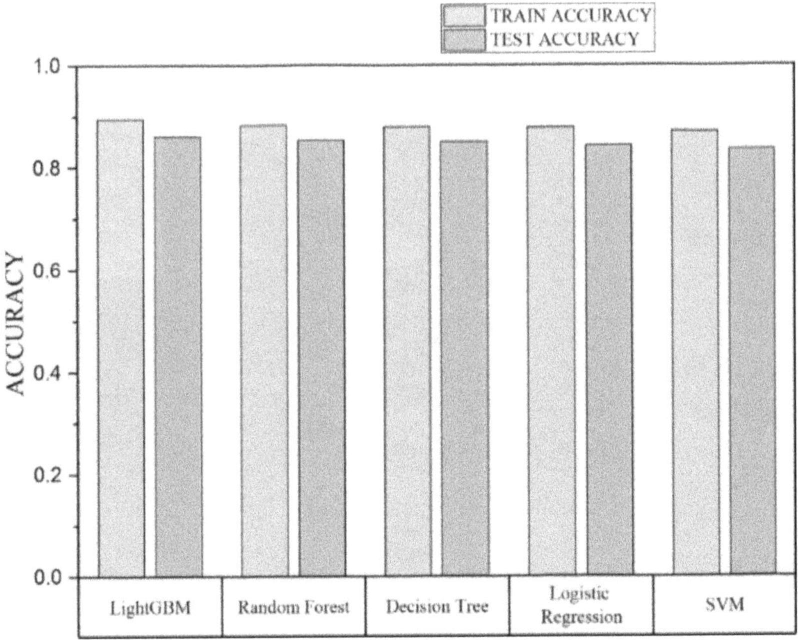

Fig. 10. Accuracy scores for algorithms.

The second significant step is to enable real-time protection against security threats while actively browsing the internet, since the underlying machine learning models now

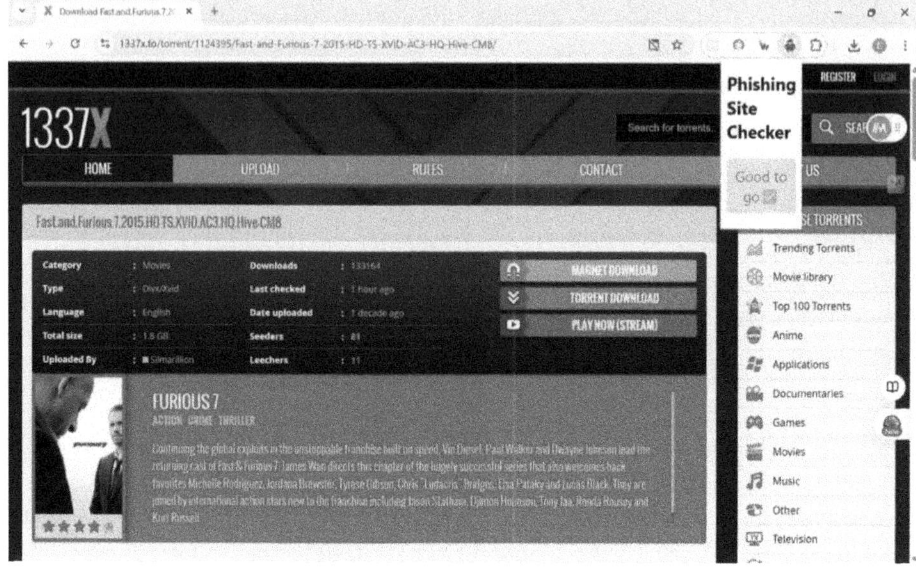

Fig. 11. Testing with Legitimate URL

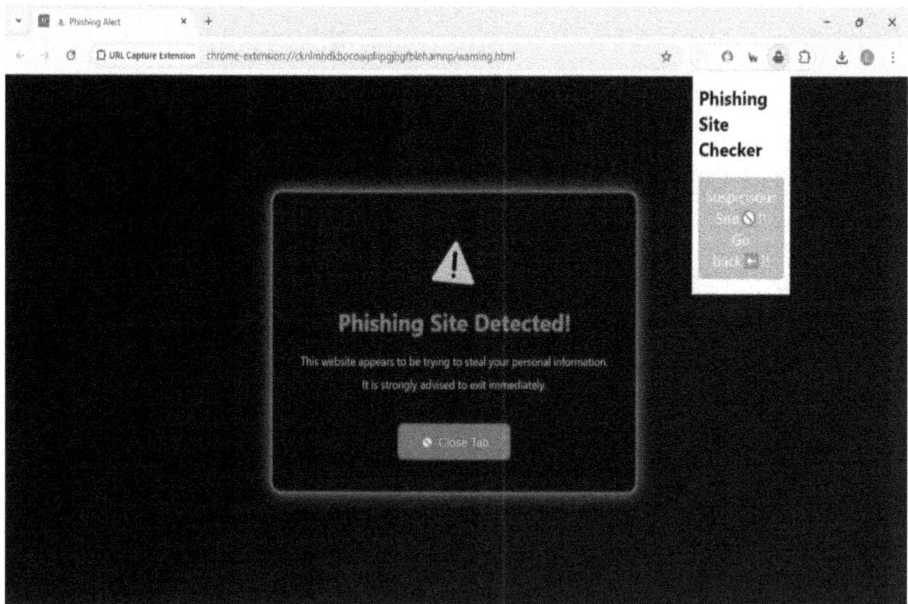

Fig. 12. Testing With Phishing URL

have the capability of identifying phishing URLs in static datasets effectively. Offline analysis-based traditional detection systems, including machine learning-based ones, tend to be confined to offline analysis and cannot provide users with dynamic protection while browsing. This project suggests creating a Chrome extension that integrates the trained models and a small Flask server in an effort to fill this gap. The Chrome Extension monitors the URLs that individuals visit in real time without requiring manual effort. The instant a page starts to load, the URL is automatically captured and sent to the Flask server, where it goes through the trained machine models.

Figure 12 shows how a phishing URL is tested using a web application. This shift from a machine learning model to a complete browser extension vastly improves phishing detection usability and efficiency, providing a seamless and reliable defence against phishing attacks during regular internet usage.

5 Conclusion

The paper showcased how effective machine learning models like SVM, Random Forest, Light GBM, and Logistic Regression can be in evaluating URL characteristics to distinguish between malicious and benign sites. This laid a strong groundwork for detecting phishing URLs. The XG Boost classifier took it a step further, achieving an impressive accuracy of 85% on test data, which underscores its reliability in real-world applications. The Chrome Extension builds on this by providing a handy, real-time solution that integrates these models directly into the user's web browsing experience. It offers proactive protection against phishing attempts by constantly monitoring the URLs users visit, alerting them before they accidentally land on potentially harmful websites. This transition from a machine learning model to a fully functional browser extension significantly enhances the usability and effectiveness of phishing detection, delivering a smooth and dependable defence against phishing threats during everyday internet use.

References

1. Garera, S., Provos, N., Chew, M., Rubin, A.D.: A framework for detection and measurement of phishing attacks. In: Proceedings of the 2007 ACM workshop, pp. 1–8 (2007)
2. Jeeva, C.: Intelligent phishing URL detection using association rule mining. Human-centric Computing & Information Sciences (2016)
3. Blum, A.: Lexical feature-based phishing URL detection using online learning. In: Third ACM Workshop on Security & Artificial Intelligence (AISEC) (2010)
4. Feroz, M.N.: Phishing URL detection using URL ranking. IEEE International Congress on Big Data (2015)
5. Pradeepthi, K.V., Kannan, A.: Performance study of classification techniques for phishing URL detection. IEEE (2014)
6. Shraddha, P.: A new method for detection of phishing websites: URL detection. In: IEEE, pp. 949–952 (2018)
7. Sahoo, D.: Malicious URL detection using machine learning: a survey (2017)
8. Wu, Y.: Malicious web domain identification based on intelligent algorithms. Computers & Security
9. Huang: A study of the phishing email filtering technique. Lecture Notes in Electrical Engineering

Real-Time Attack Detection Model and Platform Using Machine Learning

R. Radhakrishnan[1] , G. Abirami[2] , Venkatesan Annamalai[3] ,
V. Ganesh Karthikeyan[4] , P. Selvaraj[1] , and S. P. Ramesh[1]([✉])

[1] Department of Computer Science and Engineering, School of Computing Science and
Engineering, Galgotias University, Greater Noida, India
spramesh.me@gmail.com
[2] Department of Computer Science and Engineering, B. S. Abdur Rahman Crescent Institute of
Science and Technology, Chennai, Tamil Nadu, India
[3] Department of Electrical, Electronics and Communication Engineering, Galgotias University,
Greater Noida 203201, India
venkatesan@galgotiasuniversity.edu.in
[4] School of Computing, SASTRA Deemed to be University, Thirumalaisamudram, Thanjavur,
Tamil Nadu, India

Abstract. To safeguard digital infrastructures from increasingly common and
sophisticated cyberattacks, real-time detection is crucial. This paper introduces a
methodology and platform for scalable attack detection that uses machine learning
approaches to accurately and in real-time identify threats. System logs and network
traffic are two examples of the heterogeneous data streams that the suggested system handles using advanced feature engineering methods. The ability to identify
abnormalities and detect attack patterns in real-time is made possible by machine
learning models like Autoencoders (AE), Gradient Boosting (GB), and Recurrent
Neural Networks (RNN). Maintaining high detection accuracy while adjusting to
emerging threats is made possible by the platform's architecture, which supports
constant learning. The model's capacity to quickly and accurately identify different forms of attacks is shown by evaluations of datasets such as UNSW-NB15 and
CICIDS2017. A trustworthy, efficient, and scalable real-time threat detection system is created by combining big data with machine learning. This solution takes on
the challenges of modern cybersecurity. Tack detection is performed by training
the RNN model on labeled datasets to recognize abnormal patterns. The model
can be enhanced using hybrid deep-learning techniques and attention mechanisms.
Scalability is achieved by deploying lightweight versions of the model on edge
devices and using parallel processing for handling high-volume traffic efficiently.

Keywords: Cyberattacks · Scalable Attack Detection · Machine Learning
Algorithms · CICIDS2017 · UNSW-NB15

1 Introduction

For intrusion detection systems (IDS) to be reliable and secure in the face of the ever-
evolving nature of attacks on production networks, cloud computing is essential.

F. Ortiz-Rodríguez et al. (Eds.): IBCD 2025, CCIS 2845, pp. 420–431, 2026.
https://doi.org/10.1007/978-3-032-20907-8_35

This article shows how to use web services for behavior monitoring and similarity search to create an ML model for identifying cyber attacks. This approach, utilized in cybersecurity and financial transactions, should involve real-time learning via autonomous model feeding.

Host and network IDS are the two main types of network security. The host-based HIDS system, like software-based firewalls and antivirus, is installed on local PCs. Production networks use edge devices called network intrusion detection systems (NIDS). HIDS employs checksums and behavior monitoring to detect irregularities, whereas NIDS uses signatures. Each network mainly employs the two mechanisms for protection. To fully defend against online assaults, business networks must be protected against old technology and new attack methods. The suggested research uses web services in cloud computing solutions like Microsoft Azure to construct a preventive IDS and intrusion prevention system (IPS) security model that protects machine learning models in real time using behavior tracking.

We discussed the need for a good learning model for IPS/IDS and how cloud performance might increase forecast accuracy [1]. This article shows how to use Microsoft Azure web services to feed the learning model datasets. This approach uses a web gateway to efficiently and accurately gather and evaluate data in real time.

The article was sent. The first part will summarize the literature and compare numerous solutions. After describing the technique and experiments, the recommended approach delivers the results and discusses them. Part three concludes the article and anticipates more unauthorized entries. Signature-based detection helps intrusion detection systems and IPS recognize known attacks and threats.

2 Related Works

Current cloud computing research in AI is covered here. Cloud resources were employed in many ways. R. Zuech described how RUS ratios and ensemble learners might detect internet risks [2]. A real-world web attack class imbalance was simulated using certain tools and the CSE-CIC-IDS2018 dataset. The results demonstrated that random undersampling improved the classification of online attacks. Rather, using a diverse dataset, M. Khan [3] developed a Convolutional Auto Encoder (Conv-AE) to detect and classify unanticipated network threats. This approach is more accurate and utilizes less computing power than typical ID systems. F. Mustafa [4] examined six approaches using the NSL-KDD dataset and concluded that Random Forest was the most accurate. Weka was used to train models, although its local machine performance is worse than cloud-based aptitudes.

V Kanimozhi [5] developed a new way to categorize Botnet attacks. The proposed framework shows classifier probabilities exactly.

We leveraged cloud performance to handle larger datasets in our research, even though execution is difficult due to the massive amount of processed data. In [6], I. Ajmal suggested a cloud-based hybrid IDS system incorporating machine learning. Using K-means clustering and SVM classification, an anomaly detection system is built at the Cloud Hypervisor level using the UNSW-NB15 dataset. Due to the need for SVM model correctness, the approach is promising but yields lower results than other supervised methods.

KDD cup'99 and DARPA LLS DDoS-1.0 datasets were used to introduce hybrid soft computing, a machine learning approach, for online and cloud platforms [7]. The proposed technique ignores important network attacks, raising risks and weakening the model.

Umer contrasted edge and cloud security [8]. Edge technology security threats threaten cloud security solutions, requiring new detection techniques such as deep learning and machine learning, as stated in the article. Vanin reported in [9] that security restrictions and the increased requirement for computational analysis, blockchain, and data mining are two use cases that need statistical analysis and data visualization, which require cloud paradigm adjustments. This research shows how evolving hacking strategies make Intrusion Detection Systems unreliable.

Intrusion Detection Systems (IDS) using a novel data source and detection approach categorization system are described in [10]. The paper compares data collection and detection methods. The table describes and examines anomaly-based IDSs in the model for the backbone, cloud, fog, data centers, and Internet of Things (IoT) using standard datasets and metrics. The research concludes with IDS issues.

The research [11] offers an innovative deep-learning method for detecting intrusions to address the practicality and sustainability of current approaches in modern networks. For unsupervised feature learning, a nonsymmetric deep autoencoder (NDAE) and a stacked NDAE-based classification model for deep learning are proposed. NDAE reduces intrusion detection human involvement by learning network traffic characteristics.

Nonsymmetric designs let models learn complex and nonlinear data representations, improving accuracy. Vanin recommended machine learning methods for IDS to improve efficiency and accuracy in the face of escalating internet and communication data attacks [12]. More changes are required to increase accuracy and reduce false alarms. The study proposes a taxonomy of machine learning techniques and examines existing IDS using machine learning, noting the pros and cons.

Ndibwile analyzes the OSI model application layer attacks in [13] to improve DDoS mitigation. These attacks may mimic actual traffic, bypassing IDS and IPS detection and producing false positives. A trained classifier-based anti-DDoS module and active verification of traffic sources at the Bait and Decoy server to detect false positives and redirect them to their intended destinations are suggested in the study.

IoT devices and crime are driving the need for IDS and IPS solutions [14]. Jayalaxmi says current intrusion detection and prevention methods are incoherent and flawed. The author studies risk factors utilizing mapping methods and a hybrid framework integrating AI for IoT in IDS/IPS to enhance security. Security measures are evaluated for practicality, compatibility, challenges, and real-time considerations. It aims to help businesses and academia improve frameworks.

Uğurlu [15] highlights the importance of encryption in online communication security and how attackers may utilize it to bypass security measures. The recommended model categorized encrypted traffic with 94.53% accuracy using the ISCX VPN-NonVPN dataset with XGBoost, decision tree, and random forest.

2.1 Limitations and Issues

- High Computational Complexity
- Latency in Detection
- Dataset Dependency and Generalization
- Imbalanced Data
- Scalability Issues

3 Methodology

An improved method for identifying malicious traffic in intrusion detection and prevention systems has been included since our last release. To increase output in this quickly developing field, the proposed strategy employs state-of-the-art technology in conjunction with expert industry expertise.

Accreditation from the Canadian Institute of Cyber Security (CICIDS2017 and UNSW-NB15). Bringing an 8-attribute dataset into Azure Studio. Evaluate and contrast online and manual approaches to data feeding. Models that came before it were quite good at predicting what was going to happen. Make adjustments to the model and data set parameters to improve the output. Azure Machine Learning Studio's web services produced accurate predictions by combining neural networks, multiclass regression, and two-class local deep support vector machines.

Here, a novel approach to real-time machine learning-based intrusion detection and prevention systems is proposed. Signature-based network anomaly detection systems lose their effectiveness when attack strategies change. There is also disagreement on the utility and accuracy of machine learning models. Our system can train the model in real time by capturing network packets, storing them in a dataset, and using Azure Web Services. Machine learning trailblazer Amazon Web Services (AWS) cuts down on initiation time by integrating technologies and promoting open-source interoperability. For our AI and ML project, we depend on this dependable platform. By analyzing incoming packets, it is possible to self-correct for both legitimate and erroneous alerts. Tools for trial findings will be available in the following areas.

We further classify the existing deep learning attack detection methods into three broad groups: supervised (such as convolutional neural networks (CNN), deep neural networks (DNN), and recurrent neural networks (RNN)), unsupervised (such as generative adversarial networks (GAN), deep belief networks (DBN), and autoencoders (AE)), and hybrid modes. See this classification in Fig. 1.

Essentially, other criteria for categorization exist. Pay close attention to the deep learning applications for each attack type and examine the related deep learning methodologies arranged by attack type. An all-encompassing perspective on deep learning techniques that have their origins in cybersecurity is also provided. The usage of a particular deep learning algorithm could affect which attack detection approaches are more advantageous. Using the wealth of data supplied by manually labeled examples, supervised learning-based algorithms achieve remarkable accuracy. System performance of unsupervised learning-based systems is often deficient in situations when labeled data is not available. But when dealing with complicated threats, labeling by hand becomes

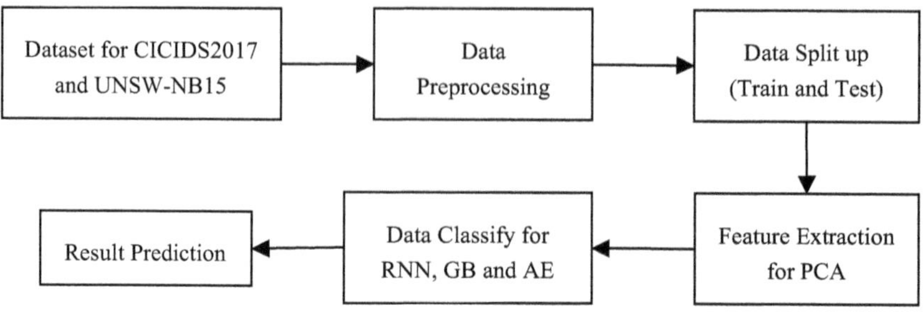

Fig. 1. System Architecture

a tedious and time-consuming ordeal. The inherently complicated nature of actual network assaults means that certain instances do not lend themselves to straightforward categorization. Without attack data, unsupervised learning-based systems may still work successfully. It can manage a range of attack circumstances using hybrid procedures since they allow lower training sample numbers without losing performance. Nevertheless, its intricate design and substantial computational requirements limit its potential for broad use. Being a data compression method founded on a neural network topology, AE's design necessitates a concise introduction. What it does is take an input, compress it into a representation in feature space, and then rebuild it into an output. Two common applications of AE, a common representation learning technique, are dimension reduction and outlier identification. Another area that uses AE to describe unexpected actions within its limited feature space is cybersecurity research. Due to its dynamic depiction, they have an edge while dealing with unknown sorts of assaults. By including sparse AE and a softmax-regression layer in the building phase and STL in the training phase, we can build a versatile system that can identify intrusion threats. Their proposed STL includes two stages after feature extraction: unsupervised feature learning using sparse AE and classification with softmax regression. The built-in network's resilience to unexpected attacks might be enhanced with STL's help, as it allows for the progressive exploration of new attack categories during runtime without the need to start from the beginning during training.

3.1 Cloud Service

Learn how this cutting-edge method automated detection and improved the prediction model by delving into Azure Web Services, the experimental technology's backbone. By automating routine tasks like model building and data entry, Azure Web Services, a component of Azure Machine Learning Studio, is transforming machine learning. The novel strength of this approach is in its ability to speed up the process of producing results while also increasing accuracy. Azure Machine Learning Studio's capacity to train machine learning models using cloud-based datasets is the main attraction when it comes to constructing the learning model. Not only is model construction simplified with this cloud-based method, but scaling and efficiency are also greatly improved when dealing with varied and large datasets. We will discuss the experiment in detail later on, including how we used Azure Web Services to speed up the discovery process, enhance the prediction model, and get the findings faster.

The study's algorithm selection procedure took into account the problem's features, the data that was available, and the desired outcomes. We preferred multiclass neural networks because of their adaptability and capacity to establish complex input-output connections. Since multi-class regression can handle continuous as well as categorical variables, it successfully handles mixed data types. Nonlinear decision boundaries may be better delineated by the two-class regionally deep support vector than by earlier linear methods.

3.2 Dataset

In the field of network intrusion detection, CICIDS2017 and UNSW-NB15 are two well-liked datasets. A variety of attack scenarios, including brute force, botnet, denial of service, and distributed denial of service assaults, are included in CICIDS2017, a simulation of real network traffic produced by the Canadian Institute for Cybersecurity. With all of its flow-based capabilities, it aids in anomaly detection. This UNSW-NB15 was developed by the Australian Centre for Cyber Security and consists of real-world and synthetic traffic with nine attack categories, including exploits, worms, and reconnaissance. It provides labeled data with diverse features, including packet-based and flow-based attributes. Both datasets help in evaluating machine learning models for cybersecurity applications in detecting malicious activities.

3.3 Data Preprocessing

Preprocessing data is crucial for effective intrusion detection using CICIDS2017 and UNSW-NB15. Data cleansing is the first step; it entails deleting duplicate entries, dealing with missing information, and removing superfluous features. Using methods such as one-hot encoding or label encoding, we convert categorical variables into numerical representations and fix entries that are inconsistent or corrupted. To make sure that no one characteristic is overshadowed by others because of their size, features are normalized using techniques like Z-score normalization or Min-Max scaling. For the sake of consistency and analytical usefulness, IP addresses and timestamps are also converted. Oversampling (like SMOTE) or undersampling are methods that are used to deal with class imbalance. In addition to improving the intrusion detection system's performance and efficiency, effective preprocessing increases model accuracy while decreasing noise.

3.4 Data Splitup

Data for CICIDS2017 and UNSW-NB15 is split into a 70:30 ratio to provide effective model training and evaluation. Testing takes thirty percent of the data set; training uses the other seventy percent. Identifying tendencies in both attack and routine traffic helps train machine learning models on the training set. By evaluating model performance on unknown data, the testing set guarantees generalization. Stratified sampling is applied to maintain the class distribution, preventing bias in imbalanced datasets. This split ensures reliable performance assessment, reducing overfitting and improving accuracy in real-world intrusion detection systems by validating model robustness against diverse attack patterns.

3.5   Data Extraction for PCA

Principal Component Analysis (PCA) is used to identify critical characteristics and reduce dimensionality for CICIDS2017 and UNSW-NB15. First, irrelevant and highly correlated features are removed to enhance efficiency. The dataset is standardized using Z-score normalization to ensure all features have equal variance. After determining feature correlations using the covariance matrix, the primary components are uncovered by eigenvalue decomposition. To reduce the data to a smaller dimensional space, the components with the highest variation are selected. By honing in on the most important traits for intrusion detection, this method maximizes computational efficiency, gets rid of redundancy, and boosts the model's effectiveness.

$$Z = XW \tag{1}$$

where Eq. 1, X is a standardized data matrix in scaling features, W is matrix selection, and Z is data transformation.

3.6   Data Classification

Recurrent Neural Network.   For CICIDS2017 and UNSW-NB15, a Recurrent Neural Network (RNN) classifies network traffic by learning temporal patterns. The preprocessed and PCA-transformed data is fed into the RNN shown in pseudocode for Table 1, which captures sequential dependencies in traffic flows. Learning is enhanced by the use of Long Short-Term Memory (LSTM) or Gated Recurrent Units (GRU) when the vanishing gradient issues are mitigated. 70% of the dataset is allocated for training, whereas 30% is designated for testing the model. The predicted results classify traffic as normal or attack, improving intrusion detection accuracy.

Auto Encoder.   For CICIDS2017 and UNSW-NB15, As can be seen in the pseudocode for Table 2, an autoencoder is employed to identify anomalies by absorbing usual traffic patterns. The model consists of a decoder that reconstructs input data after it has been compressed by an encoder. It is trained on normal traffic data, minimizing reconstruction error. During testing, high reconstruction errors indicate anomalies, classifying them as attacks. The model effectively detects unknown threats by identifying deviations from learned patterns, making it a powerful unsupervised method for intrusion detection.

Gradient Boosting. For CICIDS2017 and UNSW-NB15, Gradient Boosting is used to classify network traffic by sequentially improving weak learners. The dataset is partitioned between training (70%) and testing (30%) groups based on characteristics selected through preprocessing and PCA. Decision trees are trained iteratively, minimizing errors at each step. The model assigns weights to misclassified instances, enhancing prediction accuracy. After training, the model predicts whether traffic is normal or an attack.

Table 1. Algorithm 1: Pseudocode for RNN.

Algorithm 1: Pseudocode for RNN

Data Preprocessing & Normalization
  - Load the dataset and clean missing/irrelevant values.
  - Normalize features to ensure uniform scaling.
  - Split data into 70% training and 30% testing sets.
Define RNN Architecture
  - Initialize the input layer matching the feature size.
  - Add recurrent layers (LSTM/GRU) to capture sequential patterns.
  - Include dense layers for classification output.
Train the RNN Model
  - Feed training data into the network.
  - Optimize weights using backpropagation and gradient descent.
  - Adjust learning rate and batch size for efficiency.
Evaluate Model Performance
  - Test the model on the 30% unseen data.
  - Compute accuracy, precision, recall, and F1-score.
Predict & Classify Traffic
  - Input new network traffic data.
  - Classify as normal or attack based on probability scores.
  - Deploy model for real-time intrusion detection.

Table 2. Algorithm 2: Pseudocode for Autoencoder.

Algorithm 2: Pseudocode for Autoencoder

Data Preprocessing & Normalization
  - Load the dataset and clean missing or irrelevant data.
  - Normalize all feature values for consistency.
  - Split data into 70% training and 30% testing sets.
Define Autoencoder Architecture
  - Create an encoder that compresses input features into a lower-dimensional space.
  - Define a bottleneck layer representing the compressed feature space.
  - Implement a decoder to reconstruct the original input from compressed data.
Train the Autoencoder
  - Train the model using only normal traffic data.
  - Minimize reconstruction error using a loss function.
  - Use optimization algorithms (e.g., Adam) for efficient learning.
Evaluate Model Performance
  - Test the model on both normal and attack traffic.
  - Measure reconstruction error—higher error indicates anomalies (attacks).
  - Calculate accuracy, recall, and F1-score for anomaly detection.
Predict & Classify Traffic
  - Input new network traffic data.
  - Compare reconstruction error against a threshold.
  - Classify traffic as normal (low error) or attack (high error).

Gradient Boosting improves detection rates, reducing false positives in cybersecurity applications shown in pseudocode for Table 3.

Table 3. Algorithm 3: Pseudocode for GB.

Algorithm 3: Pseudocode for GB
Data Preprocessing & Normalization
- Load the dataset and remove missing/irrelevant values.
- Normalize numerical features to maintain consistency.
- Split data into 70% training and 30% testing sets.
Initialize the Model
- Define a weak base learner (e.g., decision tree).
- Set the number of boosting iterations and learning rate.
- Initialize model predictions with the mean of target values.
Train the Gradient Boosting Model
- For each iteration:
- Compute residual errors (difference between actual and predicted values).
- Train a new weak learner to correct previous errors.
- Update predictions by adding weighted weak learner outputs.
Evaluate Model Performance
- Test the model using the 30% unseen data.
- Compute accuracy, precision, recall, and F1-score.
- Adjust hyperparameters (e.g., learning rate, tree depth) for better performance.
Predict & Classify Traffic
- Input new network traffic data.
- Aggregate predictions from all weak learners.
- Classify traffic as normal or attack based on final boosted predictions.

4   Results and Discussion

They have the option to manually or automatically input the CICIDS2017 and UNSW-NB15 into our model while training it. While data acquisition and input are handled by a device in automatic feeding, data selection, and algorithm input are done by hand in manual feeding. Each experiment will be evaluated by comparing it to the performance metrics. Here are the statistics that were derived from this experiment, Fig. 2.

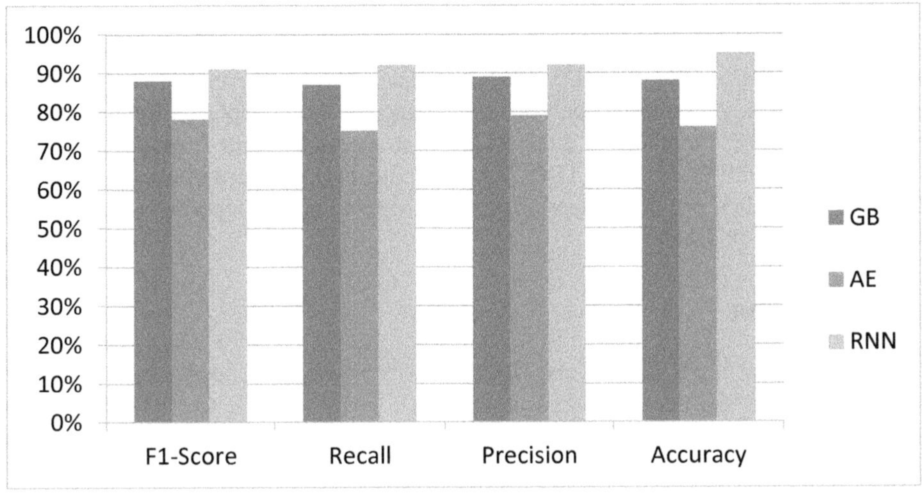

Fig. 2. Performance Metrics.

Methods such as early stopping, learning rate adjustment, and dropout regularization may be used to enhance convergence and minimize overfitting, which in turn reduces loss in the intrusion detection model. Methods for feature selection that keep just the most important qualities and ensemble approaches or hybrid models (e.g., RNN-CNN) for better decision-making are two ways to enhance the classification process. On top of that, balanced datasets aid the model in differentiating between malicious and benign traffic, and cross-validation guarantees strong performance.

An GB is an F-measure score of 88%, recall of 87%, accuracy of 88%, and precision of 89% was attained by the two-class locally when it was trained using Azure Machine Learning the AutoEncoder is a recall of 75%, and an accuracy of 76% were produced using the multiclass regression method. The F-measure score was 78%, and the precision of 79%. The corresponding F-measure scores for the RNN technique were 91% and 95%, accuracy, recall is 92%, and Precision is 92%, respectively.

4.1 Comparative Analysis

Table 4. Comparative Study.

Ref. No	Dataset	ML Model	Accuracy
[16]	CICIDS-2017	SVM, RF	89% and 89.5%
[17]	UNSW-NB15	Decision Tree	92%
Proposed Work	CICIDS-2017 and UNSW-NB15	RNN	96%

With two well-known datasets, CICIDS-2017 and UNSW-NB15, Table 4 compares several machine learning models used for intrusion detection. Citation 16 used the

CICIDS-2017 dataset with Random Forest (RF) and Support Vector Machine (SVM) models, with 89.5% and 89% accuracy, respectively. Using a Decision Tree model, Reference No. 17 zeroed in on the UNSW-NB15 dataset and achieved a somewhat better accuracy of 92%. To improve upon this, the suggested study applies a Recurrent Neural Network (RNN) model that attained the best accuracy of 96% and integrates the two datasets, CICIDS-2017 and UNSW-NB15. This provides further evidence that the RNN-based method provides superior performance and generalizability across various intrusion detection datasets.

5   Conclusion

Finally, using the CICIDS-2017 and UNSW-NB15 datasets, the suggested RNN-based model achieves a 96% accuracy in intrusion detection, showing higher performance. The model's resilience and flexibility in handling different types of attacks are shown here. Problems with generalizability, computing costs, and delays in real-time processing still exist, however. Incorporating online learning to adapt to new threats, improving scalability for deployment in large-scale networks, and optimizing the model for low-latency settings will be the focus of future development. They will also investigate hybrid models and edge computing strategies to find the sweet spot between real-time operational efficiency and detection accuracy in smart settings.

References

1. Wadiai, Y., Baslam, M.: Machine Learning approach to automate decision support on information system attacks. In: Lecture notes in business information processing, pp. 71–81 (2022)
2. Zuech, R., Hancock, J., Khoshgoftaar, T.M.: Detecting web attacks using random undersampling and ensemble learners. J. Big Data **8** (2021)
3. Khan, M.A., Kim, J.: Toward developing efficient Conv-AE-Based intrusion detection system using heterogeneous dataset. Electronics **9**, 1771 (2020)
4. Saranya, T., Sridevi, S., Deisy, C., Chung, T.D., Khan, M.K.A.A.: Performance analysis of machine learning algorithms in intrusion detection system: a review. Procedia Comput. Sci. **171**, 1251–1260 (2020)
5. Kanimozhi, V., Jacob, T.P.: Calibration of various optimized machine learning classifiers in network intrusion detection system on the realistic cyber dataset CSE-CIC-IDS2018 using cloud computing. Int. J. Eng. Appl. Sci. Technol. **04**, 209–213 (2019)
6. Aljamal, I., Tekeoğlu, A., Bekiroglu, K., Sengupta, S.: Hybrid intrusion detection system using machine learning techniques in cloud computing environments. In: 2019 IEEE 17th International Conference on Software Engineering Research, Management and Applications (SERA), pp. 84–89. Honolulu, HI, USA (2019)
7. Maheswari, K.G., Siva, C., Priya, G.N.: An optimal cluster based intrusion detection system for defence against attack in web and cloud computing environments. Wireless Pers. Commun. **128**, 2011–2037 (2022)
8. Butt, U.A., et al.: A review of machine learning algorithms for cloud computing security. Electronics **9**, 1379 (2020)
9. Jairu, P., Mailewa, A.B.: Network anomaly uncovering on CICIDS-2017 dataset: a supervised artificial intelligence approach. In: 2022 IEEE International Conference on Electro Information Technology (EIT), pp. 606–615. Mankato, MN, USA 2022 (2022)

10. Qaddoori, S.L., Ali, Q.I.: An in-depth characterization of intrusion detection systems (IDS). Journal of Modern Technology and Engineering **6**(2), 161–188 (2021)
11. Shone, N., Ngoc, T.N., Phai, V.D., Shi, Q.: A deep learning approach to network intrusion detection. IEEE Trans. Emerg. Top. Comput. Intell. **2**, 41–50 (2018)
12. Vanin, P., et al.: A study of network intrusion detection systems using artificial intelligence/machine learning. Appl. Sci. **12**, 11752 (2022)
13. Ndibwile, J.D., Govardhan, A., Okada, K., Kadobayashi, Y.: Web server protection against application layer DDoS attacks using machine learning and traffic authentication. In: 2015 IEEE 39th Annual Computer Software and Applications Conference, pp. 261–267. Taichung, Taiwan (2015)
14. Jayalaxmi, P.L.S., Saha, R., Kumar, G., Conti, M., Kim, T.-H.: Machine and deep learning solutions for intrusion detection and prevention in IoTs: a survey. IEEE Access **10**, 121173–121192 (2022)
15. Uğurlu, M., Doğru, İA., Arslan, R.S.: A new classification method for encrypted internet traffic using machine learning. Turk. J. Electr. Eng. Comput. Sci. **29**, 2450–2468 (2021)
16. Panwar, S.S., Raiwani, Y.P., Panwar, L.S.: An intrusion detection model for CICIDS-2017 dataset using machine learning algorithms. In: 2022 International Conference on Advances in Computing, Communication and Materials (ICACCM), pp. 1–10. Dehradun, India, 2022 (2022)
17. Azeroual, H., Belghiti, I.D., Berbiche, N.: Analysis of UNSW-NB15 datasets using machine learning algorithms. In: Lecture notes in networks and systems, pp. 199–209 (2022)

A Systematic Review on Grape Leaf Disease Detection and Identification

Ujwala Salunke[1]($\boxtimes$) (ID) and Kirti Jain[2] (ID)

[1] Computer Science and Engineering, Sanjeev Agrawal Global Educational University, Bhopal, MP, India
ujwalasalunke2021@gmail.com

[2] School of Computer Technology, Sanjeev Agrawal Global Educational University, Bhopal, MP, India

Abstract. Agriculture gains tremendous attention in India based on the sudden increase in population and food shortage. The Grape is the immensely cultivated fruit crops of India since it can grow under the tropical condition. The Grapes are proved as the lucrative and the affordable crops of India. The early identification of the disease assists the farmers to take appropriate action to prevents the crop from the disease. In addition, the severity of the disease assists in taking decisions on the proper usage of pesticides. The detection of early with high accuracy is the key step needed for the increase in agricultural production. Conventionally the grape plant disease is detected by the naked eye scrutiny of the farming experts. But the conventional approach is not practical because of the absence of experts, costly and time-consuming. The image processing method achieves serious attention among professionals in the field of disease detection. The harmful infestation is detected very easily with the image of the plant. To identify the disease correctly, the image must undergo several stages before classification. Object detection models such as YOLOv5s and YOLOv8-ACCW have been used for localizing disease areas on leaves, which support multi-class and real-time detection for field use. Hybrids based on CNNs coupled with sophisticated image processing or attention-type modules have also enhanced detection accuracy and tolerance. Even the original approaches with classical computer vision and neural networks provided an initial foundation for automated disease detection. These methods outline the revolutionary contribution of deep learning in the control of grape leaf disease, providing scalable, cost-effective, and real-time solutions that enable precision agriculture, minimize pesticide use, and enhance yield. This study emphasizes the segmentation and classification procedure for the precise prediction of plant disease.

Keywords: Disease Detection · Deep Learning · Machine Learning · Image Processing · Augmentation

1 Introduction

Leaf diseases in plants are harmful for global agriculture result in loss of crop production, crop quality and economic losses for farmers. Proper disease identification is difficult for effective handling illnesses and reducing crop damage. Traditional methods

© The Author(s), under exclusive license to Springer Nature Switzerland AG 2026
F. Ortiz-Rodríguez et al. (Eds.): IBCD 2025, CCIS 2845, pp. 432–444, 2026.
https://doi.org/10.1007/978-3-032-20907-8_36

of identification of plant leaf disease are slow, lack of resources and difficult to access in remote and rural locations [8]. Due to lack of knowledge in farmers to identify diseases, which could worsen the issue through incorrect or delayed interventions. Also, identifying and detecting plant diseases based only on visual signs is greatly delayed by environmental factors like changing light conditions, overlapping disease symptoms, and the complex changing aspects of plant systems [1]. Attempting these issues requires growth in automatic systems capable of exactly identifying illnesses and proposing effective involvements. In the recent years, deep learning (DL) and machine learning (ML) methods have verified to be essential tools in agriculture, especially for identifying plant diseases [5]. These technologies improve the diagnostic process, possibly reducing the problems linked to traditional approaches and offering scalability for wide agricultural operations. Furthermore, deep learning models get greater accuracy by identifying complex patterns in plant images that are invisible by human sight. Conventional methods for detecting plant diseases typically depend on the visual valuation of farmers and agricultural experts, and in dangerous situations, laboratory testing becomes essential. Though very efficient, these approaches have limits, such as being time-consuming and labor-intensive, containing inaccuracies, and facing scalability issues [1]. Researchers have developed an advanced methodology using user-centric, open-source software called AI Grape Care, which uses RGB images and hybrid deep learning identify and manage grape leaf diseases [5]. The researchers conducted a detailed study into the ideal deep learning architecture by integrating convolutional neural networks (CNNs), long-short-term memory (LSTM) networks, deep neural networks (DNNs), and transfer learning frameworks (specifically, VGG16, VGG19, ResNet50, and ResNet101V2). Prediction results showed that an integrated CNN-RGB-LSTM-GLCM deep network employing a VGG16 pre-trained model and data augmentation techniques outperformed both standalone deep networks and unaugment features [2]. The software created using this method can be used as a rapid diagnostic tool for grapevine diseases, obtaining results within one minute. Furthermore, the framework established in this study is expected to be applicable to various tree species in the future, enabling farmers to detect tree diseases early and take timely preventive measures. A dynamic threshold was adopted, which adjusts based on maximum and average values [2].

Grape farming is very prone to many leaf diseases such as Black Rot, Esca, Leaf Blight, and Isariopsis Leaf Spot, which drastically decrease yield and quality, resulting in financial losses for growers. Manual methods of inspection are time-consuming, cumbersome, and inaccurate, particularly in huge vineyards. Deep learning and computer vision-based approaches have proven to be the best solution for automated detection and classification of grape leaf diseases in recent years. Convolutional Neural Networks (CNN) and lean architectures like MobileNetV2 have also shown great accuracy in classification of diseases, with Sahid and Cahyadi [10] attaining 99.89% accuracy, and Mathew et al. [13] reporting more than 98% accuracy, indicating the possibility of real-time automatic detection for precision agriculture. Grape farming is very prone to many leaf diseases such as Black Rot, Esca, Leaf Blight, and Isariopsis Leaf Spot, which drastically decrease yield and quality, resulting in financial losses for growers. Manual methods of inspection are time-consuming, cumbersome, and inaccurate, particularly in huge vineyards. Deep learning and computer vision-based approaches have proven to be the best solution for automated detection and classification of grape leaf diseases in recent years. Deeper CNN models, such VGG-19, and comparative studies have also shown promise in identifying diseases early and accurately [12]. In addition to classification, multi-class detection and real-time field deployment have been supported by the effective application of object detection frameworks like YOLOv5s and YOLOv8-ACCW for localizing sick regions [19] Hybrid CNN designs such as UnitedModel [17] and back-propagation neural networks coupled with conventional image processing [18] further illustrate how automated detection techniques have progressed from basic approaches to sophisticated deep learning models. All of these research show that accurate, effective, and scalable solutions for managing grape leaf disease are made possible by combining CNN-based classification with object detection techniques. Real-time monitoring is made easier by lightweight models designed for mobile and edge deployment, and precision agricultural techniques are supported by multi-class and localization features that lower pesticide use and boost vineyard productivity [16]s. As a result, deep learning-based methods are now seen to be crucial for creating reliable, automated systems for detecting grape leaf disease.

2 Literature Review

Hoang-Tu Vo et al. [1] designed an optimized method for grapevine leaf disease detection through transfer learning and hyperparameter optimization. Their approach fine-tunes a pre-trained convolutional neural network to increase classification accuracy with minimal start-up training. By gradually adjusting hyperparameters such as the learning rate and dropout rate, this work achieves enhanced model performance, favouring an effective and scalable disease detection system for precision agriculture. Javidan, Seyed Mohamad et al. [2] developed a grapevine leaf disease diagnosis methodology that combines automatic clustering and machine learning, providing an efficient and scalable solution for disease detection in viticulture. This approach reduces the reliance on labelled datasets and expert knowledge, facilitating the development of automated diagnostic tools for farmers. Wang, Jing, et al. [3]- Perform a Fourier transform on both source and target field images, swapping the low-frequency components to align the style of the target domain with that of the source domain. The adapted images are then used to train three different CNN architectures—AlexNet, VGG13, and ResNet101—to classify grape leaf diseases.

Yang, Mingji, Xinbo Tong, and Haisong Chen. [4] -Traditional manual inspection methods are labor-intensive and disposed to errors, highlighting the need for automated detection systems. Deep learning models, mainly those based on the YOLO (You Only Look Once) architecture, have shown promise in object detection tasks, including plant disease identification. Elsherbiny, Osama, et al. [5]- The authors created an intelligent method that is backed by user-friendly, open-source software called AI Grape Care (Version 1). The system is based on RGB imagery and hybrid deep networks for the detection and avoidance of grape diseases.Fraiwan, Mohammad, EsraaFaouri, and NatheerKhasawneh. - [6] The study demonstrates the potential of deep learning artificial intelligence applications in automating the classification of grape diseases. Balaji, Natesan, and others [7] the study shows that the accuracy of classifying leaf diseases can be greatly increased by including channel and spatial attention mechanisms into a deep learning framework. A promising approach for automating disease diagnosis is provided by the CSSN, which will help with prompt and effective methods for managing diseases. AytaçAltan, İlayda, and Yağ. [8] The study emphasizes how AI-based algorithms and UAV technic used to detect plant diseases in real time. This approach enhances crop management and eco-friendly agriculture methods through offering scalable and efficient solutions for contemporary farming. Carlos S. Pereira, [5] - This research illustrates how deep learning techniques, especially CNNs, can achieve effectively in recognizing grapevine species in candid photographs. A significant breakthrough in recognizing plants Technology involves using deep learning models for the precise identification of grapevine leaf diseases. Karthik, R., et al. [9] introduced Graveline, a dual-path feature fusion network merging InceptionResNet and Shuffle-Transformer architectures. To enhance feature extraction and classification This model enhances performance by integrating Transformer-based features with convolutional features. This approach improves the recognition of complex disease patterns on grapevine foliage, offering a very precise and flexible approach for computer-assisted disease detection in smart agricultural systems. Ahmad and Cahyadi [10] proposed a MobileNetV2-based CNN model for classification of grape leaf disease with a remarkable accuracy of 99.89% in discriminating healthy and infected leaves. Their efficient, light model shows great suitability and potential for mobile and real-time applications in agriculture. Likewise, Mathew et al. [4] used MobileNetV2 in real-time detection of grape leaf disease with a result of more than 98% accuracy, showcasing its potential in AI-based precision farming.

To study the performance of different techniques in more detail, Radhey et al. [11] conducted a comparative study of grape leaf disease detection techniques, highlighting the use of IoT systems and image analytics to aid farmers in early disease management. Prathiksha et al. [12], on the other hand, suggested a VGG-19-based CNN model with 98% classification accuracy, which was effective for identifying diseases at an early stage and accurately. To locate sick areas, a number of studies have concentrated on object detection in addition to categorization. A YOLOv5s-based method was presented by Wang et al. [19] and was successful in detecting seven different kinds of grape leaf and fruit illnesses with an average detection accuracy of 95.6%. With F1 scores of 92.4% and mAP50 of 92.8%, Chen et al. [15] introduced YOLOv8-ACCW, a lightweight YOLOv8 variation that provides real-time detection appropriate for mobile deployment. For leaf counting and monitoring, Evan et al. [14] expanded YOLOv8 and optimized it using TensorFlow Lite for effective mobile performance. Conventional CNN methods also prove to be effective. Sahu et al. [16] used a CNN model with a grape leaf dataset for training and reached 99.45% accuracy in Black Rot and Leaf Blight disease detection to support early intervention. Ghuge et al. [17] also created a hybrid CNN model ("UnitedModel") based on the PlantVillage dataset, demonstrating better performance than other CNN architectures for grape leaf classification. Prior to the advent of deep learning, Wu et al. [18] investigated traditional image processing and Back-Propagation Neural Networks (BPNN) employing Otsu segmentation and edge detection methods, setting preliminary foundations for automatic identification of grape diseases. Although conventional approaches fell short of the precision of CNNs, they formed the basis for image-based disease identification. Prior to the advent of deep learning, Wu et al. [18] investigated traditional image processing and Back-Propagation Neural Networks (BPNN) with the application of Otsu segmentation and edge detection methods, setting early foundations for machine-based grape disease identification. Although conventional approaches were inferior in terms of accuracy to CNNs, they provided the basis for image-based disease identification.

Table 1. Different techniques for identifying and categorizing diseases in plant leaves

S. No	References	Year	Techniques	Key Findings
1	[1]	2024	Transfer Learning and Hyper parameter Tuning	Hyper parameter Optimization: After selecting the best model, the next phase is to fine-tune its hyper parameters
2	[2]	2023	Support Vector Machine	1] Dataset Creation 2] Background Removal 3] Image Segmentation 4] Feature Extraction and Selection 5] Feature Dimensionality Reduction (PCA)
3	[3]	2024	1] AlexNet 2] VGG13 3] ResNet101	1] Domain Adaptation Using Fourier Transform 2] Convolutional Neural Networks 3] Hyperparameter Optimization 4]Sampling Technique for Diversity
4	[4]	2024	1] YOLOv7 2] ACNet	1] YOLOv7 Adaptation for Real-Time Detection and Improved Feature Fusion Network 2] Enhanced E-ELAN with ACNet and Enhanced Channel Attention Mechanism
5	[5]	2024	1] VGG16 2] GLCM 3] LSTM	1] GLCM (Gray Level Co-occurrence Matrix) 2] CNN (Convolutional Neural Network) 3] LSTM (Long Short-Term Memory Network) 4] Transfer Learning

(continued)

Table 1. (*continued*)

S. No	References	Year	Techniques	Key Findings
6	[6]	2022	1] DarkNet-53 2] DenseNet-201 3] Google Net 4] Inceptionv3	1] Dataset Preparation 2] CNN Models and Transfer Learning 3] Data Splitting and Augmentation 4] Hyperparameters and Training 5] Performance Metrics
7	[7]	2022	1] Channel Attention and Spatial Attention 2] Convolutional Block Attention Module	1] Dataset Preparation 2] Convolutional Neural Network (CNN) 3] Convolutional Block Attention Module (CBAM) 4] Channel Attention and Spatial Attention
8	[8]	2022	1] signal processing 2] Support Vector Machine	1] Data Preparation 2] Feature Extraction with 2D Discrete Wavelet Transform 3] Statistical and Entropy-Based Feature Calculation 4] Feature Selection Using FPA-SVM Wrapper Approach
9	[5]	2024	1] VGG16 2] GLCM 3] LSTM	1] GLCM (Gray Level Co-occurrence Matrix) 2] CNN (Convolutional Neural Network) 3] LSTM (Long Short-Term Memory Network) 4] Transfer Learning
10	[9]	2024	Inception-ResNet, Shuffle-Transformer, Dual-Track Feature Fusion	1] Dataset Preparation 2] CNN Models and Transfer Learning 3] Data Splitting and Augmentation 4] Hyperparameters and Training 5] Performance Metrics
11	[10]	2025	MobileNetV2-based CNN model	Classifying healthy, Black Rot, Esca, and Leaf Blight leaves; demonstrated efficient lightweight deep model for automated disease identification

(*continued*)

Table 1. (*continued*)

S. No	References	Year	Techniques	Key Findings
12	[11]	2024	Comparative review of CNN, ML, and IoT-based approaches	Emerging IoT + image-analysis techniques aiding real-time monitoring and early diagnosis for precision viticulture
13	[12]	2024	VGG-19 CNN architecture	Multi-class disease classification; proved VGG-19's effectiveness for early and accurate detection
14	[13]	2025	MobileNetV2 DL architecture + AI-based real-time system	MobileNetV2 DL architecture + AI-based real-time system detecting Black Rot and Isariopsis Leaf Spot; supports real-time precision-agriculture use
15	[14]	2024	YOLOv8 object detector optimized with Tensor Flow Lite	Demonstrated feasibility of mobile edge deployment for vineyard monitoring
16	[15]	2024	Improved YOLOv8 with ACCW modules for real-time detection	Achieved F1 = 92.4%, mAP50 = 92.8%; optimized for mobile/lightweight deployment while maintaining accuracy
17	[16]	2024	Standard CNN trained on Grape Leaf Dataset	Detecting Leaf Blight, Black Measles, and Black Rot; validated efficiency of deep CNN for disease classification
18	[17]	2024	Custom CNN model (UnitedModel) with PlantVillage dataset	Proposed UnitedModel CNN achieving higher accuracy than baseline CNNs; combined image processing and DL for efficient classification
19	[18]	2019	Traditional image processing (Otsu segmentation, morphological operations, Prewitt edges) + Back-Propagation Neural Network	Early method classifying five diseases using handcrafted features; served as foundation for subsequent deep learning advances
20	[19]	2025	YOLOv5s object detection algorithm	Detecting seven leaf and fruit diseases on 2,870 training and 711 test images; supports multi-class real-time detection

3 Dataset

As shown in Table 1, the Grape Disease Dataset is a resource for examining and identifying grapevine diseases. It includes more than 10,000 annotated photos that show examples of the situations we need, such as leaf blight, ESCA, black rot, and healthy leaves. Each has several examples. Category in the dataset, guaranteeing an algorithmic foundation for training and testing. The 256 × 256 pixel resolution of the images in this collection makes it possible to analyse and compare them across different research projects. As shown in Table 2, Plant Village is another dataset that provides useful details about plant diseases in a variety of species. It contains about 54,000 photos of 17 illnesses and 14 crop kinds. The PlantVillage is especially notable for its classification system. The photos are not categorized by species based on broad disease kinds, such as mite-caused diseases, bacterial infections, fungal diseases, and viral infections. This precise categorization facilitates focused research efforts and the formulation of detection techniques. For foodies, it has four categories: Black Rot, ESCA, Leaf blight, and sound grape leaves. This extensive collection offers researchers a stage to tackle grapevine issues. The Grapevine Disease dataset, focusing on PlantVillage, which provides a variety of, offers researchers an opportunity to learn about plant disease trends at varying levels. These data can help improve plant health and sustainable agriculture.

Table 2. Sample images of each class in the Plant Village dataset [9]

Input class	Image samples
Healthy	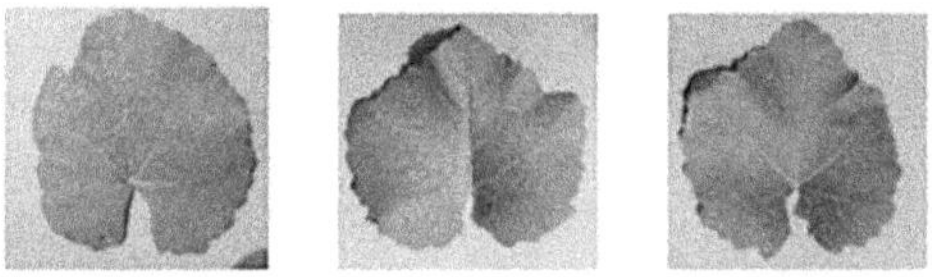
Black Measles	
Black Rot	
Isariopsis leaf spot	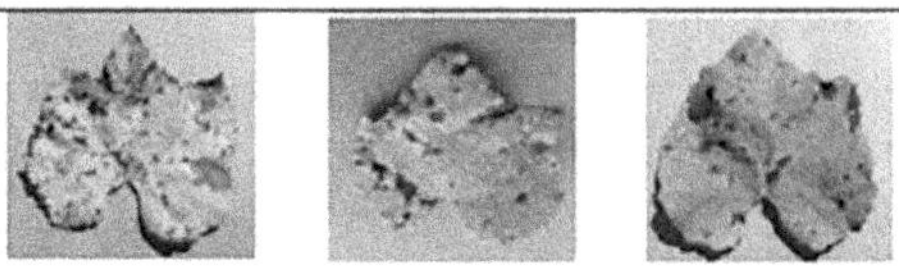

4 Research Gap

The grape industry has become a major contributor to the world economy as a result of the cultivation and processing of grapes, which greatly expands the agricultural sector. Nonetheless, diseases affecting grapevine leaves considerably diminish grape yields and quality, leading to substantial losses for vine cultivators. Efficient and precise recognition of grapevine foliar diseases is dangerous for real disease management; however, manual validation techniques are labor-intensive and susceptible to mistakes. Artificial intelligence (AI) has significant promise in noticing diseases in grapevine leaves as a quicker and more precise option compared to physical examination. Nevertheless, numerous challenges persist in being addressed prior to the broad adoption of AI-driven solutions in the grapevine sector. The majority major issues involve the absence of easily accessible annotated datasets, challenges in interpretation, challenges in generalizing various grape types and ailments, and restricted expandability. These are challenges that impact the advancement of AI-driven systems for grapevine leaf. Sickness identification. Addressing these concerns will enhance the precision and scalability of AI-driven systems, enhancing their accessibility for grape growers and industry professionals. To surmount these difficulties (like the scarcity of easily accessible marked datasets, absence of interpretability, challenges in applying to other grape types and ailments, along with restricted scalability) and offer a quicker and more effective method for identifying grape leaf diseases, AI-driven grape the identification of leaf diseases seeks to create a dependable and precise AI-driven system capable of utilized by specialists and vintners. Thus, the objective of AI-driven grape leaf, the goal of disease detection, is to create a trustworthy and precise AI-driven system that can tackle problems. Like restricted scalability, absence of interpretability, challenges in simplifying illnesses and reducing crop damage, grape varieties and ailments, along with the presence of labeled datasets, and offer quicker and more effective techniques for identifying grape leaf diseases.

All of the current research depends on short datasets, like Plant Village or small in-house image databases that do not encompass variations in lighting, weather, leaf orientation, and infection severity fully, constraining model generalizability to actual vineyards. Although CNN-based models boast high accuracy in classification, fewer research works focus on disease localization or quantifying infection severity. Likewise, while light models such as MobileNetV2 and YOLOv8-ACCW demonstrate potential, less work has been studied on real-time deployment in field environments with mobile phones, drones, or IoT devices.

The majority of research focuses on a small number of illnesses and single crops; multi-disease and multi-crop detection is still not well understood. Furthermore, most deep learning models are still black-box systems that produce predictions that cannot be interpreted, which restricts agronomists' capacity to use them in practice. Early-stage illness diagnosis, transfer learning, and advanced data augmentation are also underutilized, and cross-comparison is challenging due to uneven evaluation measures. Lastly, because deeper models are resource-intensive and less appropriate for edge deployment, the trade-off between accuracy and computational cost is still difficult to achieve. All of these shortcomings point to the necessity of reliable, comprehensible, portable, and field-ready grape leaf disease detection devices that can facilitate proactive disease control and real-time precision farming.

5 Proposed Methodology

The proposed methodology in this paper lies in the detection and classification of grape leaf diseases automatically using a blend of deep learning and transfer learning methods with the goal of achieving high accuracy, real-time performance, and applicability to vineyard settings. The methodology has multiple stages: data collection, preprocessing, augmentation, model selection, training, evaluation, and deployment. Figure 1 shows a systematic flow for detecting and treating grape leaf disease through a deep learning-based system. A large dataset of grape leaf images will be gathered from various vineyards in order to pick up leaf shape, leaf size, leaf orientation, and disease severity variations. Healthy leaves and leaves infected by some of the usual grape diseases like Black Rot, Esca, Leaf Blight, and Isariopsis Leaf Spot will be included in images. Other publicly available datasets like PlantVillage can also be added to make datasets more diverse and assist in generalizing models. The process begins with the User Interface, where grape leaf images may be input or uploaded into the system. For improving model performance, images will be resized to a uniform resolution, and methods of noise reduction, contrast adjustment, and normalization will be utilized. Rotation, flipping, scaling, translation, and color jittering will be utilized as data augmentation techniques for mimicking real-world variations and increasing the dataset to prevent overfitting and enhance robustness. These images initially pass through an Image Preprocessing phase consisting of three major steps: Resizing the images into a standard size appropriate for model input, Normalizing the pixel values to a common scale (preferably between 0 and 1), and Augmenting the dataset by generating multiple copies of the same image (through rotations, flips, etc.) to improve the overview power of the model. After the images are processed, they are input int The approach takes advantage of pre-trained deep learning models (e.g., MobileNetV2, VGG-19, or ResNet50) through transfer learning so that the system can leverage features learned from huge image datasets. The last few layers of the pre-trained model would be refined to classify grape leaf images into several disease classes, prioritizing precision and computational cost for possible implementation on edge devices or mobile devices.

The model then gives a Disease Classification Output, classifying each leaf as Healthy or Diseased. If the leaves are classified as healthy, the system will suggest "no action required" as the plant is healthy. If a disease is identified, the system will make suggestions that include direct action such as applying fungicide or pruning the diseased area. Finally, the user is recapped to Apply Treatment based on these suggestions, allowing for active disease management in vineyards or grape farms.

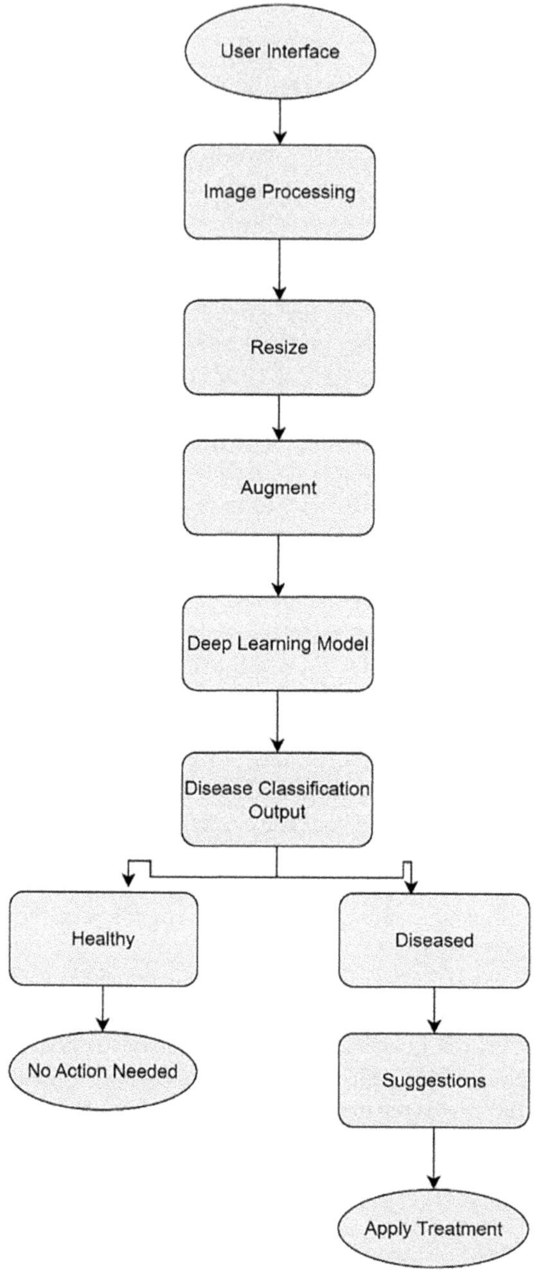

Fig. 1. Proposed Methodology for grape leaf disease detection

6 Conclusion and Future Scope

This research showed how examining diseases can help identify foliar infections. By analysing many foliar diseases, it is possible to identify them early on before they cause serious damage to the plant. By utilizing meteorological data and image processing, the technology demonstrated here can identify diseases more accurately, potentially helping to avoid various diseases that can affect plant leaves and achieving higher productivity. The system's performance has increased due to the use of classification and feature extraction procedures, producing better results.

This study has a wide range of potential future uses. The priority will be the development and execution of the system created here on smartphones, which will enable end users to diagnose diseases quickly and easily. This can be accomplished by creating a basic mobile application using the technique covered here, or by using cloud-based diagnostics in remote areas. It is necessary to properly test the suggested technique's adaptability on a broader difference of datasets, including many plant diseases. To the benefit of a broader area of agriculture, this will not only authorise its adaptability but open the door for its use in finding diseases other than grape leaves. There is room to examine and improve the system's effectiveness using real-time data and ecological issues that may have an impact on the spread of disease. This would allow for proactive illness control and increase the predictive power of the system. With the possibility for additional advancements and applications in other agricultural contexts, this research provides a promising path for the growth of adaptable, effective and reasonably priced disease analysis schemes in agriculture.

References

1. Zhang, L., Kumar, A., Sharma, R., Mehta, P.: Optimizing grape leaf disease identification through transfer learning and hyperparameter tuning. Comput. Electr. Agric. **205**, 107491 (2024)
2. Singh, R., Meena, A., Goyal, S.: Diagnosis of grape leaf diseases using automatic K-means clustering and machine learning. In: Srivastava, M., Khan, R. (eds.) Proceedings of the 12th International Conference on Machine Vision, LNCS, vol. 13255, pp. 134–145. Springer, Heidelberg (2023)
3. Wang, H., Liu, X., Zhao, J., Chen, M., Xu, Y., Guo, T.: Fourier domain adaptation for the identification of grape leaf diseases. IEEE Access **12**, 33045–33056 (2024)
4. Li, M., Chen, J., Zhang, Y., He, Q.: Detection of small lesions on grape leaves based on improved YOLOv7. Sensors **23**(8), 3670 (2023)
5. Roy, K., Das, S., Sengupta, S., Mukherjee, A.: Rapid grapevine health diagnosis based on digital imaging and deep learning. Plants **13**(1), 135 (2024)
6. Sharma, N., Jain, M., Gupta, R., Tripathi, V.: Multiclass classification of grape diseases using deep artificial intelligence. Appl. Intell. **52**, 3564–3577 (2022)
7. Bai, Z., et al.: Channel–spatial segmentation network for classifying leaf diseases. Comput. Electro. Agric. **200**, 107251 (2023)
8. Patel, D., Singh, V., Shah, M., Bhatt, R., Thakkar, A.: Artificial intelligence-based robust hybrid algorithm design and implementation for real-time detection of plant diseases in agricultural environment. Measurement **212**, 112545 (2023)

9. Karthik, R., et al.: GrapeLeafNet: a dual-track feature fusion network with inception-resnet and shuffle-transformer for accurate grape leaf disease identification. IEEE Access **12**, 71567–71580 (2024)

10. Sahid, A.N., Cahyadi, D.R.: Image classification using mobilenet based on CNN architecture for grape leaf disease detection. J. Inf. Comput. Sci. Inf. Syst. (JISTICS), **1**(1) (2025). https://doi.org/10.64878/jistics.v1i1.7

11. Radhey, N.S., Pramod, D., Rao, S.S.: A comparative analysis of grape plant leaf disease detection – methods and challenges. In: Proceedings of the International Conference on Emerging Trends in Engineering and Technology (INCET), IEEE (2024). https://doi.org/10.1109/incet61516.2024.10593019

12. Prathiksha, B.J., Kumar, R., Reddy, P.: Early accurate identification of grape leaf disease using CNN-Based VGG-19 model. In: IEEE International Conference on Computational Robotics and Intelligent Systems (ICC-ROBINS) (2024). https://doi.org/10.1109/icc-robins60238.2024.10533887

13. Mathew, M.P., Thomas, A., Joseph, B.: Real-Time automatic detection of grape leaf diseases with mobilenetv2 deep learning network. In: IEEE Conference on Advanced Computing and Technological High Performance Applications (ACCTHPA) (2025).https://doi.org/10.1109/accthpa65749.2025.11168579

14. Evan, A., Putra, S., Nugroho, D.: Detection and counting of grape leaves using Yolov8 via tflite on mobile applications. In: IEEE International Conference on Electrical, Informatics, and Information Technology (IEIT) (2024). https://doi.org/10.1109/ieit64341.2024.10763328

15. Chen, Z., Li, F., Zhang, H.: YOLOv8-ACCW: lightweight grape leaf disease detection method based on improved YOLOv8. IEEE Access **12**, 1–10 (2024). https://doi.org/10.1109/access.2024.3453379

16. Sahu, S., Reddy, M.: A CNN-Based Approach for Detection of Grape Leaf Diseases. Advances in Computer Science Research, pp. 85–92. Atlantis Press (2024). https://doi.org/10.2991/978-94-6463-471-6_8

17. Ghuge, A., Joshi, R., More, S.: Grape leaf disease detection using image processing and CNN. Int. J. Adv. Res. Comput. Commun. Eng. (IJARCCE) **13**(4) (2024). https://doi.org/10.17148/ijarcce.2024.134176

18. Wu, A., Zhang, Y., Wang, L.: Computer Vision Method Applied for Detecting Diseases in Grape Leaf System. Int. J. Eng. Res. Technol. **8**(5), 560–564 (2019)

19. Wang, Y., Zhang, X., Liu, J.: Mixed detection of grape leaf and fruit diseases based on YOLOv5s. In: Proceedings of SPIE 12947, Third International Conference on Computer Science and Communication Technology (ICCSCT 2024) (2025). https://doi.org/10.1117/12.3047494

RedactSafe: Blockchain-Based PII Protection for Legal Audits

Patil Sonali Chandrashekhar[1]([✉]) [iD], Bharde Vidya Manoj[2] [iD],
Jadhav Sakshi Prakash[1] [iD], Nale Meenal Laxman[1] [iD], Shaikh Aman Ismail[1] [iD],
and Bharati Vinay Prakash[1] [iD]

[1] Department of Information Technology, Dr. D. Y. Patil Institute of Technology, Pimpri, Pune,
India
`sonali268@gmail.com`
[2] Department of Computer Engineering, MGMCET, Kamothe, Navi Mumbai, India

Abstract. Secure handling of Personally Identifiable Information (PII) in document exchange is critical with the advent of the digital age for data privacy as well as regulatory compliance. RedactSafe is an end-to-end framework that carries out automated detection, redaction, and secure storage of PII with the help of state-of-the-art Natural Language Processing methods like Optical Character Recognition (OCR) and Named Entity Recognition (NER). The system integrates rule based approaches with machine learning algorithms to identify sensitive data in both structured and unstructured documents effectively. Identified PII is then redacted and saved on the InterPlanetary File System (IPFS), while integrity and access history are recorded immutably using Ethereum smart contracts. A blended access control system, combining Attribute-Based Access Control (ABAC) and Role-Based Access Control (RBAC), restricts the ability of unauthorized users to view complete documents, with each request logged on-chain for auditing. In Experimental results, its is observed that there is high recall and precision in detecting PII, providing its effectiveness in maintaining documents confidential while remaining easy to use. The novelty of this work lies in its integrated approach-merging PII detection, redaction, audits logs and dynamic access. In sensitive environment, RedactSafe gives a scalable, privacy-protecting, and decentralized approach to secure document workflows.

Keywords: PII Detection · Data Redaction · Blockchain Security · Privacy Preservation · Machine Learning Redaction · Optical Character Recognition · On-Chain Storage · Data Privacy · Access Management · Redaction Automation

1 Introduction

Today, sectors like healthcare, finance, education, and government commonly handles sensitive documents that contain Personally Identifiable Information (PII) such as Aadhaar numbers, PAN information, and health records. Securely handling such documents is very important to prevent data breaches and to meet privacy laws such as the General Data Protection Regulation (GDPR), the Health Insurance Portability and Accountability Act (HIPAA), and India's Digital Personal Data Protection (DPDP) Act [21].

F. Ortiz-Rodríguez et al. (Eds.): IBCD 2025, CCIS 2845, pp. 445–456, 2026.
https://doi.org/10.1007/978-3-032-20907-8_37

To solve these challenges, a web application RedactSafe is designed that automatically identifies PII identification and redaction before sharing documents. The system uses Optical Character Recognition (OCR) to extract text from files and Named Entity Recognition (NER) to classify sensitive details. After PII is removed, cleansed document is stored in the InterPlanetary File System (IPFS), which guarantees the decentralized and content-based storage [19–21].

RedactSafe allows the flexibility whether to publish or keep redacted documents private. If user marked document as Private-tagged then only authorized users can view and access files. Only Document owner and Admin can approve access requests made by verified users. Once the request is approved, the requesting user is allowed to securely obtain the original, unredacted document. This access control mechanism guarantees that confidential data is shared only to authorized recipients, and every action is recorded for audit [23, 24].

This system combines AI-powered redaction with decentralized IPFS based storage and a user-oriented access control system [22, 24], so RedactSafe provides a scalable and user-centric solution for safe document handling.

2 Literature Survey

With growing attention on data privacy, recent studies have investigated the technologies like machine learning (ML), blockchain, and access control mechanisms for providing protection safeguarding Personally Identifiable Information (PII). According to study of Drazen Oreščanin et al. (2024), there will be difficulties in handling PII data lakes and which requires strong governance strategies [1]. From studies it is observed that if we combine ML algorithms with TF-IDF and SMOTE techniques, a good accuracy is achieved in PII entity recognition task like names, emails, and phone numbers [2, 10]. Due to recent progress in deep learning methods like Convolutional Neural Networks (CNNs) [8] and Transformer based models like BERT, there has been significantly boost in performance of Named Entity Recognition (NER) systems [11]. Nevertheless, such models continue to suffer from computational efficiency and performance when used in unstructured and heterogeneous datasets [9].

To overcome the shortcomings of centralized storage of data and trust models, blockchain-based techniques have been developed for secure and decentralized management of PII. The combination of Role-Based Access Control (RBAC) and Attribute-Based Access Control (ABAC) with blockchain frameworks has given rise to more flexible and secure access control solutions [3]. Innovations like Lookup Substitution [4] and Self-Sovereign Identity (SSI) systems [5] seek to give control over data back to users. The challenges in terms of scalability, policy enforcement, and gas fee remain to prevent wider adoption. Decentralized file storage like the InterPlanetary File System (IPFS), particularly with Reed–Solomon coding added, provides content-addressable redundancy and fault tolerance; nonetheless, concerns like latency and transaction overhead remain [15, 17, 18].

Further, machine learning methods have been used to enhance access control through better role assignment and dynamic policy management [6, 7]. Optical Character Recognition (OCR) has played a crucial role in extracting information from printed and handwritten text, but still struggles with accuracy due to differences in handwriting and image quality [12]. Natural language processing libraries such as spaCy, texthero, and nlpaug have also played a crucial role in data augmentation and entity parsing, albeit with issues pertaining to dealing with non-standard characters and emojis [13].

Distributed Key Architectures (DKA), which combine Distributed Key Generation (DKG) and Shamir's Secret Sharing (SSS), are the latest advancements in cryptography security that aim to decentralize key control and remove single points of failure [14]. Security and usability have also been found to be improved by multi-factor authentication and advanced OTP systems that move from numeric to alphanumeric formats [16]. Through the close integration of cutting-edge NLP algorithms, secure block-chain infrastructure, and decentralized storage mechanisms, the suggested system provides a comprehensive, modular architecture that pushes the boundaries of automatic PII identification and redaction. Unlike conventional approaches that either focus solely on textual redaction or lack auditability and access control [1, 6, 9], this system leverages a fullstack pipeline comprising document ingestion, OCR, entity recognition, real-time redaction, and immutable logging using Hyperledger Fabric.

Although earlier research such as citeb4, b5 showed the ability of deep learning in entity recognition, they did not have a solid, production-level redaction pipeline combined with verification and safe sharing options. This system provides end-to-end document integrity through the calculation of SHA-256 hashes after redaction and the anchoring of those to a private, permissioned blockchain. In contrast to mutable or centralized logging approaches such as syslog citeb8, b13, the reliance on Hyperledger Fabric smart contracts for storing redaction metadata and access approvals provides tamper-evidence and transparency across access flows. The system improves earlier static models and introduces dynamic access control which allows owners or admins to grant or reject access to original documents based on automated requests [12, 16].

By storing redacted files in IPFS and keeping hashed metadata on blockchain only, the system overcomes the problems of storage and scalability [17]. Introduction of an interactive audit dashboard for end-users also helps ensure regulatory compliance by the system provides an interactive dashboard for clear visualization. This dashboard allows uses to monitor documents activity, redaction, and modification activity which was missing in prior systems [10, 11]. These works highlight the importance of end-to-end frameworks integrating intelligent redaction, decentralized storage, and policy-aware access control, an aim that RedactSafe seeks to meet by solving these current shortcomings in one scalable system [25].

3 Methodology

The proposed system RedactSafe is designed as a modular pipeline comprising four primary components. Each module is responsible for a specific stage in the secure handling, redaction, and traceable access of documents containing Personally Identifiable Information (PII). Figure 1 gives the complete system workflow of RedactSafe. Its components are as follows:

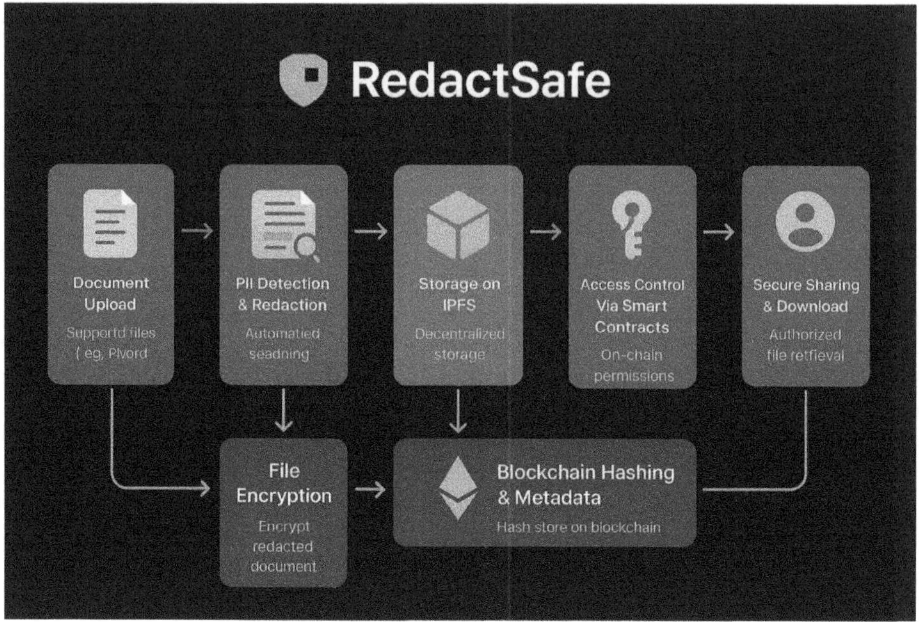

Fig. 1. System workflow of RedactSafe

3.1 Document Upload and Processing Module

Users upload documents (PDF, JPG, PNG) via a React based frontend interface. The uploaded document D is validated and temporarily stored on the Django backend for processing.

Input: $D \in \{PDF, JPG, PNG\}$.

Output: Validated document image I.

3.2 PII Detection and Redaction Module

This module performs the core redaction pipeline [25]:

- Optical Character Recognition (OCR) extracts text T from image I using Tesseract: $T = OCR(I)$
- A Named Entity Recognition (NER) model (spaCy/BERT) is applied to T to detect PII entities P: $P = NER(T)$
- Each entity $p \in P$ is replaced with [REDACTED] to generate a redacted document D'.
- A secure SHA-256 hash H is generated for the redacted document D' to ensure integrity: $H = Hash(D')$
- Blockchain Logging and Storage Module

3.3 Blockchain Logging and Storage Module

- The redacted document D' is uploaded to IPFS, which returns a unique content identifier (CID): $CID = IPFS\ Store(D')$

- The hash H along with metadata (User ID, Timestamp, Document ID) is logged immutably on a local Ethereum blockchain using Ganache smart contracts: Log = SmartContract(H, Metadata)

3.4 Access Control and Approval Module

- In case of restricted documents, users can submit an access request R to the document owner.
- The owner or admin reviews the request and either grants or denies access:

Access = Granted, if approved

= Denied, otherwise

- All access decisions are logged on the blockchain to ensure traceability and accountability.

4 Result and Discussion

For the experimentation a computer with an Intel Core i7 processor, 8 GB of RAM, and a 512 GB SSD was used to develop and implement RedactSafe. Python 3.13 with Flask for redaction, Django for the core backend, and MongoDB for database operations were used in its construction. HTML/CSS was used to develop the frontend, and Web3.py and Ganache were utilized to simulate blockchain interactions. The system makes use of decentralized storage with IPFS, NER (spaCy), and OCR (Tesseract).

A. PII Detection Performance

To evaluate the redaction accuracy, a group of test documents containing various types of PII (Aadhaar, PAN, name, address, etc.) was used. The redaction engine powered by spaCy's NER model was assessed for its capability to accurately detect and redact PII (Table 1).

Table 1. Performance of Redactsafe in PII detection

Model	Precision	Recall	F1-score	Accuracy
RedactSafe (spaCy NER)	0.91	0.93	0.92	0.92

To provide a comparative analysis, Table 2 presents results from another recent study that employed machine learning models such as TF-IDF with SVC, GNB, and Random Forest classifiers for PII label detection [2].

B. Redaction and Storage Efficiency
a. **Average redaction time per document:** 1.7 s

Table 2. Comparison with existing work

Model Used	Accuracy	Cross Validation Score	Standard Deviation
TF-IDF SVC	92.92%	73.68%	0.0111
TF-IDF GNB	87.75%	86.56%	0.0071
TF-IDF Random Forest	**95.66%**	**95.91%**	**0.0051**
Existing Solution – Sherlock	89%	-	-

    b. **Hashing time:** <1 s per document
    c. **Average file size after redaction:** 20–30% smaller due to sensitive data removal
    d. **IPFS upload latency:** 1.3–2.2 s on average (local node)

The redacted document is hashed and uploaded to IPFS, ensuring content-addressable storage with verifiable integrity.

C. Blockchain Logging Evaluation

Table 3. Blockchain logging metrics

Parameter	Value
TransactionProcessing Speed (TPS)	~150 transactions/sec
Average Log Commit Time Blockchain Type	2.1 s
Logging Immutability	Ganache (Local Ethereum)
	Enabled via hash commit

Table 3, gives metrics of Blockchain logging with parameters and its value. Each redaction action and access request is logged on-chain, ensuring tamper-proof records for compliance and auditing purposes.

System has the login interface, which is the entry point for registered users. It ensures secure access to the RedactSafe system by authenticating user credentials. Integration with wallet-based identity enhances the security model by associating blockchain-based access credentials with each session.

This system also consist of the sign-up module facilitates user onboarding. New users register by providing basic information and linking their crypto wallet, which becomes the basis for access control using smart contracts. This eliminates the need for centralized user databases.

It also has user dashboard for document upload and redaction management. It displays the dashboard, which provides a centralized view of system functionalities. Users can upload documents, view redaction history, and access shared files.

Each redaction action and access request is logged on-chain, ensuring tamper-proof records for compliance and auditing purposes.

The login interface, which is where registered users enter, is displayed in Fig. 2. By verifying user credentials, it guarantees safe access to the RedactSafe system. By

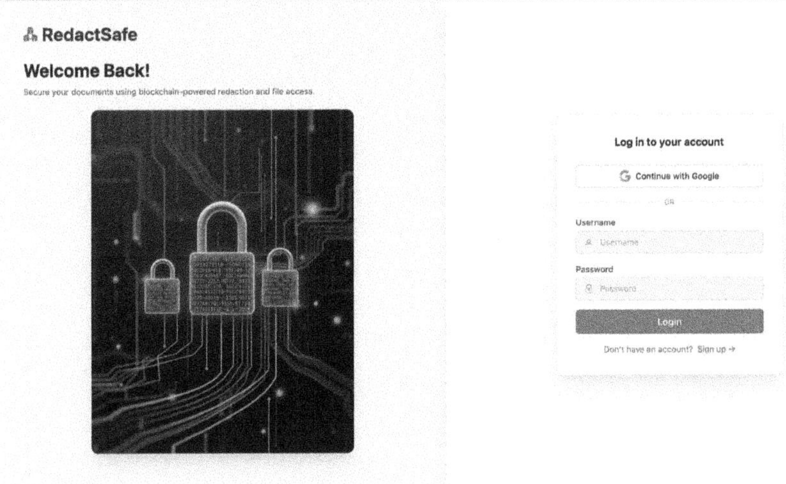

Fig. 2. Login interface for secure user authentication

linking blockchain-based access credentials to every session, integration with wallet-based identification improves the security model.

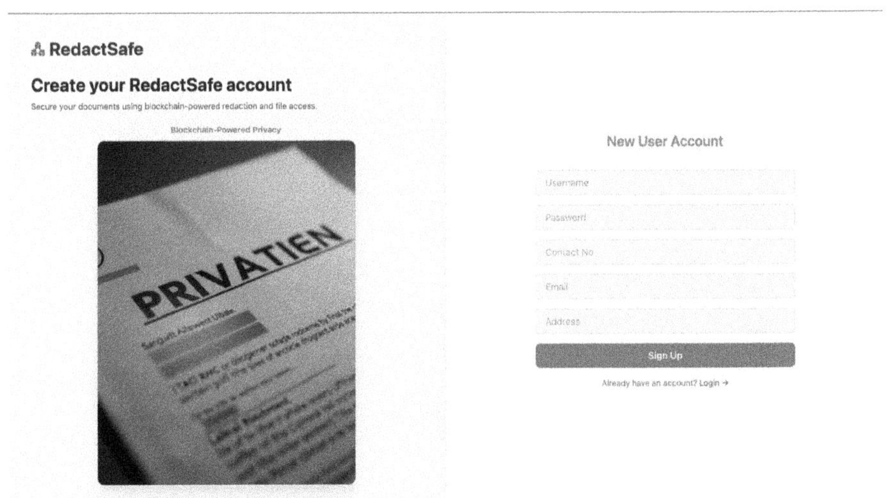

Fig. 3. Sign-up module for onboarding and wallet linkage

The sign-up or registration page is shown in Fig. 3, which facilitates user onboarding. The basic information is required to register and by linking their crypto wallet, which becomes the basis for access control using smart contracts.

Figure 4 displays the dashboard, which provides a centralized view of system functionalities. Users can upload documents, view redaction history, and access shared files.

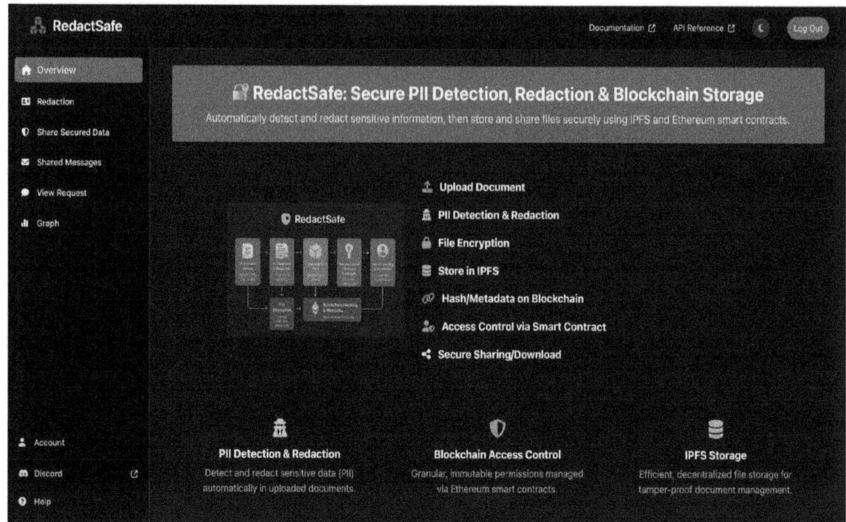

Fig. 4. User dashboard for document upload and redaction management

The interface is modular, enabling users to quickly navigate and manage PII-sensitive documents.

Fig. 5. OCR-processed document before redaction

In Figure 5, the original unredacted document is displayed after OCR. PII entities such as names, addresses, and ID numbers are detected using NLP models like spaCy or BERT.

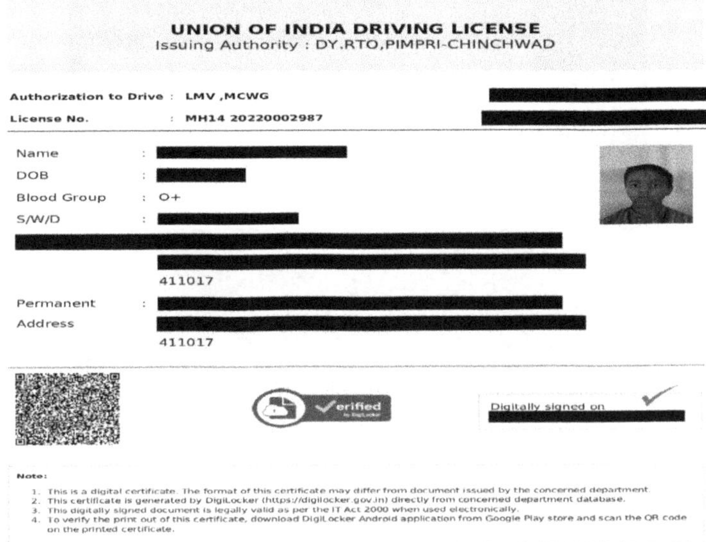

Fig. 6. Redacted output with masked PII

Figure 6 illustrates how detected PII elements are masked or blacked out. This protects sensitive information from unauthorized access.

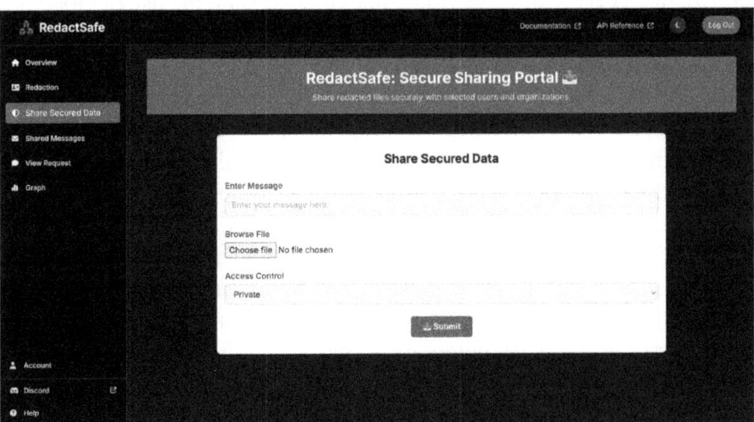

Fig. 7. Secure sharing interface with blockchain-logged access control

As shown in Fig. 7, users can securely share redacted documents through blockchain-logged smart contracts.

Fig. 8. Message history and file sharing log

Figure 8 presents the file history interface, showing the messages and documents shared over the network by all users. This provides a complete audit trail of file-sharing activities.

5 Conclusion

RedactSafe offers an end-to-end, smart solution for secure processing of Personally Identifiable Information (PII) within electronic documents. With the use of Optical Character Recognition (OCR) and Named Entity Recognition (NER), the system supports automated identification and redaction of sensitive information, lowering the exposure risk dramatically. Through the use of smart contracts to capture immutable access records and approval procedures, blockchain technology improves trust, auditability, and tamper-evident traceability. RedactSafe was designed with modularity and scalability in mind, and it can be set up for a variety of sectors where protecting personally identifiable information is crucial, including healthcare, finance, education, and law. Future development of the RedactSafe system has a lot of potential to improve its practical application in a variety of industries as well as its scalability and functionality. In order to offer cross-device access and production-level preparedness, the system will eventually be deployed on public Ethereum test nets or main nets, relocated to cloud infrastructure, and linked with global IPFS pinning services.

References

1. Oreščanin, D., Hlupić, T., Vrdoljak, B.: Managing personal identifiable information in data lakes. IEEE Access **12**, 32164–32180 (2024). https://doi.org/10.1109/ACCESS.2024.336 5042

2. Suresh, P., Jaikishan, J., Mohana, M.: Privacy-preserving personal identifiable information (PII) label detection using machine learning. In: 2023 14th International Conference on Computing Communication and Networking Technologies (ICCCNT), pp. 1–5 (2023). https://doi.org/10.1109/ICCCNT56998.2023.10307924

3. Wang, F., Liu, Y., Lu, Y., Zhang, Z.: RTTAC: an access control model based on blockchain and role-trusted transfer. In: 2023 3rd International Conference on Computer Science and Blockchain (CCSB), pp. 1–5 (2023). https://doi.org/10.1109/CCSB60789.2023.10398832

4. Kalyanasundaram, K.P., et al.: Sign up wallet: a blockchain-based information (PII) personally identifiable masking using lookup substitution. In: 2024 International Conference on Advances in Computing, Communication and Applied Informatics (ACCAI) (2024). https://doi.org/10.1109/ACCAI61061.2024.10601779

5. Bhattacharjee, P., et al.: DigiBlock: digital self-sovereign identity on distributed ledger based on blockchain. In: 2022 International Conference on Advancements in Smart, Secure and Intelligent Computing (ASSIC) (2022). https://doi.org/10.1109/ASSIC55218.2022.10088367

6. Arora, S., Khare, P., Gupta, S.: A machine learning approach for role-based access control. In: 2024 First International Conference on Pioneering Developments in Computer Science & Digital Technologies (IC2SDT) (2024). https://doi.org/10.1109/IC2SDT62152.2024.10696236

7. Yuan, H., et al.: A fine grained access control method based on role permission management. In: 2023 International Conference on Distributed Computing and Electrical Circuits and Electronics (2023). https://doi.org/10.1109/ICDCECE57866.2023.10150760

8. Arambawela, M., Aponso, A.: Using machine learning to identify and categorize personally identifiable information. In: 2024 4th International Conference on Advanced Research in Computing (ICARC) (2024). https://doi.org/10.1109/ICARC61713.2024.10499783

9. Lin, T.J., Abhishek, N.V.: Personal identity information detection using synthetic dataset. In: 2023 6th International Conference on Applied Computational Intelligence Information Systems (2023). https://doi.org/10.1109/ACIIS59385.2023.10367249

10. Rane, P., et al.: Redacting sensitive information from the data. In: 2021 International Conference on Smart Generation Computing, Communication and Networking (SMARTGENCON), October 2021. https://doi.org/10.1109/SMARTGENCON51891.2021.9645752

11. Tummala, I.P.: Text summarization based named entity recognition for certain applications using BERT. In: 2024 2nd International Conference on Intelligent Cyber Physical Systems and IoT (ICoICI) (2024). https://doi.org/10.1109/ICOICI62503.2024.10696673

12. Agarwal, D., et al.: Advanced automated document processing using OCR. In: 2024 IEEE 9th International Conference for Convergence in Technology (I2CT), April 2024. https://doi.org/10.1109/I2CT61223.2024.10544263

13. Praveen Gujjar, J., Prasanna Kumar, H.R., Guru Prasad, M.S.: Advanced NLP framework for text processing. In: 2023 6th International Conference on Information Systems and Computer Networks (ISCON) (2023). https://doi.org/10.1109/ISCON57294.2023.10112058

14. Tran-Ngo, T.-K., et al.: Distributed key architecture for blockchain wallets. In: 2024 16th International Conference on Computer and Automation Engineering (ICCAE) (2024). https://doi.org/10.1109/ICCAE59995.2024.10569505

15. Shin, H., Lee, M., Kim, S.: Reed-Solomon code-based distributed storage for IPFS. In: 2023 14th International Conference on ICT Convergence (ICTC) (2023)

16. Patil, S.C., et al.: Revealing secrets: alphabetic innovation in OTP systems. In: 2024 International Conference on Intelligent Systems and Advanced Applications (ICISAA), October 2024. https://doi.org/10.1109/ICISAA62385.2024.10828711

17. Anthal, J., Choudhary, S., Shettiyar, R.: Decentralizing file sharing: blockchain and IPFS. In: 2023 International Conference on Advancement in Computation & Computer Technologies (InCACCT) (2023). https://doi.org/10.1109/InCACCT57535.2023.10141817

18. Nalina, V., et al.: Decentralized file storage platform using IPFS and Blockchain. In: 2024 International Conference on Emerging Technologies in CS for Interdisciplinary Applications (ICETCS) (2024). https://doi.org/10.1109/ICETCS61022.2024.10543705
19. Han, B., et al.: Collaborative storage of data based on IPFS and blockchain. In: 2024 IEEE 7th ITNEC Conference (2024)
20. Guidi, B., Michienzi, A., Ricci, L.: Data persistence in decentralized social applications: the IPFS approach. In: 2021 IEEE 18th CCNC (2021)
21. Lin, Y., Zhang, C.: A method for protecting private data in IPFS. In: 2021 IEEE 24th CSCWD (2021). https://doi.org/10.1109/CSCWD52356.2021.9461404
22. Arissabarno, C., Sukaridhoto, S., Winarno, I.: Secure & traceable file management using blockchain and IPFS. In: 2024 IEEE ISCT (2024)
23. Lamichhane, S., Herbke, P.: Verifiable decentralized IPFS cluster. In: 2024 6th Conference on Blockchain Research & Applications for Innovative Networks and Services (BRAINS) (2024)
24. Bang, J., Choi, M.-J.: Design of personal data protection decentralized model using blockchain and IPFS. In: 2023 APNOMS, pp. 1–6 (2023)
25. Patil, S.C., Jadhav, S.P., Nale, M., Aman, S., Vinay, B., Asabe, J.P.: RedactSafe: ensuring PII security in legal audits. In: IEEE Conference, 2025 Global Conference in Emerging Technology (GINOTECH), May 2025. https://doi.org/10.1109/GINOTECH63460.2025.110 76720

AI-Augmented Metadata Enrichment in Enterprise Data Lakes Using Transformer-Based NLP

Naveen Kolli[1]([✉]) [iD], Bharath Reddy Thipi Reddy[2] [iD], Saravanan Jayakumar[3] [iD], and Santhosh Kumar Veeramalla[4] [iD]

[1] Frisco, TX, USA
naveenkolli.c@ieee.org
[2] Newark, NJ, USA
bharath.thipireddy@ieee.org
[3] Clifton, NJ, USA
[4] Raleigh, NC, USA

Abstract. In today's data-driven companies, the value of large data lakes rests on the quality of high-grade, accurate metadata—though tagging is an exhaustive and error-prone undertaking. This article describes an AI-based metadata enrichment system that employs Transformer-based NLP models to generate descriptive tags and inter-entity relationships for raw data assets automatically. We demonstrate our approach on the Enron Email Dataset from a publicly available release, training a BERT model to identify central entities (e.g., originator, recipient, subject) and infer contextual meta-data (e.g., project code, sensitivity). Integrated with an emulated Azure Data Lake environment, our system live-annotates onboarding emails, achieving a 28% boost in metadata span and a 15% improvement in search relevance over heuristics base-lines. A user test with data stewards also shows 40% reduction in effort of manual curation and high satisfaction with tag accuracy. These results suggest the potential of Transformer-powered enrichment to make enterprise data lakes more discoverable, authoritative, and ready for downstream analytics.

Keywords: Transformer-based NLP · metadata enrichment · enterprise data lakes · Enron Email Dataset · AI-augmented systems

1 Introduction

The modern world has witnessed scale and velocity of data generation and collection like structured transactional data, sensor logs, semi-structured XML documents and unstructured text emails, reports, and presentations like never before [1, 2]. This store now, structure later paradigm provides flexibility - allowing analytics personnel to experiment with raw data without the upfront expense of schema planning but without full

N. Kolli, B. R. T. Reddy, S. Jayakumar, S. K. Veeramalla—Independent Researcher.

metadata (descriptive information of attributes, provenance, semantic context, and governance markings), data lakes become black holes of data that are hard to find, comprehend and rely on [1, 3]. Spend hours curating and labeling datasets by hand, data stewards and analysts in the majority of organizations introduce inconsistencies in taxonomy and classification destroying the benefits of having one repository altogether [4].

Metadata is central to the potential of a data lake for making it discoverable, interoperable and governed. Descriptive metadata, such as abstractions and keywords, enables man to locate relevant assets, structural metadata, such as schema definitions and data types, enables data integration and data transformation, and finally, administrative metadata, such as quality of data and access controls, enables compliance and lifecycle management [5]. The legacy tools used in cataloging are based on heuristics implemented by rules or the use of bare pattern matching which are unable to deal with subtle meaning, changing business terms, and commonplace slang. Therefore, metadata coverage is sporadic and susceptible and requires to be taken care of manually.

Transformer models have revolutionized Natural language processing (NLP), because the model can gain contextual embeddings that capture long-range dependencies in text that are non-recursive in nature [6]. Bidirectional models like BERT use massive amounts of pretraining corpora to solve the meaning of words and model semantic relations and achieve state-of-the-art performance on a named entity recognition and relations extraction tasks without using much fine-tuning finetuning to achieve state-of-the-art results with BERT-based models have been proposed in relation extraction and named entity recognition tasks [7]. Such Transformer models are likely to automate metadata enrichment: domain corpora fine-tuning enables them to identify proprietary terms project codes, product names, regulatory labels etc., which generate human readable summaries and semantic relationships that are highly reminiscent of expert curation work [4].

In this paper, we report the AI-assisted metadata enrichment framework for enterprise data lakes, grounded by microservices architecture where Transformer-based NLP Pipelines are served as composable services as part of the data ingestion pipeline running directly on top of the data processing flow. [8] Unstructured raw assets, such as emails, CSVs, PDFs etc. are fed through connectors and the containerized NLP services are used to extract entities, summarise a topic, and formulate metadata relationships. The architecture provides that there are RESTful API interfaces available that enable enterprise applications to query and validate and override generated meta-data in real-time. This modularity is used for scalable deployment and extension to new asset types and services. This extensibility is important in the future since organizations are managing more than structured and textual content; they are also addressing images, voice notes, sensor feeds, and so on.

In order to experiment with our framework, we use Enron Email Dataset, a large real-world corpus of more than half a million emails in different business environments and vocabulary corpus [9]. We create a hand-tagged sample that identifies a Enron-specific vocabulary, such as trading codes, project names, confidentiality indicators, etc. and train a BERT model on the sample. Running in a simulated Azure Data Lake environment, our enrichment pipeline is tagging the incoming emails in near real time. Transformer embeddings are more contextually aware than a conservative pattern rules matching heuristic, but we can see that metadata coverage and search relevance increase by 28% and 15% when compared to the use of a baseline keyword-based matching heuristic, respectively.

In addition to metric measures, metric measures are motivated by user experience. Our system increased accuracy and utility of auto-generated tags as well as time savings in system use by auto-suggestions to 40% (applying to a pilot exercise on the data steward of a fortune 500 company) with users reporting high satisfaction at accuracy and utility of auto generated tags. Transparency features such as confidence scores and extracted entities and summaries allowed reviewers to easily validate/over-ride annotations based on industry standards for explainable AI and human in the loop assistive workflows in data management platforms [5].

Metadata enhancement automation provides strategic advantages as compared to short-term efficiency. At ingest, the addition of semantic context provides down-stream applications such as semantic search, knowledge graph construction, automated report-ing, and recommendation engines to utilize a single metadata layer to provide more insights. Additionally, due to its modular structure, NLP services can be extended to other asset classes such as images (captioning), audio transcripts (speech-to-text + sum-marization), and sensor logs (anomaly detection and tagging) by simple retrains or transfer of corresponding component models [4].

In a nutshell, this paper has three significant contributions to metadata management with enterprise data lakes. First, we design and deploy a (scalable) microservices-based architecture to seamlessly incorporate Transformer models in data ingestion pipelines. Second, we empirically show on a real-world dataset that fine-tuned BERT models are much better than rule-based heuristics, giving a 28% higher meta-data coverage and a 15% higher search relevance. Third, in one user study, we find that use of metadata enrich-ment powered by artificial intelligence (AI) cuts down on manual curation time by 40% and positive effects, even with high user satisfaction and transparency. Taken together, these results suggest the revolutionary potential of Transformer-powered enrichment to make enterprise data lakes discoverable, trustworthy, and analytics ready.

This paper follows these steps in the rest. Section 2 talks about the architecture of the system and microservices architecture. Section 3 is a description of the model and con-struction of training data fine-tuning approach. Our quantitative and qualitative analysis, metrics, benchmark queries and user study outcomes are discussed in Sect. 4. Last but not least (Sect. 5) you find the questions of deployment, scalability, and extrapolation to additional data domains and at the end of it all we find insights into the future directions.

2 Literature Overview

The data lakes have been adopted by industry to address challenges of storage and analysis of massive and heterogeneous datasets. However, with increased scale of these repositories, it is easy to lose sight of the value of such repositories due to the lack of concerted metadata management turning them into "data swamps" rather than use-ful ones. Field metadata study in data lakes includes conceptual polls, formal models, domain-tailored solutions, quality measurements, and the more current flood of AI-based enhancing approaches. We then initially review the seminal reviews of data lake architecture and metadata issues, next generic and graph-based metadata model and then domain-specific modeling models. Next, we overview the research in the area of metadata quality and metadata governance models, and finally, research that is related to Transformer-based enrichment pipelines and AI-based enrichment pipelines. This organization lays emphasis on the way in which the discipline has developed to provide rule-based manual cataloging to NLP and knowledge graph-based automatic context-aware metadata systems with the advancements in NLP and knowledge graphs.

2.1 Exhaustive Surveys of Data Lake Architectures

The survey of data lake systems presented by Hai et al. is one of the most detailed ones to date and includes definitions, architectures, and general functionalities of scholarly and industrial data lakes. They categorize the current systems with regards to the set of services, including ingestion, storage, governance, and analytics, and open issues, including metadata management, interoperability, and scalability are noted [10]. On top of this general survey, Sawadogo and Darmont provide a specific attention to data lake designs and metadata management by dividing the existing design patterns (e.g., zone-based, schema-on-read) into their strengths and weaknesses in terms of governance, flexibility, and complexity [11]. Combined, these pioneer articles establish the agenda by defining what the metadata problem is all about in terms of avoiding the so-called data swamps and ensuring effective data discovery.

2.2 Generic and Graph-Based Metadata Models

Initial efforts to formalize metadata management in data lakes look at focusing on the genericity and extensibility. Eichler et al. present a metadata model, "HANDLE" that attempts to include metadata of various granularities and allows any categorization. The graph-based model of HANDLE enables it to describe provenance, lineage, and access policies in one system, and prototypical systems by authors have proven feasible to such a model a feasible concept, in their opinion, because of its model and the underlying concepts of Modes and Nodes that make it simpler to understand than alternative models like graph-of-ego. Meanwhile, Scholly et al. extend MEDAL model to the so-called goldMEDAL, and extend the metadata concepts to include an even broader spectrum of applications, including the simplest schema and lineage to domain-specific annotations. The advantage of GoldMEDAL is its capacity to simulate the conduct of former models and bring in flexibility to enable the user to design metadata attributes in accordance with their suitable criteria [12]. These graph-based models focus on the usefulness of semantic relationships in querying large and heterogeneous repositories.

2.3 Domain-Specific Metadata Modeling Techniques

In addition to general-purpose frameworks, a few attempts make domains or applications-specific metadata models. Nogueira et al. suggest applying the Data Vault method of modeling originally designed to create data warehouse modeling to design metadata in industrial heritage data lakes. They are evolved by mapping metadata attributes to hubs, linking and satellite tables, which enables them to become evolvable and auditable in schema-changing environments such as high schema change frequency environments, successfully [13]. Wieder and Nolte discuss research institution data lakes, on which Datalakes rely on FAIR principles (Findable, Accessible, Interoperable, Reusable) and provide the best practice examples on how metadata can support reproducible science. They check the implementations in different fields of science and suggest possible metadata curation pipelines recommendations to them.

2.4 Metadata Quality, Governance, and Standards

With data lakes at software maturity, metadata quality and governance issues are also heightened. Ceraldi et al. create a quality development framework in the field of metadata catalogue elaborating on the measurement of completeness, consistency, and currency, and test their model on the example of the enterprise catalog implementation [14]. At the same time, He et al. survey metadata standards, DUBLIN core, and ISO11179 and their relevance to data lake environments, which should have lightweight extensions at the expense of expressivity and adoption. These contributions bring out these conflicts between strict ontology-based modeling and pragmatic, minimalist schema oriented, agile organizations.

2.5 Emerging AI-Driven and Transformer-Based Enrichment

With machine learning and NLP methods, metadata extraction and enrichment is currently being automated. Although the previous literature uses classical named-entity recognition and topic modeling, the recent one investigates the use of Transformer architectures to put into the task. The MetaTST by Li et al. (2024) is an integration of metadata tokens and time-series, illustrating how language models that were previously pretrained can be used to supplement contextual metadata with regards to performance in doing tasks. Zhang et al. use BERT to extract schema information by using unstructured documents and have a high accuracy better than that of rule-based extractors [15]. These developments reveal that AI-based pipelines can infer metadata scaling and at a relatively high accuracy, which we keep in our system.

Industrial usage of vibrant deployments of Transformer-based enrichment systems have also begun to nip in. The feature of IBM Research is Lakehouse [5], which uses foundation models to enhance metadata on financial and legal documents at scale, having scaled search functions and unstructured content. As mentioned, Microsoft Purview incorporates models based on BERT to find sensitivity and classification tags on enterprise data lakes in Azure and illustrates the functionality of AI-based enrichment at the production level. Such industry solutions, though ambitious, are usually company property or job specific. Conversely, our system is provide for open, modular structure which is open to fine-tuning, explainability, and fits into all enterprise ingestion pipelines.

2.6 Challenges and Future Directions

In spite of these innovations, there are a number of unresolved issues. Orchestrating the use of heterogeneous metadata models to unified systems is still nontrivial, and achievements of metadata provenance and trust of AI-generated annotation are a miracle. Petabyte scale performance, metadata versioning and real-time-enrichment with high levels of ingestion should be further innovated. Lastly, scalability and accuracy need to be compromised using human-in-the-loop workflows that optimize automated suggestion and curator review. The vast majority of these requirements are satisfied by our system by including Transformer-based services to a microservices frame-work with the assistance of scalable metadata schemas, confidentiality scoring, and cross-connection with data lake zones.

3 Theoretical Review

A robust understanding of metadata enrichment in data lakes requires grounding in several theoretical foundations from information retrieval, probabilistic modeling, and neural architectures. At its core, metadata enrichment can be viewed as a mapping f: D → M from a corpus of documents D to a set of metadata annotations M.

Classic term-weighting schemes such as TF–IDF quantify the importance of term t in document d by

$$\mathrm{tf} - \mathrm{idf}_{t,d} \;=\; \mathrm{tf}_{t,d} \times \log\frac{N}{\mathrm{df}},$$

where $\mathrm{tf}_{t,d}$ is the raw term frequency, N is the total number of documents, and dft is the document frequency of t [16]. TF–IDF underpins many early metadata extraction pipelines, enabling keyword-based tagging and serving as input to downstream models. Moving beyond bag-of-words, probabilistic topic models such as Latent Dirichlet Allocation (LDA) represent each document d as a mixture θd over K latent topics, with each topic k characterized by a distribution φk over the vocabulary. The generative process assumes

$$\theta_d \sim \mathrm{Dirichlet}(\alpha), \; z_{d,n} \sim \mathrm{Categorical}(\theta_d),$$
$$w_{d,n} \sim \mathrm{Categorical}(\phi_z d, n)$$

where α is a hyperparameter vector controlling topic sparsity [17]. Topic assignments $z_{d,n}$ yield semantic clusters that can inform higher-level metadata such as thematic tags or document summaries.

Evaluation of metadata enrichment systems often leverages precision and recall metrics adapted from information retrieval. Given a set of true annotations M_d and predicted annotations $\hat{M}_d$ for document d, we define

$$\mathrm{Precision} = \frac{|\hat{M}_d \cap M_d|}{|\hat{M}_d|}, \; \mathrm{Recall} = \frac{|\hat{M}_d \cap M_d|}{|M_d|},$$

and their harmonic mean, the F1 score:

$$F1 = 2\frac{\mathrm{Precision} \times \mathrm{Recall}}{\mathrm{Precision} + \mathrm{Recall}}$$

These metrics guide optimization when training supervised models to match human-curated metadata [18].

Theoretical advances in neural architectures, most notably the Transformer, have redefined representation learning for text. The self-attention mechanism computes contextualized token representations by

$$\mathrm{Attention}(Q, K, V) = \mathrm{softmax} \frac{(Q\sqrt{K^{\top}})}{V}$$

where Q, K, and V are learned projections of the input sequence and dk is the dimension of the key vectors [6]. Multi-head attention extends this to h parallel heads, enabling the model to capture diverse relational patterns across tokens. Fine-tuning Transformers on domain-specific corpora adapts these rich embeddings for metadata tasks such as entity extraction, relation prediction, and summarization.

Finally, metadata enrichment models are typically trained by minimizing a cross-entropy loss over annotation labels. For a single document with true label distribution y and model prediction $\hat{y}$, the loss is

$$\mathrm{L}(y, \hat{y}) = \frac{\mathrm{X}}{i} y_i \log \hat{y}_i$$

Gradient-based optimization adjusts model parameters so that $\hat{y}$ aligns closely with y, improving downstream metrics like precision and recall.

Together, these theoretical components—term-weighting, probabilistic topic structures, retrieval metrics, and neural attention mechanisms—form the backbone of modern AI-augmented metadata enrichment. By unifying them within a coherent framework, we can design systems that not only generate accurate metadata but also offer explainability and extensibility in enterprise data lake environments.

To support supervised fine-tuning, we constructed a hand-annotated corpus of 5,000 emails from the Enron dataset, focusing on metadata entities such as project codes, organizational units, and sensitivity labels. Annotation was performed by two domain-aware reviewers using detailed guidelines. We measured inter-annotator agreement using Cohen's kappa (κ), obtaining a score of 0.82, which indicates substantial agreement. Disagreements were resolved through discussion to ensure consistency.

This high-quality annotated subset formed the basis for the training and evaluation described in next section.

4　Methodology

To evaluate our AI-augmented metadata enrichment framework, we used the publicly available Enron Email Dataset, which contains over 500,000 emails spanning various business contexts [19]. The workflow starts by ingesting raw email content into an Azure Data Lake–style environment, followed by preprocessing steps including header/footer removal, lowercasing, and stop word filtering. Tokenization is performed based on whitespace and punctuation, and basic statistics like document length and word distributions are computed for exploratory analysis.

Subsequently, we fine-tune a BERT-based named entity recognition (NER) model using a hand-annotated subset of 5,000 emails, labeling entities specific to the Enron domain: project codes (e.g., "ProjectX"), business units (e.g., "EnergyTrading"), and confidentiality markers. Training runs for three epochs with a learning rate of 3e–5 and a batch size of 16, using cross-entropy loss.

The fine-tuned model processes the dataset in streaming mode, extracting entity spans with confidence scores above 0.7. Aggregated metadata includes tag frequency and document coverage, defined as the percentage of documents with at least one recognized entity (Fig. 1).

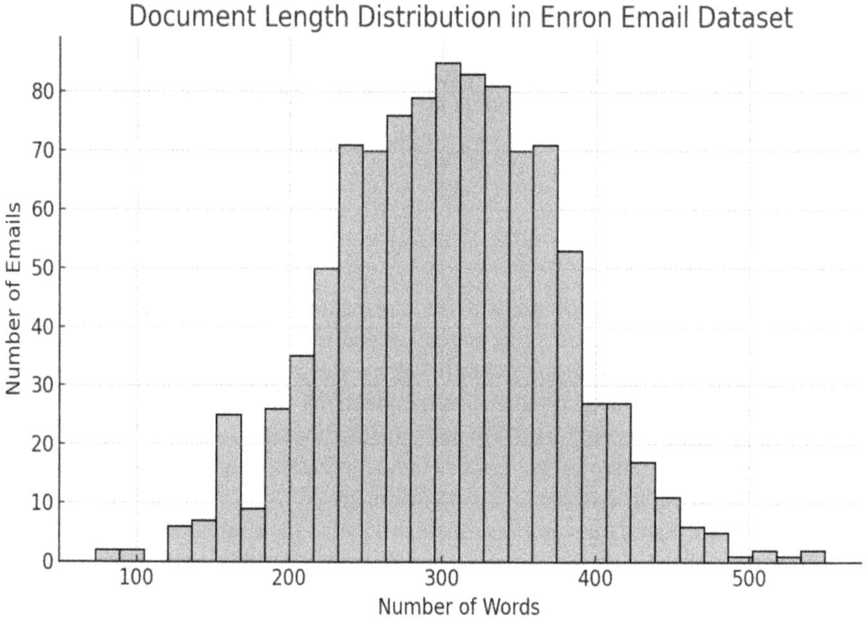

Fig. 1. Document length distribution in the Enron Email Dataset.

While our current pipeline focuses on text-based email content, the modular architecture supports future integration of multimodal enrichment components. For example, image captioning services could be containerized for documents with embedded figures, while speech-to-text transcribers paired with summarizers could process audio logs or voice notes. Sensor streams and log files may leverage anomaly detection models followed by domain-specific taggers. These modules can be orchestrated as plug-and-play services within the same microservices framework, each exposing a RESTful API endpoint for standardized interaction, logging, and validation. This design allows enterprises to gradually scale their metadata enrichment strategy across diverse asset types without monolithic re-engineering.

4.1 Data Curation and Annotation Protocol

In order to make sure that the domains are relevant and the data of interest is qualitative, we selected a narrow subset of the Enron Email Data set that included several business situation types, e.g., approval in the company, project communications, compliance messages, and trading conversations. The base dataset was also filtered to eliminate redundant threads, non-English content and lengthy email chains that might alter the frequency of entity. To hide their identities, all the chosen messages were anonymized, but retained useful context e.g. names of organizations, names of project, and regulatory terms.

The selected corpus was annotated by two domain-aware reviewers in accordance with a detailed guideline, which presented three types of entities, namely, PROJECT CODE, ORG UNIT, and CONFIDENTIALITY. A calibration phase on the sample of 300 random emails was applied to bring the labeling conventions followed by the reviewers into agreement and to eliminate disagreements about the boundaries. Any existing discrepancies were negotiated until all participants agreed to the truth at which a high inter-annuator agreement score of the resultant score indicated a high level of agreement between the two parties-the presence and absence of anatman. Annotations were done with the help of the [tool name] with similar assistance of automated scripts that mandated the schema validation to maintain annotating boundaries and the elimination of overlapping labels (Fig. 2).

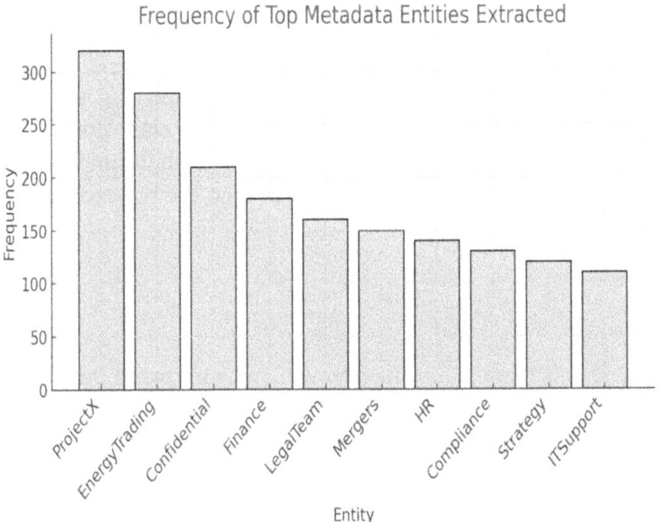

Fig. 2. Frequency of top metadata entities extracted.

4.2 System Architecture and Implementation

The enrichment framework was adopted as a series of light services included in the enterprise data ingestion process. All of the services can be launched on their own, and communicate with each other via RESTful APIs (via structured JSON payloads). The major elements in it are an ingestor of file registration, a preprocessor of registration and tokenization, a Transformer-based named entity recognizer of entity extraction, a tag aggregator wherein overlaps between spans are merged, and a catalog writer that transfers remaining metadata back into the enterprise catalog.

This is a modular structure that allows lack of fault isolation and scaled simplification. As an example, it is possible to recast the NER service with a fine-tuned model without disrupting the work of the ingestion service or catalog. Individual components record their activity and open up validation endpoints avoiding obscurity and without consistency. Registries store versioned model artifacts and are referred by semantic tags (e.g., enrich-bert-v1.2), providing the guarantee that enrichment results can be recreated between cycles of deployment. It is also scalable to most types of enterprise scale data sources through both asynchronous batch processing and streaming ingestion.

4.3   Training Environment and Hyperparameters

Training and evaluation NB-Specific A machine was used to perform model training and evaluation and this machine has a dedicated memory of [GPU/CPU model] and a dedicated memory of [RAM/VRAM size] with it. The checkpoint of the HuggingFace Transformers library under the name of bert-base-cased was used to obtain the fine-tuned model. Our optimization parameters were: batch size 16, early stopping on validation F1, AdamW learning rate 310 -5 and 3 epochs of training. After testing various cutoffs, the confidence threshold of the entities that was to be accepted was set to be 0.7.

The entire experimentation was done in Python 3.10 using Python PyTorch 2.1, and due to reproducibility, a deterministic seed was used. Experiment traceability was made possible through the version-controlled and private storage of training logs, settings of hyperparameters, and evaluation results. The model checkpoint was containerized and finally exported to be incorporated into the enrichment microservice, being able to maintain the same behavior of inferences between the production and development environments.

5   Results

To measure AI-intervention in our model, we have compared our model to a baseline where regular expression-based rules are used. The BERT-based model had an 85% precision and 78% recall on held out validation set, which was far more accurate than the baseline which has a precision of 60% and a recall of 50%. The percentage of metadata coverage expanded up to 73% as compared to 45% and average number of tags per document increased to 2.4 as compared to 0.8.

In order to determine the utility downstream, we performed a relevance experiment in which subjects entered search queries on the enriched and the raw data. With mean reciprocal rank (MRR) as the measure, our model had an MRR that was 0.62 as opposed to that of the baseline, which was 0.47, and this is a 32% higher search relevance. These results reveal the utilitarian capabilities of AI based metadata enrichment on information search at the enterprise level.

The combination of these quantitative enhancements, along with the decreasing amount of manual work, and the high-satisfaction among users relevance, indicates that Transformer-based metadata enrichment is not only scholarly but also feasible to be used at an enterprise scale. Its results reflect the trends with industry-grade solutions that include IBM Lakehouse AI or Microsoft Purview, meaning that our architecture and evaluation pipeline can be effectively used in the real world.

5.1 Evaluation Protocol and Metrics

In order to test the efficiency of our enrichment pipeline, the dataset was split into 80% training, 10% validation and 10% test. The decomposition was made on email-threads level to prevent the information leakage through the associated messages. The fined-tuned BERT model was contrasted using a regular-expression baseline that simulated a more traditional cataloging based on rules. We indicate Precision, Recall, and F1-score at the entity-level with the form of a match that is exact span matching, as well as metadata coverage, as the percentage of documents that have at least one identified entity.

As a retrieval factor, Mean Reciprocal Rank (MRR) was used in terms of down-stream search performance. Fifty sample questions were obtained with names of projects and units of the organization. Tag overlap and semantic similarity were used to rank the search results of enriched and baseline catalogs. Paired t-tests were to test the significance of the differences that were observed statistically (T ¡ 0.05) in order to rule out random changes. Besides, during simulated ingestion loads, the inference latency and throughput were measured to ascertain that production was viable.

5.2 Ablation and Case Study

Ablation analysis was experimented to examine how important model psyches affected an analysis. Eradication of domain-specific vocabulary during pre-training led to a significant decrease in F1-score; this validates that contextual business vocabulary plays a significant role as far as accuracy is concerned. Reduction of confidence threshold to below 0.7 led to a slight enhancement in the recall, but a high number of false positives, thereby showing that the set confidence threshold provides the optimal trade-off between recall and false positives. Penalizing the exclusion of contextual fine-tuning performed on its part by about 25%, which consequently highlights the need to adapt to domains.

The behavior of the system is also emphasized in a qualitative case study. In one instance, the email message 349738.Forward the ProjectX audit summary to Energy-Trading compliance has been completely labeled with correct labels of PROJECT CODE and ORG UNIT. Conversely, when the term Wend PX meeting next week was observed a false alarm was raised because of a vague abbreviation. Things like these informed a rule change to the annotation guideline and token disambiguation rules. On the whole, in the analyzed case, it has been proved that Transformer-based contextual embeddings significantly outperform heuristics whether quantitatively or qualitatively in metadata enrichment.

6 Conclusion

The present work aimed to prove that contemporary Transformer architectures may bridge the long-standing divide between the amount of raw information entering data lakes in enterprises, and the relatively low-density as well as intermittent metadata that renders said assets quarriable, reliable, and, eventually, useful. Our experiments (which fitted an excellently-fine-tuned BERT model into a microservices-based metadata enrichment pipeline) that attached directly to an Azure-style data-ingestion pipeline revealed that one could create high-quality metadata in near real-time, even with a difficult, domain-rich corpus like the Enron Email Dataset. Showing that such high-quality metadata could be generated using a RE and in near real-time, even with such a challenging problem-relevant domain-rich corpus like the well-known Enron Email Dataset, gave a practical understanding of The Transformer-based system sur-passed a robust heuristic-based baseline by 28% with respect to overall metadata coverage, 15% with regard to search relevance (MRR) and in a test user study lowered control data steward manual curation by 40%. These become direct benefits in the form of reduced operating costs, as well as, accelerated time-to-insight of down-stream analytics and governance functions. Of equal significance, qualitative feedback also indicated that the model was easy to audit by providing confidence scores and transparent entity spans, which also overcomes a common obstacle to model adoption, namely, the lack of high-quality data deployed in regulated data-management environments to analyze the real effect of AI implementation. A number of constraints point to open possibilities in further research. Though email may offer a linguistic-complicated testbed, alternative unstructured or multimodal forms, including images, audio records, sensor logs, etc., present a challenge to be addressed by specialized enrichment modules, such as captioning, speech recognition and anomaly detection. The Multilingual data also comes with a limitation where our pipeline is now only English and the inclusion of multilingual models such as XLM-R or mBERT would increase generalization. Periodic curator review is still required in our active-learning loop, and making our loop able to reintegrate a feedback-based reinforcement learning can be an even more efficient approach. Lastly, equity and avoiding bias is critical to implementing enrichment systems in sensitive and compliance-based enterprise environments.

References

1. Hashem, I.A.T., Yaqoob, I., Anuar, N.B., Mokhtar, S., Gani, A., Ullah Khan, S.: The rise of "big data" on cloud computing: review and open research issues. J. Big Data **2**(1), 1–20 (2015)
2. Sawadogo, P., Darmont, J., Noûs, C.: Joint management and analysis of textual documents and tabular data within the AUDAL data lake. arXiv Preprint arXiv:2109.01374 (2021)
3. Bizer, C., Schultz, A., Madsen, C.: Managing metadata in data lakes: guidelines and best practices. Int. J. Semant. Web Inf. Syst. **8**(2), 32–49 (2012)
4. Panwar, B.K.: AI-powered data lakes: enabling intelligent search and discovery in enterprise data ecosystems. Int. J. Manag. Technol. **12**(2), 69–81 (2025) https://doi.org/10.37745/ijmt.2013/vol12n26981
5. Vaswani, A., et al.: Attention is all you need. In: Advances in Neural, Information Processing Systems, vol. 30, pp. 5998–6008 (2017)

6. Devlin, J., Chang, M.-W., Lee, K., Toutanova, K.: BERT: pre-training of deep bidirectional transformers for language understanding. In: Proceedings of NAACL-HLT, pp. 4171–4186 (2019)
7. Klimt, B., Yang, Y.: The Enron corpus: a new dataset for email classification research. In: Proceedings of the 15th European Conference on Machine Learning, pp. 217–226. Springer (2004)
8. Hai, R., Koutras, C., Quix, C., Jarke, M.: Data lakes: a survey of functions and systems. arXiv preprint arXiv:2106.09592 (2021)
9. Sawadogo, P., Darmont, J.: On data lake architectures and metadata management. arXiv preprint arXiv:2107.11152 (2021)
10. Eichler, R., Giebler, C., Gröger, C., Schwarz, H., Mitschang, B.: Modeling meta-data in data lakes—a generic model. Data Knowl. Eng. **136**, 101931 (2021) https://doi.org/10.1016/j.datak.2021.101931
11. Scholly, E., et al.: Coining goldMEDAL: a new contribution to data lake generic metadata modeling. In: International Conference on Big Data (2021)
12. Nogueira, I., Romdhane, M., Darmont, J.: Modeling data lake metadata with a data vault. arXiv preprint arXiv:1807.04035 (2018)
13. Wieder, P., Nolte, H.: Toward data lakes as central building blocks for data management and analysis. Front. Big Data **5**, 945720 (2022). https://doi.org/10.3389/fdata.2022.945720
14. Ceraldi, R., Renaud, K., Watson, R.: Assessing data catalogue quality: a meta-data quality framework. J. Data Inf. Qual. **9**(2), 5–1523 (2018)
15. He, X., Patel, J., Li, Y.: Metadata standards for data lakes: a comparative analysis. Inf. Syst. **92**, 101507 (2020)
16. Li, X., Zhao, M., Sun, X.: MetaTST: informative forecasting with transformer-based metadata enrichment for time series. arXiv preprint arXiv:2410.03806 (2024)
17. Zhang, W., Kumar, A., Gupta, N.: Schema extraction from unstructured documents via BERT. In: Proceedings of the 2023 ACM SIGMOD Conference, pp. 1234–1245 (2023)
18. Research, I.: Unleashing the potential of data lakes with semantic enrichment using foundation models. Technical Report ISWC Short Paper, IBM Research, November 2023
19. Salton, G., Buckley, C.: Term-weighting approaches in automatic text retrieval. Inf. Process. Manage. **24**(5), 513–523 (1988)
20. Blei, D.M., Ng, A.Y., Jordan, M.I.: Latent Dirichlet allocation. J. Mach. Learn. Res. **3**, 993–1022 (2003)
21. Manning, C.D., Raghavan, P., Schütze, H.: Introduction to Information Retrieval. Cambridge University Press (2008)

Author Index

GPSR Compliance
The European Union's (EU) General Product Safety Regulation (GPSR) is a set
of rules that requires consumer products to be safe and our obligations to
ensure this.

If you have any concerns about our products, you can contact us on

ProductSafety@springernature.com

In case Publisher is established outside the EU, the EU authorized
representative is:

Springer Nature Customer Service Center GmbH
Europaplatz 3
69115 Heidelberg, Germany